ACT®
Prep Plus
2022

Lead Editor

Kathryn Sollenberger, M.Ed.

Contributing Editors

Dr. Brandon Deason, M.D.; M. Dominic Eggert; Paula L. Fleming, MA; Glen Stohr; Alexandra Strelka, MA

Special thanks to our writers and reviewers:

Laura Aitcheson, Michael Collins, Michael Cook, Maria Cuffe, Sterling Davenport, Boris Dvorkin, Mark Feery, Emily Graves, Jonathan Habermacher, Laurel Haines, Jack Hayes, Peter Haynicz-Smith, Stephanie Jolly, Samee Kirk, Jo L'Abbate, Melissa McLaughlin, Lauren Miller, Aishwarya Pillai, Gail Rivers, Anne Marie Salloum, Gordon Spector, Caroline Sykes, Heather Waite, Bonnie Wang, and Ethan Weber

Additional special thanks to

Deborah Becak, Isaac Botier, Brian Carlidge, Tim Eich, Joanna Graham, Rebecca Knauer, Camellia Mukherjee, Kristin Murner, Narender Patyal, Ashley Stussy Oscar Velazquez, Michael Wolff, Amy Zarkos, and the countless others who made this project possible.

ACT® is a registered trademark of ACT, Inc., which neither sponsors nor endorses this product.

Published by Kaplan Publishing, a division of Kaplan, Inc.
750 Third Avenue
New York, NY 10017

ISBN: 978-1-5062-7728-8
10 9 8 7 6 5 4 3 2 1

Kaplan Publishing print books are available at special quantity discounts to use for sales promotions, employee premiums, or educational purposes. For more information or to purchase books, please call the Simon & Schuster Special Sales department at 866-506-1949.

TABLE OF CONTENTS

Three Tips for ACT Success

Colleges will consider your ACT score as part of your application, so it's no surprise that it's a pretty tough test. It can feel intimidating, like a barrier you need to climb over. At Kaplan, it's our goal to help you look at the ACT as an opportunity—a chance to demonstrate your knowledge, as well as your critical thinking skills, which will be key to your success as a college student. Looking at the ACT as an opportunity will help you do better on the test.

Besides committing to a positive attitude toward the test, give yourself a head start with these tips:

- The ACT is a standardized test, meaning that scores for every testing administration mean the same thing. To achieve this reliability, the test maker must always ask questions on the same topics and in the same way. This makes the test predictable and, therefore, easier to prepare for. We've distilled how high-scoring students approach each section and every type of question into Kaplan Methods. In fact, each method gets its own chapter. Learn these simple, step-by-step methods, and you'll approach questions like an expert.

- The ACT is not like the tests you take in school. When colleges want to know how you do on tests in school, they look at your transcript. Acing the ACT requires different skills. This book highlights these skills, from taking math shortcuts to avoiding wrong-answer "traps" to managing your time. By studying this book, you'll learn to think like the test.

- Your skill level now has nothing to do with your skill level on test day. Getting some questions wrong? Having trouble with a specific topic? That just means you've found an opportunity to raise your score. Be patient with yourself! In your life so far, you've already learned thousands of things. You can learn a few more things to succeed on the ACT.

Read on to learn how your book and online resources are organized and how to make the best use of them. Good luck on the test—you're going to nail it!

Welcome to Kaplan!

Congratulations on taking this important step in your college admissions process! By studying with Kaplan, the official partner of live instruction for the ACT®, you'll maximize your score on the ACT, a major factor in your overall application.

Our experience shows that the greatest ACT score increases result from active engagement in the preparation process. Kaplan will give you direction, focus your preparation, and teach you the specific skills and effective test-taking strategies you need to know for the ACT. We will help you achieve your top performance on test day, but your effort is crucial. The more you invest in preparing for the ACT, the greater your chances of achieving your target score and getting into your top-choice college.

Are you registered for the ACT? Kaplan cannot register you for the official ACT. If you have not already registered for the upcoming ACT, visit the official website at **www.act.org** to register online and for information on registration deadlines, test sites, accommodations, and fees.

Chapter Organization

The chapters in this book follow a standard format to make this book as easy to use as possible.

How Much Do You Know?

At the beginning of most chapters, you have an opportunity to assess how much you already know about the topics by answering a set of test-like questions. If you answer most or all of the questions in a set correctly and in the most efficient way, you may want to skip one or more lessons in that chapter. If you answer some or all of the questions in a set incorrectly or in an inefficient way, you will want to review most or all of the lessons in that chapter. The answers and explanations for these sections are provided in the "Check Your Work" section immediately after the question set.

Try on Your Own

The lessons within each chapter start with a question (or passage) typical of the way the ACT tests a given topic and ends with a set of practice questions called "Try on Your Own." These sections are designed to provide immediate, targeted practice. Complete these questions and review their explanations at least once after reviewing the lesson. You might consider completing these questions multiple times if you are preparing for the ACT over an extended period of time. The answers and explanations for these sections are provided at the end of each chapter.

On Test Day

Most of the Math chapters include an "On Test Day" section that highlights one or more ways a question can be approached strategically. Complete these sections after you have reviewed the lessons but before you complete the "How Much Have You Learned?" question set.

How Much Have You Learned?

You need to reinforce what you learn in each chapter by practicing the Kaplan methods and strategies. Most chapters include a section called "How Much Have You Learned?" that features additional practice questions reinforcing the concepts explained in that chapter. The answers and explanations for these sections are provided at the end of each chapter.

Reflect

These sections can be completed during or after a chapter's completion. You might prefer to use the Reflect sections to evaluate your retention over time or reflect on the chapter as a whole when you complete all of the lessons. However you choose to reflect on your ACT studying, what's important is taking the time to do so.

The SmartPoints® System

Different topics are worth different numbers of points on the ACT because they show up more or less frequently in questions. By studying the information released by the test maker, Kaplan has been able to determine how often certain topics are likely to appear on the ACT, and therefore, predict how many points these topics are worth on test day. This means that if you master a given topic and answer all of the questions from that category correctly on test day, then you can expect to earn approximately that number of SmartPoints out of the overall 36 points total for that test.

The breakdown of SmartPoints for English, Math, Reading, and Science are summarized in the following tables. You can also see how these topics align to chapters in this book.

English SmartPoints

SmartPoints Category	# of Points	Chapter
Sentence Structure	9	Ch. 3
Agreement	10	Ch. 3
Conciseness	4	Ch. 4
Organization	4	Ch. 4
Development	9	Ch. 4
TOTAL	**36**	

Math SmartPoints

SmartPoints Category	# of Points	Chapter(s)
Number and Quantity	8	Ch. 8 and 9
Algebra	7	Ch. 10
Statistics and Probability	6	Ch. 11
Functions	4	Ch. 12
Geometry	11	Ch. 13
TOTAL	**36**	

Reading SmartPoints

SmartPoints Category	# of Points	Chapter(s)
Vocab-in-Context	3	
Function	6	
Inference	10	Ch. 17 and 18
Detail	13	
Global	4	
TOTAL	**36**	

Science SmartPoints

SmartPoints Category	# of Points	Chapter
Interpreting Data	7	Ch. 23
Applying Data	9	Ch. 23
Experimental Design	6	Ch. 24
Synthesizing Data	6	Ch. 24
Applying Core Knowledge	2	Ch. 25
Supporting Hypotheses	6	Ch. 25
TOTAL	**36**	

Practice Tests

Kaplan's practice tests are designed to mimic the actual ACT. By taking practice exams, you will prepare yourself for the actual test day experience. One of your practice tests is included in this book and the other four can be accessed online; see the "Online Resources" section to learn how to access these. Additionally, you can log into your online resources to take online versions of these practice tests. Your online study plan includes additional information about computer-based testing that will help you determine whether you should take a paper practice test or an online practice test.

We recommend you complete these practice tests as you make your way through the content of this book. If you take paper versions of the tests, you can score your tests by hand using the score conversion tables in this book, or log into your online resources for easy online scoring. When scored online, Kaplan provides you with a detailed score report. If you take the online version of the test, you will also receive this detailed report. Use this summary to help you focus and review the content areas that comprise your greatest areas of improvement.

Kaplan also provides detailed answers and explanations for the test maker's practice test. We encourage you to visit the ACT website, download and take the exam, and return to your online resources to see how you performed and review the expert explanations. Doing so will help you familiarize yourself with the official test directions.

Online Resources

GO ONLINE

To access the online resources that accompany this book, follow the steps below:

1. Go to **kaptest.com/moreonline**.

2. Have this book available as you complete the on-screen instructions.

kaptest.com/moreonline

Then whenever you want to use your online resources, go to **kaptest.com/login** and log in using the email address and password you used to register your book.

Your Kaplan *ACT Prep Plus* book comes with . . .

- A tool to make your own personalized study plan—just answer three quick questions and download a detailed week-by-week prep calendar. If your plans change, no problem—just answer the questions again and make a new schedule.

- Over 40 videos—Kaplan teachers review key topics in English, Reading, Math, and Science.
- Qbank—make custom quizzes from 250 practice questions.
- Practice tests—four more Kaplan practice tests, plus easy online scoring and detailed score reports for the tests in this book and the Official ACT Practice Test. You can also use Kaplan's proctoring video for a more realistic practice test experience.

The ACT and You

Inside the ACT

ACT Structure

The ACT, like any standardized test, is predictable. The more comfortable you are with the test structure, the more confidently you will approach each question type, thus maximizing your score.

The ACT is 2 hours and 55 minutes long, or 3 hours and 35 minutes long if you choose to complete the optional essay in the Writing Test. The ACT is made up of multiple-choice questions that test four subject areas: English, Math, Reading, and Science.

Test	Allotted time (minutes)	Question count
English	45	75
Math	60	60
Reading	35	40
Science	35	40
Writing (optional)	40	1
Total	175 OR 215 (w/writing)	215 OR 216 (w/writing)

When you take the ACT, you may take a fifth multiple-choice test. The results of this fifth test may not be reflected in your final score report, but you should treat this test as if it counts, just in case.

ACT Scoring

ACT scoring can seem a bit complex. You will receive one scaled score ranging from 1 to 36 for each required Test, and these four scores will be averaged to calculate your composite score. You will receive a separate score for the Writing Test, if you choose to take it.

In addition to your overall scores, you will receive subscores that provide a deeper analysis of your ACT performance, including STEM and, if you take the optional Writing Test, ELA scores. The ACT also gives you a percentile ranking, which allows you to compare your scores with those of other test takers. For example, a student who scored in the 63rd percentile did better than 63 percent of all others who took that test.

The scores you need depend primarily on which colleges you are planning to apply to. For example, if you want to attend an engineering school, you'll typically need a higher math score than if you want to attend a liberal arts college. Research the colleges you are interested in, find out what scores they require, and structure your ACT studying accordingly.

Superscoring

As this book goes to print, superscoring is on hold due to the Covid-19 pandemic, but once it launches, the score reports sent to colleges for students who have taken the ACT more than once will include superscores. A superscore is like a Composite Score in that it is an average of your four subject scores, but for the superscore, ACT selects your best subject score from every test administration. Therefore, your superscore is never lower than any Composite Score, and it is often higher than each of your Composite Scores. Not all schools consider the superscore in admissions, but many do, so check out the superscore policies of the colleges to which you plan to apply.

Since you can only get a superscore after you've taken more than one ACT, it's important to study for the entire test the first time around and work through as much of this book as you can before test day. However, if you're focused on only one, two, or three sections in an effort to raise your superscore, just use those units of this book.

How to Maximize Your Score

What is most important to remember while taking the test is that maximizing all the various scores and subscores depends on getting the most points you can out of every section. You'll find advice on test taking strategies below and in the section management chapters at the end of the English, Math, Reading, and Science sections of this book. However, if you still have a substantial amount of time to prepare for the ACT, the best advice we can give you is to improve the specific skills you need to answer math, verbal, and science questions correctly and efficiently. That's what this book is for. You can work through the chapters and sections in any order you like, and you can skip the lessons you don't need. You don't need to start with English or answer every single question; just use the book. Pick a lesson, read the instructional text, and work your way through the practice questions. There are hundreds of them in this book, and they are very similar to those that you will see on test day. Practice will not only improve your skills but also raise your confidence, and that's very important to test day success.

Interested in generating a personalized study schedule? If you've already registered your book, go online (**kaptest.com/login**) and log in, then click into Plan Your Path. To use Kaplan's study-planning tool, answer three quick questions and download a detailed week-by-week prep calendar. If your plans change, just answer the questions again to make a new schedule.

GO ONLINE

kaptest.com/login

When and Where to Take the ACT

For students testing in the United States or US territories, the ACT test is offered each school year on seven Saturday test dates. Typically, exams are offered in September, October, December, February, April, June, and July. You can take the ACT up to 12 times. Some states offer special administrations of the ACT on different dates, and no test centers are scheduled in California or New York for the July test date. Non-Saturday testing is available by request for students requiring religious or other exemptions.

ACT has plans to introduce section retesting. Once you have taken the four required sections of the ACT on one day, you will be able to retest one, two, or three sections at a time by testing online at an approved testing center on a national test date. Section retesting offers several benefits, but you should be sure to take your first ACT test day seriously; if that's the only time you take the full ACT, it will show up on every score report you send to colleges.

The ACT is administered at schools around the country that serve as testing centers. ACT has introduced online testing at some test centers. Your high school may or may not be a testing center, and the test center most convenient for you may not offer online testing. Check **www.actstudent.org** for a list of testing centers near you. Historically, students have needed to register for the ACT approximately one month in advance to avoid paying a late fee.

Students who are testing outside of the United States or US territories should visit the ACT website for test date and test center information.

The ACT English Test

The ACT English Test will focus on your ability to revise and edit text from a range of content areas.

ACT English Test Overview	
Timing	45 minutes
Questions	75 passage-based multiple-choice questions
Passages	5 single passages with 15 questions each
Passage Length	300–400 words per passage

The ACT English Test will contain five single passages of different genres with a variety of rhetorical situations. A passage could be an argument, an informative or explanatory text, or a narrative.

The most prevalent question format on the ACT English Test will ask you to choose the best of three alternatives to an underlined portion of the passage or to decide that the current version is already the best option. You will be asked to improve the development, organization, and diction in the passages to ensure they conform to conventional standards of English grammar, usage, and style. There are three English Test reporting categories.

Skills Tested by English Test Questions	
Production of Writing (29%–32%)	Topic development and organization, unity, and cohesion
Knowledge of Language (13%–19%)	Precision and conciseness in word choice and consistency in style and tone
Conventions of Standard English (51%–56%)	Sentence structure and formation, punctuation, and usage

The ACT Math Test

The ACT Math Test will focus on mathematical skills typically learned in required math courses before the beginning of grade 12.

ACT Math Test Overview	
Timing	60 minutes
Questions	60 multiple-choice questions

All ACT math questions are multiple-choice questions with five answer choices, and some questions will be part of a set of multiple questions related to the same graph or chart. The Math Test is divided into three reporting categories.

Skills Tested by Math Test Questions	
Preparing for Higher Mathematics (57%–60%)	Using higher-level math to answer questions in five domains: • Number and Quantity (7%–10%) • Algebra (12%–15%) • Functions (12%–15%) • Geometry (12%–15%) • Statistics and Probability (8%–12%)
Integrating Essential Skills (40%–43%)	Using essential concepts and skills to solve more complex problems, including: • Rates and percentages • Area, surface area, and volume • Solving problems using a chain of steps
Modeling (all questions counted within one of the two categories above)	Producing, interpreting, evaluating, and improving models

The ACT Reading Test

The ACT Reading Test will focus on your comprehension and reasoning skills when you are presented with challenging extended passages taken from a variety of content areas.

ACT Reading Test Overview	
Timing	35 minutes
Questions	40 passage-based multiple-choice questions
Passages	3 independent passages and 1 set of paired passages or 4 independent passages
Passage Length	750–1,000 words

Each passage is preceded by a heading that names the passage type, author, and source; this heading may also include important background information related to the passage.

The ACT Reading Test includes four types of passages: prose fiction or literary narrative, social science, humanities, and natural science. One of the four passages will consist of two shorter prose passages that are related in some way. There are three reporting categories for the Reading Test.

Skills Tested by Reading Test Questions	
Key Ideas and Details (55%–60%)	Determining central ideas and themes, summarizing information and ideas, understanding relationships between ideas, and drawing conclusions from facts stated in a passage
Craft and Structure (25%–30%)	Determining word and phrase meanings, analyzing rhetorical word choice, analyzing text structure, and understanding and analyzing purpose and point of view
Integration of Knowledge and Ideas (13%–18%)	Understanding author's claims, differentiating between facts and opinions, using evidence to make connections, analyzing how authors construct arguments, and evaluating reasoning and evidence from various sources

The ACT Science Test

The ACT Science Test will focus on your scientific reasoning ability, not your knowledge of scientific content.

ACT Science Test Overview	
Timing	35 minutes
Questions	40 passage-based multiple-choice questions
Passages	6 passages with 6–8 questions each
Passage Length	100–300 words depending on passage type

There are three passage types on the ACT Science Test:

ACT Science Test Passage Types	
Data Representation (30%–40%)	2 passages, each with multiple figures and/or tables
Research Summaries (45%–55%)	3 passages, each with one or more experiments or studies and usually at least one figure and/or table
Conflicting Viewpoints (15%–20%)	1 passage with at least two viewpoints related to a theory or phenomenon

The ACT Science Test provides three reporting categories:

Skills Tested by Science Test Questions	
Interpretation of Data (45%–55%)	Manipulating and analyzing data in tables, graphs, and diagrams
Scientific Investigation (20%–30%)	Understanding experimental tools, procedures, and design and comparing, extending, and modifying experiments
Evaluation of Models, Inferences, and Experimental Results (25%–35%)	Judging the validity of scientific information and formulating conclusions and predictions based on that information

The ACT Writing Test (Optional)

The ACT Writing Test assesses your writing skills. The Writing Test includes one prompt describing a complex issue and three perspectives related to that prompt. Your goal is to write an essay in which you present your own reasoned perspective; this perspective might—but does not need to—relate to one or more of the three perspectives in the prompt, but your essay must include a discussion of both your own perspective and at least one other. The specific perspective you decide to take will not affect your final score.

The issue discussed in the prompt might be a familiar one, but it might also be completely new to you. The Writing Test will always include a paragraph providing background on the issue because prior knowledge is not required.

The ACT Writing Test will be broken down into four categories for scoring: Ideas and Analysis, Development and Support, Organization, and Language Use and Conventions. Each of these elements will be scored on a scale of 2 to 12, and you will receive a single subject-level writing score, also on a scale of 2 to 12.

Test-Taking Strategies

The ACT is different from the tests you are used to taking in school. For example, on a test given in school, you probably go through the questions in order. You spend more time on the harder questions than on the easier ones because harder questions are usually worth more points. You also probably show your work because your teacher tells you that how you approach a question is as important as getting the correct answer.

This approach is not optimal for the ACT. On the ACT, you benefit from moving around within a section if you come across tough questions because the harder questions are worth the same number of points as the easier questions. Similarly, showing your work is unimportant. It doesn't matter how you arrive at the correct answer—only that you bubble in the correct answer choice.

The good news is that you can use the ACT's particular structure to your advantage. You have already learned about the overall structure of the ACT as well as the structures of the five Tests. The strategies outlined in this section can be applied to any of these tests.

Strategy #1: Triage the Test

You do not need to complete questions on the ACT in order. Every student has different strengths and should attack the test with those strengths in mind. Your main objective on the ACT should be to score as many points as you can. While approaching questions out of order may seem counterintuitive, it is a surefire way to achieve your best score.

Just remember, you can skip around within each Test, but you cannot work on any Test other than the one you've been instructed to work on.

To triage a Test effectively, do the following:

1. Work through all the low-difficulty questions that you can do quickly. Skip questions that are hard or time-consuming.

    *   For the Reading Test, start with the passage you find most manageable and work toward the one you find most challenging. You do not need to go in order.
    *   For the Science Test, start with the passage type you find most manageable and work toward the one you find most challenging. You do not need to go in order.

2. Work through the questions that are doable but time-consuming.

3. Work through the high-difficulty questions.

Strategy #2: Eliminate

Even though there is no wrong-answer penalty on the ACT, Elimination is still a crucial strategy. If you can determine that one or more answer choices are definitely incorrect, you can increase your chances of getting the right answer by paring the selection down.

To eliminate answer choices, do the following:

*   Read each answer choice.
*   Cross out the answer choices that are incorrect.
*   Remember: there is no wrong-answer penalty, so take your best guess.

Strategy #3: Guess

The English, Reading, and Science multiple-choice questions on the ACT have four answer choices and no wrong-answer penalty. That means if you have no idea how to approach a question, you have a 25 percent chance of randomly choosing the correct answer. Even though there's a 75 percent chance of selecting the incorrect answer, you won't lose any points for doing so. The worst that can happen on the ACT is that you'll earn zero points on a question, which means you should always at least take a guess, even when you have no idea what to do. While the probabilities are slightly different for the Math Test, which has five answer choices, the logic is the same.

When guessing on a question, do the following:

*   Try to strategically eliminate answer choices before guessing.
*   If you run out of time, or have no idea what a question is asking, pick a Letter of the Day.

A "Letter of the Day" is an answer choice letter [A/F, B/G, C/H, D/J, or (math only) E/K] that you choose before test day to select for questions you guess on. You can use the same Letter of the Day for the entire ACT or change it depending on the section, but you should always use the same Letter of the Day within an individual section.

ACT English

The Method for ACT English

How to Do ACT English

The English Test of the ACT tests a limited number of grammar errors and style or logic issues. You should feel empowered by familiarizing yourself with these recurring errors and issues and learn to spot them and address them quickly and efficiently. We'll describe the issues that you're likely to see on test day and how to deal with them in the next two chapters. In this chapter, we'll present a simple series of steps for tackling English questions.

Take a look at the passage and questions below and think about how you would approach them on test day. Then compare your approach to the recommendations that follow.

Gregory Hines, a Beloved Icon

During the last five decades of the 20th century; Gregory Hines enriched musical theater with his performances as a star of the Broadway stage. A multitalented artist, he was also employed as an actor, a director, and a producer in television and film. He had the experience of earning and receiving numerous awards, including a Tony and a Daytime Emmy.

Hines began performing as a dancer when he was five, touring professionally in nightclubs across the country with his older brother, Maurice, as a duo. Hines found inspiration in watching fellow performers such as the Nicholas Brothers and Sandman Sims. At eight, he made his Broadway debut and remained a star of the stage in a variety of musicals, including *Eubie!*, *Sophisticated Ladies*, and *Jelly's Last Jam.*

1. A. NO CHANGE
   B. century, Gregory
   C. century. Gregory
   D. century, from the 1950s to the late 1990s,

2. F. NO CHANGE
   G. had the experience of earning
   H. had the experience of receiving
   J. earned

3. Which choice provides the most specific information regarding Hines's Broadway performances?

   A. NO CHANGE
   B. which debuted at various locations among the many venues of Broadway.
   C. which opened at different times throughout Hines's considerably long career.
   D. all of which were evaluated by the rotating group of dozens of theatre professionals who are selected by the Tony Awards Administration Committee.

There is no need to read the entire passage before you start to answer questions. Instead, answer them as you read. When you see a number, finish the sentence you are reading and then look at the corresponding question. If you can answer the question based on what you've read so far, do so—this will likely be the case if the question is testing grammar. If you need more information—which may happen if the question is testing organization or relevance—keep reading until you have enough context to answer the question.

Sometimes the issue being tested will be obvious to you when you look at the underlined segment. If it isn't, glance at the answer choices to help you determine what the test maker is after. For instance, in question 1 above, a semicolon is underlined. A quick glance at the choices shows that most of them have the same words in the same order, and only the punctuation marks are different; this means that the question is testing punctuation. **Identifying the issue**, using the choices if necessary, is step 1 of the English method.

To determine the correct punctuation, use the surrounding text. "During the last five decades of the 20th century" is an introductory phrase and cannot stand on its own, so A and C are incorrect; what comes before and after either a period (choice C) or a semicolon (choice A) must be able to stand on its own as a complete sentence. **Eliminating answer choices that do not address the issue** is step 2 of the English method.

There may be more than one choice that addresses the issue. When that happens, you need to base your final response on three considerations: conciseness, relevance, and the potential of a given choice to introduce a new error. The two remaining choices are both grammatically correct and relevant to the surrounding context. However, (B) is more concise and therefore the correct answer. Choice D can be eliminated because "from the 1950s to the late 1990s" is redundant; the sentence already says "the last five decades of the 20th century." **Choosing the most concise and relevant response from those that are grammatically correct** is step 3 of the English method.

Here's what we did:

ACT ENGLISH METHOD

Step 1. Identify the issue (use the choices if need be)

Step 2. Eliminate answer choices that do not address the issue

Step 3. Plug in the remaining answer choices and select the most *correct*, *concise*, and *relevant* one

---

Some questions include errors that may not seem apparent. For example, the underlined segment in question 2 is grammatically correct but wordy. Start by **identifying the issue**, using the choices if necessary. The answer choices are shorter than the original text, so conciseness is likely the issue being tested. **Eliminating answer choices that do not address the issue** is next, and F can definitely be eliminated due to wordiness. **Finally, plugging in the remaining choices and choosing the most correct, concise, and relevant one** points you to (J): the single word *earned* expresses the same information as the much longer phrase "had the experience of earning and receiving." Choices G and H are shorter than the original, but they are not nearly as concise as (J).

Other questions may ask you to determine which answer choice provides the most specific description of a particular aspect of the passage. In those instances, **identifying the issue** is straightforward. **Eliminating answer choices that do not address the issue** is essential to answering this type of question. Question 3 requires you to determine which option provides the most specific information about Hines's Broadway performances. Eliminate B and C because they do not include specific details. **Plug in the remaining choices** and eliminate D because the process by which plays are evaluated by the Tony Awards Administration Committee is not relevant to the passage. Choice (A) is the correct answer.

Correct, **concise**, and **relevant** means that the answer choice you select:

- Has no grammatical errors
- Is as short as possible while retaining the writer's intended meaning
- Is relevant to the paragraph and the passage as a whole

Correct answers do NOT:

- Provide information that contradicts or is irrelevant to the ideas developed by the original sentence, paragraph, or passage
- Introduce new grammatical errors

How Much Have You Learned?

Directions: Take as much time as you need on these questions. Work carefully and methodically. Practice using the steps that you just learned.

Liberal Arts Education

[1]

The concept of liberal arts has existed since the time of ancient Greece, and the parameters of liberal arts study have remained largely <u>over the centuries</u> unchanged. [A] In essence, liberal arts are defined as "any study given to reflection and free inquiry," which

is a <u>lengthy</u> category that has included various subjects throughout its history.

[2]

In medieval times, the seven liberal arts were divided into two parts: the Trivium ("the three roads") and the Quadrivium ("the four roads"). [B] The Trivium consisted of grammar, rhetoric, and <u>logic, the Quadrivium</u> consisted of arithmetic, geometry, astronomy, and music. However, the description of a liberal arts college is somewhat more limiting. A liberal arts college

generally <u>awarded</u> a Bachelor of Arts degree after four years of study, primarily enrolls full-time students between the ages of 18 and 24, typically has between 800 and 1,800 students, and does not provide professional or vocational preparation.

1. The best placement for the underlined portion would be:

   A.   where it is now.
   B.   after the word *concept*.
   C.   after the word *arts*.
   D.   after the word *unchanged*.

2. Which choice best indicates that liberal arts include many disciplines?

   F.   NO CHANGE
   G.   broad
   H.   challenging
   J.   perplexing

3. A.   NO CHANGE
   B.   logic; while the Quadrivium
   C.   logic, so the Quadrivium
   D.   logic; the Quadrivium

4. F.   NO CHANGE
   G.   have awarded
   H.   award
   J.   awards

[3]

Liberal arts has been the primary focus of undergraduate education in the United States <u>since</u>
₅
the United States was only a British colony. [C] The number of liberal arts colleges in the United States

<u>steady increased</u> throughout the 20th century as private
₆
universities, state universities, and community

colleges all sought to <u>give their</u> undergraduates a broad
₇
education. [D]

[4]

The content of liberal arts study still focuses on the arts, humanities, and <u>sciences, and</u> the basic notion of
₈
forming well-rounded students in these areas is still the concept behind liberal arts education today. There

is some concern, however, that the philosophy behind liberal arts education <u>does not reflect the current times</u>
₉
<u>in which today's students are living.</u> Responding to this
₉

5. A. NO CHANGE
    B. because
    C. even though
    D. while

6. F. NO CHANGE
    G. steadily increased
    H. increased in a steady fashion
    J. increased in a steadily fashion

7. A. NO CHANGE
    B. give its
    C. giving their
    D. gave its

8. F. NO CHANGE
    G. sciences; and
    H. sciences. And
    J. sciences: and

9. A. NO CHANGE
    B. does not reflect the latest trends in education and the current times in which today's students are living.
    C. does not reflect the times in which today's students are living or the times in which future students will live.
    D. does not reflect the times in which today's students are living.

concern, <u>courses in computer science and information</u>
₁₀
<u>technology have been added to the curriculum of many</u>
₁₀
<u>colleges and universities.</u> Does this mean the end of
₁₀

10. F. NO CHANGE

    G. computer science and information technology courses have been added to the curriculum of many colleges and universities.

    H. computer science and information technology are the subject of courses that have been added to the curriculum of many colleges and universities.

    J. many colleges and universities have added courses in computer science and information technology to their curriculum.

liberal arts education as it has been practiced since the days of Martianus Capella? <u>I don't</u> believe so.
₁₁

11. A. NO CHANGE

    B. Many educators don't

    C. You wouldn't

    D. We don't

<u>Most liberal arts colleges award master's and doctoral</u>
₁₂
<u>degrees as well.</u> The study of liberal arts may have to
₁₂
evolve with the times, but its basic premise—that

12. The writer is considering deleting the underlined sentence. Should the writer make this deletion?

    F. Yes, because it contradicts information earlier in the paragraph.

    G. Yes, because it interrupts the writer's discussion of modern liberal arts education with irrelevant information.

    H. No, because it provides an example showing how liberal arts education is still relevant.

    J. No, because it makes a claim important to the writer's overall argument.

well-rounded students are well-educated students—<u>remain</u>
₁₃
as valid today as it was in medieval times.

13. A. NO CHANGE

    B. remaining

    C. remains

    D. remained

Questions 14 and 15 ask about the passage as a whole.

---

14. The writer wants to add the following sentence to the essay:

    > The late 1800s saw an expansion of liberal arts colleges as the right to education began to include minorities and women.

    If the writer were to add this sentence, it would most logically be placed at:

    F.   Point A in Paragraph 1.

    G.   Point B in Paragraph 2.

    H.   Point C in Paragraph 3.

    J.   Point D in Paragraph 3.

15. Suppose the writer's primary purpose had been to write an essay summarizing the history of higher education in the United States. Would this essay accomplish this purpose?

    A.   Yes, because it discusses the natural evolution of liberal arts, which is taught only at the collegiate level.

    B.   Yes, because it explains how most liberal arts colleges award master's and doctoral degrees as well.

    C.   No, because it does not mention higher education anywhere.

    D.   No, because it focuses exclusively on liberal arts education rather than higher education as a whole.

Reflect

Directions: Take a few minutes to recall what you've learned and what you've been practicing in this chapter. Consider the following questions, jot down your best answer for each one, and then compare your reflections to the expert responses on the following page. Use your level of confidence to determine what to do next.

1. What does an ACT expert look for when answering an ACT English question?

   _____

   _____

   _____

2. Describe at least three types of issues that could be present in English questions.

   _____

   _____

   _____

3. How does eliminating choices that do not address the issue make it easier to identify the correct answer?

   _____

   _____

   _____

4. Why do correct answers need to be grammatically correct, concise, and relevant?

   _____

   _____

   _____

Responses

1. What does an ACT expert look for when answering an ACT English question?

ACT experts look for clues in both the passage and answer choices—and question stem, if one is present—to help identify the issue and determine which choices are correct and which are incorrect. These include punctuation marks, answer choice lengths, and words such as "relevant" in the question stem.

2. Describe at least three types of issues that could be present in English questions.

Punctuation issues could involve commas, colons, parentheses, and other punctuation marks. Correct answers should be concise, so incorrect choices could use more words than necessary. Correct answers should not add information that contradicts or is irrelevant to the rest of the passage.

3. How does eliminating choices that do not address the issue make it easier to identify the correct answer?

When you identify choices that must be incorrect because they don't address the issue, you save time by eliminating them without plugging them in and checking for correctness, conciseness, and relevance.

4. Why do correct answers need to be grammatically correct, concise, and relevant?

It's not enough for an answer choice to be grammatically correct or concise or relevant. The correct answer to an ACT English question must be grammatically correct, concise, and relevant, and incorrect choices will often only meet one or two—but not all three!—of these criteria.

Next Steps

If you answered most questions correctly in the "How Much Have You Learned?" section, and if your responses to the Reflect questions were similar to those of an expert, then consider the ACT English Method an area of strength and move on to the next chapter. Do keep using the method as you work on the questions in future chapters.

If you don't yet feel confident, review those parts of this chapter that you have not yet mastered and try the questions you missed again. As always, be sure to review the explanations closely. Also, go online (**kaptest.com/login**) to watch a video about the Method for ACT English questions and to use your Qbank for more practice. If you haven't already registered your book, do so at *kaptest.com/moreonline*.

GO ONLINE

kaptest.com/login

Answers and Explanations

How Much Have You Learned?

1. D

Difficulty: Medium

Category: Sentence Structure

Getting to the Answer: The phrase "over the centuries" must be placed logically and punctuated properly. Its original position interrupts the phrase "largely unchanged," so A is incorrect. Choices B and C are incorrect because placing the phrase at the beginning of the sentence is not logical; "over the centuries" is not referring to the concept of liberal arts but rather to the parameters of liberal arts study. Placing the phrase at the end of the sentence is logical and does not require additional punctuation, so (D) is correct.

2. G

Difficulty: Medium

Category: Development

Getting to the Answer: The word *broad* means "covering a large number of subjects or areas," so (G) is correct. Choices F, H, and J are incorrect because they do not clearly express the idea that liberal arts include a variety of subjects.

3. D

Difficulty: Medium

Category: Sentence Structure

Getting to the Answer: As written, the sentence is a run-on; a comma cannot connect two independent clauses without a FANBOYS (For, And, Nor, But, Or, Yet, So) coordinating conjunction, so A is incorrect. Although there are a number of ways to correct a run-on sentence, only one answer choice will do so without introducing additional errors. Choices B, C, and (D) all address the run-on error. However, B uses a semicolon while also making the second clause dependent. The conjunction *so* in C creates a cause-and-effect relationship between the clauses that is inappropriate in context. Only (D) corrects the run-on and does not introduce new errors.

4. J

Difficulty: Medium

Category: Agreement

Getting to the Answer: Items in a list must be in parallel form. As written, this list includes four verb phrases, but they are not parallel, so F is incorrect. Choice G is incorrect because it includes present perfect tense, which does not agree with the simple present tense verb phrases in the rest of the list. Choice H is in present tense, but the plural verb *award* does not match the singular subject *college*. The present-tense singular verb *awards* agrees with both the subject and the rest of the sentence, so (J) is correct.

5. A

Difficulty: Medium

Category: Organization

Getting to the Answer: When a transition word is underlined, check that it correctly represents the relationship between the ideas it connects. In this sentence, the transition needs to convey that liberal arts have been the focus of colleges in the United States "from the time when" the country was still a British colony. *Since* does exactly that, so choice (A) is correct. Choices B, C, and D all incorrectly change the relationship between the parts of the sentence.

6. G

Difficulty: Medium

Category: Agreement

Getting to the Answer: Adjectives can modify only nouns and pronouns; all other parts of speech are modified by adverbs. As written, the sentence uses the adjective *steady* to modify the verb *increased*, so F is incorrect. Both (G) and H correct the error, but H is unnecessarily wordy, so (G) is correct. Choice J incorrectly uses the adverb *steadily* to modify the noun *fashion*.

7. A

Difficulty: Medium

Category: Agreement

Getting to the Answer: Check underlined verbs and pronouns for agreement errors. The infinitive verb *to give* is idiomatically correct with *sought*, and *their* agrees with its plural antecedent *colleges*. (A) is correct. Choices B and D pair a singular pronoun with a plural antecedent; C and D do not properly construct the infinitive verb form.

8. F

Difficulty: Medium

Category: Sentence Structure

Getting to the Answer: Carefully examine the different punctuation marks. Here, the comma is used together with a coordinating conjunction to join two independent clauses, so (F) is correct. Although the semicolon in G can join two independent clauses, it cannot be used together with a coordinating conjunction. The period in H creates a sentence fragment. Finally, J is incorrect because a colon cannot link two independent clauses.

9. D

Difficulty: Medium

Category: Conciseness

Getting to the Answer: As written, the underlined portion includes a redundancy with the words *current* and *today's*. Choice (D) corrects this error by omitting the word *current*. Choices B and C are incorrect because they are even wordier than the original.

10. J

Difficulty: Medium

Category: Sentence Structure

Getting to the Answer: An introductory clause generally modifies the noun that immediately follows it. As written, this sentence says that "courses in computer science and information technology" are "Responding to this concern." Choice F is incorrect. Choice (J) correctly puts the noun phrase, "many colleges and universities," immediately after the modifying clause. Choices G and H do not address the error.

11. B

Difficulty: Medium

Category: Agreement

Getting to the Answer: The sentence includes a pronoun that does not match the surrounding text. The author does not use the first-person pronoun *I* anywhere else in the essay, so A is incorrect. The author does not address the audience directly or use the word *we*, so C and D are incorrect. Choice (B) correctly uses "Many educators" instead of a pronoun.

12. G

Difficulty: Medium

Category: Development

Getting to the Answer: When deciding whether to delete a sentence, identify the purpose of the paragraph and determine whether the sentence supports it. This paragraph discusses concerns about liberal arts education in modern times. The sentence states that liberal arts schools also offer advanced degrees, which is not pertinent to the paragraph. Eliminate H and J. Choice (G) correctly identifies the sentence as an irrelevant interruption.

13. C

Difficulty: Medium

Category: Agreement

Getting to the Answer: A verb must agree with its subject, which may not be the noun closest to it in the sentence. Although the plural noun *students* is the closest noun to the verb *remain*, the verb's subject is actually the singular noun *premise*, so A is incorrect. Choice (C) corrects the agreement error. Choice B creates a sentence fragment, and D uses a past-tense verb that does not match the surrounding verbs, which are in present tense.

14. H

Difficulty: Medium

Category: Development

Getting to the Answer: Consider where in the essay a reference to "The late 1800s" would fit best. Choice (H) correctly places the sentence between a reference to "the United States since it was a British colony" and "the 20th century." Choices F, G, and J position the sentence illogically within the essay, either too early or too late in the history of liberal arts education.

15. D

Difficulty: High

Category: Development

Getting to the Answer: First, answer the "yes" or "no" part of the question. While the author does outline the history of liberal arts, higher education encompasses more than just "arts, humanities, and sciences." Eliminate A and B. Choice C is incorrect because the author does mention higher education throughout the essay. Choice (D) is correct.

CHAPTER 3

Spotting and Fixing Errors: Sentence Structure, Punctuation, and Agreement

LEARNING OBJECTIVES

After completing this chapter, you will be able to:

- Determine the correct punctuation and/or conjunctions to form a complete sentence
- Identify and correct inappropriate uses of semicolons
- Set off simple parenthetical elements using punctuation
- Identify and correct inappropriate uses of commas, dashes, and colons
- Identify and correct verb agreement issues
- Identify and correct pronoun agreement issues
- Identify and correct modifier agreement issues
- Identify and correct inappropriate uses of apostrophes
- Identify and correct expressions that deviate from idiomatic English

Sentence Structure: 9/36 SmartPoints® (Very high yield)

Agreement: 10/36 SmartPoints® (Very high yield)

How Much Do You Know?

Directions: Try out the questions below. The "Category" heading in the explanation for each question gives the title of the lesson that covers how to answer it. If you answered the question(s) for a given lesson correctly, you may be able to move quickly through that lesson. If you answered incorrectly, you may want to take your time on that lesson.

The Bebop Movement

For a jazz musician in New York City in the 1940s. The most interesting place to spend the hours between midnight and dawn was likely a Harlem nightclub called Minton's. After finishing their jobs at other clubs, young musicians like Charlie Parker, Dizzy Gillespie, Kenny Clarke, and Thelonious Monk would gather at Minton's and have "jam" sessions, or informal performances featuring lengthy group and solo improvisations, the all-night sessions resulted in the birth of modern jazz as these African American artists together forged a new sound, known as bebop.

Unlike "swing," the enormously popular jazz played in the 1930s, bebop was not dance music. Often it had been blindingly fast, incorporated irregular rhythms, and featured discordant sounds that jazz audiences had never heard before. The harmonic complexity of bebop distinguished it from other forms of jazz at the time. Bebop, unlike other forms of jazz, was based on a 12-note scale, thereby opening up vast new harmonic opportunities for musicians.

The musicians who pioneered bebop shared, two common elements, a vision of the new music's possibilities and astonishing improvisational skill—the ability to play or compose a musical line on the spur of

1.   A.   NO CHANGE
     B.   1940s; the
     C.   1940s, the
     D.   1940s, it was when the

2.   F.   NO CHANGE
     G.   improvisations and the all-night sessions
     H.   improvisations, the all-night sessions,
     J.   improvisations. The all-night sessions

3.   A.   NO CHANGE
     B.   was going to be blindingly fast, incorporated irregular rhythms, and featured discordant sounds
     C.   was blindingly fast, incorporated irregular rhythms, and featured discordant sounds
     D.   was blindingly fast, incorporated irregular rhythms, and featuring discordant sounds

4.   F.   NO CHANGE
     G.   shared two common elements: a vision
     H.   shared, two common elements a vision
     J.   shared two common elements a vision

the moment. As the essence of jazz, <u>providing the context</u>
<u>of a group setting for improvisation is paramount.</u>
5

5. A. NO CHANGE
   B. improvisation within the context of a group setting is paramount.
   C. paramount is improvisation within the context of a group setting.
   D. paramount is the context of a group setting for improvisation.

Parker, perhaps the <u>most great</u> instrumental genius jazz has
6
known, was a brilliant improviser. He often played twice as
fast as the rest of the band, but his solos, infused with

6. F. NO CHANGE
   G. most greatest
   H. greater
   J. greatest

creativity, <u>was</u> always in rhythm and exquisitely shaped,
7
revealing a harmonic imagination that enthralled his
listeners.

7. A. NO CHANGE
   B. is
   C. are
   D. were

   Unfortunately, the bebop movement, like many
revolutions that fought <u>its</u> way into mainstream culture,
8
initially encountered heavy resistance. Opposition came

8. F. NO CHANGE
   G. it's
   H. their
   J. there

not only from older jazz musicians initially, <u>but also, later</u>
9
<u>and more lastingly</u> from a general public alienated
9

9. A. NO CHANGE
   B. but, later and more lastingly
   C. but, later and more lastingly—
   D. but also—later and more lastingly—

by the music <u>genre's</u> complexity and sophistication.
10
Furthermore, due to the government ban on

10. F. NO CHANGE
    G. genres'
    H. genres's
    J. genres

<u>recording, that was, in effect,</u> during the early years of
11
World War II (records were made of vinyl, a petroleum
product that was essential to the war effort), the

11. A. NO CHANGE
    B. recording that was in effect
    C. recording that was; in effect
    D. recording—that was in effect

creative ferment that first produced bebop <u>most remains</u>
12
undocumented today.

12. F. NO CHANGE
    G. remains most
    H. remains mostly
    J. remain mostly

English

Check Your Work

1.   C

Difficulty: Low

Category: Sentence Structure: The Basics

Getting to the Answer: As written, the phrase before the period is a sentence fragment, so A is incorrect. Replacing the period with a semicolon does not address this issue, so B is incorrect. Choice (C) fixes the fragment by joining the dependent clause "For a jazz musician in New York City in the 1940s" and the independent clause "the most interesting place to spend the hours between midnight and dawn was likely a Harlem nightclub called Minton's" with a comma. Choice D both creates an illogical sentence structure and is unnecessarily wordy. Choice (C) is correct.

2.   J

Difficulty: Low

Category: Sentence Structure: The Basics

Getting to the Answer: As written, the underlined portion creates a run-on sentence, so F is incorrect. Eliminate G because replacing the comma with a coordinate conjunction (in this case, the word *and*) does not fix the run-on. Adding a comma after *sessions* does not fix the run-on either, so H is also incorrect. Choice (J) correctly separates the two independent clauses with a period.

3.   C

Difficulty: Medium

Category: Agreement: Verbs

Getting to the Answer: As written, the sentence includes a list of three verbs that are not in parallel form. A is incorrect. Eliminate B and D, since their verbs are also not in parallel form. Choice (C) correctly uses three past-tense verb phrases.

4.   G

Difficulty: Medium

Category: Sentence Structure: Commas, Dashes, and Colons

Getting to the Answer: Colons are used to introduce lists or short phrases, so a colon is appropriate to use after *elements*. (G) is correct. Choice F is incorrect because the phrase "two common elements" is essential to the sentence, so it should not be surrounded by commas. Choice H incorrectly separates a verb from its object, and J incorrectly omits punctuation altogether.

5.   B

Difficulty: High

Category: Agreement: Modifiers

Getting to the Answer: "As the essence of jazz" is an introductory modifying phrase, so the word(s) that immediately follow the comma must be the item(s) being modified. The word *improvisation* must come after the comma because the passage indicates that "jam" sessions, or informal performances, are the essence of jazz. (B) is correct. Choices A, C, and D do not put the word *improvisation* after the comma, so they all display modification errors.

6.   J

Difficulty: Low

Category: Agreement: Modifiers

Getting to the Answer: Eliminate F and G because "most great" and "most greatest" are idiomatically incorrect. Choice H does not create an idiom error, but the comparative form of *great* should be used only when exactly two objects or individuals are being compared. Choice (J) correctly uses the superlative form.

7.   D

Difficulty: Medium

Category: Agreement: Verbs

Getting to the Answer: If a verb is underlined, make sure that it agrees with its subject. The subject, *solos*, is plural, and the verb *was* is singular, so A is incorrect. Eliminate B because it is also singular. Choice C is plural but in the present tense. Choice (D) is plural and correctly uses the past tense, which matches the tense of the rest of the paragraph.

8.   H

Difficulty: Medium

Category: Agreement: Pronouns

Getting to the Answer: When a pronoun is underlined, check that it agrees with its antecedent, the noun to which it refers. The antecedent is the plural noun *revolutions*, so the plural pronoun *their* is needed; (H) is correct. Choice F is incorrect because *its* is singular. Choices G and J do not make sense in context; *it's* means "it is," and *there* indicates location, not possession.

9.   D

Difficulty: High

Category: Sentence Structure: Parenthetical Elements

Getting to the Answer: The phrase "later and more lastingly" is a parenthetical phrase that must be properly punctuated. Only (D) correctly sets it off from the rest of the sentence. In addition, B and C incorrectly omit the word *also*, which must be included because the sentence includes the first part of the idiomatic phrase "not only … but also."

10.   F

Difficulty: Medium

Category: Agreement: Modifiers

Getting to the Answer: The word *genre's* is a singular possessive noun. It makes sense in context because the sentence is describing the "complexity and sophistication" of a single genre of music. (F) is correct. Choices G and H are possessive, but they are both plural. In addition, H incorrectly adds an extra *s* after the apostrophe; *genres's* is considered grammatically incorrect in any context. Finally, Choice J does not show possession at all.

11.   B

Difficulty: Medium

Category: Sentence Structure: Commas, Dashes, and Colons

Getting to the Answer: When a punctuation mark is underlined, make sure that it is actually necessary. Commas, semicolons, and dashes all separate elements of the sentence into different logical units. Since the phrase "recording that was in effect" is one cohesive phrase, no punctuation of any sort should be used. Choice (B) is correct.

12.   H

Difficulty: Medium

Category: Agreement: Modifiers

Getting to the Answer: As written, the phrase *most remains* is in the wrong order. Additionally, it uses the adjective *most,* instead of the adverb *mostly,* to modify the adjective *undocumented.* Choice (H) is the only option that is in the correct order, uses an adverb, and does not introduce a new error. J incorrectly changes the singular verb *remains* to the plural verb *remain,* which does not agree with the singular subject *ferment.*

Sentence Structure: The Basics

LEARNING OBJECTIVES

After this lesson, you will be able to:

● Determine the correct punctuation and/or conjunctions to form a complete sentence

● Identify and correct inappropriate uses of semicolons

To answer a question like this:

Women's Suffrage

The struggle for women's suffrage in the United States began several decades before national legislation was <u>enacted and the</u> movement included a myriad of efforts that culminated in nationwide voting rights nearly fifty years after the birth of the women's suffrage movement.

1. A. NO CHANGE
    B. enacted, the
    C. enacted; the
    D. enacted but the

You need to know this:

Fragments and Run-ons

A complete sentence must express a complete thought and have both a subject and a verb. If any one of these elements is missing, the sentence is a **fragment**. You can recognize a fragment because the sentence will not make sense as written.

Missing Element	Example	Corrected Sentence
Subject	*Ran a marathon.*	*Lola ran a marathon.*
Verb	*Lola a marathon.*	
Complete thought	*While Lola ran a marathon.*	*While Lola ran a marathon, her friends cheered for her.*

The fragment, "While Lola ran a marathon" is an example of a dependent clause: it has a subject (Lola) and a verb (ran), but it does not express a complete thought because it starts with a subordinating conjunction (while). Notice what the word *while* does to the meaning: While Lola ran a marathon, what happened? To fix this type of fragment, eliminate the subordinating conjunction or join the dependent clause to an independent clause using a comma. Subordinating conjunctions are words and phrases such as *since*, *because*, *therefore*, *unless*, *although*, and *due to*.

Unlike a dependent clause, an independent clause can stand on its own as a complete sentence. If a sentence has more than one independent clause, those clauses must be properly joined. If they are not, the sentence is a **run-on**: *Lucas enjoys hiking, he climbs a new mountain every summer*. There are several ways to correct a run-on:

To correct a run-on	Example
Use a period	*Lucas enjoys hiking. He climbs a new mountain every summer.*
Use a semicolon	*Lucas enjoys hiking; he climbs a new mountain every summer.*
Use a colon	*Lucas enjoys hiking: he climbs a new mountain every summer.*
Make one clause dependent	*Since Lucas enjoys hiking, he climbs a new mountain every summer.*
Add a FANBOYS conjunction: For, And, Nor, But, Or, Yet, So	*Lucas enjoys hiking, so he climbs a new mountain every summer.*
Add a dash	*Lucas enjoys hiking—he climbs a new mountain every summer.*

Semicolons

Semicolons are used in one specific way on the ACT:

Use a semicolon to . . .	Example
Join two independent clauses that are not connected by a comma and a FANBOYS conjunction	*Gaby knew that her term paper would take at least four hours to write; she got started in study hall and then finished it at home.*

You need to do this:

To recognize and correct errors involving fragments, run-ons, and semicolons, familiarize yourself with the ways in which they are tested.

- Fragments
  - If a sentence is missing a subject, a verb, or a complete thought, it is a fragment.
  - Correct the fragment by adding the missing element.
- Run-ons
  - If a sentence includes two independent clauses, they must be properly joined.
  - Employ one of the following options to properly punctuate independent clauses:
    - Use a period
    - Insert a semicolon
    - Use a comma and a FANBOYS (For, And, Nor, But, Or, Yet, So) conjunction
    - Use a dash
    - Make one clause dependent by using a subordinating conjunction (since, because, therefore, unless, although, due to, etc.)
- Semicolon Use
  - A semicolon is used to join two independent clauses that are not connected by a comma and a FANBOYS conjunction.

Explanation:

The clauses before and after the word *and* are independent clauses and must be punctuated properly. Choice (C) correctly uses a semicolon to join the two clauses. Choices A, B, and D include either a comma or a coordinating conjunction but not both, so they are incorrect.

Drills

If sentence formation or semicolons give you trouble, study the information above and try out these drill questions before completing the Try on Your Own questions below. Drill answers can be found on the bottom of the next page.

a. Correct the fragment by adding a subject: Volunteered to organize the upcoming fundraiser.

b. Correct the fragment by completing the thought: Upon finding the misplaced house keys.

c. Correct the run-on sentence by adding a punctuation mark: The historic center of town was restored it once again bustled with activity.

d. Correct the run-on sentence by adding a punctuation mark: Logical thinking is essential to scientific research the irony is that scientists who make important discoveries often do so on a hunch.

e. Make one clause dependent to correct the run-on sentence: The local farms had a poor harvest last year, the price of produce at the market has risen dramatically.

Try on Your Own

Directions: Take as much time as you need on these questions. Work carefully and methodically. There will be an opportunity for timed practice at the end of the chapter.

Espresso 89

For what seemed like <u>eons; people</u> in my
₂
neighborhood complained about the lack of coffee shops in our community. The discussions at times became

<u>passionate, and it</u> seemed that my neighbors believed
₃
that a coffee shop would cure just about any problem our suburban neighborhood faced. Not a coffee drinker, I remained unconvinced that a venue to purchase coffee would make a significant difference. However, when a

coffee shop did open <u>nearby. I</u> discovered that it offered
₄
much more than warm beverages and convenient snacks. Ingrid and Gus, the owners of Espresso 89,

2.　F.　NO CHANGE

　　G.　eons, people

　　H.　eons, and people

　　J.　eons. People

3.　Which of the following replacements for the underlined segment of the sentence would NOT be acceptable?

　　A.　passionate it

　　B.　passionate; it

　　C.　passionate. It

　　D.　so passionate that it

4.　F.　NO CHANGE

　　G.　nearby, I

　　H.　nearby and

　　J.　nearby, and also I

Drill answers from previous page:

Note: These are not the only ways to correct the sentences; your answers may differ.

a. **The student** volunteered to organize the upcoming fundraiser.

b. Upon finding the misplaced house keys, **Hannah locked the front door.**

c. The historic center of town was restored. **It** once again bustled with activity.

d. Logical thinking is essential to scientific research**;** the irony is that scientists who make important discoveries often do so on a hunch.

e. The local farms had a poor harvest last year, **so** the price of produce at the market has risen dramatically.

work diligently to create an inclusive atmosphere thanks
                                        ‾‾‾‾‾‾‾‾‾‾‾‾‾‾‾
                                               5
to their dedication, their shop serves as a community

center for the area.

Espresso 89 began by inviting a local artist to

display her paintings on the walls of the shop and

holding a "gallery" opening for the occasion. Ingrid

and Gus encouraged other local artists to sign up

for future opportunities to share their work with the

coffee-drinking public. Two or three nights a week,

Espresso 89 hosts music or literary events that provide

entertainment and the opportunity for local artists

to showcase their talent. A retired elementary school

teacher conducts a weekly children's story hour she
                                          ‾‾‾‾‾‾‾‾
                                               6
offers storybook after storybook to delighted children
‾‾‾‾‾
  6
and their grateful parents.

5. A. NO CHANGE
    B. atmosphere, thanks
    C. atmosphere—thanks
    D. atmosphere so thanks

6. F. NO CHANGE
    G. hour, she offers
    H. hour; offering
    J. hour, offering

Sentence Structure: Parenthetical Elements

LEARNING OBJECTIVE

After this lesson, you will be able to:

- Set off simple parenthetical elements using punctuation

To answer a question like this:

The Nineteenth <u>Amendment which granted all</u>
₁
<u>American women the right to vote, was</u> passed by
₁
Congress on June 4, 1919.

1. A. NO CHANGE

    B. Amendment, which granted all American women the right to vote, was

    C. Amendment which granted all American women the right to vote was

    D. Amendment which granted all American women the right to vote—was

You need to know this:

Answer choices often move punctuation marks around, replace them with other punctuation marks, or remove them altogether. When underlined portions include commas, dashes, or parentheses, check to make sure the punctuation is used correctly in context.

Parenthetical Elements

Parenthetical elements may appear at the beginning, in the middle, or at the end of a sentence. They must be properly punctuated with parentheses, commas, or dashes for the sentence to be grammatically correct. A phrase such as *the capital of France* is considered parenthetical if the rest of the sentence is grammatically correct when it is removed. Do not mix and match; a parenthetical element must begin and end with the same type of punctuation.

Parenthetical element placement	Parentheses	Comma(s)	Dash(es)
Beginning	*N/A*	*The capital of France, Paris is a popular tourist destination.*	*N/A*
Middle	*Paris (the capital of France) is a popular tourist destination.*	*Paris, the capital of France, is a popular tourist destination.*	*Paris—the capital of France—is a popular tourist destination.*
End	*A popular tourist destination is Paris (the capital of France).*	*A popular tourist destination is Paris, the capital of France.*	*A popular tourist destination is Paris—the capital of France.*

You need to do this:

If the underlined portion includes punctuation, ask yourself:

- Is the punctuation used correctly?

 The commas, dashes, or parentheses need to set off a parenthetical element, be used consistently, and be placed in the correct location.

- Is the punctuation necessary?

 If you cannot identify a reason why the punctuation is included, the punctuation should be removed.

Explanation:

The phrase "which granted all American women the right to vote" is a parenthetical element that must be set off from the rest of the sentence with either two commas or two dashes. Choice (B) is correct.

Drills

If parenthetical elements give you trouble, study the information above and try out these drill questions before completing the Try on Your Own questions below. Drill answers can be found on the bottom of the next page.

a.   Use a comma to correctly punctuate the parenthetical element at the beginning of the sentence: Delayed for two hours due to a thunderstorm the baseball game started much later than fans had expected.

b.   Use parentheses to correctly punctuate the parenthetical element in the middle of the sentence: *The Heart of a Woman* originally published in 1981 is one of Maya Angelou's most popular books.

c.   Use commas to correctly punctuate the parenthetical element in the middle of the sentence: The architect a keen observer known for her meticulous attention to detail gently pointed out the error in her coworker's design.

d.   Use dashes to correctly punctuate the parenthetical element in the middle of the sentence: Contemporary Hawaiian quilts which are often featured at the Mokupāpapa Discovery Center reflect an eclectic blend of Hawaiian tradition and modern vision.

e.   Use a comma to correctly punctuate the parenthetical element at the end of the sentence: A hurricane's strength is rated on a scale of 1 to 5 depending on the speed of sustained winds.

Try on Your Own

Directions: Take as much time as you need on these questions. Work carefully and methodically. There will be an opportunity for timed practice at the end of the chapter.

Medusa

For more than two thousand <u>years; Medusa</u> has been a prominent image in the world of art and the world of myth. As far back as 200 BCE, images of

<u>Medusa—the defeated Gorgon, abounded</u>. The shield of Alexander the Great, for example, was graced with an image of the mythical Medusa with her locks of

live <u>serpents, and</u> a gaze that turned onlookers into stone.

2. F. NO CHANGE
   G. years, Medusa
   H. years Medusa
   J. years. Medusa

3. A. NO CHANGE
   B. Medusa the defeated Gorgon, abounded
   C. Medusa the defeated Gorgon abounded
   D. Medusa—the defeated Gorgon— abounded

4. F. NO CHANGE
   G. serpents;
   H. serpents,
   J. serpents and

Drill answers from previous page:

Note: These are not the only ways to correct the sentences; your answers may differ.

a. Delayed for two hours due to a thunderstorm, the baseball game started much later than fans had expected.

b. *The Heart of a Woman* (originally published in 1981) is one of Maya Angelou's most popular books.

c. The architect, a keen observer known for her meticulous attention to detail, gently pointed out the error in her coworker's design.

d. Contemporary Hawaiian quilts—which are often featured at the Mokupāpapa Discovery Center—reflect an eclectic blend of Hawaiian tradition and modern vision.

e. A hurricane's strength is rated on a scale of 1 to 5, depending on the speed of sustained winds.

Medusa was surely one of the most threatening figures of ancient Greek mythology. One of the three Gorgon <u>sisters</u> Medusa had been known for her beauty.
 5

5. A. NO CHANGE
    B. sisters,
    C. sisters because
    D. sisters was because

However, she aroused the anger of the goddess Athena, who turned <u>Medusa's, once lovely hair,</u> to snakes. With
 6
the power to turn anyone who looked upon her into stone, Medusa was feared and thought impossible to defeat.

6. F. NO CHANGE
    G. Medusa's once lovely hair
    H. Medusa's once, lovely hair
    J. Medusa's—once lovely hair—

Sentence Structure: Commas, Dashes, and Colons

LEARNING OBJECTIVE

After this lesson, you will be able to:

- Identify and correct inappropriate uses of commas, dashes, and colons

To answer a question like this:

In 1848, suffragists at the Seneca Falls Convention developed a wide array of demands, many of which were eventually considered too radical to be feasible. As a way of gaining broader support, these suffragists found it necessary to streamline and slightly alter their positions. The process was <u>tedious, but</u> necessary.
1

1. A. NO CHANGE
    B. tedious: but
    C. tedious; but
    D. tedious but

You need to know this:

Answer choices often move punctuation marks around, replace them with other punctuation marks, or remove them altogether. When underlined portions include commas, dashes, or colons, check to make sure the punctuation is used correctly in context.

Commas

There are two situations in which commas are not interchangeable with any other punctuation: when listing a series of items and when separating introductory words or phrases from the rest of the sentence.

Use commas to...	Comma(s)
Set off three or more items in a series	*Jeremiah packed a sleeping bag, a raincoat, and a lantern for his upcoming camping trip.*
Separate an introductory word or phrase from the rest of the sentence	*For example, carrots are an excellent source of several vitamins and minerals.*

Commas and Dashes

In many cases, either a comma or a dash may be used to punctuate a sentence.

Use commas or dashes to . . .	Comma(s)	Dash(es)
Separate independent clauses connected by a FANBOYS conjunction (For, And, Nor, But, Or, Yet, So)	*Jess finished her homework earlier than expected, so she started an assignment that was due the following week.*	*Jess finished her homework earlier than expected—so she started an assignment that was due the following week.*
Separate an independent and dependent clause	*Tyson arrived at school a few minutes early, which gave him time to organize his locker before class.*	*Tyson arrived at school a few minutes early—which gave him time to organize his locker before class.*
Separate parenthetical elements from the rest of the sentence (use either two commas or two dashes, not one of each)	*Professor Mann, who is the head of the English department, is known for assigning extensive projects.*	*Professor Mann—who is the head of the English department—is known for assigning extensive projects.*

Colons and Dashes

Colons and dashes are used to include new ideas that introduce or explain something or that break the flow of the sentence. Note that the clause before the colon or dash must be able to stand on its own as a complete sentence.

Use colons and dashes to...	Colon	Dash
Introduce and/or emphasize a short phrase, quotation, explanation, example, or list	*Sanjay had two important tasks to complete: a science experiment and an expository essay.*	*Sanjay had two important tasks to complete—a science experiment and an expository essay.*
Separate two independent clauses when the second clause explains, illustrates, or expands on the first sentence	*Highway 1 in Australia is one of the longest national highways in the world: it circles the entirety of the continent and connects every mainland state capital.*	*Highway 1 in Australia is one of the longest national highways in the world—it circles the entirety of the continent and connects every mainland state capital.*

Unnecessary Punctuation

Knowing when punctuation should not be used is equally important. If an underlined portion includes punctuation, take time to consider whether it should be included at all.

Do NOT use punctuation to...	Incorrect	Correct
Separate a subject from its verb	*The diligent student council, meets every week.*	*The diligent student council meets every week.*
Separate a verb from its object or a preposition from its object	*The diligent student council meets, every week.*	*The diligent student council meets every week.*
Set off elements that are essential to a sentence's meaning	*The, diligent student, council meets every week.*	*The diligent student council meets every week.*
Separate adjectives that work together to modify a noun	*The diligent, student council meets every week.*	*The diligent student council meets every week.*

You need to do this:

If the underlined portion includes punctuation, ask yourself:

- Is the punctuation used correctly?

  The punctuation needs to be the correct type (comma, dash, or colon) and in the correct location.

- Is the punctuation necessary?

If you cannot identify a reason why the punctuation is included, the punctuation should be removed.

Explanation:

A comma must be placed before *but* only if the words that follow form an independent clause. Here, only the word *necessary*, which is not an independent clause, appears after *but*, so no punctuation is needed. Choice (D) is correct.

Drills

If commas, colons, and dashes give you trouble, study the information above and try out these drill questions before completing the Try on Your Own questions below. Turn the page and look at the bottom of the page to see the answers.

Edit each sentence to correct the punctuation issue.

a. The recipe includes my favorite fruit sweet red cherries.

b. Historically popular sayings are transferred by word of mouth and rarely found in written records so there is often no definite answer to the question of their origin.

c. Paradise tree snakes subsist mostly on lizards and bats which they immobilize with mild venom.

d. As a result the United States entered an isolationist period after World War I.

e. *Hamlet* begins with two of Shakespeare's favorite ways to grab an audience's attention a supernatural phenomenon and a murder plot.

Try on Your Own

Directions: Take as much time as you need on these questions. Work carefully and methodically. There will be an opportunity for timed practice at the end of the chapter.

Music in the Park

Some people think of classical music as tedious, and unimaginative. They feel that music without lyrics is lacking in emotion or simply too complex to fully appreciate. For many years, I was among those who thought that listening to classical music was an

abysmal experience. However when a friend convinced me to attend the New York Philharmonic performance in Central Park, a free event usually scheduled twice each summer, my entire perception of orchestras and classical music changed.

I knew that there would be a large audience for the performance, but I didn't think the atmosphere would be festive. Thousands of people had spread out blankets to relax and experience the music. By the end of the first

2. F. NO CHANGE
    G. tedious; and
    H. tedious, and,
    J. tedious and

3. A. NO CHANGE
    B. However,
    C. However;
    D. However:

4. F. NO CHANGE
    G. performance; but
    H. performance; so
    J. performance, so

Drill answers from previous page:

Note: These are not the only ways to correct the sentences; your answers may differ.

a. The recipe includes my favorite fruit: sweet red cherries.

b. Historically popular sayings are transferred by word of mouth and are rarely found in written records, so there is often no definite answer to the question of their origin. OR Historically popular sayings are transferred by word of mouth and are rarely found in written records—so there is often no definite answer to the question of their origin.

c. Paradise tree snakes subsist mostly on lizards and bats, which they immobilize with mild venom.

d. As a result, the United States entered an isolationist period after World War I.

e. *Hamlet* begins with two of Shakespeare's favorite ways to grab an audience's attention—a supernatural phenomenon and a murder plot. OR *Hamlet* begins with two of Shakespeare's favorite ways to grab an audience's attention: a supernatural phenomenon and a murder plot.

piece: Mendelssohn's Symphony No. 4 in A Major—I
5
was enthralled. The second piece was Tchaikovsky's
1812 Overture, and the audience hushed their already
whispered conversations to hear the work's interplay
among the brass, strings, woodwinds, and percussion
instruments. The emotional ending, punctuated with
booming cannons and lyrical, church bells, provided the
6
opportunity for me to genuinely enjoy classical music,
albeit for the very first time.

5. A.   NO CHANGE
    B.   piece, Mendelssohn's
    C.   piece—Mendelssohn's
    D.   piece Mendelssohn's

6. F.   NO CHANGE
    G.   lyrical church
    H.   lyrical—church
    J.   lyrical: church

Agreement: Verbs

LEARNING OBJECTIVE

After this lesson, you will be able to:

● Identify and correct verb agreement issues

To answer a question like this:

Instead of arguing for equality based on principle, suffragists insisted that the difference between the two genders <u>were</u> precisely why women must be allowed
1
to participate in government. In an attempt to appease opponents, suffragists insisted that the female vote would aid in purifying politics, enacting reforms, and outweighing less-desirable votes. The positive outcome of a female voting bloc, suffragists posited, would be a government that reflected a woman's position as protector of the home, family, and society.

1. A. NO CHANGE
    B. was
    C. will be
    D. was exactly and

You need to know this:

Verb Tense

Verb tense indicates when an action or state of being took place: past, present, or future. The tense of the verb must fit the context of the passage. Each tense can express three different types of action.

Type of action	Past	Present	Future
Single action occurring only once	Connor **planted** vegetables in the community garden.	Connor **plants** vegetables in the community garden.	Connor **will plant** vegetables in the community garden.
Action that is ongoing at some point in time	Connor **was planting** vegetables in the community garden this morning before noon.	Connor **is planting** vegetables in the community garden this morning before noon.	Connor **will be planting** vegetables in the community garden this morning before noon.
Action that is completed before some other action	Connor **had planted** vegetables in the community garden every year until he gave his job to Jasmine.	Connor **has planted** vegetables in the community garden since it started five years ago.	Connor **will have planted** vegetables in the community garden by the time the growing season starts.

Subject-Verb Agreement

A verb must agree with its subject in person and number:

- Person (first, second, or third)
  - First: *I ask a question.*
  - Second: *You ask a question.*
  - Third: *She asks a question.*
- Number (singular or plural)
  - Singular: *The apple tastes delicious.*
  - Plural: *Apples taste delicious.*

The noun closest to the verb is not always the subject. Take the following sentence as an example: *The chair with the lion feet is an antique.* The singular verb in this sentence, *is*, is closest to the plural noun *feet*. However, the verb's actual subject is the singular noun *chair*, so the sentence is correct as written.

When a sentence includes two nouns, only the conjunction *and* forms a compound subject requiring a plural verb form:

- Plural: *Saliyah **and** Taylor **are** in the running club.*
- Singular: ***Either** Saliyah **or** Taylor **is** in the running club.*
- Singular: ***Neither** Saliyah **nor** Taylor **is** in the running club.*

Collective nouns are nouns that name entities with more than one member, such as *group*, *team*, and *family*. Even though these nouns represent more than one person, they are grammatically singular and require singular verb forms:

- ***The collection** of paintings **is** one of the most popular art exhibits in recent years.*
- ***The team looks** promising this year.*

Parallelism

Verbs in a list, a compound, or a comparison must be parallel in form:

Feature	Example	Parallel form
A list	*Chloe **formulated** a question, **conducted** background research, and **constructed** a hypothesis before starting the experiment.*	3 simple past verb phrases
A compound	***Hunting** and **fishing** were essential to the survival of Midwestern Native American tribes such as the Omaha.*	2 –ing verb forms
A comparison	*Garrett enjoys **sculpting** as much as **painting**.*	2 –ing verb forms

Note that parallelism may be tested using other parts of speech besides verbs. In general, any items in a list, compound, or comparison must be in parallel form. For example, if a list starts with a noun, the other items in the list must also be nouns; if it starts with an adjective, the other items must be adjectives, etc.:

Incorrect	Correct alternatives
Naomi likes **pumpkin pie and to drink coffee** on chilly weekend afternoons.	Naomi likes **pumpkin pie and coffee** on chilly weekend afternoons.
	Naomi likes **to eat pumpkin pie and to drink coffee** on chilly weekend afternoons.
Which of the dogs is the **most** docile and **better** behaved?	Which of the dogs is the **most** docile and **best** behaved?
	Which of the dogs is the **more** docile and **better** behaved?

You need to do this:

If the underlined portion includes a verb, check that the verb:

- Reflects the correct tense: Does it fit the context?
- Agrees with the subject in person and number
- Is parallel in form with other verbs in a series, list, or compound if there is one in the sentence

Explanation:

A verb must agree with its subject. In this case, the plural verb *were* does not agree with its singular subject *difference*; eliminate A. Eliminate C because the future tense does not make sense in context. The remaining choices both use the past-tense singular verb *was*, but D is unnecessarily wordy. Choice (B) is correct.

Drills

If verbs give you trouble, study the information above and try out these drill questions before completing the Try on Your Own questions below. Drill answers can be found on the bottom of the next page.

Edit each sentence to correct the verb issue.

a. Pablo present his experiment at the science fair last week.

b. The movie, with its complex plot and stirring themes, were critically acclaimed.

c. Neither the director nor the lead actor are at rehearsal today.

d. The park and wildlife refuge comprises more than 800 acres of mountains, lakes, and forests.

e. In order to pass the foreign language proficiency exam, you must be both a fluent speaker and able to read it as well.

Try on Your Own

Directions: Take as much time as you need on these questions. Work carefully and methodically. There will be an opportunity for timed practice at the end of the chapter.

Mia's Attic

I thought the tour of my friend's new house was finished as we came to a halt outside her bedroom on the third floor. However, Mia had something else in mind. "Do you want to go up to the attic?" she asked me, her eyes sparkling with mischief. "When my mom <u>inherited</u> the house from my grandmother last
₂
year, she told me that no one had gone up there for forty years!" In past situations, either Mia's mom or older

brother <u>were</u> available to help me convince Mia that her
₃
latest plan was inadvisable. Unfortunately, they were both at work and unavailable to assist me in pleading my case.

2. F. NO CHANGE
   G. inherits
   H. had inherited
   J. would have inherited

3. A. NO CHANGE
   B. was
   C. would be
   D. will have been

Drill answers from previous page:

Note: These are not the only ways to correct the sentences; your answers may differ.

a. Pablo present**ed** his experiment at the science fair last week.

b. The movie, with its complex plot and stirring themes, **was** critically acclaimed.

c. Neither the director nor the lead actor **is** at rehearsal today.

d. The park and wildlife refuge **comprise** more than 800 acres of mountains, lakes, and forests.

e. In order to pass the foreign language proficiency exam, you must be both a fluent speaker and **reader**.

I wasn't thrilled about the idea of exploring the dark, musty space overhead. In the past, I hesitated whenever Mia suggested risky or dangerous activities, but this time I just nodded, trying to appear nonchalant. Mia yanked on the cord dangling from the wooden door; a staircase unfolded, the bottom step landing directly in front of my feet. I looked up, acknowledging that seemingly endless darkness, quite possibly replete with eight-legged monsters, often <u>teem</u> with a myriad of
4
unexpected unpleasantries.

Hoping Mia wouldn't notice, I took a deep breath and <u>grip</u> the ladder. As I placed my foot on the
5
bottom rung, I wondered how my best friend had failed to take my considerable fear of spiders into account. I like arachnids about as much as I enjoy watching gory movies, enduring frightening pranks, and <u>dental appointments</u>. "The sooner you get this over
6
with, the better," I whispered to myself, trying to exude as much courage as possible.

4. F. NO CHANGE
   G. will have teemed
   H. teems
   J. to teem

5. A. NO CHANGE
   B. grips
   C. would grip
   D. gripped

6. F. NO CHANGE
   G. going to the dentist
   H. trips to the dentist
   J. dental appointments for a root canal

Agreement: Pronouns

LEARNING OBJECTIVE

After this lesson, you will be able to:

- Identify and correct pronoun agreement issues

To answer a question like this:

Despite anti-suffragist objections, the suffrage movement finally achieved its' ultimate goal, but only after offering its participants a political education and a sense of taking an active role in the nation's history, which in turn helped to convince the rest of the country of the worth of the woman's vote.

1. A. NO CHANGE
   B. their
   C. they're
   D. its

You need to know this:

Pronoun Forms

A pronoun is a word that takes the place of a noun. Pronouns can take three different forms, each of which is used based on the grammatical role it plays in the sentence.

Form	Pronouns	Example
Subjective: The pronoun is used as the subject	I, you, she, he, it, we, they, who	*Rivka is the student **who** will lead the presentation.*
Objective: The pronoun is used as the object of a verb or a preposition	me, you, her, him, it, us, them, whom	*With **whom** will Rivka present the scientific findings?*
Possessive: The pronoun expresses ownership	my, mine, your, yours, his, her, hers, its, our, ours, their, theirs, whose	*Rivka will likely choose a partner **whose** work is excellent.*

Note that a pronoun in subjective form can, logically, be the subject in a complete sentence. Pronouns that are in objective form cannot function as the subject.

When there are two pronouns or a noun and a pronoun in a compound structure, drop the other noun or pronoun to tell which form to use. For example: Leo and me walked into town. If you were talking about yourself only, you would say, "I walked into town," not "Me walked into town." Therefore, the correct form is subjective, and the original sentence should read: Leo and I walked into town.

Pronoun-Antecedent Agreement

A pronoun's antecedent is the noun it logically represents in a sentence. If the noun is singular, the pronoun must be singular; if the noun is plural, the pronoun must be plural.

Antecedent	Incorrect	Correct
selection	The selection of books was placed in **their** designated location.	The selection of books was placed in **its** designated location.
Addison	Addison fed the giraffes all of the lettuce **they** had purchased.	Addison fed the giraffes all of the lettuce **she** had purchased.
sapling	The sapling, along with dozens of flowers, was relocated to where **they** would thrive.	The sapling, along with dozens of flowers, was relocated to where **it** would thrive.
student	If a student is confused, **they** should ask for clarification.	If a student is confused, **he or she** should ask for clarification.

You need to do this:

If the underlined portion includes a pronoun, find the logical antecedent. Check that the pronoun:

- Uses the correct form
  - If the pronoun is the subject of the sentence, use a subjective pronoun such as *I, you, she, he, it, we, they,* or *who*.
  - If the pronoun is an object within the sentence, use an objective pronoun such as *me, you, her, him, it, us, they,* or *whom*.
  - If the pronoun indicates possession, use a possessive pronoun such as *my, mine, your, yours, his, her, hers, its, our, ours, their, theirs,* or *whose*.
- Agrees with its antecedent
  - A singular antecedent requires a singular pronoun; a plural antecedent requires a plural pronoun.

Explanation:

Eliminate A immediately because the word *its'* is not correct in any context. The pronoun's antecedent, the noun to which the pronoun is referring, is "the suffrage movement," which is singular. Choice (D) correctly uses the singular possessive pronoun *its*. Choice B incorrectly uses a plural possessive pronoun, and C means *they are*, which does not make sense in context.

Drills

If pronouns give you trouble, study the information above and try out these drill questions before completing the Try on Your Own questions below. Turn the page and look at the bottom of the page to see the answers.

Edit each sentence to correct the pronoun issue.

a.   The scientist, about who I had read, was more charismatic in person than I had expected.

b.   Between you and I, you are the better singer.

c.   A jaguar, with its keen senses and sharp teeth and claws, is known for their ability to dominate prey.

d.   The jar of olives is not in their regular location on the self.

e.   One cannot help but be amazed by the scientific advances in the past century, especially if you study the history of science.

Try on Your Own

Directions: Take as much time as you need on these questions. Work carefully and methodically. There will be an opportunity for timed practice at the end of the chapter.

Galloping Gertie

For four months in the fall of 1940, citizens of the Puget Sound area of Washington used one of the most illustrious, and most dangerous, suspension bridges ever built; <u>it</u> had the opportunity to travel across the Tacoma
2
Narrows Bridge, or "Galloping Gertie," which enjoyed a relatively short life compared to similar structures in the United States. "Gertie" taught important lessons on what to do—and what not to do—when building a suspension bridge.

State officials in Washington were the ones <u>whom</u>
3
identified a need for a bridge across Puget Sound. The closest point was the Tacoma Narrows, a windy 2,800-foot gap. Construction began in November of 1938, and the bridge was officially opened on July 1, 1940. Although they knew about form and structure, the bridge's engineers failed to take into account aerodynamic components, particularly the wind, and <u>it's</u> effect on the roadway. Because the roadbed
4

2. F. NO CHANGE
   G. their
   H. them
   J. they

3. A. NO CHANGE
   B. who
   C. that
   D. that spoke up and

4. F. NO CHANGE
   G. its
   H. its'
   J. their

Drill answers from previous page:

Note: These are not the only ways to correct the sentences; your answers may differ.

a. The scientist, about **whom** I had read, was more charismatic in person than I had expected.

b. Between you and **me**, you are the better singer.

c. A jaguar, with its keen senses and sharp teeth and claws, is known for **its** ability to dominate prey.

d. The jar of olives is not in **its** regular location on the self.

e. One cannot help but be amazed by the scientific advances in the past century, especially if **one studies** the history of science.

was constructed with rigid plate girders, <u>it</u> could not
5
absorb the winds of Puget Sound. Consequently, on

any windy day, the roadway buckled and contorted,

or "galloped"—hence, the nickname. The undulation

became so severe that the bridge, as <u>you</u> would hope,
6
was eventually closed to traffic.

5.   A.   NO CHANGE

       B.   they

       C.   those

       D.   these

6.   F.   NO CHANGE

       G.   we

       H.   it

       J.   one

Agreement: Modifiers

> **LEARNING OBJECTIVES**
>
> After this lesson, you will be able to:
>
> - Identify and correct modifier agreement issues
> - Identify and correct inappropriate uses of apostrophes

To answer a question like this:

Much to their surprise, <u>it was quickly apparent to</u>
₁
<u>anti-suffragists</u> that women, in fact, did not vote together
₁
as a bloc. Women voted as individuals and in smaller

proportions than men.

1. A. NO CHANGE

    B. it was quick apparent to
        anti-suffragists

    C. anti-suffragists quick found

    D. anti-suffragists quickly found

You need to know this:

A modifier is a word or phrase that describes, clarifies, or provides additional information about another part of the sentence. Modifier questions require you to identify the part of a sentence being modified and use the appropriate modifier in the proper place.

In order to be grammatically correct, the modifier must be placed as close to the word it describes as possible. Use context clues in the passage to identify the correct placement of a modifier; a misplaced modifier can cause confusion and is always incorrect on test day.

Note that a common way the ACT tests modifiers is with modifying phrases at the beginning of a sentence. Just like any other modifier, the modifying phrase grammatically modifies whatever is right next to it in the sentence. For example, consider the sentence, "While walking to the bus stop, the rain drenched Bob." The initial phrase, "While walking to the bus stop," grammatically modifies "the rain," creating a nonsense sentence; the rain can't walk to the bus stop. The writer meant that Bob was walking to the bus stop, so the sentence should read, "While walking to the bus stop, Bob was drenched by the rain."

Modifier/Modifying phrase	Incorrect	Correct
nearly	*Andre **nearly** watched the play for four hours.*	*Andre watched the play for **nearly** four hours.*
in individual containers	*The art teacher handed out paints to students **in individual containers**.*	*The art teacher handed out paints **in individual containers** to students.*
A scholar athlete	***A scholar athlete**, maintaining high grades in addition to playing soccer were expected of Maya.*	***A scholar athlete**, Maya was expected to maintain high grades in addition to playing soccer.*

Adjectives and Adverbs

Use adjectives only to modify nouns and pronouns. Use adverbs to modify everything else.

- Adjectives are single-word modifiers that describe nouns and pronouns: *Ian conducted an **efficient** lab experiment.*
- Adverbs are single-word modifiers that describe verbs, adjectives, or other adverbs: *Ian **efficiently** conducted a lab experiment.*

Note that nouns can sometimes be used as adjectives. For example, in the phrase "the fashion company's autumn line," the word *fashion* functions as an adjective modifying *company*, and the word *autumn* functions as an adjective modifying *line*.

Comparative/Superlative

When comparing similar things, use adjectives that match the number of items being compared. When comparing two items or people, use the comparative form of the adjective. When comparing three or more items or people, use the superlative form.

Comparative (two items)	Superlative (three or more items)
better, more, newer, older, shorter, taller, worse, younger	best, most, newest, oldest, shortest, tallest, worst, youngest

Possessive Nouns and Pronouns

Possessive nouns and pronouns indicate that something belongs to someone or something. In general, possessive nouns are written with an apostrophe, while possessive pronouns are not.

To spot errors in possessive noun or pronoun construction, look for...	Incorrect	Correct
Two nouns in a row	The **professors lectures** were both informative and entertaining.	The **professor's lectures** were both informative and entertaining.
Pronouns with apostrophes	The book is **her's**.	The book is **hers**.
Words that sound alike	The three friends decided to ride **there** bicycles to the park over **they're** where **their** going to enjoy a picnic lunch.	The three friends decided to ride **their** bicycles to the park over **there** where **they're** going to enjoy a picnic lunch.

Apostrophes

Use an apostrophe to...	Example
Indicate the possessive form of a single noun	My oldest **sister's soccer game** is on Saturday.
Indicate the possessive form of a plural noun	My **two** older **sisters' soccer games** are on Saturday.
Indicate a contraction (e.g., don't, can't)	**They've** won every soccer match this season.

Note that plural nouns are formed without an apostrophe.

Incorrect	Correct
Sting ray's are cartilaginous fish related to **shark's**.	**Sting rays** are cartilaginous fish related to **sharks**.
There are many **carnival's** in this area every summer.	There are many **carnivals** in this area every summer.

To check whether *it's* is appropriate, replace it in the sentence with *it is* or *it has*. If the sentence no longer makes sense, *it's* is incorrect. The following sentence is correct:

The tree frog blends perfectly into its surroundings. When it holds still, it's nearly invisible.

Note that *its'* and *its's* are never correct.

You need to do this:

If the underlined portion includes a modifier, determine whether the modifier:

- Is placed correctly
  - Is it as near as possible to the word it logically modifies?
  - If it is not in the correct place, where should it be moved?
- Agrees with the word or words it is describing
  - Does the sentence require an adjective or an adverb?
  - Does the noun or pronoun show proper possession?

If the underlined portion includes an apostrophe, make sure it correctly indicates either possession or a contraction. If an apostrophe is missing, select the answer choice that places it in the correct location.

Explanation:

"Much to their surprise" is an introductory modifying phrase, so the noun that the phrase is modifying must come immediately after the comma. Eliminate A and B because "much to their surprise" is not modifying "it." Choice C introduces a new error by changing the adverb *quickly* to *quick*, which cannot be used to modify the verb *found*. Choice (D) places the correct phrase after the comma and does not introduce any new errors.

Drills

If modifiers give you trouble, study the information above and try out these drill questions before completing the Try on Your Own questions below. Turn the page and look at the bottom of the page to see the answers.

Edit each sentence to correct the modifier or apostrophe issue.

a.   A more safely approach is to test the temperature of the water before entering.

b.   Jonas had to run to the store real quick before it closed.

c.   The new student is the better speller in the class.

d.   It took the chameleon a few weeks to acclimate to its' new habitat.

Try on Your Own

Directions: Take as much time as you need on these questions. Work carefully and methodically. There will be an opportunity for timed practice at the end of the chapter.

Basketry

Basketry may be the world's oldest handicraft. The earlier examples of basketry are 10,000 years old. These
₂

2. F. NO CHANGE
    G. more earlier
    H. most earliest
    J. earliest

ancient fragments, which have been preserved good by
₃
the dry environment of Danger Cave, Utah, show that early Native Americans mastered the art of weaving semi-rigid materials into useful objects. Notably,

3. A. NO CHANGE
    B. very good
    C. quite well and thoroughly
    D. well

the remains of baskets like the ones discovered in Utah
₄
have been found on nearly every continent.

Materials, rather than technique or decoration, are oftentimes most useful in identifying a basket's origin. Willow, just pliant enough to be either woven or plaited, is the favored basket-making material of

4. F. NO CHANGE
    G. remains' of baskets
    H. remain's of baskets
    J. remains of baskets'

Drill answers from previous page:

Note: These are not the only ways to correct the sentences; your answers may differ.

a. A **safer** approach is to test the temperature of the water before entering.

b. Jonas had to run to the store **really quickly** before it closed.

c. The new student is the **best** speller in the class.

d. It took the chameleon a few weeks to acclimate to **its** new habitat.

northern Europe. Opting for rigid materials, <u>bamboo and rattan have been used by basket makers to create sturdy baskets</u> in other regions. Africa has yielded many
5
basket-making materials, including palm leaves, tree roots, and grasses.

Not surprisingly, a basket's provenance truly depends on <u>it's</u> composite materials.
6

5. A. NO CHANGE
    B. bamboo and rattan are used to create sturdy baskets by basket makers
    C. basket makers use bamboo and rattan to create sturdy baskets
    D. sturdy baskets are made by basket makers out of bamboo and rattan

6. F. NO CHANGE
    G. its
    H. their
    J. they're

Agreement: Idioms

LEARNING OBJECTIVE

After this lesson, you will be able to:

- Identify and correct expressions that deviate from idiomatic English

To answer a question like this:

Early 20th-century women did not necessarily vote as a united caucus, but they did feel a new sense of empowerment. They were, by law, participants in a democracy that <u>couldn't hardly</u> ignore them.
1

1. A. NO CHANGE
   B. would not hardly
   C. wouldn't hardly
   D. could hardly

You need to know this:

An idiom is a combination of words that must be used together to convey either a figurative or literal meaning. Idioms are tested in three ways:

1. Proper preposition use in context: The preposition must reflect the writer's intended meaning.

   - *She waits **on** customers.*
   - *She waits **for** the bus.*
   - *She waits **with** her friends.*

2. Idiomatic expressions: Some words or phrases must be used together to be correct.

   - *Simone will **either** bike **or** run to the park.*
   - ***Neither** the principal **nor** the teachers will tolerate tardiness.*
   - *This fall, Shari is playing **not only** soccer **but also** field hockey.*

3. Implicit double negatives: Some words imply a negative and therefore cannot be paired with an explicit negative. The words *barely*, *hardly*, and *scarcely* fall into this category.

   - Incorrect: *Janie **can't hardly** wait for vacation.*
   - Correct: *Janie **can hardly** wait for vacation.*

Frequently tested prepositions	Idiomatic expressions	Words that can't pair with negative words
at	as…as	barely
by	between…and	hardly
for	both…and	scarcely
from	either…or	
of	neither…nor	
on	just as…so too	
to	not only…but also	
with	prefer…to	

You need to do this:

- If the underlined portion includes a preposition, a conjunction, or *barely/hardly/scarcely*, look for a common idiom error.
- If the underlined segment includes a commonly misused word, check the context to determine whether it is used properly.

Explanation:

Since *hardly* is implicitly negative, it cannot be paired with *not*; (D) is correct. Choices A and C include the words *couldn't* and *wouldn't*, respectively, which mean *could not* and *would not*. Choice B explicitly pairs the word *not* with *hardly*, so it is incorrect.

Drills

If idioms give you trouble, study the information above and try out these drill questions before completing the Try on Your Own questions below. Turn the page and look at the bottom of the page to see the answers.

Edit each sentence to correct the idiomatic issue.

a. Straining to hear the bird perched in the tree, Jessa stood completely still, waiting with the sound to reach her.

b. The engineer examined the malfunctioning machine closely for evidence to missing components or worn elements.

c. The protestors' bold slogans not only angered the opposition, but elicited loud reactions from bystanders.

d. Given the cold climate, farmers quickly found that they could grow neither dates or figs.

e. The writing was nearly barely legible after the rain soaked through Tia's backpack and saturated her notebook.

Try on Your Own

Directions: Take as much time as you need on these questions. Work carefully and methodically. There will be an opportunity for timed practice at the end of the chapter.

Alfred Nobel

Given that few people have had the opportunity to read their own obituaries, scientist Alfred Nobel <u>couldn't scarcely</u> believe that, in 1888, his obituary was in the daily newspaper. Alfred surmised that the newspaper editor had been either grossly

<u>misinformed, and</u> confused by a misidentification. In actuality, Alfred's brother Ludvig had died, and Ludvig was mistaken for Alfred. While Alfred was primarily known as an inventor and one of the richest people

<u>in the world at the time,</u> the paper unapologetically gave him the moniker "Merchant of Death" because of the innumerable lives that his most notable invention, dynamite, had taken.

2. F. NO CHANGE
   G. could scarcely
   H. could not scarcely
   J. not scarcely

3. A. NO CHANGE
   B. misinformed and
   C. misinformed, or
   D. misinformed or

4. F. NO CHANGE
   G. in the world for the time being
   H. on the world for the time being
   J. on the world at the time

Drill answers from previous page:

Note: These are not the only ways to correct the sentences; your answers may differ.

a. Straining to hear the bird perched in the tree, Jessa stood completely still, waiting **for** the sound to reach her.

b. The engineer examined the malfunctioning machine closely for evidence **of** missing components or worn elements.

c. The protestors' bold slogans not only angered the opposition, but **also** elicited loud reactions from bystanders.

d. Given the cold climate, farmers quickly found that they could grow neither dates **nor** figs.

e. The writing was **barely** legible after the rain soaked through Tia's backpack and saturated her notebook.

Unable to accept that dynamite—which was widely <u>used by</u> warfare—would be his enduring legacy, 5
Alfred crafted provisions in his will to create the Nobel Foundation upon his death. Nobel's foundation has not only acknowledged outstanding achievements in chemistry, economics, literature, medicine, peace, and physics, <u>but</u> raised awareness regarding crucial global 6
issues.

5. A. NO CHANGE
   B. used with
   C. used in
   D. used to

6. F. NO CHANGE
   G. it
   H. but it
   J. but also

How Much Have You Learned?

Directions: For test-like practice, give yourself 7 minutes to complete this question set. Note that this is not a test-like mix of questions; rather, these 12 questions cover the sentence structure, punctuation, and agreement issues covered in this chapter.

Be sure to study the explanations, even for questions you got correct. They can be found at the end of this chapter.

The History of Marbles

It is impossible to pinpoint the exact date when the first marble was constructed, most likely out of <u>clay, it</u> is a reasonable assumption to regard the concept [1] of marbles as nearly as old as humankind. Marbles as we know them today, however, first originated in the middle of the 19th century when they were produced in mass quantities in Europe. Originating from their appearance, material, or use, <u>an important identifying factor is often indicated by marbles' names.</u> [2]

1. A. NO CHANGE
    B. clay, nevertheless, it
    C. clay, but it
    D. clay; but it

2. F. NO CHANGE
    G. an important identifying factor is often indicated by the names of marbles.
    H. marble's names often indicate an important identifying factor.
    J. marbles' names often indicate an important identifying factor.

<u>"Alleys," for example</u> were named for their composite [3] material; the name indicates that they are made from alabaster. At least, that was the case for alleys produced at the turn of the last century. Nowadays, it's far more common for marbles to <u>consist: of</u> glass, baked clay, [4] steel, onyx, plastic, or agate.

3. A. NO CHANGE
    B. "Alleys" for example, were
    C. "Alleys," for example: were
    D. "Alleys," for example, were

4. F. NO CHANGE
    G. consist of
    H. consist—of
    J. consist, of

<u>Regardless of</u> the material with which they are [5] made, marbles can be manipulated in a variety of ways.

5. A. NO CHANGE
    B. Regardless to
    C. Regardlessly of
    D. Regardlessly to

"Knuckling" is a technique in which the knuckles of the
hand are balanced against the ground while a marble
placed against the forefinger is shot outward by the

thumb. Marbles may be thrown, rolled, and players can
even kick marbles.

Not surprisingly, there is near as many varieties
of marble games as there are ways to manipulate
marbles. The most common American version involves
winning opponents' marbles by knocking them out
of a designated area with one's own marbles. Another
popular game is taw—also known as ringtaw, or ringer,
the object of which is to shoot marbles arranged like a
cross out of a large ring. Players in a pot game such as
moshie try to knock one another's marbles into a hole.

In nineholes, or bridgeboard, players shoot our marbles
through numbered arches on the board.

The popularity of marbles crosses cultural boundaries.
The first marble games took place in antiquity. Were played
with nuts, fruit pits, or pebbles. Even the great Augustus
Caesar was known to have played marble games as a child.
During Passover, Jewish children have customarily used
filberts as marbles. Several traditional Chinese games are
also played with marbles. Indeed, while many people
consider the game of marbles to be simple, they actually
have a complex history.

6. F. NO CHANGE
   G. technique, in which,
   H. technique in, which
   J. technique in which;

7. A. NO CHANGE
   B. players can choose to kick marbles.
   C. kicked or punted.
   D. kicked.

8. F. NO CHANGE
   G. is nearly
   H. are near
   J. are nearly

9. A. NO CHANGE
   B. taw—also known as ringtaw—or ringer the object
   C. taw—also known as ringtaw or ringer—the object
   D. taw, also known as ringtaw, or ringer, the object

10. F. NO CHANGE
    G. your
    H. their
    J. its

11. A. NO CHANGE
    B. antiquity and were
    C. antiquity, and were
    D. antiquity; were

12. F. NO CHANGE
    G. they actually has
    H. it actually have
    J. it actually has

Reflect

Directions: Take a few minutes to recall what you've learned and what you've been practicing in this chapter. Consider the following questions, jot down your best answer for each one, and then compare your reflections to the expert responses on the following page. Use your level of confidence to determine what to do next.

1. Name at least three ways to correct a run-on sentence.

    _____

    _____

    _____

2. How does the ACT test subject-verb agreement and parallelism?

    _____

    _____

    _____

3. What are the three different pronoun forms? When do you use each one?

    _____

    _____

    _____

4. What is the difference between an adjective and an adverb?

    _____

    _____

    _____

5. What are the three ways that apostrophes are tested on the ACT?

    _____

    _____

    _____

Responses

1. Name at least three ways to correct a run-on sentence.

There are a number of ways to fix a run-on sentence on the ACT. The six ways that you are likely to see are: 1) use a period to create two separate sentences, 2) use a semicolon between the two independent clauses, 3) use a colon between the two independent clauses, 4) make one clause dependent, 5) add a FANBOYS conjunction after the comma, or 6) use a dash between the two independent clauses.

2. How does the ACT test subject-verb agreement and parallelism?

A subject and a verb must always agree in person (first, second, or third) and number (singular or plural). You will need to be able to spot subject-verb mismatches and correct them. Parallelism requires that all items in a list, a compound, or a comparison be in parallel form. The ACT may test lists or comparisons in which one item is in the wrong form.

3. What are the three different pronoun forms? When do you use each one?

The three forms are subjective (when the pronoun is the subject), objective (when the pronoun is the object of a verb or preposition), and possessive (when the pronoun expresses ownership).

4. What is the difference between an adjective and an adverb?

An adjective is a single word that modifies a noun or a pronoun, while an adverb is a single word that modifies a verb, an adjective, or another adverb.

5. What are the three ways that apostrophes are tested on the ACT?

Apostrophes on the ACT are used to: 1) indicate the possessive form of a singular noun ('s), 2) indicate the possessive form of a plural noun (s'), or 3) indicate a contraction (don't = do not).

Next Steps

If you answered most questions correctly in the "How Much Have You Learned?" section, and if your responses to the Reflect questions were similar to those of an expert, then consider sentence structure, punctuation, and agreement areas of strength and move on to the next chapter. Come back to these topics periodically to prevent yourself from getting rusty.

If you don't yet feel confident, review those parts of this chapter that you have not yet mastered. In particular, review punctuation usage in the Sentence Structure: The Basics and Sentence Structure: Commas, Dashes, and Colons lessons, as well as how to select the appropriate pronoun or modifier in the Agreement: Pronouns and Agreement: Modifiers lessons. Then, try the questions you missed again. As always, be sure to review the explanations closely. Then go online (**kaptest.com/login**) to watch video lessons about the highest-yield concepts in this chapter and to use your Qbank for more practice. If you haven't already registered your book, do so at *kaptest.com/moreonline*.

GO ONLINE

kaptest.com/login

Answers and Explanations

Sentence Structure: The Basics

1.   Review the Explanation portion of the Sentence Structure: The Basics lesson.

2.   **G**

Difficulty: Medium

Category: Sentence Structure

Getting to the Answer: The phrase "For what seemed like eons" is a dependent clause that must be set off from the rest of the sentence with a comma, so (G) is correct. Choices F, H, and J all create sentence fragments, since the first part of the sentence cannot stand on its own.

3.   **A**

Difficulty: Low

Category: Sentence Structure

Getting to the Answer: If a sentence includes two independent clauses, they must be properly combined. The independent clauses can be separated by a coordinating conjunction and a comma, as they currently are in the passage; separated by a semicolon, as in B; separated into two sentences, as in C; or edited so that the first part of the sentence is a dependent clause, as in D. By omitting punctuation altogether, (A) creates a run-on sentence.

4.   **G**

Difficulty: Medium

Category: Sentence Structure

Getting to the Answer: Choice F is incorrect because placing a period after *nearby* creates a sentence fragment. Changing the period to a comma creates a grammatically correct sentence with an introductory phrase followed by an independent clause. Choice (G) is correct. Choices H and J incorrectly use the coordinating conjunction *and*, which makes the resulting sentence an incomplete thought.

5.   **C**

Difficulty: High

Category: Sentence Structure

Getting to the Answer: The sentence includes two independent clauses that must be properly combined. Choice A is incorrect because it includes no punctuation whatsoever. Choice (C) correctly uses a dash to join the two clauses. Choices B and D are incorrect because both a comma and a coordinating conjunction are required to join two independent clauses. Choice B omits the conjunction, while D omits the comma.

6.   **J**

Difficulty: Medium

Category: Sentence Structure

Getting to the Answer: The underlined portion contains parts of two independent clauses that must be properly combined. Choice F includes no punctuation at all, and choice G incorrectly uses a comma without a coordinating conjunction. Both choices create a run-on sentence. Finally, eliminate H because *offering* makes the part that follows the semicolon a dependent clause. A semicolon cannot be used to separate an independent clause and a dependent clause. Choice (J) is correct because the comma properly joins the independent clause at the beginning of the sentence with the dependent clause after the comma.

Sentence Structure: Parenthetical Elements

1.   Review the Explanation portion of the Sentence Structure: Parenthetical Elements lesson.

2.   **G**

Difficulty: Low

Category: Sentence Structure

Getting to the Answer: The first part of the sentence is an introductory phrase and must be set off from the sentence with a comma. Eliminate choices F and J because they use incorrect punctuation, and eliminate H because it removes punctuation altogether. Choice (G) is correct.

3.   D

Difficulty: Medium

Category: Sentence Structure

Getting to the Answer: The underlined segment sets off the nonessential phrase "the defeated Gorgon" with one comma and one dash. Either two commas or two dashes must be used to set off this phrase; using one of each is not correct. Eliminate A. Choices B and C do not provide punctuation on both sides of the nonessential phrase, so they can be eliminated as well. Choice (D) is correct.

4.   J

Difficulty: High

Category: Sentence Structure

Getting to the Answer: As written, the sentence includes an unnecessary comma before the word *and*. Choice (J) correctly eliminates this unneeded punctuation mark. The phrase "a gaze that turned onlookers into stone" is not an independent clause. Since semicolons are used to join two independent clauses, choice G is incorrect. Finally, choice H is incorrect because it both includes the unnecessary comma and omits the necessary word *and*.

5.   B

Difficulty: Medium

Category: Sentence Structure

Getting to the Answer: "One of the three Gorgon sisters" is an introductory modifying phrase that must be followed by a comma; (B) is correct. Choice A omits the comma, and C and D add unnecessary words that do not fix the original error.

6.   G

Difficulty: High

Category: Sentence Structure

Getting to the Answer: The phrase "once lovely hair" is essential to the meaning of the sentence, so it should not be separated from the surrounding text with commas or dashes, as in choices F and J. Choice (G) is correct because no punctuation is needed. Choice H incorrectly inserts a comma into the phrase "once lovely hair." Since this phrase is one logical unit, it should not be broken up by a punctuation mark.

Sentence Structure: Commas, Dashes, and Colons

1.   Review the Explanation portion of the Sentence Structure: Commas, Dashes, and Colons lesson.

2.   J

Difficulty: Medium

Category: Sentence Structure

Getting to the Answer: When a comma is underlined, check to make sure it is necessary. The phrase "tedious and unimaginative" is one logical unit and should not be broken up by any sort of punctuation; (J) is correct.

3.   B

Difficulty: Low

Category: Sentence Structure

Getting to the Answer: *However* is a transition word that needs to be separated from the rest of the sentence with a comma; (B) is correct.

4.   F

Difficulty: Medium

Category: Sentence Structure

Getting to the Answer: The sentence includes two independent clauses properly joined with a comma and a FANBOYS (For, And, Nor, But, Or, Yet, So) conjunction, so no change is needed. Choice (F) is correct. Choice G incorrectly uses a semicolon to separate two independent clauses with a FANBOYS conjunction between them. Choices H and J are incorrect because the ideas in the two independent clauses contrast with each other. The transition word *so* indicates cause-and-effect, not contrast.

5.   C

Difficulty: Medium

Category: Sentence Structure

Getting to the Answer: The phrase "Mendelssohn's Symphony No. 4 in A Major" is a parenthetical phrase that must be set off by either two commas or two dashes. Since a dash is used at the end of the phrase, (C) is correct.

6. G

Difficulty: High

Category: Sentence Structure

Getting to the Answer: When a comma is underlined, check to make sure it is necessary. The phrase "lyrical church bells" is one logical unit and should not be broken up by any sort of punctuation; (G) is correct.

Agreement: Verbs

1. Review the Explanation portion of the Agreement: Verbs lesson.

2. F

Difficulty: Low

Category: Agreement

Getting to the Answer: When a verb is underlined, look for context clues that indicate which tense is needed. The sentence includes the phrase *last year*, so the simple past tense is appropriate; (F) is correct. Choice H is incorrect because it is in the past perfect form. This tense is used to indicate that one action happened *before* another action in the past. However, in this paragraph, the two verbs *inherited* and *told* occur at the same time. Finally, choice J contains the auxiliary verb *would*. This form is appropriate to use only when the sentence contains another clause starting with *if*.

3. B

Difficulty: High

Category: Agreement

Getting to the Answer: The idiomatic expressions *either...or* and *neither...nor* create singular subjects, and the phrase *past situations* indicates that past tense is required. Choice (B) is correct because it is the only option that uses the singular past-tense verb *was*.

4. H

Difficulty: High

Category: Agreement

Getting to the Answer: When a verb is underlined, identify its subject. The subject is *darkness*, which is singular. The singular present tense verb *teems* is needed; (H) is correct. Choice F is present tense

but plural. Choices G and J are incorrect because the future perfect tense and the infinitive form of the verb *teem* do not make sense in context.

5. D

Difficulty: Medium

Category: Agreement

Getting to the Answer: Since the verb *grip* is part of the compound verb phrase "took a deep breath and grip the ladder," the verbs *took* and *grip* must match. As written, *took* is past tense and *grip* is present tense; eliminate A. Choice (D) corrects the error by changing *grip* to *gripped*.

6. G

Difficulty: High

Category: Agreement

Getting to the Answer: All items in a list must be parallel in structure. The first two items are verb phrases, so the last item must also be a verb phrase; (G) is correct. Choices F, H, and J are all noun phrases, not verb phrases.

Agreement: Pronouns

1. Review the Explanation portion of the Agreement: Pronouns lesson.

2. J

Difficulty: Low

Category: Agreement

Getting to the Answer: When a pronoun is underlined, identify its antecedent, the noun to which it refers. The antecedent is *citizens*, so the subjective plural pronoun *they* is needed; (J) is correct. Choice F is incorrect because *it* is singular. Choices G and H are plural, but *their* is possessive and *them* is objective.

3.   B

Difficulty: High

Category: Agreement

Getting to the Answer: When deciding between *who* and *whom*, see if there is a preposition in front of the word in question. If there is, then you need the objective case *whom*. In this sentence, there is no preposition, so the subjective case *who* is required; (B) is correct. The word *that* cannot be used to refer to people, so C and D are incorrect.

4.   J

Difficulty: Medium

Category: Agreement

Getting to the Answer: The antecedent, the noun to which the pronoun refers, is *components*, so a plural pronoun is required; (J) is correct. Choice F means *it is* and H is not grammatically correct in any context. While G is a correctly written possessive pronoun, it is singular, not plural.

5.   A

Difficulty: Medium

Category: Agreement

Getting to the Answer: The underlined pronoun refers to *the roadbed*, which is singular, so the singular pronoun *it* is correct as written.

6.   J

Difficulty: Medium

Category: Agreement

Getting to the Answer: Throughout the passage, the writer does not address the reader directly, so F and G are incorrect. Choice H does not make sense in context. Choice (J) correctly uses the more formal indefinite pronoun *one*, which is grammatically correct and matches the writer's tone.

Agreement: Modifiers

1.   Review the Explanation portion of the Agreement: Modifiers lesson.

2.   J

Difficulty: Medium

Category: Agreement

Getting to the Answer: The underlined segment includes the comparative adjective *earlier*. The comparative form is used only when discussing exactly two items or people. This sentence is about all examples of basketry, so F is incorrect. Choices G and H are incorrect because the phrases *more early* and *most early* are not as concise as *earliest*. Choice (J) correctly uses the superlative adjective *earliest*.

3.   D

Difficulty: Low

Category: Agreement

Getting to the Answer: The verb phrase "have been preserved" must be modified by an adverb; eliminate A and B, which contain adjectives. Choice C is unnecessarily wordy. Choice (D) is both correct and concise.

4.   F

Difficulty: Medium

Category: Agreement

Getting to the Answer: If the sentence had used the phrase "baskets' remains," an apostrophe would be needed. However, the preposition *of* makes punctuation unnecessary; G, H, and J are incorrect. Choice (F) correctly omits all apostrophes.

5.   C

Difficulty: High

Category: Agreement

Getting to the Answer: "Opting for rigid materials" is an introductory modifying phrase, so the noun that the phrase is modifying must come immediately after the comma. Choice (C) correctly places *basket makers* after the comma. Choices A, B, and D do not feature the correct noun after the comma.

6. G

Difficulty: Medium

Category: Agreement

Getting to the Answer: The sentence requires the possessive form of the word *it*, which is written without an apostrophe; (G) is correct. The word *it's* means *it is*, so F is incorrect. Choice H is incorrect because the antecedent (the word *basket*) is singular, while the pronoun *their* is plural. Finally, J is incorrect because *they're*, which means "they are," does not fit in the context of the sentence.

Agreement: Idioms

1. Review the Explanation portion of the Agreement: Idioms lesson.

2. G

Difficulty: Medium

Category: Agreement

Getting to the Answer: Since *scarcely* is implicitly negative, it cannot be paired with *not*; (G) is correct. Choice F includes *couldn't*, which means *could not*. Choices H and J also pair the word *not* with *scarcely*, so they are incorrect.

3. D

Difficulty: Medium

Category: Agreement

Getting to the Answer: The word *either* must be paired with *or*, not *and*; eliminate A and B. The phrase "confused by a misidentification" is not an independent clause, so a comma is not needed before *or*; (D) is correct.

4. F

Difficulty: Medium

Category: Agreement

Getting to the Answer: When prepositions such as *in* and *at* are underlined, make sure they are idiomatically correct. The phrase "in the world" is correct because Alfred was a part of the world population rather than an object placed upon the Earth's surface. In addition, "at the time" is correct because the context indicates that Alfred was one of the richest people in the world during

that time period. Choice (F) is correct. The phrase "for the time being" doesn't make sense because the passage is describing past events, so G and H are incorrect. While J correctly includes "at the time," it incorrectly uses the preposition *on* instead of *in*.

5. C

Difficulty: Medium

Category: Agreement

Getting to the Answer: When a preposition is underlined, make sure that it is idiomatically correct. Warfare is an abstract concept and cannot use dynamite, so eliminate A. People use dynamite *in* war, so (C) is correct. Choice B is incorrect because dynamite is used as part of war, not alongside it. Choice D is incorrect because *used to* must be followed by a verb, which does not happen in this sentence.

6. J

Difficulty: High

Category: Agreement

Getting to the Answer: When a sentence includes the words *not only*, it must include *but also* as well. Only (J) includes *also*, so it is correct.

How Much Have You Learned?

1. C

Difficulty: Medium

Category: Sentence Structure

Getting to the Answer: As written, the sentence is a run-on, so A is incorrect. Choices B, (C), and D all attempt to fix the run-on error. Choice B is incorrect because the word *nevertheless* is not a coordinating conjunction and cannot join two sentences unless a semicolon is used as well. Choice D suffers from the opposite problem; it uses a coordinating conjunction with a semicolon instead of a comma. Only (C) corrects the run-on and does not introduce new errors.

2. J

Difficulty: High

Category: Agreement

Getting to the Answer: "Originating from their appearance, material, or use," is an introductory modifying phrase, so the item(s) that the phrase is modifying must immediately follow the comma after *use*. Eliminate F and G because the phrase is describing marbles' names, not "an important identifying factor." Choice H is incorrect because it uses the singular possessive *marble's*, which does not match the plural noun *names*. Choice (J) correctly places *marbles' names* after the modifying phrase and does not introduce new errors.

3. D

Difficulty: Medium

Category: Sentence Structure

Getting to the Answer: Parenthetical information includes words or phrases that aren't essential to the sentence structure or content and must be set off with commas. Choices A and B are incorrect because they do not include commas on both sides of the parenthetical phrase *for example*. Choice C misuses the colon, which is used to introduce a short phrase, quotation, explanation, example, or list. Choice (D) correctly sets off the nonessential phrase *for example* with two commas.

4. G

Difficulty: Medium

Category: Sentence Structure

Getting to the Answer: Since the verb *consist* and the preposition *of* form one logical unit, they should not be separated by punctuation of any sort; (G) is correct.

5. A

Difficulty: Low

Category: Agreement

Getting to the Answer: The underlined segment contains an idiom, or a phrase that must have a certain combination of words in order to be correct. The phrase *Regardless of* is idiomatically correct, so (A) is correct.

Choice B uses the incorrect preposition *to*. Choices C and D use the word *regardlessly*, which is not correct in any context.

6. F

Difficulty: Medium

Category: Sentence Structure

Getting to the Answer: Determine whether any of the tested comma rules apply to the underlined segment. Two commas are used to set off a nonessential phrase, so read the sentence without *in which* to see if the sentence still makes sense. Choice G is incorrect because the phrase *in which* is essential and thus should not be set off with commas. Choice H mistakenly places a comma between the preposition *in* and its object *which*. Finally, choice J is incorrect because the semicolon here is not joining two independent clauses. Choice (F) is correct.

7. D

Difficulty: Low

Category: Agreement

Getting to the Answer: The sentence includes items in a list that are not in parallel form, so A is incorrect. Eliminate B because it does not address the error. Choice (D) fixes the issue by using the past-tense *kicked*, which matches the other past-tense verbs in the list. Choice C includes the correct verb form but is unnecessarily wordy.

8. J

Difficulty: High

Category: Agreement

Getting to the Answer: The underlined portion has two issues. The verb *is* does not agree with its subject *varieties,* and the adverb *nearly*, not the adjective *near*, is needed. Choice (J) fixes both mistakes. None of the other options corrects both errors.

9. C

Difficulty: Medium

Category: Sentence Structure

Getting to the Answer: Although a parenthetical phrase may appear in the beginning, middle, or end of a sentence, punctuation will always separate it from the rest of the sentence. Because the sentence makes logical sense without the phrase "also known as ringtaw or ringer," two commas or two dashes are needed to set it off from the rest of the sentence. Eliminate A because using one dash and one comma is not acceptable. Eliminate B because the second dash is incorrectly placed in the middle of the parenthetical phase. Choice D uses two commas correctly but includes an unnecessary comma after *ringtaw*. Choice (C) is correct, since it uses two dashes to offset the parenthetical phrase and excludes unnecessary punctuation.

10. H

Difficulty: Low

Category: Agreement

Getting to the Answer: Pronouns must agree with their antecedents in both person and number. The antecedent here is *players*, so a third-person plural pronoun is needed; (H) is correct. Choice F is incorrect because *our* is first-person. Choice G uses a second-person pronoun, and J uses a singular pronoun.

11. B

Difficulty: Low

Category: Agreement

Getting to the Answer: The sentence that appears after the underlined period is a fragment, so A is incorrect. Choice (B) fixes the fragment by using the conjunction *and* to join the verb phrase after the period with the independent clause before the period. Choices C and D are incorrect because a semicolon or a comma and a coordinating conjunction are used to join two independent clauses, not an independent clause and a verb phrase.

12. J

Difficulty: Medium

Category: Agreement

Getting to the Answer: The underlined portion includes a pronoun and a verb. The phrase is referring to *the game*, so a singular pronoun and a singular verb are needed; (J) is correct. None of the other choices includes singular forms of both the pronoun and the verb.

Spotting and Fixing Issues: Conciseness, Organization, and Development

LEARNING OBJECTIVES

After completing this chapter, you will be able to:

- Revise wordy writing
- Determine the appropriate transition word or phrase to establish logical relationships within and between sentences
- Determine the appropriate transition sentence to establish logical relationships between paragraphs
- Determine the most logical place for a sentence in a paragraph or passage
- Identify the word that accomplishes the appropriate purpose within a sentence
- Provide an introduction or conclusion to a paragraph or passage
- Revise a sentence to accomplish a specific purpose
- Determine the relevance of a sentence within a passage
- Determine whether a passage has met a goal and state why or why not

Conciseness: 4/36 SmartPoints® (Medium yield)

Organization: 4/36 SmartPoints® (Medium yield)

Development: 9/36 SmartPoints® (Very high yield)

A Note About the Passages in This Chapter

Due to the more global nature of Organization and Development questions and the fact that ACT English passages include at least one Organization question and at least two Development questions, you will see the same passages intentionally used multiple times throughout this chapter. Each lesson will present the portion of the passage needed to answer the question(s). On test day, the various question types will be spaced throughout the passage, so you should prepare to review the entire passage, not just the underlined segments or only one or two paragraphs.

How Much Do You Know?

Directions: Try out the questions below. The "Category" heading in the explanation for each question gives the title of the lesson that covers how to answer it. If you answered the question(s) for a given lesson correctly, you may be able to move quickly through that lesson. If you answered incorrectly, you may want to take your time on that lesson.

Eva Salazar: Master Weaver

The Kumeyaay are a Native American people who have <u>developed</u> in the area now known as San Diego, California, for 12,000 years. They have retained a rich cultural and social life despite a forced split in 1875, when many Kumeyaay were driven across the border into Mexico. Now resettled in small farming communities, such as San José de la Zorra, the families have preserved their traditional way of life.

It is in this remote valley that Eva Salazar learned the ancient art of basket weaving from her tribal elders. Traditionally, Kumeyaay women have the <u>crucially necessary</u> responsibility of making baskets, which are important artifacts of everyday life. Kumeyaay baskets are tightly woven with expressive designs. They are made mostly for utilitarian purposes: cooking, storing food products, and gathering ingredients. As traditional objects of art, they are also valued for their aesthetic beauty.

1. A. NO CHANGE
   B. blossomed
   C. thrived
   D. withered

2. F. NO CHANGE
   G. crucial
   H. necessary and crucial
   J. fundamentally crucial

<u>Following in her ancestor's footsteps,</u> Eva Salazar
₃
uses native materials to weave her intricate baskets,
primarily the strong, sharp reed known as juncus, as
well as yucca, sumac, and other native plants. She colors
the reeds with black walnut, elderberry, and other
natural dyes. Eva specializes in coiled baskets, and her
shapes and decorations echo traditional forms.

<u>Though</u> she is best known for her baskets, Eva
₄
Salazar also makes dolls, willow bark skirts, nets, and
shell necklaces. Her most ambitious work is a basket
measuring almost three feet in diameter. The basket took
her two years to weave and represents a masterpiece of
Native American art.

Today, Eva is heralded as a master weaver. Now an
American citizen living in San Diego, she remains
focused on traditional tribal arts and teaches basket
weaving at local reservations and colleges. <u>Her baskets</u>
₅
<u>continue to represent the height of Kumeyaay basket-</u>
₅
<u>weaving artistry.</u>
₅

3. If the author were to delete the underlined portion, the sentence would primarily lose:

A. a counterargument regarding the authenticity of modern crafts.

B. a key detail that explains Eva Salazar's relationship to the Kumeyaay.

C. a claim that Eva Salazar will develop her own basket-weaving methods in the future.

D. a suggestion that the Kumeyaay should place greater value on Eva Salazar's work.

4. F. NO CHANGE

G. Because

H. Nonetheless

J. On the other hand

5. Which choice most effectively concludes the passage?

A. NO CHANGE

B. She is famous for not letting the Kumeyaay traditions be lost.

C. Her work has inspired countless artists to follow in her footsteps, ensuring that Kumeyaay basket weaving continues to thrive.

D. She will be remembered for her unique adaptations of the Kumeyaay traditions.

Sweat Lodges

The 21st century has seen a marked increase in the popularity of natural medicines and therapies. Among the most common of these is the sweat lodge, a practice established by some groups of indigenous peoples of the Americas. Because of the benefits this practice offers, many cultures independently evolved similar traditions, including the Finnish sauna and the Turkish steam room. The basic purpose of these therapies is to raise the body's core temperature to between 102 and 106 degrees Fahrenheit. At this temperature, bacterial and viral infections within the body cannot easily survive. The heat can also ease muscle tension and soreness, and the resulting perspiration flushes the system of toxins.

[1] In other designs, an altar barrier is positioned between the fire and the entrance to prevent participants from accidentally falling into the fire pit when they emerge from the lodge. [2] A traditional sweat lodge may be built from willow, as its bark is considered medicinal and, indeed, contains the same analgesic as aspirin. [3] Other lodges are made using a few different materials, including blankets, animal skins, and canvas. [4] In some traditions, the entrance of the sweat lodge faces east, with a clear and unobstructed view of a sacred fire pit where the stones are heated before being brought inside the lodge. 7

6. Which choice provides the best transition from the start of the paragraph into the information that follows?

F. NO CHANGE

G. Nearly every culture has adopted this practice in some form,

H. The benefits this practice offers have led many other cultures to adapt it in forms more suited to their own resources,

J. The popularity of the practice is well-earned by the many health benefits it grants to participants,

7. For the sake of the logic and coherence of this paragraph, Sentence 1 should be placed:

A. where it is now.

B. after Sentence 2.

C. after Sentence 3.

D. after Sentence 4.

The exact ceremonial process will vary, but prior to entering the lodge, <u>participants usually change into simple, traditional clothing.</u> In some versions of the
8
ceremony, the Stone People spirits are called upon and the sweat leader sounds the Water Drum once all participants have entered the lodge. A sweat might include more than one session, each lasting 30 to 45 minutes and focused on one of four distinct themes: the spirit world, cleanliness and honesty, individual prayer, and growth and healing.

Traditional sweat lodge ceremonies, which often included songs, prayers, and chants, were believed to purify not only the body <u>but also the mind as well.</u>
9
"Healing comes on a spiritual level," wrote Dr. Lewis Mehl-Madrona in his book *Coyote Medicine*. "Ceremony and ritual provide the means of making ourselves available."

8. Which of the following details best emphasizes the spiritual aspects of the sweat lodge tradition?

F. NO CHANGE

G. the sweat leader must complete years of intense training to be entrusted with the role.

H. it is important to ensure that all participants are healthy, since otherwise the intense conditions of a sweat can be harmful.

J. participants are often smudged with the smoke of burning sage, sweetgrass, or cedar to signify ritual cleanliness.

9. A. NO CHANGE

B. but also the mind in addition.

C. but also the mind.

D. but also additionally the mind.

Question 10 asks about the passage as a whole.

---

10. Suppose the author's main goal had been to write an essay describing a personal experience with a sweat lodge. Would this passage accomplish the purpose?

F. Yes, because the passage tells about the process a person goes through in a sweat.

G. Yes, because the passage explains how Dr. Lewis Mehl-Madrona feels about the ceremony.

H. No, because only the last two paragraphs discuss what happens at a sweat lodge.

J. No, because the passage describes general information about sweat lodge ceremonies, not one specific experience.

Check Your Work

1. C

Difficulty: Medium

Category: Development: Precision

Getting to the Answer: This question tests word choice. The sentence says that the Kumeyaay have lived in southern California for millennia; moreover, the sentence that follows says they maintained "a rich cultural and social life," so the correct answer must reflect that. Choices A and B both incorrectly suggest a process or change, and D is the opposite of the author's meaning. Only (C) correctly expresses the intended meaning.

2. G

Difficulty: Low

Category: Conciseness

Getting to the Answer: *Crucially necessary* is redundant. Choices F and H both include these words in different forms, so eliminate them. Choice J includes a word with a similar meaning in context, *fundamentally*, so it is also redundant. Only (G) eliminates the redundancy.

3. B

Difficulty: Medium

Category: Development: Revising Text

Getting to the Answer: The underlined portion details the relationship between Eva Salazar and the Kumeyaay. Deleting this would take away a key detail explaining her ties to the native community whose traditions she carries on through her art. Choice (B) is correct. Since the underlined segment does not provide a counterargument, claim, or suggestion, A, C, and D are incorrect.

4. F

Difficulty: Medium

Category: Organization: Transitions

Getting to the Answer: Transitions must accurately convey the relationship between ideas. The underlined transition correctly shows a contrast between what Eva is primarily known for and her other artistic creations. Choice (F) is correct. Choice G is not a contrast transition. The contrast transitions in H and J both make the first clause independent rather than dependent, turning the sentence into a run-on. Since they introduce a grammatical error, they are incorrect.

5. C

Difficulty: High

Category: Development: Introductions and Conclusions

Getting to the Answer: The final sentence must effectively conclude both the passage and the paragraph. The passage discusses Eva Salazar's dedication to preserving Kumeyaay traditions. According to the final paragraph, she has done this through learning her craft and passing her knowledge on to other artists. Choice (C) conveys how she has kept basket-weaving traditions alive through her own work and through teaching others. You may hesitate to choose this answer because it is noticeably less concise than the other options, but sometimes a long sentence is needed to convey complex ideas. Always think carefully about what a question asks to make sure the answer fulfills it. Choices B and D are incorrect because both bring up ideas outside the scope of the passage; Salazar's fame or unique adaptations of traditional art are never discussed. Choice A is factually correct but not a good conclusion because it does not emphasize the preservation of Kumeyaay artistic traditions.

6. F

Difficulty: High

Category: Organization: Transitions

Getting to the Answer: An effective transition must show the relationship between the ideas it connects. The beginning of this paragraph introduces the popularity of natural medicine, particularly sweat lodges. The information that follows briefly mentions similar practices elsewhere but primarily discusses the health benefits of such practices. Choice G does not connect sweat lodges to health benefits, so eliminate it. Choice H does connect the two, but it also brings up the topic of resources, which is not mentioned in the paragraph at all. Choice J may be tempting because it neatly connects the popularity of sweat lodges to their health benefits. However, when plugged into the sentence, it creates a modifier error in which the phrase "including the Finnish sauna and the Turkish steam room" describes *participants* instead of *examples* of similar practices. Only (F) connects sweat lodges with similar practices and with health benefits.

7. D

Difficulty: Medium

Category: Organization: Sentence Placement

Getting to the Answer: Sentence 1 does not fit well where it is now, since it jumps right into the middle of an ongoing description with specific details that have not yet been discussed, like the fire and the entrance. The paragraph would be clearer and more logical if Sentence 1 were placed after those details have been introduced in Sentence 4. Thus, (D) is the correct answer.

8. J

Difficulty: Medium

Category: Development: Revising Text

Getting to the Answer: This question asks for a detail emphasizing the spiritual aspects of the sweat lodge. Choice H discusses purely practical concerns and can be quickly eliminated. Choices F and G do not make clear whether the preparations they describe have spiritual significance or not. Choice (J) is the only answer that explicitly states that an action is undertaken for ritual, symbolic reasons, so (J) is correct.

9. C

Difficulty: Low

Category: Conciseness

Getting to the Answer: Including both *also* and *as well* makes this phrase redundant. Choices A, B, and D all include similarly redundant transition words, so (C) is correct.

10. J

Difficulty: Medium

Category: Development: Purpose

Getting to the Answer: To answer this type of question, first determine the primary purpose of the passage. This passage describes the physical and spiritual elements of Native American sweat lodge traditions. If the author's goal were to focus on an individual's experience, this passage would not be successful. Eliminate F and G. Choice H gives an incorrect reason why the passage does not fulfill the author's goal. Only (J) correctly identifies that the passage does not succeed because it gives a general description rather than tells an individual's story.

Conciseness

LEARNING OBJECTIVE

After this lesson, you will be able to:

● Revise wordy writing

To answer a question like this:

Sweat Lodges

Traditional Native American sweat lodges focus on both physical and spiritual healing. <u>Sometimes,</u> a sweat might include more than one session, each lasting 30 to 45 minutes and focused on one of four distinct themes: the spirit world, cleanliness and honesty, individual prayer, and growth and healing.

1. A. NO CHANGE
   B. More often,
   C. Occasionally,
   D. DELETE the underlined portion and capitalize the word *A*.

You need to know this:

Conciseness

A concise sentence does not include any unnecessary words. Phrasing that is wordy is considered stylistically incorrect on the ACT and needs to be revised. Each word must contribute to the meaning of the sentence; otherwise, it should be eliminated.

A *redundant* sentence says something twice: "The new policy precipitated a crisis situation." A crisis is a type of situation, so there is no need to include both *crisis* and *situation*. The sentence should be rephrased as, "The new policy precipitated a crisis." Redundancy is always incorrect on the ACT.

Wordy/Redundant sentence	Concise sentence
The superb musical score **added enhancement to the experience of** the play's development.	The superb musical score **enhanced** the play's development.
I **did not anticipate** the **surprising, unexpected** plot twist.	I **did not anticipate** the plot twist.
The students **increased some of their knowledge of** Tuscan architecture.	The students **learned about** Tuscan architecture.

You need to do this:

Choose the most concise grammatically correct option that conveys the writer's intended meaning. When answering questions about conciseness:

- Consider selecting the "DELETE the underlined portion" answer choice if there is one, according to the following guidelines:
  - If the underlined portion is wordy or redundant, delete it.
  - If the underlined portion does not enhance the intended meaning or clarity of the passage, delete it.
  - Each of the four answer choices is equally likely, so give this option the same weight as the others.
- Identify the shortest answer choice (it will not always be the correct answer, but it is an efficient place to start).
- Identify words and phrases that have the same meaning, e.g., *thoughtful* and *mindful* or *end result* and *final outcome*. Find a choice that deletes one of the redundant expressions.

Explanation:

When "DELETE the underlined portion" is an option, check whether the underlined portion contributes to the meaning of the passage. Eliminate A because the word *might* already shows that multi-session sweats do not occur all the time. *More often* and *occasionally* introduce information about frequency that is not supported by the passage, so B and C are incorrect. Because none of the other answer choices add to the meaning of the sentence, (D) is the correct answer.

Drills

If conciseness gives you trouble, study the information above and try out these drill questions before completing the Try on Your Own questions below. Turn the page and look at the bottom of the page to see the answers.

Eliminate word(s) to make the sentences more concise without losing meaning.

a. The school was founded and established in 1906.

b. I felt a sense of nervous anxiety before the curtain rose.

c. We were in agreement with each other that Naomi should be captain.

d. After a job interview, make sure to send a note of gratitude expressing thanks to your interviewer.

e. Not long after he graduated from Oxford, Oscar Wilde moved to London, a place in which he embarked on his literary career in earnest.

Try on Your Own

Directions: Take as much time as you need on these questions. Work carefully and methodically. There will be an opportunity for timed practice at the end of the chapter.

International Model United Nations

For many years, the Hague has been the stage of The European International Model United Nations (TEIMUN), <u>which is a model of the United Nations.</u>
₂
TEIMUN started in 1987, when a group of American students on an exchange program in the Netherlands organized the first conference as a part of their focus on international relations. The organizers hoped to educate participants about the workings of an international organization in order to combat <u>a growing sense of</u>
₃
<u>isolationism</u> among European youth.
₃

There were many hurdles to overcome, for students' attitudes in Europe toward simulations of the United Nations were not favorable. Hence, drumming up interest was a struggle. The Americans also wanted to

2.　F.　NO CHANGE

　　G.　being a model of the United Nations.

　　H.　which is a model UN.

　　J.　DELETE the underlined portion and change comma after *(TEIMUN)* to a period.

3.　A.　NO CHANGE

　　B.　the increasing and growing isolationism

　　C.　a growing feeling of isolationism and separation

　　D.　the increasing isolationism and sense of alienation

Drill answers from previous page:

Note: These are not the only ways to correct the sentences; your answers may differ.

a. The school was founded ~~and established~~ in 1906.

b. I felt ~~a sense of~~ nervous ~~anxiety~~ before the curtain rose.

c. We ~~were in agreement with each other~~ **agreed** that Naomi should be captain.

d. After a job interview, make sure to send a note ~~of gratitude expressing thanks~~ to **thank** your interviewer.

e. Not long after he graduated from Oxford, Oscar Wilde moved to London, ~~a place in which~~ **where** he embarked on his literary career in earnest.

ensure that <u>this new model UN would have a plan to</u> ₄ <u>help students from less-developed European countries</u> ₄ <u>with their participation.</u> ₄ Through the American students' hard work, TEIMUN prospered and attracted more participants. Over the years, the TEIMUN conference has become one of the biggest and most important model United Nations on the European continent, with participants from over 65 countries.

4. F. NO CHANGE

G. their new model United Nations had systems in place to help students from less-developed European countries participate.

H. there were rules built in to the system with the purpose of helping students from less-developed countries in their participation.

J. there were methods for helping students from less-developed countries to participate.

Organization: Transitions

LEARNING OBJECTIVES

After this lesson, you will be able to:

- Determine the appropriate transition word or phrase to establish logical relationships within and between sentences
- Determine the appropriate transition sentence to establish logical relationships between paragraphs

To answer a question like this:

International Model United Nations

Students still direct and organize each yearly conference. They seek new ways to attract enthusiastic participants, <u>since students from less-developed nations</u>
<u>are still underrepresented.</u> Countless alumni have gone
on to pursue careers in international policy after first encountering the art of diplomacy during their years in TEIMUN.

1. Which choice most effectively concludes this sentence and leads into the information that follows in the paragraph?

   A. NO CHANGE
   B. and they strongly believe that TEIMUN is a powerful avenue for fostering an interest in diplomacy among Europe's youth.
   C. even working to expand recruitment outside of Europe.
   D. and they closely follow the policies of individual countries as well as international relations in order to keep the conference up to date.

You need to know this:

Writers use transitions to show relationships such as contrast, cause and effect, continuation, emphasis, and chronology (order of events). Knowing which words indicate which type of transition will help you choose the correct answer on test day.

Contrast transitions	Cause-and-effect transitions	Continuation transitions	Emphasis transitions	Chronology transitions
although, but, despite, even though, however, in contrast, nonetheless, on the other hand, rather than, though, unlike, while, yet	as a result, because, consequently, since, so, therefore, thus	also, furthermore, in addition, moreover	certainly, in fact, indeed, that is	before, after, first (second, etc.), then, finally

You need to do this:

If a transition word is underlined, you must determine the writer's intended meaning and find the transition that best conveys this meaning. Use the surrounding text to pinpoint the appropriate word.

Explanation:

The underlined portion needs to connect the beginning of the paragraph, which discusses student organizers recruiting participants, with the last sentence, which discusses TEIMUN alumni inspired to pursue diplomatic careers. The only answer choice that does so effectively is (B).

Drills

If transitions give you trouble, study the information above and try out these drill questions before completing the Try on Your Own questions below. Turn the page and look at the bottom of the page to see the answers.

Choose the correct transition word for each sentence.

a.   (Due to/Despite) its impressive technical innovations, the small startup thrived.

b.   Cashew nuts are a popular snack worldwide; (however/moreover), they can be difficult to harvest because their shells contain a toxic resin.

c.   Izdehar is the most level-headed of my friends—(in fact/next), I think she's more reliable than some adults I know.

d.   After days of hard work, we (finally/nonetheless) finished our science fair project.

e.   The actor won an award for best supporting role this year (consequently/in addition to) releasing her first pop music album.

Try on Your Own

Directions: Take as much time as you need on these questions. Work carefully and methodically. There will be an opportunity for timed practice at the end of the chapter.

The Victorian Way of Life

The Victorian Era stretched from the coronation of Queen Victoria in 1837 to her death in 1901. Over her 63-year reign, her influence on Britain was profound. Politics and international affairs aside, manners, morals, and even dress conformed to Victoria's straightlaced concepts of what was and was not acceptable. Despite the upper classes, propriety and reputation had to be spotlessly maintained.

2. F. NO CHANGE
    G. Especially for
    H. Regardless of
    J. Occasionally among

3 In the 1840s, women's dresses were relatively simple, albeit with a number of stiff petticoats. Thirty years later, restricting corsets were worn to pull in the waist to the

3. Which of the following provides the most effective transition from the previous paragraph to this paragraph?

    A. Victoria believed modesty was particularly important for women.
    B. Lower classes were less constrained.
    C. Fashion styles were among the prescribed customs.
    D. The period's fashion innovations remain famous to this day.

Drill answers from previous page:

a. **Due to** its impressive technical innovations, the small startup thrived.

b. Cashew nuts are a popular snack worldwide; **however**, they can be difficult to harvest because their shells contain a toxic resin.

c. Izdehar is the most level-headed of my friends—**in fact**, I think she's more reliable than some adults I know.

d. After days of hard work, we **finally** finished our science fair project.

e. The actor won an award for best supporting role this year **in addition to** releasing her first pop music album.

smallest width possible <u>while</u> still leaving the wearer
room to breathe. Hats and gloves were expected for all
occasions.

Most upper-class women were educated only to the
point of literacy, with household management and
domestic arts such as needlework heavily emphasized.
<u>Because of this,</u> some women were quite well schooled,
depending on their fathers' opinion about the propriety
of educated females. Queen Victoria herself,
unsurprisingly, fell on the more educated end of the
spectrum; she spoke multiple languages and studied law
and ethics as a teenager. <u>However, her favorite subject
was history.</u>

It is a mark of the length, importance, and impact of
Queen Victoria's reign that this period of British history
is known as the Victorian Era. She left her indelible
mark not only on society and culture but also on British
influence throughout the world.

4. F. NO CHANGE
   G. rather than
   H. therefore
   J. thus

5. A. NO CHANGE
   B. Therefore,
   C. Indeed,
   D. On the other hand,

6. Given that all the choices are true, which
   one provides the best transition to the next
   paragraph?

   F. NO CHANGE
   G. This background both prepared her to
      be a world leader and influenced her
      royal policy.
   H. Her governess and varied tutors found
      her a bright but willful student.
   J. In fact, she was better educated than
      many of her prime ministers.

Organization: Sentence Placement

To answer a question like this:

Symbiotic Relationships

In the natural world, when two or more different organisms coexist, they are involved in a symbiotic relationship. Sometimes these relationships are beneficial to both organisms; other times, these relationships are beneficial to only one organism and either have no effect or are harmful to the other organism. When both organisms benefit, their relationship is known as mutualism.

[1] A classic symbiotic relationship of this kind takes place in the digestive tract of Florida wood-eating termites. [2] The protozoa provide the termite with a service necessary to its survival: they digest the cellulose in the wood that the termite consumes. [3] We think of a termite as being able to digest wood, but, in fact, it cannot. [4] The termite plays host to the protozoa, single-celled organisms that live in the termite's gut. [1]

1. For the sake of the logic and coherence of this paragraph, Sentence 2 should be placed:

   A. where it is now.

   B. before sentence 1.

   C. after sentence 3.

   D. after sentence 4.

You need to know this:

Some Organization questions will ask you to check and potentially fix the placement of a sentence within a paragraph (or a paragraph within a passage, though this is rare). Others will ask you for the best place to insert a new sentence. Your approach in both cases should be the same.

You need to do this:

Look for specific clues that indicate the best organization. Common clues include:

- Chronology: If the information is presented in order by the time when it occurred, place the sentence within the correct time frame.

- Explanation of a term or phrase: If the passage features a term, such as nuclear fusion, the writer will explain what it is (in this case, the joining of two or more nuclei to form a heavier nucleus) before using the term in other contexts.

- Introduction of a person: If the passage introduces someone, such as Grace Hopper, the writer will first refer to the person by first and last name before referring to the person by either first name (Grace) or last name (Hopper) only.

- Examples: A general statement is often followed by support in the form of examples.

- Logic: Transition words such as "however," "also," "furthermore," and "therefore" may signal the logic of the paragraph. For example, the word "therefore" indicates that a conclusion is being drawn from evidence that should logically come before it.

Explanation:

Sentence 2 discusses the function of the protozoa, but the protozoa haven't yet been introduced in the paragraph. Sentence 2 must be moved to follow the sentence that introduces the protozoa, which is Sentence 4. Choice (D) is correct.

Try on Your Own

Directions: Take as much time as you need on these questions. Work carefully and methodically. There will be an opportunity for timed practice at the end of the chapter.

Symbiotic Relationships

In the natural world, when two or more different organisms coexist, they are involved in a symbiotic relationship. Sometimes these relationships are beneficial to both organisms; other times, these relationships are beneficial to only one organism and either have no effect or are harmful to the other organism. [A] When both organisms benefit, their relationship is known as mutualism.

[1] A classic symbiotic relationship of this kind takes place in the digestive tract of Florida wood-eating termites. [2] The protozoa provide the termite with a service necessary to its survival: they digest the cellulose in the wood that the termite consumes. [3] We think of a termite as being able to digest wood, but, in fact, it cannot. [4] The termite plays host to the protozoa, single-celled organisms that live in the termite's gut.

That is far from the whole story, however. The only movement that protozoa are capable of on their own is spinning; they cannot move around inside the termite's intestine to reach the cellulose. This problem is solved by a third member of the partnership. [B] Each protozoan harbors a colony of thousands of bacteria attached to its surface. Whip-like tentacles on the bacteria (known as flagella) wave back and forth and propel each host protozoan forward. [C]

These bacteria may do more than just drive the protozoan around. Some bacteria can be found inside the protozoan and are thought to help with the digestion of tiny wood particles. [D] If this all sounds strange, consider the fact that humans have symbiotic relationships with bacteria of their own. [2]

Question 2 asks about the passage as a whole.

---

2. The writer would like to add the following sentence:

   > This allows the protozoan to move around and to continue consuming cellulose within the termite.

   The sentence would be most logically placed at:

   F. Point A in paragraph 1.
   G. Point B in paragraph 3.
   H. Point C in paragraph 3.
   J. Point D in paragraph 4.

Early 19th-Century Women in New England

In the early 19th century, the market economy expanded, and the home became a haven from the developing commercialism. [A] With men working in factories, women were responsible for housekeeping, providing religious education, and raising children.

[B] In addition to running their households, women also had opportunities for wage work. This included producing goods, such as palm-leaf hats and straw-braided items, for wider consumption. [C] Wage work provided women with the ability to live at home while earning money to supplement the family's income. [D]

[1] Shoemaking was another source of income for women, but their work was socially and physically isolated from the shoe binding that took place in cobblers' shops. [2] However, when increased demand for shoes required the use of sewing machines to speed up the pace of production, women organized a small-scale movement that trained young women to use sewing machines in their homes. [3] Despite this move, women who worked at home as shoe binders remained isolated and vulnerable to competition from the more lucrative and efficient factories. [4] Women were also denied craft status and admission into unions, which limited their influence. ⬜3

3. For the sake of logic, Sentence 4 should be placed:

   A. where it is now.
   B. before Sentence 1.
   C. before Sentence 2.
   D. before Sentence 3.

[F] Women who worked in factories were also prohibited from joining unions, allowing factories such as the Lowell Mills to exploit their labor. [G] However, female factory workers were offered a type of work outside of the home and away from their families, which provided them with a new level of independence. [H]

For many women, the changes in women's roles during the first half of the 19th century were part of a positive and liberating transformation. [J] For others, though, either their roles remained quite traditional, or their new endeavors, such as working in factories, were not as freeing as they had hoped. Women's experiences with and reactions to the changes they encountered varied, but many were eager for the journey ahead.

Questions 4–5 ask about the passage as a whole.

---

4. The writer would like to add the following sentence:

   During this time, middle-class wives and mothers in New England assumed the role of protectors and leaders of home life.

   The sentence would be most logically placed at:

   F. Point A in paragraph 1.
   G. Point B in paragraph 2.
   H. Point C in paragraph 2.
   J. Point D in paragraph 2.

5. The writer would like to add the following sentence:

   For example, they were paid half the wages given to men.

   The sentence would be most logically placed at:

   A. Point F in paragraph 4.
   B. Point G in paragraph 4.
   C. Point H in paragraph 4.
   D. Point J in paragraph 5.

Development: Precision

LEARNING OBJECTIVE

After this lesson, you will be able to:

- Identify the word that accomplishes the appropriate purpose within a sentence

To answer a question like this:

Humphrey Bogart

Although the screen appeal of Humphrey Bogart has grown immeasurably since his death in 1957, his early life was not filled with success. Born in New York City in 1899 as the son of a prominent surgeon, young Humphrey was quickly put on the track to medical school. After finishing his early schooling, he went to the prestigious Phillips Academy. Bogart, however, was not academically inclined, and during adolescence he was often described as a troublemaker. In 1918, Bogart entered the navy. It was during the service when he received an injury that partially paralyzed his upper lip, creating his <u>splendid</u> snarl.

1

1. Which of the following best conveys how the injury noticeably marked Bogart's appearance?

   A. NO CHANGE

   B. outrageous

   C. distinctive

   D. insignificant

You need to know this:

Some questions test your knowledge of the correct word to use in context. You must identify which word(s) best convey the writer's intended meaning.

Incorrect	Correct
The initial *reason the students gather in the auditorium is that it is the only location large enough for all of them.*	*The* primary *reason the students gather in the auditorium is that it is the only location large enough for all of them.*
It is common for children to perform *the actions of their parents.*	*It is common for children to* mimic *the actions of their parents.*
Zeke apologized for overstepping *when he walked into the crowded conference room.*	*Zeke apologized for* intruding *when he walked into the crowded conference room.*

You need to do this:

Read the surrounding text to deduce the author's intended meaning. Then evaluate all four answer choices. Eliminate the answer choices that:

- Create grammatical errors
- Do not make sense in context
- Do not convey the writer's intended meaning

If one or more of the words among the answer choices are unfamiliar, the process of elimination can still help you get to the correct answer. If you recognize any of the options, decide whether to keep or eliminate them. For the words that remain, use roots, prefixes and suffixes, and word charge (whether a word is positive, negative, or neutral in meaning) to make your decision. If all else fails, trust your instincts and guess; never leave a question blank.

Explanation:

The question asks for a word that approximately means *noticeably marked*. Choice D is the exact opposite, and A and B are too strongly charged—*splendid* has a strong positive charge and *outrageous* has a strong negative charge. Choice (C) is correct.

Try on Your Own

Directions: Take as much time as you need on these questions. Work carefully and methodically. There will be an opportunity for timed practice at the end of the chapter.

The History of Advertising

Over the past few decades, advertising has changed radically. In the 1990s, large companies hoped to reach their target markets through advertisements in national magazines and network television, while smaller companies <u>promoted</u> local newspapers, phone books,
2
and radio stations. Of course, companies large and small still buy advertisements in mass media outlets that reach large numbers of consumers. However, with a new

millennium came new <u>competitors,</u> including a larger
3
media outlet than previously imagined: the internet.

2. F. NO CHANGE
    G. appropriated
    H. utilized
    J. manipulated

3. Which of the following best conveys the opportunity presented by the internet?

    A. NO CHANGE
    B. circumstances,
    C. occurrences,
    D. possibilities,

Thomas Paine

As a young man, Paine worked as a corsetmaker, sailor, and minister, but he only found his true calling when he moved to the British colonies in America. Paine first gained recognition as the editor of *Pennsylvania Magazine*, and as political turmoil engulfed the colonies, he became more <u>vocal.</u> In 1776, Paine anonymously
4
published a pamphlet titled "Common Sense" that argued forcefully for American independence from Britain. The pamphlet was tremendously popular; soon there were 200,000 copies in circulation. Many historians credit the pamphlet with helping to convince the American people to fight for self-rule.

4. Which choice best conveys Paine's increased fame?

    F. NO CHANGE
    G. prominent.
    H. understandable.
    J. divisive.

Thomas Paine's influence continued far beyond sparking the Revolutionary War. Once the war began, Paine published a series of pamphlets called *The American Crisis*, which, in the midst of a bloody war, helped keep the morale of the troops up. In addition to his achievements as a writer, Thomas Paine is <u>credited</u>
5
with conceiving the name "The United States of America."

5. A. NO CHANGE
   B. tasked
   C. helped
   D. noted

Because Thomas Paine was <u>a writer,</u> Thomas
6
Jefferson and John Adams drew heavily on his work when drafting the Declaration of Independence. Later in life, Paine wrote other highly controversial works. In 1797, Paine did his part to inspire what would become Social Security. He suggested a system of social insurance for the young and the elderly in his last great work, "Agrarian Justice."

6. Which of the following replacements most effectively portrays Paine positively and describes why Jefferson and Adams used his work?

   F. an extremely talented writer,
   G. the best writer in the colonies,
   H. an adequate author,
   J. an author of controversial content,

Development: Introductions and Conclusions

LEARNING OBJECTIVE

After this lesson, you will be able to:

- Provide an introduction or conclusion to a paragraph or passage

To answer a question like this:

Early Writing Careers

Many well-known writers began their careers while they were still teenagers. Stephen King, for example, began submitting stories to science fiction magazines when he was just thirteen years old. If you are serious about a writing career, you can submit work to many publications that accept unsolicited manuscripts. It is best, however, to send a query letter first.

A query letter is a one-page document in which you introduce yourself to the editors of the publication and ask if they would like to read your work. Begin by telling the editor a little bit about yourself. Include a paragraph or two outlining the story you've written or would like to write. If you've taken any creative writing courses, won prizes for your writing, or had any work published, tell the editor about that, too. Don't forget to thank the editor for taking the time to read your letter.

You probably won't sell your first story, but don't get discouraged. Stephen King didn't sell his first submission either—or dozens after that. Nevertheless, he persisted, and he became a best-selling author.
<u>1</u>

1

1. Which choice best concludes the essay?

   A. NO CHANGE

   B. Eventually, he found an editor who liked his work, and the rest is history.

   C. Despite that, he didn't give up, and neither should you.

   D. Being a professional writer is a difficult career to break into.

You need to know this:

Some questions ask you to improve the beginning or ending of a paragraph or passage. These questions often have a question stem.

- An introduction should:
  - Explain the topic and purpose of a paragraph
  - Include information discussed later in the paragraph
  - When applicable, provide an appropriate transition from the previous paragraph or into the next paragraph

- A conclusion should:
  - Summarize the topic and purpose of a paragraph/passage
  - Include information discussed earlier in the paragraph/passage
  - When applicable, provide an appropriate transition from the previous paragraph or into the next paragraph

Note that when the question has a question stem, you are not being tested on conciseness, even when asked about deleting information. *When you see a question stem, focus on relevance rather than conciseness*. This means that you can focus on identifying the concise and relevant choice without spending time considering the grammar of each choice.

You need to do this:

- Determine the writer's intended purpose for the paragraph or essay as a whole.
- Read before and/or after the underlined segment, noting key transition words.
- Eliminate choices that do not provide an appropriate introduction or conclusion.
- For a question about the conclusion to the passage, eliminate choices that focus too much on the final paragraph and not enough on the passage as a whole or too much on the passage as a whole and not enough on the final paragraph.
- Choose the most relevant option.

Explanation:

This passage focuses on advising and encouraging aspiring young writers. The last paragraph in particular discusses the importance of not giving up and cites the example of Stephen King. Choice (C) is correct because it references both ideas and ties them together. Choice A may be tempting, but it is incorrect because it refers only to Stephen King. It does not address young writers in general.

Try on Your Own

Directions: Take as much time as you need on these questions. Work carefully and methodically. There will be an opportunity for timed practice at the end of the chapter.

Community-Supported Agriculture

This spring, my family joined our local community-supported agriculture, or CSA, association. We wanted to eat more locally-grown foods, and the CSA provided the perfect opportunity. Like other members, we bought a year's "share" of the farm's crop before the growing season began. Once it did, the farm delivered a box filled with freshly harvested fruits and vegetables every week.

We immediately discovered that fresh, in-season food is delicious. I had disliked broccoli previously, but one bunch that arrived in our second June box convinced me I'd been wrong. My younger brother, who is normally resistant to new foods, ventured to try both kale and turnips from the CSA and enjoyed both. <u>Of the four people in my family, my mother is definitely the most accomplished cook.</u>[2]

2. Given that all the choices are true, which one provides a conclusion to this paragraph that is most consistent with the other information in the paragraph?

F. NO CHANGE

G. Prior to our experience with the CSA, the most exotic vegetable he would willingly eat was a carrot—and only the orange kind.

H. The cardboard boxes are recycled each week, and the CSA even provides composting services on-site.

J. We pick up our vegetables from the farmer's delivery every Thursday afternoon.

Furthermore, we've been vexed by the outlandish
number of zucchini in our boxes. Each week in July, we
received at least six. At first, we just grilled the zucchini.
Then, we sautéed it with pasta. By the third week, when
we opened our box to find ten more zucchini, we had to
get inventive. We experimented with recipes for
zucchini soup, casserole, bread, pizza, and even
brownies. Though everything was tasty, we're all
anticipating the end of zucchini season with relief. Of
course, by then tomato season will have begun, and we'll
be looking for ways to prepare a new vegetable deluge.
I foresee more delicious experiments in the future.

Early 19th-Century Women in New England

In the early 19th century, the market economy
expanded, and the home became a haven from the
developing commercialism. During this time, middle-
class wives and mothers in New England assumed
the role of protectors and leaders of home life. With
men working in factories, women were responsible
for housekeeping, providing religious education, and
raising children.

In addition to running their households, women
became deeply involved in the labor movements of the
time. This included producing goods, such as palm-leaf
hats and straw-braided items, for wider consumption.
Wage work provided women with the ability to live at
home while earning money to supplement the family's
income.

3. Which of the following choices most effectively introduces this paragraph?

A. NO CHANGE

B. We have, however, found a minor
flaw in the CSA boxes: a profusion of
zucchini.

C. The CSA has also encouraged creative
cooking with unfamiliar produce.

D. Not all of the produce we've received
has been good, however.

4. Which choice best completes the sentence
and introduces this paragraph?

F. NO CHANGE

G. women became some of the most
important contributors to the industrial age.

H. women grew increasingly involved in
politics.

J. women also had opportunities for
wage work.

Shoemaking was another source of income for women, but their work was socially and physically isolated from the shoe binding that took place in cobblers' shops. However, when increased demand for shoes required the use of sewing machines to speed up the pace of production, women organized a small-scale movement that trained young women to use sewing machines in their homes. Despite this move, women who worked at home as shoe binders remained isolated and vulnerable to competition from the more lucrative and efficient factories. Women were also denied craft status and admission into unions, which limited their influence.

<u>Francis Cabot Lowell employed women in a new kind of factory,</u> where they were also prohibited from
5
joining unions. This allowed factories such as the Lowell Mills to exploit women's labor. For example, they were usually paid half the wages given to men. However, female factory workers were offered a type of work outside of the home and away from their families, which provided them with a new level of independence.

For many women, the changes in women's roles during the first half of the 19th century were a part of a positive and liberating transformation. For others, though, either their roles remained quite traditional, or their new endeavors, such as working in factories, were

5. Which choice provides the best introduction to this paragraph?

    A. NO CHANGE

    B. A similar tension marked women's employment in factories,

    C. Women attempted to reform laws governing factories,

    D. Some women abandoned their responsibilities at home for jobs in factories,

not as freeing as they had hoped. <u>Women's</u>
                                    6
<u>experiences with and reactions to the changes they</u>
                                    6
<u>encountered varied, but many were eager for the</u>
                                    6
<u>journey ahead.</u>
       6

6. Which of the following provides the best
    conclusion to the essay?

    F. NO CHANGE
    G. Unfortunately, discrimination and
        unfair work practices continue to
        plague women in the workplace to
        this day.
    H. Decades passed before the societal
        changes of the 19th century were
        widely accepted.
    J. This divide led to an alienation that
        plagued the women's movement of
        New England throughout the 19th and
        20th centuries.

Development: Revising Text

LEARNING OBJECTIVES

After this lesson, you will be able to:

- Revise a sentence to accomplish a specific purpose
- Determine the relevance of a sentence within a passage

To answer a question like this:

Humphrey Bogart

When Bogart was released from the navy in 1920, he turned his attention toward the theater. A family friend in the business hired him to work in a theater office in New York. Bogart eventually became a stage manager and finally procured some minor roles on the stage. <u>His inexperience showed, however, and</u> he struggled to find any substantive parts. In the early 1930s, Bogart set out for Hollywood, and although he quickly signed a contract with Fox Pictures, he appeared, marginally, in only three films.

1. If the writer were to delete the underlined portion (adjusting capitalization as necessary), the sentence would primarily lose:

   A. details about Bogart's success.
   B. a warning against changing careers.
   C. an example illustrating Bogart's lack of expertise.
   D. a reason for Bogart's slow start in the theater.

You need to know this:

Some Development questions focus on revising text in a way that affects the meaning of the passage. Most questions with this focus ask you to select the choice that:

- Accomplishes a unique, specified goal,
- Describes what would be lost if the underlined segment were deleted, or
- States why a sentence should or should not be added or deleted

For these questions, all of the answer choices are grammatically and stylistically correct. Given this fact, your task is to determine which option provides information that is most pertinent to the passage. The correct choice will relate directly to the surrounding text and could serve as support for a point, a transition to a new idea, or some other purpose.

You need to do this:

When a Development question focuses on revising text in a meaningful way, you should always consider both what information the question stem and/or underlined segment provides and whether that information (a) matches the writer's focus and (b) helps express the purpose of the sentence or paragraph. Then, refine your approach:

- When a question asks you which choice accomplishes a unique, specified goal, eliminate incorrect choices that do not accomplish this goal and confirm the correct choice using the passage. Incorrect choices:
  - Mention information that is beyond the scope of the writer's discussion,
  - Do not relate to the surrounding text, or
  - Do not help express the purpose of the sentence or paragraph

- When a question describes what would be lost if the underlined segment were deleted, treat it like a Reading question: evaluate the passage and the underlined segment and predict the answer.

- When the answer choices state why a sentence should or should not be added or deleted, decide whether the answer should include Yes or No and eliminate the two choices that don't match; then, use the passage to determine the correct reasoning.

Be sure to plug the proposed revisions back into the passage and read the full sentence (or paragraph) to best assess the change in context.

Explanation:

When asked what would be lost if a phrase were deleted, consider what the phrase adds to the surrounding text. The second half of the sentence says that Bogart "struggled to find any substantive parts," and the underlined portion supports that claim by citing his inexperience. Eliminate A because the underlined portion is about Bogart's early struggles rather than his success. Eliminate B because the paragraph describes Bogart's life without giving any advice to the reader. Choice C is incorrect because the underlined portion does not provide a specific example of Bogart's inexperience. Only (D) correctly characterizes the underlined portion and its relationship to the rest of the sentence.

Try on Your Own

Directions: Take as much time as you need on these questions. Work carefully and methodically. There will be an opportunity for timed practice at the end of the chapter.

Community Supported Agriculture

This spring, my family joined our local community-supported agriculture, or CSA, association. We wanted to eat <u>more healthy foods,</u> and the CSA provided the perfect
2
opportunity. Like other members, we bought a year's "share" of the farm's crop before the growing season began. Once it did, the farm delivered a box filled with freshly harvested fruits and vegetables every week.

We immediately discovered that fresh, in-season food is delicious. I had disliked broccoli previously, but one bunch that arrived in our second June box convinced me I'd been wrong. My younger brother, <u>who showed little interest in the CSA at first,</u> ventured
3
to try both kale and turnips from the CSA and enjoyed both. Prior to our experience with the CSA, the most exotic vegetable he would willingly eat was a carrot— and only the orange kind.

2. Which choice offers the clearest and most precise information about how the family wanted to change their diet?

   F.   NO CHANGE
   G.   more fruits and vegetables,
   H.   more locally-grown foods,
   J.   more unfamiliar fruits and vegetables,

3. Which choice best supports the paragraph's main point by showing a contrast with the information that follows in the sentence?

   A.   NO CHANGE
   B.   who is usually the most adventurous member of the family,
   C.   who has never met a food he wasn't curious about,
   D.   who is normally resistant to new foods,

The History of Advertising

Over the past few decades, advertising has changed radically. In the 1990s, large companies hoped to reach their target markets through advertisements in national magazines and network television, while smaller companies utilized local newspapers, phone books, and radio stations. Of course, companies <u>large and small</u> still
4
buy advertisements in mass media outlets that reach large numbers of consumers. However, with a new millennium came new possibilities, including a larger media outlet than previously imagined: the internet.

The internet allowed businesses to use targeted advertising, including company websites, banner advertisements, and ads generated by search engines, to reach more specific audiences. Small, local businesses in particular benefited greatly from these new marketing opportunities. 5

4. The primary purpose of the underlined portion is to provide:

   F. a connection between the advertising methods of small and large companies.

   G. information about how companies can differ in size.

   H. a description of what makes a company large or small.

   J. an opinion about the importance of maintaining a variety of business sizes.

5. The writer is considering adding the following sentence:

   > Small specialty shops were once relatively limited to serving local populations of customers, but today those same shops can have customers from around the world.

   Should the writer make this addition here?

   A. Yes, because it clarifies the kind of advertising being discussed.

   B. Yes, because it explains why small businesses benefited from internet advertising.

   C. No, because it does not explain why small shops should use internet advertising.

   D. No, because it is unnecessarily specific.

Thomas Paine

Compared to most of America's other Founding Fathers, Thomas Paine is not nearly as well known. In fact, there are many Americans who have either never even heard of him or cannot recall his significance in history. [6] Paine was born in 1737 as the son of a corsetmaker—a tailor specializing in corsets and other undergarments—and grew up in rural Thetford, England.

As a young man, Paine worked as a corsetmaker, sailor and minister, but he only found his true calling when he moved to the British colonies in America. Paine first gained recognition as the editor of *Pennsylvania Magazine*, and as political turmoil engulfed the colonies, he became more prominent. In 1776, Paine anonymously published a pamphlet titled "Common Sense" that argued forcefully for American independence from Britain. The pamphlet's popularity spread like wildfire; soon there were 200,000 copies in circulation. Many historians credit the pamphlet with helping to convince the American people to fight for self-rule. [7]

Thomas Paine's influence continued far beyond sparking the Revolutionary War. Once the war began, Paine published a series of pamphlets called *The American Crisis*, which, in the midst of a bloody war, helped keep the morale of the troops up. In addition to his achievements as a writer, Thomas Paine is credited with conceiving the name "The United States of America." Because Thomas Paine was an extremely talented writer, Thomas Jefferson and John Adams drew heavily on his work when drafting the Declaration of Independence. Later in life, Paine wrote other, highly

6. If the writer were to delete the preceding sentence, the paragraph would primarily lose:

    F. an explanation for Paine's relative obscurity.

    G. a statement supporting and elaborating on the previous sentence.

    H. a claim the writer will prove in the rest of the paragraph.

    J. an expression of the writer's disappointment in Americans' ignorance.

7. If the writer were to delete the preceding sentence, the paragraph would primarily lose:

    A. a detail that demonstrates the impact of Paine's writings.

    B. evidence that conflicts with information presented earlier in the passage.

    C. a description of the contents of Paine's pamphlet.

    D. an elaboration of Paine's goals in writing "Common Sense."

controversial works. He was even exiled from England and imprisoned in France for his writings. [8] In 1797, Paine did his part to inspire what would become Social Security. He suggested a system of social insurance for the young and the elderly in his last great work, "Agrarian Justice."

8. The writer is considering deleting the previous sentence. Should the writer make this deletion?

F. Yes, because it detracts from the focus on controversy.

G. Yes, because it does not describe the writings.

H. No, because it contributes to the focus on Paine's international relations.

J. No, because it adds an interesting detail that contributes to the purpose of the paragraph.

Early 19th-Century Women in New England

In addition to running their households, women also had opportunities for wage work. This included producing goods, such as palm-leaf hats and straw-braided items, for wider consumption. Wage work provided women with the ability to live at home while earning money to supplement the family's income.

Shoemaking was another source of income for women, and, like wage work, it allowed them to earn money from home. However, when increased demand for shoes required the use of sewing machines to speed

9. Given that all the choices are accurate, which one best emphasizes the disadvantages experienced by women working from home?

A. NO CHANGE

B. though it required more specialized tools than other goods they could produce from home.

C. but their work was socially and physically isolated from the shoe binding that took place in cobblers' shops.

D. who often sought multiple sources of income they could fit around their household responsibilities.

up the pace of production, <u>many women had to turn to</u> [10] <u>other sources of work and revenue.</u> [10] Despite this bold move, women who worked at home as shoe binders remained isolated and vulnerable to competition from the more lucrative and efficient factories. Women were also denied craft status and admission into unions, which limited their influence.

Women who worked in factories were also prohibited from joining unions, allowing factories such as the Lowell Mills to exploit their labor. However, female factory workers were offered <u>a type of work</u> [11] <u>outside of the home and away from their families,</u> [11] which provided them with a new level of independence.

10. Which of the following provides the most relevant information at this point in the essay?

F. NO CHANGE

G. few women could afford to make the switch because of the high cost of personal sewing machines.

H. women had a difficult time keeping up in addition to their responsibilities at home.

J. women organized a small-scale movement that trained young women to use sewing machines in their homes.

11. Given that all are true, which choice provides new information that helps emphasize the opportunity factory work offered for some women?

A. NO CHANGE

B. income in addition to that of their families,

C. lower wages than their male counterparts,

D. a part in the burgeoning Industrial Revolution,

Development: Purpose

> ### LEARNING OBJECTIVE
>
> After this lesson, you will be able to:
>
> - Determine whether a passage has met a goal and state why or why not

To answer a question like this:

Humphrey Bogart

Although the screen appeal of Humphrey Bogart has grown immeasurably since his death in 1957, his early life was not marked by success. Born in New York City in 1899 as the son of a prominent surgeon, young Humphrey was quickly put on the track to medical school. After finishing his early schooling, he went to the prestigious Phillips Academy. Bogart, however, was not academically inclined, and during adolescence he was often described as a troublemaker. In 1918, Bogart entered the navy. It was in the service that he received an injury that partially paralyzed his upper lip, creating his distinctive snarl.

When Bogart was released from the navy in 1920, he turned his attention toward the theater. A family friend in the business hired him to work in a theater office in New York. Bogart eventually became a stage manager and finally worked himself into some minor roles on the stage. His inexperience showed, however, and he struggled to find any substantive parts. In the early 1930s, Bogart set out for Hollywood, and although he quickly signed a contract with Fox Pictures, he appeared, marginally, in only three films.

Frustrated with his stagnant career, he returned to the Broadway stage and finally caught his break as Duke Mantee in the play *The Petrified Forest*. Bogart's performance as the quintessential tough guy soon catapulted his career. Bogart consistently created rich and complex screen images punctuated by his hangdog expressions, perennial five o'clock shadow, and world-weary attitude. From his early gangster roles to his consummate portrayal of the reluctant hero, Bogart's performances came to personify male elegance on the screen, and it is unlikely that his illustrious career will ever be forgotten.

> Question 1 asks about the passage as a whole.

1. Suppose the writer's primary purpose had been to describe the life of someone who struggled before finding success. Would this essay accomplish that purpose?

   A. Yes, because it describes Bogart's perseverance in response to people who doubted his talent.

   B. Yes, because it depicts several setbacks Bogart experienced before he found a lasting career.

   C. No, because it focuses mainly on the reasons for Bogart's success.

   D. No, because it does not describe Bogart's troubles in detail.

You need to know this:

On the ACT, some Development questions will ask you to determine why an essay does or does not achieve a given purpose. Writers select particular wording and details to support the purpose of the passage while maintaining a consistent tone and focus, so determining why a given purpose is or is not appropriate will require use of the entire passage.

Spotting and Fixing Issues: Conciseness, Organization, and Development

Only some passages will include these types of questions, but when one is present, it will be the last question in the set and preceded by a boxed-in instructional sentence:

> Question 15 asks about the passage as a whole.

You need to do this:

- Determine the author's point of view and main topic and predict the purpose.
- Ask yourself whether the given purpose is close to your prediction (Yes, because...) or not (No, because...).
- Eliminate the two choices that do not match your Yes/No conclusion.
- Examine the reasoning in the two remaining answers and use the passage to determine which is correct.

Explanation:

To determine the essay's primary purpose, summarize the passage as a whole. The passage describes Bogart's slow rise to fame, detailing the challenges he faced before and during his attempts to become a successful actor. This matches the purpose in the question stem, so eliminate C and D. The passage does not mention anyone doubting Bogart's talent, so A is incorrect. Choice (B) is correct because it accurately connects the features of the passage to the stated purpose.

Try on Your Own

Directions: Take as much time as you need on these questions. Work carefully and methodically. There will be an opportunity for timed practice at the end of the chapter.

Early Writing Careers

Many well-known writers began their careers while they were still teenagers. Stephen King, for example, began submitting stories to science fiction magazines when he was just thirteen years old. If you are serious about a writing career, you can submit work to many publications that accept unsolicited manuscripts. It is best, however, to send a query letter first.

A query letter is a one-page document in which you introduce yourself to the editors of the publication and ask if they would like to read your work. Begin by telling the editor a little bit about yourself. Include a paragraph or two outlining the story you've written or would like to write. If you've taken any creative writing courses, won prizes for your writing, or had any work published, tell the editor about that, too. Don't forget to thank the editor for taking the time to read your letter.

You probably won't sell your first story, but don't get discouraged. Stephen King didn't sell his first submission either—or dozens after that. Despite that, he didn't give up, and neither should you.

> Question 2 asks about the passage as a whole.

2. If the writer's primary goal were to write an essay about a well-known author's path to success, would this essay accomplish that purpose?

   F. Yes, because it discusses how Stephen King's career began.

   G. Yes, because it tells about the writer's path to success.

   H. No, because it doesn't give enough details about Stephen King's career path.

   J. No, because it focuses on giving advice to aspiring authors.

The History of Advertising

Over the past few decades, advertising has changed radically. In the 1990s, large companies hoped to reach their target markets through advertisements in national magazines and network television, while smaller companies utilized local newspapers, phone books, and radio stations. Of course, companies large and small still buy advertisements in mass media outlets that reach large numbers of consumers. However, with a new millennium came new possibilities, including a larger media outlet than previously imagined: the internet.

The internet allowed businesses to use targeted advertising, including company websites, banner advertisements, and ads generated by search engines, to reach more specific audiences. Small, local businesses in particular benefited greatly from these new marketing opportunities. Small specialty shops, previously limited to serving local populations of customers, were able to expand their clientele around the world.

Today, companies continue to develop ever more sophisticated methods to use the internet to reach their customers. Individually tailored advertisements appear on social media sites, in email inboxes, in the midst of streamed entertainment, and more. As internet use expands, so too will the ways businesses advertise through it.

> Question 3 asks about the passage as a whole.

3. Suppose the writer's goal had been to write an essay about how the internet has changed the world. Would this essay accomplish that goal?

    A. Yes, because it describes how businesses use the internet.

    B. Yes, because it emphasizes the broad impact the internet has had.

    C. No, because it focuses on advertising rather than the overall impact of the internet.

    D. No, because it suggests that companies would have changed without the internet.

Community-Supported Agriculture

This spring, my family joined our local community-supported agriculture, or CSA, association. We wanted to eat more locally-grown foods, and the CSA provided the perfect opportunity. Like other members, we bought a year's "share" of the farm's crop before the growing season began. Once it did, the farm delivered a box filled with freshly harvested fruits and vegetables every week.

We immediately discovered that fresh, in-season food is delicious. I had disliked broccoli previously, but one bunch that arrived in our second June box convinced me I'd been wrong. My younger brother, who is normally resistant to new foods, ventured to try both kale and turnips from the CSA and enjoyed both. Prior to our experience with the CSA, the most exotic vegetable he would willingly eat was a carrot—and only the orange kind.

We have, however, found a minor flaw in the CSA boxes: a profusion of zucchini. Each week in July, we received at least six. At first, we just grilled the zucchini. Then, we sautéed it with pasta. By the third week, when we opened our box to find ten more zucchini, we had to get inventive. We experimented with recipes for zucchini soup, casserole, bread, pizza, and even brownies. Though everything was tasty, we're all anticipating the end of zucchini season with relief. Of course, by then tomato season will have begun, and we'll be looking for ways to prepare a new vegetable deluge. I foresee more delicious experiments in the future.

> Question 4 asks about the passage as a whole.

4. If the writer's goal were to write a brief essay about the purpose and organization of community-supported agriculture, would this essay successfully accomplish that goal?

   F. Yes, because it explains how community-supported agriculture works.

   G. Yes, because it fully describes both the benefits and drawbacks of community-supported agriculture.

   H. No, because it focuses instead on one family's experience with community-supported agriculture.

   J. No, because it fails to provide an overview of how membership in a community-supported agriculture association works.

Thomas Paine

Compared to most of America's other Founding Fathers, Thomas Paine is not nearly as well known. In fact, there are many Americans who have either never even heard of him or cannot recall his significance in history. Paine was born in 1737 as the son of a corsetmaker—a tailor specializing in corsets and other undergarments—and grew up in rural Thetford, England.

As a young man, Paine worked as a corsetmaker, sailor and minister, but he only found his true calling when he moved to the British colonies in America. Paine first gained recognition as the editor of *Pennsylvania Magazine*, and as political turmoil engulfed the colonies, he became more vocal. In 1776, Paine anonymously published a pamphlet titled "Common Sense" that argued forcefully for American independence from Britain. The book's popularity spread like wildfire; soon there were 200,000 copies in circulation. Many historians credit the book with helping to convince the American people to fight for self-rule.

Thomas Paine's influence continued far beyond sparking the Revolutionary War. Once the war began, Paine published a series of pamphlets called *The American Crisis*, which, in the midst of a bloody war, helped keep the morale of the troops up. In addition to his achievements as a writer, Thomas Paine is credited with conceiving the name "The United States of America." Because Thomas Paine was an extremely talented writer, Thomas Jefferson and John Adams drew heavily on his work when drafting the Declaration of Independence. Later in life, Paine wrote other, highly controversial works. In 1797, Paine did his part to inspire what would become Social Security. He suggested a system of social insurance for the young and the elderly in his last great work, *Agrarian Justice*.

Given Thomas Paine's contributions to America, he deserves recognition as one of our most important Founding Fathers. Whether you think of him as a patriot who named an entire nation or a controversial activist who lobbied for socialist ideas, he should at the very least be remembered as a seminal figure in the development of a new, autonomous nation.

> Question 5 asks about the passage as a whole.

5. Suppose the writer's primary purpose had been to advocate placing a greater emphasis on Thomas Paine's contributions to American history. Would this essay accomplish that purpose?

   A. Yes, because it praises Paine's influence.

   B. Yes, because it is a thorough treatise on American history.

   C. No, because it does not establish that Paine's contributions were beneficial.

   D. No, because it focuses too much on the American Revolution.

How Much Have You Learned?

Directions: For test-like practice, give yourself 9 minutes to complete this question set. Be sure to study the explanations, even for questions you got correct. They can be found at the end of this chapter.

The Library System

Since the turn of the century, library systems have undergone increasing computerization, a trend that has <u>led some people to speculate about</u> the future of
₁
libraries. Some people believe that not only the card catalog but also the library stacks themselves will

eventually be rendered obsolete. <u>Many today have never</u>
₂
<u>even used a card catalog and hardly know what one is.</u>
₂

1. A. NO CHANGE
    B. brought about speculative consideration on
    C. led to speculation about
    D. brought some people to make predictions about

2. Which choice best supports the paragraph's main idea by emphasizing the changes technology is bringing to libraries?

    F. NO CHANGE
    G. It is quite likely, they say, that in the very near future, electronic data will replace books as we know them.
    H. Along with decreases in funding, this may spell trouble for libraries in the future.
    J. Young people, they say, are less and less interested in reading books, even on electronic devices like tablets.

This thought presents an interesting picture of the future. <u>Despite</u> spending a cozy evening with a good
₃

3. A. NO CHANGE
    B. While
    C. Since
    D. Instead of

book, we may be <u>looking at</u> a laptop computer. With all
                    4
the intriguing possibilities the future holds, we are

inclined to ignore the past. [A] <u>We should not ignore</u>
                                                    5
<u>the past because it helps make us who we are.</u>
                    5

Libraries may have originated as early as the third millennium BCE in Babylonia. There, clay tablets were used for record-keeping purposes and stored in <u>temples</u>
                                                          6
<u>in ancient Babylonia.</u> [B] In the seventh century BCE,
        6
the King of Assyria organized an enormous collection of records; approximately 20,000 tablets and fragments

4. Which choice best emphasizes the coziness of reading while maintaining the essay's positive tone?

   F. NO CHANGE
   G. next to
   H. stuck with
   J. curling up with

5. Given that all the choices are true, which one provides the best transition to the rest of the essay?

   A. NO CHANGE
   B. Libraries have a past as well as a future, both of which are important to keep in mind when thinking about them.
   C. The future of libraries is something perhaps none of us can fully predict, and we shouldn't try.
   D. While the future of libraries is an interesting topic, the library system's rich history is also quite intriguing.

6. F. NO CHANGE
   G. temples millennia ago in a country called Babylonia.
   H. temples.
   J. temples located in Babylonia.

have been recovered. ⟨7⟩ In the second century CE, libraries were founded in monasteries.

7. At this point, the writer is considering adding the following true statement:

> The first libraries to store books were fourth-century BCE Greek temples established in conjunction with the various schools of philosophy.

Should the writer make this addition here?

A. Yes, because it adds a relevant detail.

B. Yes, because it supports the main idea of religious contributions to libraries.

C. No, because it does not say where the temples were.

D. No, because it distracts from the emphasis on books.

[C] One of the most influential of these schools was Neoplatonism.
8

8. Given that all the statements are true, which one provides the most relevant information at this point in the essay?

F. NO CHANGE

G. It was not until the 13th century that university libraries were created.

H. The Greeks also preserved knowledge through lengthy epics memorized and recited by poets.

J. At that time, it was rare for individuals to own books.

The institution of the library continued to change over time. The emergence of a middle class, a growth in literacy, and the invention of the printing press all played a role. [D] However, wars and revolutions served to hinder the development of the
9

9. Given that all the choices are true, which one provides the best introduction to this paragraph?

A. NO CHANGE

B. Many societal changes occurred in the Renaissance.

C. During the Renaissance, a series of societal changes began to transform the library system into the form we have today.

D. The Renaissance was a rebirth of classical ideas and artistic styles.

library system in England. [10] For example, Henry VIII ordered the destruction of countless manuscripts and disbanded some monastic libraries.

In the days of King Henry, many English citizens were pondering the fate of the <u>nascent</u> library system. Today's

11
societal changes are likewise causing some of us

to <u>consider and think about</u> the same thing,

12

<u>although</u> in ways that medieval readers could never

13
have imagined. Have we progressed from clay tablets to paperbacks only to trade our paperbacks in for microchips?

10. If the writer were to delete the preceding sentence, the paragraph would primarily lose:

   F.   details that support the second sentence of the paragraph.

   G.   a link between Henry VIII's actions and libraries.

   H.   an introduction to the details in the final sentence of the paragraph.

   J.   an emphasis on library developments after the 13th century.

11.   A.   NO CHANGE

   B.   futile

   C.   delicate

   D.   immature

12.   F.   NO CHANGE

   G.   consider

   H.   consider while thinking about

   J.   consider and be thinking about

13.   A.   NO CHANGE

   B.   despite

   C.   also

   D.   consequently

Questions 14–15 ask about the passage as a whole.

---

14. The writer would like to add the following sentence:

> With the increased availability of books, patrons of scholarship founded libraries with accompanying academies of scholars in major cities throughout much of Europe.

The sentence would most logically be placed at:

   F.   Point A in paragraph 2.

   G.   Point B in paragraph 3.

   H.   Point C in paragraph 3.

   J.   Point D in paragraph 4.

15. Suppose the writer's primary purpose had been to develop a prediction about the future of libraries. Would this essay accomplish that purpose?

   A.   Yes, because it gives evidence in favor of thinking that libraries will change.

   B.   Yes, because it treats the past as unimportant.

   C.   No, because it focuses on the history of libraries.

   D.   No, because it emphasizes the struggles of libraries throughout history.

Reflect

Directions: Take a few minutes to recall what you've learned and what you've been practicing in this chapter. Consider the following questions, jot down your best answer for each one, and then compare your reflections to the expert responses on the following page. Use your level of confidence to determine what to do next.

1. When should you consider selecting "DELETE the underlined portion"?

    _____

    _____

    _____

2. How can transition words help you determine the most logical placement for a sentence?

    _____

    _____

    _____

3. Why is relevance important in determining whether a sentence should be revised, added, or deleted?

    _____

    _____

    _____

4. Name one goal of the introduction to a paragraph/passage. Name one goal of the conclusion to a paragraph/passage.

    _____

    _____

    _____

Responses

1. When should you consider selecting "DELETE the underlined portion"?

If the underlined portion is wordy/redundant, does not enhance the meaning of the sentence, or does not provide clarity, select "DELETE the underlined portion." Remember that "DELETE the underlined portion" is just as likely as any of the other three choices.

2. How can transition words help you determine the most logical placement for a sentence?

The kind of transition word that a sentence begins with (contrast, cause-and-effect, continuation, emphasis, chronology) determines the purpose the sentence should serve within the context. If the sentence does serve that purpose within the context, it is logically placed.

3. Why is relevance important in determining whether a sentence should be revised, added, or deleted?

If a sentence is missing relevant information, it needs to be revised. If you are going to add a sentence, it should be relevant to the existing information in the passage. If information is not relevant to the passage, it should be deleted.

4. Name one goal of the introduction to a paragraph/passage. Name one goal of the conclusion to a paragraph/passage.

A good introduction should explain the topic and purpose and include information that will be discussed later in the paragraph/passage. A good conclusion should summarize the topic and purpose and include information that was discussed earlier in the paragraph/passage.

Next Steps

If you answered most questions correctly in the "How Much Have You Learned" section, and if your responses to the Reflect questions were similar to those of an expert, then consider conciseness, organization, and development areas of strength and move on to the next chapter. Come back to these topics periodically to prevent yourself from getting rusty.

If you don't yet feel confident, review those parts of this chapter that you have not yet mastered. Then, try the questions you missed again. As always, be sure to review the explanations closely. Then go online (**kaptest.com/login**) to watch video lessons about the highest-yield concepts in this chapter and to use your Qbank for more practice. If you haven't already registered your book, do so at *kaptest.com/moreonline.*

GO ONLINE

kaptest.com/login

Answers and Explanations

Conciseness

1. Review the Explanation portion of the Conciseness lesson.

2. J

Difficulty: Low

Category: Conciseness

Getting to the Answer: The underlined portion in F repeats information that is already included in the name of TEIMUN. Choices G and H do so as well; (J) is the only choice that eliminates the redundancy.

3. A

Difficulty: Low

Category: Conciseness

Getting to the Answer: This question tests redundancy. Choices B, C, and D all introduce redundant language. Thus, (A) is the correct answer.

4. J

Difficulty: Medium

Category: Conciseness

Getting to the Answer: The underlined portion uses more words than is necessary to convey its meaning, as do G and H. Choice (J) is less wordy while still being clear, so it is correct.

Organization: Transitions

1. Review the Explanation portion of the Organization: Transitions lesson.

2. G

Difficulty: Medium

Category: Organization

Getting to the Answer: Transitions must accurately reflect the writer's purpose. Here, the writer's goal is to emphasize how important good manners were for the upper classes. The word *Despite* is a contrast transition, which is the opposite of the writer's intent. Eliminate F and H because they are both contrast transitions. Choice

J is incorrect because good manners were important at all times, not just occasionally. Choice (G) is correct, since *Especially for* emphasizes the point the writer is making.

3. C

Difficulty: Medium

Category: Organization

Getting to the Answer: This question asks for a transition sentence connecting the first and second paragraphs. The first is about Queen Victoria's ideas of propriety impacting culture; the second is about period fashion. The correct answer will include both ideas, and only (C) does so.

4. F

Difficulty: Medium

Category: Organization

Getting to the Answer: This sentence presents a contrast between two ideas: the desire to cinch the waist as much as possible and the fact that women still needed to breathe. Therefore, a contrast transition word is needed. Choice (F) is correct. Choices H and J are incorrect because they are cause-and-effect transition words. Finally, G is incorrect because *rather than* indicates a substitution, not a contrast.

5. D

Difficulty: Medium

Category: Organization

Getting to the Answer: The preceding sentence discusses the limited education many women received during the Victorian Era. Then the paragraph states that a minority of women were educated more fully. The difference between the two requires a contrast transition, and the current transition word does not serve that purpose. Choices B and C do not provide the appropriate contrast, so the correct answer is (D).

6. G

Difficulty: High

Category: Organization

Getting to the Answer: This question asks for a transition sentence from the third paragraph into the fourth paragraph. The third paragraph discusses women's education in the Victorian era, including Victoria's own, while the fourth paragraph discusses Victoria's lasting impact. Choices F, H, and J are all focused on her education alone and offer specific details rather than showing a connection between ideas. Choice J may be tempting because it compares her education to her prime ministers', which indirectly suggests the topic of government policy. However, the final paragraph does not mention her prime ministers, so J does not actually show the connection between these two paragraphs. Choice (G), on the other hand, clearly states the relationship between Victoria's education and her reign, so it is correct.

Organization: Sentence Placement

1. Review the Explanation portion of the Organization: Sentence Placement lesson.

2. H

Difficulty: Medium

Category: Organization

Getting to the Answer: When looking for the correct location to add a sentence, first consider the contents of the sentence to be added. The pronoun *This* at the beginning of the sentence shows that the previous sentence must reference something that "allows the protozoan to move." Choice (H) would place the new sentence after one about flagella propelling the protozoan; thus, it is correct.

3. A

Difficulty: Medium

Category: Organization

Getting to the Answer: Sentence 4 contains the continuation transition *also*. This shows that it is a logical extension of the sentence that comes immediately before it. Since Sentence 4 references craft status and unions, the sentence before Sentence 4 must also discuss these or other closely related topics. Use this to determine where Sentence 4 should go. Choice B is clearly incorrect because then the transition word *also* would have nothing from which to transition. Choices C and D are incorrect because neither contains references to anything remotely similar to craft status and unions. Thus, (A) is correct.

4. F

Difficulty: High

Category: Organization

Getting to the Answer: The sentence the writer wants to add discusses women and home life. It also starts with the phrase "During this time," which needs to make sense as a transition from the previous sentence. Choice (F) places the sentence correctly in a paragraph discussing women and home life in the 19th century. Choices G, H, and J all place it in a paragraph about women and wage work, which doesn't fit the content of the sentence.

5. B

Difficulty: Medium

Category: Organization

Getting to the Answer: The new sentence provides an example of women being treated unfairly, so it must follow and support a sentence about problems women faced at work. Choice A is incorrect because it places the example at the very beginning of the paragraph where it would not follow or support any sentence. Choices C and D place the example after sentences that describe some of the benefits of women working outside of the home. The new sentence details some of the injustices that women faced, so the two ideas do not logically belong together. Choice (B) is the only option that places the new sentence after one about difficulties women encountered, so it is correct.

Development: Precision

1. Review the Explanation portion of the Development: Precision lesson.

2. **H**

Difficulty: Medium

Category: Development

Getting to the Answer: The sentence sets up a parallel between large companies using certain outlets to advertise and small companies using others, so the underlined word needs to mean *use*. Only (H) conveys this meaning.

3. **D**

Difficulty: Medium

Category: Development

Getting to the Answer: This question tests precision in conveying nuanced meaning. While all of the answers might seem as if they could fit in the context, the question asks for one that conveys opportunity, or positive potential. Choice A, *competitors*, is too negative, while B and C are both neutral. Choice (D) highlights the positive potential of the internet and is correct.

4. **G**

Difficulty: High

Category: Development

Getting to the Answer: While each answer choice is grammatically correct, only (G) conveys Paine's increased fame.

5. **A**

Difficulty: Low

Category: Development

Getting to the Answer: When the underlined portion is a single word, make sure the word fits in the context. Because Paine lived hundreds of years ago, it does not make sense to say that he is *tasked* or is *helped* with something, so eliminate B and C. Choice D creates the phrase *is noted with. With* is not the correct preposition to use with this verb, so D is incorrect. Choice (A) is correct.

6. **F**

Difficulty: Medium

Category: Development

Getting to the Answer: Consider both the surrounding details and the author's tone to determine which phrase fits the context of the essay. Throughout, the author describes increased recognition of Paine's achievements. Eliminate H and J because they are too neutral. While G is certainly positive in tone, it goes beyond what is stated in the passage. The author says that Paine was a good writer, but this does not necessarily mean that he was the best in the colonies. Choice (F) is correct because it perfectly matches the author's positive tone regarding Paine and accurately describes why Paine's work would be used by Jefferson and Adams.

Development: Introductions and Conclusions

1. Review the Explanation portion of the Development: Introductions and Conclusions lesson.

2. **G**

Difficulty: Medium

Category: Development

Getting to the Answer: On the ACT, a strong concluding sentence will not introduce a new topic. The correct answer choice will be clearly connected to the other details in the paragraph and function as an effective summary. The paragraph describes how the narrator's family reacted positively to the CSA. Choice (G) is correct; it follows naturally from the information about the new vegetables the brother has eaten because of the family's CSA membership. The other choices are not connected to the topic of the family's positive experience with the new food from the CSA.

3.   B

Difficulty: High

Category: Development

Getting to the Answer: This paragraph describes a small problem the narrator's family has encountered with the CSA, although the narrator presents it with humor and maintains a positive tone. Choices A and D are both too negative, so eliminate them. Choice C is true but does not accurately capture the main point of the paragraph. The correct answer is (B).

4.   J

Difficulty: Medium

Category: Development

Getting to the Answer: The paragraph is primarily about women's ability to earn money by producing goods from home. Choice F, while it is about women in the workforce, brings up a topic outside the scope of the paragraph. Likewise, G makes a claim much stronger than the paragraph can actually support. Finally, H isn't about labor at all. The correct answer is (J), which introduces wage work as an opportunity for women.

5.   B

Difficulty: Medium

Category: Development

Getting to the Answer: This paragraph discusses both the negative and positive aspects of factory jobs for women. Choices A and C bring in ideas outside the scope of the paragraph and passage and are thus incorrect. Choice D, while it does discuss women working at factories, has a strong negative tone that is incompatible with the rest of the passage. On the other hand, (B) acknowledges that factory work was a mixed blessing for women, which fits well with the rest of the paragraph. The correct answer is (B).

6.   F

Difficulty: High

Category: Development

Getting to the Answer: The concluding sentence must effectively summarize both the final paragraph and the passage as a whole. The main topic of the passage is the positive and negative changes in women's roles, and

the final paragraph is a broad retrospective on those developments. Choice (F) provides the best conclusion by focusing on women's roles in the early 19th century. The other choices, G, H, and J, either bring up new ideas or look beyond the early 19th century.

Development: Revising Text

1.   Review the Explanation portion of the Development: Revising Text lesson.

2.   H

Difficulty: High

Category: Development

Getting to the Answer: This question asks for specific information about the dietary aims that the CSA helped the family fulfill. Choices F, G, and J all suggest general goals that could be easily addressed without using the CSA. Only (H) includes *locally-grown foods*, which is a precise goal that would be most effectively achieved through the CSA.

3.   D

Difficulty: High

Category: Development

Getting to the Answer: The paragraph's main point is that the produce from the CSA is especially delicious, and the latter part of the sentence supports this by saying that the narrator's brother tried and liked vegetables that the CSA supplied. The question asks for a contrast with the rest of the sentence that will support the paragraph as a whole, so the correct answer will provide information that conflicts with the brother liking the vegetables from the CSA. Choice (D) is correct.

4.   F

Difficulty: Low

Category: Development

Getting to the Answer: In the previous sentence, the author discussed how large companies advertise differently than small companies. This sentence describes what is common to both, and the underlined portion makes the connection explicit. Choice (F) is correct.

5. B

Difficulty: Medium

Category: Development

Getting to the Answer: When a question asks about adding a sentence, consider what the sentence contributes to the paragraph as a whole. This paragraph describes the advantages of internet advertising, focusing particularly on the benefits for small businesses. The additional sentence illustrates this benefit, so it should be added. Eliminate C and D. Choice A advocates adding the sentence, but for the wrong reason. The correct answer is (B).

6. G

Difficulty: High

Category: Development

Getting to the Answer: The first sentence in the paragraph says that Paine is not widely known. The sentence in question supports this claim by stating that few people today are aware of him. Choice (G) is correct. Choice F is incorrect because the fact that few people today know of him is not necessarily the reason many Americans do not know about him. Choice H is incorrect because the rest of the paragraph is not devoted to proving this claim. Finally, J is incorrect because the author's tone is neutral, not judgmental.

7. A

Difficulty: Medium

Category: Development

Getting to the Answer: The sentence in question is preceded by a sentence describing the popularity of Paine's pamphlet "Common Sense"; the sentence being considered for deletion explains the importance of that popularity by describing its influence on historical events. The correct answer is (A).

8. J

Difficulty: High

Category: Development

Getting to the Answer: The preceding sentence mentions Paine's controversial works; additional information about his being exiled and imprisoned for his writings emphasizes this controversy. Thus, (J) is correct because it helps the paragraph achieve its purpose.

9. C

Difficulty: Medium

Category: Development

Getting to the Answer: The question specifically asks for a choice that emphasizes the disadvantages of working from home. Choice (C) describes how women were isolated as a result, whereas the other choices focus on positive or neutral aspects of such work. The correct answer is (C).

10. J

Difficulty: High

Category: Development

Getting to the Answer: This sentence starts out describing a change in the shoemaking industry that affected women. The following sentence begins with "Despite this bold move" and goes on to describe how women still struggled to compete with factories. The underlined portion must describe a bold move intended to help women keep up with changes in the shoemaking industry. Choice (J) is correct.

11. A

Difficulty: High

Category: Development

Getting to the Answer: This question asks for new information that emphasizes how factory work was beneficial for women. Choices B and D both present information included earlier in the passage. Choice C gives new information, but it focuses on the downsides of factory work. Only (A) gives new information that shows how factory work could be an opportunity, so (A) is correct.

Development: Purpose

1. Review the Explanation portion of the Development: Purpose lesson.

2. J

Difficulty: Medium

Category: Development

Getting to the Answer: First determine the main idea of the passage. This passage is focused on giving advice to aspiring authors, occasionally using an established author as an example. This does not match the purpose described in the question stem, so eliminate F and G. Choice H does not accurately state why the passage does not match the described purpose. The correct answer is (J).

3. C

Difficulty: Medium

Category: Development

Getting to the Answer: This passage focuses on how advertising has changed over time, particularly with the arrival of the internet. The question's description of "how the internet has changed the world" is much more broad, so it does not match the passage. Eliminate A and B. The passage does not make the suggestion described in D, so choice (C) is correct.

4. H

Difficulty: Medium

Category: Development

Getting to the Answer: Begin by identifying the main idea of the passage. The main idea is that one family has enjoyed its experience with a CSA membership but has also experienced some drawbacks. This main idea does not match the much more general purpose given in the question, so eliminate F and G. Choice J contradicts the essay, which does provide some information on membership. Choice (H) correctly identifies the focus of the essay.

5. A

Difficulty: High

Category: Development

Getting to the Answer: When asked whether a passage accomplishes a particular purpose, consider the scope and tone of the passage. The passage focuses on

Paine's influence on the founding of the United States, and the final paragraph says that he deserves more recognition. This matches the purpose in the question stem, so eliminate C and D. Eliminate B because it incorrectly describes the scope of the passage. Choice (A) accurately reflects the scope and tone of the passage and is therefore correct.

How Much Have You Learned?

1. C

Difficulty: Low

Category: Conciseness

Getting to the Answer: The underlined portion is wordy, and B and D are even more so. Choice (C) conveys the same meaning without unnecessary words, so it is correct.

2. G

Difficulty: High

Category: Development

Getting to the Answer: The question asks for a sentence that emphasizes the changes technology is bringing to libraries. Choice F is about a change that has already happened. Choice H refers to funding, not technology. Choice J mentions electronic devices and people reading less, but technology is not cited as the cause of the change. Choice (G) is correct because it discusses how electronic data may replace physical books.

3. D

Difficulty: Medium

Category: Organization

Getting to the Answer: When a transition word is underlined, identify what ideas it connects and determine their relationship. In this sentence, the first part is about reading a book, and the second part is about using a laptop. Given the context of the passage so far, these two are likely meant to be in contrast. *Despite* and *While*, although contrast words, do not reflect the author's intended meaning that people are using laptops as an alternative to reading books, so eliminate A and B. *Instead of* is a contrast transition that makes sense in context, so (D) is correct.

4. J

Difficulty: Low

Category: Development

Getting to the Answer: When asked which choice best maintains a particular tone, eliminate answer choices that are neutral or that convey the opposite tone. Choices F and G are neutral, and H is negative. Therefore, (J) is correct.

5. D

Difficulty: Medium

Category: Development

Getting to the Answer: The current paragraph speculates about the future of libraries, and the following paragraph discusses the origin and development of libraries. The transition sentence should connect these two topics. Eliminate A because it does not discuss libraries. Choice B connects the past and the future, but it does not provide any reason to begin discussing the history of libraries. Choice C focuses only on the future, so it is not an appropriate transition. Choice (D) connects the future of libraries with their past, while giving the reader a reason to want to know more about their history, so it is correct.

6. H

Difficulty: Medium

Category: Conciseness

Getting to the Answer: The underlined phrase includes information that is already stated earlier in the paragraph. The only answer choice that eliminates all redundancy is (H).

7. A

Difficulty: High

Category: Development

Getting to the Answer: A sentence should be added only if it is relevant to the main point of the paragraph and fits well in context. The additional sentence is relevant to the discussion about the history of libraries because it helps fill in the timeline of library development. Since it should be added, eliminate C and D. While B may be tempting, the paragraph does not emphasize religious contributions to libraries; it merely mentions that a few of the developments took place in temples and monasteries. Choice (A) correctly states the reason for adding the sentence.

8. G

Difficulty: High

Category: Development

Getting to the Answer: The paragraph is about the historical development of libraries, so the correct answer will supply more information about that topic. Choice (G) is correct.

9. C

Difficulty: Medium

Category: Development

Getting to the Answer: An introductory sentence should give the reader a broad idea of the paragraph's topic and flow well into the sentence that immediately follows it. Because the next sentence lists societal factors that "played a role," the introductory sentence should relate these factors to the history of libraries. Choice (C) is correct because it both introduces the societal changes and continues the timeline of library development from the preceding paragraph.

10. H

Difficulty: Medium

Category: Development

Getting to the Answer: Look for the answer choice that accurately describes how the sentence in question relates to the surrounding sentences. Because the sentence begins with *However*, we know that it contrasts with the preceding sentence; therefore, F can be eliminated. Choice G is incorrect because the passage establishes the link between Henry VIII's actions and libraries in the sentence *after* the one in question. Finally, the entire paragraph deals with library developments after the 13th century, so J is not specific enough. The correct answer is (H).

11. A

Difficulty: High

Category: Development

Getting to the Answer: This question tests word choice. The rest of the sentence states that the fate of the library system was in question, and the previous paragraph describes circumstances that hindered its growth and development. The correct answer will reflect this context. Choice B, *futile*, is too strongly negative. Choice C, *delicate*, does not capture the idea that the library system was growing and changing. Finally, D, *immature*, is used to describe a person's emotional state and cannot be meaningfully used to describe an inanimate object. *Nascent* captures the meaning that the library system was just beginning and the course of its development was still unknown; (A) is correct.

12. G

Difficulty: Low

Category: Conciseness

Getting to the Answer: When one answer choice is noticeably shorter than the others, the question may be testing conciseness. Since *consider* and *think about* mean the same thing, F, H, and J are all unnecessarily repetitive. Therefore, (G) is correct.

13. A

Difficulty: Medium

Category: Organization

Getting to the Answer: When a transition word is underlined, check that it is logically and grammatically correct. Logically, the connected ideas are in contrast. People may consider questions similar to those considered by English citizens under Henry VIII, but they think about these questions in very different ways. Eliminate C and D. Since the word *despite* can introduce only a noun phrase, B is incorrect. Choice (A) fits with both the logic and grammatical structure of the sentence, so it is correct.

14. J

Difficulty: Medium

Category: Organization

Getting to the Answer: When considering where to add a sentence, first examine its content. This sentence says that books became more available and patrons founded libraries throughout Europe, so it must go in one of the paragraphs about the history of libraries. Paragraph 2 does not discuss this topic, so eliminate F. Paragraph 3 is about the historical development of the first libraries, but paragraph 4 describes their proliferation, so both G and H can be eliminated. Choice (J) correctly places the new sentence in the paragraph discussing the development of libraries in Europe, including the invention of the printing press.

15. C

Difficulty: Medium

Category: Development

Getting to the Answer: When asked whether the passage accomplishes a particular purpose, first check whether the stated purpose is too narrow or too broad. While the passage does discuss predictions about the future of libraries, it focuses mostly on the historical development of libraries. Thus, the stated purpose is too narrow. Eliminate A and B. The passage does not go into detail about the struggles of libraries, so D is incorrect. The correct answer is (C).

CHAPTER 5

ACT English: Timing and Section Management Strategies

LEARNING OBJECTIVE

After completing this chapter, you will be able to:

- Move quickly and efficiently through the English Test so that you have a fair chance at every question

Timing

You have 45 minutes to complete 5 passages with 15 questions each, so you need to complete each passage and accompanying questions in 9 minutes. This means that after about 20 minutes, you should be working through your third passage. When the proctor informs you that there are 5 minutes remaining, you should have a little more than half of a passage to finish.

Section Management

While you do want to spend approximately the same amount of time on each passage, you definitely do not need to spend the same amount of time on each question. Every question counts for the same number of points, so be sure to complete the questions you find easiest to answer first. If a particular question is challenging, take a guess and come back to it if you have time. The test rewards students for conciseness, so when you guess, choosing the shortest option is a good idea. It won't always be the correct answer, but it certainly is a good option.

Moving efficiently through this section is important, but that does not mean that you should skip over any text. Even if sections of a passage may not be underlined, you need an understanding of the passage as a whole to answer certain questions. Reading all of the text in the passage is essential to answering questions efficiently and accurately.

There is a full-length English passage in the "How Much Have You Learned?" section that comes next. Use it to practice timing: skip questions you find too time-consuming, return to them if you have time, and keep an eye on the clock. When you are finished, check your work—and reflect on how well you managed the timing. Then keep practicing these timing strategies when you take full-length tests, both in your book and online.

How Much Have You Learned?

Directions: For test-like practice, give yourself 9 minutes to complete this question set. Be sure to study the explanations, even for questions you got correct. They can be found at the end of this chapter.

Frankenstein

The character of Frankenstein did not originate in Hollywood. Rather, the legendary mad scientist <u>whom sought to reanimate</u> lifeless bodies was the creation of Mary Wollstonecraft Shelley, who was married to famed poet Percy Bysshe Shelley. *Frankenstein: The Modern Prometheus*, Mary Shelley's novel published in 1818, is considered <u>one of the greater</u> horror tales of all time.

1. A. NO CHANGE
   B. whom seeks to reanimate
   C. who sought in reanimating
   D. who sought to reanimate

2. F. NO CHANGE
   G. one of her greater
   H. one of the greatest
   J. the greatest

Mary Shelley created her <u>desperate</u> subject in response to a bet. [A] She, her husband, Lord Byron, and Byron's physician had a contest to see who could

3. Which choice best emphasizes that the work is a horror story?
   A. NO CHANGE
   B. offensive
   C. nightmarish
   D. dangerous

write the best ghost story. Although <u>the writing project began whimsical,</u> her tale became a serious examination of the fate of an individual who decides to overstep moral and social bounds. [B]

4. F. NO CHANGE
   G. the writing project was begun whimsical,
   H. the writing project began whimsically, but
   J. the writing project began whimsically,

Shelley's novel tells the story of a scientist,

Dr. Victor <u>Frankenstein, who</u> discovers the secret of
₅

bringing corpses back to life and creates a monster <u>with</u>
₆
<u>material from graveyards, dissecting rooms, and</u>
₆
<u>slaughterhouses.</u>
₆

<u>Similar to</u> his gruesome appearance, the monster is
₇
basically good. [C] After being rejected by

Dr. Frankenstein and all other people with whom he

comes into contact, the monster becomes violent.

One by one, the monster murders the people

Dr. Frankenstein cares for the most: <u>his younger</u>
₈
<u>brother, and his best friend, and he even killed</u>
₈
<u>his wife.</u> [D] The tale ends with Dr. Frankenstein
₈

chasing the monster to the North Pole, <u>where each</u>
₉
<u>of them eventually die.</u>
₉

5. A. NO CHANGE
   B. Dr. Victor Frankenstein–who
   C. Dr. Victor Frankenstein: who
   D. Dr. Victor Frankenstein, he

6. If the writer were to delete the underlined portion, the paragraph would primarily lose:

   F. information that emphasizes the grisliness of how Frankenstein acquired his materials.
   G. details about the sources from which Mary Shelley drew inspiration for her story.
   H. an explanation of why Frankenstein's monster ultimately became dangerous.
   J. a description that shows Frankenstein's dedication to his work.

7. A. NO CHANGE
   B. Although
   C. Despite
   D. Because of

8. F. NO CHANGE
   G. his younger brother, and his best friend, and his wife.
   H. his younger brother, best friend, and his wife.
   J. his younger brother, his best friend, and his wife.

9. A. NO CHANGE
   B. where both of them eventually dies.
   C. where each of them eventually have died.
   D. where each of them eventually dies.

It is a horror story, Mary Shelley's *Frankenstein* is
respected by many as a literary classic. The critical
acclaim and continued popularity of the story are also
evidenced by the numerous films that have been based

on it. Some versions like *Young Frankenstein,* provide a
humorous retelling of the story. Other versions, like the
most recent *Mary Shelley's Frankenstein,* attempt to be

faithful and true to the original.

The many adaptations demonstrate that Mary Shelley's
story of overreach and its dark consequences remains
compelling to this day.

10. F. NO CHANGE
    G. Although it is a horror story,
    H. It is a horror story, for
    J. The horror story,

11. A. NO CHANGE
    B. Some versions, like *Young Frankenstein,* provide
    C. Some versions, like *Young Frankenstein*; provide
    D. Some versions–like *Young Frankenstein,* provide

12. F. NO CHANGE
    G. faithful to
    H. faithful and closely follow
    J. accurate and faithful reproductions of

13. Which choice provides the most effective conclusion to the paragraph and the passage?
    A. NO CHANGE
    B. Some film adaptations, however, bear little resemblance to the original book beyond sharing a title with it.
    C. Mary Shelley would be pleased by the lasting appeal of a book she wrote for a wager.
    D. Hollywood, it seems, never tires of creating new interpretations of this story.

Questions 14 and 15 ask about the passage as a whole.

14. The writer wants to add the following sentence to the essay:

    > The monster, who is nameless, only becomes evil when his creator refuses to accept and care for him.

    The sentence would most logically be placed at:

    F. Point A in Paragraph 2.
    G. Point B in Paragraph 2.
    H. Point C in Paragraph 3.
    J. Point D in Paragraph 3.

15. Suppose the writer's primary purpose had been to write an essay analyzing the film adaptations of Mary Shelley's *Frankenstein*. Would this essay accomplish this purpose?

    A. Yes, because it compares and contrasts various film versions of the story.
    B. Yes, because it critiques how closely film versions follow the original story.
    C. No, because it only focuses on one type of film adaptation of the story.
    D. No, because the film adaptations are one point in an overall discussion of the story.

Answers and Explanations

1. D

Difficulty: Medium

Category: Agreement

Getting to the Answer: A subjective pronoun performs the action in a sentence; an objective pronoun is the receiver of the action in a sentence. The pronoun in the underlined segment, *whom*, is an objective pronoun. However, the verbs in the answer choices require the subjective pronoun *who*. Eliminate A and B. Choice C introduces an idiom error, since "sought in reanimating" is not grammatically correct English. The correct answer is (D).

2. H

Difficulty: Medium

Category: Agreement

Getting to the Answer: The adjective *greater* is used only when comparing two items or people. The passage compares Shelley's novel to all other horror tales. The superlative adjective form is needed, so F and G are incorrect. If J is plugged back into the sentence, it creates the illogical phrase "considered the greatest horror tales of all time." The correct answer is (H).

3. C

Difficulty: Medium

Category: Development

Getting to the Answer: This question tests word choice. Although all of the answer choices are grammatically correct, the question asks for one that particularly emphasizes horror. *Desperate*, *offensive*, or *dangerous* subjects do not necessarily inspire horror, so A, B, and D are incorrect. Only *nightmarish* has connotations of horror, so the correct answer is (C).

4. J

Difficulty: Medium

Category: Agreement

Getting to the Answer: Recall that adverbs modify verbs, while adjectives modify nouns. Since the word being modified is the verb *began*, it must be modified by an adverb. The word *whimsical* is an adjective, so eliminate F and G. Choice H correctly contains an adverb

but disrupts the structure of the sentence with the extra conjunction *but*. The correct answer is (J).

5. A

Difficulty: Medium

Category: Sentence Structure

Getting to the Answer: The underlined section includes a comma that sets off nonessential information—the name of the scientist. The punctuation at the beginning and end of the nonessential information must match. Since the opening punctuation is a comma, the closing punctuation must be a comma as well; eliminate B and C. Choice D keeps the comma, but introduces a new error by changing *who* to *he*, which makes the sentence a run-on. The sentence is correct as written, so (A) is the answer.

6. F

Difficulty: High

Category: Development

Getting to the Answer: This question asks what would be lost if the underlined portion were deleted. The underlined portion is a list of places from which Dr. Frankenstein gathered body parts. Including these details emphasizes the morbid nature of the story. Choice (F) is correct. There is nothing in the passage that suggests that Mary Shelley was inspired by these locations or that the monster became dangerous because of his origins; in fact, evidence elsewhere in the passage contradicts both G and H. Choice J is incorrect because showing Frankenstein's dedication to his work is not the primary effect of the underlined portion.

7. C

Difficulty: Medium

Category: Organization

Getting to the Answer: This sentence asks for a transition word that contrasts the monster's *gruesome appearance* with his good nature. The transitions *Similar to* and *Because of* do not convey this contrast, so eliminate A and D. Choice B contains the contrast word *Although*, but it creates a fragment when plugged back into the original sentence. The correct answer is (C).

8. J

Difficulty: Low

Category: Sentence Structure

Getting to the Answer: When a list is underlined, ensure that all items of the list have parallel structure. Choices F and H both contain elements that do not match each other, so they are incorrect. The list items in choice G match, but the *and* before the phrase "his best friend" is unnecessary. The correct answer is (J).

9. D

Difficulty: High

Category: Agreement

Getting to the Answer: The subject of the verb *die* is *each*, which requires a singular verb. Eliminate A and C, which contain plural verbs. Choice B includes the singular verb *dies* but introduces a different subject, *both*, which is plural. Only (D) matches a singular subject with a singular verb. The correct answer is (D).

10. G

Difficulty: Medium

Category: Sentence Structure

Getting to the Answer: This sentence includes two independent clauses incorrectly joined with a comma, forming a run-on sentence. Eliminate F. Choice H correctly contains a coordinating conjunction that joins the two independent clauses, but it creates the wrong logical relationship between the clauses—being a horror story is not a result of the book being viewed as a classic. Choice J changes the sentence structure completely and introduces a comma error. Choice (G) makes the first clause dependent by using a subordinating conjunction that correctly captures the logical relationship between the clauses. The correct answer is (G).

11. B

Difficulty: Low

Category: Sentence Structure

Getting to the Answer: The phrase "like *Young Frankenstein*" is nonessential information that must be set off from the rest of the sentence with either two commas or two dashes. Only (B) has the same punctuation mark at both the beginning and end of the phrase, so (B) is correct.

12. G

Difficulty: Low

Category: Conciseness

Getting to the Answer: The underlined phrase is redundant. Eliminate F. Choices H and J are also unnecessarily wordy, so eliminate them, too. Only (G) is free of redundancy, so (G) is correct.

13. A

Difficulty: High

Category: Development

Getting to the Answer: A concluding sentence must summarize both the entire passage and the last paragraph. The passage discusses Mary Shelley's *Frankenstein*, including its origin, substance, and critical reception. The last paragraph focuses on critical responses to and interpretations of the book. The closing sentence of the passage must incorporate both, which (A) does effectively. Choice B introduces new ideas, and D is too narrowly focused on the final paragraph. Choice C, while it returns to an earlier part of the passage, is also too narrowly focused on one particular detail. The correct answer is (A).

14. H

Difficulty: High

Category: Organization

Getting to the Answer: This sentence focuses on the monster's transition from good to evil. Paragraph 2 does not discuss the monster at all, so you can eliminate F and G. Choice J would put the sentence too late in paragraph 3, after the monster has already committed evil acts. Choice (H) is the correct answer.

15. D

Difficulty: High

Category: Development

Getting to the Answer: While the passage does examine various film adaptations of *Frankenstein*, the essay focuses mostly on how the classic horror story was created and what it means. Eliminate A and B. Eliminate C because the reasoning is not correct; the essay does explore different types of films, even though discussing the films is not the author's main purpose. The correct answer is (D).

PART 3

ACT Math

CHAPTER 6

Prerequisite Skills and Calculator Use

LEARNING OBJECTIVES

After completing this chapter, you will be able to:

- Identify skills you need to develop to obtain the full benefits of the math sections of this book

- Distinguish ACT problems on which a calculator will be helpful or unhelpful

Math Fundamentals

> **LEARNING OBJECTIVE**
>
> After this lesson, you will be able to:
>
> * Identify skills you need to develop to obtain the full benefits of the math sections of this book

Course Prerequisites

This course focuses on the skills that are tested on the ACT. It assumes a working knowledge of arithmetic, algebra, and geometry. Before you dive into the subsequent chapters, where you'll try test-like questions, there are a number of concepts—ranging from basic arithmetic to geometry—that you should master. The following sections contain a brief review of these concepts.

Order of Operations

The **order of operations** is one of the most fundamental of all arithmetic rules. A well-known mnemonic device for remembering this order is PEMDAS: Please Excuse My Dear Aunt Sally. This translates to Parentheses, Exponents, Multiplication/Division, Addition/Subtraction. Perform multiplication and division from left to right (even if it means division before multiplication) and treat addition and subtraction the same way.

$$(14 - 4 \div 2)^2 - 3 + (2 - 1)$$
$$= (14 - 2)^2 - 3 + (1)$$
$$= 12^2 - 3 + 1$$
$$= 144 - 3 + 1$$
$$= 141 + 1$$
$$= 142$$

Subtracting a positive number is the same as adding its negative. Likewise, subtracting a negative number is the same as adding its positive.

$$r - s = r + (-s) \rightarrow 22 - 15 = 7 \text{ and } 22 + (-15) = 7$$
$$r - (-s) = r + s \rightarrow 22 - (-15) = 37 \text{ and } 22 + 15 = 37$$

The Commutative, Associative, and Distributive Properties

Three basic properties of number (and variable) manipulation—commutative, associative, and distributive—will assist you with algebra on test day.

* **Commutative:** Numbers can swap places and still provide the same mathematical result. This is valid only for addition and multiplication.

$$a + b = b + a \rightarrow 3 + 4 = 4 + 3$$
$$a \times b = b \times a \rightarrow 3 \times 4 = 4 \times 3$$

BUT: $3 - 4 \neq 4 - 3$ and $3 \div 4 \neq 4 \div 3$

* **Associative:** Different number groupings will provide the same mathematical result. This is valid only for addition and multiplication.

$$(a + b) + c = a + (b + c) \rightarrow (4 + 5) + 6 = 4 + (5 + 6)$$
$$(a \times b) \times c = a \times (b \times c) \rightarrow (4 \times 5) \times 6 = 4 \times (5 \times 6)$$

BUT: $(4 - 5) - 6 \neq 4 - (5 - 6)$ and $(4 \div 5) \div 6 \neq 4 \div (5 \div 6)$

- **Distributive:** A number that is multiplied by the sum or difference of two other numbers can be rewritten as the first number multiplied by the two others individually. This does not work with division.

$$a(b + c) = ab + ac \rightarrow 6(x + 3) = 6x + 6(3)$$
$$a(b - c) = ab - ac \rightarrow 3(y - 2) = 3y + 3(-2)$$

$$\text{BUT: } 12 \div (6 + 2) \neq 12 \div 6 + 12 \div 2$$

Note: When subtracting an expression in parentheses, such as in $4 - (x + 3)$, distribute the negative sign outside the parentheses first: $4 + (-x - 3) \rightarrow 1 - x$.

Prime Factorization

A **prime number** is a positive integer that is divisible without a remainder by only 1 and itself. The number 2 is the smallest prime number and the only even prime number; 1 is not considered prime.

To find the prime factorization of an integer, use a factor tree to keep breaking the integer up into factors until all the factors are prime numbers. To find the prime factorization of 36, for example, you could begin by breaking it into 4×9. Then break 4 into 2×2 and break 9 into 3×3. The prime factorization of 36 is $2 \times 2 \times 3 \times 3$.

Manipulating Fractions

You should be comfortable manipulating both proper and improper fractions.

- To add and subtract fractions, first find a common denominator, then add the numerators together.

$$\frac{2}{3} + \frac{5}{4} \rightarrow \left(\frac{2}{3} \times \frac{4}{4}\right) + \left(\frac{5}{4} \times \frac{3}{3}\right) = \frac{8}{12} + \frac{15}{12} = \frac{23}{12}$$

- Multiplying fractions is straightforward: Multiply the numerators together, then repeat for the denominators. Cancel when possible to simplify the answer.

$$\frac{5}{8} \times \frac{8}{3} = \frac{5}{\cancel{8}} \times \frac{\cancel{8}}{3} = \frac{5 \times 1}{1 \times 3} = \frac{5}{3}$$

- Dividing by a fraction is the same as multiplying by its reciprocal. Once you've rewritten a division problem as multiplication, follow the rules for fraction multiplication to simplify.

$$\frac{3}{4} \div \frac{3}{2} = \frac{\cancel{3}}{\cancel{4}} \times \frac{\cancel{2}}{\cancel{3}} = \frac{1 \times 1}{2 \times 1} = \frac{1}{2}$$

Evaluating Expressions and Equations

Whatever you do to one side of an equation, you must do to the other. For instance, if you multiply one side by 3, you must multiply the other side by 3 as well.

The ability to solve straightforward, one-variable equations is critical on the ACT. Here's an example:

$$\frac{4x}{5} - 2 = 10$$

$$\frac{4x}{5} = 12$$

$$\frac{5}{4} \times \frac{4x}{5} = 12 \times \frac{5}{4}$$

$$x = 15$$

Number Lines

Absolute value refers to the distance a number is from 0 on a number line. Because absolute value is a distance, it is always positive or 0. Absolute value can never be negative.

$$|-17| = 17, \ |21| = 21, \ |0| = 0$$

Fraction/Decimal/Percent Conversion

Percent means "out of a hundred." For example, $27\% = \frac{27}{100}$. You can also write percents as decimals, e.g., $27\% = 0.27$.

The ability to recognize a few simple fractions masquerading in decimal or percent form will save you time on test day, as you won't have to turn to your calculator to convert them. Memorize the content of the following table.

Fraction	Decimal	Percent
$\frac{1}{10}$	0.1	10%
$\frac{1}{5}$	0.2	20%
$\frac{1}{4}$	0.25	25%
$\frac{1}{3}$	$0.333\overline{3}$	$33.3\overline{3}\%$
$\frac{1}{2}$	0.5	50%
$\frac{3}{4}$	0.75	75%

You will encounter **irrational numbers,** such as common radicals and π, on test day. You can carry an irrational number through your calculations as you would a variable (e.g., $4 \times \sqrt{2} = 4\sqrt{2}$). Only convert to a decimal when you have finished any intermediate steps and when the question asks you to provide an *approximate* value.

Graphing

Basic two-dimensional graphing is performed on a coordinate plane. There are two axes, x and y, that meet at a central point called the origin. Each axis has both positive and negative values that extend outward from the origin at evenly spaced intervals. The axes divide the space into four sections called quadrants, which are labeled I, II, III, and IV. Quadrant I is always the upper-right section, and the rest follow counterclockwise.

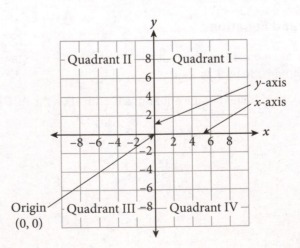

To plot points on the coordinate plane, you need their coordinates. The *x*-coordinate is where the point falls along the *x*-axis, and the *y*-coordinate is where the point falls along the *y*-axis. The two coordinates together make an ordered pair written as (*x,y*). When writing ordered pairs, the *x*-coordinate is always listed first (think alphabetical order). Four points are plotted in the following figure as examples.

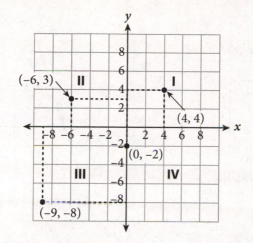

When two points are vertically or horizontally aligned, calculating the distance between them is easy. For a horizontal distance, only the *x*-value changes; for a vertical distance, only the *y*-value changes. Take the positive difference of the *x*-coordinates (or *y*-coordinates) to determine the distance—that is, subtract the smaller number from the larger number so that the difference is positive. Two examples are presented here:

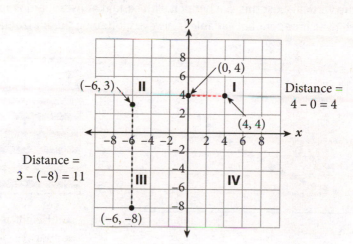

Math

Two-variable equations have an independent variable (input) and a dependent variable (output). The dependent variable (often y), depends on the independent variable (often x). For example, in the equation $y = 3x + 4$, x is the independent variable; any y-value depends on what you plug in for x. You can construct a table of values for the equation, which can then be plotted.

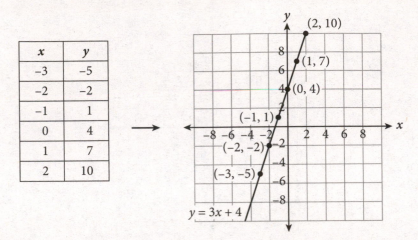

x	y
−3	−5
−2	−2
−1	1
0	4
1	7
2	10

You may be asked to infer relationships from graphs. In the first of the following graphs, the two variables are time and population. Clearly the year does not depend on how many people live in the town; rather, the population increases over time and thus depends on the year. In the second graph, you can infer that plant height depends on the amount of rain; thus, rainfall is the independent variable. Note that the independent variable for the second graph is the vertical axis; this can happen with certain nonstandard graphs. On the standard coordinate plane, however, the independent variable is always plotted on the horizontal axis.

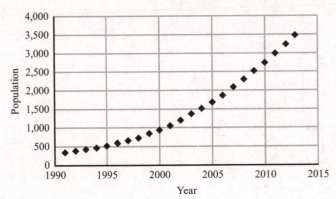

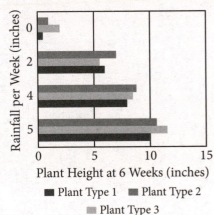

Lines and Angles

When two straight lines are graphed simultaneously, one of three possible scenarios will occur:

- The lines will not intersect at all (no solution).
- The lines will intersect at one point (one solution).
- The lines will lie on top of each other (infinitely many solutions).

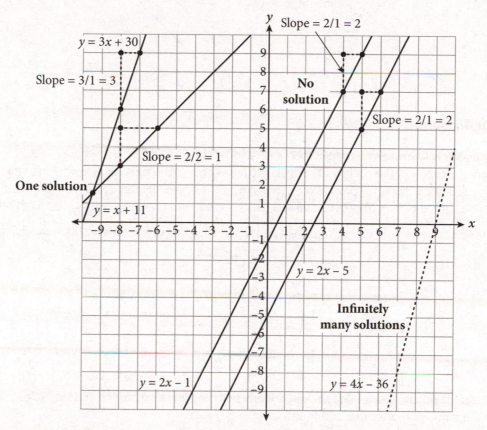

Adjacent angles can be added to find the measure of a larger angle. The following diagram demonstrates this:

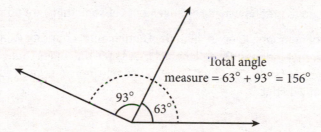

Total angle
measure = 63° + 93° = 156°

93°

63°

Two angles that sum to 90° are called complementary angles. Two angles that sum to 180° are called supplementary angles.

Two distinct lines in a plane will either intersect at one point or extend indefinitely without intersecting. If two lines intersect at a right angle (90º), they are perpendicular and are denoted with ⊥. If the lines never intersect, they are parallel and are denoted with ||.

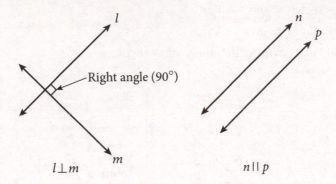

Radius and Diameter

A circle's perimeter is known as its circumference (C) and is found using $C = 2\pi r$, where r is the radius (distance from the center of the circle to its edge). The area of a circle is given by $A = \pi r^2$. The strange symbol is the lowercase Greek letter pi (π, pronounced "pie"), which is approximately 3.14. As mentioned in the algebra section, you should carry π throughout your calculations without rounding unless instructed otherwise.

A tangent line touches a circle at exactly one point and is perpendicular to a circle's radius at the point of contact.

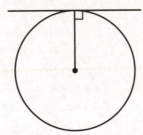

The presence of a right angle opens up the opportunity to draw otherwise hidden shapes, so pay special attention to tangents when they're mentioned.

Simple Counting Techniques

Counting techniques are used to find how many arrangements of something are possible.

When dealing with groups of numbers, keep in mind the **Fundamental Counting Principle**: If an event has m possible outcomes, and another independent event has n possible outcomes, then there are mn ways for the two events to occur together (multiply). You'll know to use this principle when you see phrases like "how many different" or "how many distinct."

Here's a good general strategy to follow:

- Step 1: Draw a blank to represent each position.
- Step 2: Fill in the number of possibilities for each position.
- Step 3: Multiply.

Factorials (!) are sometimes used when counting is happening. A factorial is a term with an exclamation mark following it; the exclamation mark means that instead of just the term shown, you need to calculate the value of term $\times$ (term $-$ 1) $\times$ (term $-$ 2) $\times \ldots \times$ 1. So, the value of 4! is $4 \times 3 \times 2 \times 1 = 24$. On the ACT, factorials within a fraction are a clue that you can cancel common terms before multiplying.

Mental Math

Even if you're a math whiz, you need to adjust your thought process in regard to the ACT to give yourself the biggest advantage you can. Knowing a few extra things will boost your speed on test day.

- Don't abuse your calculator by using it to calculate basic facts you can probably memorize, such as $15 \div 3$; it's far too easy to type in the incorrect number or operator without noticing. You can save time on test day by reviewing multiplication tables in particular. At a minimum, work up through the 10s. If you know them through 12 or 15, that's even better. Comfort with basic multiplication can go a long way toward improving your overall confidence on test day.
- You can save a few seconds of number crunching by memorizing perfect squares. Knowing perfect squares through 10 is a good start; go for 15 or even 20 if you have the time and motivation.
- Advanced formulas and identities will be provided, but memorizing certain relationships, such as $\cos(x) + \sin(x) = 1$, could save you valuable time on high-difficulty questions.

If you're comfortable with these concepts, read on for tips on calculator use. If not, frequently review this lesson and remember to refer to it for help if you get stuck in a later chapter.

Math

Calculator Use

LEARNING OBJECTIVE

After this lesson, you will be able to:

- Distinguish ACT problems on which a calculator will be helpful or unhelpful

---

Calculators and the ACT

Educators and parents believe that calculators serve a role in solving math questions, but they are sometimes concerned that students rely too heavily on calculators. They believe this dependence weakens students' overall ability to think mathematically. While the ACT does have a calculator policy that prohibits some models of calculators, they do allow you to have access to your permissible calculator during the entire ACT Math Test.

However, just because you can use your calculator doesn't mean you should. Many students never stop to ask whether using a calculator is the most efficient way to solve a problem. This chapter will show you how the strongest test takers use their calculators strategically; that is, they carefully evaluate when to use the calculator and when to skip it in favor of a more streamlined approach. As you will see, even though you can use a calculator, sometimes it's more beneficial to save your energy by approaching a question more strategically. Work smarter, not harder.

Which Calculator Should You Use?

The ACT allows most four-function, scientific, and graphing calculators, but you should visit ACT's website to confirm your ability to use your usual calculator. Due to the wide range of mathematics topics you'll encounter on test day, we recommend using a graphing calculator, such as the TI-83/84, but remember to confirm that your favorite graphing calculator model isn't prohibited, such as the TI-89.

No matter which calculator you choose, start practicing with it now; you don't want to waste valuable time on test day looking for the exponent button or figuring out how to correctly graph equations. If you don't already own one, see if you can borrow one from your school's math department or a local library.

A graphing calculator's capabilities extend well beyond what you'll need for the test, so don't worry about memorizing every function. The next few pages will cover which calculator functions you'll want to know how to use for the ACT. If you're not already familiar with your graphing calculator, you'll want to get the user manual; you can find this on the internet by searching for your calculator's model number. Identify the calculator functions necessary to answer various ACT Math questions, then write down the directions for each to make yourself a handy study sheet.

When Should You Use a Calculator?

Some ACT question types are designed based on the idea that students will do some or all of the work using a calculator. As a master test taker, you want to know what to look for so you can identify when calculator use is advantageous. Questions involving statistics, determining roots of complicated quadratic equations, and other topics are generally designed with calculator use in mind.

Other questions aren't intentionally designed to involve calculator use. Solving some with a calculator can save you time and energy, but you'll waste both if you go for the calculator on others. You will have to decide which method is best when you encounter the following topics:

- Graphing quadratics and circles
- Simplifying exponents and radicals and calculating roots
- Plane and coordinate geometry

Practicing long computations by hand and with the calculator will not only boost your focus and mental math prowess, but it will also help you determine whether it's faster to do the work for a given question by hand or reach for the calculator on test day.

Graphing quadratic equations may be a big reason you got that fancy calculator in the first place; it makes answering these questions a snap! This is definitely an area where you need to have an in-depth knowledge of your calculator's functions. The key to making these questions easy using the calculator is being meticulous when entering the equation. Also, be aware that some equations, such as the equation of a circle, might be more time-consuming to graph on your calculator than to sketch on paper.

Another stressful area for many students is radicals, especially when the answer choices are written as decimals. Those two elements are big red flags that trigger a reach for the calculator. Beware: not all graphing calculators have a built-in radical simplification function, so consider familiarizing yourself with this process.

Geometry can also be a gray area for students when it comes to calculator use. Consider working by hand when dealing with angles and lines, specifically when filling in information on complementary, supplementary, and congruent angles. You should be able to work fluidly through those questions without using your calculator, but feel free to reach for your calculator when operating on large numbers.

If you choose to use trigonometric functions to get to the answer on triangle questions, make sure you have your calculator set to degrees or radians as required by the question.

To Use or Not to Use?

A calculator is a double-edged sword on the ACT: using one can be an asset for verifying your work if you struggle when doing math by hand, but turning to it for the simplest computations will cost you time that you could devote to more complex questions. Practice solving questions with and without a calculator to get a sense of your personal preference as well as your strengths and weaknesses with and without one. Think critically about when a calculator saves you time and when mental math is faster. Use the exercises in this book to practice your calculations so that by the time test day arrives, you'll be in the habit of using your calculator as effectively as possible!

CHAPTER 7

The Method for ACT Math Questions

LEARNING OBJECTIVE

After completing this chapter, you will be able to:

- Effectively and efficiently apply the ACT Math Method

How to Do ACT Math

ACT Math questions can seem more difficult than they actually are, especially when you are working under time pressure. The method we are about to describe will help you answer ACT Math questions, whether you are comfortable with the math content or not. This method is designed to give you the confidence you need to get the right answers on the ACT by helping you think through a question logically, one piece at a time.

Take a look at this question and spend a minute thinking about how you would attack it if you saw it on test day.

> A certain television set is discounted 20% on Monday and then discounted another 25% on Tuesday. What is the total percent discount applied to the price of the television on Monday and Tuesday?
>
> A. 22.5%
>
> B. 40%
>
> C. 45%
>
> D. 50%
>
> E. 60%

Many test takers will see a question like this and panic. Others will waste a great deal of time reading and rereading without a clear goal. You want to avoid both of those outcomes.

Start by defining clearly for yourself **what the question is actually asking**. What do the answer choices represent? In this question, they represent total percent discount.

Next, **examine the information** that you have and organize it logically. The question asks about the total percent discount applied to the price of the television on Monday and Tuesday. You are given the percent discount on Monday (20%) and the discount on Tuesday (25%). However, you can't just add the two percents to get the total percent discount. Watch out for C, which is a distractor. You need to use the discounted price on Monday to calculate the discounted price on Tuesday in order to calculate the total percent change.

Now, **make a strategic decision** about how to proceed. You aren't given the original price of the television set, so this is a perfect question for Picking Numbers. When Picking Numbers for percents problems for which the initial value is unknown, you should usually start with 100 to make your calculations easier: pick $100 as the original cost. Then Monday's cost is 80% of that, or $100(0.8) = $80, and Tuesday's cost is 75% of the new amount, or $80(0.75) = $60. The total amount of the discount is $100 − $60 = $40. Now use the percent change formula:

$$\text{percent change} = \frac{\text{new price} - \text{original price}}{\text{original price}} \times 100\%$$

$$= \frac{\$60 - \$100}{\$100} \times 100\%$$

$$= \frac{-\$40}{\$100} \times 100\%$$

$$= -40\%$$

Finally, **confirm** that you answered the right question: you want the total percent discount applied to the price of the television on Monday and Tuesday. Great! You're done; the correct answer is (B).

Here's what we did:

ACT MATH METHOD

Step 1. State what the question is asking

Step 2. Examine the given information

Step 3. Choose your approach

Step 4. Confirm that you answered the right question

You can think of these steps as a series of questions to ask yourself:

1. What do they want?
2. What are they giving me to work with?
3. How should I approach this?
4. Did I answer the right question?

Not all ACT Math questions will require that you spend time on all the steps. The question above required a fair amount of analysis in steps 1 and 2 because it is a word problem. Other questions will require very little thought in steps 1 and 2. Carefully deciding on the appropriate strategy in step 3 will allow you to effectively answer questions. Step 4 is quick, but you should always do it: just make sure you answered the question that was actually asked before you bubble in your response. Doing so will save you from speed mistakes on questions that you know how to do and should be getting credit for.

There are several approaches you can choose from in step 3: Picking Numbers; Backsolving; doing the traditional math; eliminating; or taking a strategic guess.

Note that since the answer choices in the question above were numbers and did not contain variables, you were done once you found a match. However, when using the **Picking Numbers** strategy for questions with variables in the question stem *and* the answer choices, it is always possible that another answer choice can produce the same result, so check all the answer choices to be sure there isn't another match. Choose a number(s) to substitute for the variable(s) in the question and then substitute the same number(s) for the variable(s) in the choices to see which one matches. If there is more than one match, go back and pick another number to distinguish between the choices that match.

When Picking Numbers, use numbers that are permissible and manageable. That is, use numbers that are allowed by the stipulations of the question and that are easy to work with. A small positive integer is usually the best choice in this situation. Here is an example:

Which of the following expressions will produce an odd number for any integer a?

F. a^2

G. $a^2 + 1$

H. $a^2 + 2$

J. $2a^2 + 1$

K. $3a^2 + 1$

Step 1: What do they want? The choice that is always odd.

Step 2: What do they give you? a is any integer.

Step 3: What approach will you use?

Rather than trying to think this one through abstractly, it may be easier to Pick Numbers for a. The question states that a is any integer, so it could be even or odd. Try an even value for a. Let $a = 2$ and plug the value into the answer choices. Eliminate choices that are not odd:

Choice F: $a^2 = 2^2 = 4$ Eliminate.

Choice G: $a^2 + 1 = 2^2 + 1 = 5$ Keep.

Choice H: $a^2 + 2 = 2^2 + 2 = 6$ Eliminate.

Choice (J): $2a^2 + 1 = 2(2)^2 + 1 = 9$ Keep.

Choice K: $3a^2 + 1 = 3(2)^2 + 1 = 13$ Keep.

Choices G, (J), and K all give an odd result. Go back and try an odd value for a, like 3, for the remaining choices.

Choice G: $a^2 + 1 = 3^2 + 1 = 10$ Eliminate.

Choice (J): $2a^2 + 1 = 2(3)^2 + 1 = 19$ Keep.

Choice K: $3a^2 + 1 = 3(3)^2 + 1 = 28$ Eliminate.

Only (J) is odd for any integer a, so (J) is correct.

In the next example, you'll see Backsolving in action:

A physics midterm has 60 questions. The test is scored as follows: for each correct answer, 2 points are awarded; for each incorrect answer, $\frac{2}{3}$ of a point is subtracted; for unanswered questions, points are neither added nor subtracted. If Denise scored a 68 and did not answer 2 of the questions, how many questions did she answer correctly?

A. 34

B. 36

C. 38

D. 40

E. 42

Step 1: What do they want? The number of questions Denise answered correctly.

Step 2: What do they give you? The total number of questions answered $(60 - 2 = 58)$, the number of points for correct (2) and incorrect $\left(-\frac{2}{3}\right)$ answers, and Denise's midterm score (68).

Step 3: What approach will you use?

Here's a chance to practice Backsolving: plug the choices in for the unknown and see which one works. It often makes sense to start with C/H when you can tell from the context whether you'll need a larger or smaller answer choice if the one you're testing fails. If the question asks for the smallest or largest value, start with A/F or E/K.

For this question, start with the middle answer choice, C. If Denise answered 38 of the questions correctly and skipped 2, then she answered $60 - 38 - 2 = 20$ questions incorrectly. She gets 2 points for every correct question and loses $\frac{2}{3}$ of a point for every incorrect question, so do the calculations to determine her total points:

$$38(2) - 20\left(\frac{2}{3}\right) = 76 - \frac{40}{3}$$
$$= \frac{228}{3} - \frac{40}{3}$$
$$= \frac{188}{3}$$
$$= 62\frac{2}{3}$$

This is too low, so eliminate both A and B, and try the next-largest choice: 40. If Denise answered 40 questions correctly, she earned $40(2) - 18\left(\frac{2}{3}\right) = 80 - 12 = 68$ points.

Step 4: Did you solve for the right thing? You found the number of questions Denise answered correctly to earn a score of 68 points, so yes. Choice (D) is the correct answer. You do not need to evaluate the other answer choices.

Here's an example using the elimination strategy.

Suppose line *PQ* is perpendicular to line *RS* and *Q* is a point on line *RS*. If *L* is in the interior of $\angle PQS$, which of the following could be the measure of $\angle LQR$?

F.   110°

G.   90°

H.   70°

J.   50°

K.   30°

Step 1: What do they want? The measure of $\angle LQR$.

Step 2: What do they give you? *PQ* is perpendicular to *RS* and *Q* is a point on *RS*. *L* is in the interior of $\angle PQS$.

Step 3: What approach will you use?

When the question does not provide a figure, draw one yourself.

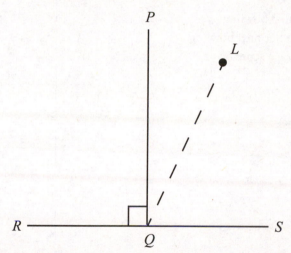

Because lines *PQ* and *RS* are perpendicular, $\angle PQR$ must form a 90° angle. If point *L* is in the interior of $\angle PQS$, the measure of $\angle LQR$ must be greater than 90°. You can eliminate all choices that are less than or equal to 90°. Only (F) is greater than 90°, so it is correct.

Step 4: Did you solve for the right thing? You found the measure of $\angle LQR$, so yes. Choose (F) and move on.

Now it's your turn. Be deliberate with the questions in the next section. If there is analysis to do up front, do it. If there is more than one way to do a question, consider carefully before choosing your approach, and be sure to check whether you answered the right question. Forming good habits now, in slow and careful practice, will set you up for confidence on test day.

How Much Have You Learned?

Directions: Take as much time as you need on these questions. Work carefully and methodically. There will be opportunities for timed practice in future chapters.

Math

1. Let z equal $3x - 2y + 1$. If the value of x is increased by 2 and the value of y is decreased by 3, what will happen to the value of z?

    A. It will decrease by -13.
    B. It will decrease by -12.
    C. It will be unchanged.
    D. It will increase by 12.
    E. It will increase by 13.

B.

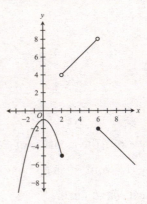

2. Deepa scored 150, 195, and 160 in 3 bowling games. What should she score on her next bowling game if she wants to have an average score of exactly 175 for the 4 games?

    F. 205
    G. 195
    H. 185
    J. 175
    K. 165

C.

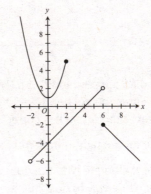

3. Which of the following is the graph for the function defined below?

    $$f(x) = \begin{cases} x^2 + 1 & \text{for} \quad x \leq 2 \\ x - 4 & \text{for} \quad 2 < x < 6 \\ 2 - x & \text{for} \quad x \geq 6 \end{cases}$$

D.

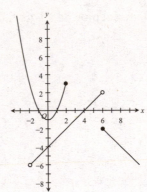

A.

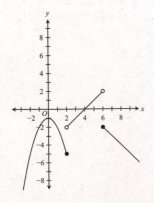

E.

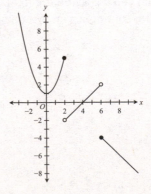

Questions 4–5 refer to the following information.

A scientist measured all of the trees in an area that was once a waste dump and is now being returned to nature. The scientist made the following histogram to show the heights of the trees.

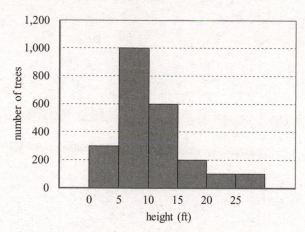

4. Which range of heights contains the median of the data?

    F. 0–4
    G. 5–9
    H. 10–14
    J. 15–19
    K. Cannot be determined from the information.

5. The scientist decides to present the data in a circle graph (pie chart). To the nearest degree, what is the measure of the central angle of the sector for 15–19?

    A. 16°
    B. 31°
    C. 47°
    D. 94°
    E. 157°

6. On the number line below, point G is the midpoint of FH and $HJ = JK$. If $HK = 18$, what is the length of GJ?

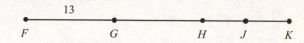

    F. 13
    G. 18
    H. 22
    J. 26
    K. 31

7. What is the period of the function $f(x) = 2\sin(3x - \pi)$?

    A. $\dfrac{\pi}{3}$
    B. $\dfrac{\pi}{2}$
    C. $\dfrac{2\pi}{3}$
    D. $\dfrac{5\pi}{6}$
    E. π

8. In 1992, the cost of a school lunch was $1.20. In 2017, the cost of a school lunch was $2.90. Assuming the cost increased linearly, what was the cost of a school lunch in 2002?

    F. $1.30
    G. $1.52
    H. $1.70
    J. $1.88
    K. $2.20

9. Viktor owns a car dealership. The numbers of different types of vehicles on his car lot are given in the following table. If a vehicle is selected at random, what is the probability that it is NOT a luxury vehicle or SUV?

Vehicle type	Number on lot
Subcompact	64
Compact	35
Midsize	61
Full-size	58
Luxury	32
SUV	43
Truck	27
Total	320

   A. $\dfrac{7}{32}$

   B. $\dfrac{15}{64}$

   C. $\dfrac{101}{320}$

   D. $\dfrac{49}{64}$

   E. $\dfrac{7}{8}$

10. If the sum of five consecutive even integers is equal to their product, what is the greatest of the five integers?

   F. 4

   G. 10

   H. 14

   J. 16

   K. 20

Reflect

Directions: Take a few minutes to recall what you've learned and what you've been practicing in this chapter. Consider the following questions, jot down your best answer for each one, and then compare your reflections to the expert responses on the following page. Use your level of confidence to determine what to do next.

1. Think about your current habits when attacking ACT questions. Are you a strategic test taker? Do you take the time to think through what would be the fastest way to the answer?

   _____

   _____

   _____

2. Do word problems give you trouble? If so, what can you do?

   _____

   _____

   _____

3. What are the steps of the ACT Math Method, and why is each step important?

   _____

   _____

   _____

Responses

1. Think about your current habits when attacking ACT questions. Are you a strategic test taker? Do you take the time to think through what would be the fastest way to the answer?

If yes, good for you! If not, we recommend doing questions more than one way whenever possible as part of your ACT prep. If you can discover now, while you're still practicing, that Picking Numbers is faster for you on certain types of questions but not on others, you'll be that much more efficient on test day.

2. Do word problems give you trouble? If so, what can you do?

If word problems are difficult for you, get into the habit of taking an inventory, before you do any math, of what the question is asking for and what information you have.

3. What are the steps of the ACT Math Method, and why is each step important?

Here are the steps:

Step 1. *State what the question is asking*

Step 2. *Examine the given information*
(Taking an inventory is especially important in word problems.)

Step 3. *Choose your approach*
(Taking a moment to decide what approach will be the fastest way to the answer will ultimately save you time.)

Step 4. *Confirm that you answered the right question*
(Making sure you solved for the right thing will save you from losing points to speed mistakes on questions that you know how to do and should be getting credit for.)

Next Steps

If you answered most questions correctly in the "How Much Have You Learned" section, and if your responses to the Reflect questions were similar to those of an expert, then consider the ACT Math Method an area of strength and move on to the next chapter. Do keep using the method as you work on the questions in future chapters.

If you don't yet feel confident, review those parts of this chapter that you have not yet mastered, and try the questions you missed again. As always, be sure to review the explanations closely. Then go online (**kaptest.com/login**) to watch a video about the Kaplan Method for ACT Math and use your Qbank for more practice. If you haven't already registered your book, do so at *kaptest.com/moreonline*.

GO ONLINE

kaptest.com/login

Answers and Explanations

1.   D

Difficulty: Medium

Category: Number and Quantity

Getting to the Answer: The question asks for the value of z after x is increased by 2 and y is decreased by 3. You are given $z = 3x - 2y + 1$. The new value of x is $x + 2$ and the new value of y is $y - 3$. Substitute these new values into the expression, $3x - 2y + 1$, to find the new value of z: $3(x + 2) - 2(y - 3) + 1$. This gives $3x + 6 - 2y + 6 + 1$, which equals $3x - 2y + 13$. Since z is $3x - 2y + 1$, the expression in terms of z is $(3x - 2y + 1) + 12$. Thus, the value of z will increase by 12. You found the change in z. (D) is correct.

Alternatively, you could Pick Numbers for x and y. If $x = 1$ and $y = 2$, then $z = 3(1) - 2(2) + 1 = 0$. Increasing x by 2 and decreasing y by 3 gives $x + 2 = 1 + 2 = 3$ and $y - 3 = 2 - 3 = -1$. Thus, the new value of z is $3(3) - 2(-1) + 1 = 9 + 2 + 1 = 12$. The change is $12 - 0 = 12$. Since the change is positive, z will increase by 12. This matches (D).

2.   G

Difficulty: Medium

Category: Statistics and Probability

Getting to the Answer: The question asks what score a bowler must get for her next game to attain an average score of 175 for 4 games, and gives the scores of her first 3 games. The average of a group of numbers is the sum of the values divided by the number of values. You can either set up an equation involving the missing score or use Backsolving to plug each of the possible scores into the question stem to see which one works.

Backsolving is often a great way to solve questions about averages, especially ones that give you the average and ask for a missing number. If you Backsolve, remember to start with the middle number:

Choice H: $\dfrac{150 + 195 + 160 + 185}{4} = \dfrac{690}{4} = 172.5$

Too low? Try the next-largest number:

Choice (G): $\dfrac{150 + 195 + 160 + 195}{4} = \dfrac{700}{4} = 175$

Choice (G) is correct.

To answer the question algebraically, call the missing score x and set up the average equation:

$$\frac{150 + 195 + 160 + x}{4} = 175$$
$$505 + x = 700$$
$$x = 195$$

This approach also shows that (G) is correct.

Alternatively, if you know how to use the balance approach for averages, you could determine that the 150 score was 25 less than the desired average, the 195 score was 20 greater, and the 160 score was 15 less, for a total of 20 less. Thus, the fourth score would need to be $175 + 20 = 195$ to raise the average to 175. Remember, step 3 is all about figuring out which approach works best for you, so be sure to practice approaching questions in multiple ways.

3.   E

Difficulty: Medium

Category: Functions

Getting to the Answer: The question asks which of the graphs in the choices correctly shows the piecewise function given. To identify which graph matches the piecewise-defined function, evaluate each piece of the function for the given domain.

When $x \leq 2$, the function is $f(x) = x^2 + 1$. This is an upward-facing parabola since the coefficient of x^2 is positive. Eliminate A and B. An easy point to evaluate is $x = 0$, at which point $f(0) = 1$. Eliminate C.

Evaluate the next piece of the function, $f(x) = x - 4$. Note that the domain of this piece of the function is $2 < x < 6$, which matches (E). Graph D does not match since the domain of the line $x - 4$ is $-2 < x < 6$. There is no need to consider the third piece of the function.

4. G

Difficulty: Medium

Category: Statistics and Probability

Getting to the Answer: The question asks which range of the histogram contains the median value. The median of a set of data is the middle value when the data is written in ascending order. This means that half of the data is less than the median and half is greater.

The total number of data values is the sum of the number of trees in each group: $300 + 1,000 + 600 + 200 + 100 + 100 = 2,300$. Half of that is 1,150. From left to right, the first bar contains 300 data values and the second bar contains 1,000 more, for a total of 1,300 data values. The middle value for all the data must therefore lie within the interval represented by the second bar, making (G) correct. Note that it is not possible to determine the exact median, only the interval within which it lies. Be certain that you used the correct total when determining the median.

5. B

Difficulty: Medium

Category: Geometry

Getting to the Answer: The question asks what the central angle of the 15–19 range would be if the same data were shown as a circle graph. According to the histogram, approximately 200 trees are in the 15–19 group. The total number of trees is the sum of the number of trees in each group: $300 + 1,000 + 600 + 200 + 100 + 100 = 2,300$. Thus, the fraction of trees that is in the 15–19 group is $\frac{200}{2300} = \frac{2}{23}$.

Since there are 360° in a circle, to find the measure of the central angle of the sector for the 15–19 group, multiply 360° by the fraction above: $360°\left(\frac{2}{23}\right) = 31.3°$. Choice (B) is correct; the number of values in the range is slightly more than $\frac{1}{12}$ th of the total number of values, and 31° is slightly more than $\frac{1}{12}$ th of 360°.

6. H

Difficulty: Medium

Category: Number and Quantity

Getting to the Answer: The question asks for the length of segment GJ on the line segment shown. Point G bisects segment FH and point J bisects segment HK. The length of FG is 13 and the length of HK is 18.

Since G is the midpoint of FH, $GH = FG = 13$. Also, since $HK = 18$ and $HJ = JK$, $HJ = JK = 9$. Line segment $GJ = GH + HJ$, which is $13 + 9 = 22$. The correct choice is (H). Check that you answered the question that was asked; G is HK, J is FH, and K is GK.

7. C

Difficulty: High

Category: Functions

Getting to the Answer: The question asks for the period of the function $2\sin(3x - \pi)$. Recall that the period of sin, cos, sec, and csc graphs is 2π, which means that the function values repeat themselves every full rotation around a circle, which is 2π radians.

For the general function $a\sin(bx - c) + d$, a affects the amplitude or vertical stretch, b affects the period or horizontal stretch, b and c together affect the horizontal shift, and d affects the vertical shift.

Since only b affects the period, you can think of this function as just $\sin(3x)$. Multiplying the value inside the parentheses "speeds up" the process of completing the full circle, which shortens the period and results in a horizontal contraction. Thus, multiplying the x by 3 means that the function will cycle through its values 3 times as quickly as $\sin(x)$. The function will make three cycles every 2π radians, or one cycle every $\frac{2\pi}{3}$ radians. Choice (C) is correct.

8.   J

Difficulty: Medium

Category: Algebra

Getting to the Answer: The question asks for the cost of a school lunch in 2002. You are given the costs in 1992 and 2017 and the fact that the cost increased linearly during that time span. Since the cost increased linearly, determine the constant rate at which the cost of a school lunch increased per year. The constant rate, or slope, is $\frac{\$2.90 - \$1.20}{2017 - 1992} = \frac{\$1.70}{25} = \$0.068$ per year. Thus, the cost in 2002 (10 years after 1992) is $\$1.20 + \$0.068(10) = \$1.88$. Choice (J) is correct.

9.   D

Difficulty: Medium

Category: Statistics and Probability

Getting to the Answer: The question asks for the probability that a vehicle selected at random from the cars shown in the table will not be either a luxury vehicle or an SUV. Recall the fundamental probability formula: probability $= \frac{\#\text{desired outcomes}}{\#\text{ total outcomes}}$. Also remember that the probability of an event NOT occurring is 1 minus the probability of that event occurring. Since calculating the probability of selecting a luxury vehicle or SUV involves less number-crunching, determine that probability and then subtract it from 1 to find the probability of NOT selecting a luxury vehicle or SUV:

Viktor has 320 cars in his lot. The probability of selecting a luxury vehicle or SUV is $\frac{32 + 43}{320} = \frac{75}{320} = \frac{15}{64}$. Thus, the probability of NOT selecting a luxury vehicle or SUV is $1 - \frac{15}{64} = \frac{64}{64} - \frac{15}{64} = \frac{49}{64}$. Choice (D) is correct.

10.   F

Difficulty: Medium

Category: Number and Quantity

Getting to the Answer: The question asks for the greatest of five consecutive even integers whose product is equal to their sum. First, put the question into words you can more easily understand. It says that when you add up the five consecutive even integers, you get the same thing as when you multiply them. The word *even* tells you that the difference between each integer in the sequence is 2. Finally, the answer choices themselves represent numbers that could be the final term of this sequence.

You could model the situation with an equation: $x + (x - 2) + (x - 4) + (x - 6) + (x - 8) = x(x - 2)$ $(x - 4)(x - 6)(x - 8)$. However, that's a very difficult equation to solve algebraically; try Backsolving instead. The question asks for the greatest of the integers, so you have to start with the greatest answer choice, K. If you start with any other, you won't know whether it's the largest, even if it works.

Choice K: $20 + 18 + 16 + 14 + 12 = 80$. Unfortunately, $20 \times 18 \times 16 \times 14 \times 12$ is way too big. Try H. If H is too small, then J is correct.

Choice H: $14 + 12 + 10 + 8 + 6 = 50$. The product $14 \times 12 \times 10 \times 8 \times 6$ is still way too big! Jump to (F); if it is too small, then G must be the correct answer.

Choice (F): $4 + 2 + 0 + (-2) + (-4) = 0$ and the product $4 \times 2 \times 0 \times -2 \times -4 = 0$.

Choice (F) is correct.

CHAPTER 8

Number and Quantity

LEARNING OBJECTIVES

LEARNING OBJECTIVES

After completing this chapter, you will be able to:

- Apply exponent rules
- Add, subtract, multiply, and divide numbers written in scientific notation
- Apply radical rules
- Solve absolute value equations
- Identify a specific term in an arithmetic or geometric sequence
- Perform arithmetic operations on imaginary and complex numbers
- Perform arithmetic operations using matrices

Number and Quantity: 8/36 SmartPoints® (Very high yield)

How Much Do You Know?

Try out the questions below. Show your work so that you can compare your solutions to the ones found on the next page. The "Category" heading in the explanation for each question gives the title of the lesson that covers how to solve it. If you answered the question(s) for a given lesson correctly, and if your scratchwork looks like the explanations, you may be able to move quickly through that lesson. If you answered incorrectly or used a different approach, you may want to take your time on that lesson.

1. What is the value of $\dfrac{10^5 \times 100^7}{1,000^6}$?

   A.   1
   B.   10
   C.   100
   D.   1,000
   E.   10,000

2. Which of the following is equivalent to $\sqrt{24} + \sqrt{150}$?

   F. $\sqrt{174}$
   G. $7\sqrt{6}$
   H. $29\sqrt{6}$
   J. $36\sqrt{7}$
   K. $36\sqrt{29}$

3. If $x = 4$, evaluate $\left| \dfrac{x-8}{2x+2} \right|$.

   A. $-\dfrac{1}{2}$
   B. $-\dfrac{2}{5}$
   C. $\dfrac{2}{5}$
   D. $\dfrac{1}{2}$
   E. $\dfrac{3}{4}$

4. If the first term in a geometric sequence is 4 and the third term is 100, what is the common ratio (r) ?

   F.   3
   G.   4
   H.   5
   J.   6
   K.   7

5. Write $(3i + 4) - (5i + 3)$ in $a + bi$ form.

   A. $1 - 2i$
   B. $7 - 2i$
   C. $7 + 8i$
   D. $5 + 2i$
   E. $4 - 5i$

Answers and explanations are on the next page. ▶ ▶ ▶

Check Your Work

1. B

Difficulty: Low

Category: Number and Quantity: Exponents

Getting to the Answer: To perform the arithmetic efficiently, begin by rewriting every term in the expression as 10 raised to some power:

$$\frac{10^5 \times \left(10^2\right)^7}{\left(10^3\right)^6}$$

Apply exponent rules and simplify. Remember that when you divide, you subtract the exponents, and when you raise one exponent to another, you multiply:

$$\frac{10^5 \times 10^{14}}{10^{18}} = \frac{10^{19}}{10^{18}} = 10^{19-18} = 10$$

Therefore, (B) is correct.

2. G

Difficulty: Low

Category: Number and Quantity: Radicals

Getting to the Answer: Simplify each radical by looking for two numbers that multiply to equal the radicand (the number under the radical sign). Numbers that are perfect squares are optimal. Then combine like terms:

$$\sqrt{24} + \sqrt{150}$$
$$\sqrt{4}\sqrt{6} + \sqrt{25}\sqrt{6}$$
$$2\sqrt{6} + 5\sqrt{6}$$
$$7\sqrt{6}$$

Choice (G) is correct.

3. C

Difficulty: Low

Category: Number and Quantity: Absolute Value

Getting to the Answer: You need to find the value of the expression. To do so, plug in the value for x and simplify.

Remember that the final answer is positive since the entire expression is inside absolute value brackets:

$$\left|\frac{(4)-8}{2(4)+2}\right| = \left|\frac{-4}{10}\right|$$
$$= \frac{4}{10}$$
$$= \frac{2}{5}$$

Choice (C) is correct.

4. H

Difficulty: Medium

Category: Number and Quantity: Sequences

Getting to the Answer: The question asks for the common ratio in a sequence. Since the sequence is geometric, you multiply each term by some constant (r) to get to the next term. The best way to solve this question is to plug in the answer. Since the first and third terms of the sequence are given, multiply the first term by the common ratios given in the answer choices twice. Whichever one results in 100 is the correct answer.

$$\text{F)} \ 4 \times 3 \times 3 = 36$$
$$\text{G)} \ 4 \times 4 \times 4 = 64$$
$$\text{H)} \ 4 \times 5 \times 5 = 100$$

You can stop here: (H) is correct.

5. A

Difficulty: Low

Category: Number and Quantity: Imaginary Numbers

Getting to the Answer: Combine like terms, being careful to distribute the negative on the outside of the parentheses.

$$(3i + 4) - (5i + 3)$$
$$3i + 4 - 5i - 3$$
$$-2i + 1$$
$$1 - 2i$$

Choice (A) is correct.

Exponents

To answer a question like this:

Which of the following is equivalent to $\dfrac{(3.0 \times 10^4)(8.0 \times 10^9)}{1.2 \times 10^6}$?

A. 2.0×10^5

B. 2.0×10^6

C. 2.0×10^7

D. 2.0×10^8

E. 2.0×10^9

You need to know this:

Exponents

Rule	Example
When multiplying two terms with the same base, add the exponents.	$a^b \times a^c = a^{(b+c)} \rightarrow 4^2 \times 4^3 = 4^{(2+3)} = 4^5$
When dividing two terms with the same base, subtract the exponents.	$\dfrac{a^b}{a^c} = a^{(b-c)} \rightarrow \dfrac{4^3}{4^2} = 4^{(3-2)} = 4^1$
When raising a power to another power, multiply the exponents.	$(a^b)^c = a^{(bc)} \rightarrow (4^3)^2 = 4^{(3 \times 2)} = 4^6$; $(y^2)^3 = y^{(2 \times 3)} = y^6$
When raising a product to a power, apply the power to all factors in the product.	$(2m)^3 = 2^3 \times m^3 = 8m^3$
Any non-zero term raised to the zero power equals 1.	$a^0 = 1 \rightarrow 4^0 = 1$
A base raised to a negative exponent can be rewritten as the reciprocal raised to the positive of the original exponent.	$a^{-b} = \dfrac{1}{a^b} \rightarrow 4^{-2} = \dfrac{1}{4^2}$; $\dfrac{1}{a^{-b}} = a^b \rightarrow \dfrac{1}{5^{-3}} = 5^3$
A negative number raised to an even exponent will produce a positive result; a negative number raised to an odd exponent will produce a negative result.	$(-2)^4 = 16$, but $(-2)^3 = -8$

Scientific Notation

Scientific notation is used to express very large or very small numbers.

- A number written in scientific notation is a number that is greater than or equal to 1, but less than 10, raised to a power of 10.
  - 3.64×10^8 is written in scientific notation, while 36.4×10^7 is not.
  - The two numbers are equivalent, but the second doesn't meet the definition of scientific notation because 36.4 is not between 1 and 10.
- To write a number in scientific notation, move the decimal point (to the right or to the left) until the number is between 1 and 10.
  - Count the number of places you moved the decimal point—this tells you the power of 10 that you'll need.
  - If the original number was a tiny decimal number (which means you had to move the decimal to the right), the exponent will be negative.
  - If the original number was a large number (which means you had to move the decimal point to the left), the exponent will be positive.
- You can add and subtract numbers written in scientific notation as long as the power of 10 in each term is the same; simply add (or subtract) the numbers and keep the same power of 10.
- You can multiply and divide numbers written in scientific notation using rules of exponents; simply multiply (or divide) the numbers and add (or subtract) the powers of 10.

You need to do this:

- Identify the appropriate rule by looking at the operation.
- Apply the rule.
- Repeat as necessary.

Straightforward ACT exponent questions should be quick points, but it's more likely you'll apply exponent rules as one step in solving a medium or high-difficulty question. Make sure you memorize the rules in the table on the previous page before test day.

Explanation:

You'll need several exponent rules to answer the scientific notation question at the beginning of this lesson. Work through this problem slowly and methodically.

First, simplify the numerator by multiplying the 3.0 and 8.0: $3 \times 8 = 24.0$. Then, determine the product of 10^4 and 10^9 by adding the exponents: $10^4 \times 10^9 = 10^{(4+9)} = 10^{13}$. Now, the numerator has a value of 24.0×10^{13}.

Since the values in both the numerator and the denominator are being multiplied, you can simplify the fraction by dividing the similar terms. First, divide the first terms of the expressions: $24.0 \div 1.2 = 20.0$. To find the value of $10^{13} \div 10^6$, subtract the exponents: $10^{(13-6)} = 10^7$. Combine these terms: 20.0×10^7.

Finally, convert the result into standard scientific notation. All of the choices start with 2.0, so factor out 10 from the first term ($20.0 \div 10 = 2.0$) and multiply the second term (10^7) by that 10, which can also be written as 10^1:

$$\frac{\left(3.0 \times 10^4\right)\left(8.0 \times 10^9\right)}{1.2 \times 10^6} = \frac{24.0 \times 10^{13}}{1.2 \times 10^6}$$

$$= 20.0 \times 10^7$$

$$= 2.0 \times 10^7 \times 10^1$$

$$= 2.0 \times 10^8$$

Therefore, (D) is correct.

Drills

If exponents or scientific notation gives you trouble, study the information above and try out these drill questions before completing the Try on Your Own questions below. Simplify each expression, and if the answer involves numbers only, write your answer in scientific notation. Turn the page and look at the bottom of the page to see the answers.

a. $820{,}000{,}000 + 500{,}000{,}000$

b. $(3.5 \times 10^5) \times (4.0 \times 10^3)$

c. $\dfrac{4.2 \times 10^8}{2.0 \times 10^5}$

d. $x^4 \times x^3$

e. $\dfrac{y^{10}}{y^4}$

Try on Your Own

Directions: Take as much time as you need on these questions. Work carefully and methodically. There will be an opportunity for timed practice at the end of the chapter.

1. What is the value of $\dfrac{3{,}200{,}000 - 2{,}300{,}000}{3{,}000}$?

    A. 3.0×10^2

    B. 3.0×10^3

    C. 3.0×10^4

    D. 3.0×10^5

    E. 3.0×10^6

2. Simplify $\dfrac{z^9 y^4 x^6}{x y^6 z^3}$.

    F. $\dfrac{y^2}{xz^6}$

    G. $\dfrac{x^5 z^6}{y^2}$

    H. $\dfrac{z^8 x^3}{y^2}$

    J. $\dfrac{y^2}{z^8 x^3}$

    K. $z^8 y^2 x^3$

3. Evaluate $\dfrac{\left(2.0 \times 10^4\right)\left(6.0 \times 10^7\right)}{4.0 \times 10^2}$ and write in scientific notation.

    A. 3.0×10^8

    B. 3.0×10^9

    C. 3.5×10^8

    D. 4.0×10^8

    E. 4.0×10^9

4. Which of the following is equivalent to $\dfrac{a^{-7} c^2 b^{-4}}{b^2 c^{-3} a^{-3}}$?

    F. $\dfrac{c^5}{a^4 b^6}$

    G. $\dfrac{a^{-10} b^{-4}}{c^5}$

    H. $\dfrac{a^{10} b^6}{c^5}$

    J. $\dfrac{c^{-5}}{a^{-10} b^{-6}}$

    K. $\dfrac{a^5 b}{c}$

HINT: For Q5, remember the definition of scientific notation. What must be true about the first part?

---

5. Write $\dfrac{2.1 \times 10^{-12}}{\left(2.0 \times 10^4\right)\left(5.0 \times 10^3\right)}$ in scientific notation.

    A. 0.21×10^{-4}

    B. 0.21×10^{-5}

    C. 2.1×10^{-6}

    D. 2.1×10^{-19}

    E. 2.1×10^{-20}

Drill answers from previous page:

a. 1.32×10^9 d. x^7

b. 1.4×10^9 e. y^6

c. 2.1×10^3

Radicals

LEARNING OBJECTIVE

After this lesson, you will be able to:

- Apply radical rules

To answer a question like this:

Which of the following expressions is equivalent to $\dfrac{4x}{10 - \sqrt{5}}$?

A. $\dfrac{40x + 4x\sqrt{5}}{95}$

B. $\dfrac{40x + 4x\sqrt{5}}{105}$

C. $\dfrac{44x - 77}{95}$

D. $\dfrac{44x - 77}{105}$

E. $\dfrac{4x - 7}{10 + \sqrt{5}}$

You need to know this:

Rule	Example
When a fraction is under a radical, you can rewrite it using two radicals: one containing the numerator and the other containing the denominator.	$\sqrt{\dfrac{a}{b}} = \dfrac{\sqrt{a}}{\sqrt{b}} \rightarrow \sqrt{\dfrac{4}{9}} = \dfrac{\sqrt{4}}{\sqrt{9}} = \dfrac{2}{3}$
Two factors under a single radical can be rewritten as separate radicals multiplied together.	$\sqrt{ab} = \sqrt{a} \times \sqrt{b} \rightarrow \sqrt{75} = \sqrt{3 \times 25}$ $= \sqrt{3} \times 5$ $= 5\sqrt{3}$
A radical can be written using a fractional exponent.	$\sqrt{a} = a^{\frac{1}{2}} \rightarrow \sqrt{289} = 289^{\frac{1}{2}} \quad \sqrt[3]{a} = a^{\frac{1}{3}} \rightarrow \sqrt[3]{729} = 729^{\frac{1}{3}}$
When you have a fractional exponent, the numerator is the power to which the base is raised, and the denominator is the root to be taken.	$a^{\frac{b}{c}} = \sqrt[c]{a^b} \rightarrow 5^{\frac{2}{3}} = \sqrt[3]{5^2}$
When a number is squared, the original number can be positive or negative, but the square root of a number can only be positive.	If $a^2 = 81$, then $a = \pm 9$, BUT $\sqrt{81} = 9$ only.
Cube roots of negative numbers are negative.	$\sqrt[3]{-27} = -3$
To rationalize a fraction containing a radical combined with a number or variable in the denominator, multiply both the numerator and the denominator by the conjugate of the denominator. (The conjugate of a binomial uses the same terms but the opposite sign between them.)	$\dfrac{3}{2+\sqrt{5}} \rightarrow$ the conjugate of $\left(2+\sqrt{5}\right)$ is $\left(2-\sqrt{5}\right)$ $\dfrac{3}{2+\sqrt{5}} \times \dfrac{2-\sqrt{5}}{2-\sqrt{5}} = \dfrac{3\left(2-\sqrt{5}\right)}{\left(2+\sqrt{5}\right)\left(2-\sqrt{5}\right)}$ $= \dfrac{6-3\sqrt{5}}{4-2\sqrt{5}+2\sqrt{5}-\sqrt{5}\times 5}$ $= \dfrac{6-3\sqrt{5}}{4-\sqrt{25}}$ $= \dfrac{6-3\sqrt{5}}{4-5}$ $= \dfrac{6-3\sqrt{5}}{-1}$ $= -6+3\sqrt{5}$

You need to do this:

- Identify the appropriate rule by looking at the answer choices. What form do you need to get the expression into? What rule do you need to apply to get there?
- Apply the rule.
- Repeat as necessary.

Straightforward ACT radicals questions should be quick points. Make sure you memorize the rules in the table on the previous page before test day.

Explanation:

Notice that four of the answer choices have no radicals in the denominator; this suggests that the denominator most likely needs to be rationalized. Multiply both the numerator and denominator by the conjugate of the denominator since this will eliminate any radicals in the denominator.

$$\frac{(4x)(10 + \sqrt{5})}{(10 - \sqrt{5})(10 + \sqrt{5})} = \frac{40x + 4x\sqrt{5}}{100 - 5} = \frac{40x + 4x\sqrt{5}}{95}$$

Choice (A) is correct.

Drills

If radicals give you trouble, study the information above and try out these drill questions before completing the Try on Your Own questions below. Turn the page and look at the bottom of the page to see the answers.

a. $\dfrac{1}{\sqrt{3}} + \dfrac{8}{\sqrt{2}}$

b. $9^{-\frac{3}{2}}$

c. $\sqrt{0.0016x^2}$

d. $\left(5\sqrt{3}\right)^2$

e. $13x\sqrt{5} - 4x\sqrt{5}$

Try on Your Own

Directions: Take as much time as you need on these questions. Work carefully and methodically. There will be an opportunity for timed practice at the end of the chapter.

1. What is the greatest integer smaller than $\sqrt{160}$?

    A. 12

    B. 13

    C. 14

    D. 15

    E. 16

2. Which of the following is equivalent to $\left(\sqrt{8}+\sqrt{6}\right)\left(\sqrt{8}-\sqrt{6}\right)$?

    F. 1

    G. 2

    H. $\sqrt{7}$

    J. $\sqrt{14}$

    K. 7

3. Which of the following is equivalent to the product $\sqrt{3} \times \sqrt[6]{3}$?

    A. $\sqrt[6]{3}$

    B. $\sqrt[7]{3}$

    C. $\sqrt[6]{6}$

    D. $\sqrt[3]{9}$

    E. Cannot be determined from the given information

4. Which of the following values of n satisfies the inequality $\frac{4}{5} < n < 1$?

    F. $\frac{\sqrt{10}}{5}$

    G. $\frac{\sqrt{14}}{5}$

    H. $\frac{\sqrt{18}}{5}$

    J. $\frac{\sqrt{26}}{5}$

    K. $\frac{\sqrt{30}}{5}$

HINT: For Q5, is there an alternative to the radicals presented in the question stem and answer choices that could make the algebra easier to manage?

---

5. Which of the following is equivalent to $\dfrac{\sqrt[5]{x^3}\,\sqrt{z^5}\,\sqrt[3]{y^4}}{z^2\,\sqrt[3]{y}\,\sqrt[5]{x^2}}$?

    A. $\sqrt[3]{x^2}\,\sqrt[5]{y^3}\,\sqrt[5]{z^4}$

    B. $\dfrac{x^5}{zy^2\,\sqrt[4]{z}\,\sqrt[5]{y^3}}$

    C. $\dfrac{zy^2\,\sqrt[4]{z}\,\sqrt[5]{y^3}}{x^5}$

    D. $\dfrac{x\sqrt[6]{y^{17}}}{\sqrt[3]{z^{10}}}$

    E. $y\sqrt[5]{x}\,\sqrt{z}$

Drill answers from previous page:

a. $\dfrac{\sqrt{2}+8\sqrt{3}}{\sqrt{6}}$

b. $\dfrac{1}{27}$

c. $\pm 0.04x$

d. 75

e. $9x\sqrt{5}$

Absolute Value

To answer a question like this:

Evaluate $\left|\dfrac{5-9}{8-6}\right| - |4-8|$.

A. -4

B. -2

C. 0

D. 2

E. 4

You need to know this:

- Absolute value means the distance a number is from 0 on a number line.
- Because absolute value is a distance, it is always positive or 0.
- Absolute value symbols function as grouping symbols (like parentheses or brackets) in the order of operations.

You need to do this:

- Follow the order of operations and simplify the expression from the inside set of parentheses or absolute value brackets out.
- Collect and combine like terms.
- Be careful with your positive and negative signs.

Explanation:

There are two sets of absolute value brackets, but they are not nested, so you can calculate them independently. First, simplify the terms within the grouping symbols; then, determine the absolute value and complete the subtraction. To account for the absolute value brackets, make each term positive after you simplify it.

$$\left|\frac{5-9}{8-6}\right| - |4 - 8| = \left|\frac{-4}{2}\right| - |-4|$$
$$= |-2| - 4$$
$$= 2 - 4$$
$$= -2$$

Hence, (B) is correct.

Drills

If absolute values give you trouble, study the information above and try out these drill questions before completing the Try on Your Own questions below.

a. $\big|\,|-4 + 3| - |7 - 10|\,\big|$

b. $\left|\dfrac{-7 \times 4}{6 \times 2}\right|$

c. Given $x = -2$, evaluate $-|x - 4| + 5x$.

d. Given $x = 3$, evaluate $-\left|\dfrac{4x - 10}{-x - 2}\right|$.

e. Given $x = -3$ and $y = 4$, evaluate
$$|xy + 5| - \left|\dfrac{y}{2} - 1\right|.$$

Try on Your Own

Directions: Take as much time as you need on these questions. Work carefully and methodically. There will be an opportunity for timed practice at the end of the chapter.

1. What is the value of $\dfrac{|5 - 2x| - 13}{-x}$ when $x = 3$?

   A.   3

   B.   4

   C. $\dfrac{14}{3}$

   D.   6

   E. $\dfrac{19}{3}$

2. If $a = -2$, then which of the following is equivalent to $-2|5a - 4|$?

   F. -28

   G. -12

   H.   0

   J.   12

   K.   28

3. When $t = 8$, what is the value of $-4\left|\dfrac{t}{2} - 4\right| + 4$?

   A. -8

   B. -4

   C.   0

   D.   4

   E.   8

4. Which of the following is equivalent to $-\left|\dfrac{-4 \times 10}{3 \times 5}\right|$?

   F. $-\dfrac{8}{3}$

   G. $-\dfrac{4}{3}$

   H.   1

   J. $\dfrac{4}{3}$

   K. $\dfrac{8}{3}$

> HINT: For Q5, take the time to familiarize yourself with both the question and the information provided. Which two answer choices can be marked incorrect without doing any substitution or algebra?

5. Given that $b = 3$ and $d = 1$, which of the following is equivalent to $\left|\dfrac{2b - 3}{-4d + 1}\right|$?

   A. -2

   B. -1

   C.   0

   D.   1

   E.   2

Drill answers from previous page:

a. 2

b. $\dfrac{7}{3}$

c. -16

d. $-\dfrac{2}{5}$

e. 6

Math

Sequences

LEARNING OBJECTIVE

After this lesson, you will be able to:

- Identify a specific term in an arithmetic or geometric sequence

---

To answer a question like this:

If the first term in a geometric sequence is 3, the third term is 48, and all the terms are positive integers, what is the ELEVENTH term?

A.   228
B.   528
C.   110,592
D.   3,145,728
E. 12,582,912

You need to know this:

A **sequence** is a list of numbers or expressions in which there is a pattern.

- Each number in a sequence is called a term and is named by, or is a function of, its position in the sequence.
- The first term in a sequence is called a_1, the nth term is called a_n, the term right after the nth term is called a_{n+1}, and so on. So a general sequence looks like $a_1, a_2, a_3, \ldots a_{n-1}, a_n, a_{n+1}, \ldots$.
- You can also write a sequence using function notation: $f(1), f(2), f(3), \ldots, f(n-1), f(n), f(n+1), \ldots$.
- A sequence can be arithmetic, geometric, or neither. For example, the sequence $1, 8, 27, 64, 125, \ldots$ has a pattern (perfect cubes) but is neither arithmetic nor geometric.

An **arithmetic sequence** is a sequence in which the same number is added to get from one term to the next.

- The difference between any two terms is called the common difference and is usually represented by the variable d.
- You can find the nth term in an arithmetic sequence using this formula: $a_n = a_1 + (n-1)d$.

A **geometric sequence** is a sequence in which the same number is multiplied to get from one term to the next.

- The number that you're multiplying by is called the common ratio and is usually represented by the variable r.
- You can find the nth term in a geometric sequence using this formula: $a_n = a_1 r^{(n-1)}$.

You need to do this:

- Look for clues in the question stem to help you determine the type of sequence.
- Use any given terms to calculate the common difference or common ratio.
- Use Backsolving or the appropriate formula as needed to calculate the missing value.

Explanation:

To find the next term in a geometric sequence, multiply the current term by a constant r. You are told that $a_1 = 3$ and $a_3 = 48$, so find r by creating the equation $a_1 \times r \times r = a_3$. Plugging in the given values yields $3 \times r \times r = 48$. Thus, $r^2 = 16$ and $r = 4$. Finally, use the general form of a geometric sequence, $a_n = a_1 r^{(n-1)}$, to solve for a_{11}.

$$a_{11} = a_1 (r)^{(11-1)}$$
$$= 3(4^{10})$$
$$= 3,145,728$$

Choice (D) is correct.

Math

Try on Your Own

Directions: Take as much time as you need on these questions. Work carefully and methodically. There will be an opportunity for timed practice at the end of the chapter.

1. Four numbers are in a sequence with 8 as the first term and 36 as the last term. The first three numbers form an arithmetic sequence with a common difference of -7. The last three numbers form a geometric sequence. What is the common ratio of the last three terms of the sequence?

   A. -10
   B. -6
   C. 0
   D. 10
   E. 32

HINT: For Q2, how can you determine the common difference without consecutive terms?

---

2. What three numbers should be placed in the blanks below so that the difference between consecutive numbers is the same?

$$12, \underline{\quad}, \underline{\quad}, \underline{\quad}, 32$$

   F. $16, 22, 28$
   G. $17, 22, 27$
   H. $20, 22, 30$
   J. $22, 24, 30$
   K. $23, 29, 31$

3. If the first and second terms of a geometric sequence are 3 and 12, what is an expression for the value of the TWENTY-FOURTH (24th) term of the sequence?

   A. $a_{24} = 3^4 \times 12$
   B. $a_{24} = 3^4 \times 23$
   C. $a_{24} = 4^3 \times 12$
   D. $a_{24} = 4^{23} \times 3$
   E. $a_{24} = 4^{24} \times 3$

4. If the first four terms of an arithmetic sequence are 25, 21, 17, and 13 respectively, what is the TWENTIETH (20th) term of the sequence?

   F. -55
   G. -51
   H. -47
   J. -43
   K. -39

5. If the fifth and the sixth terms of a geometric sequence are 3 and 1, respectively, what is the FIRST term of the sequence?

   A. -5
   B. $\dfrac{1}{27}$
   C. 11
   D. 27
   E. 243

Imaginary Numbers

> **LEARNING OBJECTIVE**
>
> After this lesson, you will be able to:
>
> - Perform arithmetic operations on imaginary and complex numbers

To answer a question like this:

Given a positive integer n such that $i^n = -1$, which of the following statements about n must be true? (Note: $i^2 = -1$)

A. When n is divided by 4, the result is a multiple of 0.

B. When n is divided by 4, the result is a multiple of $\frac{1}{3}$.

C. When n is divided by 4, the result is a multiple of $\frac{1}{2}$.

D. When n is divided by 4, the result is a multiple of 1.

E. When n is divided by 4, the result is a multiple of 2.

You need to know this:

The square root of a negative number is not a real number but an **imaginary number**.

To take the square root of a negative number, use i, which is defined as $i = \sqrt{-1}$. For example, to simplify $\sqrt{-49}$, rewrite $\sqrt{-49}$ as $\sqrt{-1 \times 49}$, take the square root of -1 (which is by definition i), and then take the square root of 49, which is 7. The end result is $7i$.

When a number is written in the form $a + bi$, where a is the real component and b is the imaginary component (and i is $\sqrt{-1}$), it is referred to as a **complex number**.

Solving ACT questions that involve complex numbers in the denominator of a fraction will require the use of a conjugate number. Complex numbers and the conjugates that go with them are binomials, so you can use FOIL to multiply complex numbers by their conjugate numbers. Review this skill in chapter 10 if needed.

The powers of i follow a predictable pattern that can help you work more efficiently on the ACT.

When you have ...	... it becomes ...
i^1	i
i^2	$\sqrt{-1} \times \sqrt{-1} = -1$
i^3	$i^2 \times i = -1 \times i = -i$
i^4	$i^2 \times i^2 = -1 \times -1 = 1$

So, the cycles of i are i, -1, $-i$, 1, then repeat (try a few more if you're not convinced). When you have i raised to an exponent greater than 4, divide the exponent by 4. The remainder will dictate the final answer.

- Take i^{63} as an example.
- Divide 63 by 4 to get 15 with a remainder of 3.
- This means that $i^{63} = (i^4)^{15} \times i^3 = 1^{15} \times i^3$.
- Because $i^3 = -i$, i^{63} becomes $-i$.

You need to do this:

Add, subtract, multiply, and divide complex numbers just as you do real numbers.

- To add (or subtract) complex numbers, simply add (or subtract) the real parts and then add (or subtract) the imaginary parts.
- To multiply complex numbers, treat them as binomials and use FOIL. To simplify the product, use the simplification $i^2 = -1$ and combine like terms.
- To divide complex numbers, write them in fraction form and multiply the numerator and denominator by the **conjugate** of the complex number in the denominator. To form the conjugate, change the sign in the complex number. For example, the conjugate of $2 + i$ is $2 - i$.
- Use FOIL as needed to multiply complex numbers by their conjugates.

Explanation:

The statement $i^n = -1$ will be satisfied when $n = 2, 6, 10, 14, \ldots$ because there are four stages in the cycle of i and the definition of i is that $i^2 = -1$. Every answer asks what happens when n is divided by 4. Divide each of the values of n above by 4 and see if you can spot a pattern.

$\frac{n}{4} = \frac{1}{2}, \frac{3}{2}, \frac{5}{2}, \frac{7}{2}, \ldots$ All of these numbers are multiples of $\frac{1}{2}$, so (C) is correct.

Try on Your Own

Directions: Take as much time as you need on these questions. Work carefully and methodically. There will be an opportunity for timed practice at the end of the chapter.

HINT: For Q1, what quadratic process can help you multiply the complex numbers in the question?

1. Given that $i = \sqrt{-1}$, which of the following is equal to $(11 + 4i)(2 - 5i)$?

   A. 2

   B. 42

   C. $2 - 75i$

   D. $22 - 20i$

   E. $42 - 47i$

2. Which of the following is the correct simplification of the expression $(2 + 7i) - (4 - 3i)$?

   F. $-2 - 10i$

   G. $-2 - 4i$

   H. $-2 + 10i$

   J. $2 - 4i$

   K. $2 + 10i$

3. The complex number i is defined such that $i^2 = -1$. What is the value of $(2i - 3)^2$?

   A. -13

   B. 5

   C. $-3 - 4i$

   D. $9 + 4i$

   E. $5 - 12i$

4. If $i^2 = -1$, which of the following is a square root of $8 - 6i$?

   F. $3 + i$

   G. $3 - i$

   H. $3 - 4i$

   J. $4 + 3i$

   K. $4 - 3i$

5. Which of the following numbers is NOT a real number?

   A. $-\sqrt{9}$

   B. 3^{-2}

   C. $\sqrt{-9}$

   D. $\sqrt{3}$

   E. $(-3)^2$

Matrices

LEARNING OBJECTIVE

After this lesson, you will be able to:

- Perform arithmetic operations using matrices

To answer a question like this:

If $\begin{bmatrix} 1 & 2 & 3 \end{bmatrix} \begin{bmatrix} x \\ 2x \\ 3x \end{bmatrix} = 42$, what is the value of x?

A. 2

B. 3

C. 4

D. 6

E. 7

You need to know this:

A **matrix** (*plural: matrices*) is a rectangular arrangement of numbers, symbols, or expressions, formatted in rows and columns.

- You can think of matrices as tables with no borders around the cells.

- The ACT tests matrices mostly in basic ways—addition, subtraction, and perhaps a multiplication problem here or there.

- To add (or subtract) matrices, the matrices must be exactly the same size. Add (or subtract) the corresponding entries (the numbers that sit in the same spots).

- You can multiply an entire matrix by a number by multiplying each entry in the matrix by that number.

- Often, a high-difficulty matrix question will appear as one of the final 10 questions.

  - These questions are more difficult because they typically require algebraic and critical thinking skills as opposed to straightforward calculations.

  - The definition of the determinant of matrix $\begin{bmatrix} a & b \\ c & d \end{bmatrix}$ (which is equal to $ad - bc$) will be provided when needed.

You need to do this:

Carefully determine whether the question is asking for:

- a missing value within a matrix?
- the sum or difference of two or more matrices?
- the product of a matrix and a number?
- something else, potentially unfamiliar?

Examine the given information:

- How many matrices are there?
- Are you given a specified piece of information, such as the definition of the discriminant, to use in some way?
- How many variables are there? How many do you need?

Choose your approach:

- Can you Backsolve using the answer choices?
- Can you use algebra to find a requested combination?
- If so, what equation can you set up to find a missing value?
- If you're stuck or know the approach will take a long time, mark the question to return to later if you have time remaining.

Explanation:

When multiplying matrices, the number of columns in the first matrix must match the number of rows in the second matrix. Here, you are multiplying a 1×3 matrix and 3×1 matrix. These match up, so multiply the rows of the first matrix by the columns of the second matrix. This creates a simple equation in x.

$$(1)(x) + (2)(2x) + (3)(3x) = 42$$
$$x + 4x + 9x = 42$$
$$14x = 42$$
$$x = 3$$

Choice (B) is correct.

Try on Your Own

Directions: Take as much time as you need on these questions. Work carefully and methodically. There will be an opportunity for timed practice at the end of the chapter.

1. If $A = \begin{bmatrix} 4 & 0 & 3 \\ 0 & -2 & 1 \end{bmatrix}$ and $B = \begin{bmatrix} 1 & 5 & -2 \\ 0 & 0 & 4 \end{bmatrix}$, then $2A + B = ?$

   A. $\begin{bmatrix} 9 & 5 & 4 \\ 0 & -4 & 6 \end{bmatrix}$

   B. $\begin{bmatrix} 9 & 5 & 4 \\ 0 & 0 & 4 \end{bmatrix}$

   C. $\begin{bmatrix} 9 & 5 & 4 \\ 0 & -2 & 4 \end{bmatrix}$

   D. $\begin{bmatrix} 8 & 0 & 6 \\ 0 & -4 & 2 \end{bmatrix}$

   E. $\begin{bmatrix} 5 & 5 & 1 \\ 0 & -2 & 5 \end{bmatrix}$

2. From the four matrices shown below, which of the following products is NOT possible?

   $A = \begin{bmatrix} 1 & 2 \\ 3 & 4 \end{bmatrix}$ $B = \begin{bmatrix} 5 & 6 & 7 \\ 8 & 9 & 0 \end{bmatrix}$ $C = \begin{bmatrix} 2 \\ 4 \end{bmatrix}$ $D = \begin{bmatrix} 3 & 5 \end{bmatrix}$

   F. AB

   G. AC

   H. BC

   J. CD

   K. DA

3. The product of $\begin{bmatrix} 1 & 2 & 3 \end{bmatrix} \begin{bmatrix} -1 \\ -2 \\ -3 \end{bmatrix}$ is

   A. -14

   B. 0

   C. 14

   D. $\begin{bmatrix} -1 & 0 & 0 \\ 0 & -4 & 0 \\ 0 & 0 & -9 \end{bmatrix}$

   E. $\begin{bmatrix} 0 & 1 & -1 \\ 2 & 0 & -2 \\ 3 & -3 & 0 \end{bmatrix}$

4. Evaluate $2x + y + 4z$, given $\begin{bmatrix} 4 & y & 8 \end{bmatrix} \begin{bmatrix} x \\ 2 \\ z \end{bmatrix} = 10$.

   F. 1

   G. 2

   H. 3

   J. 4

   K. 5

HINT: For Q5, how can you calculate the values of the four variables?

---

5. What is the value of $zy - xw$, given

   $\begin{bmatrix} 3x & 3 \\ 2w & 2z \end{bmatrix} + \begin{bmatrix} 6 & -2y \\ -4 & -6 \end{bmatrix} = \begin{bmatrix} 9 & 4 \\ 6 & 10 \end{bmatrix}$?

   A. -9

   B. -1

   C. 3

   D. 6

   E. 7

On Test Day

Remember that the ACT doesn't ask you to show your work. If you find the math in a question challenging, there may be another way to get to the answer.

Try out this question first using straightforward math and then using the Backsolving strategy from earlier in this chapter. Which approach do you find easier? There's no right or wrong answer—just remember your preferred approach and try it first if you see a question like this on test day.

1. What is the greatest integer smaller than $\sqrt{250}$?

    A. 15
    B. 16
    C. 17
    D. 19
    E. 20

The correct answer and both ways of solving can be found at the end of this chapter.

How Much Have You Learned?

Directions: For test-like practice, give yourself 10 minutes to complete this question set. Be sure to study the explanations, even for questions you got correct. They can be found at the end of this chapter.

1. The number $5^{\frac{5}{2}}$ is equal to which of the following?

   A.   5
   B.   12.5
   C.   25
   D. $\sqrt[5]{25}$
   E. $\sqrt{5^5}$

2. If $i^2 = -1$, which of the following represents $\dfrac{1}{3-i}$ written in $a + bi$ form?

   F. $\dfrac{3}{10} + \dfrac{1}{10}i$
   G. $\dfrac{1}{3} - \dfrac{1}{i}$
   H. $\dfrac{3}{8} + \dfrac{1}{8}i$
   J. $3 + i$
   K. $3 - i$

3. Evaluate $\dfrac{\left|14 + |2x - 4|\right|}{5x + 6}$ when $x = -2$.

   A. -12
   B. $-\dfrac{11}{2}$
   C. -2
   D. $\dfrac{9}{4}$
   E. $\dfrac{11}{2}$

4. The first four terms of a geometric sequence are $-2, 4, -8,$ and 16. What is the NINTH term of the geometric sequence?

   F. -512
   G. -256
   H. 128
   J. 256
   K. 512

5. If $m = 2n$, then for what positive value of n does the determinant of $\begin{bmatrix} m & 8 \\ 4 & n \end{bmatrix}$ equal 0?

   (Note: The determinant of matrix $\begin{bmatrix} a & b \\ c & d \end{bmatrix}$ equals $ad - bc$.)

   A.   4
   B. $4\sqrt{2}$
   C.   8
   D. $8\sqrt{2}$
   E.   There is no such value of n.

6. Which of the following is equivalent to $\dfrac{10}{7 - 2\sqrt{5}}$?

   F. $\dfrac{70 - 47\sqrt{55}}{29}$
   G. $\dfrac{70 + 47\sqrt{71}}{69}$
   H. $\dfrac{70 + 20\sqrt{5}}{29}$
   J. $\dfrac{27 + \sqrt{5}}{45}$
   K. $\dfrac{25 - \sqrt{55}}{45}$

7. Which of the following is equivalent to $\dfrac{\left(xy^2\right)^{-4} z^3}{z^{-1} y^2 x^{-3}}$?

   A. z^4

   B. $\dfrac{1}{z^4}$

   C. $\dfrac{x^3 y^2}{z^4}$

   D. $\dfrac{z^2}{x^4 y^3}$

   E. $\dfrac{z^4}{xy^{10}}$

8. When the imaginary number i is defined as $i = \sqrt{-1}$, it follows that $i^2 = -1$. Based on this information, which of the following is equivalent to $\dfrac{i^3 + 4i}{\sqrt{-9}}$?

   F. -1

   G. 1

   H. 3

   J. i

   K. $3i$

9. Which of the following expresses the value of $530{,}000{,}000 - 442{,}000{,}000$ in scientific notation?

   A. 8.8×10^5

   B. 8.8×10^6

   C. 8.8×10^7

   D. 8.8×10^8

   E. 88×10^6

10. If $\begin{bmatrix} x & 6 \\ 13 & x \end{bmatrix} + \begin{bmatrix} 2 & 3y \\ 5 & y \end{bmatrix} = \begin{bmatrix} 6 & 12 \\ 18 & z \end{bmatrix}$, what is the value of z ?

    F. -6

    G. 6

    H. 8

    J. 22

    K. 24

Reflect

Directions: Take a few minutes to recall what you've learned and what you've been practicing in this chapter. Consider the following questions, jot down your best answer for each one, and then compare your reflections to the responses on the following page. Use your level of confidence to determine what to do next.

1. How do you add, subtract, multiply, and divide terms that involve exponents? What must be true in order to complete these operations?

_____

_____

_____

2. How are exponents and radicals related?

_____

_____

_____

3. When you answer questions involving absolute value, what is the most important thing to pay attention to?

_____

_____

_____

4. How can the algebraic skill FOIL help you answer tough imaginary number questions?

_____

_____

_____

Responses

1. How do you add, subtract, multiply, and divide terms that involve exponents? What must be true in order to complete these operations?

To combine terms that involve exponents, the terms must have the same base. To add or subtract, keep the base and the exponent the same and add or subtract the coefficients (e.g., $2x^2 + 3x^2 = 5x^2$). To multiply, keep the base the same and add the exponents (e.g., $x^2x^3 = x^5$). To divide, keep the base the same and subtract the exponents (e.g., $x^8 \div x^2 = x^6$).

2. How are exponents and radicals related?

Radicals are fractional, or inverse, exponents.

3. When you answer questions involving absolute value, what is the most important thing to pay attention to?

When solving an equation like $|x| = 8$, there are two possibilities for x: 8 and -8. Do not forget that the answer could be negative!

4. How can the algebraic skill FOIL help you answer tough imaginary number questions?

To multiply two imaginary numbers in $a + bi$ form, you must FOIL. Simplify, collect like terms, and remember that $i^2 = -1$.

Next Steps

If you answered most questions correctly in the "How Much Have You Learned" section, and if your responses to the Reflect questions were similar to those of an expert, then consider Number and Quantity an area of strength and move on to the next chapter. Come back to this topic periodically to prevent yourself from getting rusty.

If you don't yet feel confident, review those parts of this chapter that you have not yet mastered. Then, try the questions you missed again. As always, be sure to review the explanations closely. Then go online (**kaptest.com/login**) to watch video lessons about the highest-yield concepts in this chapter and to use your Qbank for more practice. If you haven't already registered your book, do so at *kaptest.com/moreonline*.

GO ONLINE

kaptest.com/login

Answers and Explanations

Exponents

1. A

Difficulty: Low

Category: Number and Quantity

Getting to the Answer: Simplify the numerator and divide. Then convert into scientific notation.

$$\frac{3,200,000 - 2,300,000}{3,000} = \frac{900,000}{3,000}$$

$$300 = 3.0 \times 10^2$$

Choice (A) is correct.

2. G

Difficulty: Medium

Category: Number and Quantity

Getting to the Answer: Combine like terms and apply exponent rules to simplify. Remember that when you divide, you subtract the exponents.

$$\frac{x^6 y^4 z^9}{x y^6 z^3} = x^5 y^{-2} z^6 = \frac{x^5 z^6}{y^2}$$

Choice (G) is correct.

3. B

Difficulty: Low

Category: Number and Quantity

Getting to the Answer: First, simplify the numerator. Divide the numbers without exponents (12.0 and 4.0) first. Then, apply exponent rules to determine the correct power of 10: add the exponents when multiplying the same bases and subtract the exponents when dividing the same bases.

$$\frac{(2.0 \times 10^4)(6.0 \times 10^7)}{4.0 \times 10^2} = \frac{12.0 \times 10^{11}}{4.0 \times 10^2} = 3.0 \times 10^9$$

Choice (B) is correct.

4. F

Difficulty: Medium

Category: Number and Quantity

Getting to the Answer: Remember that you can make a term with a negative exponent have a positive exponent by taking the reciprocal of the term. To make this expression easier to understand, begin by making all the exponents positive. Then apply exponent rules to simplify.

$$\frac{a^{-7} c^2 b^{-4}}{b^2 c^{-3} a^{-3}} = \frac{a^3 c^2 c^3}{a^7 b^2 b^4} = \frac{c^5}{a^4 b^6}$$

Choice (F) is correct.

5. E

Difficulty: Medium

Category: Number and Quantity

Getting to the Answer: Simplify the denominator and divide. Make sure that the answer is written in correct scientific notation.

$$\frac{2.1 \times 10^{-12}}{(2.0 \times 10^4)(5.0 \times 10^3)} = \frac{2.1 \times 10^{-12}}{10.0 \times 10^7}$$

$$\frac{2.1 \times 10^{-12}}{10^8} = 2.1 \times 10^{-20}$$

Thus, (E) is correct.

Radicals

1. A

Difficulty: Low

Category: Number and Quantity

Getting to the Answer: The best way to find the biggest integer smaller than $\sqrt{160}$ is to square each answer choice. The largest one that, when squared, is still smaller than 160 is correct.

$$A) 12^2 = 144$$

$$B) 13^2 = 169$$

Since the answer choices are listed in increasing order, all other choices will be even larger than 169. Thus, (A) is correct.

2. G

Difficulty: Medium

Category: Number and Quantity

Getting to the Answer: Use the FOIL method to simplify. Notice that the terms being multiplied are conjugates, which means that the cross terms will cancel out. If you observe this, you can save some time by multiplying only the first and last terms.

$$\left(\sqrt{8} + \sqrt{6}\right)\left(\sqrt{8} - \sqrt{6}\right) = 8 - \sqrt{48} + \sqrt{48} - 6 = 2$$

Choice (G) is correct.

3. D

Difficulty: Medium

Category: Number and Quantity

Getting to the Answer: Because the radicals have different roots, you can't use the basic radical properties. Instead, change each radical into exponent form. Since you are multiplying two terms with the same base, add the exponents. Finally, change the expression back into radical form.

$$\sqrt{3} \times \sqrt[6]{3} = 3^{\frac{1}{2}} \times 3^{\frac{1}{6}}$$
$$= 3^{\frac{3}{6}} \times 3^{\frac{1}{6}}$$
$$= 3^{\frac{4}{6}}$$
$$= 3^{\frac{2}{3}}$$
$$= \sqrt[3]{3^2}$$
$$= \sqrt[3]{9}$$

Choice (D) is correct.

4. H

Difficulty: Low

Category: Number and Quantity

Getting to the Answer: Your task is to find the fraction between $\frac{4}{5}$ and 1. Notice that all the answer choices have radicals in the numerator and 5 in the denominator. Manipulate the given inequality to get it into the same form.

$$\frac{4}{5} < n < 1$$
$$\frac{4}{5} < n < \frac{5}{5}$$
$$\frac{\sqrt{16}}{5} < n < \frac{\sqrt{25}}{5}$$

Since 18 is between 16 and 25, (H) is correct.

5. E

Difficulty: High

Category: Number and Quantity

Getting to the Answer: First, change the radicals into exponent form. Next, apply exponent rules to simplify, adding exponents when multiplying and subtracting exponents when dividing. Remember that you need common denominators to add or subtract fractions. Finally, convert the exponents back into radical form.

$$\frac{\sqrt[5]{x^3}\,\sqrt{z^5}\,\sqrt[3]{y^4}}{z^2\,\sqrt[3]{y}\,\sqrt[5]{x^2}} = \frac{x^{\frac{3}{5}}z^{\frac{5}{2}}y^{\frac{4}{3}}}{z^2 y^{\frac{1}{3}}x^{\frac{2}{5}}}$$
$$\frac{x^{\frac{3}{5}}y^{\frac{4}{3}}z^{\frac{5}{2}}}{x^{\frac{2}{5}}y^{\frac{1}{3}}z^{\frac{4}{2}}} = x^{\frac{1}{5}}yz^{\frac{1}{2}}$$
$$x^{\frac{1}{5}}yz^{\frac{1}{2}} = y\sqrt[5]{x}\sqrt{z}$$

Choice (E) is correct.

Absolute Value

1. B

Difficulty: Low

Category: Number and Quantity

Getting to the Answer: Plug in 3, the value given for x, and simplify. Remember that absolute-value brackets change negative numbers into positive numbers.

$$\frac{|5 - 2x| - 13}{-x} = \frac{|5 - 6| - 13}{-3}$$
$$= \frac{|-1| - 13}{-3}$$
$$= \frac{1 - 13}{-3}$$
$$= \frac{-12}{-3}$$
$$= 4$$

Choice (B) is correct.

2. F

Difficulty: Medium

Category: Number and Quantity

Getting to the Answer: Start by plugging in -2, the given value. Simplify and make sure to utilize the absolute value.

$$-2|5a - 4| = -2|5(-2) - 4|$$
$$= -2|-14|$$
$$= -28$$

Thus, (F) is correct. Do not be tricked by choice K: this would be the answer without using the absolute value.

3. D

Difficulty: Medium

Category: Number and Quantity

Getting to the Answer: First, plug in the given value of 8 and simplify inside of the absolute value. Make sure the number inside the absolute value is not negative before moving on to the next simplifying steps.

$$-4\left|\frac{t}{2} - 4\right| + 4 = -4\left|\frac{(8)}{2} - 4\right| + 4$$
$$= -4|0| + 4$$
$$= 4$$

Choice (D) is correct.

4. F

Difficulty: Medium

Category: Number and Quantity

Getting to the Answer: First simplify the numerator and denominator, then reduce the resulting fraction. The fraction inside the absolute value will be positive. Then multiply the negative outside of the absolute value.

$$-\left|-\frac{40}{15}\right| = -\left|-\frac{8}{3}\right| = -\frac{8}{3}$$

Choice (F) is correct. K is a trap answer; it is the expression's result if the absolute value were absent.

5. D

Difficulty: Medium

Category: Number and Quantity

Getting to the Answer: Plug in the given values ($b = 3$ and $d = 1$) and simplify the numerator and denominator. After you divide, make sure that the resulting number is positive because of the absolute value.

$$\left|\frac{2b - 3}{-4d + 1}\right| = \left|\frac{2(3) - 3}{-4(1) + 1}\right|$$
$$= \left|\frac{3}{-3}\right|$$
$$= |-1|$$
$$= 1$$

Choice (A) is correct. Be careful; B would be the answer if there were no absolute value brackets.

Sequences

1. B

Difficulty: Medium

Category: Number and Quantity

Getting to the Answer: Your task is to find r, the common ratio of a geometric sequence. Since you are told that the first three terms form an arithmetic sequence with a common difference of -7, you can find the second and third term in the sequence by subtracting 7. So, $a_1 = 8$, $a_2 = 1$, and $a_3 = -6$. You are also told that $a_4 = 36$ and that the last three terms form a geometric sequence. $1 \times r = -6$ and $-6 \times r = 36$, so the ratio is -6. Choice (B) is correct.

2. G

Difficulty: Medium

Category: Number and Quantity

Getting to the Answer: The question gives you the first and fifth terms of an arithmetic sequence. The task is to figure out the middle three terms. Use the arithmetic sequence formula with $n = 5$ and $a_1 = 12$ to solve for the common difference.

$$a_5 = a_1 + (n-1)d$$
$$32 = 12 + (5-1)d$$
$$32 = 12 + 4d$$
$$4d = 20$$
$$5 = d$$

Starting at 12 and repeatedly adding 5 yields 12, 17, 22, 27, 32.

Hence, (G) is correct. Note that you can also solve this problem by Backsolving. Choices H, J, and K are themselves not arithmetic sequences, so they're incorrect. Choice F doesn't work because the difference between 12 and 16 is 4, whereas the difference between 16 and 22 is 6. This leaves (G) as the only choice that works.

3. D

Difficulty: Low

Category: Number and Quantity

Getting to the Answer: Since the first and second terms are given, find the common ratio r by setting $3r = 12$. This yields $r = 4$. The question asks for the 24th term, so plug $r = 4$, $n = 24$, and $a_1 = 3$ into the geometric sequence formula.

$$a_n = a_1 r^{(n-1)}$$
$$a_{24} = 3 \times 4^{(24-1)}$$
$$a_{24} = 3 \times 4^{23}$$

Terms can be multiplied in any order, so $a_{24} = 3 \times 4^{23} = 4^{23} \times 3$. Therefore, (D) is correct.

4. G

Difficulty: Low

Category: Number and Quantity

Getting to the Answer: It is too laborious to calculate the 20th term of this sequence by hand, so plug $d = -4$, $n = 20$, and $a_1 = 25$ into the arithmetic sequence formula.

$$a_n = a_1 + (n-1)d$$
$$a_{20} = 25 + (20-1)(-4)$$
$$a_{20} = 25 - 76$$
$$a_{20} = -51$$

Therefore, (G) is correct.

5. E

Difficulty: Low

Category: Number and Quantity

Getting to the Answer: Since the fifth and sixth terms of the sequence are given, you can find the common ratio r by setting $3r = 1$. This yields $r = \frac{1}{3}$. Now plug $r = \frac{1}{3}$, $a_6 = 1$, and $n = 6$ into the geometric sequence formula and solve for a_1.

$$a_n = a_1 r^{(n-1)}$$
$$a_6 = a_1 \left(\frac{1}{3}\right)^{(6-1)}$$
$$1 = a_1 \left(\frac{1}{3}\right)^5$$
$$1 = a_1 \left(\frac{1}{243}\right)$$
$$243 = a_1$$

Therefore, (E) is correct.

Imaginary Numbers

1. E

Difficulty: Medium

Category: Number and Quantity

Getting to the Answer: FOIL the given expression and remember that $i^2 = -1$. Simplify by combining like terms. Finally, make sure that your answer is in $a + bi$ form.

$$
\begin{aligned}
(11 + 4i)(2 - 5i) &= 22 - 55i + 8i - 20i^2 \\
&= 22 - 47i - 20(-1) \\
&= 22 - 47i + 20 \\
&= 42 - 47i
\end{aligned}
$$

Choice (E) is correct.

2. H

Difficulty: Low

Category: Number and Quantity

Getting to the Answer: Combine like terms, being careful to distribute the negative outside the parentheses.

$$
\begin{aligned}
&2 + 7i - (4 - 3i) \\
&2 + 7i - 4 + 3i \\
&-2 + 10i
\end{aligned}
$$

Choice (H) is correct.

3. E

Difficulty: Medium

Category: Number and Quantity

Getting to the Answer: Since the term in parentheses is squared, write out both terms and FOIL. Remember that $i^2 = -1$.

$$
\begin{aligned}
&(2i - 3)(2i - 3) \\
&4i^2 - 6i - 6i + 9 \\
&4i^2 - 12i + 9 \\
&4(-1) - 12i + 9 \\
&-4 - 12i + 9 \\
&5 - 12i
\end{aligned}
$$

Choice (E) is correct.

4. G

Difficulty: Medium

Category: Number and Quantity

Getting to the Answer: The square root of n is a number that yields n when it is multiplied by itself. It is difficult to take the square root of $8 - 6i$ directly because the number has both a real and an imaginary component, so approach the question strategically. Square each answer choice: the one that equals $8 - 6i$ is the square root.

$$
\begin{aligned}
(3 + i)(3 + i) &= 8 + 6i \\
(3 - i)(3 - i) &= 8 - 6i \\
(3 - 4i)(3 - 4i) &= -7 - 24i \\
(4 + 3i)(4 + 3i) &= 7 + 24i \\
(4 - 3i)(4 - 3i) &= 7 - 24i
\end{aligned}
$$

Therefore, (G) is correct. Note that if you go in order, you can stop after you see that (G) is correct: there is no need to waste time doing math on test day if you've already found the answer.

5. C

Difficulty: Low

Category: Number and Quantity

Getting to the Answer: The imaginary number i is defined as $i = \sqrt{-1}$. The only answer that has a negative number under a radical sign is (C).

Matrices

1.   A

Difficulty: Medium

Category: Number and Quantity

Getting to the Answer: To add or subtract matrices, both matrices need to have the same dimensions. Both A and B are 2×3 matrices, so they are compatible. To compute $2A$, multiply each entry in A by 2. To add A and B, add each corresponding component in A and B.

$$2\begin{bmatrix} 4 & 0 & 3 \\ 0 & -2 & 1 \end{bmatrix} + \begin{bmatrix} 1 & 5 & -2 \\ 0 & 0 & 4 \end{bmatrix}$$

$$\begin{bmatrix} 8 & 0 & 6 \\ 0 & -4 & 2 \end{bmatrix} + \begin{bmatrix} 1 & 5 & -2 \\ 0 & 0 & 4 \end{bmatrix}$$

$$\begin{bmatrix} 9 & 5 & 4 \\ 0 & -4 & 6 \end{bmatrix}$$

Thus, (A) is correct.

2.   H

Difficulty: Low

Category: Number and Quantity

Getting to the Answer: When multiplying matrices, the number of columns of the first matrix must match the number of rows in the second matrix. BC is not possible because the 3 columns in B do not match the 2 rows in C.

Choice (H) is correct.

3.   A

Difficulty: Low

Category: Number and Quantity

Getting to the Answer: When multiplying matrices, the number of columns in the first matrix must match the number of rows in the second matrix. Here, you are multiplying a 1×3 matrix and 3×1 matrix. The product matrix will have the same number of rows as the first matrix and the same number of columns as the second matrix. This means that the resulting matrix is 1×1.

Eliminate D and E immediately. Finally, multiply the two matrices by multiplying the rows of the first matrix by the columns of the second matrix.

$$\begin{bmatrix} 1 & 2 & 3 \end{bmatrix}\begin{bmatrix} -1 \\ -2 \\ -3 \end{bmatrix}$$

$$1(-1) + 2(-2) + 3(-3)$$
$$-1 - 4 - 9$$
$$-14$$

Choice (A) is correct.

4.   K

Difficulty: Medium

Category: Number and Quantity

Getting to the Answer: Remember that you multiply two matrices by multiplying the columns of the first matrix by the rows of the second matrix.

$$\begin{bmatrix} 4 & y & 8 \end{bmatrix}\begin{bmatrix} x \\ 2 \\ z \end{bmatrix} = 10$$

$$4(x) + 2(y) + 8(z) = 10$$
$$4x + 2y + 8z = 10$$

Notice that your end goal is very similar to the equation above. Divide both sides by 2 to obtain $2x + y + 4z = 5$.

Thus, (K) is correct.

5.   A

Difficulty: High

Category: Number and Quantity

Getting to the Answer: Matrices can be added only if their dimensions are the same. Here, all the matrices are 2×2, so add the matrices component-wise.

$$\begin{bmatrix} 3x + 6 & 3 - 2y \\ 2w - 4 & 2z + -6 \end{bmatrix} = \begin{bmatrix} 9 & 4 \\ 6 & 10 \end{bmatrix}$$

Next, write out four equations and solve for each variable.

$$3x + 6 = 9 \Rightarrow x = 1$$
$$2w - 4 = 6 \Rightarrow w = 5$$
$$3 - 2y = 4 \Rightarrow y = -\frac{1}{2}$$
$$2z + -6 = 10 \Rightarrow z = 8$$

Finally, plug these values into $zy - xw$.

$$zy - xw$$
$$8\left(-\frac{1}{2}\right) - 1(5)$$
$$-4 - 5$$
$$-9$$

Choice (A) is correct.

On Test Day

1.   A

Difficulty: Low

Category: Number and Quantity

Getting to the Answer: Using straightforward math, you will use your calculator to approximate the square root of 250: 15.8114. This is between the integers 15 and 16, and 16 is not smaller than 15.8114, so (A) is correct.

Another way to find the biggest number smaller than $\sqrt{250}$ is to Backsolve and square each answer choice. The largest one that is still smaller than $\sqrt{250}$ is correct:

$$A) \ 15^2 = 225$$
$$B) \ 16^2 = 256$$

Since the answer choices are listed in increasing order, all other choices will be even larger than 256. Thus, (A) is correct.

How Much Have You Learned?

1.   E

Difficulty: Medium

Category: Number and Quantity

Getting to the Answer: Recall that with a fractional exponent, the top number represents the power, while the bottom number represents the root. Thus, an exponent of $\frac{5}{2}$ involves raising a number to the 5th power and taking a square root. The base of the exponent is 5, so raise it to the 5th power and take the square root. The only choice that does this is (E), so (E) is correct.

2.   F

Difficulty: Medium

Category: Number and Quantity

Getting to the Answer: For this question, you need to rearrange an expression, not solve an equation. When there are imaginary numbers in the denominator of a fraction, multiply both the numerator and denominator by the conjugate of the denominator to make sure all imaginary numbers are eliminated in the denominator.

$$\frac{1}{3-i} \cdot \frac{(3+i)}{(3+i)} = \frac{3+i}{9-i^2}$$
$$\frac{3+i}{10} = \frac{3}{10} + \frac{1}{10}i$$

Choice (F) is correct.

3.   B

Difficulty: Medium

Category: Number and Quantity

Getting to the Answer: Plug in -2, the value for x, and simplify. Make sure that any number that comes out of an absolute value is positive.

$$\frac{\big|14 + |2x - 4|\big|}{5x + 6} = \frac{\big|14 + |2(-2) - 4|\big|}{5(-2) + 6}$$
$$= \frac{\big|14 + |-4 - 4|\big|}{-10 + 6}$$
$$= \frac{|14 + 8|}{-4}$$
$$= \frac{22}{-4}$$
$$= -\frac{11}{2}$$

Choice (B) is correct. Be wary of E; the numerator has absolute value symbols, but the full fraction does not.

4. F

Difficulty: Medium

Category: Number and Quantity

Getting to the Answer: Since you are working with a geometric sequence, first find r by comparing the first and second terms.

$$-2r = 4$$
$$r = -2$$

Then plug $r = -2$ and $n = 9$ into the geometric sequence formula to solve for the ninth term, a_9.

$$a_n = -2r^{(n-1)}$$
$$a_9 = -2(-2)^{(9-1)}$$
$$= -2(-2)^8$$
$$= -2^9$$
$$= -512$$

Choice (F) is correct.

5. A

Difficulty: High

Category: Number and Quantity

Getting to the Answer: The question asks for the value of n that makes the determinant of the given matrix equal 0. You are given the formula for calculating the determinant. Substitute m for a, 8 for b, 4 for c, and n for d, and set the resulting expression equal to 0.

$$ad - bc = 0$$
$$mn - 8(4) = 0$$
$$mn - 32 = 0$$
$$mn = 32$$

The question states that $m = 2n$. Substitute $2n$ for m and solve for n:

$$(2n)n = 32$$
$$2n^2 = 32$$
$$n^2 = 16$$
$$n = \pm 4$$

The question asks for the positive value of n, so (A) is correct.

6. H

Difficulty: Medium

Category: Number and Quantity

Getting to the Answer: On the ACT, square roots normally do not appear in the denominators of fractions in answer choices. Rationalize the denominator by multiplying the top and bottom by the conjugate.

$$\frac{(10)}{(7 - 2\sqrt{5})} \times \frac{(7 + 2\sqrt{5})}{(7 + 2\sqrt{5})} = \frac{70 + 20\sqrt{5}}{49 - 4(5)}$$
$$= \frac{70 + 20\sqrt{5}}{29}$$

Choice (H) is correct.

7. E

Difficulty: Medium

Category: Number and Quantity

Getting to the Answer: Remember that when an exponent is raised to another exponent, the exponents are multiplied. Simplify and combine like terms.

$$\frac{\left(xy^2\right)^{-4} z^3}{z^{-1}y^2x^{-3}} = \frac{x^{-4}y^{-8}z^3}{z^{-1}y^2x^{-3}} = \frac{x^{-1}y^{-10}z^4}{1} = \frac{z^4}{xy^{10}}$$

Choice (E) is correct.

8. G

Difficulty: High

Category: Number and Quantity

Getting to the Answer: Rather than solving an equation, you are manipulating an expression using properties of i. Simplify the expression using the information given in the question stem.

$$\frac{i^3 + 4i}{\sqrt{-9}} = \frac{i^2(i) + 4i}{\sqrt{9}\sqrt{-1}} = \frac{-i + 4i}{3i} = \frac{3i}{3i} = 1$$

Choice (G) is correct.

9. C

Difficulty: High

Category: Number and Quantity

Getting to the Answer: Your task is to select the answer choice that expresses the difference in scientific notation. Write each number in scientific notation, then solve.

$$530,000,000 = 5.3 \times 10^8$$
$$442,000,000 = 4.42 \times 10^8$$
$$5.3 \times 10^8 - 4.42 \times 10^8 = 0.88 \times 10^8$$

However, this is not the final answer. To be in scientific notation, the number before the multiplication sign must be between 1 and 10. Adjust the value to 8.8×10^7, and you find that the answer is (C).

10. G

Difficulty: Medium

Category: Number and Quantity

Getting to the Answer: Your task is to find z. Although writing an equation for z only involves the bottom right numbers in the matrices, doing so will give you $x + y = z$, so you will need the rest of the matrix to determine the missing variables.

First, add the two matrices. Remember that matrix addition is performed component-wise—add the numbers that sit in the same spots:

$$\begin{bmatrix} x & 6 \\ 13 & x \end{bmatrix} + \begin{bmatrix} 2 & 3y \\ 5 & y \end{bmatrix} = \begin{bmatrix} x+2 & 6+3y \\ 13+5 & x+y \end{bmatrix}$$

Next, set the matrix sum equal to the third matrix:

$$\begin{bmatrix} x+2 & 6+3y \\ 18 & x+y \end{bmatrix} = \begin{bmatrix} 6 & 12 \\ 18 & z \end{bmatrix}$$

You can now write out three equations and solve for each variable:

$$x + 2 = 6 \Rightarrow x = 4$$
$$6 + 3y = 12 \Rightarrow y = 2$$
$$x + y = z \Rightarrow z = 6$$

Choice (G) is correct.

CHAPTER 9

Rates, Ratios, Proportions, and Percents

LEARNING OBJECTIVES

After completing this chapter, you will be able to:

- Solve math questions with real-world scenarios using one or more rates
- Create a ratio to represent the relationship between two numbers
- Set up a proportion and solve to find a missing value
- Calculate percents
- Calculate percent change

subset of Number and Quantity: 8/36 SmartPoints® (Very high yield)

How Much Do You Know?

Directions: Try out the questions below. Show your work so that you can compare your solutions to the ones found on the next page. The "Category" heading in the explanation for each question gives the title of the lesson that covers how to solve it. If you answered the question(s) for a given lesson correctly, and if your scratchwork looks like ours, you may be able to move quickly through that lesson. If you answered incorrectly or used a different approach, you may want to take your time on that lesson.

1. Muna bikes to school every morning. It takes her 20 minutes to travel 3 miles. What is Muna's average rate of speed, in miles per hour, on her trip to school?

   A.   7
   B.   8
   C.   9
   D.   10
   E.   11

2. The ratio of seniors to juniors in a class is 3:5. If the class has 32 total students who are exclusively juniors and seniors, how many more juniors are there than seniors?

   F.   2
   G.   5
   H.   8
   J.   12
   K.   20

3. Tyrone is reading a road map. On the map, $\frac{1}{4}$ inch represents 12 miles. Approximately how many miles apart are two cities that are $3\frac{1}{2}$ inches apart on Tyrone's map?

   A.   12
   B.   48
   C.   96
   D.   132
   E.   168

4. If 125% of a number is 470, what is 50% of the number?

   F.   168
   G.   188
   H.   208
   J.   228
   K.   248

5. There are green, red, and blue marbles in a bag in a ratio of 1:2:3. The total number of marbles in the bag is 42. All the red marbles are taken and moved into a new bag with different marbles. After the addition of the red marbles, the second bag contains 52 marbles. How many marbles were in the second bag before the addition of the red marbles?

   A.   17
   B.   24
   C.   31
   D.   38
   E.   45

Answers and explanations are on the next page. ▶ ▶ ▶

Check Your Work

1.   C

Difficulty: Low

Category: Number and Quantity: Rates, Ratios, and Proportions

Getting to the Answer: The question asks for a bicyclist's average speed and provides distance in miles and time in minutes. Notice that all of the answer choices are in miles per hour, so start by converting the time from minutes into hours:

$$20 \text{ minutes} \times \frac{1 \text{ hour}}{60 \text{ minutes}} = \frac{20}{60} \text{ hours} = \frac{1}{3} \text{ hours}$$

Now use the formula $d = rt$ to solve for r.

$$d = rt$$
$$3 = r\left(\frac{1}{3}\right)$$
$$9 = r$$

The question asks for r, so (C) is correct.

2.   H

Difficulty: Medium

Category: Number and Quantity: Rates, Ratios, and Proportions

Getting to the Answer: Read carefully; the question asks how many more juniors than seniors are in a class. The stem provides the number of *total* students and the ratio of seniors to juniors. Convert the part-to-part ratio to a part-to-whole ratio of seniors to total students: $\frac{3}{3+5} = \frac{3}{8}$. Then, set up a proportion and cross-multiply to solve for the number of seniors:

$$\frac{3}{8} = \frac{s}{32}$$
$$3(32) = 8s$$
$$96 = 8s$$
$$12 = s$$

Since there are 12 seniors in a class of 32 total students, there must be $32 - 12 = 20$ juniors. The question asks how many more juniors there are than seniors, so the correct answer is $20 - 12 = 8$, (H).

3.   E

Difficulty: Medium

Category: Number and Quantity: Rates, Ratios, and Proportions

Getting to the Answer: The question asks you to determine the mileage between two cities. You are given their distance apart on a road map and the scale used for the map. Set up a proportion and cross-multiply. Convert $3\frac{1}{2}$ into the improper fraction $\frac{7}{2}$ to make the calculations easier.

$$\frac{\frac{1}{4} \text{ inch}}{12 \text{ miles}} = \frac{\frac{7}{2} \text{ inch}}{x \text{ miles}}$$
$$\frac{1}{4}x = 12\left(\frac{7}{2}\right)$$
$$\frac{1}{4}x = 42$$
$$x = 168$$

The question asks for x, so (E) is correct.

4.   G

Difficulty: Medium

Category: Number and Quantity: Percents

Getting to the Answer: This question asks for the value of 50% of a number given the value of 125% of that number. Translate carefully from English into math. In a word problem, "of" means multiply, "a number" means a variable, and "is" means equals. Translate the first part of the question and solve for x. Remember that $125\% = 1.25$.

$$1.25x = 470$$
$$x = 376$$

Finally, because it's what the question asks for, take 50% of x.

$$(0.50)x = (0.50)(376)$$
$$= 188$$

Choice (G) is correct.

5.   D

Difficulty: Medium

Category: Number and Quantity: Rates, Ratios, and Proportions

Getting to the Answer: The question asks for the original number of marbles in the second bag. You are given the final number of marbles in that bag, the ratio of different colors of marbles, and the total number of marbles in the first bag from which the red marbles were taken. Use the ratio to find the number of red marbles and subtract that from the total number of marbles in the second bag.

Since the ratio of green to red to blue marbles in the first bag is 1:2:3, the ratio of red marbles to total marbles is 2:6. Set up a proportion and cross-multiply to solve for the number of red marbles in the first bag:

$$\frac{2}{6} = \frac{r}{42}$$
$$\frac{1}{3} = \frac{r}{42}$$
$$42 = 3r$$
$$14 = r$$

Since there are 52 marbles in the second bag after the addition of the red marbles from the first bag, there must have been $52 - 14 = 38$ marbles originally in the second bag. This is the value you need, so (D) is correct.

Rates, Ratios, and Proportions

> **LEARNING OBJECTIVES**
>
> After this lesson, you will be able to:
>
> - Solve math questions with real-world scenarios using one or more rates
> - Create a ratio to represent the relationship between two numbers
> - Set up a proportion and solve to find a missing value

To answer a question like this:

A construction team is building a house from blueprints that are made to scale. Every 0.5 inch on the blueprint corresponds to 5 feet that the construction team needs to build. One wall the team is currently working on is 4.5 inches tall in the blueprint. Approximately how many *feet* tall does the wall need to be?

A. 15

B. 27

C. 38

D. 45

E. 63

You need to know this:

A **rate** is any "something per something"—days per week, miles per hour, dollars per gallon, etc.

- Pay close attention to the units of measurement; the rate could be given in one measurement in the question and a different measurement in the answer choices.
  - This means you would need to convert the units in the first rate to the units in the desired rate before you answer the question.
  - On the ACT, unit conversion is usually tested in conjunction with geometry, so you should review chapter 13 for instruction on this skill.
- Rate questions will often use the DIRT formula: Distance Is Rate × Time, or $d = rt$. The rate will always be the something per something, the distance value will match the units in the first part of the rate ("something per . . . "), and the time value will match the units in the second part of the rate (" . . . per something").

A **ratio** is a comparison of one quantity to another.

- When writing ratios, you can compare one part of a group to another part of that group, or you can compare a part of the group to the whole group.
  - If you have a bowl of apples and oranges, you can write ratios that compare apples to oranges (part to part), apples to total fruit (part to whole), and oranges to total fruit (part to whole).
- Ratios can be expressed using colons (3:5), fractions $\left(\dfrac{3}{5}\right)$, or words (3 to 5).

- Ratios are typically expressed in lowest terms and convey relative amounts—not necessarily actual amounts.
  - If there are 10 apples and 6 bananas in a bowl, the ratio of apples to bananas would likely be expressed as $\frac{5}{3}$ on the ACT rather than as $\frac{10}{6}$.
  - If you know the ratio of apples to bananas and either the actual number of apples or the total number of pieces of fruit, you can find the actual number of bananas by setting up a proportion, but if you only know ratios and no actual numbers, you cannot calculate any actual numbers.
  - If the ratio of apples to bananas is $\frac{5}{3}$ and there are 10 apples, then you can use the common multiplier 2 (because $5 \times 2 = 10$) to determine that there must be $3 \times 2 = 6$ bananas.
  - If the ratio of apples to bananas is $\frac{5}{3}$ and there are 16 pieces of fruit, you can set up a proportion to find the number of bananas:

$$\frac{3 \text{ bananas}}{5 \text{ apples}} \rightarrow \frac{3 \text{ bananas}}{8 \text{ total fruit}}$$

$$\frac{3 \text{ bananas}}{8 \text{ total fruit}} = \frac{b \text{ bananas}}{16 \text{ total fruit}}$$

$$3(16) = 8b$$

$$48 = 8b$$

$$6 = b$$

  - If the only information provided is that the ratio of apples to bananas is $\frac{5}{3}$ and the ratio of apples to total fruit is $\frac{5}{8}$, then there is not enough information to determine the actual numbers of apples or bananas or the total number of fruit.

A **proportion** is simply two ratios set equal to each other, e.g., $\frac{a}{b} = \frac{c}{d}$.

- Proportions are an efficient way to solve certain problems, but you must exercise caution when setting them up.
- Noting the units of each piece of the proportion will help you put each piece of the proportion in the right place.
- Cross-multiplication allows you to easily convert a proportion into an often easy-to-solve equation:

$$\frac{a}{b} \bowtie \frac{c}{d} \rightarrow ad = bc$$

- If you know any three numerical values in a proportion, you can solve for the fourth.
  - For example: say a fruit stand sells 3 peaches for every 5 apricots, and you need to calculate the number of peaches sold on a day when 20 apricots were sold.
  - You could use this information to set up a proportion and solve for the unknown:

$$\frac{3}{5} = \frac{p}{20}$$

- You can now solve for the number of peaches sold, p, by cross-multiplying:

$$60 = 5p$$

$$p = 12$$

- Alternatively, you could use the common multiplier to solve for p: the numerator and denominator in the original ratio must be multiplied by the same value to arrive at their respective terms in the new ratio.
- To get from 5 to 20 in the denominator, you multiply by 4, so you also have to multiply the 3 in the numerator by 4 to arrive at the actual number of peaches sold: $4(3) = 12$.

You need to do this:

- Identify the quantities and units used in any rates, ratios, or proportions in the question stem or answer choices.
- When needed, convert between part:part and part:whole ratios.
- When helpful, convert ratios that use colons into ratios that use fractions.
- Use common multipliers to calculate common ratios.
- Set up a proportion using two ratios and solve for the unknown either by cross-multiplying or by using the common multiplier.

Explanation:

The question asks how many feet tall a wall must be and gives the blueprint scale in inches. Use the given information to set up a proportion to solve for the actual height of the wall. Make sure that the units on both sides of the equal sign match up:

$$\frac{0.5 \text{ inch}}{5 \text{ feet}} = \frac{4.5 \text{ inch}}{x \text{ feet}}$$

$$0.5x = 4.5(5)$$

$$0.5x = 22.5$$

$$x = 45$$

Thus, the wall must be 45 feet tall, and choice (D) is correct.

Drills

If rates, ratios, and proportions give you trouble, study the information above and try out these drill questions before completing the Try on Your Own questions below. Determine the value of the variable for each part. Drill answers can be found on the bottom of the next page.

a. $\dfrac{2}{10} = \dfrac{x}{15}$

b. $\dfrac{7}{2} = \dfrac{7}{x}$

c. $\dfrac{a}{12} = \dfrac{6}{8}$

d. $\dfrac{\frac{1}{2}}{w} = \dfrac{\frac{1}{4}}{\frac{5}{2}}$

e. $\dfrac{2.5}{5} = \dfrac{z}{4}$

Try on Your Own

Directions: Take as much time as you need on these questions. Work carefully and methodically. There will be an opportunity for timed practice at the end of the chapter.

1. Which of the following values of x satisfies the proportion $\dfrac{5(x-2)}{9} = \dfrac{4}{3}$?

   A. $\dfrac{18}{15}$

   B. $\dfrac{33}{15}$

   C. $\dfrac{42}{15}$

   D. $\dfrac{51}{15}$

   E. $\dfrac{66}{15}$

HINT: For Q2, fractions inside of fractions can look confusing, but the cross-multiplication still works the same way. Which terms should you multiply together?

---

2. What is the value of $x - y$ if $y = 4$ and $\dfrac{\frac{3}{5}}{\frac{1}{2}} = \dfrac{x}{10}$?

   F. 4

   G. 8

   H. 10

   J. 12

   K. 16

3. At the end of the season, a team's ratio of wins to losses was 3:5. If there were no ties, what percentage of its games did the team win?

   A. $33\frac{1}{3}\%$

   B. $37\frac{1}{2}\%$

   C. 40%

   D. $62\frac{1}{2}\%$

   E. 75%

4. Four liters of water are mixed with 6 juiced lemons to make lemonade. How many liters of water should be mixed with 10 juiced lemons to obtain the same result?

   F. $4\frac{2}{3}$

   G. $5\frac{1}{3}$

   H. $6\frac{1}{3}$

   J. $6\frac{2}{3}$

   K. $8\frac{1}{3}$

Drill answers from previous page:

a. 3

b. 2

c. 9

d. 5

e. 2

5. For a certain company, a train coming from New York to Washington, D.C., takes 3 hours to travel 228 miles. A new train company is able to complete the same journey in only 2.5 hours. How much faster is the new company's train in terms of miles per hour (mph)?

   A.   7.5
   B.   11.7
   C.   15.2
   D.   17.3
   E.   21.4

6. Two packages of strawberries are sold for $10. How many packages could you buy with $25 ?

   F.   3
   G.   4
   H.   5
   J.   6
   K.   7

7. Which of the following is equivalent to $\dfrac{x^2y}{2zw} = \dfrac{4xy^2}{3z^3w}$?

   A. $y = \dfrac{3xz^2}{8}$

   B. $x = \dfrac{3yz^2}{8}$

   C. $z = \dfrac{3xy^2}{8}$

   D. $w = \dfrac{3xz^2}{8}$

   E. $\dfrac{3}{8} = yxz^2$

HINT: For Q8, do you have part:part or part:whole ratios? What actual numbers are you given? What are you trying to find?

---

8. The ratio of students to faculty on the First Year College Experience Committee at a certain university is 1.2:1. If there are 22 people on the committee, how many faculty are on the committee?

   F.   3
   G.   7
   H.   10
   J.   15
   K.   19

9. The school newspaper staff is selling cookies to raise money for the next school year. The first student who sells 252 boxes earns a laptop. Eva sells on average 7 boxes per hour, while Sylvia sells on average 3 boxes every 30 minutes. How much time, in hours, will pass until at least one of the students sells enough boxes to earn a laptop?

   A.   10
   B.   15
   C.   23
   D.   36
   E.   42

10. Carmen and Eduardo are building a tree house. Their mother constructs a drawing to scale that uses only two different lengths of wood pieces. The ratio, in inches, of the wood pieces is 2:3. If the longer wood piece is 5.5 feet, then how long is the shorter wood piece? (12 inches = 1 foot)

   F.   3 feet, 8 inches
   G.   3 feet, 10 inches
   H.   4 feet
   J.   4 feet, 2 inches
   K.   8 feet, 3 inches

Percents

LEARNING OBJECTIVES

After this lesson, you will be able to:

- Calculate percents
- Calculate percent change

To answer a question like this:

In 1960, scientists estimated a certain animal population in a particular geographical area to be 6,400. In 2000, the population had risen to 7,200. If this animal population experiences the same percent increase over the next 40 years, what will the approximate population be in 2040?

A. 7,200

B. 8,000

C. 8,100

D. 8,500

E. 9,000

You need to know this:

To calculate percents, use this basic equation:

$$\text{percent} = \frac{\text{part}}{\text{whole}} \times 100\%$$

Alternatively, use this statement: [blank] percent of [blank] is [blank]. Translating from English into math, you get [blank]% × [blank] = [blank].

You may sometimes need to calculate percent change on the ACT. You can determine the percent change in a given situation by applying this formula:

$$\text{percent change} = \frac{\text{amount of change}}{\text{original amount}} \times 100\%$$

If the change is positive, the amount of change will be positive. If the change is negative, the amount of change will be negative. So, a change in population might be a 3% change, while the change in a sales price might be −40%.

Sometimes more than one change will occur. Be careful here, as it can be tempting to take a "shortcut" by just adding two percent changes together (which will almost always lead to an incorrect answer). Instead, you'll need to find the total amount of the increase or decrease and then apply the formula.

You need to do this:

To use the basic percents equation:

- Plug in the values for any two parts of the formula and solve for the third.
- In some calculations, it may be more convenient to express percents as decimals. To do this, use the formula above, but stop before you multiply by 100% at the end.

To calculate a percent change:

- Calculate the actual increase or decrease.
- Divide by the original amount (not the new amount!).
- Multiply by 100%.

Explanation:

Use the percent change formula to find the percent change from 1960 to 2000.

$$\text{percent change} = \frac{\text{amount of change}}{\text{original amount}} \times 100\%$$

Plug in the values given in the question stem.

$$\frac{7,200 - 6,400}{6,400} = \frac{800}{6,400} = 0.125 \times 100\% = 12.5\%$$

Finally, apply this same percent increase to the population in the year 2000. Remember that $12.5\% = 0.125$.
$7,200 + 7,200(0.125) = 8,100$. Hence, (C) is correct.

Drills

If percents give you trouble, study the information above and try out these drill questions before completing the Try on Your Own questions below. Drill answers can be found on the bottom of the next page.

a. Calculate 25% of 200.

b. Calculate $1.8 \times 75\%$.

c. Express $\frac{11}{15}$ as a percent.

d. Express 1.3×0.4 as a percent.

e. Express 150% of 60% as a percent.

Try on Your Own

Directions: Take as much time as you need on these questions. Work carefully and methodically. There will be an opportunity for timed practice at the end of the chapter.

1. A school admits applicants only if they are able to pass a written and oral exam. Past records have shown that 60% of the applicants pass the written exam, and 80% of the applicants who pass the written exam go on to pass the oral exam. If there are 1,500 applicants, how many students will be admitted?

   A.   500
   B.   720
   C.   900
   D.   1,000
   E.   1,200

2. The managers of a restaurant calculated their business expenditures for the previous month. Overhead cost was \$4,800, food cost was \$8,000, and wages paid to employees were \$6,500. What percent of the total expenditures did the greatest expense comprise? Round your answer to the nearest whole percent.

   F.   25%
   G.   29%
   H.   35%
   J.   41%
   K.   46%

3. 12% of 50 is $\frac{3}{5}$ of what number?

   A.   7
   B.   8
   C.   9
   D.   10
   E.   11

4. What number is 16% of 25 ?

   F.   4
   G.   5
   H.   6
   J.   7
   K.   8

HINT: Questions like Q5 can be quick and easy to solve if you translate carefully from English to math.

---

5. 40% of 24 is $\frac{5}{2}$ of what number?

   A.   2.76
   B.   3.35
   C.   3.84
   D.   4.52
   E.   5.12

Drill answers from previous page:

a. 50

b. 1.35

c. 73.33%

d. 52%

e. 90%

On Test Day

When a question features multiple percentages, you have to make a key strategic decision: Can you do the arithmetic on the percentages themselves and get the answer right away, or do you have to calculate each percentage individually and do the arithmetic on the actual values?

For example, suppose a car traveling 50 miles per hour increases its speed by 20 percent and then decreases its speed by 20 percent. Can you just say that its final speed is 50 miles per hour since $+20\% - 20\% = 0$? No, because after a 20% increase, the car's speed becomes 120% of the original: $1.2(50) = 60$. When the car "decreases its speed by 20 percent," that 20 percent is calculated based on the new speed, 60, not the original speed, and 20 percent of 60 is greater than 20 percent of 50. Thus, the car's final speed is lower than its starting speed: $50(1.2)(0.8) = 48$ miles per hour.

By contrast, suppose you have to find how many more pet owners than non-pet owners live in a certain region where there are 13,450 residents, 32 percent of whom don't own a pet and 68 percent of whom do. It may be tempting to find 32 percent of 13,450 ($0.32 \times 13{,}450 = 4{,}304$), then find 68 percent of 13,450 ($0.68 \times 13{,}450 = 9{,}146$), and finally subtract those two numbers to get the answer ($9{,}146 - 4{,}304 = 4{,}842$). This is a waste of time, even though it will give you the correct answer. Instead, you can quickly find the difference between the two percentages ($68 - 32 = 36$) and take 36 percent of the total to get the answer in one step: $13{,}450 \times 0.36 = 4{,}842$, which is the same answer because the totals are the same.

If you can do arithmetic using the percentages but choose to do arithmetic on the raw numbers instead, you'll waste time doing unnecessary work. But if you can't do arithmetic on the percentages (as in the first example) but try anyway, you'll get the wrong answer. Being able to tell whether you can or can't do the arithmetic on the percentages is a useful skill.

Luckily, the fundamental principle is simple: you can do arithmetic on the percentages as long as the percentages are out of the same total. If the totals are different, then you must convert the percentages into actual values. Practice applying this principle to this question from earlier in this chapter:

1. A school admits applicants only if they are able to pass a written and oral exam. Past records have shown that 60% of the applicants pass the written exam, and 80% of the applicants who pass the written exam go on to pass the oral exam. If there are 1,500 applicants, how many students will be admitted?

   A. 500

   B. 720

   C. 900

   D. 1,050

   E. 1,200

The answer and explanation can be found at the end of this chapter.

How Much Have You Learned?

Directions: For test-like practice, give yourself 10 minutes to complete this question set. Be sure to study the explanations, even for questions you got correct. They can be found at the end of this chapter.

1. Which of the following will result in an odd integer for any integer n?

    A. n^2

    B. $3n^2$

    C. $4n^2$

    D. $3n^2 + 1$

    E. $4n^2 + 1$

2. Yeong-Ho owns two dogs. Each day, one dog eats $1\frac{1}{2}$ scoops of dog food, and the other eats $2\frac{3}{4}$ scoops of the same dog food. If one bag of this dog food contains about 340 scoops, how many days should it last the two dogs?

    F.   80

    G.   85

    H.   92

    J.   100

    K.   120

3. If $a{:}b = 2{:}5$ and $b{:}c = 4{:}3$, what is the ratio of $a{:}c$?

    A.   4:1

    B.   2:3

    C.   5:3

    D.   8:15

    E.   15:8

4. If 12 inches equal 30.48 centimeters, how many centimeters are in 36 inches?

    F.   91.44

    G.   92.33

    H.   93.48

    J.   93.89

    K.   94.52

5. A construction company is building a group of houses that all have the same ratio of length to width. If one house has a ratio of 10:3 and another house has a ratio of 5:a, then what is the value of $2a + 4$?

    A. -4

    B. $\frac{3}{2}$

    C.   7

    D.   8

    E.   12

Math

6. At a factory, Taj produces 23 toys per hour and Rosa produces 47 toys per hour. How many hours will it take for Taj and Rosa to produce 490 toys?

F. 4

G. 5

H. 6

J. 7

K. 8

7. Ernesto is shopping at a store that is having a clearance sale. The price of everything in the store is discounted by 25%. If Ernesto buys a shirt originally priced at $22.00 and a 6% sales tax is added, what will be the total price of the shirt?

A. $29.15

B. $23.10

C. $18.66

D. $17.49

E. $16.50

8. Atiya bought pants that were on clearance for 40% off the original price. She paid the cashier a total of $29.70 after sales tax. If sales tax is 10%, what was the original price of the pants?

F. $39.52

G. $41.80

H. $45

J. $48

K. $52.18

9. Ryan and Kamini can make 30 gallons of chocolate milk in 5 hours. Ryan can make 2 gallons of chocolate milk every hour. How many gallons of chocolate milk can Kamini make every hour?

A. 1

B. 2

C. 3

D. 4

E. 5

10. A 12 foot metal alloy bar weighs 114 pounds. What is the weight in pounds of a bar made out of the same alloy, with the same width and height, that is 3 feet 8 inches long?

F. $27\frac{1}{2}$

G. $34\frac{5}{6}$

H. $41\frac{2}{3}$

J. $49\frac{1}{6}$

K. $58\frac{1}{4}$

Reflect

Directions: Take a few minutes to recall what you've learned and what you've been practicing in this chapter. Consider the following questions, jot down your best answer for each one, and then compare your reflections to the responses on the following page. Use your level of confidence to determine what to do next.

1. What is a ratio, and how is it different from a proportion?

    _____

    _____

    _____

2. If you're given a ratio of one quantity to another, what can you say about the total number of quantities?

    _____

    _____

    _____

3. Suppose the value of something increases by 20 percent. How can you calculate the final value in the fewest number of steps? What if the value decreases by 20 percent?

    _____

    _____

    _____

4. What is the percent change formula, and what is the biggest pitfall to avoid when using it?

    _____

    _____

    _____

Math

Responses

1. What is a ratio, and how is it different from a proportion?

A ratio is the relative comparison of one quantity to another. For example, if the ratio of dogs to cats in an animal shelter is 3 to 5, then there are 3 dogs for every 5 cats. A proportion is two ratios set equal to each other.

2. If you're given a ratio of one quantity to another, what can you say about the total number of quantities?

Given a ratio, you know that the total must be a multiple of the sum of the ratio's parts. For example, if the ratio of dogs to cats is 3 to 5, then the total number of dogs and cats must be a multiple of 3 + 5, or 8. This means that when the ACT gives you one ratio, it's actually giving you several. If you're told that dogs:cats = 3:5, then you also know that dogs:total = 3:8 and cats:total = 5:8. You can use this "hidden" knowledge to your advantage.

3. Suppose the value of something increases by 20 percent. How can you calculate the final value in the fewest number of steps? What if the value decreases by 20 percent?

The fastest way to increase a value by 20 percent is to multiply it by 1.2, which is 100% + 20% = 120%. Similarly, to decrease something by 20 percent, you multiply it by 0.8, as that is 100% − 20% = 80%.

4. What is the percent change formula, and what is the biggest pitfall to avoid when using it?

The percent change formula is:

$$\text{percent change} = \frac{\text{amount of change}}{\text{original amount}} \times 100\%$$

A common mistake is to put the new amount on the bottom of the fraction rather than the original amount.

Next Steps

If you answered most questions correctly in the "How Much Have You Learned" section, and if your responses to the Reflect questions were similar to those of an expert, then consider ratios and the related topics in this chapter an area of strength and move on to the next chapter. Come back to this topic periodically to prevent yourself from getting rusty.

If you don't yet feel confident, review those parts of this chapter that you have not yet mastered, and try the questions you missed again. As always, be sure to review the explanations closely. Then go online (**kaptest.com/login**) to watch video lessons about the highest-yield concepts in this chapter and to use your Qbank for more practice. If you haven't already registered your book, do so at *kaptest.com/moreonline*.

GO ONLINE

kaptest.com/login

Answers and Explanations

Rates, Ratios, and Proportions

1.   E

Difficulty: Medium

Category: Number and Quantity

Getting to the Answer: The question asks for the value of x and provides a proportion in which one term is x. Cross-multiply and simplify to solve for x:

$$\frac{5(x-2)}{9} = \frac{4}{3}$$
$$15(x-2) = 36$$
$$x - 2 = \frac{36}{15}$$
$$x = \frac{36}{15} + 2$$
$$x = \frac{36}{15} + \frac{30}{15}$$
$$x = \frac{66}{15}$$

You don't need to do anything with x, so (E) is correct.

2.   G

Difficulty: High

Category: Number and Quantity

Getting to the Answer: The question asks for the value of $x - y$. The value of y is provided, and x is part of a proportion with stacked fractions. Fractions inside of fractions can look confusing, but the cross-multiplication still works the same way:

$$\frac{\frac{3}{5}}{\frac{1}{2}} = \frac{x}{10}$$
$$\frac{3}{5}(10) = \frac{1}{2}x$$
$$6 = \frac{1}{2}x$$
$$12 = x$$

Remember that you need to find $x - y$. Since $x = 12$ and $y = 4$, $x - y = 8$, choice (G) is the correct answer.

3.   B

Difficulty: Low

Category: Number and Quantity

Getting to the Answer: The question gives you a team's win-loss ratio and asks for the percentage of games that the team won. Since there were no ties, you can convert the given part-to-part ratio of 3:5 to the part-to-whole ratio of 3:8. (Note that the 8 comes from the fact that $3 + 5 = 8$.) To find the percentage of games won, convert that ratio to a percentage: $\frac{3}{8} \times 100\% = 37.5\%$.

This is the percentage of games won, so (B) is correct. Be careful; D is the percentage of games *lost* and is therefore incorrect.

4.   J

Difficulty: Low

Category: Number and Quantity

Getting to the Answer: The question asks how many liters of water should be mixed with the juice from 10 lemons to create lemonade with the same concentration as mixing 4 liters of water with the juice from 6 lemons. Set up a proportion using the given information and designate the number of liters of water as w. Cross-multiply and solve for w:

$$\frac{w \text{ liters of water}}{10 \text{ lemons}} = \frac{4 \text{ liters of water}}{6 \text{ lemons}}$$
$$6w = 40$$
$$w = \frac{40}{6}$$
$$w = \frac{20}{3} = 6\frac{2}{3}$$

The question asks for w, so (J) is correct.

5. C

Difficulty: Medium

Category: Number and Quantity

Getting to the Answer: The question asks how much faster one train is than another. The choices are stated in terms of mph. You are given the distance of a certain trip and the time it takes each train to complete the journey. Calculate each rate separately by plugging the given distance and time into the $d = rt$ equation.

$$d_1 = r_1 t_1 \qquad d_2 = r_2 t_2$$
$$228 = r_1(3) \qquad 228 = r_2(2.5)$$
$$76 = r_1 \qquad 91.2 = r_2$$

The question asks for the difference between the rates, which is $91.2 - 76 = 15.2$ mph, (C).

6. H

Difficulty: Low

Category: Number and Quantity

Getting to the Answer: The question asks how many packages of strawberries can be bought for $25 and gives the price for 2 packages of strawberries. Set up a proportion using the given information. Cross-multiply and solve for p.

$$\frac{2 \text{ packages}}{10 \text{ dollars}} = \frac{p \text{ packages}}{25 \text{ dollars}}$$
$$10p = 50$$
$$p = 5$$

This is the number of packages that you could buy with $25, so (H) is correct.

7. A

Difficulty: High

Category: Number and Quantity

Getting to the Answer: The question asks which choice is equivalent to the given proportion. Since the choices are stated in terms of different variables, your strategy is to cross-multiply and isolate for one variable at a time, then compare your results to the corresponding choice. You may have to do this multiple times until you find something that matches an answer choice.

$$\frac{x^2 y}{2zw} = \frac{4xy^2}{3z^3 w}$$
$$3x^2 yz^3 w = 8xy^2 zw$$
$$3xz^2 = 8y$$
$$\frac{3xz^2}{8} = y$$

This question relies on trial and error, so you may not arrive at this answer immediately. When you isolate y, the resulting expression matches choice (A), so that is the correct answer.

8. H

Difficulty: High

Category: Number and Quantity

Getting to the Answer: The question asks how many faculty are on a committee. You are given the total number of committee members and the ratio of students to faculty, which is 1.2:1.

Convert the part-to-part ratio to a part-to-whole ratio and use this ratio to solve for the number of faculty.

$$\frac{1 \text{ faculty}}{1 + 1.2 \text{ total}} = \frac{f \text{ faculty}}{22 \text{ total}}$$
$$(22)(1) = 2.2f$$
$$22 = 2.2f$$
$$10 = f$$

There are 10 faculty on the committee. Hence, (H) is correct.

9. D

Difficulty: Medium

Category: Number and Quantity

Getting to the Answer: The question asks how long it will take the more efficient of the two students selling cookies to reach a specific sales goal. You are given the rates at which both students are selling, but these rates are in different units. First, check to see which student is selling boxes at a faster rate. Sylvia sells 3 boxes every 30 minutes, or 6 boxes every hour. Eva sells 7 boxes per hour, so she will reach the goal first.

Now use the $d = rt$ equation to solve for t to determine how long it will take her to sell 252 boxes:

$$d = rt$$
$$252 = 7t$$
$$36 = t$$

This is how long it will take the faster student to sell the cookies, so (D) is correct. Note that E is how many hours it would take Sylvia, the student who sells at a slower rate, to sell the 252 boxes.

10. F

Difficulty: Medium

Category: Number and Quantity

Getting to the Answer: The question gives you the ratio of the lengths of two pieces of wood and asks for the length of the shorter piece. Set up a proportion and cross-multiply to solve.

$$\frac{2 \text{ in}}{3 \text{ in}} = \frac{x \text{ ft}}{5.5 \text{ ft}}$$
$$2(5.5) = 3x$$
$$11 = 3x$$
$$\frac{11}{3} = x$$

Finally, convert $\frac{11}{3}$ into a mixed number of feet and inches.

$$\frac{11}{3} \text{ ft} = 3\frac{2}{3} \text{ ft}$$
$$\frac{2}{3} \text{ ft} \times \frac{12 \text{ in}}{\text{ft}} = 8 \text{ in}$$

This is the length of the shorter piece, so (F) is correct. Choice K is a strong distractor that you would choose if you reversed the ratio.

Percents

1. B

Difficulty: Medium

Category: Number and Quantity

Getting to the Answer: The question asks how many students will be admitted to a certain school. You're given the total number of applicants, the percent who pass the written exam, and the percent (of those who pass the written exam) who pass the oral exam. Start by multiplying the total number of applicants by the percent of applicants who pass the written exam.

$$1,500 \, (0.60) = 900$$

Then multiply by the percent of applicants who pass the oral exam.

$$900 \, (0.80) = 720$$

This gives the number of admitted applicants, so (B) is correct.

2. J

Difficulty: Low

Category: Number and Quantity

Getting to the Answer: The question asks you to find the greatest expenditure and calculate what percent of the total it was. Recall that percent $= \frac{\text{part}}{\text{whole}} \times 100\%$. The question asks about the highest expenditure, which is food cost. The total expenditure is $4,800 + $8,000 + $6,500 = $19,300. Plug these numbers into the percent formula.

$$\text{percent} = \frac{8,000}{19,300} \times 100\%$$
$$= 0.41451 \times 100\%$$
$$= 41.451\%$$

Round to the nearest whole number to get 41%, choice (J).

Math

3. D

Difficulty: Medium

Category: Number and Quantity

Getting to the Answer: To understand what the question asks, translate carefully from English into math. Recall that "of" means multiply, "is" means equals, and "what number" means x. First convert 12% to 0.12.

$$0.12(50) = \frac{3}{5}x$$
$$6 = \frac{3}{5}x$$
$$6\left(\frac{5}{3}\right) = x$$
$$10 = x$$

You chose x to represent the number the question asked for, so (D) is correct.

4. F

Difficulty: Low

Category: Number and Quantity

Getting to the Answer: To understand what the question asks, translate carefully from English into math. Recall that "what number" means x, "is" means equals, and "of" means multiply. Convert 16% to 0.16.

$$x = (0.16)(25)$$
$$x = 4$$

This is the number that was asked for, so (F) is correct.

5. C

Difficulty: Medium

Category: Number and Quantity

Getting to the Answer: To understand what the question asks, translate carefully from English into math. Recall that "of" means multiply, "is" means equals, and "what number" means x.

$$0.40 \times 24 = \frac{5}{2}x$$
$$9.6 = \frac{5}{2}x$$
$$9.6\left(\frac{2}{5}\right) = x$$
$$3.84 = x$$

This is the value you need, so (C) is correct.

On Test Day

1. B

Difficulty: Medium

Category: Number and Quantity

Getting to the Answer: The question asks how many students will be admitted to a certain school. You're given the total number of applicants, the percent who pass the written exam, and the percent (of those who pass the written exam) who pass the oral exam. Start by multiplying the total number of applicants by the percent of applicants who pass the written exam:

$$1,500\,(0.60) = 900$$

Then multiply by the percent of applicants who pass the oral exam:

$$900\,(0.80) = 720$$

This gives the number of admitted applicants, so (B) is correct.

The students who pass the written exam and the students who pass the oral exam are separate groups, but the number of students who pass the oral exam is a subset of the number of students who pass the written exam. This means that the totals are different, and thus, you must calculate each percent independently. Someone who chooses to average the percents will end up with $1,500(0.7) = 1,050$, D, which is incorrect. Skipping the first percent and directly finding 80% of the original total (instead of 80% of those who pass the written exam) will also yield an incorrect answer, E: $1,500(0.8) = 1,200$.

How Much Have You Learned?

1. B

Difficulty: High

Category: Number and Quantity

Getting to the Answer: You need to find the expression that will always yield an odd integer. The question states that n is an integer, but it could be positive or negative or zero, and it could be even or odd. The answers contain variables, so Picking Numbers is an option.

Each choice contains an n^2, so start with that. Remember, n can be any integer, so you may as well pick an easy number to start with.

If $n = 2$, then:

$n^2 = 2^2 = 4$, even. Eliminate A.

$3n^2 = 3(4) = 12$, even. Eliminate B.

$4n^2 = 4(4) = 16$, even. Eliminate C.

$3n^2 + 1 = 12 + 1 = 13$, odd. Keep D.

$4n^2 + 1 = 16 + 1 = 17$, odd. Keep E.

To decide between D and E, pick another value for n. This time, try an odd value. (You can then try negative numbers if using an odd number doesn't help you narrow it down to the correct answer.)

If $n = 3$, then:

$3n^2 + 1 = 3(9) + 1 = 28$, even. Eliminate D.

Choice (E) is correct.

2. F

Difficulty: Medium

Category: Number and Quantity

Getting to the Answer: The question asks how many days it will take two dogs to consume a dog food bag of a certain size. You are told how much food each dog eats every day and how much food is in the bag. Since the dogs are eating out of the same bag of food, add the number of scoops each dog eats per day to find how many total scoops per day are being eaten.

$$1\frac{1}{2} + 2\frac{3}{4}$$

$$\frac{3}{2} + \frac{11}{4}$$

$$\frac{6}{4} + \frac{11}{4}$$

$$\frac{17}{4}$$

Since you are given a rate and asked to solve for time, use the $d = rt$ equation.

$$340 = \frac{17}{4}t$$

$$340\left(\frac{4}{17}\right) = t$$

$$80 = t$$

Because t represents the number of days the food will last, (F) is correct.

3. D

Difficulty: Medium

Category: Number and Quantity

Getting to the Answer: The question asks for the ratio of a to c and provides the ratios of a to b and b to c. Notice that $\left(\frac{a}{b}\right)\left(\frac{b}{c}\right) = \frac{a}{c}$. To find $\frac{a}{c}$, simply multiply the two given ratios together.

$$\left(\frac{2}{5}\right)\left(\frac{4}{3}\right) = \frac{8}{15}$$

This is the ratio of a to c, so (D) is correct. Be certain that you answered the question that was asked. Choice (E) is the ratio of c to a.

4. F

Difficulty: Low

Category: Number and Quantity

Getting to the Answer: The question asks how many centimeters are equivalent to 36 inches. You are given the number of centimeters in 12 inches. Set up a proportion and cross-multiply to solve for c, the number of centimeters in 36 inches.

$$\frac{12 \text{ inches}}{30.48 \text{ centimeters}} = \frac{36 \text{ inches}}{c \text{ centimeters}}$$

$$12c = (30.48)36$$

$$12c = 1,097.28$$

$$c = 91.44$$

Because c is the variable you chose to represent the answer, (F) is correct.

5. C

Difficulty: Medium

Category: Number and Quantity

Getting to the Answer: The question asks for the value of $2a + 4$ and provides two equivalent ratios, one of which contains a. Begin by solving for a. Set up a proportion and cross-multiply:

$$\frac{10}{3} = \frac{5}{a}$$
$$10a = 15$$
$$a = \frac{3}{2}$$

You're not done yet, though. The question asks for $2a + 4$, so plug in $a = \frac{3}{2}$ to find the value of this expression.

$$2a + 4 = 2\left(\frac{3}{2}\right) + 4$$
$$= 3 + 4$$
$$= 7$$

This is the final answer, so (C) is correct. Be certain that you answered the question that was asked; choice B is the value of a.

6. J

Difficulty: Medium

Category: Number and Quantity

Getting to the Answer: The question asks how long, in hours, it will take for two workers to produce 490 toys. You are given the rates at which each worker produces toys. Since both workers' rates are given in toys per hour, you can add the two rates together to find how many toys both workers make per hour: $23 + 47 = 70$. Plug this rate and the total number of toys needed into the $d = rt$ equation.

$$490 = 70t$$
$$7 = t$$

This is how long it will take the workers to produce 490 toys, so (J) is correct.

7. D

Difficulty: Medium

Category: Number and Quantity

Getting to the Answer: The question asks what price Ernesto paid for a shirt. You are given the original price, a discount percentage, and a sales tax percentage. First determine the price of the shirt after the 25% discount. Recall that $22 - 22(0.25) = 22(0.75)$.

$$22\,(0.75) = 16.50$$

Now add the 6% sales tax by multiplying the price of the shirt by 1.06 (again, note that $100\% + 6\% = 106\% = 1.06$):

$$16.50\,(1.06) = 17.49$$

This is the final price of the shirt, so (D) is correct. Be certain that you considered everything stated in the question; E is the price without the sales tax added.

8. H

Difficulty: High

Category: Number and Quantity

Getting to the Answer: The question asks for the original price of a pair of pants for which Atiya paid $29.70. You are given the discount rate and the sales tax rate in percents. If Atiya bought her pants at a 40% discount, then she must have paid 60% of what the original price was. Call the original price P:

$$0.60P$$

Additionally, Atiya was taxed 10% on this purchase. Recall that $0.60P + 0.60P(0.10) = 1.10(0.60P)$:

$$1.10\,(0.60P)$$

Finally, you are told that she paid the cashier $29.70. Create an equation and solve for P:

$$1.10\,(0.60P) = 29.70$$
$$0.66P = 29.70$$
$$P = 45$$

The original price of the pants was $45, so (H) is correct.

9.   D

Difficulty: Medium

Category: Number and Quantity

Getting to the Answer: The question asks how much chocolate milk Kamini can make per hour. You are given the rate at which Ryan makes chocolate milk and told that Ryan and Kamini working together can make 30 gallons in 5 hours. Since both rates are given as gallons per hour, the rates can be added. Kamini's rate is not known, so call it k. Plug the given information into to the $d = rt$ equation. Simplify and solve for k.

$$30 = (2 + k)5$$
$$6 = 2 + k$$
$$4 = k$$

This is Kamini's rate, so (D) is correct.

10.   G

Difficulty: Medium

Category: Number and Quantity

Getting to the Answer: The question asks for the weight of a metal bar that is 3 feet 8 inches long. You are given the weight of the same type of bar that is 12 feet long. Before setting up a proportion, convert the 8 inches of the 3 feet 8 inch bar into feet.

$$8 \text{ inches} \left(\frac{1 \text{ foot}}{12 \text{ inches}} \right)$$
$$\frac{8}{12} \text{ foot}$$
$$\frac{2}{3} \text{ foot}$$

Thus, 3 feet + 8 inches = 3 feet + 2/3 feet = $3\frac{2}{3}$ feet = $\frac{11}{3}$ feet. Now set up the proportion and cross-multiply to solve for the weight of the bar.

$$\frac{12 \text{ feet}}{114 \text{ lbs}} = \frac{\frac{11}{3} \text{ feet}}{w \text{ lbs}}$$
$$12 w = 114 \left(\frac{11}{3} \right)$$
$$12 w = 38(11)$$
$$w = \frac{38(11)}{12}$$
$$w = \frac{209}{6}$$

This is the final answer, but unfortunately, none of the answer choices are improper fractions. Convert into a mixed number to match the format of the choices: $\frac{209}{6} = 34\frac{5}{6}$. The answer is (G).

CHAPTER 10

Algebra

LEARNING OBJECTIVES

After completing this chapter, you will be able to:

- Add, subtract, multiply, and factor polynomials
- Isolate a variable
- Calculate the slope or midpoint of a line given two points
- Write the equation of a line in slope-intercept form
- Solve an inequality for a range of values
- Identify the graph of an inequality
- Determine the inequality given a graph
- Identify solutions to quadratic equations
- Solve systems of equations
- Translate word problems into equations and/or inequalities and solve

---

Algebra: 7/36 SmartPoints®

How Much Do You Know?

Directions: Try out the questions below. Show your work so that you can compare your solutions to the ones found on the next page. The "Category" heading in the explanation for each question gives the title of the lesson that covers how to solve it. If you answered the question(s) for a given lesson correctly, and if your scratchwork looks like ours, you may be able to move quickly through that lesson. If you answered incorrectly or used a different approach, you may want to take your time on that lesson.

1. What is the slope of the line given by the equation $-12x - 2y = 14$?

    A. -7
    B. -6
    C. $-\dfrac{1}{6}$
    D. $\dfrac{1}{6}$
    E. 6

2. At a certain toy store, tiny stuffed zebras cost \$3 and giant stuffed zebras cost \$14. The store doesn't sell any other sizes of stuffed zebras. If the store sold 29 stuffed zebras and made \$208 in revenue in one week, how many tiny stuffed zebras were sold?

    F. 8
    G. 11
    H. 14
    J. 18
    K. 21

3. Which of the following expressions is equivalent to $\dfrac{2}{3}a(12a - 6b - 6a + 9b)$?

    A. $6a^2b$
    B. $9ab$
    C. $2a^2 + ab$
    D. $4a^2 + 2ab$
    E. $8a^2 - 4ab - 4a + 6b$

4. What is the midpoint of a line segment with endpoints $(4,-4)$ and $(-2,6)$?

    F. $(-1,5)$
    G. $(0,4)$
    H. $(1,1)$
    J. $\left(\sqrt{5},\sqrt{13}\right)$
    K. $\left(2\sqrt{5},2\sqrt{13}\right)$

5. Brandy has a collection of comic books. If she adds 15 to the number of comic books in her collection and multiplies the sum by 3, the result will be 65 less than 4 times the number of comic books in her collection. How many comic books are in her collection?

    A. 50
    B. 85
    C. 100
    D. 110
    E. 145

6. Which of the following graphs represents the solution set for $5x - 10y > 6$?

F.
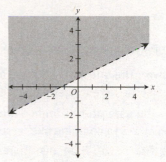

G.
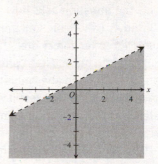

H.
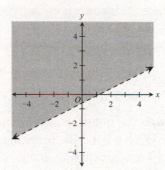

J.
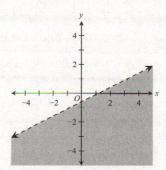

K.
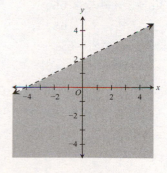

7. What is the solution for x in the system of equations below?

$$\begin{cases} 3x + 4y = 31 \\ 3x - 4y = -1 \end{cases}$$

A. 4
B. 5
C. 6
D. 9
E. 10

8. Which of the following are solutions to the quadratic equation $(x + 1)^2 = \dfrac{1}{25}$?

F. $x = -6, x = 4$

G. $x = -\dfrac{24}{25}$

H. $x = -\dfrac{6}{5}, x = -\dfrac{4}{5}$

J. $x = -\dfrac{4}{5}, x = \dfrac{6}{5}$

K. $x = \dfrac{4}{5}, x = \dfrac{6}{5}$

9. Which of the following inequalities is equivalent to $-2 - 4x \le -6x$?

A. $x \ge -2$
B. $x \ge 1$
C. $x \ge 2$
D. $x \le -1$
E. $x \le 1$

10. Which value(s) of x satisfies the equation $5|2x - 6| + 3 = 13$?

F. -2
G. 2
H. 4
J. -2 and 4
K. 2 and 4

Check Your Work

1. B

Difficulty: Low

Category: Algebra: Linear Graphs

Getting to the Answer: To find the slope of a line given by an equation in standard form, rewrite the equation in slope-intercept form: $y = mx + b$. In this form, the coefficient of x gives you the slope, so manipulate the equation in the question to put it in slope-intercept form:

$$-12x - 2y = 14$$
$$-2y = 12x + 14$$
$$y = \frac{12x}{-2} + \frac{14}{-2}$$
$$y = -6x - 7$$

The slope of the equation is -6, which is (B).

2. J

Difficulty: Medium

Category: Algebra: Systems of Equations

Getting to the Answer: The question asks how many tiny stuffed zebras were sold. Carefully translate from English into math. Because both toys are zebras, z is likely to be a confusing choice for a variable. Instead, use t for tiny and g for giant.

$$t + g = 29$$
$$3t + 14g = 208$$

You now have a system of equations. You want to find t, so use combination to eliminate g. Multiply the first equation by -14 and add the result to the second equation. Then solve for t.

$$-14t - 14g = -406$$
$$+\ \ \underline{3t + 14g =\ \ \ 208}$$
$$-11t = -198$$
$$t =\ \ \ 18$$

Don't waste time finding the value of g. The question asks only for the number of tiny stuffed zebras, so you're done. Choice (J) is correct.

3. D

Difficulty: Low

Category: Algebra: Polynomials

Getting to the Answer: The question asks you to simplify the expression. Resist the urge to distribute the $\frac{2}{3}a$ to each term inside the parentheses immediately; instead, first use PEMDAS to combine like terms inside the parentheses: $\frac{2}{3}a(6a + 3b)$. Then, distribute the $\frac{2}{3}a$: $4a^2 + 2ab$. Choice (D) is correct.

4. H

Difficulty: Low

Category: Algebra: Linear Graphs

Getting to the Answer: The question asks for the midpoint of the two given points. The coordinates of the midpoint of a line segment with endpoints (x_1, y_1) and (x_2, y_2) are $\left(\frac{x_1 + x_2}{2}, \frac{y_1 + y_2}{2}\right)$. Plug the points $(4, -4)$ and $(-2, 6)$ into the midpoint equation: $\left(\frac{4 + -2}{2}, \frac{-4 + 6}{2}\right) = (1, 1)$. Choice (H) is correct.

5. D

Difficulty: Medium

Category: Algebra: Word Problems

Getting to the Answer: The question asks how many comic books are in Brandy's collection. Call the number of comic books in Brandy's collection c. Then, translate methodically from English into math. First, "she adds 15 to the number" means $c + 15$. Then she "multiplies the sum by 3," so you have $3(c + 15)$. "The result will be" indicates an equal sign, and "65 less than 4 times the number" is $4c - 65$. So this scenario can be modeled by the equation $3(c + 15) = 4c - 65$. Now solve for c:

$$3(c + 15) = 4c - 65$$
$$3c + 45 = 4c - 65$$
$$45 = c - 65$$
$$110 = c$$

Brandy has 110 comic books in her collection. Choice (D) is correct.

6. H

Difficulty: Medium

Category: Algebra: Graphing Inequalities

Getting to the Answer: The question asks you to match the given inequality to the correct graph. Start with straightforward math by rewriting the inequality in slope-intercept form. Remember that the inequality symbol flips when you divide by a negative:

$$5x - 10y > 6$$
$$-10y > -5x + 6$$
$$\frac{-10y}{-10} < \frac{-5x}{-10} + \frac{6}{-10}$$
$$y < \frac{1}{2}x - \frac{3}{5}$$

The y-intercept is $-\frac{3}{5}$, so you can eliminate F, J, and K immediately. The "less than" symbol indicates that the shading should be below the dashed line (use the y-axis values to determine what's "less than" as needed), so (H) must be correct.

7. B

Difficulty: Low

Category: Algebra: Systems of Equations

Getting to the Answer: The question asks you to solve for the x-value in the system of equations. Any system of equations with the same number of equations as variables can be solved with either combination or substitution, but one approach will often be easier than the other. Because this system already has $+4y$ and $-4y$, combination is the better choice here:

$$\begin{array}{r} 3x + 4y = 31 \\ +\ 3x - 4y = -1 \\ \hline 6x = 30 \\ x = 5 \end{array}$$

The question asks for the value of x, so (B) is correct. There is no need to find the value of y.

8. H

Difficulty: Medium

Category: Algebra: Quadratics

Getting to the Answer: The question asks you to solve for the solutions of the given quadratic. Both sides of this equation are already perfect squares, so take the square roots of both sides instead of FOILing the left side. Then, solve the resulting equations. Remember that there will be two equations to solve as a result of the square root step, both a positive case and a negative case:

$$(x + 1)^2 = \frac{1}{25}$$
$$\sqrt{(x + 1)^2} = \sqrt{\frac{1}{25}}$$
$$x + 1 = \frac{1}{5}$$
$$x = -\frac{4}{5}$$

Now simplify each equation:

$$x = -1 + \frac{1}{5} = -\frac{5}{5} + \frac{1}{5} = -\frac{4}{5}$$

and

$$x = -1 - \frac{1}{5} = -\frac{5}{5} - \frac{1}{5} = -\frac{6}{5}$$

The solutions are $x = -\frac{6}{5}$ and $-\frac{4}{5}$. Choice (H) is correct.

9.   E

Difficulty: Low

Category: Algebra: Solving Inequalities

Getting to the Answer: The question asks you to solve for the given inequality. You solve an inequality the same way you solve an equation, but with one difference: if you multiply or divide by a negative number, you must reverse the direction of the inequality symbol. To keep things simple, try to move the terms in such a way that you don't end up with negatives:

$$-2 - 4x \leq -6x$$
$$-2 + 2x \leq 0$$
$$2x \leq 2$$
$$x \leq 1$$

The values of x are less than or equal to 1. Choice (E) is correct.

10.   K

Difficulty: Medium

Category: Algebra: Solving Equations

Getting to the Answer: The question asks you to solve for the values of x. Isolate x by first subtracting 3 from both sides and then dividing by 5:

$$5|2x - 6| + 3 = 13$$
$$5|2x - 6| = 10$$
$$|2x - 6| = \frac{10}{5}$$
$$|2x - 6| = 2$$

Recall that if $|x| = a$, then $x = a$ and $x = -a$. Therefore, you must split the absolute value equation into two separate equations and solve for x:

$$2x - 6 = 2$$
$$2x = 8$$
$$x = 4$$
$$\text{and}$$
$$2x - 6 = -2$$
$$2x = 4$$
$$x = 2$$

Therefore, $x = 2$ and $x = 4$. Choice (K) is correct.

Polynomials

LEARNING OBJECTIVE

After this lesson, you will be able to:

- Add, subtract, multiply, and factor polynomials

To answer a question like this:

Which of the following expressions is equivalent to $x(x - 6) - 8(2 - x)$?

A. $3x - 16$

B. $6x - 16$

C. $x^2 - 14x - 16$

D. $x^2 + 2x - 16$

E. $2x^2 - 4x - 16$

You need to know this:

A **polynomial** is an expression composed of variables, exponents, and coefficients. By definition, a polynomial cannot have a variable in a denominator, and all exponents must be integers. Here are some examples of polynomial and non-polynomial expressions:

Polynomials	Non-Polynomials
$23x^2$	$\dfrac{10}{z} + 13$
$\dfrac{x}{5} - 6$	$x^3 y^{-6}$
$y^{11} - 2y^6 + \dfrac{2}{3} xy^3 - 4x^2$	$x^{\frac{1}{2}}$
$z + 6$	$\dfrac{4}{y - 3}$

You need to do this:

To add and subtract polynomials, start by identifying like terms—that is, terms in which both the types of variables and their exponents match. For example, x^2 and $3x^2$ are like terms; adding them would give $4x^2$ and subtracting them would give $x^2 - 3x^2 = -2x^2$. Note that you cannot add or subtract unlike terms. For example, there is no way to simplify $x^2 + y$. You can, however, multiply unlike terms: $x^2 \cdot y = x^2y$.

To multiply two polynomials, multiply each term in the first factor by each term in the second factor, then combine like terms.

To factor a polynomial, find a value or variable that divides evenly into each term. For example: $2x^3 + 2x^2 + 2x = 2x(x^2 + x + 1)$.

Explanation:

The question asks you to simplify the given expression. First, distribute the x and -8: $x^2 - 6x - 16 + 8x$. Then combine like terms: $x^2 + 2x - 16$. Choice (D) is correct.

Try on Your Own

Directions: Take as much time as you need on these questions. Work carefully and methodically. There will be an opportunity for timed practice at the end of the chapter.

1. The expression $3(x + 4) - 7(2x - 5)$ is equivalent to:

    A. $-6x - 5$

    B. $-6x + 19$

    C. $-6x - 23$

    D. $-11x - 23$

    E. $-11x + 47$

2. Which of the following expressions is equivalent to $\frac{1}{4}x(-8x - 12y + 4x + 4y)$?

    F. $-x + 2xy$

    G. $-4x - 8xy$

    H. $-x^2 - 2y$

    J. $-x^2 - 2xy$

    K. $2x^2 + x - 2xy$

3. $\left(x^2 - 3x + 2\right) - \left(3x^2 - 3x - 2\right)$ is equivalent to:

    A. $-2x^2$

    B. $-2x^2 - 6$

    C. $-2x^2 + 4$

    D. $-2x^2 - 6x + 4$

    E. $-2x^2 + 6x - 4$

HINT: For Q4, is there anything you can factor out to make the algebra easier?

---

4. For $x \neq 0$, $\dfrac{8x^6 - 16x^2}{2x^2} = ?$

    F. $4x^3 - 8$

    G. $4x^3 - 16x^2$

    H. $4x^4 - 8$

    J. $4x^4 - 8x$

    K. $4x^4 - 16x^2$

HINT: For Q5, what is the most efficient way to approach this question?

---

5. If $a = 4$, what is the value of $\dfrac{4a^4 + 64b}{16}$?

    A. $\frac{1}{4} + 4b$

    B. $4 + 16b$

    C. $64 + 4b$

    D. $32 + 16b$

    E. $16 + 64ba$

Math

Solving Equations

LEARNING OBJECTIVE

After this lesson, you will be able to:

- Isolate a variable

To answer a question like this:

If $5x = -17(3 - x)$, then $x = ?$

A. $-4\dfrac{1}{4}$

B. $-4\dfrac{1}{12}$

C. $-2\dfrac{7}{22}$

D. $4\dfrac{1}{3}$

E. $4\dfrac{1}{4}$

You need to know this:

Isolating a variable means getting that variable by itself on one side of the equation. To do this, use inverse operations to manipulate the equation, remembering that whatever you do to one side of the equation, you must do to *both* sides.

If needed, review the order of operations information in chapter 7 before continuing on with this lesson.

You need to do this:

It usually makes sense to proceed in this order:

- Eliminate any fractions.
- Collect and combine like terms.
- Divide to leave the desired variable by itself.

Explanation:

The question asks you to solve for the given equation. First, distribute the -17 to each term inside the parentheses: $-51 + 17x$. Then solve for x:

$$5x = -51 + 17x$$
$$-12x = -51$$
$$x = \frac{51}{12}$$

Convert the improper fraction to a mixed fraction: $\frac{51}{12} = 4\frac{3}{12}$, which reduces to $4\frac{1}{4}$. Choice (E) is correct.

Drills

If you find isolating a variable to be challenging, try out these drills before proceeding to the Try on Your Own set. Isolate the variable in each equation. Turn the page and look at the bottom of the page to see the answers.

a. $2(a + 5) = 11 - (3 - 6a)$

b. $4(3 - r) = 2r + 18$

c. $\dfrac{2t}{3} - \dfrac{5t}{2} = \dfrac{5}{6}$

d. Isolate F: $C = \dfrac{5}{9}(F - 32)$

e. Isolate b: $A = \dfrac{1}{2}bh$

Math

Try on Your Own

Directions: Take as much time as you need on these questions. Work carefully and methodically. There will be an opportunity for timed practice at the end of the chapter.

1. What is the value of x that satisfies the equation $15(x + 9) = -21$?

    A. $-\dfrac{52}{5}$

    B. -2

    C. 2

    D. $\dfrac{114}{15}$

    E. $\dfrac{52}{5}$

2. If $9(a - 3) = 15a$, then $a = ?$

    F. $-4\dfrac{1}{2}$

    G. $-1\dfrac{1}{8}$

    H. $-\dfrac{2}{9}$

    J. $\dfrac{8}{9}$

    K. $6\dfrac{3}{4}$

3. The two solutions to $|7x - 1| + 2 = 4$ are equal to which of the following pairs of equations?

    A. $7x + 1 = 4$
       $7x + 1 = -4$

    B. $7x - 1 = 2$
       $-(7x - 1) = 2$

    C. $7x + 1 = 2$
       $-7x + 1 = 4$

    D. $7x - 1 = 6$
       $-(7x - 1) = 6$

    E. $7x - 1 = 2$
       $-(7x - 1) = 6$

Drill answers from previous page:

a. $2(a + 5) = 11 - (3 - 6a)$
$2a + 10 = 11 - 3 + 6a$
$2a + 10 = 8 + 6a$
$2 = 4a$
$\dfrac{1}{2} = a$

b. $4(3 - r) = 2r + 18$
$12 - 4r = 2r + 18$
$-6 = 6r$
$-1 = r$

c. $\left(\dfrac{2}{2}\right)\dfrac{2t}{3} - \left(\dfrac{3}{3}\right)\dfrac{5t}{2} = \dfrac{5}{6}$
$\dfrac{4t}{6} - \dfrac{15t}{6} = \dfrac{5}{6}$
$-\dfrac{11t}{6} = \dfrac{5}{6}$
$6\left(-\dfrac{11t}{6}\right) = 6\left(\dfrac{5}{6}\right)$
$-11t = 5$
$t = -\dfrac{5}{11}$

d. $\dfrac{9}{5} \times C = \dfrac{9}{5} \times \dfrac{5}{9}(F - 32)$
$\dfrac{9}{5}C = F - 32$
$\dfrac{9}{5}C + 32 = F$

e. $A = \dfrac{1}{2}bh$
$2(A) = 2\left(\dfrac{1}{2}bh\right)$
$2A = bh$
$\dfrac{2A}{h} = b$

HINT: For Q4, when absolute value is involved, what must be true?

---

4. Which of the following values of x satisfy the equation $|-x+3| = -2$?

   F. -1

   G. 1

   H. 5

   J. 1 and 5

   K. There are no values of x for which the equation is true.

5. If $8(x-2y) = 16x$, then what is x in terms of y ?

   A. $-8y$

   B. $-2y$

   C. $-\frac{2}{3}y$

   D. $2y$

   E. $4y$

Linear Graphs

> **LEARNING OBJECTIVES**
>
> After this lesson, you will be able to:
>
> - Calculate the slope or midpoint of a line given two points
> - Write the equation of a line in slope-intercept form

To answer a question like this:

Which of the following is an equation of the line that crosses through $(-3,4)$ and $(3,6)$?

A. $x + 3y = -15$

B. $x - 3y = -15$

C. $\frac{1}{3}x - y = 5$

D. $3x + y = 5$

E. $-3x + y = 5$

You need to know this:

The answer choices in this question are written in slope-intercept form: $y = mx + b$. In this form of a linear equation, m represents the slope of the line and b represents the y-intercept. You can think of the slope of a line as how steep it is. The y-intercept is the point at which the line crosses the y-axis and can be written as the ordered pair $(0,y)$.

You can calculate the slope of a line if you know any two points on the line. The formula is $m = \frac{y_2 - y_1}{x_2 - x_1}$, where (x_1,y_1) and (x_2,y_2) are the coordinates of the two points on the line.

A line that moves from the bottom left to the top right has a positive slope. A line that moves from the top left to the bottom right has a negative slope. A horizontal line has a slope of zero, and a vertical line has an undefined slope.

Some ACT questions ask about parallel or perpendicular lines. Parallel lines have the same slope, while perpendicular lines have negative reciprocal slopes.

You need to do this:

- Find the slope of the line.
- Write the equation in slope-intercept form, substituting the value of the slope you found and one of the known points for x and y.
- Solve for the y-intercept.

Explanation:

The question asks you to solve for the given equation. The equation of a line is given by $y = mx + b$, where m is the slope of the line and b is the y-intercept. First, use the two points to find the slope:

$$m = \frac{y_2 - y_1}{x_2 - x_1}$$

$$= \frac{6 - 4}{3 - (-3)}$$

$$= \frac{2}{6} = \frac{1}{3}$$

Then use the slope to find the y-intercept. Plug in $m = \frac{1}{3}$ and either of the given points for x and y:

$$y = mx + b$$

$$4 = \frac{1}{3}(-3) + b$$

$$4 = -1 + b$$

$$5 = b$$

The slope-intercept form of the line is $y = \frac{1}{3}x + 5$. The answer choices are written in standard form, so rewrite the equation:

$$y = \frac{1}{3}x + 5$$

$$3(y) = 3\left(\frac{1}{3}x + 5\right)$$

$$3y = x + 15$$

$$-x + 3y = 15$$

$$x - 3y = -15$$

The line that goes through the given points is $x - 3y = -15$. This matches (B).

Try on Your Own

Directions: Take as much time as you need on these questions. Work carefully and methodically. There will be an opportunity for timed practice at the end of the chapter.

1. If the equation of a line is $4x - 7y = 14$, what is the slope of the line?

   A. -7

   B. $-\dfrac{4}{7}$

   C. $\dfrac{4}{7}$

   D. $\dfrac{7}{4}$

   E. 7

HINT: For Q2, what equation can you create that will help you easily identify the *y*-intercept?

---

2. What is the *y*-intercept of the line that passes through the points $(1,-13)$ and $(-10,31)$?

   F. -9

   G. -4

   H. 0

   J. 4

   K. 9

3. Given point $A(-3,-8)$, if the midpoint of segment AB is $(1,-5)$, what are the coordinates of point B ?

   A. $(5,-2)$

   B. $(4,-2)$

   C. $(-1,-6.5)$

   D. $(-2,-2)$

   E. $(-1,-1.5)$

4. The following graph represents which of the following equations?

   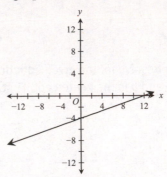

   F. $y = -3x + 4$

   G. $y = -3x - 4$

   H. $y = -\dfrac{1}{3}x + 4$

   J. $y = \dfrac{1}{3}x - 4$

   K. $y = 3x - 4$

HINT: For Q5, how can the format of the answer choices help you decide how to answer this question?

---

5. Which of the following equations best describes the linear relationship shown in the table, where *r* represents the number of pounds of rice sold and *d* represents the price in dollars of one pound of rice?

Price of One Pound	Projected Number of Pounds Sold
$1.20	15,000
$1.40	12,500
$1.60	10,000
$1.80	7,500
$2.00	5,000
$2.20	2,500

   A. $r = 1.2d + 12,500$

   B. $r = 12,500d + 15,000$

   C. $r = -12,500d + 17,500$

   D. $r = 12,500d + 30,000$

   E. $r = -12,500d + 30,000$

Solving Inequalities

LEARNING OBJECTIVE

After this lesson, you will be able to:

- Solve an inequality for a range of values

To answer a question like this:

Which of the following represents all the values of x that satisfy the inequality $2 \leq 3 - \frac{x}{4} \leq 4$?

A. $x \leq -16$

B. $x \geq 4$

C. $x \geq 16$

D. $-4 \leq x \leq 4$

E. $x \leq -4$ or $x \geq 4$

You need to know this:

Linear inequalities are similar to linear equations but have two differences:

- You are solving for a **range of values** rather than a single value.
- If you multiply or divide both sides of the inequality by a negative, you must **reverse the inequality sign**.

You need to do this:

- Eliminate any fractions.
- Collect and combine like terms.
- Divide to leave the desired variable by itself.
  - If you multiply or divide both sides of the inequality by a negative, reverse the inequality sign.
  - If possible, avoid moving the variable terms in such a way that the coefficients become negative.

Explanation:

The question asks you to solve for the given inequality. This is a compound inequality, so whatever you do to one piece, you must do to all three pieces. First add 3, and then multiply all three parts by -4.

$$2 \leq 3 - \frac{x}{4} \leq 4$$

$$-1 \leq -\frac{x}{4} \leq 1$$

$$-4(-1) \geq -4\left(-\frac{x}{4}\right) \geq -4(1)$$

$$4 \geq x \geq -4$$

Don't forget to flip the entire inequality to more easily match it with the correct answer: $-4 \leq x \leq 4$. Choice (D) is correct.

Try on Your Own

Directions: Take as much time as you need on these questions. Work carefully and methodically. There will be an opportunity for timed practice at the end of the chapter.

1. Which of the following is equivalent to the inequality $-8x + 2y \leq 14$?

    A. $y \geq -4x - 7$
    B. $y \geq -4x + 7$
    C. $y \leq -4x + 7$
    D. $y \geq 4x - 7$
    E. $y \leq 4x + 7$

2. Which of the following represents the solution set for $-15 \leq 2x - 13 < 3$?

    F. $-1 \leq x < 8$
    G. $-2 \leq x < 16$
    H. $-5 \leq x < -1$
    J. $-14 \leq x < 8$
    K. $-28 \leq x < 16$

3. If $-3x + 7y \leq 4y + 6$ and x is an integer, which of the following statements must be true?

    A. $x \geq -y - 2$
    B. $x \geq -y + 2$
    C. $x \leq y - 2$
    D. $x \geq y - 2$
    E. $x \leq y + 2$

HINT: For Q4, if $|x| = a$, then what are the possible values for x?

4. Which of the following values of x satisfies the inequality $|2x + 5| < 11$?

    F. $-8 < x < 3$
    G. $-8 > x > 3$
    H. $-3 < x < -8$
    J. $-3 < x < 8$
    K. $-3 > x > 8$

5. Which of the following is the set of x such that $x + 2 > x + 1$?

    A. The empty set
    B. The set containing all real numbers
    C. The set containing all negative real numbers
    D. The set containing all positive real numbers
    E. The set containing only zero

Graphing Inequalities

To answer a question like this:

The solution to which inequality is represented in the graph shown?

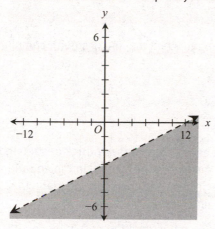

A. $x + 4y < -12$

B. $x + 4y > -12$

C. $x - 4y < 12$

D. $x - 4y > 12$

E. $4x + y < -3$

You need to know this:

Linear inequalities in one variable are graphed on a number line as a point that is or is not filled in ("closed" or "open," respectively), with an arrow representing the location of the solutions as either less than or greater than the point.

- Use a closed circle (●) for inequalities with ≤ or ≥ signs because the point itself is included in the solution set.
- Use an open circle (○) for inequalities with < or > signs because the point itself is not included in the solution set.

While linear equations in two variables graph as simple lines, inequalities in two variables are graphed as shaded regions.

- Use solid lines for inequalities with ≤ or ≥ signs because the line itself is included in the solution set.
- Use dashed lines for inequalities with < or > signs because, in these cases, the line itself is not included in the solution set.
- The shaded region represents all points that make up the solution set for the inequality.

You need to do this:

To graph a linear inequality in one variable, start by isolating the variable.

- For $x \leq a$ and $x \geq a$, use a closed circle (●).
- For $x < a$ and $x < a$, use an open circle (○).
- For $x < a$ and $x \leq a$, draw an arrow pointing to the left of the circle.
- For $x > a$ and $x \geq a$, draw an arrow pointing to the right of the circle.

To graph an inequality in two variables, start by writing the inequality in slope-intercept form, then graph the solid or dashed line.

- For $y > mx + b$ and $y \geq mx + b$, shade the region above the line.
- For $y < mx + b$ and $y \leq mx + b$, shade the region below the line.

If it's hard to tell which region is above/below the line (which can happen when the line is steep), compare the y-values on both sides of the line.

Explanation:

The question asks you to match the correct inequality with the given graph. Don't answer this question too quickly! The shading is below the line, but that does not necessarily mean that the symbol in the equation will be the less than symbol ($<$). Start by writing the equation of the dashed line shown in the graph in slope-intercept form. Then use the shading to determine the correct inequality symbol.

The slope of the line shown in the graph is $\frac{1}{4}$ and the y-intercept is -3, so the equation of the dashed line is $y = \frac{1}{4}x - 3$. The graph is shaded below the boundary line, so use the $<$ symbol. When written in slope-intercept form, the inequality is $y < \frac{1}{4}x - 3$. The inequalities in the answer choices are written in standard form ($Ax + By = C$), so rewrite your answer in this form.

$$y < \frac{1}{4}x - 3$$

$$-\frac{1}{4}x + y < -3$$

Multiply everything by -4 to get integer coefficients, and don't forget to reverse the inequality symbol: $x - 4y > 12$. Choice (D) is correct.

Drills

If graphing inequalities gives you trouble, study the information above and try out these drill questions before completing the Try on Your Own questions below. Drill answers can be found on the bottom of the next page.

Graph the following inequalities.

a. $-1 < x \leq 3$

b. $|x + 1| \leq 3$

c. $y > 2x$

d. $y + 2 \leq x$

e. $x - 1 < y \leq x + 1$

Try on Your Own

Directions: Take as much time as you need on these questions. Work carefully and methodically. There will be an opportunity for timed practice at the end of the chapter.

HINT: For Q1, how do you solve an inequality that includes absolute value?

---

1. Which of the following represents the solution to the inequality $|2x - 5| > 11$?

   A.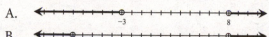

   B.

   C.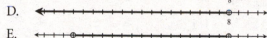

   D.

   E.

2. For the number line shown, which of the following inequalities describes the range of possible values for some number w ?

   F. $|w - 2| \leq 2$

   G. $|w - 2| \leq 4$

   H. $|w + 2| \leq -4$

   J. $|w + 2| \leq 2$

   K. $|w + 2| \leq 4$

3. Which of the following systems of inequalities includes the shaded region in the graph below?

   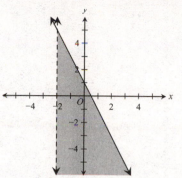

   A. $\begin{cases} x < -2 \\ y \leq -\frac{1}{2}x + 1 \end{cases}$

   B. $\begin{cases} x > -2 \\ y \leq -2x + 1 \end{cases}$

   C. $\begin{cases} x > -2 \\ y \leq -\frac{1}{2}x + 1 \end{cases}$

   D. $\begin{cases} y > -2 \\ y \leq -2x + 1 \end{cases}$

   E. $\begin{cases} y > -2 \\ y \geq -2x + 1 \end{cases}$

Drill answers from previous page:

a.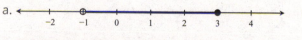

b.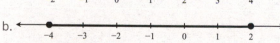

c.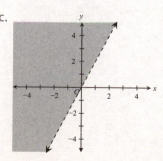

d.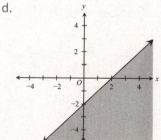

e.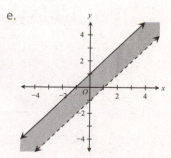

4. Which of the following graphs represents the region $2 < y - x < 3$ in the standard (x,y) coordinate plane?

F.

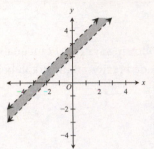

G.

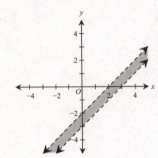

H.

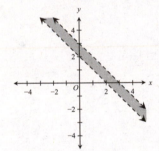

J.

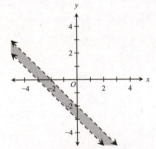

K.

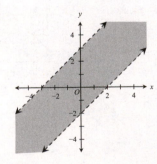

HINT: For Q5, how can thinking about absolute value as a distance help you approach this question more efficiently?

5. If the following number line shows the range of possible values for some number b, which of the following inequalities shows the same possible values for b ?

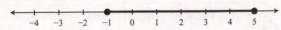

A. $|b - 5| \leq 1$

B. $|b - 5| \leq 2$

C. $|b - 2| \leq 5$

D. $|b - 2| \leq 3$

E. $|b - 1| \leq 5$

Quadratics

To answer a question like this:

If $x^2 + 8x = 48$ and $x > 0$, what is the value of $x - 5$?

A. -9

B. -1

C. 4

D. 7

E. 9

You need to know this:

A **quadratic** expression is a second-degree polynomial—that is, a polynomial containing a squared variable. You can write a quadratic expression as $ax^2 + bx + c$.

The **FOIL** acronym (which stands for First, Outer, Inner, Last) will help you remember how to multiply two binomials to create a quadratic expression: multiply the first terms together (ac), then the outer terms (ad), then the inner terms (bc), and finally the last terms (bd):

$$(a + b)(c + d) = ac + ad + bc + bd$$

FOIL can also be done in reverse if you need to go from a quadratic expression to its factors. To solve a quadratic equation by factoring, the quadratic expression must be set equal to zero. For example:

$$x^2 + x - 56 = 0$$
$$(x + 8)(x - 7) = 0$$

From the binomial factors, you can find the solutions, also called roots or zeros, of the equation. For two factors to be multiplied together and produce zero as the result, one or both of those factors must be zero. In the example above, either $x + 8 = 0$ or $x - 7 = 0$, which means that $x = -8$ or $x = 7$.

The quadratic formula can be used to solve any quadratic equation. It yields solutions to any quadratic equation that is written in standard form, $ax^2 + bx + c = 0$:

$$x = \frac{-b \pm \sqrt{b^2 - 4ac}}{2a}$$

The term under the square root, $b^2 - 4ac$, can help you determine how many real solutions there are. When the term is negative, there are no real solutions for x because negative numbers have no real square roots. When the term is 0, then the value of x will be $\frac{-b}{2a}$, which yields only one solution. Finally, when the term is positive, x will have two solutions because of the $\pm$ symbol.

Memorizing the following classic quadratic equations may save you time on test day:

- $x^2 - y^2 = (x + y)(x - y)$
- $x^2 + 2xy + y^2 = (x + y)^2$
- $x^2 - 2xy + y^2 = (x - y)^2$

You need to do this:

Here are the steps for solving a quadratic equation by factoring:

- Set the quadratic expression equal to zero.
- Factor the squared term. For factoring, it's easiest when a, the coefficient in front of x^2, is equal to 1.
- Make a list of the factors of c. Remember to include negatives.
- Find the factor pair that, when added, equals b, the coefficient in front of x.
- Write the quadratic as the product of two binomials.
- Set each binomial equal to zero and solve.

To solve a quadratic using the quadratic formula, start by getting the quadratic equation into the form $ax^2 + bx + c = 0$. Then substitute a, b, and c into the quadratic formula and simplify.

When you see a pattern that matches the left or the right side of a classic quadratic equation, simplify by substituting its equivalent form. For example, say you need to simplify the following:

$$\frac{a^2 - 2ab + b^2}{a - b}$$

You would substitute $(a - b)(a - b)$ for the numerator and cancel to find that the expression simplifies to $a - b$:

$$\frac{a^2 - 2ab + b^2}{a - b} = \frac{(a - b)(a - b)}{a - b} = \frac{a - b}{1} = a - b$$

Explanation:

The question asks you to first solve for x and then evaluate $x - 5$. When solving a quadratic equation, always start by rewriting the equation to make it equal to 0 (unless both sides of the equation are already perfect squares). Then, take a peek at the choices. If they are all integers, then factoring is probably the quickest method for solving the equation. If the answers include messy fractions or square roots, then the quadratic formula may be a better choice.

To make the original equation equal to 0, subtract 48 from both sides to get $x^2 + 8x - 48 = 0$. The choices are all integers, so try to factor the equation. Look for two numbers whose product is -48 and whose sum is 8: -4 and 12. This means the factors are $(x - 4)$ and $(x + 12)$.

Now, set each factor equal to 0 and solve to obtain $x = 4$ and $x = -12$. The question states that $x > 0$, so x must equal 4. Before selecting an answer, check that you answered the right question! The question asks for the value of $x - 5$, not just x, so the correct answer is $4 - 5 = -1$. (B) is correct.

Try on Your Own

Directions: Take as much time as you need on these questions. Work carefully and methodically. There will be an opportunity for timed practice at the end of the chapter.

1. If $x^2 - 4x - 6 = 6$, what are the possible values for x?

   A. -6 and -2

   B. -6 and 2

   C. 6 and -2

   D. 4 and 12

   E. 6 and 2

2. For all a and b, what is the product of $(b - a)$ and $(a + b)$?

   F. $-a^2 + b^2$

   G. $a^2 - b^2$

   H. $a^2 + b^2$

   J. $a^2 - 2ab + b^2$

   K. $-a^2 - 2ab + b^2$

HINT: For Q3, how are the answer choices formatted?

---

3. Which of the following are the roots of the equation $x^2 + 8x - 3 = 0$?

   A. $-8 \pm \sqrt{19}$

   B. $-4 \pm \sqrt{19}$

   C. $-4 \pm \sqrt{3}$

   D. $4 \pm \sqrt{19}$

   E. $8 \pm \sqrt{19}$

4. Which of the following is the simplified form of $\dfrac{x^2 - 4x + 4}{2x^2 + 4x - 16}$?

   F. $\dfrac{1}{2}$

   G. $\dfrac{x}{x + 4}$

   H. $\dfrac{x - 2}{2(x + 4)}$

   J. $\dfrac{x + 2}{2(x - 8)}$

   K. $\dfrac{x^2 - 4x + 1}{x^2 + 2x - 4}$

HINT: For Q5, what does "how long will it take the projectile to hit the ground" mean in terms of h and t?

---

5. A projectile is launched from a cannon on top of a building. The height of the projectile in feet can be modeled using the quadratic equation $h = -16t^2 + 128t + 320$, where h represents the height and t represents the number of seconds after the projectile was launched. After it is launched, how long will it take the projectile to hit the ground?

   A. 2 seconds

   B. 4 seconds

   C. 8 seconds

   D. 10 seconds

   E. 12 seconds

Systems of Equations

To answer a question like this:

Which of the following pairs is a solution to the following system of equations:

$$\begin{cases} -x + 3y = 9 \\ 2x + 5y = 4 \end{cases}$$

A. $(-15, -2)$

B. $(-15, 2)$

C. $(-3, 2)$

D. $(3, -2)$

E. $(15, 2)$

You need to know this:

A **system** of two linear equations is the set of equations of two lines. "Solving" a system of two linear equations usually means finding the point where the two lines intersect.

- A system of linear equations may have one solution, infinitely many solutions, or no solution.
- If a system of equations represents two lines that intersect, then the system will have exactly one solution (in which the x- and y-values correspond to the point of intersection).
- If a system of equations has infinitely many solutions, the two equations actually represent the same line. For example, $2x + y = 15$ and $4x + 2y = 30$ represent the same line. If you divide the second equation by 2, you arrive at the first equation. Every point along this line is a solution.
- If a system of equations has no solution, the lines are parallel: there is no point of intersection.

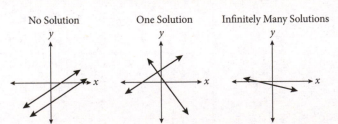

There are two algebraic ways to solve a system of linear equations: substitution and combination, a strategy fundamentally the same as elimination. For some ACT questions, substitution is faster; for others, combination is faster.

Substitution involves substituting the value for one variable into that variable's location in a second equation. Combining two equations means adding or subtracting them, usually with the goal of either eliminating one of the variables or solving for a combination of variables, e.g., $5n + 5m$.

You need to do this:

To solve a system of two linear equations by substitution:

- Isolate a variable (ideally, one whose coefficient is 1) in one of the equations.
- Substitute the result into the other equation.

To solve a system of two linear equations by combination:

- Make sure that the coefficients for one variable have the same absolute value. (If they don't, multiply one equation by an appropriate constant. Sometimes, you'll have to multiply both equations by constants.)
- Either add or subtract the equations to eliminate one variable.
- Solve for the remaining variable, then substitute its value into either equation to solve for the other variable.

Explanation:

The question asks you to solve for the given system of equations. You can solve this system by either substitution or combination. To use combination, multiply the first equation by 2 and then add it to the second equation to cancel out the x terms:

$$\begin{aligned} -2x + 6y &= 18 \\ 2x + 5y &= 4 \\ \hline 11y &= 22 \\ y &= 2 \end{aligned}$$

Then substitute $y = 2$ into one of the original equations to solve for x:

$$\begin{aligned} -x + 3(2) &= 9 \\ -x &= 9 - 6 \\ -x &= 3 \\ x &= -3 \end{aligned}$$

Therefore, $(-3, 2)$ is a solution for the system of equations. Choice (C) is correct.

To use substitution, solve the first equation for x in terms of y and then plug that expression into the second equation:

$$\begin{aligned} -x + 3y &= 9 \\ -x &= 9 - 3y \\ x &= -9 + 3y \end{aligned}$$

$$\begin{aligned} 2(-9 + 3y) + 5y &= 4 \\ -18 + 6y + 5y &= 4 \\ 11y &= 22 \\ y &= 2 \end{aligned}$$

Finally, substitute $y = 2$ into one of the original equations to get $x = -3$.

Try on Your Own

Directions: Take as much time as you need on these questions. Work carefully and methodically. There will be an opportunity for timed practice at the end of the chapter.

1. What is the sum of the solutions for the following system of equations?

$$\begin{cases} 6x = 20 \\ 3y + 7 = 14 \end{cases}$$

A. 1

B. $2\dfrac{5}{6}$

C. 3

D. $5\dfrac{2}{3}$

E. $7\dfrac{7}{9}$

2. If A and B are polynomial expressions such that $A = 24xy + 13$ and $B = 8xy + 1$, how much greater is A than B?

F. $32xy - 14$

G. $16xy - 14$

H. $16xy + 12$

J. $32xy + 12$

K. $32xy + 14$

3. If $2x + 5y = 49$ and $5x + 3y = 94$, then the product of x and $y =$?

A. 17

B. 34

C. 42

D. 48

E. 51

HINT: For Q4, which is likely to be more efficient: substitution or combination? Why?

---

4. You are given the following system of equations:

$$\begin{cases} x + 9y = 11 \\ 2x - 7y = -3 \end{cases}$$

What is the value of $4x - 5y$?

F. -6

G. 1

H. 2

J. 3

K. 13

HINT: For Q5, what part of the quadratic formula provides information about the number of roots for a quadratic equation or function?

---

5. You are given the following system of equations:

$$\begin{cases} y = x \\ -py + qx^2 = r \end{cases}$$

where p, q, and r are integers. For which of the following expressions will there be more than one real solution?

A. $p^2 - 4qr < 0$

B. $p^2 + 4qr < 0$

C. $p^2 + 4qr > 0$

D. $q^2 - 4pr > 0$

E. $q^2 + 4pr > 0$

Word Problems

LEARNING OBJECTIVE

After this lesson, you will be able to:

- Translate word problems into equations and/or inequalities and solve

---

To answer a question like this:

At a school trivia competition, contestants can answer two kinds of questions: easy questions and hard questions. Easy questions are worth 3 points, and hard questions are worth 5 points. Chantrea knows that she correctly answered 21 questions and that she had a total of 79 points. How many hard questions did she answer correctly?

A. 7
B. 8
C. 12
D. 13
E. 15

You need to know this:

The ACT likes to test your understanding of how to describe real-world situations using math equations. For some questions, it will be up to you to extract and solve an equation; for others, you'll have to interpret an equation in a real-life context. The following table shows some of the most common phrases and mathematical equivalents you're likely to see on the ACT.

Word Problems Translation Table	
English	**Math**
equals, is, equivalent to, was, will be, has, costs, adds up to, the same as, as much as	$=$
times, of, multiplied by, product of, twice, double	$\times$
divided by, out of, ratio	$\div$
plus, added to, sum, combined, increased by	$+$
minus, subtracted from, smaller than, less than, fewer, decreased by, difference between	$-$
a number, how much, how many, what	x, n, etc.

You need to do this:

When translating from English to math, start by *defining the variables*, choosing letters that make sense. Then, *break the question down into small pieces*, writing down the translation for one phrase at a time.

Math

Explanation:

The question asks you to solve for how many hard questions Chantrea answered correctly. Both Backsolving and straightforward algebra work well here.

To solve algebraically, set up a system of equations with one equation that represents the number of questions of each type (e for easy and h for hard) and another that represents the number of points that Chantrea earned. Because she correctly answered 21 questions, $e + h = 21$. The number of points that she earned is $3e + 5h = 79$. Substitute $e = 21 - h$ into the second equation and solve for h:

$$3(21 - h) + 5h = 79$$
$$63 - 3h + 5h = 79$$
$$2h = 16$$
$$h = 8$$

To Backsolve, start with C. Remember that the choices represent the number of *hard* questions, not the number of *easy* questions. If Chantrea got 12 hard questions right, then she got $21 - 12 = 9$ easy questions right for a total of $9(3) + 12(5) = 27 + 60 = 87$ points. This is too many points, so she must have gotten fewer hard questions right.

Try (B). If she got 8 hard questions right, then she got $21 - 8 = 13$ easy questions right. This would give her a total of $13(3) + 8(5) = 39 + 40 = 79$ points, so (B) is correct.

Drills

If word problems give you trouble, study the information above and try out these drill questions before completing the Try on Your Own questions below. Drill answers can be found on the bottom of the next page.

Translate the following into math.

a.   If n is greater than m, the positive difference between twice n and m

b.   A quarter of the sum of a and b is 4 less than a.

c.   The product of y and 9 decreased by the sum of x and 7 is the same as dividing x decreased by z by 7 decreased by x.

d.   The ratio of $4q$ to $7p$ is 5 to 2.

e.   If \$500 is taken from F's salary, then the combined salaries of F and G will be double what F's salary would be if it were increased by 50%.

Try on Your Own

Directions: Take as much time as you need on these questions. Work carefully and methodically. There will be an opportunity for timed practice at the end of the chapter.

1. An aquarium contains dolphins, sharks, and whales. There are twice as many dolphins as whales and 8 fewer sharks than dolphins and whales combined. If there are w whales, which of the following represents the number of sharks?

    A. $5w$

    B. $3w - 8$

    C. $10 + w$

    D. $3w^2 - 8w$

    E. $3\sqrt{2w - 8}$

2. If paintbrushes cost $1.50 each and canvases cost 6 times that much, which of the following represents the cost, in dollars, of p paintbrushes and c canvases?

    F. $7.5pc$

    G. $10.5pc$

    H. $7.5(p + c)$

    J. $9c + 1.5p$

    K. $10.5(p + c)$

3. The toll for driving a segment of a certain freeway is $1.50 plus 25 cents for each mile traveled. Joy paid a $25.00 toll for driving a segment of the freeway. How many miles did she travel?

    A. 75

    B. 94

    C. 96

    D. 100

    E. 106

4. At a local theater, adult tickets cost $8 and student tickets cost $5. At a recent show, 500 tickets were sold for a total of $3,475. How many adult tickets were sold?

    F. 125

    G. 200

    H. 325

    J. 400

    K. 450

HINT: For Q5, what do the 20 pints of glaze represent in relation to v?

---

5. A ceramist uses $\left(v^2 + v\right)$ pints of glaze for v porcelain vases. What is the maximum number of vases the ceramist can glaze with 20 pints of glaze?

    A. 2

    B. 4

    C. 5

    D. 10

    E. 20

Drill answers from previous page:

a. $2n - m$

b. $\frac{1}{4}(a + b) = a - 4$

c. $9y - (x + 7) = \frac{(x - z)}{7 - x}$

d. $\frac{4q}{7p} = \frac{5}{2}$

e. $F - 500 + G = 2(F + 0.50F)$

Math

On Test Day

Remember that the ACT doesn't ask you to show your work; if you find the algebra in a question challenging, there is often another way to get to the answer.

Try out this new question, first using algebra and then using the Backsolving strategy you learned in chapter 7. Time yourself both times. Which approach do you find easier? Which one was faster? Did you get the correct answer both times? Remember your preferred approach and try it first if you see a question like this on test day.

1. Which of the following values of x satisfies the equation $|2x - 6| = -4$?

    A. -1

    B. 1

    C. 5

    D. 1 and 5

    E. There are no values of x for which the equation is true.

The correct answer and both ways of solving can be found at the end of this chapter.

How Much Have You Learned?

Directions: For test-like practice, give yourself 10 minutes to complete this question set. Be sure to study the explanations, even for questions you got correct. They can be found at the end of this chapter.

1. How many distinct real roots does the equation $3x^3 + 30x^2 + 75x = 0$ have?

    A. 0
    B. 1
    C. 2
    D. 3
    E. 5

2. Point $P(-3,5)$ and point $Q(0,1)$ are points on the (x,y) coordinate plane. What is the midpoint between points P and Q?

    F. $(-3,1)$
    G. $\left(-\frac{3}{2},1\right)$
    H. $\left(-\frac{3}{2},3\right)$
    J. $(1,3)$
    K. $\left(1,\frac{1}{2}\right)$

3. What is the y-intercept of the line that passes through the points $(1,21)$ and $(4,42)$?

    A. 0
    B. 7
    C. 9
    D. 14
    E. 19

4. What is the solution set for the equation $|2x - 3| = 13$?

    F. $\{-8\}$
    G. $\{-8, 8\}$
    H. $\{-5\}$
    J. $\{-5, 8\}$
    K. $\{5, -8\}$

5. Bye Bye Bugs charges a $275 annual fee for quarterly service plus $20 per additional visit. Pest Be Gone charges a $200 annual fee for quarterly service plus $25 per additional visit. For how many additional visits in a year would the total charges from each exterminator be equal?

    A. 2
    B. 5
    C. 15
    D. 50
    E. 95

6. Which of the following systems of inequalities includes the shaded region in the graph shown?

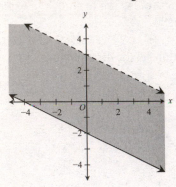

F. $-\frac{1}{2}x - 2 \le y < -\frac{1}{2}x + 3$

G. $-\frac{1}{2}x - 2 < y \le -\frac{1}{2}x + 3$

H. $-\frac{1}{2}x - 2 \ge y > -\frac{1}{2}x + 3$

J. $-2x - 2 \le y < -2x + 3$

K. $-2x - 2 < y \le -2x + 3$

7. Which of the following expressions is equivalent to $\frac{1}{5}p(7q - p + 8q + 11p)$?

A. $5p^2q$

B. $25pq$

C. $3pq + 2p^2$

D. $15pq + 10p$

E. $\frac{7}{5}pq - \frac{1}{5}p + \frac{8}{5}q^2 + \frac{11}{5}p^2$

8. For the system of equations below, which of the following gives the solutions for x ?

$$\begin{cases} y = x^2 \\ 24 + y = 10x \end{cases}$$

F. -12 and 2

G. -6 and -4

H. -2 and 12

J. 3 and 8

K. 4 and 6

9. The 2 solutions to $|4x + 3| - 1 < 8$ are equal to which of the following pairs of inequalities?

A. $4x + 3 < 7$
    $4x + 3 > -7$

B. $4x + 3 < 7$
    $4x + 3 < -9$

C. $4x + 3 < 9$
    $4x + 3 < -9$

D. $4x + 3 < 9$
    $4x + 3 < 7$

E. $4x + 3 < 9$
    $4x + 3 > -9$

10. Rasheed is contemplating whether to buy a membership for a trampoline park, which is \$50 a year. As a member, Rasheed receives a 15% discount on jump tickets. If the non-membership price for a jump ticket is \$12 per hour, for how many hours does Rasheed need to jump in order for the cost of the membership to be less than the total cost of buying jump tickets at the non-membership price?

F. 22

G. 23

H. 25

J. 27

K. 28

Reflect

Directions: Take a few minutes to recall what you've learned and what you've been practicing in this chapter. Consider the following questions, jot down your best answer for each one, and then compare your reflections to the expert responses on the following page. Don't be intimidated by the number of reflection questions here. Answer them at your own pace, then use your level of confidence to determine what to do next.

1. How do you multiply two polynomials?

2. What should you do to isolate a particular variable in an equation?

3. What is the most useful equation for a line in the coordinate plane? Why?

4. When the ACT gives you two points on a line, what can you figure out?

5. How are parallel and perpendicular lines related to each other?

6. What types of key words should you look for when translating English into math?

7. What is the difference between a linear inequality and a linear equation?

_____

_____

_____

8. The rules for manipulating an inequality are very similar to those for manipulating an equation. What is the major difference?

_____

_____

_____

9. Which form of a quadratic equation gives its y-intercept?

_____

_____

_____

10. When is substitution a good choice for solving a system of equations?

_____

_____

_____

11. When is combination a good choice for solving a system of equations?

_____

_____

_____

12. What does it mean if a system of equations has no solution? Infinitely many solutions?

_____

_____

_____

13. How do you solve a system of one linear and one quadratic equation?

_____

_____

_____

Responses

1. How do you multiply two polynomials?

Distribute each term in the first set of parentheses to each term in the second set, then combine like terms.

2. What should you do to isolate a particular variable in an equation?

Perform inverse operations until the variable is by itself on one side of the equal sign. If the equation has fractions, make them disappear by multiplying both sides of the equation by the denominator(s). If like terms appear on different sides of the equation, collect them on the same side so that you can combine them.

3. What is the most useful equation for a line in the coordinate plane? Why?

The best equation is slope-intercept form, $y = mx + b$, *because it tells you the slope (m) and the y-intercept (b). Conversely, if you need to derive an equation yourself, you can plug the slope and y-intercept into slope-intercept form and you're done.*

4. When the ACT gives you two points on a line, what can you figure out?

If you know two points, you can figure out the slope of the line with the equation $m = \dfrac{y_2 - y_1}{x_2 - x_1}$. *From there, you can plug one of the points and the slope into slope-intercept form and find the y-intercept.*

5. How are parallel and perpendicular lines related to each other?

Parallel lines never intersect, and they have equal slopes. Perpendicular lines intersect at a 90° angle, and they have negative reciprocal slopes.

6. What types of key words should you look for when translating English into math?

Look for key words that signal equality ("is," "has," "was"), variable names ("Marina's age," "the cost of one bathtub"), or one of the four arithmetic operations (addition, subtraction, multiplication, and division).

7. What is the difference between a linear inequality and a linear equation?

A linear equation is solved for a single value, whereas a linear inequality is solved for a range of values.

8. The rules for manipulating an inequality are very similar to those for manipulating an equation. What is the major difference?

When solving an inequality, you can do the same thing to both sides, just as you can for an equation. The big difference is that if you divide or multiply both sides of an inequality by a negative number, you have to flip the inequality sign.

9. Which form of a quadratic equation gives its *y*-intercept?

The vertex form is $y = a(x - h)^2 + k$. *The constant k is the y-value at the vertex, which occurs at the maximum or minimum.*

10. When is substitution a good choice for solving a system of equations?

Substitution works best when at least one of the variables has a coefficient of 1, making the variable easy to isolate. This system, for example, is well suited for substitution:

$$a + 3b = 5$$
$$4a - 6b = 21$$

That's because in the first equation, you can easily isolate the a as a = 5 − 3b and plug that result in for a in the other equation. By contrast, substitution would not be a great choice for solving this system:

$$2a + 3b = 5$$
$$4a - 6b = 21$$

If you used substitution now, you'd have to work with fractions, which is messy.

11. When is combination a good choice for solving a system of equations?

Combination is often a good choice. It is at its worst in systems such as this one:

$$2a + 3b = 5$$
$$3a + 5b = 7$$

Neither a-coefficient is a multiple of the other, and neither b-coefficient is a multiple of the other, so to solve this system with combination, you'd have to multiply both equations by a constant (for example, multiplying the first equation by 3 and the second equation by 2 to create a 6a term in both equations). But substitution wouldn't be stellar in this situation, either.

Note that combination may be particularly effective when the ACT asks for a combination of variables. For example, if a question based on the previous system of equations asked for the value of 5a + 8b, then you could find the answer instantly by adding the equations together because 2a + 3a = 5a and 3b + 5b = 8b.

12. What does it mean if a system of equations has no solution? Infinitely many solutions?

A system of equations with no solution represents two parallel lines, which never cross. The coefficient of a variable in one equation will match the coefficient of the same variable in the other equation, but the constants will be different. For example, this system has no solution:

$$2x + 3y = 4$$
$$2x + 3y = 5$$

Subtracting one equation from the other yields the equation 0 = −1, which makes no sense.

If a system of equations has infinitely many solutions, then the two equations represent the same line. For example, this system has infinitely many solutions:

$$2x + 3y = 4$$
$$4x + 6y = 8$$

Dividing the second equation by 2 yields 2x + 3y = 4, so while the two equations look different, they are actually the same.

13. How do you solve a system of one linear and one quadratic equation?

Put the linear equation in the form $y = mx + b$ *and the quadratic equation in the form* $y = ax^2 + bx + c$. *Set the right sides of the equations equal to each other, and solve.*

Next Steps

If you answered most questions correctly in the "How Much Have You Learned" section, and if your responses to the Reflect questions were similar to those of an expert, then consider Algebra an area of strength and move on to the next chapter. Come back to this topic periodically to prevent yourself from getting rusty.

If you don't yet feel confident, review those parts of this chapter that you have not yet mastered. Then, try the questions you missed again. As always, be sure to review the explanations closely. Then go online (**kaptest.com/login**) to watch video lessons about the highest-yield concepts in this chapter and to use your Qbank for more practice. If you haven't already registered your book, do so at *kaptest.com/moreonline*.

GO ONLINE

kaptest.com/login

Math

Answers and Explanations

Polynomials

1. E

Difficulty: Low

Category: Algebra

Getting to the Answer: The question asks you to simplify the given expression. First, distribute the 3 and -7: $3x + 12 - 14x + 35$. Then combine the like terms: $-11x + 47$. Choice (E) is correct.

2. J

Difficulty: Low

Category: Algebra

Getting to the Answer: The question asks you to simplify the given expression. Before distributing $\frac{1}{4}x$ to each term inside the parentheses, combine like terms inside the parentheses: $\frac{1}{4}x(-4x - 8y)$. Then distribute the $\frac{1}{4}x$: $-x^2 - 2xy$. Choice (J) is correct.

3. C

Difficulty: Low

Category: Algebra

Getting to the Answer: The question asks you to simplify the given expression. First, distribute the -1 to each of the terms in the second set of parentheses: $-3x^2 + 3x + 2$. Now combine like terms: $x^2 - 3x + 2 - 3x^2 + 3x + 2 = -2x^2 + 4$. Choice (C) is correct.

4. H

Difficulty: Medium

Category: Algebra

Getting to the Answer: The question asks you to simplify the given expression. Notice that you can factor out a $2x^2$ from each term in the numerator:

$$\frac{2x^2\left(4x^4 - 8\right)}{2x^2}$$

Then cancel the $2x^2$, since it appears in both the numerator and denominator:

$$\frac{2x^2\left(4x^4 - 8\right)}{2x^2}$$

$$4x^4 - 8$$

$4x^4 - 8$ is equivalent to the given expression; (H) is correct.

5. C

Difficulty: Medium

Category: Algebra

Getting to the Answer: The question asks you to simplify the given expression with the known value of a. Simplifying before plugging in $a = 4$ will save you valuable time on test day. Notice that you can factor out 4 from each term in the numerator:

$$\frac{4\left(a^4 + 16b\right)}{16}$$

Then cancel the 4, since it appears in both the numerator and the denominator:

$$\frac{a^4 + 16b}{4}$$

Now plug in $a = 4$ and simplify:

$$\frac{4^4 + 16b}{4} = \frac{256 + 16b}{4}$$

$$= \frac{256}{4} + \frac{16b}{4}$$

$$= 64 + 4b$$

The given expression simplifies to $64 + 4b$. Choice (C) is correct.

Solving Equations

1.   A

Difficulty: Low

Category: Algebra

Getting to the Answer: The question asks you to solve for the given equation. Distribute the 15 to each term in the parentheses: $15x + 135$. Then solve for x:

$$15x + 135 = -21$$
$$15x = -156$$
$$x = -\frac{156}{15}$$

Reduce $-\frac{156}{15}$ to $-\frac{52}{5}$. Choice (A) is correct.

2.   F

Difficulty: Low

Category: Algebra

Getting to the Answer: The question asks you to solve for the given equation. First, distribute the 9 to the two terms inside the parentheses: $9a - 27$. Then solve for a:

$$9a - 27 = 15a$$
$$-27 = 6a$$
$$-\frac{27}{6} = a$$

Since $-\frac{27}{6}$ is not an answer, reduce it to $-\frac{9}{2}$. Then, write it as a mixed number: $-\frac{9}{2} = -4\frac{1}{2}$. This matches (F).

3.   B

Difficulty: Medium

Category: Algebra

Getting to the Answer: The question asks you to solve for the given equation. Recall that if $|x| = a$, $x = a$ and $-x = a$. In this question, $|7x - 1| + 2 = 4$ simplifies to $|7x - 1| = 2$. Therefore, $7x - 1 = 2$ and $-(7x - 1) = 2$. This matches (B).

4.   K

Difficulty: Medium

Category: Algebra

Getting to the Answer: The question asks you to solve for the given equation, so there is no math necessary here! If you remember that absolute value represents distance on a number line and therefore cannot be negative, you'll immediately see that there are no values of x for which the equation is true because the right-hand side is -2. Choice (K) is correct.

5.   B

Difficulty: Low

Category: Algebra

Getting to the Answer: The question asks you to solve for x. First, distribute the 8 to each of the terms in the parentheses: $8x - 16y$. Then isolate x:

$$8x - 16y = 16x$$
$$-16y = 8x$$
$$-2y = x$$

x in terms of y is $x = -2y$. The correct answer is (B).

Linear Graphs

1.   C

Difficulty: Low

Category: Algebra

Getting to the Answer: The question asks for the slope of the given line equation. The equation of a line is $y = mx + b$, where m is the slope and b is the y-intercept. Rewrite the given equation to get y in terms of x.

$$4x - 7y = 14$$
$$-7y = -4x + 14$$
$$y = \frac{4}{7}x - 2$$

The slope of the line given by this equation is the coefficient of x, which is $\frac{4}{7}$. Choice (C) is correct.

2. F

Difficulty: Medium

Category: Algebra

Getting to the Answer: The question asks for the y-intercept of the line that passes through the given points. Here is another type of question in which you need to use the slope-intercept form of a line, $y = mx + b$. First, use the two given points and the slope formula to find the slope of the line:

$$m = \frac{y_2 - y_1}{x_2 - x_1} = \frac{31 - (-13)}{-10 - 1} = \frac{44}{-11} = -4$$

Now, plug this slope and the values of either point into $y = mx + b$ to find b (the y-intercept). Using $(1, -13)$, the result is $-13 = -4(1) + b$. Simplify the equation to get $b = -9$, which is (F).

Notice that G is a distractor; it's the slope of the line, not the y-intercept. Double-check that you're answering the right question before you make your selection.

3. A

Difficulty: Low

Category: Algebra

Getting to the Answer: The question asks for the endpoint of the line with the given endpoint and midpoint. The coordinates of the midpoint of a line segment with endpoints (x_1, y_1) and (x_2, y_2) are $\left(\frac{x_1 + x_2}{2}, \frac{y_1 + y_2}{2} \right)$. Setting $x_1 = -3$ and $y_1 = -8$, solve for x_2 and y_2.

First, $1 = \frac{-3 + x_2}{2}$, or $2 = -3 + x_2$. Add 3 to both sides to get $x_2 = 5$. You can already select (A) based on this because none of the other x-coordinates are correct.

If you have extra time to confirm your choice or have more than one choice remaining, find y_2 using the same process: $-5 = \frac{-8 + y_2}{2}$, or $-10 = -8 + y_2$. Add 8 to both sides to get $y_2 = -2$. Choice (A) is correct.

4. J

Difficulty: Low

Category: Algebra

Getting to the Answer: The question asks you to match one of the given line equations with the given graph. Use the graph to determine the y-intercept and the slope of the line. Then write an equation in slope-intercept form: $y = mx + b$. Once you have your equation, look for the answer choice that matches. The line crosses the y-axis at $(0, -4)$, so the y-intercept (b) is -4. The line rises 1 unit for every 3 units that it runs to the right, so the slope (m) is $\frac{1}{3}$. The equation of the line is thus $y = \frac{1}{3}x - 4$, which matches (J).

5. E

Difficulty: High

Category: Algebra

Getting to the Answer: The question asks you to solve for the line equation that models the given table; start by looking at the answer choices. The equations are given in slope-intercept form, so start by finding the slope. Substitute two pairs of values from the table (pick small numbers if possible) into the slope formula, $m = \frac{y_2 - y_1}{x_2 - x_1}$.

Keep in mind that the projected number of pounds sold depends on the price, so the price is the independent variable (x) and the projected number of pounds is the dependent variable (y). Using the points $(1.2, 15,000)$ and $(2, 5,000)$, the slope is calculated as follows:

$$m = \frac{5,000 - 15,000}{2 - 1.20}$$
$$= \frac{-10,000}{0.8}$$
$$= -12,500$$

Eliminate A, B, and D because the slope is not correct. To choose between C and (E), you could find the y-intercept of the line, but this is a fairly time-consuming process. Instead, choose the simplest pair of values from the table, $(2, 5,000)$, and substitute them into both C and (E). Choice (E) is correct because the equation $5,000 = -12,500(2) + 30,000$ is true.

Solving Inequalities

1.   E

Difficulty: Low

Category: Algebra

Getting to the Answer: The question asks you to solve for the given inequality. Since all of the choices are y in terms of x, solve for y:

$$-8x + 2y \le 14$$
$$2y \le 14 + 8x$$
$$y \le 7 + 4x$$

The inequality simplifies to $y \le 4x + 7$. Choice (E) is correct.

2.   F

Difficulty: Medium

Category: Algebra

Getting to the Answer: The question asks you to solve for the solution set of the given inequality. Straightforward algebra is the best approach here. Don't forget—whatever you do to one piece, you must do to all three pieces:

$$-15 \le 2x - 13 < 3$$
$$-2 \le 2x < 16$$
$$\frac{-2}{2} \le \frac{2x}{2} < \frac{16}{2}$$
$$-1 \le x < 8$$

The solution set is numbers greater than or equal to -1 but less than 8. Choice (F) is correct.

3.   D

Difficulty: Medium

Category: Algebra

Getting to the Answer: The question asks you to solve for the given inequality. Since all of the choices are x in terms of y, solve for x. Remember that you need to flip the inequality when multiplying or dividing by a negative number:

$$-3x + 7y \le 4y + 6$$
$$-3x \le -3y + 6$$
$$x \ge y - 2$$

The inequality solved for x in terms of y is $x \ge y - 2$. Choice (D) is correct.

4.   F

Difficulty: High

Category: Algebra

Getting to the Answer: The question asks you to solve for the given inequality. If $|x| = a$, then $x = a$ and $x = -a$. Accordingly, if $|x| < a$, $x < a$ and $x > -a$ because the direction of the inequality flips when multiplying or dividing by a negative. Therefore, $|2x + 5| < 11$ can be written as $2x + 5 < 11$ and $2x + 5 > -11$. Solve each inequality for x:

$$2x + 5 < 11$$
$$2x < 6$$
$$x < 3$$

$$2x + 5 > -11$$
$$2x > -16$$
$$x > -8$$

Thus, $-8 < x < 3$. Choice (F) is correct.

5.   B

Difficulty: Medium

Category: Algebra

Getting to the Answer: The question asks you to solve for the given inequality. To find x such that $x + 2 > x + 1$, subtract x from both sides to obtain $2 > 1$. This inequality is true for any value of x, so the set of x is the set of all real numbers. Choice (B) is correct.

Graphing Inequalities

1.   A

Difficulty: High

Category: Algebra

Getting to the Answer: The question asks you to solve for the given inequality. Whenever you encounter an absolute value inequality, you must rewrite it without the absolute value signs. The symbol here is $>$, so this will become two inequalities separated by an "or." Split $|2x - 5| > 11$ into $2x - 5 > 11$ or $2x - 5 < -11$ and solve each inequality separately.

$$2x - 5 > 11$$
$$2x > 16$$
$$x > 8$$
$$\text{or}$$
$$2x - 5 < -11$$
$$2x < -6$$
$$x < -3$$

Find the number line that matches. Choice (A) is correct.

2.   K

Difficulty: Medium

Category: Algebra

Getting to the Answer: The question asks you to choose the correct inequality that matches the given number line. The shaded region in the number line shows a range from -6 to 2. The center is $\frac{-6 + 2}{2} = -2$, with -6 and 2 each 4 units away from the center. Recall that $|x - b| \leq a$ represents all numbers up to and including a units away from the center b. Thus, the absolute value inequality is $|w - (-2)| \leq 4$ or $|w + 2| \leq 4$. This matches choice (K).

You can check your choice by solving for w algebraically:

$$w + 2 \leq 4$$
$$w \leq 2$$

$$w + 2 \geq -4$$
$$w \geq -6$$

The range of w is $-6 \leq w \leq 2$, which exactly matches the number line.

3.   B

Difficulty: Medium

Category: Algebra

Getting to the Answer: The question asks you to match the correct system of inequalities with the given graph. First, determine the equations of the lines in the graph. Then, determine the signs of the inequalities. The vertical line is dashed and passes through $x = -2$. The area to the right of the line is shaded, so the inequality is $x > -2$. Eliminate A, D, and E. The other line is solid and has a slope of -2 (it moves down 2 units for every increase of 1 unit to the right) and a y-intercept of 1. The area below the line is shaded, so the inequality is $y \leq -2x + 1$. Choice (B) is correct.

4.   F

Difficulty: Medium

Category: Algebra

Getting to the Answer: The question asks you to match the correct graph with the given inequality. Start by rewriting the compound inequality as two separate inequalities. Then write the inequalities in slope-intercept form, $y = mx + b$, where m is the slope and b is the y-intercept. Solving each one for y yields:

$$2 < y - x$$
$$y > x + 2$$

$$y - x < 3$$
$$y < x + 3$$

The two lines are parallel lines with a positive slope of 1. Thus, the lines must be increasing (going up) from left to right. Eliminate H and J. To decide between the remaining choices, consider the y-intercepts of the lines. One line has a y-intercept of 2, and the other has a y-intercept of 3. This matches (F).

5.   D

Difficulty: High

Category: Algebra

Getting to the Answer: The question asks you to solve for the possible values of b. One approach to this question is to solve each of the answer choices algebraically to get a range of values for b and then see which one gives you the same range as that shown in the figure. However, a faster method is to think of absolute value as a distance. The center of the shaded region is $\frac{-1+5}{2} = 2$, with -1 and 5 each 3 units away from the center. Therefore, the distance between b and 2 must be less than or equal to 3, so $|b - 2| \leq 3$. Choice (D) is correct.

You can confirm your choice by rewriting the absolute value inequality as a compound inequality and solving for b:

$$|b - 2| \leq 3$$
$$-3 \leq b - 2 \leq 3$$
$$-1 \leq b \leq 5$$

This inequality matches the number line exactly.

Quadratics

1.   C

Difficulty: Low

Category: Algebra

Getting to the Answer: The question asks you to solve for the given quadratic equation. All of the choices are integers, so factoring is likely the quickest route to the answer. Start by setting the equation equal to 0.

$$x^2 - 4x - 6 = 6$$
$$x^2 - 4x - 12 = 0$$

Now find two numbers whose product is -12 and whose sum is -4. That's -6 and 2: $(x - 6)(x + 2) = 0$. Solving for x yields:

$$(x - 6) = 0 \rightarrow x = 6$$
$$(x + 2) = 0 \rightarrow x = -2$$

The possible values of x are -2 and 6. Choice (C) is correct.

2.   F

Difficulty: Low

Category: Algebra

Getting to the Answer: The question asks you to multiply two expressions and simplify. Although there are variables in the question stem and the choices, using the Picking Numbers strategy will be laborious. The more straightforward route is to use FOIL:

$$(b - a)(a + b) = ba + b^2 - a^2 - ab$$
$$= b^2 - a^2$$

Note that the ab terms cancel out. Rearranging $b^2 - a^2$ gives you $-a^2 + b^2$, which is (F).

3.   B

Difficulty: High

Category: Algebra

Getting to the Answer: The question asks you to solve for the given quadratic equation. The choices contain radicals, so use the quadratic formula. First, jot down the values for a, b, and c. You should also write down the formula itself so you're not trying to remember it and plug in values at the same time.

$$x = \frac{-b \pm \sqrt{b^2 - 4ac}}{2a}$$
$$a = 1, b = 8, c = -3$$

Carefully substitute the values into the formula and simplify.

$$x = \frac{-(8) \pm \sqrt{(8)^2 - 4(1)(-3)}}{2(1)}$$
$$= \frac{-8 \pm \sqrt{64 + 12}}{2}$$
$$= \frac{-8 \pm \sqrt{76}}{2}$$

This is not one of the choices, which tells you that you need to simplify the radical. To simplify the radical, look for a perfect square that divides evenly into 76.

$$x = \frac{-8 \pm \sqrt{4}\sqrt{19}}{2}$$
$$= \frac{-8 \pm 2\sqrt{19}}{2}$$
$$= -4 \pm \sqrt{19}$$

The roots of the given quadratic are $-4 \pm \sqrt{19}$, so (B) is correct.

4. H

Difficulty: Medium

Category: Algebra

Getting to the Answer: The question asks you to simplify the given expression. Factor the numerator and denominator. For the denominator, first factor out a 2 to get 1 for the x^2 coefficient. Then factor the quadratic as usual. If the numerator and denominator have any factors in common, cancel those factors.

$$\frac{x^2 - 4x + 4}{2x^2 + 4x - 16} = \frac{(x-2)(x-2)}{2(x^2 + 2x - 8)}$$

$$= \frac{(x-2)(x-2)}{2(x+4)(x-2)}$$

$$= \frac{x-2}{2(x+4)}$$

This is the most simplified form of the given expression; (H) is correct.

5. D

Difficulty: High

Category: Algebra

Getting to the Answer: The question asks how long it will take for the projectile to hit the ground after launch. To find the amount of time it takes for the projectile to hit the ground, find the value of t for which $h = 0$. The fact that 16 divides evenly into 32 (and therefore into 320) is a big hint that you'll be able to factor.

$$0 = -16t^2 + 128t + 320$$

$$0 = -16(t^2 - 8t - 20)$$

$$0 = t^2 - 8t - 20$$

$$0 = (t - 10)(t + 2)$$

Setting each factor equal to 0 gives $t = 10$ or $t = -2$. However, because time cannot be negative, the answer is $t = 10$ seconds. Choice (D) is correct.

Systems of Equations

1. D

Difficulty: Low

Category: Algebra

Getting to the Answer: The question asks you to solve for the sum of the given system of equations. Solve for x and y individually, and then add them together to find the final answer.

$$6x = 20$$

$$x = \frac{20}{6}$$

$$x = \frac{10}{3}$$

$$3y + 7 = 14$$

$$3y = 7$$

$$y = \frac{7}{3}$$

The sum is $x + y = \frac{10}{3} + \frac{7}{3} = \frac{17}{3}$. Writing $\frac{17}{3}$ as a mixed number yields $5\frac{2}{3}$, which matches (D).

2. H

Difficulty: Low

Category: Algebra

Getting to the Answer: The question asks how much greater A is than B. Determining how much greater A is than B means finding the difference between the two, $A - B$:

$$(24xy + 13) - (8xy + 1)$$

$$24xy + 13 - 8xy - 1$$

$$16xy + 12$$

A is $16xy + 12$ greater than B. Choice (H) is correct.

3.   E

Difficulty: Medium

Category: Algebra

Getting to the Answer: The question asks you to solve for the product of x and y. First, solve for x and y individually. Then multiply them together to find their product.

To solve using combination, you will need to multiply each equation by a constant. Suppose you want to eliminate x. The coefficients of the x terms are 2 and 5, so you need to multiply the equations by numbers that will give you -10 and 10 as your new x term coefficients. To do this, multiply the first equation by -5 and the second equation by 2:

$$-5(2x + 5y = 49)$$
$$2(5x + 3y = 94)$$

Now add the resulting equations:

$$\begin{array}{r} -10x - 25y = -245 \\ +\ \ 10x + 6y = \ \ \ 188 \\ \hline -19y = -57 \\ y = 3 \end{array}$$

Next, plug $y = 3$ back into either equation and solve for x. This yields $x = 17$. Finally, multiply x and y together to obtain 51, which is (E).

4.   J

Difficulty: High

Category: Algebra

Getting to the Answer: The question asks you to solve for the value of $4x - 5y$. To determine the value of $4x - 5y$, first find the solution to the system of equations. You can solve by either substitution or combination/elimination. However, since it is easy to isolate x in the first equation, substitution is preferred. Solve the first equation for x and then substitute it into the second equation to solve for y:

$$x = 11 - 9y$$

$$2(11 - 9y) - 7y = -3$$
$$22 - 18y - 7y = -3$$
$$-25y = -25$$
$$y = 1$$

Then plug $y = 1$ into $x = 11 - 9y$ to find x:
$x = 11 - 9(1) = 2$. Thus, $4x - 5y = 4(2) - 5(1) = 8 - 5 = 3$. Choice (J) is correct.

5.   C

Difficulty: High

Category: Algebra

Getting to the Answer: The question asks you to choose the inequality that will have more than one real solution. Substitute $y = x$ into the second equation and set the equation equal to 0:

$$-py + qx^2 = r$$
$$-px + qx^2 - r = 0$$
$$qx^2 - px - r = 0$$

Recall that the quadratic formula for a quadratic equation in the form $ax^2 + bx + c = 0$ is $x = \dfrac{-b \pm \sqrt{b^2 - 4ac}}{2a}$. The term under the square root, $b^2 - 4ac$, determines how many real solutions there are. When the term is negative, there are no real solutions for x because negative numbers have no real square roots. When the term is 0, then the value of x will be $\dfrac{-b}{2a}$, which yields only one solution. Finally, when the term is positive, x will have two solutions because of the $\pm$ symbol.

Thus, there will be more than one solution if the term under the square root is greater than 0. Here $a = q$, $b = -p$ and $c = -r$. Substitute accordingly and solve:

$$b^2 - 4ac > 0$$
$$(-p)^2 - 4q(-r) > 0$$
$$p^2 + 4qr > 0$$

$p^2 + 4qr$ will produce more than one real solution. Choice (C) is correct.

Word Problems

1. B

Difficulty: Medium

Category: Algebra

Getting to the Answer: The question asks for the correct expression of the number of sharks in terms of whales and dolphins. If w represents the number of whales, then the phrase "twice as many dolphins as whales" means that there are $2w$ dolphins. Therefore, "dolphins and whales combined" is $2w + w$, or $3w$. Because there are 8 fewer sharks than dolphins and whales combined, you need to subtract 8 from $3w$, which makes (B) correct.

You can also answer this question by using the Picking Numbers strategy. Pick a small, positive number, like 5, for the number of whales. If there are 5 whales and "twice as many dolphins as whales," then there must be 10 dolphins. Combine the number of whales and dolphins and subtract 8 from that sum to find the number of sharks: $(5 + 10) - 8 = 15 - 8 = 7$. Plug in $w = 5$ to determine which answer choice gives you a value of 7:

Choice A: $5(5) = 25$ Eliminate.

Choice (B): $3(5) - 8 = 15 - 8 = 7$ Keep.

Choice C: $10 + 5 = 15$ Eliminate.

Choice D: $3(5)^2 - 8(5) = 75 - 40 = 35$ Eliminate.

Choice E: $3\sqrt{2(5) - 8} = 3\sqrt{2} \neq 7$ Eliminate.

Choice (B) is the only answer that works.

2. J

Difficulty: Low

Category: Algebra

Getting to the Answer: The question asks for the expression that represents the cost, in dollars, of p paintbrushes and c canvases. The total cost of the two kinds of items is the cost of the paintbrushes multiplied by the number of paintbrushes purchased plus the cost of the canvases multiplied by the number of canvases purchased. Because a canvas costs "6 times" the cost of a paintbrush, a canvas costs $6(\$1.50) = \$9$.

Total cost of paintbrushes: $1.50 \times p = 1.5p$
Total cost of canvases: $9 \times c = 9c$
Sum of both: $9c + 1.5p$

$9c + 1.5p$ represents the expression for costs in dollars. Therefore, (J) is correct.

3. B

Difficulty: Medium

Category: Algebra

Getting to the Answer: The question asks you to determine how many miles Joy traveled. Backsolving works well on many word problems with integers in the choices. Start with the middle choice, C. If Joy drove 96 miles, she would have paid $\$1.50 + \$0.25(96) = \$25.50$. This is too much, so try (B). If she drove 94 miles, she would have paid $\$1.50 + \$0.25(94) = \$25.00$. Choice (B) is correct.

You could also set up an equation and solve algebraically. If m is the number of miles traveled, then the toll is $\$1.50 + \$0.25m$. Joy paid a total of $\$25.00$, so solve this equation:

$$\$1.50 + \$0.25m = \$25.00$$
$$\$0.25m = \$23.50$$
$$m = 94$$

This confirms that (B) is correct.

4. H

Difficulty: Medium

Category: Algebra

Getting to the Answer: The question asks how many adult tickets were sold. Algebra and Backsolving both work well on word problems like this one. Use the method with which you are more comfortable.

To solve this problem algebraically, first translate it into a system of equations. At $8 per adult ticket and $5 per student ticket, the total amount of money collected can be written as $8a + 5s = 3,475$. Because there were 500 tickets total, $a + s = 500$. Plug $s = 500 - a$ into the first equation and solve for a:

$$8a + 5(500 - a) = 3,475$$
$$8a + 2,500 - 5a = 3,475$$
$$3a = 975$$
$$a = 325$$

Choice (H) is correct.

To Backsolve, start with (H). If there are 325 adult tickets, then there are $500 - 325 = 175$ student tickets. The total amount of money collected would be $325(8) + \$175(5)$, or $\$2,600 + \$875 = \$3,475$. Because this is the total given in the question stem, (H) is correct.

5. B

Difficulty: High

Category: Algebra

Getting to the Answer: The question asks for the maximum number of vases the ceramist can glaze with 20 pints of glaze. Because you want to know the value of v when the given expression is at most 20, set up an inequality and solve for v:

$$v^2 + v \leq 20$$
$$v^2 + v - 20 \leq 0$$
$$(v + 5)(v - 4) \leq 0$$
$$v \leq -5 \text{ and } 4$$

Thus, the maximum number of vases the ceramist can glaze is 4. (B) is correct.

On Test Day

1. E

Difficulty: Medium

Category: Algebra

Getting to the Answer: A strategic "guess" is actually the best approach for this question; the question asks you to solve for the given equation, so there is no math actually necessary here. If you remember that absolute value represents distance on a number line and therefore cannot be negative, you'll immediately see that there are no values of x for which the equation is true because the right-hand side is -4. Choice (E) is correct.

However, you might not spot this shortcut, or the question might not provide such an easy way to eliminate 4 out of 5 choices. In that case, you'll want to consider algebra or Backsolving as alternative approaches.

To solve this equation algebraically, follow the order of operations, making sure you create two equations when you account for the absolute value symbols:

$$|2x - 6| = -4$$
$$2x - 6 = +(-4) \quad \text{or} \quad 2x - 6 = -(-4)$$
$$2x = 6 + (-4) \qquad\qquad 2x = 6 + 4$$
$$2x = 2 \qquad\qquad\qquad 2x = 10$$
$$x = 1 \qquad\qquad\qquad x = 5$$

Be careful! Plug these values back into the equation to ensure success. At this point, you'll notice that neither value works:

$$|2x - 6| = -4$$
$$|2(1) - 6| = -4 \quad \text{or} \quad |2(5) - 6| = -4$$
$$|3 - 6| = -4 \qquad\qquad |10 - 6| = -4$$
$$|-3| = -4 \qquad\qquad |4| = -4$$
$$3 \neq -4 \qquad\qquad 4 \neq -4$$

If you choose to solve this question by Backsolving, consider the answer choices carefully. If you start with B and prove that $x \neq 1$, then you can eliminate both B and D:

$$|2(1) - 6| = -4$$
$$|3 - 6| = -4$$
$$|-3| = -4$$
$$3 = -4$$

Then, plug in both A and C:

$$A: |2(-1) - 6| = -4 \quad C: |2(5) - 6| = -4$$
$$|-2 - 6| = -4 \qquad |10 - 6| = -4$$
$$|-8| = -4 \qquad\qquad |4| = -4$$
$$8 \neq -4 \qquad\qquad 4 \neq -4$$

Since neither value is a solution, (E) must be correct.

How Much Have You Learned?

1. C

Difficulty: High

Category: Algebra

Getting to the Answer: The question asks how many distinct roots the given equation has. The equation is a polynomial in one variable, so the greatest number of roots (solutions) it can have is equal to the highest power of the variable, which is 3. This means that you can eliminate E right away. That doesn't mean the answer is 3, however, because you are counting the number of *distinct* real solutions. To solve the equation, start by factoring out the GCF, which is $3x$. Then factor:

$$3x^3 + 30x^2 + 75x = 0$$
$$3x(x^2 + 10x + 25) = 0$$
$$3x(x + 5)(x + 5) = 0$$

Setting each factor equal to 0 and solving for x yields $x = 0$, $x = -5$, and $x = -5$. There are only two distinct real solutions, 0 and -5, so (C) is correct.

2. H

Difficulty: Low

Category: Algebra

Getting to the Answer: The question asks for the coordinate of the midpoint between the two points given. The coordinates of the midpoint of a line segment with endpoints (x_1, y_1) and (x_2, y_2) are $\left(\dfrac{x_1 + x_2}{2}, \dfrac{y_1 + y_2}{2}\right)$. Plug the points $(-3,5)$ and $(0,1)$ into the formula: $\left(\dfrac{-3 + 0}{2}, \dfrac{5 + 1}{2}\right) = \left(-\dfrac{3}{2}, 3\right)$. Choice (H) is correct.

3. D

Difficulty: Low

Category: Algebra

Getting to the Answer: The question asks for the y-intercept of the line that passes through the given points. You are looking for the y-intercept, so use the slope-intercept form, $y = mx + b$. Unfortunately, you must find m before you can find b.

$$m = \frac{y_2 - y_1}{x_2 - x_1} = \frac{42 - 21}{4 - 1} = \frac{21}{3} = 7$$

Plug in $m = 7$ and the (x,y) values of either point to find b. It's typically easier to work with smaller numbers, so use $(1,21)$.

$$y = mx + b$$
$$21 = 7(1) + b$$
$$21 = 7 + b$$
$$14 = b$$

You don't need to write out the full equation of the line, since you are interested in b only. Choice (D) is correct.

4.   J

Difficulty: Medium

Category: Algebra

Getting to the Answer: The question asks for the solution set for the given equation. To solve an absolute value equation, you must always consider the two possibilities: If $|2x - 3| = 13$, then the expression inside the absolute value signs could equal either 13 or -13:

$$2x - 3 = 13$$
$$2x = 16$$
$$x = 8$$

and

$$2x - 3 = -13$$
$$2x = -10$$
$$x = -5$$

Together, the two solutions form the solution set $\{-5, 8\}$, which is (J).

5.   C

Difficulty: Medium

Category: Algebra

Getting to the Answer: The question asks for the number of additional visits in a year that that would yield the same cost for both exterminators. Carefully translate from English into math.

Bye Bye Bugs: $\$275 + \$20 \times$ number of additional visits

Pest Be Gone: $\$200 + \$25 \times$ number of additional visits

Call v the number of additional visits and set the two equations equal to each other:

$$275 + 20v = 200 + 25v$$
$$75 = 5v$$
$$15 = v$$

It will take 15 additional visits for the cost of both exterminators to be equal. Choice (C) is correct.

6.   F

Difficulty: Medium

Category: Algebra

Getting to the Answer: The question asks you to choose the inequality that matches the given graph. First, determine the equations of the lines in the graph. Then, determine the sign of the inequality. The dashed line has a slope of $-\frac{1}{2}$ and a y-intercept of 3. The area below the dashed line is shaded, so $y < -\frac{1}{2} + 3$. The solid line also has a slope of $-\frac{1}{2}$ and a y-intercept of -2. The area above the solid line is shaded, so $y \geq -\frac{1}{2}x - 2$. Thus, $-\frac{1}{2}x - 2 \leq y < -\frac{1}{2}x + 3$. Choice (F) is correct.

7.   C

Difficulty: Low

Category: Algebra

Getting to the Answer: The question asks you to simplify the given expression. Before distributing the $\frac{1}{5}p$, combine like terms inside the parentheses: $\frac{1}{5}p(15q + 10p)$. Then distribute the $\frac{1}{5}p$: $3pq + 2p^2$. Choice (C) is correct.

8.   K

Difficulty: High

Category: Algebra

Getting to the Answer: The question asks for the solutions of x. First, substitute $y = x^2$ into the second equation.

$$24 + x^2 = 10x$$

You now have a quadratic equation. Set it equal to 0, factor, and solve for x.

$$24 + x^2 = 10x$$
$$x^2 - 10x + 24 = 0$$
$$(x - 4)(x - 6) = 0$$

Thus, $x = 4$ and $x = 6$. Choice (K) is correct.

9. E

Difficulty: Medium

Category: Algebra

Getting to the Answer: The question asks for the two solutions of the given inequality. If $|x| = a$, then $x = a$ and $x = -a$. Similarly, for $|x| < a$, $x < a$ and $x > -a$. Recall that the direction of the inequality sign flips when you multiply or divide by a negative. Therefore, $|4x + 3| - 1 < 8$ can be written as $4x + 3 < 9$ and $4x + 3 > -9$. This matches (E).

10. K

Difficulty: High

Category: Algebra

Getting to the Answer: The question asks you to determine how many hours Rasheed needs to jump in order for the cost of the membership to be less than the total cost of buying jump tickets at the non-membership price. An individual non-membership ticket costs $12, so if Rasheed jumps for h hours, the total cost will be $12h$.

If Rasheed buys the membership, then the total cost will be the membership fee plus the discounted rate of the jump ticket per hour. The discounted ticket is $12 - (0.15 \times 12)$, or $12 \times 0.85 = 10.2$.

Set up an inequality to solve for the minimum number of hours, h, Rasheed needs to jump in order for the cost of the membership to be less than the total cost of buying jump tickets at the non-membership price.

$$50 + 10.2h < 12h$$
$$50 < 1.8h$$
$$27.8 < h$$

The smallest whole number greater than 27.8 is 28, so the answer is (K).

CHAPTER 11

Tables, Graphs, Statistics, and Probability

LEARNING OBJECTIVES

After completing this chapter, you will be able to:

- Draw inferences about data presented in a variety of graphical formats
- Calculate mean, median, mode, range, and expected value
- Calculate probabilities based on data sets

Statistics and Probability: 6/36 SmartPoints® (High yield)

How Much Do You Know?

Directions: Try out the questions below. Show your work so that you can compare your solutions to the ones found on the next page. The "Category" heading in the explanation for each question gives the title of the lesson that covers how to solve it. If you answered the question(s) for a given lesson correctly, and if your scratchwork looks like the explanations, you may be able to move quickly through that lesson. If you answered incorrectly or used a different approach, you may want to take your time on that lesson.

1. Jamal has a suitcase that contains 2 white socks (and no other socks). He wants to add enough black socks so that the probability of randomly selecting a white sock is $\frac{1}{5}$. How many black socks should Jamal add to the suitcase?

   A. 6
   B. 7
   C. 8
   D. 9
   E. 10

2. What is the distance, on a number line, between the median and the range of the set $\{-9, -6, -2, 0, 4, 9\}$?

   F. −1
   G. 0
   H. 1
   J. 18
   K. 19

3. Jasmin's goal is to collect 200 cans of food during a food drive. During her first 4 days, she averages 10 cans per day. With 10 days remaining, Jasmin must average how many cans per day to meet her goal?

   A. 12
   B. 14
   C. 16
   D. 18
   E. 20

4. The following frequency chart shows the number of Ms. Kirkham's English students whose test scores fell within certain score ranges. All test scores are whole numbers. How many students have a test score in the interval 71–75?

Score range	Cumulative number of students
60–65	1
60–70	3
60–75	8
60–85	9
60–100	12

   F. 1
   G. 3
   H. 4
   J. 5
   K. 8

5. A certain baseball stadium has 12,000 seats. Based on several previous years' attendance rates, the owners of the stadium constructed the following table showing the daily attendance rates, expressed as decimals, and their probabilities of occurring for the coming baseball season. Based on the probability distribution in the table below, what is the expected number of seats that will be occupied on any given day during the coming baseball season?

Attendance rate	Probability
0.40	0.15
0.50	0.25
0.60	0.35
0.70	0.15
0.80	0.10

- A. 5,400
- B. 6,240
- C. 6,960
- D. 7,080
- E. 7,200

6. The data set $\{1, 3, -8, x, 10\}$ has a mean of 7. What is the median of this data set?

- F. −8
- G. 1
- H. 3
- J. 10
- K. 29

7. Zaina's bookshelf contains 10 horror novels, 10 romance novels, 10 true crime books, and no other books. If Zaina chooses 2 books from the shelf at random to take with her on vacation, what is the probability that the two books she chooses will belong to the same genre?

- A. $\frac{9}{87}$
- B. $\frac{1}{6}$
- C. $\frac{9}{29}$
- D. $\frac{56}{87}$
- E. $\frac{2}{3}$

8. The average of a list of 4 numbers is 100. If the first number is increased by 4, the second number decreased by 5, the third number increased by 6, and the fourth number increased by 1, what will the average be?

- F. 95
- G. 97.5
- H. 100
- J. 101.5
- K. 102

9. Janelle is planning to go out of town for 2 consecutive days and needs to create a watering schedule for her garden. During her time out of town, there is a 50% chance of rain each day. Assuming that the chance of rain is independent of the day, what is the probability that it will rain both days that she is gone?

   A. 0.20

   B. 0.25

   C. 0.50

   D. 0.75

   E. 1.00

10. A researcher is looking to evaluate the impact on blood pressure levels of stroking various types of pets. Her 120 research participants were grouped by the one type of pet they would be interacting with during the study.

   If 1 person from this research group is randomly selected, what is the probability that this person will interact with a dog or a cat?

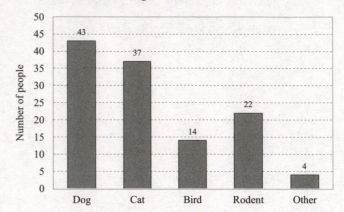

   F. $\dfrac{37}{120}$

   G. $\dfrac{40}{120}$

   H. $\dfrac{43}{120}$

   J. $\dfrac{37}{43}$

   K. $\dfrac{80}{120}$

Check Your Work

1. C

Difficulty: Low

Category: Statistics and Probability: Probability

Getting to the Answer: The question asks how many black socks Jamal should add to a suitcase so that the probability of randomly selecting a white sock is $\frac{1}{5}$. In order for the probability of selecting one of the 2 white socks to be $\frac{1}{5}$, there must be 10 total socks in the suitcase, since $\frac{1}{5} = \frac{2}{10}$. Currently, the only socks in the suitcase are the 2 white socks, so Jamal must add $10 - 2 = 8$ black socks to the suitcase to bring the total to 10. Choice (C) is correct.

2. K

Difficulty: Medium

Category: Statistics and Probability: Statistics

Getting to the Answer: The question asks for the distance between the median and the range of the given set. In a set with an even number of values, the median is the average of the two middle numbers. The values are already in ascending order, so the two middle numbers are -2 and 0. The median is thus -1. This is not the answer to the question, though.

The range of a set of numbers is the biggest number minus the smallest number. The range is thus $9 - (-9) = 9 + 9 = 18$. This still is not the answer to the question; keep going.

The distance between -1 and 18 on a number line is $18 - (-1)$, or $18 + 1 = 19$. Choice (K) is correct.

3. C

Difficulty: Medium

Category: Statistics and Probability: Statistics

Getting to the Answer: The question asks how many cans per day Jasmin must collect in her remaining 10 days to meet her goal. Use the average formula:

$$\text{average} = \frac{\text{sum of terms}}{\text{number of terms}}$$

You are told that the average for the first 4 days is 10. Plug these values into the formula:

$$10 = \frac{\text{sum of terms}}{4}$$

The total number of cans that Jasmin collected in the first 4 days is therefore $10 \times 4 = 40$. Jasmin wants to collect 200 cans in all, so she needs to collect another $200 - 40 = 160$ cans. There are 10 days left, so use the average formula a second time:

$$\text{average} = \frac{160}{10}$$

Jasmin needs to average $\frac{160}{10} = 16$ cans per day to reach her goal. Choice (C) is correct.

4. J

Difficulty: Medium

Category: Statistics and Probability: Tables and Graphs

Getting to the Answer: The question asks how many students have a test score in the interval 71–75, but the interval 71–75 does not appear in the frequency chart. However, you can deduce the number of students in this interval by comparing the number of students in the 60–70 and 60–75 intervals.

According to the chart, there are 3 students in the 60–70 interval, and there are 8 students in the 60–75 interval. Since both intervals have the 60–70 range in common, the 5 additional students must have come from the 71–75 range.

Choice (J) is correct.

5. C

Difficulty: High

Category: Statistics and Probability: Probability

Getting to the Answer: The question asks for the expected number of seats that will be occupied on any given day during the coming baseball season. To calculate the expected value, multiply each value by its probability and add up the results:

$$
\begin{aligned}
(0.40 \times 0.15) & \quad\quad 0.060 \\
(0.50 \times 0.25) & \quad\quad 0.125 \\
(0.60 \times 0.35) \longrightarrow & \quad\quad 0.210 \\
(0.70 \times 0.15) & \quad\quad 0.105 \\
+ (0.80 \times 0.10) & \quad\quad + 0.080 \\
\hline
& \quad\quad 0.580
\end{aligned}
$$

Be careful! This value represents the expected *attendance rate*, but the question asks for the expected number of *seats*. To find the expected number of seats, multiply the expected attendance rate by the total number of seats in the stadium, 12,000:

$$12,000(0.58) = 6,960$$

Choice (C) is correct.

6. H

Difficulty: Low

Category: Statistics and Probability: Statistics

Getting to the Answer: The question asks for the median of the given data set. To find the median, you must first find *x*. Apply the average formula to solve for *x*.

$$\text{average} = \frac{\text{sum of terms}}{\text{number of terms}}$$
$$7 = \frac{1 + 3 - 8 + x + 10}{5}$$
$$7 = \frac{6 + x}{5}$$
$$35 = 6 + x$$
$$29 = x$$

The median is the middle number when the data set is arranged in increasing order:

$$\{-8, 1, 3, 10, 29\}$$

3 is the median, and (H) is correct.

7. C

Difficulty: High

Category: Statistics and Probability: Probability

Getting to the Answer: The question asks for the probability that Zaina picks two books of the same genre. Use the probability formula:

$$\text{probability} = \frac{\text{\# of desired outcomes}}{\text{\# of possible outcomes}}$$

After Zaina chooses her first book, there will be $10 - 1 = 9$ books of that type left. Thus, the "desired" number of books is 9. There are $10 + 10 + 10 = 30$ total books to start with. After Zaina takes one, 29 books remain. Thus, the total number of possibilities is 29. Plugging these values into the probability formula yields $\frac{9}{29}$. Answer choice (C) is correct.

8. J

Difficulty: Medium

Category: Statistics and Probability: Statistics

Getting to the Answer: The question asks for the average of a list of 4 numbers after some changes are made. This scenario may look intimidating, but start with what you know: "the average of a list of 4 numbers is 100" can be written mathematically as:

$$\frac{a + b + c + d}{4} = 100$$

You don't know the individual variables' values, but that information is not necessary to answer this question. If you multiply both sides of the equation by 4, you can determine the sum of the four variables: $a + b + c + d = 400$. Then, use the numbers in the question stem to calculate the new sum: $400 + 4 - 5 + 6 + 1 = 406$. The new average, then, will be this new sum divided by the number of values: $406 \div 4 = 101.5$. Choice (J) is correct.

9. B

Difficulty: Medium

Category: Statistics and Probability: Probability

Getting to the Answer: Your task is to calculate the probability that it will rain two days in a row. The probability that multiple independent events will all occur is the product of their individual probabilities. The probability of rain each day is 50%, or 0.5. The probability of getting rain on both days is therefore $0.5 \times 0.5 = 0.25$, choice (B).

10. K

Difficulty: Low

Category: Statistics and Probability: Probability

Getting to the Answer: Probability is the ratio of the number of desired outcomes to the number of possible outcomes. Here, the desired outcome is that a participant has a dog or a cat. According to the graph, this is $43 + 37 = 80$ participants. The question states that there are 120 participants, which is the number of possible outcomes. So the probability that one randomly selected person will have either a dog or a cat is 80 out of 120, or $\frac{80}{120}$, which is (K).

Tables and Graphs

LEARNING OBJECTIVE

After this lesson, you will be able to:

- Draw inferences about data presented in a variety of graphical formats

To answer a question like this:

Callum is playing a game in which he draws cards out of a standard 52-card deck. If he draws an odd number, he awards himself 2 points. If he draws an even number, he awards himself 3 points. If he draws a face card (jack, queen, king, or ace) he awards himself 4 points. Let the random variable x represent the total number of points awarded on any draw from the deck. What is the expected value of x? (Note: A standard deck of cards contains four copies of the numbers 2 through 10 and four copies of each of the face cards.)

A. 2

B. 2.85

C. 3

D. 3.57

E. 4

You need to know this:

The ACT uses some straightforward methods of representing data sets that you are probably already familiar with, such as **tables** and **bar graphs**. There are, however, some less common types of tables or graphs that show up from time to time that can be confusing at first glance.

Histograms, piecewise graphs, and circle graphs could all show up on the Math Test. They shouldn't be difficult to interpret, but it's helpful to keep in mind that the test maker often includes more information than you actually need. It's important to consider what the question asks for so that you find only the information that you need.

- **Histograms** look a lot like bar charts and can be read in the same way, but they show how many times a certain value shows up in a number range (as opposed to showing counts of various groups).
  - The numbers on the x-axis provide the boundaries for each bar's range.

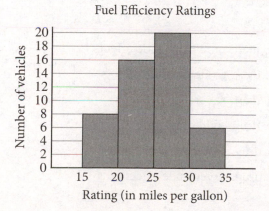

Fuel Efficiency Ratings

- **Piecewise graphs** are graphs created from functions that are defined, literally, by multiple pieces.
  - The domain, the set of *x*-values, is what determines the breaks between pieces.
  - The pieces can be similar or vastly different. All of the pieces could be horizontal segments of the same length that "jump" *y*-coordinates at designated *x*-values. Alternatively, one piece could be part of a linear function, one piece could be part of a quadratic function, one piece could be a single *y*-value, etc.

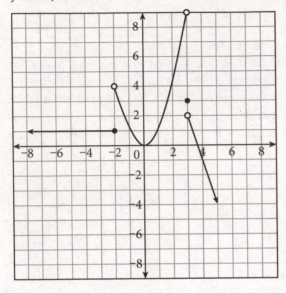

$$f(x) = \begin{cases} 1, & \text{if } x \leq -2 \\ x^2, & \text{if } -2 < x < 3 \\ 3, & \text{if } x = 3 \\ -3x + 11, & \text{if } x > 3 \end{cases}$$

- **Circle graphs** (also called **pie graphs**) represent data as parts of a circle where relative percentages dictate the portions of the circle.
  - When displaying data in a circle graph, find the measures of the central angles for each sector of the circle. To do this, multiply each percent by 360°.
  - For example, a sector that represents 35% of the data should have a central angle that measures approximately $0.35(360°) = 126°$.
  - When you're done, the percentages should sum to 100%, and the angle measures should sum to 360°.

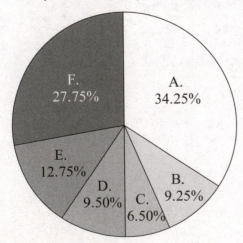

A. inert, mild or no side effects

B. inert, moderate side effects

C. inert, severe side effects

D. drug, mild or no side effects

E. drug, moderate side effects

F. drug, severe side effects

You need to do this:

When presented with a question that uses a graph or table to present information, first inspect the format of the graph or table. What kind of graph or table is it? What information is presented on each axis? What information do you need to find in order to answer the question?

Find the information you need from the table or graph, and then use the information for any calculation the question might require, such as taking the average, finding the median, or determining the expected value.

Explanation:

The question asks for the expected value of x. There is a lot of information in this question, so make a table to organize it:

Draw	Points
Odd	2
Even	3
Face	4

Next, determine the probability of drawing an odd, even, or face card. Remember that there are 4 odd numbers and 5 even numbers in each of the 4 suits:

Draw	Probability
Odd	$\frac{16}{52}$
Even	$\frac{20}{52}$
Face	$\frac{16}{52}$

Next, update the first table with the probabilities you found in the second table:

Draw	Probability	Points
Odd	$\frac{16}{52}$	2
Even	$\frac{20}{52}$	3
Face	$\frac{16}{52}$	4

Finally, calculate the expected value. Think of expected value as a weighted average: multiply the number of points Callum earns by the probability of getting these points and then adding those products together. Expected value is designed to give an idea of the "long term" behavior of the probability distribution: how many points Callum would expect to earn per card if he kept drawing cards for years and years.

$$\frac{16}{52}(2) + \frac{20}{52}(3) + \frac{16}{52}(4)$$

$$\frac{32}{52} + \frac{60}{52} + \frac{64}{52}$$

$$\frac{156}{52}$$

$$3$$

The expected value of x is 3, so (C) is correct. This makes intuitive sense, since 3 points is the midpoint between 2 and 4.

Try on Your Own

Directions: Take as much time as you need on these questions. Work carefully and methodically. There will be an opportunity for timed practice at the end of the chapter.

HINT: Expected value is really just a weighted average. Review the first question and associated explanation from earlier in this lesson if needed to answer Q1.

---

1. Dr. Li has taught 1,520 university students over the past 10 years. The grade points (0–4) earned by past students and their corresponding probabilities are recorded in the table shown. Based on this probability distribution, what is the expected number of grade points that a randomly selected student in her class this semester can expect to earn?

Grade points	Probability
4	0.20
3	0.35
2	0.30
1	0.10
0	0.05

A. 1.85

B. 2.0

C. 2.25

D. 2.55

E. 3

Use the following information to answer questions 2 and 3.

The following table shows the number of infants born in a certain hospital in August 2016. The table categorizes the births by gender and whether the infant was below, above, or within the healthy weight range, as defined by the World Health Organization.

	Below range	Within range	Above range	Total
Male	1	56	10	67
Female	8	48	5	61
Total	9	104	15	128

2. Approximately what percent of the infants born at this hospital in August 2016 were below the healthy weight range?

F. 7%

G. 8%

H. 9%

J. 12%

K. 15%

3. A neonatal care company conducted a study on the female infants born at this hospital in August 2016 who were either below or above the healthy weight range. If an infant is randomly selected from females born at this hospital in August 2016, what is the probability that the infant is one of those who were included in the study?

A. $\dfrac{5}{128}$

B. $\dfrac{5}{61}$

C. $\dfrac{13}{128}$

D. $\dfrac{13}{61}$

E. $\dfrac{61}{128}$

Use the following information to answer questions 4 and 5.

Phase I clinical trials are run to determine the safety of an investigational drug. Dr. Gibbons is overseeing a treatment-resistant influence Phase I trial with 400 healthy participants. Half are given the drug, and half are given an inert pill. The circle graph below shows a distribution of the severity of common side effects.

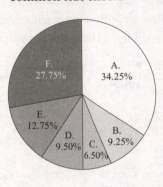

A. inert, mild or no side effects
B. inert, moderate side effects
C. inert, severe side effects
D. drug, mild or no side effects
E. drug, moderate side effects
F. drug, severe side effects

5. How many more participants experienced mild or no side effects than severe side effects?

    A. 10

    B. 38

    C. 42

    D. 50

    E. 64

4. What percent of the participants experienced severe side effects?

    F. 6.50%

    G. 21.25%

    H. 27.75%

    J. 34.25%

    K. 65.75%

Statistics

LEARNING OBJECTIVE

After this lesson, you will be able to:

- Calculate mean, median, mode, range, and expected value

To answer a question like this:

The average of a list of 3 distinct numbers is 20. A new list of 3 distinct numbers has the same median as the original list and the same largest number as the original list. The range of the new list is 3 greater than the range of the original list. What is the average of this new list of numbers?

A. 19

B. 20

C. 21

D. 22

E. 23

You need to know this:

Suppose a nurse took a patient's pulse at different times of day and found it to be 75, 78, 71, 71, and 68. Here are four fundamental statistics figures you can determine for this data set:

- **Mean** (also called arithmetic mean or average): The sum of the values divided by the number of values. For this data set, the mean pulse is $\frac{75 + 78 + 71 + 71 + 68}{5} = \frac{363}{5} = 72.6$.

  - When a question involves the mean, or average, it is often helpful to write out the average formula and use it to determine the missing piece(s):

  $$\text{average} = \frac{\text{sum of values}}{\text{\# of values}}$$

- **Median:** The value that is in the middle of the set when the values are arranged in ascending order. The pulse values in ascending order are 68, 71, 71, 75, and 78. The middle term is the third term, making the median 71. (If the list consists of an even number of values, the median is the average of the middle two values.)

- **Mode:** The value that occurs most frequently. The value that appears more than any other is 71, which appears twice (while all other numbers appear only once), so it is the mode.

  - If more than one value appears the most often, that's okay; a set of data can have multiple modes. For example, if the nurse took the patient's pulse a sixth time and it was 68, then both 71 and 68 would be modes for this data set.

  - A set of data can also have no mode. For example, if the nurse had accidentally written down the 71 twice and removed one, the new data set would not have any number that occurs the most frequently, and therefore, there would not be a mode.

- **Range:** The difference between the highest and lowest values. In this data set, the lowest and highest values are 68 and 78, respectively; so the range is $78 - 68 = 10$.

You need to do this:

When a question involves averages or modes, the order of the values does not matter. To determine a missing value, write out the sum in the average formula as shown below:

$$\text{average} = \frac{\text{value 1} + \text{value 2} + \text{value 3} + \text{value 4}}{4}$$

Then, fill in the information given in the question stem and use algebra to solve.

To find the median, arrange all values in order. In a histogram, that means finding the group with the middle value.

Explanation:

The question asks for the average of the new list after changes are made to the original list of numbers. Recall that $\text{average} = \frac{\text{sum of terms}}{\text{number of terms}}$. "The average of a list of 3 numbers is 20" can therefore be written as:

$$\frac{a + b + c}{3} = 20$$
$$a + b + c = 60$$

The new list contains the same median and the same largest number as the original list, so it also contains b and c. However, you are told that the range of the new list is 3 greater than the original list. This means that the smallest element of the new list is 3 smaller than a:

$$x = a - 3$$

Plug these numbers into the average formula and simplify. Remember that $a + b + c = 60$:

$$\text{average} = \frac{x + b + c}{3}$$
$$= \frac{(a - 3) + b + c}{3}$$
$$= \frac{(a + b + c) - 3}{3}$$
$$= \frac{60 - 3}{3}$$
$$= \frac{57}{3}$$
$$= 19$$

The average of the new list is 19, so choice (A) is correct.

Try on Your Own

Directions: Take as much time as you need on these questions. Work carefully and methodically. There will be an opportunity for timed practice at the end of the chapter.

1. What is the average of the expressions $2x + 5$, $5x - 6$, and $-4x + 2$?

   A. $x - \dfrac{1}{3}$

   B. $x + \dfrac{1}{4}$

   C. $x + \dfrac{1}{3}$

   D. $3x + 3$

   E. $3x - 3$

HINT: For Q2, what information do you need to determine the range of a data set?

---

2. The list of numbers 21, 31, 5, x, y, 12 has a median of 14. What is the range of the list?

   F. 5

   G. 26

   H. 27.25

   J. 31

   K. Cannot be determined from the given information

3. The following table gives the frequency of grades in certain grade intervals for 25 test grades in an AP Statistics class. Which interval contains the median of the grades?

Grade interval	Frequency
A (91–100)	5
B (81–90)	7
C (71–80)	7
D (61–70)	4
F (60 and below)	2

   A. A (91–100)

   B. B (81–90)

   C. C (71–80)

   D. D (61–70)

   E. F (60 and below)

4. Lunenburg County has 4 public parks. The following pictograph shows the number of trees in each park. What is the average number of trees per park in Lunenburg County?

Number of Trees in Public Parks in Lunenburg County

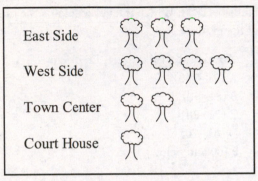

F.   50

G.   75

H.   125

J.   150

K.   200

5. The list of numbers 3, 6, 7, $2x + 1$, $x - 12$ has an arithmetic mean of 1.6. What is the mode of this list of numbers?

A.   −9

B.   1

C.   3

D.   4

E.   7

Probability

LEARNING OBJECTIVE

After this lesson, you will be able to:

- Calculate probabilities based on data sets

To answer a question like this:

Alicia is playing a game in which she draws marbles from a box. There are 50 marbles, numbered 1 through 50. Alicia draws one marble from the box and sets it aside, then draws a second marble. If both marbles have the same units digit, then Alicia wins. If the first marble she draws is numbered 25, what is the probability that Alicia will win on her next draw?

- A. $\frac{1}{50}$

- B. $\frac{1}{49}$

- C. $\frac{2}{25}$

- D. $\frac{4}{49}$

- E. $\frac{9}{49}$

You need to know this:

Probability is a fraction or decimal between 0 and 1 comparing the number of desired outcomes to the number of total possible outcomes.

- The formula is:

$$\text{probability} = \frac{\text{number of desired outcomes}}{\text{number of total possible outcomes}}$$

- A probability of 0 means that an event will not occur; a probability of 1 means that it definitely will occur.
  - For instance, if you roll a six-sided die, each side showing a different number from 1 to 6, the probability of rolling a number higher than 4 is $\frac{2}{6} = \frac{1}{3}$ because there are two numbers higher than 4 (5 and 6) and six numbers total (1, 2, 3, 4, 5, and 6).
  - To find the probability that an event will not happen, subtract the probability that the event will happen from 1.
  - Continuing the previous example, the probability of not rolling a number higher than 4 would be $1 - \frac{1}{3} = \frac{2}{3}$.
- The ACT tests probability in the context of data tables. Using a table, you can find the probability that a randomly selected data value (be it a person, object, etc.) will fit a certain profile.

- Expected value is the weighted average of all possible values that the variable can take on; for the ACT, you will need to have a basic understanding of what expected value is and a strong understanding of how to calculate it based on a probability distribution table.

  - Calculating expected value from a probability distribution table is very straightforward: simply multiply each outcome by its corresponding probability and add the results.

  - Word problems that involve expected value will often call it something different, so look out for questions involving weighted averages and follow this process when needed.

You need to do this:

- Determine the number of desired and total possible outcomes by looking at the table.
- Read the question carefully when determining the number of possible outcomes: Do you need the entire set or a subset?
- Calculate probabilities and expected values based on the data in the table(s).

Explanation:

The question outlines a game scenario and asks for the probability that Alicia wins on her next draw. Recall that $\text{probability} = \frac{\text{desired}}{\text{total}}$. Since Alicia has already drawn a 25, there are 49 marbles left in the box. She needs a 5, 15, 35, or 45 to match the units digit of 5 and win, so there are 4 desired numbers.

$$\text{probability} = \frac{\text{desired}}{\text{total}} = \frac{4}{49}$$

Choice (D) is correct.

Try on Your Own

Directions: Take as much time as you need on these questions. Work carefully and methodically. There will be an opportunity for timed practice at the end of the chapter.

HINT: For Q1, are the probabilities dependent or independent? What does that mean for your calculations?

1. In 3 fair coin tosses, what is the probability of obtaining at least 2 heads? (Note: In a fair coin toss, the 2 outcomes of heads and tails are equally likely.)

    A. $\frac{1}{8}$

    B. $\frac{3}{8}$

    C. $\frac{1}{2}$

    D. $\frac{2}{3}$

    E. $\frac{7}{8}$

2. Two events are *dependent* if the outcome of one event affects the outcome of the other event. One of the following statements describes dependent events. Which one?

    F. A king is drawn from a deck of cards and set aside. Then a coin lands heads up.

    G. A coin lands heads up. Then an ace is drawn from a deck of cards.

    H. A coin lands tails up. Then a 6-sided die lies with a 5 face up.

    J. A 6-sided die lies with a 3 face up. Then a queen is drawn from a deck of cards.

    K. A king is drawn from a deck of cards and set aside. Then a queen is drawn from the same deck.

3. The following figure shows the number of people enrolled in different divisions in a local powerlifting meet. If 1 person is randomly selected out of the 150 total lifters, what is the probability that this person is a member of either the Class I or the Elite division?

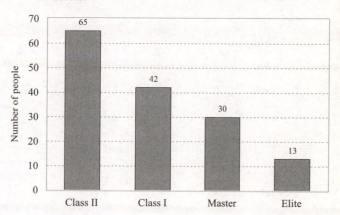

    A. $\frac{13}{150}$

    B. $\frac{31}{150}$

    C. $\frac{42}{150}$

    D. $\frac{55}{150}$

    E. $\frac{95}{150}$

4. To be admitted into the Springfield Technological Academy, applicants must pass both a written and an oral test. Academy records show that 50% of applicants pass the written test, and 20% of the applicants who pass the written test pass the oral test. Based on these figures, how many persons in a random group of 800 applicants would you expect to be admitted to Springfield Technological Academy?

   F.   80

   G.   120

   H.   240

   J.   400

   K.   560

HINT: For Q5, don't stop too soon. Completing all of the steps for this question will take some time and careful calculator use.

5. In a darts tournament, Lorena and her friends use a scoring system that awards points only when the player hits the same number that is announced before throwing. Landing a dart anywhere within a number's "wedge" counts as a hit and earns a score of that number. No points are awarded for hitting a different number. The following table shows the probability of hitting the announced number and how many throws Lorena attempted. What is Lorena's expected total score from the tournament?

Number, n, announced	Probability of hitting n in a throw	Number of throws Lorena attempted
15	0.25	12
16	0.70	20
17	0.80	15
18	0.75	24
19	0.80	30
20	0.85	60

   A.   122

   B.   161

   C.   1,020

   D.   2,273

   E.   2,983

On Test Day

The ACT tests the concept of average fairly heavily. The average formula will serve you well on questions that ask about a sum of values or the average of a set of values, but for questions that give you the average and ask for a missing value in the data set, there is an alternative that can be faster: the balance approach.

The balance approach is based on the idea that if you know what the average is, you can find the totals on both sides of the average and then add the missing value that makes both sides balance out. This approach is especially helpful if the values are large and closely spaced. Imagine that a question gives you the set $\{976, 980, 964, 987, x\}$ and tells you that the average is 970. You would reason as follows: 976 is 6 over the average, 980 is 10 over, 964 is 6 under, and 987 is 17 over. That's a total of $6 + 10 - 6 + 17 = 27$ over, so x needs to be 27 under the average, or $970 - 27 = 943$.

Try solving this question from chapter 7's "How Much Have You Learned?" section (reprinted below) both ways, using first the average formula and then the balance approach. If you find the latter to be fast and intuitive, add it to your test day arsenal.

1. Deepa scored 150, 195, and 160 in 3 bowling games. What should she score on her next bowling game if she wants to have an average score of exactly 175 for the 4 games?

    A. 205
    B. 195
    C. 185
    D. 175
    E. 165

The correct answer and both ways of solving can be found at the end of the chapter.

How Much Have You Learned?

Directions: For test-like practice, give yourself 10 minutes to complete this question set. Be sure to study the explanations, even for questions you got right. They can be found at the end of this chapter.

Use the table below to answer questions 1 and 2.

The following table shows the number of students in Jordan High School. The table categorizes students by grade level and whether or not they are taking Driver's Education.

	Freshman	Sophomore	Junior	Senior	Total
Enrolled in Driver's Ed	98	381	200	85	764
Not Enrolled in Driver's Ed	491	118	251	355	1,215
Total	589	499	451	440	1,979

1. Approximately what percent of juniors are NOT enrolled in Driver's Ed?

   A. 10%
   B. 13%
   C. 26%
   D. 44%
   E. 56%

2. A research group is conducting a study about freshmen and seniors who choose not to enroll in Driver's Ed. If two students are randomly selected one at a time from the students not enrolled in Driver's Ed, what is the approximate probability that the first student will be a senior and the second student will be a freshman?

   F. 0.06
   G. 0.12
   H. 0.43
   J. 0.70
   K. 0.82

3. Laisha works as a software salesperson. The following graph shows Laisha's sales for the year 2018. What is her median number of sales per month?

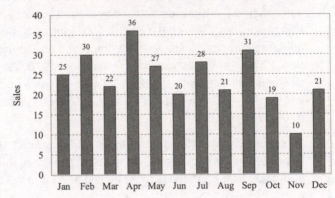

   A. 22
   B. 23
   C. 23.5
   D. 24.5
   E. 25

4. The average of a list of 5 numbers is 110. A new list of 5 numbers has the same first 3 numbers as the original list. The average of the last two numbers in the original list is 70, and the average of the last two numbers in the new list is 75. What is the average of this new list of numbers?

   F. 111
   G. 112
   H. 112.5
   J. 113.5
   K. 115

5. If you randomly pick an integer between 1 and 25, inclusive, what is the probability that it is both odd and prime?

   A. $\dfrac{1}{5}$

   B. $\dfrac{7}{25}$

   C. $\dfrac{8}{25}$

   D. $\dfrac{9}{25}$

   E. $\dfrac{17}{25}$

6. The list of integers 15, 20, 26, x, y, 32 has a mode of 26 and an arithmetic mean of 27. What is the median of the list of numbers?

   F. 15

   G. 23

   H. 23.5

   J. 26

   K. 32

7. Roman is playing a game in which he draws cards from a standard 52-card deck. Roman draws one card from the deck, sets it aside, then draws a second card. Roman wins if the color of the first card is the same as the color of the second card. If the first card that Roman draws is red, what is the probability that he will win on his next draw? (Note: A standard deck of cards contains 26 red cards and 26 black cards.)

   A. $\dfrac{25}{104}$

   B. $\dfrac{25}{52}$

   C. $\dfrac{25}{51}$

   D. $\dfrac{1}{2}$

   E. $\dfrac{50}{51}$

8. At the state fair, Mai plays a game in which she rolls a pair of fair 6-sided dice. She is awarded 10 points if the sum of the numbers on the dice is either 2 or 12. She is awarded 5 points if the sum of the numbers on the dice is between 3 and 5, inclusive, or 9 and 11, inclusive. Finally, she is awarded 3 points if the sum of the numbers on the dice is between 6 and 8, inclusive. Let the random variable x represent the total number of points awarded on any given roll of the dice. What is the approximate expected value of x? (Note: A fair 6-sided die has six sides numbered 1 through 6. When a fair die is rolled, each of the six outcomes is equally likely.)

   F. 3.55

   G. 4.39

   H. 5

   J. 6.79

   K. 9.27

9. Jin's Xtreme Xscape Rooms includes 3 keys to the doors out of the room. To make the puzzle more challenging, Jin adds 5 other keys that do not open any door. Jin puts all of the keys together in a bag. If you walk into the escape room and select a key at random, what is the probability that it will NOT open any door?

   A. $\dfrac{3}{8}$

   B. $\dfrac{1}{2}$

   C. $\dfrac{3}{5}$

   D. $\dfrac{5}{8}$

   E. $\dfrac{7}{8}$

10. Consider the data set $\{1, 6, -1, 9, -5\}$. What is the positive difference between its range and its median?

    F. 1

    G. 5

    H. 8

    J. 13

    K. 15

Math

Reflect

Directions: Take a few minutes to recall what you've learned and what you've been practicing in this chapter. Consider the following questions, jot down your best answer for each one, and then compare your reflections to the expert responses on the following page. Use your level of confidence to determine what to do next.

1. What are some common ways the ACT may present data?

    _____

    _____

    _____

2. What is the difference between median, mode, and range?

    _____

    _____

    _____

3. What is expected value?

    _____

    _____

    _____

4. What are two ways to calculate the probability of a single event?

    _____

    _____

    _____

Responses

1. What are some common ways the ACT may present data?

The ACT may present data in tables, bar graphs, histograms, pie graphs, and piecewise graphs.

2. What is the difference between median, mode, and range?

The median of a set is the middle value, whereas the mode is the most common value. The range of a set is the distance between the smallest value and the largest one.

3. What is expected value?

Expected value is the weighted average of all possible values that the variable can take on.

4. What are two ways to calculate the probability of a single event?

The fundamental probability formula is:

$$\text{probability} = \frac{\# \text{ desired}}{\# \text{ total}}$$

Alternatively, the probability that an event happens is 1 minus the probability that it doesn't happen.

Next Steps

If you answered most questions correctly in the "How Much Have You Learned" section, and if your responses to the Reflect questions were similar to those of an expert, then consider tables and graphs, statistics, and probability an area of strength and move on to the next chapter. Come back to this topic periodically to prevent yourself from getting rusty.

If you don't yet feel confident, review those parts of this chapter that you have not yet mastered, then try the questions you missed again. As always, be sure to review the explanations closely. Then go online (**kaptest.com/login**) to watch video lessons about the highest-yield concepts in this chapter and to use your Qbank for more practice. If you haven't already registered your book, do so at *kaptest.com/moreonline*.

GO ONLINE

kaptest.com/login

Answers and Explanations

Tables and Graphs

1.   D

Difficulty: High

Category: Statistics and Probability

Getting to the Answer: The question asks for the expected number of grade points that a random student in Dr. Li's class will earn. Recall from the first question in this lesson that expected value is really a weighted average: calculate it by multiplying the grade points by the probability of getting these points and then adding everything together at the end.

$$4(0.20) + 3(0.35) + 2(0.30) + 1(0.10)$$
$$= 0.80 + 1.05 + 0.60 + 0.10$$
$$= 2.55$$

Choice (D) is correct.

2.   F

Difficulty: Low

Category: Statistics and Probability

Getting to the Answer: The question asks for the percent of infants who were born below the healthy weight range. According to the table, 9 infants were born below the healthy weight range in August 2016. The table also shows that a total of 128 infants were born in August 2016. Plug these two numbers into the percent formula.

$$\text{percent} = \frac{\text{part}}{\text{whole}} \times 100\%$$
$$= \frac{9}{128} \times 100\%$$
$$\approx 0.07 \times 100\%$$
$$\approx 7\%$$

Choice (F) is correct.

3.   D

Difficulty: Medium

Category: Statistics and Probability

Getting to the Answer: Read the question carefully! An infant is being randomly selected, not from the *total* number of infants, but from the *females* only. This means that you should look only at the second row of the table and ignore everything else.

According to the table, 8 females were below the healthy weight range and 5 females were above the healthy weight range. There were a total of 61 females born in this hospital in August 2016. Plug these numbers into the probability formula and simplify.

$$\text{probability} = \frac{\text{desired \#}}{\text{total \#}}$$
$$= \frac{8 + 5}{61}$$
$$= \frac{13}{61}$$

Choice (D) is correct.

Be sure that you answered the question that was being asked; C is the probability of selecting an infant from *all* of the infants, not the females alone.

4.   J

Difficulty: Low

Category: Statistics and Probability

Getting to the Answer: Look carefully at the graph's legend. Categories C and F are both marked as severe side effects. Add these two percents together to get the total percentage of participants with severe side effects: $6.5\% + 27.75\% = 34.25\%$.

Choice (J) is correct.

5.   B

Difficulty: Medium

Category: Statistics and Probability

Getting to the Answer: The question asks how many more participants experienced mild or no side effects than severe side effects. According to the graph, $34.25\% + 9.5\% = 43.75\%$ of participants experienced mild or no side effects. Since there were 400 total participants in the study, $400(0.4375) = 175$ participants experienced mild or no side effects.

Similarly, $6.5\% + 27.75\% = 34.25\%$ of participants experienced severe side effects. Therefore, $400(0.3425) = 137$ participants experienced severe side effects.

Don't stop too soon, though. The question asks how many more participants experienced mild or no side effects than severe side effects, so subtract these two numbers: $175 - 137 = 38$.

Choice (B) is correct.

Statistics

1.   C

Difficulty: Medium

Category: Statistics and Probability

Getting to the Answer: The question asks for the average of the given expressions, and all of the choices contain the variable x. Don't let this intimidate you, though. Just apply the average formula and simplify:

$$\text{average} = \frac{\text{sum of terms}}{\text{number of terms}}$$
$$= \frac{(2x + 5) + (5x - 6) + (-4x + 2)}{3}$$
$$= \frac{3x + 1}{3}$$
$$= \frac{3x}{3} + \frac{1}{3}$$
$$= x + \frac{1}{3}$$

Choice (C) is correct.

2.   K

Difficulty: High

Category: Statistics and Probability

Getting to the Answer: The question asks you to calculate the range of the given list, which includes two variables. Recall that the range is the biggest number in the list minus the smallest number in the list. The median is the middle number when the data set is arranged in increasing order. Since there are an even number of terms, the median is the average of the two middle terms.

In a question like this that allows for many possibilities for x and y, try Picking Numbers to see if you can find values that yield a median of 14.

One way is to let $x = 7$ and $y = 16$. This gives a median of 14 because $\frac{12 + 16}{2} = 4$. When the data set is arranged in increasing order, it looks like:

$$5, 7, 12, 16, 21, 31$$

The range of this data set is $31 - 5 = 26$.

Notice that letting $y = 16$ gives you considerable freedom for what you can pick for x. As long as x is less than 12, the median will still be 14. There is thus the possibility of obtaining a different value for the range. With this in mind, let $x = 3$ and $y = 16$. When the data set is arranged in increasing order, it looks like:

$$3, 7, 12, 16, 21, 31$$

The range of this data set is $31 - 3 = 28$.

Since there at least two possibilities for the range, it cannot be determined from the information given. Choice (K) is correct.

3.   C

Difficulty: Medium

Category: Statistics and Probability

Getting to the Answer: The question asks which interval contains the median of the grades. Recall that the median is the middle number when the data set is arranged in increasing order. Since there are 25 total terms, the median is the 13th term. Working upward from the lowest grades, there are 2 F's, 4 D's, and 7 C's, so the 13th term is in the C interval.

Choice (C) is correct.

4.   H

Difficulty: Low

Category: Statistics and Probability

Getting to the Answer: The question asks for the average number of trees in the parks based on the pictograph. Since each tree in the pictograph represents 50 real trees, East Side contains 150 trees, West Side 200 trees, Town Center 100 trees, and Court House 50 trees. Plug these numbers into the average formula.

$$\text{average} = \frac{150 + 200 + 100 + 50}{4}$$
$$= \frac{500}{4}$$
$$= 125$$

Choice (H) is correct.

5. C

Difficulty: Medium

Category: Statistics and Probability

Getting to the Answer: The question asks for the mode of the given list of numbers. Don't let the variables intimidate you; just apply the average formula and solve for x:

$$\frac{3 + 6 + 7 + (2x + 1) + (x - 12)}{5} = 1.6$$
$$3 + 6 + 7 + 2x + 1 + x - 12 = 8$$
$$5 + 3x = 8$$
$$3x = 3$$
$$x = 1$$

Next, plug $x = 1$ back in to see what the data set looks like.

$$3, 6, 7, 3, -11$$

Finally, recall that the mode is the most frequently occurring number in the data set. The mode is thus 3, and (C) is correct.

Probability

1. C

Difficulty: High

Category: Statistics and Probability

Getting to the Answer: The question asks for the probability of obtaining at least 2 heads when a coin is flipped 3 times. Since the coin is being flipped 3 times, the phrase "at least 2 heads" means either 2 heads or 3 heads. Consider each situation separately:

First, think about the different ways in which you could get 2 heads. It is helpful to write down the different possibilities for each coin:

$$HHT$$
$$HTH$$
$$THH$$

Now think about the ways in which you could get 3 heads. This is much simpler:

$$HHH$$

All together, there are $3 + 1 = 4$ different ways to obtain at least 2 heads.

Next, calculate the total number of possible outcomes of flipping a coin 3 times. Since each flip has exactly 2 possibilities (heads or tails), there are $(2)(2)(2) = 8$ possible outcomes.

Finally, plug these numbers into the probability formula:

$$\text{probability} = \frac{\#\text{ of desired outcomes}}{\#\text{ of total possible outcomes}}$$
$$= \frac{1 + 3}{8}$$
$$= \frac{4}{8}$$
$$= \frac{1}{2}$$

Choice (C) is correct.

Be certain that you answered the question that was being asked. Choice B is the probability of obtaining exactly 2 heads rather than 2 or more heads.

2. K

Difficulty: Low

Category: Statistics and Probability

Getting to the Answer: The question defines dependent events and then asks you to find an example. Work through each answer choice systematically.

Drawing a card and flipping a coin are two completely separate processes and do not affect each other in any way. Therefore, F and G are incorrect.

Similarly, flipping a coin and rolling a die are independent events. Eliminate H.

Finally, rolling a die and drawing a card are also independent. Choice J is incorrect.

By process of elimination, (K) must be correct.

3. D

Difficulty: Low

Category: Statistics and Probability

Getting to the Answer: The question asks for the probability of randomly selecting a person who is competing in either the Class I or the Elite division. Recall that $\text{probability} = \frac{\#\text{ of desired outcomes}}{\#\text{ of total possible outcomes}}$. Since there are 150 lifters in the competition, the total is 150. There are 42 lifters in the Class I division and

13 lifters in the Elite division, so the number of desired lifters is $42 + 13 = 55$. Plug these numbers into the probability formula.

$$\text{probability} = \frac{\text{desired}}{\text{total}} = \frac{55}{150}$$

Choice (D) is correct.

Be certain that you answered the question that was asked. Choice E is the probability that the selected contestant is in the Class II or Master division.

4. F

Difficulty: Low

Category: Statistics and Probability

Getting to the Answer: You are being asked for the total number of students who will be admitted from a group of 800 applicants. First, calculate the number who pass the written test. Then determine the number who pass the oral test as well.

The number of applicants who pass the written test is $800(0.50) = 400$. Out of these 400, only 20% pass the oral test. Thus, $400(0.20) = 80$ pass both the written and oral tests.

Choice (F) is correct.

Be certain that you correctly interpreted the question. If you added the percentages to get a 70% pass rate, you would have incorrectly chosen K.

5. D

Difficulty: High

Category: Statistics and Probability

Getting to the Answer: Lorena's expected total score can be calculated by multiplying the number, n, by the probability of hitting n by the number of attempted throws:

- $0.25 \times 12 \times 15 = 45$
- $0.70 \times 20 \times 16 = 224$
- $0.80 \times 15 \times 17 = 204$
- $0.75 \times 24 \times 18 = 324$
- $0.80 \times 30 \times 19 = 456$
- $0.85 \times 60 \times 20 = 1020$

These values represent Lorena's expected score based on the number announced. Lorena's expected total score, then, is the sum of these values: $45 + 224 + 204 + 324 + 456 + 1,020 = 2,273$ points, (D).

On Test Day

1. B

Difficulty: Medium

Category: Statistics and Probability

Getting to the Answer: The question asks what score a bowler must get for her next game to attain an average score of 175 for 4 games and gives the scores of her first 3 games. The average of a group of numbers is the sum of the values divided by the number of values. You can either set up and solve an equation involving the missing score or use the balance approach.

To answer the question algebraically, call the missing score x and set up the average equation:

$$\frac{150 + 195 + 160 + x}{4} = 175$$
$$505 + x = 700$$
$$x = 195$$

Choice (B) is correct.

Using the balance approach for averages, you could determine that the 150 score was 25 less than the desired average, the 195 score was 20 greater, and the 160 score was 15 less, for a total of 20 less. Thus, the fourth score would need to be $175 + 20 = 195$ to raise the average to 175. This approach also shows that (B) is correct.

How Much Have You Learned?

1. E

Difficulty: Low

Category: Statistics and Probability

Getting to the Answer: The question asks what percent of juniors are not enrolled in Driver's Ed. Recall that $\text{Percent} = \frac{\text{part}}{\text{whole}} \times 100\%$. Since the question asks "what percent of juniors," the total number of juniors, 451, is the needed whole. According to the table, 251 juniors are not enrolled in Driver's Ed. Plug these numbers into the percent formula and simplify.

$$\text{Percent} = \frac{\text{part}}{\text{whole}} \times 100\%$$
$$= \frac{251}{451} \times 100\%$$
$$= 0.566 \times 100\%$$
$$= 56.6\%$$

Choice (E) is correct.

Be certain that you answered the question that was asked! Choice D is the percentage of juniors that *are* enrolled in Driver's Ed.

2. G

Difficulty: Medium

Category: Statistics and Probability

Getting to the Answer: The question asks for the probability of selecting a senior and then a freshman from the students who are not enrolled in Driver's Ed. First, find the probability of selecting a senior from the students who are not enrolled in Driver's Ed.

$$\text{Probability} = \frac{\text{desired}}{\text{total}} = \frac{355}{1,215} = 0.292$$

Now find the probability that the second student selected will be a freshman. Since you already picked out one senior, you must reduce the denominator by 1.

$$\text{Probability} = \frac{\text{desired}}{\text{total}} = \frac{491}{1,214} = 0.404$$

In probability problems involving multiple events, the word "and" means to multiply. To find the probability of the first student being a senior *and* the second student being a freshman, multiply the two individual probabilities together.

$$(0.292)(0.404) = 0.118$$

Since the question asks for the approximate probability, (G) is correct.

3. C

Difficulty: Low

Category: Statistics and Probability

Getting to the Answer: The question asks for the median of Laisha's sales in 2018. Recall that the median is the middle number when the data are arranged in increasing order. Since this data set is not in order, put it in order:

10, 19, 20, 21, 21, 22, 25, 27, 28, 30, 31, 36

This data set contains an even number of terms, so there are actually two middle numbers: 22 and 25. The median is the average of these two numbers.

$$\frac{22 + 25}{2} = \frac{47}{2} = 23.5$$

The median of Laisha's sales from 2018 is 23.5. Choice (C) is correct.

4. G

Difficulty: High

Category: Statistics and Probability

Getting to the Answer: The question asks for the average of the new list after changes are made to the original list. At its heart, this question is nothing more than a repeated application of the average formula:

$$\text{Average} = \frac{\text{sum of terms}}{\text{number of terms}}$$

Methodically translate from English into math. "The average of a list of 5 numbers is 110" can be written as:

$$\frac{a + b + c + d + e}{5} = 110$$

This statement allows you to conclude that the sum of the variables $a + b + c + d + e$ is 550.

"A new list of 5 numbers has the same first 3 numbers as the original list" means that the new list includes a, b, and c. To avoid confusion, call the fourth and fifth numbers in the new list x and y.

Now, compare the averages of the last two numbers in each list. In the original list, the average of these two numbers is 70; this can be translated from English to math:

$$\frac{d + e}{2} = 70$$

This means the sum of $d + e = 140$, so the sum of $a + b + c = 550 - 140 = 410$.

Next, calculate the sum of the last two numbers in the new list. Fill in the average formula:

$$\frac{x + y}{2} = 75$$

This means that $x + y = 150$. Finally, "What is the average of this new list of numbers?" tells you what the question is asking for:

$$\frac{a + b + c + x + y}{5} = \text{average}$$

Since you determined that $a + b + c = 410$ and $x + y = 150$, you can plug these values into the formula:

$$\frac{410 + 150}{5} = \frac{560}{5} = 112$$

The average of the new list is 112. Choice (G) is correct.

5.   C

Difficulty: Medium

Category: Statistics and Probability

Getting to the Answer: The question asks for the probability that a randomly selected integer between 1 to 25 inclusive will be both prime and odd. Recall that probability $= \frac{\text{desired}}{\text{total}}$. You are choosing out of a group of 25 numbers, so "total" is 25. To find "desired," simply write down all of the odd numbers between 1 and 25 and cross out the ones that are not prime, which leaves: 3, 5, 7, 11, 13, 17, 19, and 23. "Desired" is thus 8. Finally, plug these numbers into the probability formula.

$$\text{probability} = \frac{\text{desired}}{\text{total}} = \frac{8}{25}$$

Choice (C) is correct.

Be sure that you answered the correct question! You are asked about the numbers that are both odd and prime. You would arrive at D if you simply counted the number of primes between 1 and 25, not specifically the odd primes.

6.   J

Difficulty: High

Category: Statistics and Probability

Getting to the Answer: The question asks for the median of the list of numbers. Recall that the mode of a data set is the number that occurs the most frequently. Thus, either $x = 26$, $y = 26$, or $x = y = 26$. At this point, you cannot tell.

Fortunately, you are also given that the arithmetic mean is 27. Set up an equation to obtain more information about x and y.

$$\frac{15 + 20 + 26 + x + y + 32}{6} = 27$$
$$15 + 20 + 26 + x + y + 32 = 162$$
$$93 + x + y = 162$$
$$x + y = 69$$

Since $26 + 26 = 52$, there is no way that x and y could *both* be 26. If $x = 26$, then $y = 69 - 26 = 43$. Thus, the list looks like:

$$15, 20, 26, 26, 32, 43$$

Recall that the median is the middle number when the data are arranged in increasing order. This data set contains an even number of terms, so there are actually two middle numbers: 26 and 26. The median is the average of these two numbers, which is just 26.

Thus, (J) is correct.

7.   C

Difficulty: Medium

Category: Statistics and Probability

Getting to the Answer: The question asks for the probability that Roman will draw another red card, assuming that his first draw was also a red card. Recall that probability $= \frac{\text{desired}}{\text{total}}$. Since Roman has already picked out one card, there are 51 cards left in the deck. Similarly, since he has already set aside a red card, there are 25 red cards left. Plug these two numbers into the probability formula.

$$\text{probability} = \frac{\text{desired}}{\text{total}} = \frac{25}{51}$$

Choice (C) is correct.

Be sure to read the question carefully! If you didn't remember that the first card drawn was not replaced in the deck, you would have picked B.

8.   G

Difficulty: High

Category: Statistics and Probability

Getting to the Answer: This question outlines a game scenario and asks for the expected value. There is a lot of information here, so make a table to organize it:

Roll Total	Points
2 or 12	10
3, 4, 5, 9, 10, or 11	5
6, 7, or 8	3

Next, determine the probability of actually getting these rolls. Since there are two dice to keep track of, this is also best visualized with a table:

Roll Total	(Die 1, Die 2)	Probability
2	(1, 1)	$\frac{1}{36}$
3	(1, 2) (2, 1)	$\frac{2}{36}$
4	(1, 3) (2, 2) (3, 1)	$\frac{3}{36}$
5	(1, 4) (2, 3) (3, 2) (4, 1)	$\frac{4}{36}$
6	(1, 5) (2, 4) (3, 3) (4, 2) (5, 1)	$\frac{5}{36}$
7	(1, 6) (2, 5) (3, 4) (4, 3) (5, 2) (1, 6)	$\frac{6}{36}$
8	(2, 6) (3, 5) (4, 4) (5, 3) (6, 2)	$\frac{5}{36}$

Roll Total	(Die 1, Die 2)	Probability
9	(3, 6) (4, 5) (5, 4) (6, 3)	$\frac{4}{36}$
10	(4, 6) (5, 5) (6, 4)	$\frac{3}{36}$
11	(5, 6) (6, 5)	$\frac{2}{36}$
12	(6, 6)	$\frac{1}{36}$

Next, update the first table with the probabilities you found in the second table. Remember that if you want to find the probability of rolling a 3, 4, or 5, you must add these individual probabilities together:

Roll Total	Probability	Points
2 or 12	$\frac{2}{36}$	10
3, 4, 5, 9, 10, or 11	$\frac{18}{36}$	5
6, 7, or 8	$\frac{16}{36}$	3

Finally, calculate the expected value. Think of this as a weighted average: multiply the number of points Mai earns by the probability of getting these points and then add those products together.

$$10\left(\frac{2}{36}\right) + 5\left(\frac{18}{36}\right) + 3\left(\frac{16}{36}\right)$$

$$\frac{20}{36} + \frac{90}{36} + \frac{48}{36}$$

$$\frac{158}{36}$$

$$4.388$$

The expected value of x is 4.388, so (G) is correct. This makes sense since half of the results are 5 points, but there are more 3-point outcomes than 10-point outcomes. You would thus expect the result to be less than 5.

9. D

Difficulty: Low

Category: Statistics and Probability

Getting to the Answer: The question asks for the probability that a randomly selected key will not open any door. Recall that probability $= \frac{\text{desired}}{\text{total}}$. Since there were 3 keys originally and Jin added another 5, there are now 8 total. You are asked for the probability that a key does *not* open a door, so the desired number of keys is 5. Plug these numbers into the probability formula.

$$\text{probability} = \frac{\text{desired}}{\text{total}} = \frac{5}{8}$$

Choice (D) is correct.

Double-check that you answered the question that was asked. Choice A is the probability that the key *will* open a door.

10. J

Difficulty: Medium

Category: Statistics and Probability

Getting to the Answer: The question asks for the difference between the range and median of the given data set. The range is the difference between the highest and lowest values of the data set.

$$\text{range} = 9 - (-5) = 14$$

The median is the middle number when the numbers are arranged in increasing order.

$$\{-5, -1, 1, 6, 9\}$$

The median is 1.

The question asks for the difference between the range and the median, so subtract the two: $14 - 1 = 13$. Choice (J) is correct.

Be sure that you subtract the two values when finding the range. If you added 14 and 1, you would have picked K.

CHAPTER 12

Functions

LEARNING OBJECTIVES

After completing this chapter, you will be able to:

- Apply function notation

- Define the domain and range of a function

- Evaluate the output of a function for a given input

- Interpret the graph of a function

- Write a function to describe a rule or data set

- Find coordinates of a point that is translated, reflected over an axis, or rotated about the origin

- Match graphs of basic trigonometric functions with their equations

- Use trigonometric concepts and basic identities to solve problems

- Given an equation or function, find an equation or function whose graph is a translation

---

Functions: 4/36 SmartPoints® (Medium yield)

How Much Do You Know?

Directions: Try out the questions below. Show your work so that you can compare your solutions to the ones found on the next page. The "Category" heading in the explanation for each question gives the title of the lesson that covers how to solve it. If you answered the question(s) for a given lesson correctly, and if your scratchwork looks like ours, you may be able to move quickly through that lesson. If you answered incorrectly or used a different approach, you may want to take your time on that lesson.

1. In the figure shown, what is the approximate value of $f(0) + g\left(\frac{1}{2}\right)$?

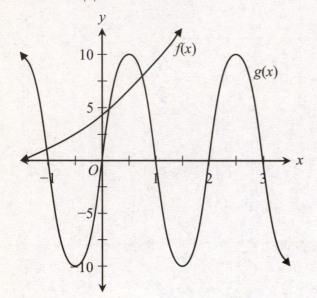

A. −4
B. 4
C. 6
D. 10
E. 14

2. The following graph shows a transformation of the absolute value function, $f(x) = |x|$. Which equation best describes the transformation?

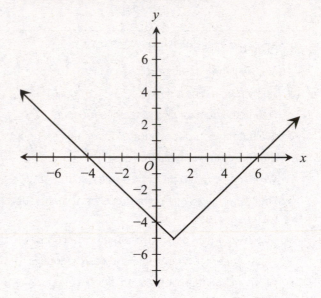

F. $y = f(x + 1) - 5$
G. $y = f(x - 1) - 5$
H. $y = f(x - 1) + 5$
J. $y = -f(x + 1) - 5$
K. $y = -f(x - 1) - 5$

3. If $a(x) = \sqrt{x^2 + 7}$ and $b(x) = x^3 - 7$, then what is the value of $\dfrac{a(3)}{b(2)}$?

   A. $\dfrac{\sqrt{11}}{20}$

   B. $\dfrac{1}{4}$

   C. $\sqrt{11}$

   D. 4

   E. $4\sqrt{11}$

4. The following graph of $f(x)$ is a quadratic equation. Which of the following represents the domain and range of the function?

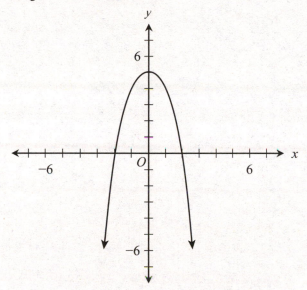

   F. Domain: $f(x) \geq 5$; range: all real numbers

   G. Domain: $f(x) \leq 5$; range: all real numbers

   H. Domain: all real numbers; range: $f(x) \geq 5$

   J. Domain: all real numbers; range: $f(x) \leq 5$

   K. Domain: all real numbers; range: all real numbers

5. Which of the following correctly describes the range of the function $h(x) = 4x^2 - 9$?

   A. All real numbers

   B. All real numbers greater than $-3/2$

   C. All real numbers greater than or equal to -9

   D. All real numbers between $-3/2$ and $3/2$

   E. All real numbers between and including -9 and 9

6. If $p(x) = x^2 - 4x + 8$ and $q(x) = x - 3$, what is the value of $\dfrac{q(p(5))}{p(q(5))}$?

   F. 0

   G. 0.4

   H. 1

   J. 2.5

   K. 10

7. What is the amplitude of the function $f(x) = 4\sin(2x + \pi)$?

   A. $\dfrac{1}{4}$

   B. $\dfrac{1}{2}$

   C. 2

   D. π

   E. 4

8. If $-2 \leq x \leq 2$, the maximum value of $f(x) = 1 - x^2$ is which of the following?

   F. 2

   G. 1

   H. 0

   J. -1

   K. -2

9. For the function $g(x) = 3x^2 - 5x - 7$, what is the value of $g(-2)$?

    A. -29

    B. -9

    C. -5

    D. 15

    E. 39

10. Suppose a polynomial function $p(x)$ has roots of -4 and 7. If $q(x)$ is a translation of $p(x)$ such that $q(x) = p(x - 2)$, through which two points must the graph of $q(x)$ pass?

    F. $(-4,0)$ and $(7,0)$

    G. $(-4,2)$ and $(7,2)$

    H. $(-4,-2)$ and $(7,-2)$

    J. $(-2,0)$ and $(9,0)$

    K. $(-6,0)$ and $(5,0)$

Check Your Work

1.   E

Difficulty: Low

Category: Functions: Graphs of Functions

Getting to the Answer: The question asks for the approximate sum of the values of the two functions on the graph at two specified points. Use the graph to find the y-values for the given x-values. For the graph f, when $x = 0$, $y = 4$. For the graph g, when $x = \frac{1}{2}$, $y = 10$. So, $f(0) + g\left(\frac{1}{2}\right) = 4 + 10 = 14$.

Thus, (E) is correct. Be certain that you answered the question that was asked. Choice C is $f\left(\frac{1}{2}\right) + g(0)$.

2.   G

Difficulty: Medium

Category: Functions: Transformations

Getting to the Answer: The question asks for the choice that represents the transformation shown in the graph. Adding or subtracting inside of the function parentheses moves the function left or right. If you subtract 1 from x, the function shifts 1 to the right. The way the function moves is actually opposite of the sign; eliminate F and J.

Moving the function up or down is much more straightforward. The addition or subtraction *outside* of the parentheses moves the function vertically in the direction of the sign. In the above example, the function shifts down by 5 so the function should have -5 in the equation. Eliminate H.

The last difference is the positive or negative sign in front of the $f(x - 1)$. A negative sign reflects, or flips, the function around the x-axis. Since the absolute value graph is opening upward, the sign should be positive. Eliminate J.

Therefore, (G) is correct. You can quickly confirm your choice by plugging $x = 1$ into $f(x)$.

3.   D

Difficulty: Low

Category: Functions: Function Notation

Getting to the Answer: This question asks for the value of the function $a(3)$ divided by the function $b(2)$. The question defines the two functions, so merely plug in the values:

$$\frac{a(3)}{b(2)} = \frac{\sqrt{(3)^2 + 7}}{(2)^3 - 7} = \frac{\sqrt{16}}{1} = 4$$

Hence, (D) is correct. Be certain that you answered the correct question; B is the reciprocal of the correct value.

4.   J

Difficulty: Medium

Category: Functions: Graphs of Functions

Getting to the Answer: The question asks for the domain and range of the function shown in the graph. Domain refers to the x-values on the graph, and range refers to the y-values on the graph. It is easy to find the range a quadratic equation because its minimum or maximum value always occurs at its vertex. In the figure above, the parabola's vertex is located at $(0, 5)$. Notice that the parabola never goes above the vertex. Thus, the greatest that y can be is 5. Since $y = f(x)$, you can conclude that the range of f is $f(x) \leq 5$.

At this point, you can see that the answer must be (J). But, just to confirm, the domain is all real numbers because of the arrows on the parabola. These lines extend infinitely and thus will eventually pass through every x-value. Be certain that you correctly used domain and range since G reverses these.

5.   C

Difficulty: Medium

Category: Functions: Function Notation

Getting to the Answer: The question asks which choice correctly describes the range of a given function. Range refers to the y-values on the graph (the "output" of the function). The function $4x^2 - 9$ is simply a transformed version of the more basic function x^2, an upward-opening parabola whose vertex is $(0,0)$. Thinking about this more elementary function can help you understand the graph of $4x^2 - 9$.

Since the parabola x^2 opens upward, its minimum value is $y = 0$. Multiplying the x^2 by 4 makes the parabola "skinnier," but it will not affect its range. The -9 represents a downward shift. Thus, the minimum value is no longer 0, but -9. This means that the range is greater than or equal to -9.

Choice (C) is correct. Since you didn't have to do much calculating, be certain that your logic is correct.

6.   J

Difficulty: Medium

Category: Functions: Function Notation

Getting to the Answer: The question asks for the value of dividing one nested combination of two functions by another and provides the equations for the functions. When evaluating nested functions, start with the innermost parentheses and work your way out. First, find $p(5)$ and $q(5)$.

$$p(5) = (5)^2 - 4(5) + 8 \quad q(5) = (5) - 3$$
$$p(5) = 25 - 20 + 8 \qquad q(5) = 2$$
$$p(5) = 13$$

Now plug these values into the given expression and simplify.

$$\frac{q(p(5))}{p(q(5))} = \frac{q(13)}{p(2)} = \frac{(13) - 3}{(2)^2 - 4(2) + 8}$$
$$= \frac{10}{4 - 8 + 8}$$
$$= \frac{10}{4}$$
$$= 2.5$$

Choice (J) is correct. Be certain that you answered the exact question that was asked; G is the reciprocal of the correct value.

7.   E

Difficulty: Medium

Category: Functions: Trigonometry on the Coordinate Plane

Getting to the Answer: The question asks for the amplitude of a given sine function. Think of the amplitude as the "height" of the sine function—the maximum difference from 0. The maximum value of $\sin(x)$ is 1, so its amplitude is 1. However, this question asks us to consider $4\sin(2x + \pi)$.

Think about the rules of translation: expressions inside the function parentheses affect horizontal shifts, while expressions outside the function parentheses affect vertical shifts. Since you are interested in the height of the sine function, the terms inside the function parentheses are irrelevant. The 4 on the outside vertically stretches the sine function by a factor of 4. Thus, the amplitude is $4(1) = 4$.

Choice (E) is correct.

8.   G

Difficulty: Medium

Category: Functions: Function Notation

Getting to the Answer: The question asks for the maximum value of $f(x) = 1 - x^2$. You are given the allowable domain of x. The function $1 - x^2$ is simply a transformed version of the more basic function x^2, an upward-opening parabola whose vertex is $(0,0)$. Thinking about this more elementary function can help you understand the graph of $1 - x^2$.

The negative sign in front of the x^2 term means that the parabola opens downward. Since the parabola x^2 opens downward, its maximum value is $y = 0$. The $+1$ shifts the function up by 1. Thus, the vertex is now at $(0,1)$, and the maximum value is 1.

Choice (G) is correct.

9. D

Difficulty: Low

Category: Functions: Function Notation

Getting to the Answer: The question asks for the value of $g(x)$ when $x = 2$ and provides the equation for the function. Plug in $x = -2$ and simplify.

$$g(-2) = 3(-2)^2 - 5(-2) - 7$$
$$g(-2) = 3(4) - (-10) - 7$$
$$g(-2) = 12 + 10 - 7$$
$$g(-2) = 15$$

Hence, (D) is correct. Be certain that you used the correct value for x. Using $x = 2$ rather than $x = -2$ would result in choosing C.

10. J

Difficulty: High

Category: Functions: Transformations

Getting to the Answer: The question asks through which two points in the choices the graph of $q(x)$ passes. You are given that $q(x) = p(x - 2)$ and that $p(x)$ has roots of -4 and 7. Thus, the points $(-4, 0)$ and $(7, 0)$ lie on its graph.

Adding or subtracting inside of the function parentheses moves the function left or right. If you subtract 2 from x, the function shifts 2 to the right. Moving 2 to the right corresponds to *adding* 2 to the x-coordinate of every point on the graph of $p(x)$.

$$(-4 + 2, 0) = (-2, 0)$$
$$(7 + 2, 0) = (9, 0)$$

Thus, (J) is correct. K is a distractor as these points would result from shifting the graph 2 units to the left instead of 2 units to the right.

Function Notation

> ### LEARNING OBJECTIVES
>
> After this lesson, you will be able to:
>
> - Apply function notation
> - Define the domain and range of a function
> - Evaluate the output of a function for a given input

To answer a question like this:

If $f(x) = x^2 + \frac{x}{2}$, then $f(a + 2) =$

A. $a^2 + \frac{a}{2}$

B. $a^2 + \frac{5a}{2} + 2$

C. $a^2 + \frac{5a}{2} + 5$

D. $a^2 + \frac{9a}{2} + 2$

E. $a^2 + \frac{9a}{2} + 5$

You need to know this:

A **function** is a rule that generates one unique output for a given input. In function notation, the x-value is the input and the y-value, designated by $f(x)$, is the output. Be sure to note that other letters besides x and f may be used.

A linear function has the same form as the slope-intercept form of a line; just think of $f(x)$ as y:

$$f(x) = mx + b$$

In questions that describe real-life situations, the y-intercept will often be the starting point for the function. You can think of it as $f(0)$, or the value of the function where $x = 0$.

The set of all possible x-values is called the **domain** of the function, while the set of all possible y-values is called the **range**.

You need to do this:

- To find $f(x)$ for some value of x, substitute the concrete value in for the variable and do the arithmetic.
- For questions that ask about the domain of a function, check whether any inputs are not allowed, such as those that would cause division by zero.
- For questions that ask about a function of a function, e.g., $g(f(x))$, start on the inside and work your way out.

Explanation:

The notation $f(a+2)$ means that you should plug in $a+2$ everywhere you see an x in the expression $x^2 + \frac{x}{2}$.

$$f(a+2) = (a+2)^2 + \frac{(a+2)}{2}$$

Simplify and collect like terms.

$$(a+2)(a+2) + \frac{(a+2)}{2} = a^2 + 4a + 4 + \frac{(a+2)}{2}$$
$$= a^2 + 4a + 4 + \frac{a}{2} + \frac{2}{2}$$
$$= a^2 + 4a + 4 + \frac{a}{2} + 1$$
$$= a^2 + \frac{8a}{2} + 4 + \frac{a}{2} + 1$$
$$= a^2 + \frac{9a}{2} + 5$$

Choice (E) is correct.

Math

Try on Your Own

Directions: Take as much time as you need on these questions. Work carefully and methodically. There will be an opportunity for timed practice at the end of the chapter.

1. What is $f(g(x+2))$ if $f(x) = x^2 - 4x + 7$ and $g(x) = 7x - 3$?

   A. $49x^2 + 126x + 84$

   B. $63x^2 - 80x + 52$

   C. $25x^2 + 75x - 33$

   D. $-16x^2 - 22x + 5$

   E. $-17x^2 + 61x - 10$

2. Doctors use the function shown below to calculate the concentration, in parts per million, of a certain drug in a patient's bloodstream after t hours. How many more parts per million of the drug are in the bloodstream after 20 hours than after 10 hours?

   $$c(t) = -0.05t^2 + 2t + 2$$

   F. 5

   G. 7

   H. 12

   J. 17

   K. 22

HINT: For Q3, what do the numbers in the answer choices represent? What could cause you to stop too soon or go too far when calculating the answer to this question?

---

3. A company uses the function below to determine how much profit the company will make when it sells 150 units of a certain product that sells for x dollars per unit. How much more profit per unit will the company make if it charges \$25 for the product than if it charges \$20?

   $$p(x) = 150x - x^2$$

   A. \$3.50

   B. \$35

   C. \$52.50

   D. \$350

   E. \$525

4. If $h(x) = 3x - 1$, what is the value of $h(5) - h(2)$?

   F. 5

   G. 8

   H. 9

   J. 12

   K. 14

5. If $f(x) = 3\sqrt{x^2 + 3x + 4}$, what is the value of $f(4)$?

   A. 4

   B. $3\sqrt{2}$

   C. $4\sqrt{2}$

   D. 12

   E. $12\sqrt{2}$

Graphs of Functions

LEARNING OBJECTIVES

After this lesson, you will be able to:

- Interpret the graph of a function
- Write a function to describe a rule or data set

To answer a question like this:

A pep club is keeping track of how many students show up to home football games wearing their school colors. To encourage participation, there is a prize giveaway at each game. As the prizes get more exciting, participation begins to increase.

If x represents the game number and $f(x)$ represents the number of students wearing school colors at game x, which of the following functions best models the information in the table below?

Game	1	2	3	4	5	6	7	8
Number of students	5	11	21	35	53	75	101	131

A. $f(x) = x + 4$

B. $f(x) = 2x + 3$

C. $f(x) = 6x - 1$

D. $f(x) = x^2 + 4$

E. $f(x) = 2x^2 + 3$

You need to know this:

Interpreting graphs of functions is similar to interpreting graphs of equations. For example:

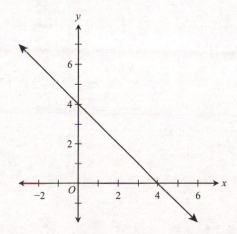

Say the graph above represents the function $f(x)$, and you're asked to find the value of x for which $f(x) = 6$. Because $f(x)$ represents the output value, or range, you can translate this to, "When does the y value equal 6?" To answer the question, find 6 on the y-axis, then trace over to the function (the line). Read the corresponding x value: It's -2, so when $f(x) = 6$, x must be -2.

Math

The ACT may sometimes ask about a function's **maximum** or **minimum**. These terms mean the greatest and least value of the function, respectively. This graph of $f(x)$ does not have a maximum or minimum, as the arrows on the line indicate that it continues infinitely in both directions.

Modeling real-life situations using functions is the same as modeling them using equations; the only difference is the function notation and the rule that each input has only one output.

You need to do this:

- Treat $f(x)$ as the y-coordinate on a graph.
- The maximum and minimum refer to a function's greatest and least y-coordinates, respectively.
- In word problems involving function notation, translate the math equations exactly as you learned in chapter 10 in the Word Problems lesson, but substitute $f(x)$ for y.

Explanation:

This is not a linear expression because the y-values, or number of students, do not increase by the same number for each individual game. Eliminate A, B, and C. Since only two answer choices are left, start plugging in x values and eliminate the equation that is not true. When $x = 1$, both equations equal 5. However, when $x = 2$, D equals 8 and (E) equals 11. Since 11 matches the data in the table, (E) is correct.

Try on Your Own

Directions Take as much time as you need on these questions. Work carefully and methodically. There will be an opportunity for timed practice at the end of the chapter.

1. What is the domain of the following function?

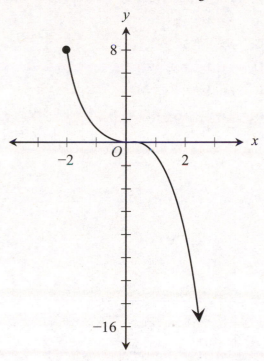

A. All real numbers

B. All real numbers less than or equal to 8

C. All real numbers greater than or equal to -2

D. All real numbers between -2 and 2

E. All real numbers between and including 2 and 8

The graph that follows shows $h(x)$, which represents a portion of a polynomial function.

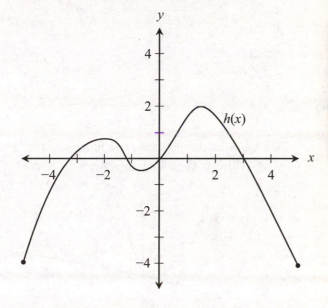

Use the graph for questions 2–3.

2. What is the range of $h(x)$?

F. All real numbers

G. All real numbers greater than or equal to -5

H. All real numbers greater than or equal to -4

J. All real numbers between and including -5 and 5

K. All real numbers between and including -4 and 2

HINT: For Q3, what does $h(x) = 0$ mean in terms of the graph?

3. Given that $-5 \leq x \leq 5$, for how many values of x does $h(x) = 0$?

    A. 0

    B. 1

    C. 2

    D. 3

    E. 4

5. Which of the following is the equation that represents the data given in the table shown here?

x	-3	-2	-1	0	1	2	3	4
$f(x)$	-11	-7	-3	1	5	9	13	17

    A. $y = -2x - 11$

    B. $y = 4x + 1$

    C. $y = x + 5$

    D. $y = 2x^2 + 9$

    E. $y = 3x^2 - 7$

4. The following graph shows two functions, $f(x)$ and $g(x)$. Which of the following statements is true?

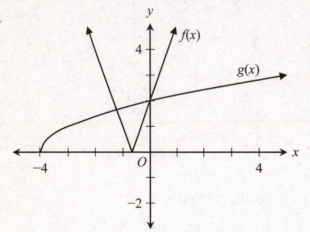

    F. $f(0) = -4$

    G. $g(2) = 0$

    H. $f(x) > g(x)$ for all values of x

    J. $(0,2)$ is a solution for $f(x) = g(x)$

    K. $f(x) = 0$ has exactly two solutions

Transformations

LEARNING OBJECTIVE

After this lesson, you will be able to:

- Find coordinates of a point that is translated, reflected over an axis, or rotated about the origin

---

To answer a question like this:

Which of the following transformations, when applied to the parent function $y = |x|$, results in the graphs of $y = |x + 4| - 2$?

A. Translation to the right 4 coordinate units and up 2 coordinate units

B. Translation to the left 4 coordinate units and down 2 coordinate units

C. Translation down 4 coordinate units and to the right 2 coordinate units

D. Translation up 4 coordinate units and to the left 2 coordinate units

E. Reflection across the line $x = -2$

You need to know this:

A **family of functions** is a group of functions that have the same basic shape and characteristics.

- The simplest function in a family is called the parent function.
- Learning the basic shapes of these parent functions can help you to recognize or write equations for more complex functions in the same family.

Equation family	Graph	Equation family	Graph
linear: $f(x) = x$		absolute value: $f(x) = |x|$	
quadratic: $f(x) = x^2$		square root: $f(x) = \sqrt{x}$	
cubic: $f(x) = x^3$		cube root: $f(x) = \sqrt[3]{x}$	
exponential: $f(x) = b^x$		logarithmic: $f(x) = \log_b x$	

A **transformation** occurs when a change is made to the function's equation or graph. The most commonly tested transformations are translations (moving a graph up/down, left/right) and reflections (flips about an axis or other line). How do you know which is occurring? The table on the following page provides some rules for altering the cubic function $f(x) = x^3$.

Algebraic change	Corresponding graphical change	Graph
$f(x + a)$ $f(x - a)$	$f(x)$ moves left a units $f(x)$ moves right a units	
$f(x) + a$ $f(x) - a$	$f(x)$ moves up a units $f(x)$ moves down a units	
$f(-x)$ $-f(x)$	$f(x)$ is reflected over the y-axis (left to right) $f(x)$ is reflected over the x-axis (top to bottom)	
$af(x)$	$f(x)$ is stretched or compressed vertically (the y-values are multiplied by a)	

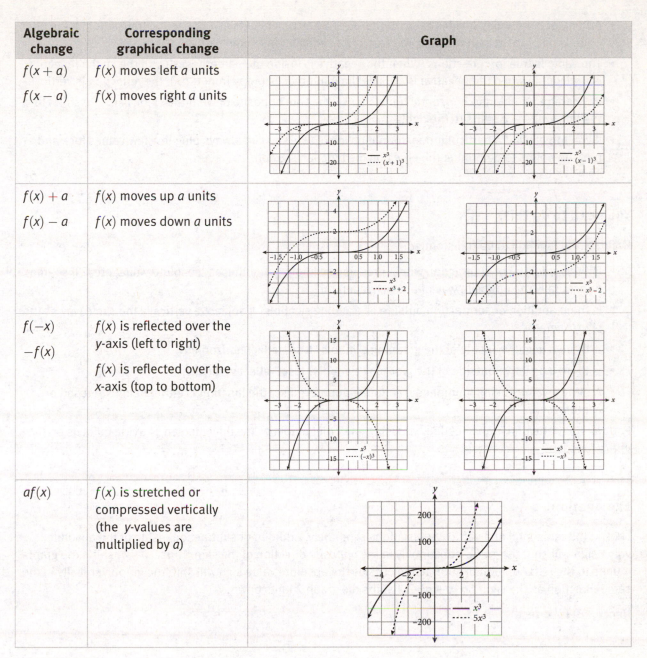

- Adding or subtracting inside the parentheses of a function results in a horizontal translation. If the alteration is outside the parentheses, the result is a vertical translation.
- The same is true for reflections. When the negative is inside the parentheses (with the x), the reflection is horizontal; when the negative is outside the parentheses (away from the x), the reflection is vertical.
- Pay careful attention to horizontal translations—they are opposite of what they look like: $+a$ shifts to the left, while $-a$ shifts to the right.
- If you forget what a particular transformation looks like, you can always plug in a few values for x and plot the points to determine the effect on the function's graph.

You need to do this:

Evaluate the function to be transformed:

- Is there addition or subtraction within grouping symbols (parentheses, absolute value, etc.)? If so, move horizontally the opposite way of the sign/operator.
- Is there addition or subtraction outside of grouping symbols? If so, move vertically the same way as the sign/operator.
- Is there a negative inside of the grouping symbols? If so, reflect horizontally.
- Is there a negative outside of the grouping symbols? If so, reflect vertically.
- Are the y-values being multiplied by another number? If so, the function is either being stretched or compressed.

Perform the transformations needed, choosing one point to follow at a time instead of trying to focus on the entire function.

Explanation:

Look at the horizontal and vertical translations separately. Addition or subtraction inside of the absolute value sign will shift the graph horizontally in the *opposite* direction of the sign. Thus, $|x+4|$ shifts the graph 4 units to the left. Addition or subtraction outside the absolute value sign will shift the graph vertically in the same direction as the sign. So $|x+4|-2$ shifts the graph 2 units down.

Hence, (B) is correct.

Try on Your Own

Directions: Take as much time as you need on these questions. Work carefully and methodically. There will be an opportunity for timed practice at the end of the chapter.

1. The vertex of an upward-facing parabola is at $(-3,4)$. Which of the following represents the coordinates of the vertex after the parabola has been reflected about the x-axis?

    A. $(-3,-4)$
    B. $(-3,4)$
    C. $(0,0)$
    D. $(3,-4)$
    E. $(3,4)$

2. The graph of $f(x) = 2x^3$ is translated 3 units to the right and 2 units down. Which of the following represents the equation of the graph after this translation?

    F. $(x-3)^3 - 2$
    G. $2(x+3)^3 + 2$
    H. $(x-3)^3 + 2$
    J. $(x+3)^3 - 2$
    K. $2(x-3)^3 - 2$

3. The function $f(x)$ passes through the point (x,y). The function $g(x)$ is obtained by translating $f(x)$ 3 units to the left and 4 units up. Through which one of the following points must $g(x)$ pass?

    A. $(x-4, y+3)$
    B. $(x-3, y-4)$
    C. $(x-3, y+4)$
    D. $(x+3, y-4)$
    E. $(x+4, y+3)$

4. The function $g(x)$ is translated 4 units to the right and 1 unit down to form $f(x)$. If $g(x) = \sqrt{x-5} + 3$, which of the following represents $f(x)$?

    F. $f(x) = \sqrt{x-6} + 7$
    G. $f(x) = \sqrt{x-1} + 4$
    H. $f(x) = \sqrt{x-4} - 1$
    J. $f(x) = \sqrt{x-9} + 2$
    K. $f(x) = \sqrt{x-5} + 8$

HINT: For Q5, the functions may look more complicated than usual, but the standard transformation rules apply.

---

5. If $f(x) = e^x$ and $g(x) = e^{(x+3)} - 2$, which of the following describes the translation from $f(x)$ to $g(x)$?

    A. Translation to the left 3 coordinate units and down 2 coordinate units
    B. Translation to the left 2 coordinate units and down 3 coordinate units
    C. Translation to the right 2 coordinate units and down 3 coordinate units
    D. Translation to the left 3 coordinate units and up 2 coordinate units
    E. Translation to the right 3 coordinate units and up 2 coordinate units

Math

Trigonometry on the Coordinate Plane

LEARNING OBJECTIVES

After this lesson, you will be able to:

- Match graphs of basic trigonometric functions with their equations
- Use trigonometric concepts and basic identities to solve problems
- Given an equation or function, find an equation or function whose graph is a translation

To answer a question like this:

The graph of $g(x) = \cos(3x)$ is shown below. Which of the following lists represents the values of x for which $g(x) = 0$?

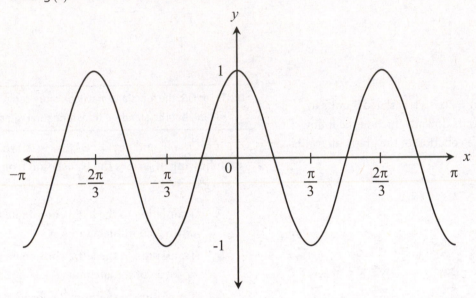

A. $-180°, -120°, -60°, 60°, 120°, 180°$

B. $-165°, -105°, -45°, 45°, 105°, 165°$

C. $-150°, -90°, -30°, 30°, 90°, 150°$

D. $-120°, -80°, -40°, 40°, 80°, 120°$

E. $-105°, -90°, -75°, 75°, 90°, 105°$

You need to know this:

The ACT may ask you to recognize the graphs of the **sine, cosine,** and **tangent functions,** which are presented in the table below. You may also be asked to apply transformations to these graphs.

Sine	Cosine	Tangent
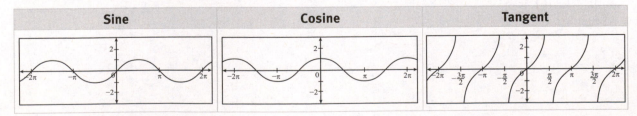		

The domain of the sine and cosine functions is all real numbers, but notice that their graphs oscillate (bounce back and forth) between $y = -1$ and 1.

- This means the range of $y = \sin x$, and also $y = \cos x$ is $-1 \leq y \leq 1$.
- This is not true for tangent, which has a range of all real numbers.
- In other words, the maximum value of a standard sine or cosine function is 1 and the minimum value is -1, while the tangent function has no maximum or minimum.

When trigonometric functions are graphed, the horizontal axis is almost always measured in **radians**.

- The conversion rate is simple: $180° = \pi$ radians.
- Use this relationship as a conversion factor to convert degrees into radians: $90° \times \dfrac{\pi \text{ radians}}{180°} = \dfrac{\pi}{2}$ radians.
- You can also use this relationship to convert radians into degrees: $\dfrac{\pi}{2} \times \dfrac{180°}{\pi \text{ radians}} = 90°$.

You are also likely to see words such as **amplitude** and **period** in questions about trig functions.

- The amplitude of a wave function (such as sine or cosine) is the vertical distance from the center line (the horizontal at rest line) to the maximum or minimum value.
- For the standard sine and cosine functions, the amplitude is 1.
- The period of the standard sine and cosine functions is 2π because their graphs repeat every 2π units.
- The period of the standard tangent function is π.

There are three reciprocal trig functions: secant (sec), cosecant (csc), and cotangent (cot). Their values are the reciprocals of the sine, cosine, and tangent functions:

$$\csc x = \frac{1}{\sin x}$$

$$\sec x = \frac{1}{\cos x}$$

$$\cot x = \frac{1}{\tan x}$$

To find the value of one of these functions, flip the relationships given by SOHCAHTOA (which are covered in the Geometry chapter):

$$\csc x = \frac{\text{hypotenuse}}{\text{opposite}}$$

$$\sec x = \frac{\text{hypotenuse}}{\text{adjacent}}$$

$$\cot x = \frac{\text{adjacent}}{\text{opposite}}$$

Two other particularly useful trigonometric relationships include $\tan x = \dfrac{\sin x}{\cos x}$ and the Pythagorean identity: $\sin^2 x + \cos^2 x = 1$ (notice that it resembles the Pythagorean theorem).

You need to do this:

- Identify the trigonometric information needed to answer the question.
- Use transformation rules or trig properties and relationships to determine unknown values.
- Use the x- and y-intercepts strategically to help eliminate choices or determine the correct answer.

Explanation:

The question asks you to find the *x*-intercepts of the graph. Notice that the *x*-intercepts are already marked by dots on the graph. The graph is in radians while the answer choices are in degrees, so you must convert from radians to degrees. Begin with the smallest *x*-intercept.

$$\frac{-5\pi \text{ radians}}{6}\left(\frac{180 \text{ degrees}}{\pi \text{ radians}}\right) = \frac{-900 \text{ degrees}}{6} = -150 \text{ degrees}$$

Since all of the answer choices begin with different values, you can conclude that (C) is correct.

Try on Your Own

Directions: Take as much time as you need on these questions. Work carefully and methodically. There will be an opportunity for timed practice at the end of the chapter.

1. What is the period of the function $f(x) = 2\sin\left(\frac{x}{4} - \pi\right) + 3$?

    A. $-\pi$

    B. $\dfrac{\pi}{4}$

    C. $\dfrac{\pi}{2}$

    D. 4π

    E. 8π

2. The functions $f(x) = \cos(x)$ and $g(x) = a\cos(x + b)$ have the same minimum value and are graphed in the standard (x,y) coordinate plane as shown. Which one of the following statements could be true?

    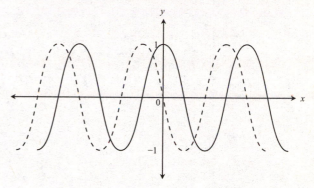

    F. $a = 1$ and $b = 0$

    G. $a < 1$ and $b > 0$

    H. $a = 1$ and $b > 0$

    J. $a < 1$ and $b = 0$

    K. Cannot be determined from the given information

HINT: Some trigonometry on the coordinate plane questions can be answered using basic function transformation rules. Use what you know about translations, reflections, and scaling on the coordinate plane to answer a question like Q3.

3. One of the following graphs is the graph of $y = \frac{1}{2}\sin(2x) + 4$. Which one?

A.

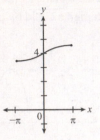

B.

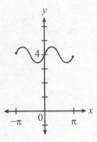

C.

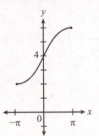

D.

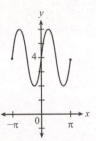

E.

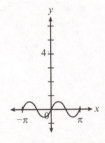

4. What is the amplitude of the function $f(x) = 2\cos(4x - \pi)$?

F. 1

G. $\frac{\pi}{2}$

H. 2

J. π

K. $\frac{3\pi}{2}$

5. The graph of $y = a\cos(bx)$ is shown. One of the following values is equal to b. Which one?

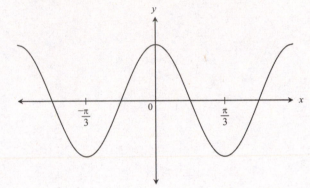

A. $\frac{1}{6}$

B. $\frac{1}{3}$

C. 1

D. 3

E. 6

On Test Day

The ACT likes to test the modeling of real-life situations. Get comfortable with function notation in these questions. Remember that you can write the equation of a line as $y = mx + b$ or as $f(x) = mx + b$, where m is the slope and b is the y-intercept. Both mean the same thing.

In a formula using function notation, the slope indicates rate of change. Often, in questions asking about real-life situations, the x-variable indicates time. In that case, the y-intercept (that is, the value of the function at $x = 0$, or $f(0)$) indicates the starting point. Practice interpreting this principle using this question from earlier in this chapter.

1. Doctors use the function shown below to calculate the concentration, in parts per million, of a certain drug in a patient's bloodstream after t hours. How many more parts per million of the drug are in the bloodstream after 20 hours than after 10 hours?

$$c(t) = -0.05t^2 + 2t + 2$$

    A. 5
    B. 7
    C. 12
    D. 17
    E. 22

The correct answer and an explanation can be found at the end of this chapter.

How Much Have You Learned?

Directions: For test-like practice, give yourself 10 minutes to complete this question set. Be sure to study the explanations, even for questions you got right. They can be found at the end of this chapter.

1. Which of the following functions represents the data given below?

x	0	1	2	3	4	5	6	7
$f(x)$	-19	-11	-3	5	13	21	29	37

  A. $f(x) = 8x - 19$

  B. $f(x) = x^2 - 4$

  C. $f(x) = -8x + 19$

  D. $f(x) = (x - 4)^2 - 19$

  E. $f(x) = 4x + 2$

2. The graph of a function $h(x)$ is found by translating the graph of the function $g(x)$ up 4 units and left 3 units. If $g(x) = (x - 1)^2$, then $h(x) = $?

  F. x^2

  G. $(x - 3)^2 + 4$

  H. $(x + 2)^2 + 4$

  J. $(x + 3)^2 + 4$

  K. $(x + 4)^2 - 3$

3. Several values for the functions $g(x)$ and $h(x)$ are shown in the following table. What is the value of $g(h(3))$?

x	$g(x)$		x	$h(x)$
-6	-3		0	6
-3	-2		1	-4
0	-1		2	2
3	0		3	0
6	1		4	-2

  A. -1

  B. 0

  C. 1

  D. 3

  E. 6

4. If $f(x) = x^2 + 1$ and $g(x) = 3x + 1$, which of the following expressions represents $f(g(x))$?

  F. $3x^2 + 2$

  G. $3x^2 + 4$

  H. $9x^2 + 2$

  J. $9x^2 + 3x + 4$

  K. $9x^2 + 6x + 2$

5. If $f(x) = x^2 + 3x - 5$, what is the value of $f(x + h)$?

  A. $x^2 + 3x - 5 - h$

  B. $x^2 + 3x - 5 + h$

  C. $x^2 + 3x - 5 + 2h$

  D. $x^2h^2 + 2xh + 3x + 3h - 5$

  E. $x^2 + 2xh + 3x + h^2 + 3h - 5$

6. The rule of translation from $f(x)$ to $g(x)$ is $(x,y) \rightarrow (x - 1.5, y + 2.8)$. If $f(x)$ passes through $(-2.3, -1.2)$, which coordinate pair must $g(x)$ pass through?

  F. $(-0.8, -3.8)$

  G. $(0.8, 1.6)$

  H. $(2.7, -3.8)$

  J. $(-3.8, 1.6)$

  K. $(3.8, 1.6)$

7. If $x > 0$, $a = x\cos\theta$, and $b = x\sin\theta$, then which of the following is equivalent to $\sqrt{a^2 + b^2}$?

    A. 1
    B. x
    C. $2x$
    D. $x(\cos\theta + \sin\theta)$
    E. $x\cos\theta\,\sin\theta$

8. If $f(x) = -4x + 1$ and $g(x) = \sqrt{x} + 2.5$, what is the value of $f\left(g\left(\frac{1}{4}\right)\right)$?

    F. -11
    G. -2
    H. 0
    J. 2.5
    K. 3

9. What is the range of the function shown here?

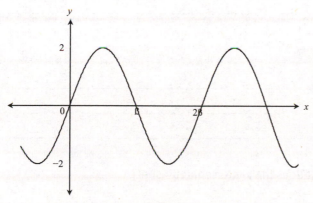

    A. All real numbers between and including -2 and 2
    B. All real numbers less than or equal to 2
    C. All real numbers greater than or equal to -2
    D. All real numbers between 0 and 2π
    E. All real numbers

10. Which trigonometric function could be represented by the following graph?

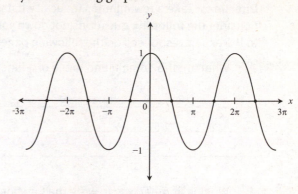

    F. $g(x) = \sin(x - \pi)$
    G. $g(x) = \sin(x + \pi)$
    H. $g(x) = \sin(x + 2\pi)$
    J. $g(x) = \sin\left(x - \frac{\pi}{2}\right)$
    K. $g(x) = \sin\left(x + \frac{\pi}{2}\right)$

Math

Reflect

Directions: Take a few minutes to recall what you've learned and what you've been practicing in this chapter. Consider the following questions, jot down your best answer for each one, and then compare your reflections to the expert responses on the following page. Use your level of confidence to determine what to do next.

1. What are the domain and range of a function?

   _____

   _____

   _____

2. What is another way to write the function $f(x) = x + 4$?

   _____

   _____

   _____

3. In the function above, what does x represent? What does $f(x)$ represent?

   _____

   _____

   _____

4. What will the above function look like when graphed?

   _____

   _____

   _____

5. In a function whose x-value represents time, what does the y-intercept represent?

   _____

   _____

   _____

Responses

1. What are the domain and range of a function?

The domain of a function indicates the possible x-values, and the range of a function indicates the possible y-values. For example, in the function $f(x) = x^2$*, the domain is all real numbers because any number can be squared, and the range is any number greater than or equal to 0, because* x^2 *can't be negative.*

2. What is another way to write the function $f(x) = x + 4$?

When you graph the function on the xy-coordinate plane, you can replace $f(x)$ *with y. This function is equivalent to* $y = x + 4$*.*

3. In the function above, what does *x* represent? What does $f(x)$ represent?

In this function, x is the input and $f(x)$ *is the output.*

4. What will the above function look like when graphed?

The slope of the line is 1 and its y-intercept is 4, so it will move from the lower left to the upper right and cross the y-axis at $y = 4$*.*

5. In a function whose *x*-value represents time, what does the *y*-intercept represent?

The y-intercept represents the initial quantity when $t = 0$*. Say a function represents the progress of a machine manufacturing widgets at a rate of 6 widgets per hour. The machine adds the widgets it makes to a growing pile that consisted of 12 widgets when the machine started working. If this function were graphed as a function of time, the y-intercept would be 12—the pile of 12 widgets that was there when the machine started its task.*

Next Steps

If you answered most questions correctly in the "How Much Have You Learned" section, and if your responses to the Reflect questions were similar to those of an expert, then consider Functions an area of strength and move on to the next chapter. Come back to this topic periodically to prevent yourself from getting rusty.

If you don't yet feel confident, review those parts of this chapter that you have not yet mastered. All four lessons in this chapter cover question types that are fairly common on the ACT, and it is to your advantage to have a firm grasp on this material, so go back over it until you feel more confident. Then, try the questions you missed again. As always, be sure to review the explanations closely. Then go online (**kaptest.com/login**) to watch video lessons about high-yield ACT Math concepts and to use your Qbank for more practice. If you haven't already registered your book, do so at *kaptest.com/moreonline*.

GO ONLINE

kaptest.com/login

Answers and Explanations

Function Notation

1. A

Difficulty: Medium

Category: Functions

Getting to the Answer: The question asks for the value of two nested functions in terms of the variable x. Calculate this from the inside out, just like you would for any set of nested parentheses. First, calculate $g(x + 2)$ by substituting $x + 2$ wherever you see an x in the g function:

$$g(x + 2) = 7(x + 2) - 3$$
$$g(x + 2) = 7x + 14 - 3$$
$$g(x + 2) = 7x + 11$$

Then, plug this value of $g(x + 2)$ into the f function, $f(x) = x^2 - 4x + 7$:

$$f(g(x + 2)) = f(7x + 11)$$
$$= (7x + 11)^2 - 4(7x + 11) + 7$$
$$= (7x + 11)(7x + 11) - 28x - 44 + 7$$
$$= 49x^2 + 77x + 77x + 121 - 28x - 37$$
$$= 49x^2 + 126x + 84$$

Thus, (A) is correct.

2. F

Difficulty: Medium

Category: Functions

Getting to the Answer: The question is asking you to calculate $c(20) - c(10)$ for the given function since, in word problems, the phrase "how many more" indicates subtraction. Calculate $c(20)$ and $c(10)$ individually and then subtract:

$$c(20) = -0.05(20^2) + 2(20) + 2$$
$$= -0.05(400) + 40 + 2$$
$$= -20 + 40 + 2$$
$$= 22$$

$$c(10) = -0.05(10^2) + 2(10) + 2$$
$$= -0.05(100) + 20 + 2$$
$$= -5 + 20 + 2$$
$$= 17$$

Since $c(20) - c(10) = 22 - 17 = 5$, (F) is correct. Be certain that you answered the question that was asked since J and K are the individual values for $c(20)$ and $c(10)$.

3. A

Difficulty: High

Category: Functions

Getting to the Answer: Pay careful attention to the wording of this question. You are being asked NOT for the difference in profit but for the difference in profit *per unit*.

Begin by calculating $P(25)$ and $P(20)$ individually.

$$p(25) = 150(25) - (25)^2$$
$$= 3,750 - 625$$
$$= 3,125$$

$$p(20) = 150(20) - (20)^2$$
$$= 3,000 - 400$$
$$= 2,600$$

However, the question is asking for profit *per unit*, so you must divide 525 by 150:

$$\frac{525}{150} = 3.5$$

Choice (A) is correct. Confirm that you answered the question that was asked. Since $P(25) - P(20) = 3,125 - 2,600 = 525$, it may be tempting to select E.

4. H

Difficulty: Low

Category: Functions

Getting to the Answer: The question asks for the difference between the two outputs of the function $h(x)$ when the given values of x are used as inputs. First, calculate $h(5)$ and $h(2)$ individually:

$$h(5) = 3(5) - 1$$
$$= 15 - 1$$
$$= 14$$
$$h(2) = 3(2) - 1$$
$$= 6 - 1$$
$$= 5$$

Since $h(5) - h(2) = 14 - 5 = 9$, (H) is correct. Confirm that you answered the question that was asked; F and K are the individual values of the function.

5.　E

Difficulty: Low

Category: Functions

Getting to the Answer: The question asks for the value of $f(4)$ given that $f(x) = 3\sqrt{x^2 + 3x + 4}$. The notation $f(4)$ means that you should plug in a 4 everywhere there is an x in the equation $3\sqrt{x^2 + 3x + 4}$.

$$f(4) = 3\sqrt{(4)^2 + 3(4) + 4}$$
$$= 3\sqrt{16 + 12 + 4}$$
$$= 3\sqrt{32}$$
$$= 3\sqrt{16}\sqrt{2}$$
$$= 3(4)\sqrt{2}$$
$$= 12\sqrt{2}$$

Choice (E) is correct. Confirm that you used the correct values given in the question.

Graphs of Functions

1.　C

Difficulty: Low

Category: Functions

Getting to the Answer: The question asks for the values of the domain of the function shown on the graph. Remember that domain is another word for x-values, which are shown on the horizontal axis of the graph. The leftmost point on the graph is the minimum value of the domain. This occurs at $x = -2$. Eliminate choices A and B.

Now find the maximum value of the domain by looking for the rightmost point. The arrow on the point $(2, -8)$ indicates that the graph keeps going towards infinity. Eliminate D and E.

Thus, choice (C) is correct.

2.　K

Difficulty: Medium

Category: Functions

Getting to the Answer: The question asks for the range of the function shown on the graph. Remember that range is another word for y-values, which are shown on the vertical axis of the graph. The lowest y-value occurs at $y = 4$ because the dots indicate that the curve terminates at those points. The highest y-value is 2. Thus, the range of $h(x)$ is from -4 to 2.

Choice (K) is correct. Be certain that you determined the range; the domain is J.

3.　E

Difficulty: Low

Category: Functions

Getting to the Answer: The question asks for the number of points on the graph at which the function equals 0. Remember that $y = h(x)$. Thus, the question is asking how many times $y = 0$. Look at the graph and see that this occurs 4 times. Therefore, (E) is correct. Be certain that you answered the question that was asked. Choice B is the number of points where $x = 0$.

4.　J

Difficulty: Medium

Category: Functions

Getting to the Answer: The question asks which of the choices is true based on the graph of the two functions. Work through each choice systematically.

Eliminate F, since $f(0) = 2$.

Eliminate G, since $g(2) \approx 2.5$.

Eliminate H, since $g(x) > f(x)$ roughly between $x = -1.2$ and $x = 0$.

Recall that a solution for $f(x) = g(x)$ occurs when the graphs of the functions touch or cross each other. Since one of the points where the two functions cross is at $(0,2)$, (J) is correct.

For the record, K is incorrect because $f(x)$ has only one solution, at approximately $(-0.75, 0)$. Confirm that you answered the question that was asked.

5. B

Difficulty: Medium

Category: Functions

Getting to the Answer: The question asks which of the choices is the equation for the data given in the table. First, determine whether the data are in a linear or non-linear relationship. Since all the *x*-values increase by 1, the *y*-values should increase or decrease proportionally. Notice that the *y*-values always increase by 4 throughout the table, so this is indeed a linear relationship. Eliminate D and E.

The slope of the line is the coefficient of *x* in the linear equation. Since *y* increases by 4 for every 1 unit increase in *x*, that value is 4, and (B) is correct. You can confirm this by plugging 4 into the equation to obtain the *y*-value of 17.

Transformations

1. A

Difficulty: Medium

Category: Functions

Getting to the Answer: The question asks for the coordinates of the vertex of the given parabola after it is reflected about the *x*-axis. Reflecting about the *x*-axis will not change the *x*-coordinate but will reverse the sign of the *y*-coordinate. So, $(-3, 4)$ becomes $(-3, -4)$.

Therefore, (A) is correct. Be certain that you answered the question that was asked. Reflection about the *y*-axis would result in the vertex being E.

2. K

Difficulty: Low

Category: Functions

Getting to the Answer: The question asks which of the choices is the expression for $f(x)$ after performing the given horizontal and vertical translation. Addition or subtraction inside of the function parentheses will shift the graph horizontally in the *opposite* direction of the sign. Thus, a translation of 3 units to the right is obtained by subtracting 3 from inside the function parentheses so the function becomes $2(x - 3)^3$.

Addition or subtraction outside of the function parentheses will shift the graph vertically in the same direction of the sign. Thus, a translation of 2 units down

is obtained by subtracting 2 from outside the function parentheses: $2(x - 3)^3 - 2$.

Choice (K) is correct. Be certain that you followed the correct procedures for translation; J shifts the function 3 units to the left.

3. C

Difficulty: Medium

Category: Functions

Getting to the Answer: The question asks which of the choices is a point through which $f(x)$ must pass after performing the given horizontal and vertical translation. Translating 3 units to the left means subtracting 3 from the *x*-coordinate: $x - 3$. Translating 4 units up means adding 4 to the *y*-coordinate: $y + 4$. Thus, (C) is correct. You can readily verify this by noticing that (C) is the only choice with the term $y + 4$.

4. J

Difficulty: Medium

Category: Functions

Getting to the Answer: The question asks which of the choices is the given function translated 4 units to the right and 1 unit down. Translate the square root sign to the $\frac{1}{2}$ power. Addition or subtraction inside of the function parentheses will shift the graph horizontally in the *opposite* direction of the sign. Thus, a translation of 4 units to the right is obtained by subtracting 4 inside the parentheses. Translating 1 unit down subtracts 1 from the constant outside the radical.

So, $\sqrt{x - 5} + 3 = (x - 5)^{\frac{1}{2}} + 3$. After translation, this becomes $(x - 5 - 4)^{\frac{1}{2}} + 3 - 1 = (x - 9)^{\frac{1}{2}} + 2$. When returned to radical format, this matches (J). Ensure that you translated in the correct direction; G is a translation 4 units right and 1 unit up.

5. A

Difficulty: Medium

Category: Functions

Getting to the Answer: The question asks which of the choices describes the transformation of $f(x)$ to $g(x)$ and provides the exponential expressions for each function. Do not be intimidated by the exponential function! The same translation rules still apply.

Addition or subtraction inside of the function parentheses will shift the graph horizontally in the *opposite* direction of the sign. Here, the exponential function e acts like function parentheses. Thus, $e^{(x+3)}$ represents a translation of 3 units to the left. Eliminate B, C, and E.

Addition or subtraction outside of the function parentheses will shift the graph vertically in the same direction of the sign. Thus, $e^{(x+3)} - 2$ represents a translation of 2 units down. Eliminate D.

Thus, (A) is correct. Be certain that you correctly applied the translation rules and used the proper signs.

Trigonometry on the Coordinate Plane

1.   E

Difficulty: Medium

Category: Functions

Getting to the Answer: To answer this question, use function transformation rules. The period of a sine function is determined by the coefficient of x, so you can ignore the 2, π, and 3 values. When the coefficient of x is 1, the period of a sine function is 2π. When the coefficient of x is larger than 1, the graph is horizontally compressed, so the period of a sine function gets smaller. When the coefficient is smaller than 1, the graph is horizontally expanded, so the period of a sine function gets larger. In this function, the coefficient of x is $\frac{1}{4}$, so the period will be 4 times as big: $2\pi \times 4 = 8\pi$. Choice (E) is correct.

You could also use a trigonometry rule to answer this question. When a sine function has the setup $a \sin(bx)$, the period is $\frac{2\pi}{b}$. In this equation, $b = \frac{1}{4}$, so the period of the function is $\frac{2\pi}{\frac{1}{4}} = 8\pi$.

2.   H

Difficulty: Medium

Category: Functions

Getting to the Answer: The question asks which of the choices could be true and refers to the given graph of two functions of $\cos(x)$, one of which appears to be the other shifted horizontally. The most basic form of the cosine function is $f(x) = \cos(x)$. Since the minimum and maximum values of both functions are the same, there is no scaling from $f(x)$ to $g(x)$. You can therefore deduce that $a = 1$. Since the graph does shift horizontally, $b \neq 0$. With the given information, b could be either positive or negative, but not 0. Hence, (H) is correct.

3.   B

Difficulty: High

Category: Functions

Getting to the Answer: Use function transformation rules to answer this question. The graph of a basic sine function crosses both the x- and y-axes at (0,0) and has a period of 2π and an amplitude of 1. The sine function in the question has a vertical expansion (from the $\frac{1}{2}$), a horizontal compression (from the 2), and a vertical shift (from the 4).

Eliminate E because it does not include a vertical shift. Eliminate C and D because they do involve a vertical compression (the amplitude is smaller than 1) instead of a vertical expansion (the amplitude is bigger than 1). Choice (B) is correct because it has a horizontal compression (the period is smaller than 2π), whereas A has a horizontal expansion (the period is bigger than 2π).

Math

4. H

Difficulty: Medium

Category: Functions

Getting to the Answer: The question asks for the amplitude of the given function. Think of the amplitude as the "height" of the cosine function. The maximum value of $\cos(x)$ is 1, so its amplitude is 1. However, this question asks for the value of $2\cos(4x - \pi)$.

Think back to the rules of translation. Expressions inside the function parentheses affect horizontal shifts, while expressions outside the function parentheses affect vertical shifts. Since you are interested in the height of the cosine function, the terms inside the function parentheses are irrelevant. The 2 on the outside vertically stretches the cosine function by a factor of 2. Thus, the amplitude is $2(1) = 2$.

Choice (H) is correct. Since the question asks for amplitude, be certain that you considered only the y-value of the function.

5. D

Difficulty: Medium

Category: Functions

Getting to the Answer: The question asks about the value of b in the graph $y = a\cos(bx)$ based on the graph. The coefficient in front of x indicates a horizontal compression or expansion. The graph of a basic cosine function crosses the y-axis at $(0,1)$ and has a period of 2π and an amplitude of 1. The period of this graph is $\frac{2\pi}{3}$, which means that this graph has undergone a horizontal compression as the period is smaller than 2π. Thus, b is greater than 1. Eliminate A, B, and C.

As b is the coefficient in front of x, the period of the function can be calculated as $\frac{2\pi}{b}$. Set up the equation $\frac{2\pi}{3} = \frac{2\pi}{b}$, and recognize that $b = 3$. Choice (D) is correct.

On Test Day

1. A

Difficulty: Medium

Category: Functions

Getting to the Answer: The question is asking you to calculate $c(20) - c(10)$ for the given function since, in word problems, the phrase "how many more" indicates subtraction. Calculate $c(20)$ and $c(10)$ individually and then subtract:

$$c(20) = -0.05\left(20^2\right) + 2(20) + 2$$
$$= -0.05(400) + 40 + 2$$
$$= -20 + 40 = 2$$
$$= 22$$

$$c(10) = -0.05\left(10^2\right) + 2(10) + 2$$
$$= -0.05(100) + 20 + 2$$
$$= -5 + 20 + 2$$
$$= 17$$

Since $c(20) - c(10) = 22 - 17 = 5$, (A) is correct. Be certain that you answered the question that was asked since D and E are the individual values for $c(20)$ and $c(10)$.

So what does $c(0)$ represent? Since $c(t)$ represents the amount of the drug in parts per million present in the bloodstream after t hours, $c(0)$ represents the amount of the drug in parts per million present in the bloodstream after 0 hours—at the beginning of the treatment.

How Much Have You Learned?

1. A

Difficulty: Medium

Category: Functions

Getting to the Answer: The question asks for the function that creates the values shown in the table. First, determine whether the data are in a linear or a non-linear relationship. Since all the x-values increase by 1, the changes in the y-values will be consistent if it is a linear relationship. Notice that the y-values always increase by 8 throughout the table, so this is indeed a linear relationship. Eliminate B and D.

Since the *y*-values increase by 8 and the *x*-values increase by 1 at every point, the slope is 8. This is the value of the *x*-coefficient, so you can eliminate C and E. Thus, (A) is correct. You can plug any of the *x*-values into that equation to get the matching *y*-value in order to verify that it is the correct choice.

2.   H

Difficulty: Medium

Category: Functions

Getting to the Answer: The question asks for the translation of $g(x)$ 4 units upward and 3 units to the left. Addition or subtraction inside of the function parentheses will shift the graph horizontally in the *opposite* direction of the sign. Thus, a translation of 3 units to the left is obtained by adding 3 inside the function parentheses. This means $(x - 1)^2$ becomes $(x + 2)^2$.

On test day, you could stop here since only (H) has the correct expression inside the parentheses. However, for the sake of completeness, recall that addition or subtraction outside of the function parentheses will shift the graph vertically in the same direction of the sign. Thus, a translation of 4 units up is obtained by adding 4 outside the parentheses.

Therefore, (H) is correct. Be certain that you used the correct values for the original function; using *x* rather than $x - 1$ would result in the expression in J.

3.   A

Difficulty: Low

Category: Functions

Getting to the Answer: The question asks for the value of nested functions for $x = 3$, and you are given tables showing various *x*- and *y*-values for the two functions. Work from the inside out. Before trying to determine the equations for the functions, see if the tables already contain the values that you require. Find the *y*-value of the *h* function when $x = 3$. The table indicates that $h(3) = 0$.

Now evaluate $g(0)$ in the same way. The *y*-value when $x = 0$ is -1.

Choice (A) is correct. Be certain that you answered the question that was asked; reversing the functions would result in the value in E.

4.   K

Difficulty: Medium

Category: Functions

Getting to the Answer: The question asks for the value of $f(g(x))$ in terms of *x* and provides both expressions. Calculate $f(g(x))$ by plugging $g(x) = 3x + 1$ into the *f* function.

$$
\begin{aligned}
f\big(g(x)\big) &= (3x + 1)^2 + 1 \\
&= (3x + 1)(3x + 1) + 1 \\
&= 9x^2 + 3x + 3x + 1 + 1 \\
&= 9x^2 + 6x + 2
\end{aligned}
$$

Therefore, (K) is correct. Be certain that you evaluated the correct expression; $g(f(x))$ is G.

5.   E

Difficulty: Medium

Category: Functions

Getting to the Answer: The question asks for the value of $f(x + h)$ given that $f(x) = x^2 + 3x - 5$. Calculate $f(x + h)$ by plugging in $x + h$ everywhere you see an *x* in the *f* function.

$$
\begin{aligned}
f(x + h) &= (x + h)^2 + 3(x + h) - 5 \\
&= (x + h)(x + h) + 3x + 3h - 5 \\
&= x^2 + xh + xh + h^2 + 3x + 3h - 5 \\
&= x^2 + 2xh + 3x + h^2 + 3h - 5
\end{aligned}
$$

Thus, (E) is correct.

Math

6. J

Difficulty: Medium

Category: Functions

Getting to the Answer: The question asks which of the coordinate pairs is a valid value of $g(x)$. You are given the translation operations from $f(x)$ to $g(x)$ in terms of x- and y-coordinates, and the coordinates of a point through which $f(x)$ passes. Take the given point, subtract 1.5 from the x-coordinate, and add 2.8 to the y-coordinate:

$$(-2.3, -1.2)$$
$$(-2.3 - 1.5, -1.2 + 2.8)$$
$$(-3.8, 1.6)$$

Choice (J) is correct. Be certain that you used the correct values given in the question.

7. B

Difficulty: Medium

Category: Functions

Getting to the Answer: The question asks which of the choices is equivalent to $\sqrt{a^2 + b^2}$ and gives you the equations for a and b. Plug in the given values and simplify. Remember the Pythagorean identity: $\cos^2\theta + \sin^2\theta = 1$.

$$\sqrt{a^2 + b^2} = \sqrt{(x\cos\theta)^2 + (x\sin\theta)^2}$$
$$= \sqrt{x^2\cos^2\theta + x^2\sin^2\theta}$$
$$= \sqrt{x^2(\cos^2\theta + \sin^2\theta)}$$
$$= \sqrt{x^2(1)}$$
$$= x$$

Choice (B) is correct. Be certain that you used all the given values; omitting the x term results in choice A.

8. F

Difficulty: Medium

Category: Functions

Getting to the Answer: The question asks for the value of nested functions when $x = \frac{1}{4}$ and provides the equations for both functions. Start by evaluating $g\left(\frac{1}{4}\right)$:

$$g\left(\frac{1}{4}\right) = \sqrt{\frac{1}{4}} + 2.5$$
$$= \frac{1}{2} + 2.5$$
$$= 3$$

Now evaluate $f(3)$:

$$f(3) = -4(3) + 1$$
$$= -12 + 1$$
$$= -11$$

Thus, (F) is correct. Be certain that you answered the question that was asked. Determining $g\left(f\left(\frac{1}{4}\right)\right)$ results in the value in J.

9. A

Difficulty: Medium

Category: Functions

Getting to the Answer: The question asks for the range of the function shown in the graph. Range refers to the maximum and minimum of the y-values of a function. Notice that the function never goes above 2 or below -2. Since the minimum value is -2 and the maximum value is 2, the range is all real numbers between -2 and 2, including those endpoints. Choice (A) is correct. Be certain that you found the range rather than the domain.

10. K

Difficulty: Medium

Category: Functions

Getting to the Answer: The question asks which trigonometric function could be shown on the graph. Notice that all the answer choices are of the form $\sin(x + k)$. Compare the parent function, $\sin(x)$, to the given graph and solve for the horizontal shift k.

Observe that the y-intercept of the graph is 1. Since the y-intercept occurs when $x = 0$, plug $x = 0$ into the equation $\sin(x + k) = 1$ and solve for k.

$$\sin(x + k) = 1$$
$$\sin(0 + k) = 1$$
$$\sin(k) = 1$$

Since $\sin\left(\frac{\pi}{2}\right) = 1$, you can conclude that $k = \frac{\pi}{2}$.

Therefore, (K) is correct.

CHAPTER 13

Geometry

LEARNING OBJECTIVES

After completing this chapter, you will be able to:

- Identify equal angles when two parallel lines are crossed by a transversal
- Identify supplementary and vertical angles and determine missing angle measures
- Determine an unknown angle measure in a polygon using line and angle properties
- Calculate the value of the third angle in a triangle given the other two angle measures
- Identify similar triangles and apply their properties
- Apply relationships between side lengths and angle measures in a triangle
- Calculate the length of the third side of a right triangle given the other two side lengths
- Given one side length of a 45–45–90 or 30–60–90 triangle, calculate the other two
- Calculate the area or perimeter of a polygon or complex figure
- Perform unit conversions
- Answer math questions about circles using relationships among angles, arcs, distances, and area
- Relate properties of a quadratic function to its graph and vice versa
- Identify and calculate measurements within a complex figure
- Transfer information among multiple figures
- Calculate the volume and surface area of common three-dimensional (3D) figures
- Apply basic trigonometric ratios and formulas to answer questions involving right triangles

Geometry: 11/36 SmartPoints® (Very high yield)

How Much Do You Know?

Directions: Try out the questions below. Show your work so that you can compare your solutions to the ones found on the next page. The "Category" heading in the explanation for each question gives the title of the lesson that covers how to solve it. If you answered the question(s) for a given lesson correctly, and if your scratchwork looks like the explanations, you may be able to move quickly through that lesson. If you answered incorrectly or used a different approach, you may want to take your time on that lesson.

1. In the figures shown, $\triangle ABC$ is similar to $\triangle DEF$. $\angle A$ corresponds to $\angle D$, $\angle B$ corresponds to $\angle E$, and $\angle C$ corresponds to $\angle F$. If the given lengths are of the same unit of measure, what is the value of x ?

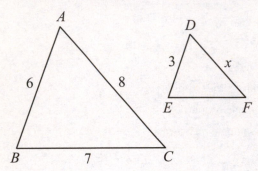

A. 3

B. 3.5

C. 4

D. 5

E. 6

2. What is the area, in square centimeters, of the polygon in the figure shown here?

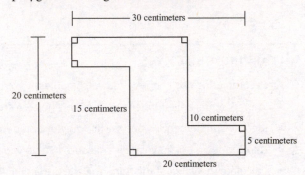

F. 100

G. 225

H. 300

J. 550

K. 600

3. In the following figure, O is the center of the circle, and the ratio of the area of sector $OABC$ to the area of sector $OCDA$ is 3 to 5. What is the value of x?

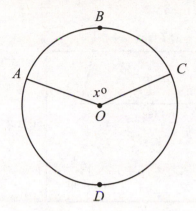

A. 120°

B. 135°

C. 144°

D. 150°

E. 216°

4. In the following figure, line t crosses parallel lines m and n. What is the degree measure of $\angle x$?

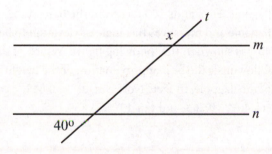

F. 40

G. 50

H. 60

J. 130

K. 140

5. In the figure shown, $ABCD$ is a square, and $\overline{AB}$ is a diameter of the circle centered at O. If $\overline{AD}$ is 10 units long, what is the area, in square units, of the shaded region?

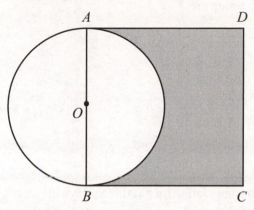

A. $100 - 50\pi$

B. $100 - 25\pi$

C. $100 - \dfrac{25}{2}\pi$

D. $100 - 10\pi$

E. $100 - \dfrac{5}{2}\pi$

6. If an isosceles right triangle has a hypotenuse of 4 inches, what is the perimeter, in inches, of the triangle?

F. $4\sqrt{2}$

G. $4 + 4\sqrt{2}$

H. $4 + 8\sqrt{2}$

J. 8

K. $8 + 4\sqrt{2}$

7. A certain rectangle is $(x + 3)$ units long and $(x + 7)$ units wide. If a square with sides of length x is removed from the interior of the rectangle, which of the following is an expression for the remaining area?

    A. 10

    B. 21

    C. $2x + 10$

    D. $10x + 21$

    E. $x^2 + 10x + 21$

8. A rectangular prism has three faces with areas of 28, 20, and 35 square centimeters. What is the volume of this solid in cubic centimeters?

    F. 83

    G. 140

    H. 166

    J. 196

    K. 19,600

9. Elizabeth plans to install artificial grass around the patio and fountain in her backyard as shown in the following figure. How many square feet of artificial grass does she need?

    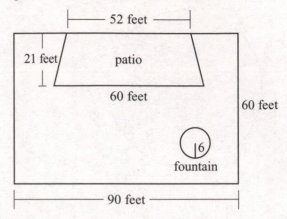

    A. $4140 - 6\pi$

    B. $4140 - 12\pi$

    C. $4140 - 36\pi$

    D. $4224 - 12\pi$

    E. $4224 - 36\pi$

10. Armando wants to determine the height of a flagpole. He stands 100 feet from the base of the flagpole and measures the angle of elevation to be $40°$, as shown in the following figure. Which of the following is the best approximation of the height of the flagpole, in feet? Note: $\sin 40° = 0.643$, $\cos 40° = 0.766$, and $\tan 40° = 0.839$.

    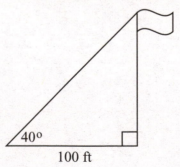

    F. 40

    G. 50

    H. 64

    J. 77

    K. 84

Check Your Work

1. C

Difficulty: Low

Category: Geometry: Triangle Properties

Getting to the Answer: You need to find the value of x. You are told that the triangles are similar and are given a figure with labeled side lengths. In similar triangles, corresponding sides are proportional. $\overline{DE}$ corresponds to $\overline{AB}$, and $\overline{DF}$ corresponds to $\overline{AC}$. Use this relationship to set up a proportion. Cross-multiply to solve for x.

$$\frac{\overline{AB}}{\overline{DE}} = \frac{\overline{AC}}{\overline{DF}}$$
$$\frac{6}{3} = \frac{8}{x}$$
$$6x = 3(8)$$
$$6x = 24$$
$$x = 4$$

You found the value of x, so you are done. Choice (C) is correct.

2. H

Difficulty: Medium

Category: Geometry: Complex Two-Dimensional Figures

Getting to the Answer: The area of the polygon can be found by dividing the polygon into two 5 cm × 20 cm rectangles and one 10 cm × 10 cm square. The area of the polygon is thus the sum of the areas of the rectangles and square: $2(5 \times 20) + (10 \times 10) = 300$ square centimeters. Choice (H) is correct.

Alternatively, the area of the polygon can be found by subtracting the two 10 cm × 15 cm rectangles from the larger 30 cm × 20 cm rectangle: $20 \times 30 - 2(10 \times 15) = 300$ square centimeters.

3. B

Difficulty: Medium

Category: Geometry: Circles and Parabolas

Getting to the Answer: You need to find the value of x. You are given a circle that is divided into two sectors. You are also given the ratio of the areas of the sectors: $\frac{OABC}{OCDA} = \frac{3}{5}$. Because the only angle measure you know is the whole circle (360°), you need to rewrite the given part-to-part ratio as a part-to-whole ratio:
$$\frac{OABC}{OABC + OCDA} = \frac{3}{3+5} = \frac{3}{8}.$$

Now use what you know about the parts of a circle: the ratio between the interior angle of a sector and 360° is the same as the ratio between the area of a sector and the area of the whole circle. This means that you can use the part-to-whole ratio from the areas to find the missing angle measure by setting up a proportion.

$$\frac{\text{area of sector}}{\text{area of circle}} = \frac{\text{central angle}}{360°}$$
$$\frac{3}{8} = \frac{x}{360°}$$
$$360(3) = 8x$$
$$1080 = 8x$$
$$135 = x$$

You found the value of x. Choice (B) is correct.

4. K

Difficulty: Low

Category: Geometry: Lines and Angles

Getting to the Answer: When a transversal crosses parallel lines, the four acute angles formed are all equal, the four obtuse angles formed are all equal, and any angles that are not equal are supplementary. The angle marked x is obtuse, so it is supplementary to the given 40° angle. Since $180 - 40 = 140$, the answer is (K).

5. C

Difficulty: Medium

Category: Geometry: Complex Two-Dimensional Figures

Getting to the Answer: You are looking for the area of the shaded region. You are given a figure and told that $\overline{AB}$ is a diameter of the circle and that $\overline{AD}$ (one side of the square) is 10 units long.

First, determine which area you are actually looking for. Describe it in words first, and then apply the correct formulas. Finally, fill in the dimensions given in the question stem. The side of the square is 10 units. The radius of the circle is half the diameter, or 5.

$$\text{shaded region} = \text{square} - \text{semicircle}$$

$$A_{shaded} = s^2 - \frac{1}{2}\pi r^2$$

$$A_{shaded} = 10^2 - \frac{1}{2}\pi (5)^2$$

$$= 100 - \frac{1}{2}(25\pi)$$

$$= 100 - \frac{25}{2}\pi$$

Stop! Look back at the answer choices before you waste time trying to simplify. You already have a match. Choice (C) is correct.

6. G

Difficulty: Medium

Category: Geometry: Right Triangles

Getting to the Answer: An isosceles right triangle is a 45-45-90 triangle, which has sides in the ratio $x:x:x\sqrt{2}$. If the hypotenuse has a length of 4 inches, then the sides are each $\frac{4}{\sqrt{2}}$ or $2\sqrt{2}$ inches long. This means that the perimeter of the triangle is $2\sqrt{2} + 2\sqrt{2} + 4 = 4 + 4\sqrt{2}$, which is (G).

7. D

Difficulty: Medium

Category: Geometry: Polygons

Getting to the Answer: If you have trouble keeping track of the variables, you can Pick Numbers. However, many students find it slightly faster to work with variables in a question like this.

Use FOIL to find that the rectangle has an area of $(x + 3)(x + 7) = x^2 + 10x + 21$. The square that is being removed has an area of x^2, so the area after removing the square is $x^2 + 10x + 21 - x^2 = 10x + 21$, which is (D).

8. G

Difficulty: High

Category: Geometry: Three-Dimensional Figures

Getting to the Answer: To answer this question, sketch an "unfolded" drawing of the solid and add dimensions to your sketch as you reason through the information provided in the question:

Opposite faces of a rectangular solid are congruent, so there are six faces with the corresponding areas shown above. Look for factors that will produce the given areas. These factors are the dimensions of the solid. Since $7 \times 4 = 28$, $7 \times 5 = 35$, and $4 \times 5 = 20$, the dimensions are 7 cm, 4 cm, and 5 cm. Finally, use the volume formula to arrive at the correct answer: $V = lwh = 7 \times 5 \times 4 = 140$ cubic centimeters, which is (G).

9.   E

Difficulty: High

Category: Geometry: Complex Two-Dimensional Figures

Getting to the Answer: To determine the amount of artificial grass Elizabeth needs, subtract the area of the patio and the area of the fountain from the total area of the backyard. The total area of the backyard is 60 ft $\times$ 90 ft = 5,400 ft^2. The patio is in the shape of a trapezoid, so its area is $\frac{1}{2}(b_1 + b_2)h = \frac{1}{2}(52 + 60)21 = 1,176$ square feet. The area of the fountain represented by a circle is $\pi r^2 = \pi 6^2 = 36\pi$ square feet. Thus, the amount of artificial grass Elizabeth needs is $5,400 - 1,176 - 36\pi = 4,224 - 36\pi$ square feet. Choice (E) is correct.

10. K

Difficulty: High

Category: Geometry: Triangles and Trigonometry

Getting to the Answer: Don't try to do questions like these in your head. Set up an equation that relates the thing you're looking for to the things that you know and then solve.

You know the angle of elevation and the distance from the base of the flagpole, and you're looking for the height of the flagpole. In other words, you know one angle and the length of the side adjacent to it, and you're looking for the length of the side opposite it. Which trig function describes the relationship between an angle and the opposite and adjacent sides? Tangent does: $\tan 40° = \frac{h}{100}$, where h is the height of the flagpole.

Therefore, $100 \tan 40° = h$. The question tells you that $\tan 40°$ is approximately 0.839, so h is approximately $100(0.839) = 83.9$. The best approximation of this is (K).

Lines and Angles

To answer a question like this:

Lines E, F, and G are parallel lines cut by transversal H as shown. What is the value of $a + b + c + d$?

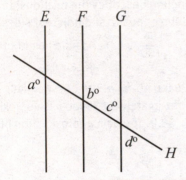

A. 180°

B. 270°

C. 360°

D. 540°

E. Cannot be determined from the given information

You need to know this:

Adjacent angles can be added to find the measure of a larger angle. The following diagram demonstrates this.

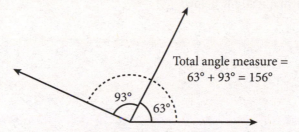

Two angles that sum to 90° are called **complementary angles**. Two angles that sum to 180° are called **supplementary angles**.

Two distinct lines in a plane will either intersect at one point or extend indefinitely without intersecting. If two lines intersect at a right angle (90°), they are **perpendicular** and are denoted with ⊥. If the lines never intersect, they are **parallel** and are denoted with ‖.

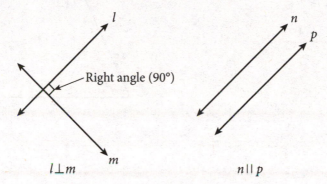

When a third line crosses two parallel lines, it creates two points of intersection and eight angles. This line is called a transversal. When a question involves parallel lines and one or more transversal lines, corresponding and supplementary angle relationships will help you identify missing angle measures.

You need to do this:

- If the question does not include an image, draw one.
- Label the figure.
- Look for line and angle relationships that will allow you to determine new information.
- Add more information to the figure(s) as needed to answer the question.

Explanation:

The question asks for the value of $a + b + c + d$. You are told that line H is a transversal through the parallel lines E, F, and G. There are no angle measures given, so you need to think about properties of parallel lines. The angles labeled a and b are obtuse angles; the angles labeled c and d are acute angles. Thus, angle a must be supplementary to angle d, and angle b must be supplementary to angle c. In other words, $a + d = 180$ and $b + c = 180$. Thus, $a + b + c + d = 180 + 180 = 360$. You found the sum of the four angle measures, so you are done. Choice (C) is correct.

Drills

If lines and angles give you trouble, study the information above and try out these drill questions before completing the Try on Your Own questions below.

Solve for the variable.

a.

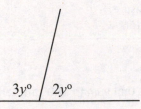

d.

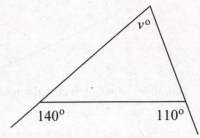

b.   For the following figure, lines *l* and *m* are parallel and lines *n* and *o* are parallel.

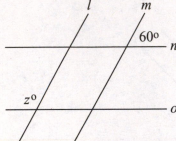

e.

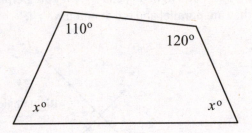

c.

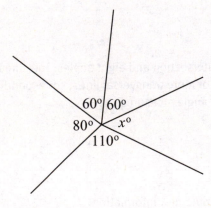

Try on Your Own

Directions: Take as much time as you need on these questions. Work carefully and methodically. There will be an opportunity for timed practice at the end of the chapter.

1. In the following figure, $\overline{CD}$ is parallel to $\overline{AB}$, and $\overline{PQ}$ intersects $\overline{CD}$ at R and $\overline{AB}$ at T. If the measure of $\angle CRP$ is 110°, what is the measure of $\angle ATQ$?

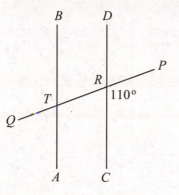

A. 30°

B. 50°

C. 70°

D. 90°

E. 110°

2. In the following figure, lines a and b are perpendicular, and line c passes through their point of intersection. What is the measure of y in terms of x ?

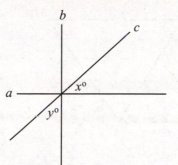

F. $x°$

G. $(45 + x)°$

H. $(90 - x)°$

J. $(90 + x)°$

K. $(180 - x)°$

Drill answers from previous page:

a. 36°   d. 70°

b. 120°   e. 65°

c. 50°

Math

3. What is the value of $b - c$ in the figure
    shown given the equalities listed here?
    $\overline{LM} = \overline{MN} = \overline{NO} = \overline{OL} = \overline{LN}$

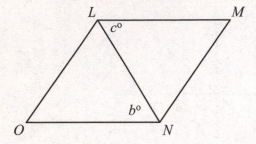

    A. $-30°$
    B. $-10°$
    C. $0°$
    D. $10°$
    E. $30°$

4. The following figure shows quadrilateral $ABCD$.
    The measure of $\angle B$ is $2x°$ and the measure of $\angle D$ is
    $3x°$. What is the measure of $\angle A$ in terms of x?

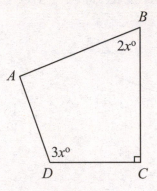

    F. $(90 + 5x)°$
    G. $(180 - 5x)°$
    H. $(180 + 5x)°$
    J. $(270 - 5x)°$
    K. $(270 - 5x)°$

5. In the following figure, $\angle ABC = 45°$ and
    $\angle CDE = 155°$. What is $\angle BCD$?

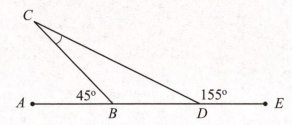

    A. $15°$
    B. $20°$
    C. $25°$
    D. $30°$
    E. $35°$

Triangle Properties

LEARNING OBJECTIVES

After this lesson, you will be able to:

- Calculate the value of the third angle in a triangle given the other two angle measures
- Identify similar triangles and apply their properties
- Apply relationships between side lengths and angle measures in a triangle

---

To answer a question like this:

In the following figure, K, L, N, and O lie on the same line. If $\overline{LM} = \overline{MN}$ and $\angle NOP$ and $\angle OPN$ are as marked, what is the measure of $\angle KLM$?

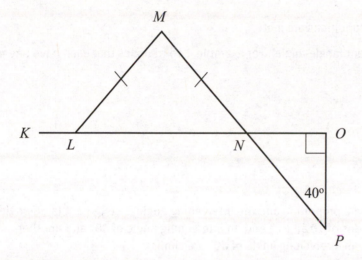

A. 125°

B. 130°

C. 135°

D. 140°

E. 150°

You need to know this:

The **interior angles** of a triangle sum to 180°. If you know any two interior angles, you can calculate the third.

The corresponding angles and side lengths of **congruent triangles** are equal. **Similar triangles** have the same angle measurements and proportional sides. In the figure below, △ABC and △DEF have the same angle measurements, so the side lengths can be set up as the following proportion: $\frac{A}{D} = \frac{B}{E} = \frac{C}{F}$.

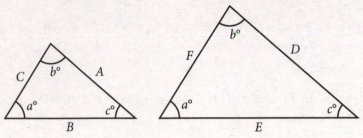

Two triangles are similar if three specific conditions are met:

- Two of their three angles are congruent (angle-angle). For example, two triangles that each have one 40° and one 55° angle are similar.

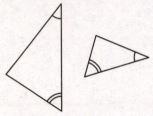

- Two of their three sides are in the same proportion and the intervening angle is congruent (side-angle-side). For example, a triangle with sides of 10 and 12 and an intervening angle of 40° and another triangle with sides of 20 and 24 and an intervening angle of 40° are similar.

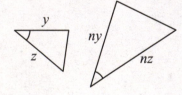

- Their three sides are in the same proportion (side-side-side). For example, a triangle with sides of 5, 6, and 8 and a triangle with sides 15, 18, and 24 are similar.

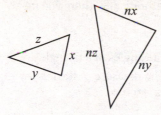

You need to do this:

- Use line and angle properties to determine missing triangle angle measures.
- Determine whether two triangles are similar by checking for angle-angle, side-angle-side, or side-side-side relationships.
- Find a missing side length by setting up a proportion.

Explanation:

You are trying to find $\angle KLM$, but you have very little information about this part of the figure. However, you do have a lot of information about $\triangle NOP$, so start there. Since there are 180 degrees in a triangle, $\angle ONP$ is $180° - 40° - 90° = 50°$. Angles ONP and MNL are vertical, so they are equal. Recall that angles that are opposite equal sides in a triangle are equal. Thus, $\angle MLN$ is also $50°$. Finally, since $\angle MLN$ and $\angle KLM$ lie on a straight line, they are supplementary. Thus, $\angle KLM = 180° - 50° = 130°$ and (B) is correct.

Try on Your Own

Directions: Take as much time as you need on these questions. Work carefully and methodically. There will be an opportunity for timed practice at the end of the chapter.

1. In the following figure, $\overline{DE}$ is parallel to $\overline{AC}$. If $\overline{DF} = \overline{DE} = \overline{FE}$, then what is the measure of $\angle DAB$?

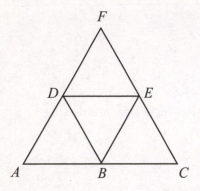

   A. 20°
   B. 30°
   C. 45°
   D. 60°
   E. 70°

2. In isosceles triangle ABC, $\overline{AB}$ and $\overline{BC}$ are congruent. If $m\angle CAB = 27°$, what is the measure of $\angle ABC$?

   F. 27°
   G. 54°
   H. 90°
   J. 126°
   K. 153°

3. If the measures of the angles of a triangle are in the ratio 2:3:7, what is the measure of the largest angle?

   A. 15°
   B. 30°
   C. 45°
   D. 84°
   E. 105°

4. In the figure shown, what is the length of the altitude that passes through vertex X in $\triangle YXZ$?

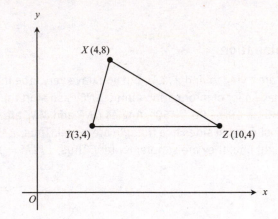

   F. $\sqrt{5}$
   G. 4
   H. $2\sqrt{5}$
   J. $2\sqrt{13}$
   K. 7

HINT: For Q5, how does the dotted line segment *d* help you
answer this question?

---

5. $\triangle PQR$ has side lengths *a*, *b*, and *c*, as shown in the
    following figure. A dotted line segment, *d*, origi-
    nates at point *P* and is perpendicular to $\overline{QR}$. What
    is the ratio of the length of *d* to the length of $\overline{PQ}$?

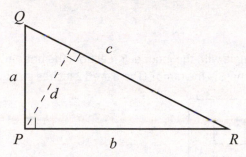

A. $\dfrac{a}{c}$

B. $\dfrac{b}{c}$

C. 1

D. $\dfrac{a}{b}$

E. $\dfrac{b}{a}$

Right Triangles

LEARNING OBJECTIVE

After this lesson, you will be able to:

• Calculate the length of the third side of a right triangle given the other two side lengths

• Given one side length of a 45–45–90 or 30–60–90 triangle, calculate the other two

To answer a question like this:

The ramp shown in the following figure is placed at a 30° angle with the ground, 8 feet from the bottom step in front of the building. Approximately how long, in inches, is the ramp? (There are 12 inches in 1 foot.)

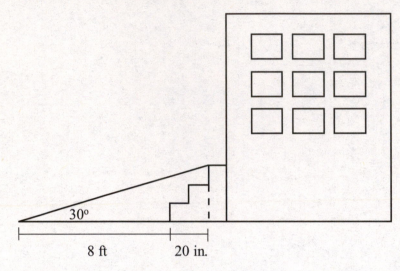

A.   67

B.   84

C. 116

D. 128

E. 134

You need to know this:

The Pythagorean theorem states that in any right triangle (and only in right triangles), the square of the hypotenuse (the longest side) is equal to the sum of the squares of the legs (the shorter sides). If you know the lengths of any two sides of a right triangle, you can use the Pythagorean equation, $a^2 + b^2 = c^2$, to find the length of the third. In this equation, a and b are the legs of the triangle and c is the hypotenuse, the side across from the right angle of the triangle.

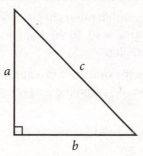

Consider an example: a right triangle has a leg of length 9 and a hypotenuse of length 14. To find the missing leg, plug the known values into the Pythagorean equation: $9^2 + b^2 = 14^2$. This simplifies to $81 + b^2 = 196$, which becomes $b^2 = 115$. Take the square root of both sides to find that $b = 115$.

Some right triangles have side lengths that are all integers. These sets of integer side lengths are called Pythagorean triples. The two most common Pythagorean triples on the ACT are 3-4-5 and 5-12-13. Look for multiples of these (for example, 6-8-10 and 10-24-26) as well. Memorizing these triples now can save you valuable calculation time on test day.

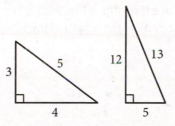

Special right triangles are defined by their angles. As a result, the ratios of their side lengths are always the same.

- If you know the length of any one of the three sides of a special right triangle, you can find the lengths of the other two.

- The ratio of the sides of a 45-45-90 triangle is $x:x:x\sqrt{2}$, where x is the length of each leg and $x\sqrt{2}$ is the length of the hypotenuse.

- The ratio of the sides of a 30-60-90 triangle is $x:x\sqrt{3}:2x$, where x is the shorter leg, $x\sqrt{3}$ is the longer leg, and $2x$ is the hypotenuse.

- These side length ratios are not provided to you on the ACT, so you should memorize them, especially if you are working to earn a top score.

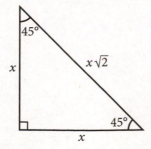
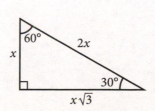

You need to do this:

- Keep in mind that the Pythagorean theorem applies only to right triangles.
- When you need to find a side length of a right triangle, look first for the common Pythagorean triples or their multiples.
- If you cannot identify any Pythagorean triples, substitute any two known side lengths into the equation $a^2 + b^2 = c^2$, where c represents the hypotenuse, to find the third.
- Look for hidden special right triangles within other shapes. For example, an equilateral triangle can be bisected (cut in half) to form two congruent 30-60-90 triangles, and a square can be divided with a diagonal into two congruent 45-45-90 triangles.
- Use one known side length to deduce the other two in a special right triangle. For example, if the shorter leg of a 30-60-90 triangle has a length of 5, then the longer leg has a length of $5\sqrt{3}$, and the hypotenuse has a length of $5(2) = 10$.

Explanation:

Two of the angles in the triangle have degree measures of 30 and 90, which means that the third angle must measure 60 degrees. Thus, you can use the properties of 30-60-90 triangles to help you. In a 30-60-90 triangle, the sides are always in the ratio $x:x\sqrt{3}:2x$ (short leg:long leg:hypotenuse). The only length that you know is the long leg, the side represented by the ground and the width of the bottom two steps. Convert feet into inches so that the units are the same. The ramp is to be placed 8 feet $\times \dfrac{12\text{ inches}}{1\text{ foot}} = 96$ inches from the bottom step, and the steps themselves account for an additional 20 inches. This means that this leg of the triangle is $96 + 20 = 116$ inches long. Use the ratio of the sides given above to set up a proportion to find the length of the hypotenuse, which corresponds to the length of the ramp, r.

$$\frac{\sqrt{3}}{2} = \frac{116}{r}$$
$$\sqrt{3}r = 232$$
$$r = 133.94$$

The result is approximately 134 inches, which matches (E).

Try on Your Own

Directions: Take as much time as you need on these questions. Work carefully and methodically. There will be an opportunity for timed practice at the end of the chapter.

1. The hypotenuse of $\triangle ABC$ is 20 meters and $\angle ABC$ is 30°. What is the length, in meters, of AB?

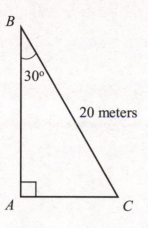

A. 10
B. $10\sqrt{2}$
C. $10\sqrt{3}$
D. 20
E. $20\sqrt{3}$

2. The diagonal measure of a square tile is 18 inches. What is the side length, in inches, of the tile?

F. $6\sqrt{3}$
G. 9
H. $9\sqrt{2}$
J. $9\sqrt{3}$
K. $18\sqrt{2}$

3. The longer leg of a right triangle is twice the length of the shorter leg. If the length of the shorter leg is 6 inches, what is the length, in inches, of the hypotenuse?

A. $3\sqrt{5}$
B. 12
C. $6\sqrt{5}$
D. $9\sqrt{2}$
E. 18

4. A playground slide is 10 feet long, and the base of the slide is 8 feet from the base of a ladder, as shown in the following figure. If the ladder is perpendicular to the ground, what is the height, in feet, of the ladder?

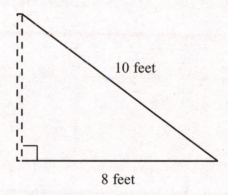

F. 3
G. 4
H. 5
J. 6
K. 7

HINT: There are two approaches you can take to answer Q5.
Which one is more efficient for you?

---

5.   What is the length, in units, of side *AB* in the following diagram?

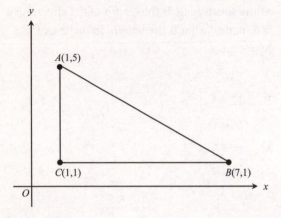

A. $\sqrt{13}$

B.   4

C.   6

D. $2\sqrt{13}$

E.   8

Polygons

LEARNING OBJECTIVES

After this lesson, you will be able to:

- Calculate the area or perimeter of a polygon or complex figure
- Perform unit conversions

To answer a question like this:

Jayden plans to order a rectangular rug for his dorm room. His roommate wants a rug that has a perimeter of 14 yards and covers an area of 12 square yards. What are the dimensions of the rug, in feet? (Note: 1 yard = 3 feet)

A. 3 by 36

B. 4 by 27

C. 6 by 18

D. 7 by 14

E. 9 by 12

You need to know this:

Perimeter and area are basic properties that all two-dimensional shapes have.

- The **perimeter** of a polygon can easily be calculated by adding the lengths of all its sides.
- **Area** is the amount of two-dimensional space a shape occupies.

Parallelograms are quadrilaterals with two pairs of parallel sides.

- Rectangles and squares are subsets of parallelograms.
- The area of a parallelogram is $A = bh$.
- Remember, base and height must be perpendicular when using geometric formulas.

A **trapezoid** is a quadrilateral with only one set of parallel sides.

- Those parallel sides form the two bases.
- To find the area, average those bases and multiply by the height.

Unit Conversion

You can set up a proportion to perform unit conversions. This is especially useful when there are multiple conversions or when the units are unfamiliar. On the ACT, you may see unit conversion involve scale factors related to maps or blueprints.

For example, though these units of measurement are no longer commonly used, there are 8 furlongs in a mile and 3 miles in a league. Say you're asked to convert 4 leagues to furlongs. A convenient way to do this is to set up a proportion so that equivalent units cancel:

$$4 \text{ leagues} \times \frac{3 \text{ miles}}{1 \text{ league}} \times \frac{8 \text{ furlongs}}{1 \text{ mile}} = 4 \times 3 \times 8 = 96 \text{ furlongs}$$

Notice that all the units cancel out except the furlongs, which is the unit you want.

You need to do this:

- If a figure is not provided as part of the question, draw one.
- Label the figure with given information.
- Use angle and line properties to determine missing values, such as base or height.
- Double-check the units in the question and the units in the choices to plan for any necessary unit conversion.
- When unit conversion is necessary, set up a proportion to make equivalent units cancel.
  - Keep track of the units by writing them down next to the numbers in the proportion.
  - You should be left with the units you're converting into.

Explanation:

You can approach this question by setting up a system of equations using the formulas for the area and perimeter of a rectangle. The area is $l \times w$, and the perimeter is $l + l + w + w$ or $2l + 2w$.

$$l \times w = 12$$
$$2l + 2w = 14$$

Solve the second equation for l: $l = 7 - w$. Then substitute it into the first equation to solve for w:

$$(7 - w)w = 12$$
$$7w - w^2 = 12$$
$$0 = w^2 - 7w + 12$$
$$0 = (w - 3)(w - 4)$$
$$3 \text{ and } 4 = w$$

Thus, $l = 4$ and 3, respectively. Finally, use the 1 yard = 3 feet conversion factor to convert 3 and 4 yards into feet:

$$3 \text{ yards} \times \frac{3 \text{ feet}}{1 \text{ yard}} = 9 \text{ feet}$$

and

$$4 \text{ yards} \times \frac{3 \text{ feet}}{1 \text{ yard}} = 12 \text{ feet}$$

Choice (E) is correct.

Alternatively, you could Backsolve. All of the choices except D yield an area of

length (feet) × width (feet) = area (square feet) = 108 ft^2, and 108 ft$^2 \times \frac{1 \text{ yd}}{3 \text{ ft}} \times \frac{1 \text{ yd}}{3 \text{ ft}} = 12$ yd^2, so D is

incorrect. The perimeters in choices A, B, and C are larger than 14 yards $\times \frac{3 \text{ feet}}{1 \text{ yard}} = 42$ feet. Only (E) works.

Drills

If polygons and unit conversion gives you trouble, study the information above and try out these drill questions before completing the Try on Your Own questions below. Drill answers can be found on the bottom of the next page.

Solve the following.

a.   What is the perimeter?

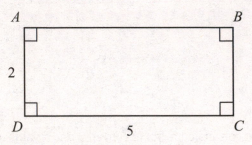

b.   If the perimeter is 48, $x = $?

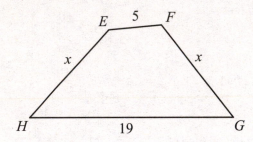

c.   What is the area?

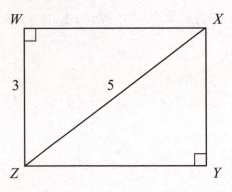

d.   What is the area?

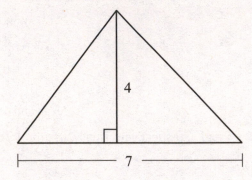

e.   What is the area?

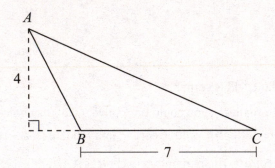

Try on Your Own

Directions: Take as much time as you need on these questions. Work carefully and methodically. There will be an opportunity for timed practice at the end of the chapter.

1. Triangle *PQR* has a base of 16 centimeters and an altitude of 10 centimeters. If the area of square *ABCD* is twice the area of △*PQR*, what is the length, in centimeters, of a side of the square *ABCD*?

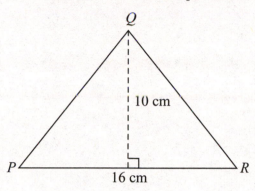

    A. 4
    B. $4\sqrt{5}$
    C. $4\sqrt{10}$
    D. $8\sqrt{5}$
    E. 8

2. As shown in the following figure , points $(-2,2)$, $(4,2)$, $(0,5)$, and $(6,5)$ are the vertices of a parallelogram. What is the area, in square units, of the parallelogram?

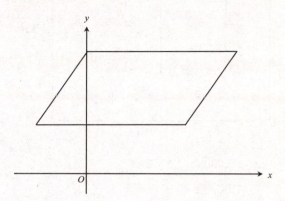

    F. 12
    G. 18
    H. $6\sqrt{13}$
    J. 24
    K. 30

Drill answers from previous page:

a. 14   d. 14

b. 12   e. 14

c. 12

HINT: For Q3, how can you calculate the
missing side lengths?

---

3. In the polygon shown, all angles are right angles.
    What is the perimeter, in centimeters?

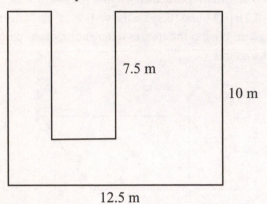

7.5 m

10 m

12.5 m

A. 3,000
B. 4,500
C. 6,000
D. 9,700
E. 12,500

4. In the figure shown, $\overline{BE}$ is perpendicular to $\overline{AD}$,
    and the lengths of $\overline{AB}$, $\overline{BC}$, $\overline{CD}$, and $\overline{BE}$ are given
    in inches. What is the area, in square inches, of
    trapezoid $ABCD$?

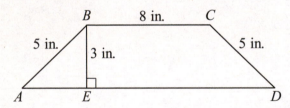

B   8 in.   C

5 in.

3 in.   5 in.

A   E   D

F. 24
G. 30
H. 32
J. 34
K. 36

5. For the area of a square to triple, the new side
    lengths must be the old side lengths multiplied by
    which of the following?

A. $\sqrt{3}$
B. 3
C. 9
D. $\sqrt{27}$
E. 27

Circles and Parabolas

LEARNING OBJECTIVES

After this lesson, you will be able to:

- Answer math questions about circles using relationships among angles, arcs, distances, and area
- Relate properties of a quadratic function to its graph and vice versa

To answer a question like this:

A circle centered at (2,2) has a radius of 5. A parabola on the same coordinate plane has a vertex at (0,3) and passes through (−2,7). At how many points do the circle and parabola intersect?

A. 0

B. 1

C. 2

D. 3

E. 4

You need to know this:

On the ACT, you might see a question with a system of equations that involves one parabola and one circle. This system is usually solved using a coordinate plane. Use the information in the following sections to graph and interpret circles and parabolas.

Circles

The equation of a circle in the coordinate plane is as follows:

$$(x - h)^2 + (y - k)^2 = r^2$$

In this equation, called **standard form**, r is the radius of the circle, and h and k are the x- and y-coordinates of the circle's center, respectively: (h,k).

You might also see what is referred to as **general form**:

$$x^2 + y^2 + Cx + Dy + E = 0$$

In the general form, the fact that there are x^2 and y^2 terms with coefficients of 1 is an indicator that the equation does indeed graph as a circle. To convert to standard form, complete the square for the x terms, then repeat for the y terms. Refer to chapter 10 for a quadratics review if needed.

The ACT may also ask you about the following parts of circles: arcs, central angles, and sectors. The ability to set up ratios and proportions correctly is essential for these questions. Review chapter 9 for more information on rates, ratios, proportions, and percents.

- An **arc** is part of a circle's circumference. If the circumference is divided into exactly two arcs, the smaller one is called the minor arc, and the larger one is called the major arc. If a diameter cuts the circle in half, the two arcs formed are called semicircles. An arc length can never be greater than the circle's circumference.

- An angle formed by two radii is called a **central angle**. Because a full circle contains 360°, a central angle measure cannot be greater than this.

- The part of a circle's area defined by a central angle is called a **sector**. The area of a sector cannot be greater than the circle's total area.

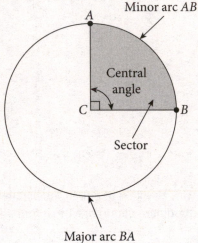

Minor arc *AB*

Central angle

Sector

Major arc *BA*

Here's a summary of the ratios formed by these three parts and their whole counterparts:

$$\frac{\text{central angle}}{360°} = \frac{\text{arc length}}{\text{circumference}} = \frac{\text{sector area}}{\text{circle area}}$$

Notice that all of these ratios are equal. Intuitively, this should make sense: when you slice a pizza into four equal slices, each piece should have $\frac{1}{4}$ of the cheese, crust, and sauce. If you slice a circle into four equal pieces, the same principle applies: each piece should have $\frac{1}{4}$ of the degrees, circumference, and area.

Parabolas

As defined in the Functions chapter, a quadratic function is a quadratic equation set equal to y or $f(x)$ instead of 0.

- Remember that the solutions (also called "roots" or "zeros") of any polynomial function are the same as the x-intercepts.
- To solve a quadratic function, substitute 0 for y, or $f(x)$, then solve algebraically.
- Alternatively, you can plug the equation into your graphing calculator and read the x-intercepts from the graph.

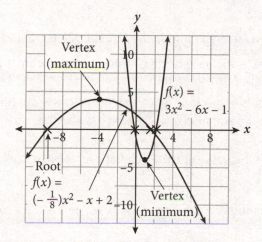

The graph of every quadratic equation (or function) is a **parabola**, which is a symmetric U-shaped graph that opens either upward or downward.

- To determine which way a parabola will open, examine the value of a in the equation.
- If a is positive, the parabola will open upward.
- If a is negative, it will open downward.
- Take a look at the examples above to see this graphically.

Like quadratic equations, quadratic functions will have zero, one, or two real solutions, corresponding to the number of times the parabola crosses the x-axis. Graphing is a powerful way to determine the number of solutions a quadratic function has:

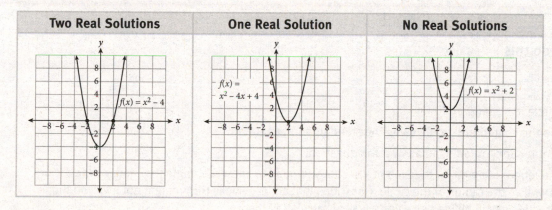

There are three algebraic forms that a quadratic equation can take: standard, factored, and vertex. Each is provided in the following table along with the graphical features that are revealed by writing the equation in that particular form:

Standard	Factored	Vertex
$y = ax^2 + bx + c$	$y = a(x - m)(x - n)$	$y = a(x - h)^2 + k$
y-intercept is c	Solutions are m and n	Vertex is (h,k)
In real-world contexts, starting quantity is c	x-intercepts are m and n	Minimum/maximum of function is k
Format needed to solve via quadratic formula	Vertex is halfway between m and n	Axis of symmetry is given by $x = h$

You've already seen standard and factored forms in the Algebra chapter, but vertex form might be new to you.

- In vertex form, a is the same as the a in standard form, and h and k are the coordinates of the **vertex** (h,k).
- If a quadratic function is not in vertex form, you can still find the x-coordinate of the vertex by plugging the appropriate values into the equation $h = \frac{-b}{2a}$, which is also the equation for the axis of symmetry (see graph that follows).
- Once you determine h, plug this value into the quadratic function and solve for y to determine k, the y-coordinate of the vertex.

The equation of the **axis of symmetry** of a parabola is $x = h$, where h is the x-coordinate of the vertex.

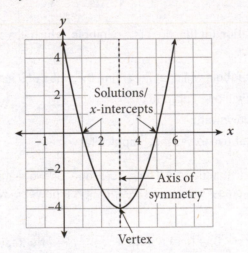

You need to do this:

Circles

- Get the circle into standard form.
- Determine the center and radius using the standard form equation.
- Use the center and/or radius to answer the question.
- To find the length of an arc or the area of a sector, you need to know the angle that defines the arc or sector as well as the radius of the circle. Questions that are especially tricky might not give you those values directly but will instead give you a way of calculating them.

Parabolas

- To find the vertex of a parabola, get the function into vertex form: $y = a(x - h)^2 + k$, or use the formula $h = \frac{-b}{2a}$.
- To find the y-intercept of a quadratic function, plug in 0 for x.
- To determine whether a parabola opens upward or downward, look at the coefficient of a.
  - If a is positive, it opens upward.
  - If a is negative, it opens downward.
- To determine the number of x-intercepts, set the quadratic function equal to 0 and solve or examine its graph.

To answer a question involving a system of equations with a parabola and a circle, take it one figure at a time until you find the point(s) of intersection and/or gather the information you need to answer the question.

Explanation:

Sketch the circle and parabola to visualize the situation and make the question easier to answer. Since the circle is centered at $(2,2)$ and has a radius of 5, the vertex of the parabola $(0,3)$ lies within the circle. Since the parabola passes through $(-2,7)$, it opens upward and intersects the circle at two distinct points:

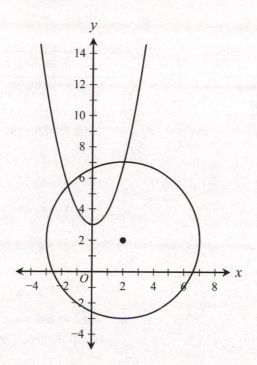

Choice (C) is correct.

Try on Your Own

Directions: Take as much time as you need on these questions. Work carefully and methodically. There will be an opportunity for timed practice at the end of the chapter.

1. What is the area, in square inches, of a circle that has a circumference of 8π inches?

    A. 4π
    B. 8π
    C. 16π
    D. 32π
    E. 64π

2. The two circles shown are tangent to each other. The radius of the larger circle is 75% greater than that of the smaller circle. What is the area, in square feet, of the shaded region?

    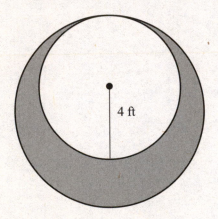

    4 ft

    F. 6π
    G. 9π
    H. 10π
    J. 16π
    K. 33π

HINT: What information in the question stem for Q3 is useful in determining the correct answer?

---

3. Earth makes one complete rotation about its axis every 24 hours, at a fairly constant rate. Assuming the Earth is a perfect sphere, through how many degrees would Quito, Ecuador, which lies on the Earth's equator, rotate from 12:00 noon on January 1 to 3:00 p.m. on January 2 ?

    A. $340°$
    B. $370°$
    C. $385°$
    D. $405°$
    E. $415°$

HINT: For Q4, what does the distance of 5 represent?

---

4. Which of the following equations describes the set of all points (x,y) in the coordinate plane that are a distance of 5 units from the point $(-3,4)$?

    F. $(x+3) + (y-4) = 5$
    G. $(x-3) + (y+4) = 5$
    H. $(x+3)^2 + (y-4)^2 = 5$
    J. $(x+3)^2 + (y-4)^2 = 25$
    K. $(x-3)^2 + (y+4)^2 = 25$

5. If the equation for a parabola is $y = (x+3)^2 - 1$, which of the following best describes the solutions for x ?

    A.   2 distinct negative real solutions
    B.   2 distinct positive real solutions
    C.   1 positive real solution and 1 negative real solution
    D.   2 real solutions that are not distinct
    E.   2 distinct solutions that are not real

Complex Two-Dimensional Figures

LEARNING OBJECTIVES

After this lesson, you will be able to:

- Identify and calculate measurements within a complex figure
- Transfer information among multiple figures

To answer a question like this:

The following figure shows a rectangular basketball court that is symmetric about the mid-court line (the vertical line with a shaded circle located in the middle of the figure). The shaded area is approximately what percent of the full court?

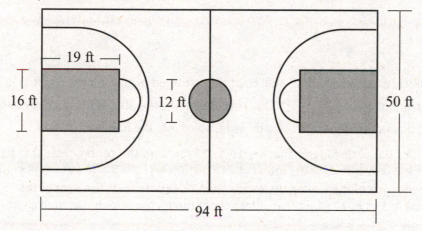

A. 13.7

B. 15.3

C. 22.6

D. 37.4

E. 61.7

You need to know this:

Some ACT math questions will combine multiple 2D figures, especially quadrilaterals, circles, and triangles.

- These questions can involve multiple formulas or steps.
- They can require other math skills, such as percent calculations.

You need to do this:

- If a figure is not provided as part of the question, draw one.
- Label the figure with the given information.
- Use angle and line properties to determine missing values, such as base or height.
- Share information among figures when permissible.
- Double-check the units in the question and the units in the choices to plan for any necessary unit conversion.
- When unit conversion is necessary, set up a proportion to make equivalent units cancel.
- Pause for an extra moment before selecting your answer to confirm you really did answer the right question.
- Look out for other math skills needed to answer these questions.

Explanation:

You are asked to find approximately what percent of the full court is constituted by the shaded regions. To do so, you need to use the percent formula, $\% = \frac{\text{part}}{\text{whole}} \times 100\%$. First, determine the area of the shaded regions. Next, find the area of the full basketball court. Finally, plug these numbers into the formula.

The shaded areas include the two equal rectangles that are 16 by 19 feet and the center circle that has a diameter of 12 feet. Use $2 \times l \times w$ to calculate the area of the 2 rectangles: $2 \times 16 \times 19 = 608$ square feet. Use $A = \pi r^2$ to calculate the area of the center circle: $\pi(6)^2 \approx 113$ square feet. The sum of the areas is thus approximately $608 + 113 = 721$ feet. The total area of the rectangular basketball court is $50 \times 94 = 4{,}700$ square feet.

Now plug these numbers into the $\% = \frac{\text{part}}{\text{whole}} \times 100\%$ formula to calculate approximately what percent the shaded region is of the full court: $\frac{721}{4700} \times 100\% = 15.3\%$. Choice (B) is correct.

Try on Your Own

Directions: Take as much time as you need on these questions. Work carefully and methodically. There will be an opportunity for timed practice at the end of the chapter.

1. Lorenzo is deciding between two examination room layouts for his new clinic. The cross-sectional area of each square chair is 2 square feet, and the cross-sectional areas of the circle chair and exam table are π and 4.9 square feet, respectively. What is the difference in the areas, in square feet, of the shaded portion between the two layouts?

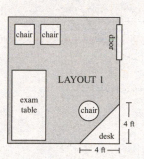
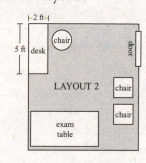

A. 2

B. 4

C. 6

D. 8

E. 10

2. The following figure shows a scale drawing of the table layout for Yan's upcoming graduation party ($\frac{3}{4}$ inch = 9 feet). What is the area, in square inches, of each table in the scale drawing?

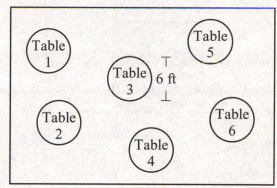

F. $\frac{1}{16}\pi$

G. $\frac{1}{4}\pi$

H. $\frac{4}{9}\pi$

J. $\frac{1}{2}\pi$

K. 2π

3. A circle with radius 5 is inscribed in a square. What is the difference between the area of the square and the area of the circle?

A. 25π

B. 50π

C. $50 - 25\pi$

D. $100 - 25\pi$

E. 100

4. In the figure shown, the shaded region is a square with an area of 12 square units, inscribed inside equilateral triangle *ABC*. What is the perimeter of △*ABC* ?

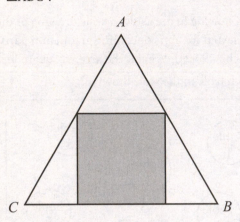

F. $18\sqrt{3}$

G. $4 + \sqrt{3}$

H. $4 + 6\sqrt{3}$

J. $8 + 6\sqrt{3}$

K. $12 + 6\sqrt{3}$

HINT: For Q5, what additional line segments can you add to the figure to help you get closer to determining the distance between $\overline{YZ}$ and $\overline{WX}$?

---

5. The semicircle shown has a radius of *r* inches, and chord $\overline{YZ}$ is parallel to diameter $\overline{WX}$. If the length of $\overline{YZ}$ is 25% shorter than the length of $\overline{WX}$, what is the shortest distance between $\overline{YZ}$ and $\overline{WX}$ in terms of *r* ?

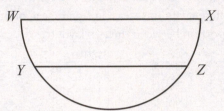

Note: Figure not drawn to scale

A. $\frac{1}{4}\pi r$

B. $\frac{3}{4}\pi r$

C. $\frac{5}{4}\pi r$

D. $\frac{\sqrt{2}}{4}r$

E. $\frac{\sqrt{7}}{4}r$

Three-Dimensional Figures

To answer a question like this:

A rectangular box with an open top is constructed from cardboard to have a square base of area x^2 and height h. If the volume of this box is 50 cubic units, how many square units of cardboard, in terms of x, are needed to build the box?

A. $5x^2$

B. $6x^2$

C. $\dfrac{200}{x} + x^2$

D. $\dfrac{200}{x} + 2x^2$

E. $\dfrac{250}{x} + 2x^2$

You need to know this:

Three-dimensional (3D) shapes are also called solids. There are several different types of solids that might appear on test day—rectangular solids, cubes, cylinders, prisms, spheres, cones, and pyramids—and knowing their structures will help you on test day.

The following diagram shows the basic anatomy of a 3D shape:

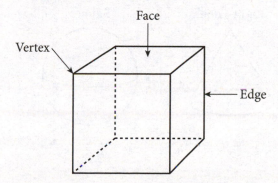

A **face** (or **surface**) is a two-dimensional (2D) shape that acts as one of the sides of the solid. Two faces meet at a line segment called an **edge**, and three faces meet at a single point called a **vertex**.

Volume

Volume is the amount of 3D space occupied by a solid. Volume is analogous to the area of a 2D shape. You can find the volume of many 3D shapes by finding the area of the base and multiplying it by the height: ($V = A_{base} \times h$). In the table of formulas, the pieces that represent the areas of the bases are enclosed in parentheses.

Rectangular Solid	Cube	Right Cylinder
$V = (l \times w) \times h$	$V = (s \times s) \times s = s^3$	$V = (\pi \times r^2) \times h$

These three 3D shapes are **prisms**. Almost all prisms on the ACT are right prisms; that is, all faces are perpendicular to those with which they share edges. You might see less common prisms, such as a triangular or a hexagonal prism, but don't worry: the volume of any right prism can be calculated by finding the area of the base and multiplying it by the height.

When you are not explicitly given the area of the base of a prism, you'll need to rely on your two-dimensional geometry knowledge to find it before calculating the volume of the prism.

More complicated 3D shapes include the right pyramid, right cone, and sphere. The vertex of a right pyramid or right cone will always be centered above the middle of the base. Their volume formulas are similar to those of prisms, albeit with different coefficients.

Some of these formulas might look daunting, but you won't have to memorize them for test day; they'll be provided in the question stem if they are needed.

Right Rectangular Pyramid	Right Cone	Sphere
$V = \frac{1}{3} \times (l \times w) \times h$	$V = \frac{1}{3} \times \left(\pi \times r^2\right) \times h$	$V = \frac{4}{3} \times \pi \times r^3$

A right pyramid can have any polygon as its base, but the square variety is the one you're most likely to see on the ACT. Also note that the vertex above the base of a right pyramid or cone is not necessarily formed by an intersection of exactly three faces, as in prisms, but it is still a single point and is still called a vertex.

Surface Area

Surface area is the sum of the areas of all faces of a solid. To calculate the surface area of a solid, simply find the area of each face using your 2D geometry skills, then add them all together.

You won't be expected to know the surface area formulas for right pyramids, right cones, and spheres. They'll be provided at the beginning of each Math section. However, you could be asked to find the surface area of a prism, in which case you'll be given enough information to find the area of each surface of the solid.

You might think that finding the surface area of a solid with many sides, such as a right hexagonal prism, is a tall order. However, you can save time by noticing a vital trait: this prism has two identical hexagonal faces and six identical rectangular faces. Don't waste time finding the area of each of the eight surfaces. Find the area of one hexagonal face and one rectangular face only. Then multiply the area of the hexagonal face by 2 and the area of the rectangular face by 6, add the products together, and you're done. The same is true for other 3D shapes such as rectangular solids (including cubes), other right prisms, and certain pyramids.

You need to do this:

- To answer questions that involve regular solids, look for ways to find the area of the base and the height.
- To answer questions that involve solids that are not regular, look up and apply the appropriate formula.
- To answer questions that involve surface area, look for surfaces that are the same. Calculate the area of each kind of surface once, and then multiply by the number of identical surfaces in the solid.

Explanation:

Use the given volume, 50, to get h in terms of x:

$$\text{volume} = \text{length} \times \text{width} \times \text{height}$$

$$50 = x^2 h$$

$$\frac{50}{x^2} = h$$

Since the box has an open top, the area you're looking for is equal to four lateral faces and one bottom face.

Each lateral face has area $xh = x\left(\dfrac{50}{x^2}\right) = \dfrac{50}{x}$ square units, and the base has area x^2 square units. Thus, the total area you're looking for is:

$$4\left(\frac{50}{x}\right) + x^2 = \frac{200}{x} + x^2$$

Choice (C) is correct.

Try on Your Own

Directions: Take as much time as you need on these questions. Work carefully and methodically. There will be an opportunity for timed practice at the end of the chapter.

1. In the figure that follows, a wooden plank is shown with its dimensions in inches. If Hawanatu wants to spray-paint every surface of the plank, how much paint, in square inches, will Hawanatu need?

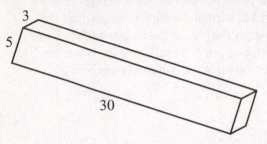

A. 38
B. 76
C. 240
D. 450
E. 510

HINT: How can the fact that the figure in Q2 is half of a cube help you determine the answer more efficiently?

---

2. If the solid shown is half of a cube that has been cut in half along the diagonal, from one edge to the opposite edge, what is its volume?

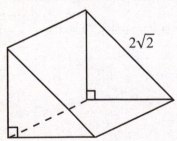

2√2

F. 4
G. 4√2
H. 8
J. 8√2
K. 12

3. What is the volume, in cubic inches, of the cylinder shown?

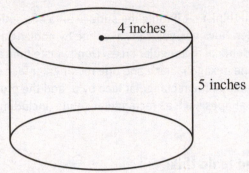

4 inches

5 inches

A. 20π
B. 40π
C. 60π
D. 80π
E. 100π

HINT: For Q4, which surfaces will you actually be covering with wrapping paper?

4. Mali bought several right cylindrical candles as party favors and plans to wrap them such that the gift paper wraps around the candle exactly once with no overlap. She wants to leave an extra 3 inches of wrapping paper past each end of the candles so she can tie both ends with a bit of ribbon. If each candle has a diameter of 4 inches and is 8 inches tall, how many square inches of wrapping paper will Mali need to wrap one candle?

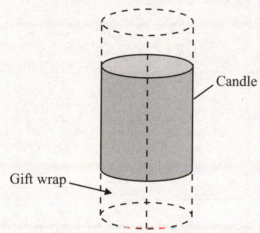

Candle

Gift wrap

F. 32π
G. 40π
H. 44π
J. 56π
K. 64π

5. Noelle submerges a figurine into a tank of water to determine the volume of the figurine. The tank is 10 inches by 13 inches, and the water is filled to a depth of 5 inches. If the water level rises 0.4 inches when the figurine is submerged, what is the volume, in cubic inches, of the object?

A. 4
B. 52
C. 130
D. 650
E. 702

Math

Triangles and Trigonometry

LEARNING OBJECTIVE

After this lesson, you will be able to:

● Apply basic trigonometric ratios and formulas to answer questions involving right triangles

To answer a question like this:

In the following figure, a surfboard is propped up against a rectangular box. If the board is 7 feet long, which of the following is closest to the height, in feet, of the box?

(Note: sin 23° ≈ 0.3907, cos 23° ≈ 0.9205, tan 23° ≈ 0.4245)

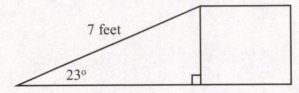

A. 2.7

B. 3.0

C. 4.3

D. 5.6

E. 6.4

You need to know this:

The ACT tests three trigonometric functions: **sine, cosine**, and **tangent**.

- All three are simply the ratios of side lengths within a right triangle.
- The notation for sine, cosine, and tangent functions always includes a reference angle; for example, cos x or cos θ. That's because you'll need to refer to the given angle within a right triangle to determine the appropriate side ratios.

There is a common mnemonic device for the sine, cosine, and tangent ratios: SOHCAHTOA (commonly pronounced: sew-kuh-TOE-uh). Here's what it represents:

- **S**ine is **O**pposite over **H**ypotenuse
- **C**osine is **A**djacent over **H**ypotenuse
- **T**angent is **O**pposite over **A**djacent.

See the triangle and the table below for a summary of the ratios and what each equals for $\angle A$ in $\triangle CAB$:

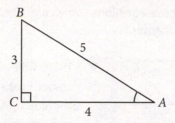

Sine (sin)	Cosine (cos)	Tangent (tan)
$\dfrac{\text{opposite}}{\text{hypotenuse}}$	$\dfrac{\text{adjacent}}{\text{hypotenuse}}$	$\dfrac{\text{opposite}}{\text{adjacent}}$
$\dfrac{3}{5}$	$\dfrac{4}{5}$	$\dfrac{3}{4}$

Complementary angles have a special relationship relative to sine and cosine:

- $\sin x° = \cos(90° - x°)$
- $\cos x° = \sin(90° - x°)$
- In other words, the sine of an acute angle is equal to the cosine of the angle's complement and vice versa. For example, $\cos 30° = \sin 60°$, $\cos 45° = \sin 45°$, and $\cos 60° = \sin 30°$.

You need to do this:

Apply the appropriate trigonometric ratio to a right triangle, or use the relationship between the sine and cosine of complementary angles.

Explanation:

You need to find the height of the box. You are given a figure that includes a right triangle and an angle measure, as well as the length of the surfboard. You are also given three trig values, which you may or may not need. Let x equal the height of the triangle (which is also the height of the box). Now, look at the triangle. You know the length of the hypotenuse, and you're looking for the side opposite the given angle. This tells you which trig function to use: $\sin x = \dfrac{\text{opp}}{\text{hyp}}$. The question states that $\sin 23° \approx 0.3907$. Use this information to solve for x:

$$\sin 23° = \frac{x}{7}$$
$$0.3907 = \frac{x}{7}$$
$$0.3907 \times 7 = x$$
$$2.7349 = x$$

The height of the box is approximately 2.7 feet, so choice (A) is correct.

Try on Your Own

Directions: Take as much time as you need on these questions. Work carefully and methodically. There will be an opportunity for timed practice at the end of the chapter.

HINT: The unit circle will help you answer Q1, a high-difficulty question, more confidently.

---

1. If $0 \leq \theta \leq \pi$, what are the values of θ when $\sin\theta = \frac{1}{2}$?

    A. $\frac{\pi}{6}$ and $\frac{2\pi}{3}$

    B. $\frac{\pi}{6}$ and $\frac{5\pi}{6}$

    C. $\frac{\pi}{4}$ and $\frac{3\pi}{4}$

    D. $\frac{\pi}{3}$ and $\frac{4\pi}{3}$

    E. $\frac{7\pi}{6}$ and $\frac{11\pi}{6}$

2. In a right triangle with angle measure β, $\cos\beta = \frac{36}{39}$ and $\sin\beta = \frac{15}{39}$. What is the value of $\tan\beta$?

    F. $\frac{15}{36}$

    G. $\frac{36}{15}$

    H. $\frac{39}{36}$

    J. $\frac{39}{15}$

    K. Cannot be determined from the given information

3. In the following figure, $\triangle ABC$ has an area of 60 square centimeters. If $\angle ABC$ is reduced to $45°$ and the length of $\overline{AC}$ is shortened accordingly, what is the new area, in square centimeters, of $\triangle ABC$? (Note: The area of a triangle is $\frac{1}{2}ab\sin x$, where a and b are the lengths of the sides and x is the angle between them.)

    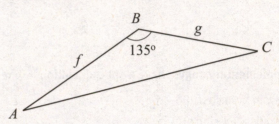

    A. 20

    B. 30

    C. 40

    D. 50

    E. 60

4. Eric is a glass collector. The following figure is one of the triangular glass fragments that Eric collected. Which of the following expressions is the value of z? (Note: The law of sines states that for a triangle with sides of lengths a, b, and c and opposite angles of measure A, B, and C, respectively, $\frac{\sin A}{a} = \frac{\sin B}{b} = \frac{\sin C}{c}$).

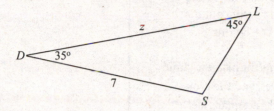

F. $\dfrac{7\sin 35°}{\sin 45°}$

G. $\dfrac{7\sin 35°}{\sin 100°}$

H. $\dfrac{7\sin 45°}{\sin 100°}$

J. $\dfrac{7\sin 100°}{\sin 35°}$

K. $\dfrac{7\sin 100°}{\sin 45°}$

HINT: Q5 looks complicated, but the question stem gives you the formulas you need to answer the question correctly.

5. Triangle EFG is shown in the following figure. What is the length, in inches, of $\overline{FG}$? (Note: For a triangle with side lengths a, b, and c and opposite angles A, B and C, respectively, $\frac{\sin A}{a} = \frac{\sin B}{b} = \frac{\sin C}{c}$, and $c^2 = a^2 + b^2 - 2ab \cos C$.)

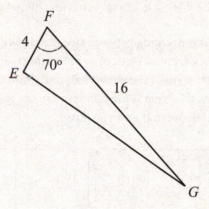

A. $4 \sin 70°$

B. $16 \sin 70°$

C. $\sqrt{16^2 - 4^2 - 2(16)(4)\cos 70°}$

D. $\sqrt{16^2 + 4^2 - 2(16)(4)\cos 70°}$

E. $\sqrt{16^2 + 4^2 + 2(16)(4)\cos 70°}$

Math

Math

On Test Day

Occasionally, a question will give you more information than you need to determine the correct answer. Think about what information you really need to arrive at the answer before you begin your calculations so that you don't get sidetracked and spend time doing unnecessary work.

As you read through this question from earlier in this chapter, plan your strategy to get the correct value and identify what information you need to carry out that strategy. Note if there is any unnecessary information that you can ignore.

1. Lorenzo is deciding between two examination room layouts for his new clinic. The cross-sectional area of each square chair is 2 square feet, and the cross-sectional areas of the circle chair and exam table are π and 4.9 square feet, respectively. What is the difference in the areas, in square feet, of the shaded portion between the two layouts?

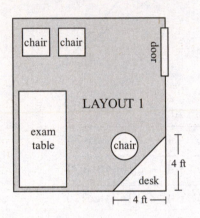 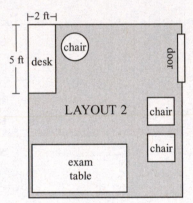

A.   2

B.   4

C.   6

D.   8

E.   10

The explanation appears at the end of this chapter.

How Much Have You Learned?

Directions: For test-like practice, give yourself 10 minutes to complete this question set. Be sure to study the explanations, even for questions you got right. They can be found at the end of this chapter. Note that this question set includes foundational topics in geometry covered in Math Fundamentals in chapter 6.

1. In the following figure, N is the intersection of segments $\overline{MO}$ and $\overline{LP}$. If $\overline{LM} = \overline{MN} = \overline{NL}$, what is the measure of $\angle NPO$?

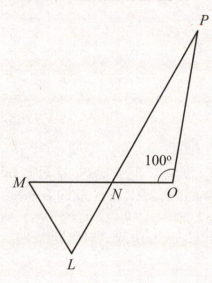

    A. 10°
    B. 15°
    C. 20°
    D. 25°
    E. 30°

2. The ratio of the perimeters of two similar triangles is 4:7. The sides of the larger triangle are 10, 12, and 13 cm, respectively. What is the perimeter, in centimeters, of the smaller triangle?

    F. 7
    G. 11
    H. 12
    J. 20
    K. 26

3. During a hiking trip, Keesha and Dwayne decide to climb a mountain using two different routes to the top. Keesha takes the hiking route that travels 5 miles south, 6 miles east, 7 miles south, and 2 miles west to the summit; Dwayne uses the climbing route that starts at the same point as the hiking route but goes directly from there to the summit. Approximately how many miles in all will the two hike on the way to the summit?

    A. 12.65
    B. 29.42
    C. 32.65
    D. 33.42
    E. 34.00

4. The following figure shows $\triangle WXY$ in which Z is the midpoint of $\overline{WY}$ and $\overline{WX}$ is perpendicular to $\overline{YX}$. What is the length, in inches, of $\overline{WZ}$?

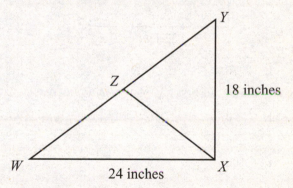

    F. 13
    G. 15
    H. 21
    J. 30
    K. 32

5. In the following figure, $\overline{CD} = \overline{BD}$ and $\angle BED$ is 17°. What is the measure, in degrees, of $\angle ABC$?

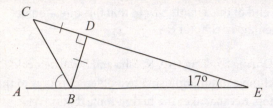

    A. 30
    B. 45
    C. 54
    D. 62
    E. 107

6. The following figure shows the floor dimensions of Akanksha's living room. She wants to install floor molding along the perimeter of the floor. How many feet of molding does she need?

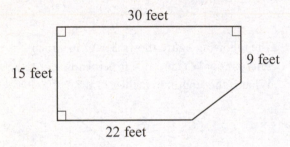

    F. 76
    G. 86
    H. 90
    J. 96
    K. 100

7. Yesenia has a rectangular orchard that she would like to divide into two triangular fields—one for planting orange trees and one for planting grapefruit trees—by building a fence from one corner of the field to the opposite corner. If the area of the field is 540 square feet and the length of the field is 36 feet, how many feet of fence will Yesenia need to create the divider?

    A. 39
    B. 51
    C. 60
    D. 81
    E. 102

8. In the following figure, the diameter of the smallest circle is 2 inches, and each of the other circles has a radius 1 inch larger than the previous. What percent of the total area is the area of the shaded region?

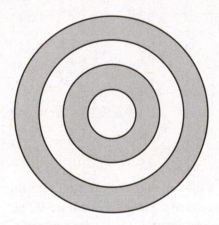

    F. 25
    G. 37.5
    H. 50
    J. 62.5
    K. 75

9. The opening of a perfectly cylindrical sewer tunnel has a circumference of 8π. The tunnel has a volume of $2{,}048\pi$ cubic feet. How many feet long is the tunnel?

   A.   44

   B.   62

   C.   84

   D.   128

   E.   156

10. In the following figure, point C is the center of the circle, and the measure of angle D is $37°$. Which of the following expresses the length of the radius?

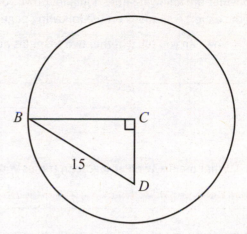

   F. $15 \sin 53°$

   G. $15 \sin 37°$

   H. $15 \cos 37°$

   J. $15 \tan 53°$

   K. $15 \tan 37°$

Math

Reflect

Directions: Take a few minutes to recall what you've learned and what you've been practicing in this chapter. Consider the following questions, jot down your best answer for each one, and then compare your reflections to the expert responses on the following page. Use your level of confidence to determine what to do next.

1. How can you tell whether two triangles are similar?

   _____

   _____

   _____

2. What are the two Pythagorean triples you are most likely to see on test day?

   _____

   _____

   _____

3. What are the ratios of the side lengths of a 45-45-90 triangle? Of a 30-60-90 triangle?

   _____

   _____

   _____

4. When doing unit conversions, how can you make sure you're doing them correctly?

   _____

   _____

   _____

5. What is the standard form for the equation of a circle?

   _____

   _____

   _____

6. What is the relationship of a circle's central angle to the arc and sector the angle defines?

    _____

    _____

    _____

7. How would you find the surface area of a right triangular prism with equilateral triangles as its bases?

    _____

    _____

    _____

Responses

1. How can you tell whether two triangles are similar?

There are three ways to tell:

*   *Two of their three angles are congruent (angle-angle).*
*   *Two of their three sides are in the same proportion and the intervening angle is congruent (side-angle-side).*
*   *Their three sides are in the same proportion (side-side-side).*

2. What are the two Pythagorean triples you are most likely to see on test day?

The two most common Pythagorean triples on the ACT are 3:4:5 and 5:12:13. You may also see multiples of these, e.g., 6:8:10 or 10:24:26.

3. What are the ratios of the side lengths of a 45-45-90 triangle? Of a 30-60-90 triangle?

The side lengths of a 45-45-90 triangle are always in the ratio of $x:x:x\sqrt{2}$. The side lengths of a 30-60-90 triangle are always in the ratio of $x:x\sqrt{3}:2x$. Remember that the shortest side of any triangle is across from the smallest angle, and the longest side is across from the greatest angle.

4. When doing unit conversions, how can you make sure you're doing them correctly?

To do unit conversions correctly, set up the conversion in whichever way makes units cancel. For example, to convert 3 feet into inches, you multiply 3 feet by 12 inches per foot, because it cancels out the feet unit. If instead you multiplied 3 feet by 1 foot per 12 inches, then the resulting units would be "feet squared per inch," which makes no sense.

5. What is the standard form for the equation of a circle?

The equation of a circle in the coordinate plane is $(x - h)^2 + (y - k)^2 = r^2$, where r is the radius of the circle, and (h,k) is the ordered pair representing its center.

6. What is the relationship of a circle's central angle to the arc and sector the angle defines?

The central angle, the arc, and the sector are all in proportion to the full circle:

$$\text{central angle} = \frac{\text{arc length}}{\text{circumference}} = \frac{\text{sector area}}{\text{circle area}}$$

7. How would you find the surface area of a right triangular prism with equilateral triangles as its bases?

Calculate the area of one of the equilateral triangles and multiply by 2. Calculate the area of one of the rectangular faces and multiply by 3. Then add the results.

Next Steps

If you answered most questions correctly in the "How Much Have You Learned" section, and if your responses to the Reflect questions were similar to those of an expert, then consider Geometry an area of strength and move on to the next chapter. Come back to this topic periodically to prevent yourself from getting rusty.

If you don't yet feel confident, review those parts of this chapter that you have not yet mastered. In particular, review the lessons on triangles, as these are important shapes on the ACT. Then, try the questions you missed again. As always, be sure to review the explanations closely. Then go online (**kaptest.com/login**) to watch video lessons about the highest-yield concepts in this chapter and to use your Qbank for more practice. If you haven't already registered your book, do so at *kaptest.com/moreonline*.

GO ONLINE

kaptest.com/login

Answers and Explanations

Lines and Angles

1. C

Difficulty: Low

Category: Geometry

Getting to the Answer: To answer questions about angles formed when a transversal cuts parallel lines, figure out which angles are equal and which are supplementary. Remember that when a transversal crosses two parallel lines, all the acute angles are equal and all the obtuse angles are equal. Here, $\angle CRP = \angle ATR$ because $\overline{CD}$ and $\overline{AB}$ are parallel. $\angle ATR$ and $\angle ATQ$ are supplementary, so the measure of $\angle ATQ = 180° - 110° = 70°$. Choice (C) is correct.

2. H

Difficulty: Low

Category: Geometry

Getting to the Answer: Because lines a and b are perpendicular, the lines form four 90° angles. Line c, which passes through the intersection of lines a and b, creates two sets of vertical angles. The angle across from the angle that is $y°$ also equals $y°$, and the angle across from the angle that is $x°$ equals $x°$. Thus, $x° + y° = 90°$. Solving for y in terms of x gives $y = (90 - x)°$. Choice (H) is correct.

3. C

Difficulty: Medium

Category: Geometry

Getting to the Answer: Because $\overline{OL} = \overline{NM}$ and $\overline{LM} = \overline{ON}$, $\overline{LM}$ and $\overline{ON}$ must be parallel lines, making $\overline{LN}$ a transversal. Angles b and c are opposite interior angles, which means that they have congruent angle measures. Although you can calculate the actual values of b and c, the fact that $b = c$ means that $b - c$ will always equal 0, regardless of the actual angle measures. Choice (C) is correct.

4. J

Difficulty: Low

Category: Geometry

Getting to the Answer: In a quadrilateral, the sum of the interior angles is 360°. Thus, $\angle A + 2x° + 90° + 3x° = 360°$. Solving for $\angle A$ in terms of x gives $\angle A = 360° - 90° - 2x° - 3x°$. Thus, $\angle A = 270° - 5x°$, and (J) is correct.

5. B

Difficulty: Low

Category: Geometry

Getting to the Answer: Use the properties of supplementary angles to find the measures of $\angle DBC$ and $\angle BDC$: $\angle DBC = 180° - 45° = 135°$ and $\angle BDC = 180° - 155° = 25°$. The sum of the interior angles in a triangle equals 180°, so $\angle BCD = 180° - (135° + 25°) = 20°$. Choice (B) is correct.

Triangle Properties

1. D

Difficulty: Medium

Category: Geometry

Getting to the Answer: Since $\overline{DF} = \overline{DE} = \overline{FE}$, $\triangle DFE$ is an equilateral triangle and all the interior angles are 60°. $\overline{DE}$ is parallel to $\overline{AC}$, so $\angle FDE$ and $\angle DAB$ are corresponding angles. Thus, $\angle DAB$ is also 60°. Choice (D) is correct.

Math

2. J

Difficulty: Low

Category: Geometry

Getting to the Answer: The question asks for the measure of $\angle ABC$. You know that $\overline{AB}$ and $\overline{BC}$ are congruent sides of $\triangle ABC$ and that $m\angle CAB = 27°$. Sketch out $\triangle ABC$ to visualize this information.

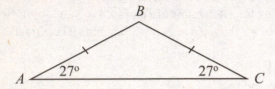

Because $\overline{AB}$ and $\overline{BC}$ are congruent, $m\angle ACB$ must also equal 27°. The sum of the measures of the interior angles of a triangle is 180°. Therefore, find $m\angle ACB$ by subtracting $2 \times 27°$ from 180°: $m\angle ABC = 180° - 54° = 126°$. You found the measure of $\angle ABC$, so you are done. Choice (J) is correct.

3. E

Difficulty: Medium

Category: Geometry

Getting to the Answer: The measures of the angles of a triangle sum to 180°. You can use the given ratio to represent the relative sizes of the angles. For example, if x equals one "part," the measures of the angles can be represented by $2x$, $3x$, and $7x$. To find the size of one part, solve the equation $2x + 3x + 7x = 180°$. This simplifies to $12x = 180°$, or $x = 15°$. Be careful; this is not the answer. The question asks for the measure of the largest angle, which is $7x = 7(15) = 105°$. Choice (E) is correct.

4. G

Difficulty: Low

Category: Geometry

Getting to the Answer: The altitude is the perpendicular line from a vertex to the opposite side of the triangle. Thus, the length of the altitude from X to $\overline{YZ}$ is 4. Choice (G) is correct.

5. B

Difficulty: High

Category: Geometry

Getting to the Answer: When two triangles have two equal angles, they are similar triangles. When you notice a triangle within a triangle, like the one in this figure, pay special attention to the angles that are shared by both triangles.

The triangle with hypotenuse b that is formed by the dotted line is similar to $\triangle PQR$. This is because they both contain a right angle and both have angle R in common. The sides of this smaller triangle, therefore, will be in proportion to the sides of $\triangle PQR$. Your job is to evaluate the answer choices to find which ratio describes the ratio of the smaller triangle to $\triangle PQR$.

Side d is the shortest side of the smaller triangle, and a is the shortest side of $\triangle PQR$. Side c is the longer leg of the smaller triangle, and b is the longer leg of $\triangle PQR$. Therefore, the ratio between the two pairs of sides is the same, and $\frac{d}{a} = \frac{b}{c}$. Choice (B) is correct.

Right Triangles

1. C

Difficulty: Medium

Category: Geometry

Getting to the Answer: Triangle ABC is a 30-60-90 triangle, and side AB is across from the 60° angle. Set up a proportion using the ratio of the sides in a 30-60-90 triangle, $x:x\sqrt{3}:2x$, to find the length of AB:

$$\frac{\sqrt{3}}{2} = \frac{AB}{20}$$
$$20\sqrt{3} = 2AB$$
$$10\sqrt{3} = AB$$

Choice (C) is correct.

2.   H

Difficulty: Medium

Category: Geometry

Getting to the Answer: The diagonal of the square tile is also the hypotenuse of two 45-45-90 triangles.

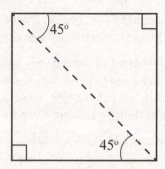

Use the ratio of the sides in a 45-45-90 triangle, $x:x:x\sqrt{2}$, to set up a proportion to determine the side length of the square. Let s be the side of the square:

$$\frac{s}{18} = \frac{1}{\sqrt{2}}$$

$$\sqrt{2}s = 18$$

$$s = \frac{18}{\sqrt{2}}$$

Rationalize this expression by multiplying the numerator and denominator by $\sqrt{2}$: $\frac{18}{\sqrt{2}} \times \frac{\sqrt{2}}{\sqrt{2}} = \frac{18\sqrt{2}}{2} = 9\sqrt{2}$. Choice (H) is correct.

3.   C

Difficulty: Low

Category: Geometry

Getting to the Answer: Since the length of the shorter leg is 6 inches and the length of the longer leg is twice the length of the shorter leg, the length of the longer leg is $2 \times 6 = 12$. Use the Pythagorean theorem, $a^2 + b^2 = c^2$, to find the hypotenuse c:
$c = \sqrt{6^2 + 12^2} = \sqrt{36 + 144} = \sqrt{180} = 6\sqrt{5}$. Choice (C) is correct.

4.   J

Difficulty: Low

Category: Geometry

Getting to the Answer: The figure shown is a right triangle. The length of the hypotenuse equals the length of the slide, which is 10 feet, and the length of the long leg equals the distance between the base of the slide and the ladder, which is 8 feet. Since you are given two of the sides, you can use the Pythagorean theorem, $a^2 + b^2 = c^2$, to determine the third side. Let a equal the height of the ladder:

$$a = \sqrt{c^2 - b^2}$$
$$= \sqrt{10^2 - 8^2}$$
$$= \sqrt{36}$$
$$= 6$$

Choice (J) is correct.

If you recognized that the sides were a multiple of the Pythagorean triple 3:4:5, then you could avoid using the Pythagorean theorem and quickly see that the third side must be $3 \times 2 = 6$.

5.   D

Difficulty: Medium

Category: Geometry

Getting to the Answer: In the figure above, $\overline{AB}$ is the hypotenuse of a right triangle. $\overline{AC}$ is 4 units and $\overline{CB}$ is 6 units, so use the Pythagorean theorem, $a^2 + b^2 = c^2$, to find the length of $\overline{AB}$:

$$c = \sqrt{a^2 + b^2}$$
$$= \sqrt{4^2 + 6^2}$$
$$= \sqrt{52}$$
$$= \sqrt{4}\sqrt{13}$$
$$= 2\sqrt{13}$$

Choice (D) is correct.

Alternatively, you could use the distance formula, which is derived from the Pythagorean theorem: $d = \sqrt{(y_2 - y_1)^2 + (x_2 - x_1)^2}$. The distance between points A and B is therefore
$d = \sqrt{(1 - 5)^2 + (7 - 1)^2} = 2\sqrt{13}$.

Polygons

1. C

Difficulty: Medium

Category: Geometry

Getting to the Answer: First, use $A_{triangle} = \frac{1}{2}bh$ to calculate the area of $\triangle PQR$: $A_{PQR} = \frac{1}{2}(16)(10) = 80$.

Then, determine the area of the square. Since the area of square $ABCD$ is twice the area of $\triangle PQR$, the area of square $ABCD$ is $2 \times 80 = 160$. Use $A_{square} = s^2$ to determine the length of a side: $s = \sqrt{160} = \sqrt{16}\sqrt{10} = 4\sqrt{10}$, which is (C).

2. G

Difficulty: Low

Category: Geometry

Getting to the Answer: Use the formula $A = bh$ to determine the area of the parallelogram. The length of the base, b, is the distance between -2 and 4, which is 6. The height, h, is the perpendicular distance from the base to the top of the parallelogram, which is the change in the y-coordinate values: $5 - 2 = 3$. Thus, the area is $6 \times 3 = 18$ square units, which matches (G).

3. C

Difficulty: Low

Category: Geometry

Getting to the Answer: Imagine moving the short horizontal side to the top of the polygon to form a rectangle that is 10 meters by 12.5 meters. Then, add the perimeter of that rectangle to the two sides that are 7.5 meters to get the perimeter of the polygon: $2(10) + 2(12.5) + 2(7.5) = 60$ m. Finally, use 1 meter $=$ 100 centimeters to convert 60 meters to centimeters: $60 \text{ m} \times \frac{100 \text{ cm}}{1 \text{ m}} = 6{,}000$ cm. Choice (C) is correct.

4. K

Difficulty: Medium

Category: Geometry

Getting to the Answer: The formula for the area of a trapezoid is $A = \left(\frac{b_1 + b_2}{2}\right)h$, where b_1 and b_2 are the lengths of the parallel sides. You could also think of this formula as the height times the average of the bases.

You are given the height (3 inches), one base (8 inches), and enough information to determine the other base. Notice that $\triangle ABE$ is a 3-4-5 triangle, so $AE = 4$ inches. And if you were to drop an altitude down from point C, you'd get another 3-4-5 triangle on the right:

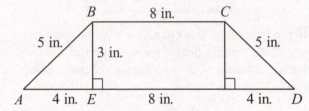

Now you can see that the bottom base is 16 inches. Plug these numbers into the area formula:

$$
\begin{aligned}
A &= \left(\frac{b_1 + b_2}{2}\right)h \\
&= \left(\frac{8 + 16}{2}\right) \times 3 \\
&= 12 \times 3 \\
&= 36
\end{aligned}
$$

The answer is (K).

If you don't remember the area formula on test day, you can also just find the areas of the two side triangles and the rectangle in the middle and add them all up.

5. A

Difficulty: Medium

Category: Geometry

Getting to the Answer: Picking Numbers can make a theoretical question like this much more concrete. If you are not sure which answer choice makes the most sense, assume that each side starts with length 1 and try each answer choice out. The area starts as $1 \times 1 = 1$, so triple the area is 3. Begin testing with the middle answer choice:

C: area $= (1 \times 9)(1 \times 9) = 81$. This is too big, so try a smaller choice.

B: area $= (1 \times 3)(1 \times 3) = 9$. Still too big.

(A): area $= (1 \times \sqrt{3})(1 \times \sqrt{3}) = \sqrt{3} \times \sqrt{3} = 3$.

Choice (A) is correct.

Circles and Parabolas

1. C

Difficulty: Medium

Category: Geometry

Getting to the Answer: You need to find the area of the circle, and you are given the circumference of the circle. As with most circle questions, the first thing you need to do is find the radius. Use the given circumference and the circumference formula to find r.

$$C = 2\pi r$$
$$8\pi = 2\pi r$$
$$4 = r$$

Now you can use the radius to find the area:
$A = \pi r^2 = \pi(4)^2 = 16\pi$. You found the area, 16π, so you are done. Choice (C) is correct.

2. K

Difficulty: Medium

Category: Geometry

Getting to the Answer: The area of the shaded region can be determined by subtracting the area of the smaller circle from the area of the larger circle. First, find the radius of the larger circle. Then, use $A = \pi r^2$ to calculate the area of each circle. Finally, find the difference in areas.

Since the radius of the larger circle is 75% greater than that of the smaller circle, the radius of the larger circle is $4 + 4 \times 0.75 = 7$. The area of the smaller circle is $\pi(4)^2 = 16\pi$, and the area of the larger circle is $\pi(7)^2 = 49\pi$. This means the area of the shaded region is $49\pi - 16\pi = 33\pi$ square feet. Choice (K) is correct.

3. D

Difficulty: High

Category: Geometry

Getting to the Answer: Think logically to answer this question. Because Earth makes a complete rotation about its axis in 24 hours, any point on the equator must rotate through 360° during that time.

Quito rotates 360° in the 24 hours from noon on January 1 to noon on January 2. There are 3 hours between noon on January 2 and 3:00 p.m. on January 2, so it rotates an additional $\frac{3}{24} \times 360° = 45°$, for a total of $360° + 45° = 405°$. Choice (D) is correct.

4. J

Difficulty: High

Category: Geometry

Getting to the Answer: The set of points described in the question stem form a circle centered at $(-3,4)$. The distance of 5 represents the length of its radius. This means that you have everything you need to use the standard equation for a circle with center (h,k) and radius r. The equation is:

$$(x - h)^2 + (y - k)^2 = r^2$$
$$(x - (-3))^2 + (y - 4)^2 = 5^2$$
$$(x + 3)^2 + (y - 4)^2 = 25$$

The answer is (J).

5.   A

Difficulty: Medium

Category: Geometry

Getting to the Answer: To find the solutions for *x*, set the equation equal to 0 and solve for *x*.

$$0 = (x+3)^2 - 1$$
$$1 = (x+3)^2$$
$$\sqrt{1} = x + 3$$
$$\pm 1 = x + 3$$
$$-4 \text{ and } -2 = x$$

Both values of *x* are negative, so (A) is correct.

Alternatively, you could graph the equation. The solutions for *x* are the *x*-intercepts of the graph. In this graph, the parabola intersects the *x*-axis in two places, both to the left of the origin. This means that the equation has two different negative real solutions:

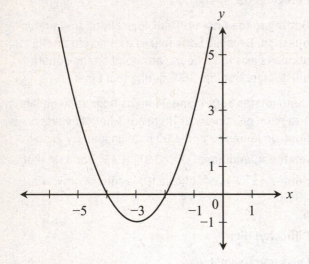

Choice (A) is correct.

Complex Two-Dimensional Figures

1.   A

Difficulty: High

Category: Geometry

Getting to the Answer: The difference in areas of the shaded portion between the two layouts arises solely from the different desk shapes. Thus, you need to calculate the difference in the cross-sectional area of the desks only. The triangular desk in Layout 1 has an area of $\frac{1}{2}bh = \frac{1}{2}(4)(4) = 8$ square feet. The rectangular desk in Layout 2 has an area of $l \times w = 5 \times 2 = 10$ square feet. The difference in the areas of the desks, and therefore of the shaded portions between the layouts, is $10 - 8 = 2$ square feet, which matches (A).

2.   F

Difficulty: Medium

Category: Geometry

Getting to the Answer: A scale can be written in the form of a fraction. The question states that the scale here is $\frac{3}{4}$ inches to 9 feet, which can be written as $\frac{\frac{3}{4}}{9}$. To find the area, in square inches, of each table in the scale drawing, first set up a proportion to solve for the diameter of the table in the scale drawing.

$$\frac{\frac{3}{4} \text{ inch}}{9 \text{ feet}} = \frac{x \text{ inch}}{6 \text{ feet}}$$
$$\frac{18}{4} = 9x$$
$$\frac{1}{2} = x$$

The diameter is *x*, so the radius is $\frac{1}{2} \div 2 = \frac{1}{4}$. Finally, calculate the area of a table using πr^2:
$A = \pi \left(\frac{1}{4}\right)^2 = \frac{1}{16}\pi$. Choice (F) is correct.

3.   D

Difficulty: Medium

Category: Geometry

Getting to the Answer: Because the problem does not provide you with a figure, draw one to visualize what you are being asked.

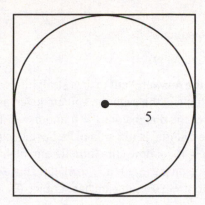

The circle is inscribed within the square, so its radius is half the side of the square. The circle has a radius of 5, so the square has a side of $2 \times 5 = 10$. Therefore, the area of the circle is $5^2\pi = 25\pi$, and the area of the square is $10^2 = 100$. The difference between the area of the square and the area of the circle is thus $100 - 25\pi$, which is (D).

4.   K

Difficulty: High

Category: Geometry

Getting to the Answer: You want to find the perimeter of the triangle. Unfortunately, you do not have much concrete information about it yet. Instead, start with what you know about the shaded square. Because its area is 12, each side must be $\sqrt{12} = \sqrt{4}\sqrt{3} = 2\sqrt{3}$. Jot this down because you'll need it later.

Triangle *ABC* is an equilateral triangle, so each of its interior angles measures 60°. This means that the two vertical sides of the square each represent the longer leg of a 30-60-90 triangle (the small white triangles on the sides).

Use the ratio of the sides, $x:x\sqrt{3}:2x$, to determine the length of the short leg. Since the length of the long leg is $2\sqrt{3}$, the short legs are each 2. You now have the length of the base of the large equilateral triangle: $2 + 2\sqrt{3} + 2 = 4 + 2\sqrt{3}$.

Because the triangle is equilateral, each side of the triangle has length $4 + 2\sqrt{3}$. The perimeter is the sum of all three sides, so multiply the side length by 3 to get $12 + 6\sqrt{3}$. Choice (K) is correct.

5.   E

Difficulty: High

Category: Geometry

Getting to the Answer: You need to determine the shortest distance between the two chords in terms of *r*. You are told that $\overline{WX}$ is the diameter and that $\overline{YZ}$ is 25% smaller than $\overline{WX}$. One of the simplest ways to discover new information in tough geometry questions is to draw additional lines. Start with an additional radius (call it *r*) that extends from the center of the diameter of the semicircle to $\overline{YZ}$. Then add a line that represents the shortest distance between the two chords. This creates a right triangle.

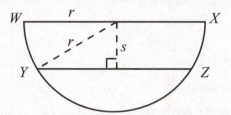

You know that $\overline{YZ}$ is 25% shorter than $\overline{WX}$, so $\overline{YZ} = \frac{3}{4}\overline{WX}$. Since $\overline{WX}$ is the diameter of the circle, $\overline{WX} = 2r$. Combine these two equations to determine the other side of the right triangle, $\frac{1}{2}\overline{YZ}$:

$$\overline{YZ} = \frac{3}{4}\overline{WZ}$$
$$\overline{YZ} = \frac{3}{4}(2r)$$
$$\overline{YZ} = \frac{3}{2}r$$
$$\frac{1}{2}\overline{YZ} = \frac{3}{4}r$$

You now have two of the three sides of the right triangle and can solve for the third using the Pythagorean theorem.

$$\left(\frac{3}{4}r\right)^2 + s^2 = r^2$$
$$\frac{9}{16}r^2 + s^2 = r^2$$
$$s^2 = \frac{16}{16}r^2 - \frac{9}{16}r^2$$
$$s^2 = \frac{7}{16}r^2$$
$$s = \pm\frac{\sqrt{7}}{4}r$$

Distance can't be negative, so (E) is the correct answer.

Three-Dimensional Figures

1. E

Difficulty: Medium

Category: Geometry

Getting to the Answer: You need to determine the amount of paint that Hawanatu needs in square inches. You are given a rectangular prism with several dimensions. Jot these down: $l = 30$, $w = 3$, $h = 5$. The amount of paint needed to cover the surface is the same as the total surface area of the solid. Use $SA = 2(wl + hl + hw)$ to find the amount of paint needed: $2[3(30) + 5(30) + 5(3)] = 2(90 + 150 + 15) = 510$ square inches. Choice (E) is correct.

2. F

Difficulty: High

Category: Geometry

Getting to the Answer: You need to find the volume of the solid. You are told that the solid is half a cube, and you are given the length of one part. Since the shape is half a cube, the perpendicular edges are equal and form the legs of a 45-45-90 triangle. Use the ratio of the sides, $x:x:x\sqrt{2}$, to determine the length of the legs (and the edges of the half cube). Since the hypotenuse is $2\sqrt{2}$, the length of the leg is 2.

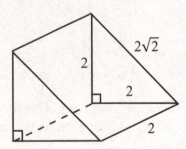

The volume of the whole cube is $V_{cube} = s^3 = (2)^3 = 8$. Thus, the volume of the half-cube figure is 4. Choice (F) is correct.

3. D

Difficulty: Medium

Category: Geometry

Getting to the Answer: Your task is straightforward: find the volume of the cylinder. You are given a figure that includes the dimensions $r = 4$ and $h = 5$. The volume of a cylinder is the area of its base (a circle) times its height. Jot down the formula and fill in the given dimensions: $V = \pi r^2 h = \pi(4)^2(5)$. This expression simplifies to $V = 80\pi$ cubic inches. Choice (D) is correct.

4. J

Difficulty: High

Category: Geometry

Getting to the Answer: You need to find the amount of wrapping paper required to wrap one candle. You are given a figure and the dimensions of the candle. You are also told that there will be extra paper on each end. Covering a 3D shape with gift wrap means that you are working with surface area.

Recall that the formula for the surface area of a cylinder is $2\pi r^2 + 2\pi rh$, but be careful. The circular top and bottom of the candle will not be covered, so the surface area of the gift wrap is just $2\pi rh$. You are given that the diameter of the candle is 4 inches, so assuming the thickness of the gift wrap is negligible, $r = 2$ inches. Since Mali wants the gift wrap to be 3 inches past the top and bottom of the candle, the height of the gift wrap is $h = 3 + 8 + 3 = 14$ inches. Plug these numbers into $2\pi rh$ and simplify: $2\pi(2)(14) = 56\pi$ square inches. Check that your answer is in the correct units. Choice (J) is correct.

5. B

Difficulty: Medium

Category: Geometry

Getting to the Answer: To find the volume of the figurine, you need to find the change in the volume of the water after placing the figurine in the water. After the figurine is submerged, the height of the water rises 0.4 inches, but the length and width do not change. You can multiply these dimensions by a height of 0.4 to find the volume of the figurine: $10 \times 13 \times 0.4 = 52$ cubic inches. Choice (B) is correct.

Alternatively, you could determine the volume before and after the figurine is submerged and then calculate the difference:

$$V_{before} = 10(13)(5)$$
$$= 650$$
$$V_{after} = 10(13)(5.4)$$
$$= 702$$
$$V_{after} - V_{before} = 702 - 650$$
$$= 52$$

As expected, this matches (B).

Triangles and Trigonometry

1. B

Difficulty: High

Category: Geometry

Getting to the Answer: The question asks you to find the values of θ when $\sin\theta = \frac{1}{2}$. Use the unit circle to determine that for θ between 0 and π, $\sin\theta = \frac{1}{2}$ occurs when $\theta = \frac{\pi}{6}$ and $\frac{5\pi}{6}$. This matches (B).

If you do not know the unit circle by memory, draw a sketch. Since θ is between 0 and π, draw θ in Quadrants I and II.

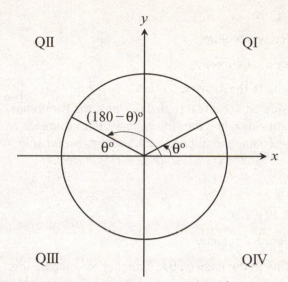

Recall that the definition of sine is $\frac{\text{opposite}}{\text{hypotenuse}}$. Form a right triangle using θ and label the opposite side 1 and the hypotenuse 2. Note that these sides correspond to those of a 30-60-90 triangle. Use the ratio of the sides, $x : x\sqrt{3} : 2x$, to determine θ. The angle opposite 1 is 30°. Thus, $\theta = 30°$ and $180° - 30° = 150°$.

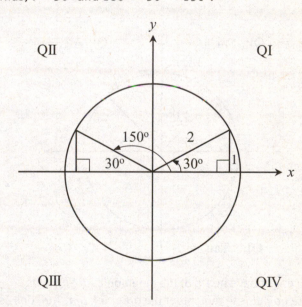

Convert your answer into radians using the conversion factor $180° = \pi$ radians: $30° = \frac{\pi}{6}$ and $150° = \frac{5\pi}{6}$. Finally, double-check that you used the correct interval for θ. Choice (B) is correct.

2. F

Difficulty: Medium

Category: Geometry

Getting to the Answer: Since $\cos = \frac{\text{adj}}{\text{hyp}}$ and $\sin = \frac{\text{opp}}{\text{hyp}}$, the side adjacent to β is 36 units long, the hypotenuse is 39 units long, and the side opposite is 15 units long. To determine the value of tanβ, use the relationship $\tan = \frac{\text{opp}}{\text{adj}}$: $\tan\beta = \frac{15}{36}$, so choice (F) is correct.

3. E

Difficulty: High

Category: Geometry

Getting to the Answer: Use $\frac{1}{2}ab\sin x$ to compare the areas of the original and new triangles. The area of the original triangle is $\frac{1}{2}fg\sin 135°$, and the area of the new triangle is $\frac{1}{2}fg\sin 45°$. The only difference is the angle.

On the unit circle, 45°, which is between 0° and 90°, is in Quadrant I, and 135°, which is between 90° and 180°, is in Quadrant II. Note that $180° - 135° = 45°$.

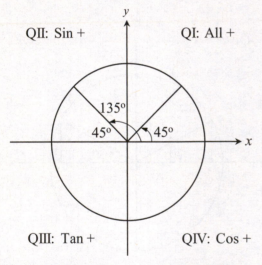

You might have heard of the mnemonic *All Students Take Calculus* to remember the order *All, Sin, Tan, Cos* as you move counter-clockwise around the unit circle; like PEMDAS, there are multiple mnemonics that can be used to remember this information. In Quadrants I and II, sin is positive. Therefore, $\sin(135°) = \sin(45°)$, and the areas are equal. The new area is also 60 square centimeters, so (E) is correct.

4. K

Difficulty: High

Category: Geometry

Getting to the Answer: On test day, be on the lookout for questions that simply ask you to plug values into a given formula. They may look tough, but they don't require you to do much thinking.

Here, the question is asking for the expression that represents the value of z. Since you know the values of two of the three angles in the triangle, you can deduce that the unmarked angle has a measure of $180° - 35° - 45° = 100°$. You are given the length of $\overline{DS}$ along with its opposite angle, so plug that information into the law of sines to solve for z:

$$\frac{\sin 45°}{7} = \frac{\sin 100°}{z}$$
$$z\sin 45° = 7\sin 100°$$
$$z = \frac{7\sin 100°}{\sin 45°}$$

Choice (K) is correct.

5. D

Difficulty: High

Category: Geometry

Getting to the Answer: For $\triangle EFG$, $\overline{FG} = 16$, $\overline{EF} = 4$, and $\angle F = 70°$. Use the second formula, $c^2 = a^2 + b^2 - 2ab\cos C$, to find $\overline{EG}$:

$$\overline{EG} = \sqrt{e^2 + g^2 - 2eg\cos F}$$
$$= \sqrt{16^2 + 4^2 - 2(16)(4)\cos 70°}$$

This matches (D).

On Test Day

1. A

Difficulty: High

Category: Geometry

Getting to the Answer: The difference in the areas of the shaded portion between the two layouts arises solely from the different desk shapes. Thus, you need to calculate the difference in the cross-sectional area of the desks only; ignore the other furniture. The triangular desk in Layout 1 has an area of $\frac{1}{2}bh = (4)(4) = 8$ square feet. The rectangular desk in Layout 2 has an area of $l \times w = 5 \times 2 = 10$ square feet. The difference in the areas of the desks, and therefore of the shaded portions between the layouts, is $10 - 8 = 2$ square feet, which matches (A).

How Much Have You Learned?

1. C

Difficulty: Medium

Category: Geometry

Getting to the Answer: Since $\overline{LM} = \overline{MN} = \overline{NL}$, ΔMNL is an equilateral. Thus, each interior angle is 60°. Vertical angles are congruent, so $\angle PNO$, which is opposite $\angle MNL$, also has a measure of 60°. The sum of the measures of the interior angles of a triangle is always 180°. Therefore, $\angle NOP = 180° - 60° - 100° = 20°$, which is (C).

2. J

Difficulty: Low

Category: Geometry

Getting to the Answer: The corresponding sides in similar triangles are proportional. Since the perimeter is the sum of all the sides, the perimeters are proportional as well. Set up the following equation to solve for the perimeter of the smaller triangle, denoted by x: $\frac{\text{perimeter smaller}}{\text{perimeter larger}} = \frac{4}{7} = \frac{x}{10 + 12 + 13}$.

$$\frac{4}{7} = \frac{x}{35}$$
$$140 = 7x$$
$$20 = x$$

The correct answer is (J).

3. C

Difficulty: Medium

Category: Geometry

Getting to the Answer: You are asked to find the number of miles that Keesha and Dwayne will hike on their way to the summit. You are given verbal descriptions of the hikers' paths to the summit, but it is much easier to understand the situation if you draw a diagram of Keesha and Dwayne's routes. After drawing and labeling the diagram with the information given, look for a way to create a right triangle by drawing in additional lines. Then, fill in the lengths of any new segments that you draw.

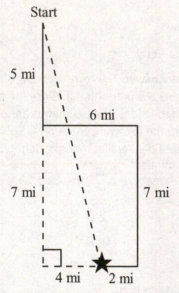

Use the Pythagorean theorem to calculate the distance that Dwayne hikes.

$$c^2 = (5 + 7)^2 + 4^2$$
$$c^2 = 144 + 16$$
$$c^2 = 160$$
$$c = \sqrt{160}$$

You're not done yet! The question asks you to find the total distance the two hikers travel. Keesha traveled $5 + 6 + 7 + 2 = 20$ miles. So, the total distance is $\sqrt{160} + 20 = 32.65$ miles. Choice (C) is correct.

4. G

Difficulty: Medium

Category: Geometry

Getting to the Answer: Before you rush to the Pythagorean theorem, note that 18 and 24 fit the pattern of a 3:4:5 Pythagorean triple that has been multiplied by 6: $(3:4:5) \times 6 = 18:24:30$. This means that $\overline{WY}$ is 30, but the question asks for the length of $\overline{WZ}$. Since Z is the midpoint of $\overline{WY}$, $\overline{WZ}$ is half of 30, or 15. Choice (G) is correct.

5. D

Difficulty: Medium

Category: Geometry

Getting to the Answer: Since $\angle CDB$ and $\angle BDE$ are on a straight line, they are supplementary. Because $\angle CDB$ is 90°, $\angle BDE$ is also 90°. The sum of the interior angles of a triangle equals 180°, so $\angle EBD$ is $180° - 90° - 17° = 73°$. Because $\overline{CD} = \overline{BD}$, $\triangle CDB$ is a 45-45-90 triangle. Thus, $\angle DBC = 45°$. Angles ABC, DBC, and EBD are supplementary, so $\angle ABC = 180° - 73° - 45° = 62°$. This matches (D).

6. G

Difficulty: Low

Category: Geometry

Getting to the Answer: To determine the total amount of molding needed, find the perimeter of the floor. Notice that the diagonal is the hypotenuse of a triangle that has a height of $15 - 9 = 6$ feet and a base of $30 - 22 = 8$ feet.

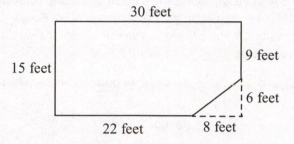

If you do not recognize the Pythagorean triple $(3{:}4{:}5) \times 2 = 6{:}8{:}10$, use the Pythagorean theorem $\left(a^2 + b^2 = c^2\right)$ to calculate the hypotenuse.

$$c^2 = 8^2 + 6^2$$
$$c^2 = 100$$
$$c = 10$$

Add up all the sides to calculate the total length of molding Akanksha needs: $15 + 9 + 30 + 22 + 10 = 86$ feet. Choice (G) is correct.

7. A

Difficulty: Low

Category: Geometry

Getting to the Answer: You need to find the length of the fence. You are told that the orchard is rectangular and that Yesenia will split it diagonally into two triangles. You're also given some dimensions: $A = 540$ square feet and $l = 36$ feet.

Draw and label a figure to visualize the situation.

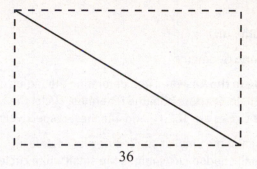

The area of a rectangle is the product of its length and width. Because you know the length and the area, you can find the width:

$$A = lw$$
$$540 = 36w$$
$$15 = w$$

Add the width to the diagram. Now you know that the fence is the hypotenuse of a right triangle with legs of lengths 15 and 36. Before turning to the Pythagorean theorem, look for a Pythagorean triplet to save time. Indeed, this is a 5-12-13 triangle multiplied by 3. Therefore, the hypotenuse—and the amount of fence needed—is $13 \times 3 = 39$ feet, which is (A).

If you didn't recognize this fact, you could also have plugged these numbers into the Pythagorean theorem, $a^2 + b^2 = c^2$.

$$c^2 = 15^2 + 36^2$$
$$c^2 = 225 + 1296$$
$$c = \sqrt{1521}$$
$$= 39$$

8. J

Difficulty: High

Category: Geometry

Getting to the Answer: First, determine the radius of each circle. Starting from the innermost circle, the radii for the circles are 1, 2, 3, and 4 inches, respectively.

The area of the smaller shaded ring is the area of the small shaded circle minus the small white circle: $4\pi - \pi = 3\pi$ square inches. The area of the larger shaded ring is the area of the larger shaded circle minus the larger white circle: $16\pi - 9\pi = 7\pi$ square inches.

The total area of the shaded region is therefore the sum of the shaded areas: $3\pi + 7\pi = 10\pi$ square inches.

Finally, calculate the percent of the total area the shaded area represents using the formula $\frac{part}{whole} \times 100\%$. Thus, the percent is $\frac{10\pi}{16\pi} \times 100\% = \frac{5}{8} \times 100\% = 62.5\%$. Choice (J) is correct.

9. D

Difficulty: Medium

Category: Geometry

Getting to the Answer: The question tells you that the circumference of the opening (which is a circle) is 8π, so substitute this value into the formula for circumference and solve for r:

$$C = 2\pi r$$
$$8\pi = 2\pi r$$
$$4 = r$$

You can now find h, which represents the length of the tunnel. Use the formula $V = \pi r^2 h$:

$$2{,}048\pi = \pi(4)^2(h)$$
$$2{,}048 = 16h$$
$$128 = h$$

The tunnel is 128 feet long, which is (D).

10. G

Difficulty: High

Category: Geometry

Getting to the Answer: Remembering the acronym SOHCAHTOA can get you through a lot of trig questions. This question is asking for the length of $\overline{BC}$. The only length you are given is that of the hypotenuse of the triangle, so start by checking for either a cosine or sine relationship (since the tangent part of the acronym, TOA, does not involve the hypotenuse). Since $\overline{BC}$ is opposite $\angle D$, the $37°$ angle, you can set up an equation involving $\sin 37°$:

$$\sin = \frac{\text{opp}}{\text{hyp}}$$
$$\sin(37°) = \frac{BC}{15}$$
$$15\sin(37°) = BC$$

Choice (G) is correct.

CHAPTER 14

ACT Math Timing and Section Management Strategies

ACT Math: Timing and Section Management Strategies

The Math Test has 60 questions to be completed in 60 minutes, which means you'll have one minute per question. This is an average, though. Some questions will be straightforward, meaning that you can get the correct answer in 30 seconds or less. Others will be more difficult and time-consuming. Test takers who start at the beginning of the section, attempt the questions in order, and only move on to the next question when the previous one is complete often find that they get bogged down and don't make it to the end of the section, potentially missing questions that they could have answered correctly. Flexibility can earn you more points.

A better approach is to make your way through the section with a plan to deal with each question. Each time you read a new question, take a moment to gauge your gut reaction:

- Does this question seem quick and easy? Do it immediately.
- Does this question seem time-consuming but manageable? Skip it for now. Put a circle around it, and try it on a second pass through the section.
- Does this question look confusing or difficult? Skip it. Don't worry about circling or marking questions like this. You'll approach them only after you have worked on the other questions in the section, and only if you have time.

Try to make this decision quickly. The more you practice, the easier it will be to recognize which questions are easier and which are more challenging for you.

When you approach a test section this way, you'll end up taking two or three passes through it. This technique ensures that you'll get all of the easy points first, and if you run out of time, you'll know that the questions you didn't attempt were the hardest in the section and would have been tougher to get right anyway.

Before the end of the section, make sure you have something bubbled in for every question since there is no penalty for guessing. Also, be very careful when bubbling your answers. It's easy to skip a question but then forget to skip a line on the grid and bubble your answer to the next question in the wrong place.

The questions in the Math Test will be in approximate order of difficulty, with the easiest questions at the beginning of the section and the most difficult questions at the end of the section.

If you tend to finish the Math sections early but find that you are making speed mistakes, you may consider pausing at the confirmation step to check your logic and calculations before bubbling your response to each question.

How Much Have You Learned?

Directions: Use this question set to practice effective question triage. Skip those questions that you feel will take too long; come back to them if you have time. Try to get as many questions correct as you can in 15 minutes. As always, be sure to study the explanations, even for questions you got right. They can be found at the end of this chapter.

1. What are the roots of $3x^2 + 5x - 3$?

   A. $\dfrac{5 \pm \sqrt{11}}{3}$

   B. $\dfrac{3 \pm \sqrt{51}}{6}$

   C. $\dfrac{-3 \pm \sqrt{61}}{6}$

   D. $\dfrac{-5 \pm \sqrt{11}}{3}$

   E. $\dfrac{-5 \pm \sqrt{61}}{6}$

2. $\triangle XYZ$ is similar to $\triangle UVW$. If $\overline{XY} = 10$, $\overline{YZ} = 6$, and $\overline{UV} = 15$, then what is the length of $\overline{VW}$?

   F. 3

   G. 6

   H. 9

   J. 17

   K. 25

3. Which of the following is equivalent to $(3 - 8i)(5 + 3i)$?

   A. $39 - 31i$

   B. $-9 - 31i$

   C. $39 + 49i$

   D. $-9 + 49i$

   E. $11 + 3i$

4. A customer of a retail store purchases an item for $23.10 after the 10% tax. If the item was discounted by 30%, what was the original price of the item in dollars?

   F. 24

   G. 26

   H. 28

   J. 30

   K. 33

5. Which of the following is equivalent to tan E ?

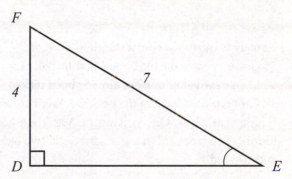

   A. $\dfrac{4}{7}$

   B. $\dfrac{4}{\sqrt{33}}$

   C. $\dfrac{7}{4}$

   D. $\dfrac{7}{\sqrt{33}}$

   E. $\dfrac{\sqrt{33}}{4}$

6. If the first term of an arithmetic sequence is 3 and the 32nd term is 127, what is the 17th term?

   F. 59

   G. 63

   H. 67

   J. 71

   K. 75

7. A circle has a diameter of 8 feet. If the circle's area were tripled, what would its new radius be in feet?

   A. 5

   B. 6

   C. $4\sqrt{3}$

   D. $8\sqrt{3}$

   E. $\sqrt{30}$

8. Kareem is learning about a standard deck of 52 cards. What is the likelihood that he will pick a red face card after one has already been picked and not replaced back in the deck? (A face card is classified as a Jack, Queen, King, or Ace. There are four of each face card in a standard deck: two black and two red.)

   F. $\dfrac{7}{51}$

   G. $\dfrac{7}{52}$

   H. $\dfrac{8}{51}$

   J. $\dfrac{2}{13}$

   K. $\dfrac{4}{51}$

9. If $a{:}b = 3{:}7$ and $c{:}b = 4{:}5$, what is the ratio of a to c ?

   A. 3:4

   B. 3:5

   C. 15:20

   D. 15:28

   E. 28:15

Use the table below for questions 10–12.
---

x	-2	-1	0	1	2
$f(x)$	-6	-2	2	6	10
$g(x)$	4	2	0	-2	-4

10. Which of the following equations describes $f(x)$?

    F. $f(x) = -2x^2 + 5x - 2$

    G. $f(x) = 4x + 2$

    H. $f(x) = 3x^2 - 2x + 4$

    J. $f(x) = -2x - 2$

    K. $f(x) = 3x$

11. What is the value of $f(g(1))$?

    A. -6

    B. -2

    C. 0

    D. 4

    E. 6

12. If the equation for function g is $g(x) = -2x$, then what is the solution that satisfies both $f(x)$ and $g(x)$?

    F. $\left(-\dfrac{4}{3}, -\dfrac{2}{3}\right)$

    G. $\left(-\dfrac{2}{3}, -\dfrac{1}{3}\right)$

    H. $\left(-\dfrac{1}{3}, \dfrac{2}{3}\right)$

    J. $\left(\dfrac{1}{3}, -\dfrac{2}{3}\right)$

    K. $\left(\dfrac{2}{3}, \dfrac{1}{3}\right)$

13. Suppose $f(x) = x^2$ and $g(x) = (x+4)^2 - 2$. Which of the following points lies on $g(x)$ if $(-2,4)$ lies on $f(x)$?

    A. $(-6,-2)$
    B. $(-6,2)$
    C. $(-4,0)$
    D. $(0,8)$
    E. $(2,6)$

14. Given the data set $\{-5, 8, 6, -3, -1\}$, what is the positive difference between the arithmetic mean and median?

    F. 1
    G. 2
    H. 3
    J. 4
    K. 5

15. If the base of a scale model is 12 inches by 18 inches and the shorter side of the real object is 14 feet, then how long in feet is the longer side of the real object?

    A. 9
    B. 14
    C. 18
    D. 21
    E. 26

Answers and Explanations

How Much Have You Learned?

1.   E

Difficulty: Medium

Category: Algebra

Getting to the Answer: The question asks you to find the roots, or solutions, of the given quadratic equation. Because all the answer choices are in quadratic formula form, the best strategy is to use the quadratic formula. Write down that $a = 3$, $b = 5$, and $c = -3$, and plug into the quadratic formula.

$$x = \frac{-(5) \pm \sqrt{(5)^2 - 4(3)(-3)}}{2(3)}$$
$$= \frac{-5 \pm \sqrt{25 + 36}}{6}$$
$$= \frac{-5 \pm \sqrt{61}}{6}$$

Hence, (E) is correct. Be very careful and keep track of all negative signs when plugging in: the other choices could be correct if values were incorrectly plugged in.

2.   H

Difficulty: Medium

Category: Geometry

Getting to the Answer: This question asks for the length of the segment $\overline{VW}$ in the second triangle given certain lengths of two similar triangles. Look carefully at the order in which the vertices of the similar triangles are stated, as that will tell you which segments correspond to each other. With the given segments, $\overline{XY}$ corresponds to $\overline{UV}$ while $\overline{YZ}$ corresponds to $\overline{VW}$. Create an equation with proportions to solve for $\overline{VW}$.

$$\frac{6}{10} = \frac{x}{15}$$
$$10x = 90$$
$$x = 9$$

$\overline{VW} = 9$, so (H) is correct. Be careful of K, as this could be an answer if the proportions were set up incorrectly.

3.   A

Difficulty: Medium

Category: Number and Quantity

Getting to the Answer: This question asks you to evaluate an expression that contains imaginary numbers. Use FOIL, and take care to keep track of the negative signs while multiplying. Plug in the value $i^2 = -1$ when appropriate.

$$(3 - 8i)(5 + 3i) = 15 + 9i - 40i - 24i^2$$
$$= 15 - 31i + 24$$
$$= 39 - 31i$$

Choice (A) is correct. Notice that B is the answer you would get if you plugged in 1 for i^2 instead of -1.

4.   J

Difficulty: High

Category: Number and Probability

Getting to the Answer: The question asks for the original price of an item before a 30% discount and a 10% tax. First, calculate the discounted price before the tax by using the equation $x + 0.1x = 23.10 \rightarrow 1.1x = 23.10 \rightarrow x = 21$. Set up another equation that shows that when the original price is reduced by 30%, it equals $21. Use the complement of 30%, which is 70%, to get $0.7x = 21 \rightarrow x = 30$. The original price of the item is $30, which matches (J).

5.   B

Difficulty: Medium

Category: Geometry

Getting to the Answer: The question asks you to solve for tan E. Because tangent = opposite over adjacent, use the Pythagorean theorem to solve for the adjacent side: $a^2 + (4)^2 = (7)^2 \rightarrow a^2 = 33 \rightarrow a = \sqrt{33}$. So, $\tan E = \frac{4}{\sqrt{33}}$, and (B) is correct.

Another way to find the answer is to use Elimination. The side opposite angle E is 4, so 4, or one of its factors, should be in the numerator of the answer. This eliminates C, D, and E. The adjacent side can't be 7, because that's the hypotenuse. Thus, A is wrong. Only (B) is left, so it must be the answer.

6.   H

Difficulty: High

Category: Number and Quantity

Getting to the Answer: The question asks you to solve for a_{17} given information about the arithmetic sequence. Use the arithmetic sequence equation $a_n = a_1 + (n-1)d$ and plug in all the given information to solve for d, the common difference between each term:

$$a_{32} = a_1 + (32-1)d$$
$$(127) = (3) + 31d$$
$$124 = 31d$$
$$4 = d$$

Now use the same equation to solve for a_{17}:

$$a_{17} = (3) + (17-1)(4)$$
$$= 3 + (16)(4)$$
$$= 3 + 64$$
$$= 67$$

The 17th term in the arithmetic sequence is 67. Thus, (H) is correct. Be certain that you used $n-1$ rather than n in your calculations.

7.   C

Difficulty: Medium

Category: Geometry

Getting to the Answer: The question asks what the radius of a circle with an 8-foot diameter would become if its area were tripled. First, use the diameter given to calculate the radius of the circle: $d = 2r \to 8 = 2r \to 4 = r$. Next, use the area formula for a circle, $A = \pi r^2$, to find the area: $A = \pi(4)^2 = 16\pi$. The question states that the circle's area is tripled, so its new area is $(3)16\pi = 48\pi$. Use the area of the larger circle to calculate the radius: $(48\pi) = \pi r^2 \to 48 = r^2 \to \sqrt{48} = 4\sqrt{3} = r$. Therefore, (C) is correct. Notice that D is a trap since this is the calculation using the diameter.

8.   F

Difficulty: High

Category: Statistics and Probability

Getting to the Answer: The question asks how likely it is to pick a red face card after one has already been picked with no replacement. Use the probability formula: probability $= \frac{\text{desired}}{\text{total}}$. There are 8 red face cards in a

standard deck of 52 cards. After one is picked, only 7 red face cards and 51 total cards remain, so the probability is $\frac{7}{51}$. Hence, (F) is correct. If you did not remember to decrease the denominator by the card that was already drawn, you would have answered G.

9.   D

Difficulty: High

Category: Statistics and Probability

Getting to the Answer: Between the two ratios, there are three variables, which means this is a three-part ratio. If you have two ratios, $a{:}b$ and $c{:}b$, you can derive $a{:}c$ by finding a common multiple of the b terms to make them the same. Here, a common multiple is 35. Multiply each ratio by the factor that will get you to $b = 35$. Use 5 for $a{:}b$ and 7 for $c{:}b$. The result is $5(3{:}7) = 15{:}35$ and $7(4{:}5) = 28{:}35$. Now that the b terms are the same, $a{:}b = 15{:}35$ and $c{:}b = 28{:}35$, you can rewrite the ratio $a{:}b{:}c$ as $15{:}35{:}28$. This means the ratio of $a{:}c$ is $15{:}28$, which is (D).

Alternatively, you can recognize that $\frac{a}{b} \times \frac{b}{c} = \frac{a}{c}$ and plug in the given values (inverting $c{:}b$ to get $b{:}c$) to determine that $\frac{a}{c} = \frac{3}{7} \times \frac{5}{4} = \frac{15}{28}$.

10.   G

Difficulty: Medium

Category: Algebra

Getting to the Answer: This question asks for the definition of $f(x)$ that is consistent with the data in the table. Notice that all the choices are either quadratic or linear, so check the table to see which relationship fits $f(x)$. All the x-values increase by one, while all the y-values increase by 4. This means that the table represents a linear equation, so eliminate the quadratic choices F and H. Calculate the slope or y-intercept to eliminate further choices: the point $(0,2)$ is the y-intercept, which eliminates choices J and K. Thus, (G) is correct. The slope can be calculated by choosing two points, such as $(0,2)$ and $(1,6)$, and plugging them into the slope formula:

$$m = \frac{y_2 - y_1}{x_2 - x_1}$$
$$= \frac{6-2}{1-0}$$
$$= \frac{4}{1}$$
$$= 4$$

Only (G) has a slope of 4.

11. A

Difficulty: Low

Category: Algebra

Getting to the Answer: This question asks you to solve for the composite function using the given data table. Use the table and make sure to work from the inside out, starting with solving for $g(1)$: for function g, when $x = 1$, $f(x) = -2$. Now you can solve for $f(-2)$: for function f, when $x = -2$, $f(x) = -6$. Therefore, (A) is correct. Note that if you had incorrectly used the value of $g(-2)$, you would have selected D.

12. H

Difficulty: Low

Category: Algebra

Getting to the Answer: This question asks for the solution to the system of equations $f(x)$ and $g(x)$. Use the given equation and the equation for $f(x)$ that you figured out earlier. Substitution is the easiest method.

$$-2x = 4x + 2$$
$$-6x = 2$$
$$x = -\frac{1}{3}$$

This means that the lines intersect when $x = -\frac{1}{3}$. Note that (H) is correct since it is the only choice with that x-value. If you needed to calculate the y-value, you could plug in $x = -\frac{1}{3}$ to either equation and simplify.

13. B

Difficulty: Medium

Category: Algebra

Getting to the Answer: The question asks which of the choices lies on the graph $g(x)$. You could plug the x-coordinate of each choice into $g(x)$ and see which one produces the matching y-coordinate, but you will find the answer more quickly if you apply the properties of function transformations. Notice that, compared to $f(x)$, $g(x)$ translates 4 units to the left and 2 units down. You can confirm this by setting the inside of what is being squared to zero and solving: $x + 4 = 0 \rightarrow x = -4$. This is reason for the horizontal shift of 4 units to the left. The term on the right side is the vertical shift, which

is more straightforward: the function shifts 2 units down because of the subtraction of 2. Take the given point on f, subtract 4 from the x-coordinate, and subtract 2 from the y-coordinate: $(-2 - (4), 4 - (2)) = (-6, 2)$. Thus, (B) is correct.

14. G

Difficulty: Medium

Category: Statistics and Probability

Getting to the Answer: The question asks for the positive difference between the arithmetic mean and median of the given data set. First, calculate the mean by adding all the given numbers and dividing by the total amount of numbers.

$$\frac{-5 + 8 + 6 - 3 - 1}{5} = \frac{5}{5} = 1$$

Next, find the median by arranging the list in ascending order and locating the middle number. $\{-5, 8, 6, -3, -1\} \rightarrow \{-5, -3, -1, 6, 8\}$, so -1 is the median. Remember that the question asks for the positive difference between the two values, which is $1 - (-1) = 1 + 1 = 2$. Thus, (G) is correct.

15. D

Difficulty: Medium

Category: Number and Quantity

Getting to the Answer: The question asks for the length of the longer side of the real object given information about the scale model. Notice that the scale model is given in inches, while the choices are given in feet. However, because units often cancel when you set up a proportion, don't waste time converting everything into feet. Immediately set up a proportion and solve:

$$\frac{12}{18} = \frac{14}{x}$$
$$12x = 14 \times 18$$
$$x = \frac{14 \times 18}{12}$$
$$x = 21$$

The longer side of the real object is 21 feet. Therefore, (D) is correct. Choice A would be the answer if the proportion were set up incorrectly.

PART 4

ACT Reading

CHAPTER 15

The Method for ACT Reading

LEARNING OBJECTIVE

After completing this chapter, you will be able to:

- Apply the ACT Reading Passage Strategy
- Apply the ACT Reading Question Method

How to Do ACT Reading

The ACT Reading Test is usually made up of three independent passages and one Paired Passage set, but it is possible to see four independent passages. Each independent passage or passage set has 750–1,000 words and 10 questions, resulting in a total of 40 questions for you to read and answer before the 35 minutes is up. ACT Reading questions focus more on the author's purpose (*why* she wrote this passage) and the passage's structure (*how* the author makes and supports her points) than on the details or facts of the subject matter (*what* this passage is about).

You have probably heard the misconception that you should read the questions before the passage when you get to the ACT Reading Test. While this may be true for some reading tests you've seen before, it is definitely not true for the ACT Reading Test because of the way the test is designed. Trying to remember the 10 specific questions while you read just to start over again with the next passage is unnecessary and almost always a waste of time.

Instead, the key to maximizing correct answers on the ACT Reading Test is learning the five types of questions that the test is designed to include. You can answer these predictable questions more confidently when you start by noting *how* the author uses certain words or examples and *why* the author wrote the passage.

In this chapter, we'll give you an overview of how to tackle Reading passages and questions. The other chapters in this unit will help you become a stronger reader and present the five ACT Reading question types as well as tips for improving your approach for literature and paired passages.

To see the ACT Reading Question Method in action, try the passage and questions that follow on your own. Then, compare your approach to our recommendations for how to approach ACT Reading. Finally, reflect on how you can become a more efficient test taker.

SOCIAL SCIENCE: The following passage is adapted from an article in a travel journal on tourism in Mexico.

Before tourism became a mainstay of the economy, the value of terrain in Mexico was defined by the arability of the land. To many Americans, tropical tourist-oriented beach towns
5   such as Acapulco and Puerto Vallarta characterize Mexico. These may be the most common sorts of destinations for foreign travelers, but they certainly are not the most representative areas of the country itself. These cities, and others like them, are set
10 up to be attractive to the tourist trade, for better or worse. But the land and culture are vastly different from those of the *altiplano*, or high plain. The function and appearance of each type of terrain dictate this divergence.

15   A tropical beach is a specialized area, not only because it cannot be found outside of specific latitude measurements; any living thing must be highly specialized to survive there or else must acclimate quickly. This is the least livable area:
20 the closer a land dweller moves to the ocean, the fewer the resources necessary to sustain life, and vice versa. Specialized areas in nature are analogous to the settlements of indigenous people in forbidding environments, untouched by
25 modern society. Surroundings dictate the life of a consumer—human or otherwise—and, through adaptation, one is nearly defined by the other. In sharp contrast is the tourist in the tropics, who has likely settled upon a destination by how different it
30 looks from home. In order to appeal to such tourists, the beach towns often contain deliberate marks of earlier civilizations, but these contrivances do not characterize the history or culture of the portions of the country inhabited for function rather than beauty.

35   Mexico's beach towns import resources to accommodate a great number of people, but the terrain itself generally lacks certain basic human necessities: soil suitable for plant cultivation and sufficient reserves of drinking water, both of
40 which occur naturally in the temperate and fertile *altiplano* region. A traveler in Acapulco would learn no more about the foundations of Mexican agriculture than a visitor to Yellowstone Park would learn about New York City. While the tourist often
45 delights in the year-round heat and humidity of the coast, the Mayan people, the first known to flourish in coastal Mexico, are considered to have been brilliant in their eschewing of the natural hazards and barrenness of tropical beaches rather
50 than reveling in this environment. The Mayans relied on the discovery and utilization of *cenotes*, natural springs that provided fresh water. Without a *cenote* nearby, the Mayans would not settle in a locale, no matter how picturesque.

55   The tropical coast is uniformly regulated by the ocean, but the *altiplano* is a tapestry of microclimates that vary from one mile to the next. The coast extends laterally, breaking only for the mouth of a river or the edge of a mountain range,
60 where cliffs are slowly eroding into future beaches. The *altiplano*, on the other hand, expands in all directions and gradually fades into the mountains. The coast presents a border; the *altiplano* is expansive and indefinite. The difference is akin to
65 that between a gymnasium and an open market. A gymnasium is set up to provide a basic range of functions, and because of this, a person familiar with one gymnasium will find similar equipment and be able to obtain a similar experience at
70 another. The gymnasium is equipped to sustain its patrons for a short period of time. It presents a widely understood and repeatable experience to visitors. Any great variance would do customers a disservice. The market, conversely, represents the
75 surroundings through products and vendors. When there are avocados at a market, there are avocados in fields nearby. If one product is found in a disproportionately large number of vendors' stands, it is likely well suited for cultivation or popular
80 with local consumers. The local residents set the tone for both what is available and what is popular. A different market keeps only the conventions of the seller and buyer; the local residents and agricultural terrain dictate price, product, and

85 appearance. The traveler's preferences are not
addressed. An unseasoned cut of meat may not be
available, and its replacement may include an array
of flavors completely new to a foreign palate. A
desired apple could be a rare and exotic indulgence
90 and may give way to the ubiquitous guava.

   The best way to experience foreign lands,
therefore, is a less conventional way: through areas
defined by local culture rather than by tourists,
avoiding both the prepared environments and the
95 artificial familiarity that defines them.

1. Which of the following best states the main idea of
the passage?

  A. More people ought to visit the *altiplano* regions of Mexico instead of its tropical beaches.

  B. Without the contributions of the *altiplano*,
Mexico's beach resort towns would not be able
to sustain themselves or their visitors.

  C. The *altiplano* is more diverse and rich in life
than tropical beaches.

  D. Although tropical beaches are popular tourist
destinations, the *altiplano* provides a truer
experience of Mexican culture.

2. According to the passage, what makes a tropical
beach a specialized area?

  F. It cannot exist outside of particular longitudes.

  G. It resembles a gymnasium.

  H. Land-based life has difficulty finding the
resources to survive there.

  J. One tropical beach is much like any other
tropical beach.

3. As it is used in line 25, the word *dictate* most nearly
means:

  A. command action.

  B. speak for recording.

  C. forbid response.

  D. shape development.

4. The passage most strongly suggests that the Mayan
people were the first to flourish in coastal Mexico
because they:

  F. adapted to thrive in the year-round heat and
humidity.

  G. successfully discovered enough *cenotes* to
support the population.

  H. conveniently avoided the risks of living on the
coastline.

  J. avoided confrontations with others by using
the coast as a border.

5. The comparison between a gymnasium and an
open market in paragraph 4 is meant to:

  A. contrast tourists who visit the coast with those
who visit the *altiplano*.

  B. show that inland areas are better equipped
than beach towns to accommodate the needs
of visitors.

  C. emphasize that beach resorts are set up to cater
to visitors in a way that the *altiplano* is not.

  D. indicate that consumer goods are less available
on the coast than inland.

Reading

Strategic Reading

The ACT Reading Test is an open-book test: the passage is right there for you to reference. Moreover, ACT Reading questions actively test your skill in looking up details. Because of the way the test is constructed, it is in your best interest to read fairly quickly, noting the outline of the passage as you go and marking up the page as you read with margin notes. Your goal is to get a solid understanding of the main idea without wasting time memorizing details.

Be sure to read the pre-passage blurb, the short introduction that comes before the passage. Identify any information that helps you to understand the topic of the passage or to anticipate what the author will discuss. For the passage above, the blurb states the topic (tourism) and announces that the passage is an excerpt from "a travel journal on tourism in Mexico." That's an invitation to keep your eye out for a perspective on tourism in Mexico as you read.

Remember, you should not read even the question stems until you after you've read the passage. There is only one exception to this approach: when you encounter a new passage with less than five minutes remaining, you will probably start with the questions. For more on what to do in this situation, review chapter 21.

You'll learn all the skills you need to **read strategically** in chapter 16, but for now, here's an example of an expert's strategic thinking and passage map notes. Don't worry if your notes don't look exactly like this (or even anything like this, yet). Follow the expert's thought process in the discussion that follows the passage to see what he was thinking and asking as he read the passage.

SOCIAL SCIENCE: The following passage is adapted from an article in a travel journal on tourism in Mexico.

Before tourism became a mainstay of the economy, the value of terrain in Mexico was defined by the arability of the land. To many Americans, tropical tourist-oriented beach towns
5 such as Acapulco and Puerto Vallarta characterize Mexico. These may be the most common sorts of destinations for foreign travelers, but they certainly are not the most representative areas of the country itself. These cities, and others like them, are set
10 up to be attractive to the tourist trade, for better or worse. But the land and culture are vastly different from those of the *altiplano*, or high plain. The function and appearance of each type of terrain dictate this divergence.

beach towns vs. altiplano; beaches = tourism

ANALYSIS

Pre-passage blurb: The passage will address tourism in Mexico.

¶1 introduces a contrast in how land in Mexico is valued, based on tourism or arability. The author connects tourism with tropical beach cities but says these areas are not "representative" of Mexico. The author then contrasts this with the altiplano (note the "But" at the beginning of the sentence in line 11). It seems like coming paragraphs will discuss how "function and appearance" lead to this contrast.

15   A tropical beach is a specialized area, not only
because it cannot be found outside of specific
latitude measurements; any living thing must be
highly specialized to survive there or else must
acclimate quickly. This is the least livable area:
20   the closer a land dweller moves to the ocean,
the fewer the resources necessary to sustain
life, and vice versa. Specialized areas in nature
are analogous to the settlements of indigenous
people in forbidding environments, untouched by
25   modern society. Surroundings dictate the life of
a consumer—human or otherwise—and, through
adaptation, one is nearly defined by the other. In
sharp contrast is the tourist in the tropics, who has
likely settled upon a destination by how different it
30   looks from home. In order to appeal to such tourists,
the beach towns often contain deliberate marks of
earlier civilizations, but these contrivances do not
characterize the history or culture of the portions of
the country inhabited for function rather than beauty.

35   Mexico's beach towns import resources to
accommodate a great number of people, but the
terrain itself generally lacks certain basic human
necessities: soil suitable for plant cultivation and
sufficient reserves of drinking water, both of
40   which occur naturally in the temperate and fertile
altiplano region. A traveler in Acapulco would
learn no more about the foundations of Mexican
agriculture than a visitor to Yellowstone Park would
learn about New York City. While the tourist often
45   delights in the year-round heat and humidity of
the coast, the Mayan people, the first known to
flourish in coastal Mexico, are considered to have
been brilliant in their eschewing of the natural
hazards and barrenness of tropical beaches rather
50   than reveling in this environment. The Mayans
relied on the discovery and utilization of *cenotes*,
natural springs that provided fresh water. Without
a *cenote* nearby, the Mayans would not settle in a
locale, no matter how picturesque.

beaches require adaptation; tourists just want good looks

altiplano has better resources than beach; Maya smart for avoiding beach

¶2 discusses function and appearance of tropical beaches. They are "specialized" environments; organisms must adapt to survive. "In sharp contrast"—the author wants to make a point—tourists are attracted by appearance, not function.

¶3 emphasizes the necessity of basic resources. The author again contrasts beaches and altiplano, saying that the beach lacks resources available in the "temperate and fertile" altiplano. The author clearly favors the altiplano. The second part of the paragraph contains another contrast ("While," line 44), this time between the tourists and the Maya, "brilliant" for settling only where they could find resources.

Reading

55   The tropical coast is uniformly regulated
by the ocean, but the *altiplano* is a tapestry of
microclimates that vary from one mile to the next.
The coast extends laterally, breaking only for the
mouth of a river or the edge of a mountain range,
60   where cliffs are slowly eroding into future beaches.
The *altiplano*, on the other hand, expands in all
directions and gradually fades into the mountains.
The coast presents a border; the *altiplano* is
expansive and indefinite. The difference is akin to
65   that between a gymnasium and an open market.
A gymnasium is set up to provide a basic range of
functions, and because of this, a person familiar
with one gymnasium will find similar equipment
and be able to obtain a similar experience at
70   another. The gymnasium is equipped to sustain
its patrons for a short period of time. It presents
a widely understood and repeatable experience to
visitors. Any great variance would do customers a
disservice. The market, conversely, represents the
75   surroundings through products and vendors. When
there are avocados at a market, there are avocados
in fields nearby. If one product is found in a
disproportionately large number of vendors' stands,
it is likely well suited for cultivation or popular
80   with local consumers. The local residents set the
tone for both what is available and what is popular.
A different market keeps only the conventions
of the seller and buyer; the local residents and
agricultural terrain dictate price, product, and
85   appearance. The traveler's preferences are not
addressed. An unseasoned cut of meat may not be
available, and its replacement may include an array
of flavors completely new to a foreign palate. A
desired apple could be a rare and exotic indulgence
90   and may give way to the ubiquitous guava.

    The best way to experience foreign lands,
therefore, is a less conventional way: through areas
defined by local culture rather than by tourists,
avoiding both the prepared environments and the
95   artificial familiarity that defines them.

---

altiplano is
varied and
extensive;
gym/market
analogy

¶4 expands on the contrast between beach
and *altiplano*. There's more information about
the *altiplano*, shown as a series of contrasts
with the beach. Again, the author's language
choices favor the *altiplano*, describing it as a
"tapestry" that "expands in all directions."
Then, the author presents an extended analogy
comparing the beach to a gym—limited and
uniform, catering to its customers—and the
altiplano to a market—varied and expansive, a
product of many local factors.

*au: altiplano
better
to visit*

¶5 states the author's opinion: that foreign
visitors should seek out local culture, not
artificial sculpted environments.

To sum up **the big picture**, pause for a moment after reading to consider the passage's main idea and the author's purpose for writing it.

BIG PICTURE SUMMARY

Main idea: Although most tourists opt to visit Mexico's resort towns, the author argues that these towns are not representative of the country as a whole.

Author's purpose: To compare the experiences of tourists who visit the Mexican coast and those who visit the *altiplano*

As you consider the overall purpose of strategic reading, think back to what you saw the ACT expert accomplish in each step as he tackled the tourism passage and its questions:

> ### ACT READING PASSAGE STRATEGY
>
> Step 1. Extract everything you can from the pre-passage blurb
>
> Step 2. Read each paragraph actively
>
> Step 3. Summarize the passage's big picture

Don't worry if your notes don't look exactly like the ones in this book. When you review a set of strategic thinking notes, focus on comparing your overall thought process and main takeaways to those of a strategic test taker and determine at least one way you can read more effectively and efficiently next time. When you take the time to read strategically first, you are more likely to answer questions both efficiently and correctly.

The ACT Reading Question Method

Once you've read the passage strategically, you're ready for the questions. Because different question types require different strategies, start by **unpacking the information in the question stem** and identifying the question type while ignoring the answer choices. Remember, there are only five types of questions in the Reading Test, so knowing what type of question you're answering will help you decide where to look for your answer. You'll learn how to do this important step in chapter 17.

Based on the type of question, **research the passage** or consult your passage map to get the information you need. The incorrect answer choices on a multiple-choice test actually have a name: distractors. If the incorrect choices were written to be obviously incorrect, everyone would be able to identify the correct answers. Instead, distractors are carefully crafted to sound correct and distract you from the correct choice, so if you read all of the answer choices as soon as you finish examining the question stem, you risk getting distracted from what's actually supported by the passage. With the relevant part of the passage in mind, **predict** what the correct answer will say before you look at the answer choices.

Finally, use your prediction to evaluate the choices and **find the one correct answer**. Notice that experts don't merely read or look at the answers; they *evaluate* them, knowing that only one of them answers the question correctly and that the other three are demonstrably incorrect in some way. Because ACT experts arm themselves with strong predictions in Step 3, they can often zero in on the correct response without wasting time by rereading or hunting around in the passage to check each answer. You'll go over the strategies and tactics that experts use for Steps 2–4 in chapter 18.

Here's what we did:

ACT READING QUESTION METHOD

Step 1. Unpack the question stem

Step 2. Research the answer

Step 3. Predict the answer

Step 4. Find the one correct answer

Take a look at a strategic approach to the questions from the tourism in Mexico passage. Look for at least one way per question that your original approach could have been faster and more confident.

Question	Explanation
1. Which of the following best states the main idea of the passage? A. More people ought to visit the *altiplano* regions of Mexico instead of its tropical beaches. B. Without the contributions of the *altiplano*, Mexico's beach resort towns would not be able to sustain themselves or their visitors. C. The *altiplano* is more diverse and rich in life than tropical beaches. D. Although tropical beaches are popular tourist destinations, the *altiplano* provides a truer experience of Mexican culture.	The question stem for the first question includes the phrase *main idea*, which indicates that it is a Global question. To answer this type of question, you should review the main idea summary in your notes. Predict that the correct answer will involve a contrast between the tropical beach, which is specialized to cater to tourism, and the *altiplano*, which displays the diversity of the local population. Choice (D) matches this prediction and is correct. Choices B and C, while factually accurate, do not fully capture the main idea of the whole passage. Choice A is too extreme, making a stronger statement than the passage does.

Question	Explanation
2. According to the passage, what makes a tropical beach a specialized area? F. It cannot exist outside of particular longitudes. G. It resembles a gymnasium. H. Land-based life has difficulty finding the resources to survive there. J. One tropical beach is much like any other tropical beach.	The question stem includes the phrase "According to the passage," which indicates that it is a Detail question. The tropical beach as a specialized area is discussed in paragraph 2, which describes the beach as "the least livable area: the closer a land dweller moves to the ocean, the fewer the resources necessary to sustain life." Predict that these regions are specialized because it is hard to live there due to the lack of resources. Choice (H) is correct. Choice F is a distortion; the passage states that tropical beaches cannot exist outside of certain *latitudes*, not *longitudes*. Choice G is a misused detail; while the author does compare tropical beach towns to gymnasiums, the resemblance is not the reason why such locations are specialized. Finally, choice J does not address what makes these areas specialized.
3. As it is used in line 25, the word *dictate* most nearly means: A. command action. B. speak for recording. C. forbid response. D. shape development.	The question stem includes the clues "As used in line" and "the word . . . most nearly means" that indicate that it is a Vocab-in-Context question. To answer a question like this, read a little bit above and below line 25 and think about what the word *dictate* means here. Predict that the environment *impacts* or *molds* the living things that dwell there. Choice (D) is correct. Choices A, B, and C are all other meanings of *dictate* that do not fit the context of the sentence: surroundings cannot *command*, *orate*, or *forbid*.
4. The passage most strongly suggests that the Mayan people were the first to flourish in coastal Mexico because they: F. adapted to thrive in the year-round heat and humidity. G. successfully discovered enough *cenotes* to support the population. H. conveniently avoided the risks of living on the coastline. J. avoided confrontations with others by using the coast as a border.	The question stem includes the phrase "most strongly suggests" that indicates that it is an Inference question. Tropical beaches' inhospitable nature is discussed in paragraph 3, which states that tropical beaches usually lack basic necessities like drinking water. It goes on to discuss the brilliance of the Maya in avoiding barren tropical coasts in favor of *cenotes*, which provided the fresh water they needed. Predict that this is the likely reason why they flourished in coastal regions when others had not. Choice (G) is correct. Choice F is a distortion; the passage says that tourists enjoy the heat and humidity in order to contrast them with the Maya. Choice H is vague and does not specifically explain how the Mayans succeeded. Finally, choice J is out of scope; the passage does not mention any potential conflicts with others.

Question	Explanation
5. The comparison between a gymnasium and an open market in paragraph 4 is meant to: A. contrast tourists who visit the coast with those who visit the *altiplano*. B. show that inland areas are better equipped than beach towns to accommodate the needs of visitors. C. emphasize that beach resorts are set up to cater to visitors in a way that the *altiplano* is not. D. indicate that consumer goods are less available on the coast than inland.	The question stem includes the clue "is meant to" that indicates that it is a Function question. Paragraph 4 says that a gymnasium provides a predictable and repeatable experience for its patrons, whereas the open market offers whatever happens to be available at a given time. Predict that the reference is meant to show that the beach resort towns are set up more specifically for the needs of visitors than the *altiplano* is. Choice (C) is correct. Choice A is out of scope; there is no comparison between different types of tourists. Choice B is opposite; the author says that the beach towns, not the *altiplano*, are set up for tourists. Finally, choice D is out of scope; the passage never compares the quantities of consumer goods in the different areas.

Putting It All Together

As you use the ACT Reading Passage Strategy and ACT Reading Question Method repeatedly, they will become second nature. You won't have to say "step 1, step 2, . . . " in your head; you'll just be performing them, and you'll be improving your score on the ACT Reading Test as you do. Take a moment to go over these steps in action one more time and imagine applying them to the next passage you'll try.

ACT READING PASSAGE STRATEGY

Step 1. Extract everything you can from the pre-passage blurb

Step 2. Read each paragraph actively

Step 3. Summarize the passage's big picture

Strategic test takers . . .

- Never skip the pre-passage blurb. They quickly assess it to gather any information that provides context for the passage or that helps them anticipate what the author will cover.

- Determine the author's purpose for writing each paragraph and anticipate the passage's next paragraph. They "map" the passage by jotting down a short note for each paragraph. They might also circle or underline key words that indicate the author's opinion, details the author highlighted or emphasized, and comparisons and contrasts made in the text.

- Pause for a moment after reading the passage to summarize the big picture. They do this by quickly noting the passage's main idea and the author's primary purpose in writing it.

ACT READING QUESTION METHOD

Step 1. Unpack the question stem

Step 2. Research the answer

Step 3. Predict the answer

Step 4. Find the one correct answer

Strategic test takers . . .

- Step 1.
  - Determine the kind of question being asked, which indicates the kind of thinking and research the question requires.
  - Look for clues in the question stem to tell them where in the passage to find the correct answer.
  - In Chapter 17, you'll learn the characteristics of five types of questions found in the ACT Reading section, and you'll learn how to spot the most common research clues.
- Step 2.
  - Use the passage text or their summaries of it to answer questions.
  - Avoid rereading most or all of the passage.
- Step 3.
  - Predict, specifically or generally, what the correct answer will say.
  - Use their research or big-picture summaries to establish the criteria for the correct answer when a prediction is difficult to make.
- Step 4.
  - Avoid comparing answer choices to each other.
  - Avoid rereading portions of the passage after each answer choice.
  - Confidently choose the answer that matches their prediction and rephrase their predictions when necessary to match the criteria for a correct answer.

In the next section, you'll see another ACT Reading passage, this time with 10 questions. Try to apply the ACT Reading Passage Strategy and the ACT Reading Question Method presented in this lesson to read and answer the questions as quickly and confidently as possible.

Reading

How Much Have You Learned?

Directions: Take as much time as you need on these questions. Work carefully and methodically. There will be opportunities for timed practice in future chapters.

PROSE FICTION: The following passage is a work of fiction based on the real experiences of Wilma Mankiller, the first female principal chief of the Cherokee Nation.

During an interview for a literary magazine, I was asked why my autobiography, titled *Mankiller: A Chief and Her People*, contained so much history of the Cherokee, history that occurred almost five
5 centuries before I was born. That answer is a very simple one for me to give, but may be difficult to understand. The person that I am has been defined by my people and their experiences, whether it was a week ago or centuries ago. When I ran for
10 Deputy Chief in 1985, I ran as a Cherokee, not as a Cherokee woman. I was shocked by how much my gender played a role in the election, because it never once entered my mind when I made the decision to run. My decision to run for office was founded on
15 the desire to help my people recognize their own strength and realize they had the power to rebuild their lives and their communities because they had been able to accomplish these goals in the past.

I am proud to be a Cherokee and I am proud of
20 my people, both past and present. Everything that has happened in our past has affected our present and will affect our future. But one theme remains constant: survival. Our history has been full of obstacles and hardships, yet we persevere. In the
25 late 1830s, the Cherokee were forced to relocate from their homelands throughout the Southeast to Indian Territory in what later became Oklahoma. We were stripped of our land, our homes, and our possessions and then forced to walk to the new
30 territory. Many others may have simply succumbed to the hardships and ceased to exist. Instead, we rebuilt our tribe and our community with a new constitution, a new tribal government including our own judicial system, businesses, schools for
35 both girls and boys, and even newspapers printed in both Cherokee and English. This renewal occurred within seven years of our arrival in Indian Territory. These accomplishments alone show the limitless tenacity of the Cherokee People.

40 It becomes even more clear when the story continues and the history of the early 1900s includes the destruction of everything we had rebuilt in the previous fifty years. Our schools and our courts were closed down. Our sovereignty was
45 stripped away. From 1906 to 1971, we could not even elect our own tribal leaders. But the Cherokee did what we had always done: we survived. This second rebirth took much longer than the first, but we found the strength to do what had been done
50 before. You may wonder why I use "we" when I speak of Cherokee history. Again, I return to the idea that as a Cherokee, my tribe's history has defined me, just as it has defined all Cherokee.

In fact, some of my personal experiences parallel
55 the experiences of my ancestors. In 1956, my parents, siblings, and I were moved to California as part of the Bureau of Indian Affairs relocation program. We were moved away from our family, our tribe, and our community in an effort to
60 improve our lives. Unlike the forced removal of the 1830s, the program was voluntary, but it had the same effect on the tribe as a whole. It divided us and showed us that the federal government believed we could not improve our lives without aid. But
65 just as my ancestors survived the hardships, so did my family. We found a new community at the San Francisco Indian Center. We found a place where we belonged and where we could find strength in sharing experiences with other Native Americans.

70 In 1977, I began working for the Cherokee Nation as an economic stimulus coordinator. I was charged with the task of getting university training in environmental science and health for as many Cherokee students as possible so that they could
75 return to their communities and provide service for their people. All around me, I saw a rebuilt Cherokee government working hard to restore the tribe to its earlier glory. One project in particular was a shining example of how the Cherokee are capable
80 of finding and implementing our own solutions—the

Bell Project. Bell was a small rural community where violence was a method of solving problems, where indoor plumbing was a luxury, and where many houses were on the brink of falling down.

85 We entered the community and asked them what needed to be done and what their dreams for the future included. We asked them to define the problems, then worked with them to decide how they could rebuild their community. As a community,

90 they decided to build a water system, rehabilitate twenty of their existing houses, and build twenty-five new ones. They would provide volunteer labor while we would provide the materials and technical resources by soliciting financial support for

95 the project.

1. According to the passage, Wilma Mankiller included so much Cherokee history in her autobiography because:

    A. her people's history has had a deep impact on her.

    B. being Cherokee is the most important part of her identity.

    C. it helps explain why she ran for Deputy Chief.

    D. she wanted to be viewed as a Cherokee, not as a Cherokee woman.

2. The author mentions the forced relocation of the Cherokee in lines 24–27 in order to:

    F. provide an example of an insurmountable obstacle faced by her people.

    G. describe a personal experience that defined her identity as a Cherokee.

    H. emphasize the Cherokee people's perseverance in the face of hardships.

    J. indicate the motivation behind the Bell Project.

3. The passage states that among the Cherokee tribe's accomplishments in the mid- to late 1800s was:

    A. establishing a court system.

    B. creating trade alliances with neighboring tribes.

    C. building a new water system.

    D. moving the entire tribe to Oklahoma.

4. When Mankiller states "we found the strength to do what had been done before," she's most clearly referring to:

    F. surviving relocation.

    G. creating Cherokee newspapers.

    H. building lodgings and infrastructure.

    J. constructing a new tribal government.

5. As depicted in the passage, the attitude of the Bureau of Indian Affairs in carrying out the relocation program can best be described as:

    A. malicious: the Bureau damaged the Cherokee tribe by separating its communities.

    B. altruistic: the Bureau set out to improve the lives of the Cherokee.

    C. patronizing: the Bureau believed it knew what would best help the Cherokee.

    D. repentant: the Bureau sought to right the wrongs committed in earlier relocations.

6. The author's attitude toward the Bureau of Indian Affairs relocation program in lines 54–64 can best be described as:

    F. resigned.

    G. dismayed.

    H. inspired.

    J. agreeable.

7. The author introduces the San Francisco Indian Center in lines 66–69 in order to:

   A. show where her family found a community after their relocation to California.

   B. illustrate the size of the San Francisco Native American community.

   C. describe how the government helped the author's family after their relocation.

   D. emphasize the need for community centers outside of the Native American tribal lands.

8. As it is used in line 72, the phrase *charged with* most nearly means:

   F. rushed alongside.

   G. burdened with.

   H. entrusted with.

   J. accused of.

9. Which of the following events mentioned in the passage happened first chronologically?

   A. Mankiller ran for Deputy Chief as a Cherokee.

   B. Mankiller moved to California as part of a relocation program.

   C. Mankiller worked as an economic stimulus coordinator.

   D. Mankiller participated in the Bell Project.

10. Which of the following statements best captures why the Bell Project exemplified Wilma Mankiller's vision of the Cherokee?

    F. A community suffered hardship and broke down as a result of violence.

    G. A community received financial and material aid from a larger governing organization.

    H. A community facing difficult challenges decided for itself how to address them and did so.

    J. A community restored its infrastructure in order to improve life for its members.

Reading

Reflect

Directions: Take a few minutes to recall what you've learned and what you've been practicing in this chapter. Consider the following questions, jot down your best answer for each one, and then compare your reflections to the expert responses on the following page. Use your level of confidence to determine what to do next.

1. Describe active, or strategic, reading on ACT passages.

   _____

   _____

   _____

2. What do ACT experts mean by summarizing the big picture of a passage?

   _____

   _____

   _____

3. How can writing brief "margin notes" help you answer ACT Reading questions more effectively?

   _____

   _____

   _____

4. What does an ACT expert look for in the question stem of an ACT Reading question?

   _____

   _____

   _____

5. Why do expert test takers predict or characterize the correct answer to each ACT Reading question before assessing the answer choices?

   _____

   _____

   _____

6. What will you do differently on future passages and their questions?

   _____

   _____

   _____

Reading

Responses

1.   Describe active, or strategic, reading on ACT passages.

Because the ACT asks many questions about why an author has written the passage or about how the author makes a point, expert test takers read for the author's purpose and main idea. Noting key words that indicate a shift or contrast in points of view or that indicate opinions and emphases helps keep ACT experts on point as they anticipate where the passage will go.

2.   What do ACT experts mean by summarizing the big picture of a passage?

To read for the big picture means to be able to accurately summarize the main idea of a passage and note the author's purpose for writing it. The big picture summary helps you answer Global questions and questions that ask about the author's opinion or point of view.

3.   How can writing brief "margin notes" help you answer ACT Reading questions more effectively?

Jotting down margin notes provides a reference "map" to the subject or purpose of each paragraph in the passage. It helps you locate specific subjects or opinions expressed in the passage when they are called out in the questions.

4.   What does an ACT expert look for in the question stem of an ACT Reading question?

Each question stem indicates the type of question and contains clues as to whether the answer will come from researching the passage text or from our big picture summary. Many question stems have specific clues (for example, line numbers or references to details from the passage) that tell you precisely where to research.

5.   Why do expert test takers predict or characterize the correct answer to each ACT Reading question before assessing the answer choices?

Predicting or characterizing the correct answer allows you to evaluate each answer choice one time and avoid rereading for every answer choice. Wrong answers often distort what the passage said or misuse details from the passage, so it's best to research the passage once to know what the correct answer must say before diving into the choices.

6.   What will you do differently on future passages and their questions?

There is no one-size-fits-all answer to this question. Each student has his or her own initial strengths and opportunities in the Reading section. What's important here is that you're honestly self-reflective. Take what you need from the expert's examples and strive to apply it to your own performance. Many test takers convince themselves that they'll never get faster or more confident in ACT Reading, but the truth is, many test takers who now routinely ace the Reading section were much slower and more hesitant before they learned to approach this section systematically and strategically.

Next Steps

If you answered most questions correctly in the "How Much Have You Learned?" section, and if your responses to the Reflect questions were similar to those of an expert, then consider the ACT Reading Question Method an area of strength and move on to the next chapter. Come back to this topic periodically to prevent yourself from getting rusty.

If you don't yet feel confident, review the material in "How to Do ACT Reading" and then try the questions you missed again. As always, be sure to review the explanations closely. Then go online (**kaptest.com/login**) to watch a video lessons about the Kaplan Method for ACT Reading and use your Qbank for more practice. If you haven't already registered your book, do so at *kaptest.com/moreonline*.

GO ONLINE

kaptest.com/login

Answers and Explanations

How Much Have You Learned?

PROSE FICTION: The following passage is a work of fiction based on the real experiences of Wilma Mankiller, the first female principal chief of the Cherokee Nation.

During an interview for a literary magazine, I was asked why my autobiography, titled *Mankiller: A Chief and Her People*, contained so much history of the Cherokee, history that occurred almost five
5 centuries before I was born. That answer is a very simple one for me to give, but may be difficult to understand. The person that I am has been defined by my people and their experiences, whether it was a week ago or centuries ago. When I ran for
10 Deputy Chief in 1985, I ran as a Cherokee, not as a Cherokee woman. I was shocked by how much my gender played a role in the election, because it never once entered my mind when I made the decision to run. My decision to run for office was founded on
15 the desire to help my people recognize their own strength and realize they had the power to rebuild their lives and their communities because they had been able to accomplish these goals in the past.

I am proud to be a Cherokee and I am proud of
20 my people, both past and present. Everything that has happened in our past has affected our present and will affect our future. But one theme remains constant: survival. Our history has been full of obstacles and hardships, yet we persevere. In the
25 late 1830s, the Cherokee were forced to relocate from their homelands throughout the Southeast to Indian Territory in what later became Oklahoma. We were stripped of our land, our homes, and our possessions and then forced to walk to the new
30 territory. Many others may have simply succumbed to the hardships and ceased to exist. Instead, we rebuilt our tribe and our community with a new constitution, a new tribal government including our own judicial system, businesses, schools for
35 both girls and boys, and even newspapers printed in both Cherokee and English. This renewal occurred within seven years of our arrival in Indian Territory. These accomplishments alone show the limitless tenacity of the Cherokee People.

identifies as a Cherokee, not a woman

Cherokee survive

ANALYSIS

Pre-passage blurb: The blurb tells you that you are about to read an extract from an autobiography from the first female chief of the Cherokee Nation. Expect a personal and emotionally-nuanced tone.

¶1 When the author is asked why she included so much Cherokee history in her autobiography, she replies that the experiences of the tribe as a whole have shaped her. For her, Cherokee history is personal and vital, not a collection of facts that happened a long time ago.

¶2 The author states that the great theme in Cherokee history is survival. Despite suffering numerous injustices and material setbacks in the 19th century, the tribe rebuilt its government and school system.

40　　It becomes even more clear when the story continues and the history of the early 1900s includes the destruction of everything we had rebuilt in the previous fifty years. Our schools and our courts were closed down. Our sovereignty was
45　stripped away. From 1906 to 1971, we could not even elect our own tribal leaders. But the Cherokee did what we had always done: we survived. This second rebirth took much longer than the first, but we found the strength to do what had been done
50　before. You may wonder why I use "we" when I speak of Cherokee history. Again, I return to the idea that as a Cherokee, my tribe's history has defined me, just as it has defined all Cherokee.

　　In fact, some of my personal experiences parallel
55　the experiences of my ancestors. In 1956, my parents, siblings, and I were moved to California as part of the Bureau of Indian Affairs relocation program. We were moved away from our family, our tribe, and our community in an effort to
60　improve our lives. Unlike the forced removal of the 1830s, the program was voluntary, but it had the same effect on the tribe as a whole. It divided us and showed us that the federal government believed we could not improve our lives without aid. But
65　just as my ancestors survived the hardships, so did my family. We found a new community at the San Francisco Indian Center. We found a place where we belonged and where we could find strength in sharing experiences with other Native Americans.

70　　In 1977, I began working for the Cherokee Nation as an economic stimulus coordinator. I was charged with the task of getting university training in environmental science and health for as many Cherokee students as possible so that they could
75　return to their communities and provide service for their people. All around me, I saw a rebuilt Cherokee government working hard to restore the tribe to its earlier glory. One project in particular was a shining example of how the Cherokee are capable
80　of finding and implementing our own solutions—the Bell Project. Bell was a small rural community where violence was a method of solving problems, where indoor plumbing was a luxury, and where many houses were on the brink of falling down.

tribal challenges　¶3 Around the turn of the 20th century, the Cherokee nation suffered another blow. Its sovereignty as an independent nation was stripped away, and the schools and government systems described in the previous paragraph ceased to function.

personal challenges　¶4 Here, the author explicitly connects the history of her tribe with her personal story. Like her tribe, she too moved to a new land and initially felt isolated. However, she eventually became comfortable with her new home and community in San Francisco.

85 We entered the community and asked them what
    needed to be done and what their dreams for the
    future included. We asked them to define the prob-
    lems, then worked with them to decide how they
    could rebuild their community. As a community,
90 they decided to build a water system, rehabilitate
    twenty of their existing houses, and build twenty-
    five new ones. They would provide volunteer labor
    while we would provide the materials and technical
    resources by soliciting financial support for
95 the project.

Bell Project

¶5 The author ties together the two big themes of the essay—hardship and survival—in the example of the Bell Project. The people in Bell worked together with the Cherokee nation to rebuild their town. Crucially, they did not rely on federal aid but did everything themselves.

BIG PICTURE SUMMARY

Main idea: The author looks to Cherokee history as a source of inspiration for her own life.

Author's purpose: To explain how the Cherokee Nation has survived many challenges in the past and how its history continues to influence the future of its people

---

1.   A

Difficulty: Low

Category: Detail

Getting to the Answer: The phrase "According to the passage" in the question stem shows that this is a Detail question. In the first paragraph, Wilma Mankiller states that she has been *defined by* her people's experiences. You can predict that she included the history in her autobiography because she felt it was integral to her life story. This fits (A), which is correct.

Beware of B, which is extreme; although being Cherokee is clearly important to her, the passage never says that it is the most important part of her identity. Choice C is a distortion; the history may relate to why she ran for Deputy Chief, but that is not the main reason that she included it. Finally, D is a misused detail; the author does say that gender "never once entered my mind when I made the decision to run," but this does not explain why she put so much history in her autobiography.

2.   H

Difficulty: Medium

Category: Function

Getting to the Answer: The wording "The author mentions . . . in order to" indicates that this is a Function question. The text immediately before the lines in the question asserts that the Cherokee survive hardships through their perseverance. The information about the forced relocation supports this assertion. Choice (H) closely matches this prediction and is correct.

Choice F is too extreme. The author states that the obstacles were overcome; thus, they were not insurmountable. Choices G and J are misused details; the forced relocation occurred in the 1830s and was not part of the author's personal experience, and the Bell Project happened after 1977 and was not directly related to this forced relocation.

3.   A

Difficulty: Low

Category: Detail

Getting to the Answer: The phrase "the passage states" in the question shows that this is a Detail question. The Cherokee's achievements in the mid- to late 1800s must take place between the forced relocation of the late 1830s and the shutdown of the tribal government in the early 1900s. Lines 31–36 present a list of what the Cherokee accomplished during this time period. Only (A) matches any of these accomplishments.

Choice B is out of scope; neither trade nor neighboring tribes are discussed in the passage. Choice C is a misused detail; building a new water system takes place in Bell over a century later. Choice D is opposite; moving the tribe was something they were forced to do, not an accomplishment.

4.   J

Difficulty: High

Category: Inference

Getting to the Answer: The phrase "most clearly referring to" in the question stem indicates that this is an Inference question, since what it asks for is not directly stated in the passage. Read around the line in the question to find what it refers to. Immediately before this line, the passage states "the second rebirth took much longer than the first," so "what had been done before" must refer to a rebirth. Earlier in the paragraph, the speaker explains that the Cherokee's independent government, schools, and courts were shut down. According to the previous paragraph, these were first built after the Cherokee's forced relocation to Indian Territory. Thus, the line quoted in the question must refer to the Cherokee rebuilding their government and society again. Choice (J) is correct.

Choices F, G, and H all reference other things that the Cherokee did at some point in their history but don't actually answer the question at hand. There is no indication that the Cherokee were relocated in this particular instance, so F is incorrect. Choices G and H are incorrect because the paragraph is focused on government, not newspapers or infrastructure.

5.   C

Difficulty: High

Category: Inference

Getting to the Answer: The clues "Bureau of Indian Affairs" and "attitude . . . best be described as" along with a narrow content reference—the relocation program—show that this is an Inference question. The passage says that the program was an attempt to improve the Cherokee's lives, but it actually harmed them and reinforced the idea that they couldn't help themselves. Predict that the answer will involve failing to be helpful. The correct answer is (C).

Choices B and D are both too positive; although the BIA may have intended to help and the relocation was voluntary instead of forced, there is insufficient evidence in the passage to demonstrate that the BIA acted out of altruism or repentance. On the other hand, A is too negative; although the BIA caused harm, there is not enough evidence in the passage to show that the BIA's intent was malicious.

6.   G

Difficulty: Medium

Category: Global

Getting to the Answer: Although this question references a specific paragraph, it asks about the "author's attitude," which pervades the passage as a whole. Therefore, this is a Global question. Mankiller characterizes the BIA relocation as a hardship, similar to her ancestors' removal to the Indian Territory. Predict something like distressed or disturbed. These predictions match (G).

Choice F is a distortion; the author is not resigned to the situation but believes that her people are capable of helping themselves without government assistance. Choices H and J are opposites; both are too positive.

7. A

Difficulty: Medium

Category: Function

Getting to the Answer: The phrase "The author introduces . . . in order to" indicates that this is a Function question. The author leads into this reference by describing her family's relocation experience. She explains how her family found a sense of belonging at this San Francisco community center. This matches answer choice (A).

Choices B, C, and D are all out of scope; the author does not mention community size, government help after relocation, or other community centers.

8. H

Difficulty: Medium

Category: Vocab-in-Context

Getting to the Answer: This question has the distinctive wording of a Vocab-in-Context question. Read the sentence to determine how *charged with* is used in this particular instance. Since it relates to Mankiller's job duties, you can predict that it means assigned or given to. Choice (H) matches this prediction and is correct.

Choices F and J are both other meanings of charge that do not fit in this context. Choice G could describe job duties, but *burdened* is too negative to correctly reflect the author's positive feelings about her position.

9. B

Difficulty: Easy

Category: Detail

Getting to the Answer: The clues "mentioned in the passage" and "chronologically" show that this is a Detail question. Locate the events referenced in the answer choices and determine when they took place. Wilma Mankiller ran for Deputy Chief in 1985, relocated to California in 1956, worked as an economic stimulus coordinator starting in 1977, and participated in the Bell Project during her time as an economic stimulus coordinator. The correct answer is (B); all of the other events happened after Mankiller moved to California as a child.

10. H

Difficulty: Medium

Category: Global

Getting to the Answer: Mankiller's "vision of the Cherokee" is described throughout the passage, making this a Global question. Consult your notes to see that she repeatedly emphasizes the indomitable spirit of the Cherokee nation. Predict that the Bell Project embodies this view because a town going through hardships worked together to resolve the problems it faced. The correct answer is (H).

Choice F is incorrect because Mankiller certainly does not see her people as breaking down under hardships. Choices G and J are factually correct but do not sufficiently highlight the Cherokee's resolve.

ACT Reading Passage Strategies

How Much Do You Know?

Directions: In this chapter, you'll learn how ACT experts actively read the passage, take notes, and summarize the main idea to prepare themselves to answer all of the passage's questions quickly and confidently. You saw this kind of reading modeled in the previous chapter. To get ready for the current chapter, take five minutes to actively read the following passage by:

1. noting the key words that indicate the author's point of view and the passage's structure

2. jotting down a quick description next to each paragraph

3. summarizing the big picture (the passage's main idea and the author's purpose for writing it)

When you're done, compare your work to the explanations on the following page.

HUMANITIES: This passage explores the relationship between the immigrant experience and one person's career choice.

My grandfather was born in a turbulent time in Russia. His non-communist lineage made him unwelcome before he had left the womb. His father, an officer in the Russian army, was considered
5 an enemy of the communist Bolsheviks, so my grandfather lived less than a year in what was his native Moscow and spent most of his younger years moving across Asia. Despite this, he had pride in being Russian, associated with Russians throughout
10 his life, and would frequently quiz me on Russian history. This all in tribute to a country that ended up under hostile rule during the time his mother was pregnant with him.

As a child, exiled to Siberia, my grandfather
15 heard his father tell of the greatness that existed within the country that had forced the family into exile. It was known that, first with his parents, and later as an adult, my grandfather was going to have to seek a new place to call home.
20 Despite this foregone conclusion, Russia was still romanticized, and my grandfather learned to treat the country with reverence. This was in contrast to the sentiments found in other recently exiled Russians, who would not simply lament the actions
25 taken by the country but disparage all eight million square miles. In my family's search for a place to settle, attempting to forge a consistent identity was nearly impossible, as no one knew whether the next location would hold for a month, let alone a year.
30 All hoped for an unattainable "new Moscow."

The first long-term refuge was found, ironically, in China, which would have its own communist revolution. After several years of relative stability, this revolution precipitated the move to the
35 United States. Upon arrival in San Francisco, my grandfather, along with my grandmother and their young son, my father, found other Russian immigrants who were also new to the country. "*Ya amerikanets*," people would say, and despite the fact
40 that they were recent immigrants who associated primarily with those of shared ethnicity and circumstance, they would play the role they desired and repeat "*ya amerikanets*"—"I am American." They would share many stories about their native
45 land, but did not repeat "*ya russkiy*," because being Russian went without saying. While it was clear that this would be the last country my grandfather would reside in and that he wished to become more American, it was perhaps the most confusing
50 of times. It was less a problem of acclimating to an adopted setting and more of dealing with a permanent setting at all. The only consistency throughout the first thirty years of my grandfather's life was the knowledge that every "home" was
55 temporary, and now this was no longer the case. I often wonder if his successful career in the real estate business had anything to do with what must have been a rare transformation of circumstance.

Not only was my grandfather interested in real
60 estate, he was ardent about the importance of ownership, a naturally discordant view to that of the then Soviet Union. Thus, selling homes became a purpose in addition to an occupation.

Part of his success in real estate was owed to strategic compromise. Considering American sentiments regarding Russia during the Cold War, there were times that he was sure he lost certain house sales due to his last name and accent. However, to those willing to listen, he found advantages to informing people that he was an exiled Russian who ardently disagreed with the communist government. He would also point out his pride in being a new American and allow a potential buyer to degrade Russia without blinking.

Fortunately, the 1950s were a time of settling across the country, and this made real estate a very lucrative profession. It wasn't just this that attracted my grandfather, though; he also saw it as an opportunity to give tiny parts of the country to other people—returning the favor, in a way.

Yet, it always seemed that something vital still rested in the opposite hemisphere. Once communism fell, he began returning to Russia yearly. He and my grandmother never showed the family pictures from Russia the way they would from the various cruise ships they traveled on; it could be deduced that returning to Russia was a journey of personal necessity for him rather than pleasure, and the encounter elucidated his existence in a way that being solely American could not. In selling real estate, my grandfather had worked to make this unnecessary. I believe that he wished for people to keep those houses and pass them down to later generations, giving the space a sort of familial permanence rather than a fleeting stay.

For most, the thought of real estate agents conjures up images of smiling advertisements on benches and buses and the skill of selling something so important. Many are wary of salespeople in general, questioning the practice of convincing people something is in their best interest when the salesperson stands to personally benefit. My grandfather did financially benefit from sales, but there was more to it: his realization of the American dream only made him want to be a part of others reaching for the same thing, whether their native home was around the block or thousands of miles away.

Reading

Check Your Work

HUMANITIES: This passage explores the relationship between the immigrant experience and one person's career choice.

My grandfather was born in a turbulent time in Russia. His non-communist lineage made him unwelcome before he had left the womb. His father, an officer in the Russian army, was considered

5 an enemy of the communist Bolsheviks, so my grandfather lived less than a year in what was his native Moscow and spent most of his younger years moving across Asia. Despite this, he had pride in being Russian, associated with Russians throughout

10 his life, and would frequently quiz me on Russian history. This all in tribute to a country that ended up under hostile rule during the time his mother was pregnant with him.

As a child, exiled to Siberia, my grandfather

15 heard his father tell of the greatness that existed within the country that had forced the family into exile. It was known that, first with his parents, and later as an adult, my grandfather was going to have to seek a new place to call home.

20 Despite this foregone conclusion, Russia was still romanticized, and my grandfather learned to treat the country with reverence. This was in contrast to the sentiments found in other recently exiled Russians, who would not simply lament the actions

25 taken by the country but disparage all eight million square miles. In my family's search for a place to settle, attempting to forge a consistent identity was nearly impossible, as no one knew whether the next location would hold for a month, let alone a year.

30 All hoped for an unattainable "new Moscow."

The first long-term refuge was found, ironically, in China, which would have its own communist revolution. After several years of relative stability, this revolution precipitated the move to the

35 United States. Upon arrival in San Francisco, my grandfather, along with my grandmother and their young son, my father, found other Russian immigrants who were also new to the country. "*Ya amerikanets*," people would say, and despite the fact

40 that they were recent immigrants who associated primarily with those of shared ethnicity and

grandfather, chaotic childhood

still loves Russia

ANALYSIS

Pre-passage blurb: From this blurb, you learn that the passage will focus on one person's career choice and, in particular, how that person's career choice is impacted by being an immigrant.

¶1 The author introduces his grandfather and gives some background, focusing in particular on his grandfather's chaotic and unstable childhood.

¶2 This paragraph provides additional context about why the author's grandfather still feels positively toward Russia, despite his unstable, chaotic childhood.

circumstance, they would play the role they desired
and repeat *"ya amerikanets"*—"I am American."
They would share many stories about their native
45 land, but did not repeat *"ya russkiy,"* because being
Russian went without saying. While it was clear
that this would be the last country my grandfather
would reside in and that he wished to become
more American, it was perhaps the most confusing
50 of times. It was less a problem of acclimating to
an adopted setting and more of dealing with a
permanent setting at all. The only consistency
throughout the first thirty years of my grandfather's
life was the knowledge that every "home" was
55 temporary, and now this was no longer the case.
I often wonder if his successful career in the real
estate business had anything to do with what must
have been a rare transformation of circumstance.

Not only was my grandfather interested in real
60 estate, he was ardent about the importance of
ownership, a naturally discordant view to that of
the then Soviet Union. Thus, selling homes became
a purpose in addition to an occupation.

Part of his success in real estate was owed to
65 strategic compromise. Considering American
sentiments regarding Russia during the Cold War,
there were times that he was sure he lost certain
house sales due to his last name and accent.
However, to those willing to listen, he found
70 advantages to informing people that he was an
exiled Russian who ardently disagreed with the
communist government. He would also point out
his pride in being a new American and allow a
potential buyer to degrade Russia without blinking.

75 Fortunately, the 1950s were a time of settling
across the country, and this made real estate a
very lucrative profession. It wasn't just this that
attracted my grandfather, though; he also saw it as
an opportunity to give tiny parts of the country to
80 other people—returning the favor, in a way.

Yet, it always seemed that something vital
still rested in the opposite hemisphere. Once
communism fell, he began returning to Russia
yearly. He and my grandmother never showed the
85 family pictures from Russia the way they would
from the various cruise ships they traveled on; it

*moves
to US,
becomes
real estate
agent*

¶3 In this paragraph, the author's grandfather
starts to find stability: first in China, then in
the United States. There, the author's grandfather finds a group of immigrants like him, and
the author reflects on his grandfather's journey. At the end of this paragraph, it's revealed
that his grandfather is a real estate agent.

*real estate
is his
vocation*

¶4 The author expands on his grandfather's
career choice, adding a deeper meaning
behind the choice.

*allows
people
to insult
Russia*

¶5 The author opens by discussing his grandfather's willingness to strategically compromise, even if it meant degrading the home
country he felt so positively about.

*wants to
give back*

¶6 Selling homes was not just a career or a
source of income for the author's grandfather;
rather, it was a way for him to help others in
the way he felt he had been helped.

Reading

could be deduced that returning to Russia was a journey of personal necessity for him rather than pleasure, and the encounter elucidated his existence

90 in a way that being solely American could not. In selling real estate, my grandfather had worked to make this unnecessary. I believe that he wished for people to keep those houses and pass them down to later generations, giving the space a sort of familial

95 permanence rather than a fleeting stay.

For most, the thought of real estate agents conjures up images of smiling advertisements on benches and buses and the skill of selling something so important. Many are wary of

100 salespeople in general, questioning the practice of convincing people something is in their best interest when the salesperson stands to personally benefit. My grandfather did financially benefit from sales, but there was more to it: his realization of the

105 American dream only made him want to be a part of others reaching for the same thing, whether their native home was around the block or thousands of miles away.

visits Russia every year

¶7 Now that Russia is more open than it was in the author's grandfather's past, he makes a point to visit yearly but does not share these journeys with his family. The author has a sense that his grandfather uses this annual trip to remind himself of his motivations.

wants to give people a home

¶8 Real estate agent may not have seemed like an obvious career choice for the author's grandfather, but his motivation to help others find their own *native homes*, wherever that may be, resulted in both his own financial success and his success in an unexpected career.

BIG PICTURE SUMMARY

Main idea: A Russian immigrant attempts to make a life and find a purpose in his new homeland through real estate.

Author's purpose: To reminisce about his grandfather's life experiences, memories, and impact

---

ACT Reading Strategies: Key Words, Margin Notes, and the Big Picture Summary

LEARNING OBJECTIVES

After this lesson, you will be able to:

- Identify key words that promote active reading and relate passage text to the questions
- Create short, accurate margin notes that help you research the text efficiently
- Summarize the big picture of the passage

To read and map a passage like this:

NATURAL SCIENCE: This passage is adapted from an essay about astrobiology.

Astrobiology, also known as exobiology, is a complex, multidisciplinary science dedicated to studying the possibility of life outside the confines of Earth. Humanity has speculated for centuries
5 about whether or not we are alone in the universe, but with the advent of space exploration in the 1950s and 1960s, for the first time in human history there was the possibility of actually exploring the surface of alien planets. Scientists
10 and engineers worked together to build what they called landers, spacecraft capable not only of landing on other planets, but also of exploring and photographing them.

When the first of the two Viking landers touched
15 down on Martian soil on July 20, 1976, and began to send camera images back to Earth, the scientists at the Jet Propulsion Laboratory could not suppress a certain nervous anticipation. Like people who hold a ticket to a lottery, they had a one-in-a-million chance
20 of winning. The first photographs that arrived, however, did not contain any evidence of life. They revealed merely a barren landscape littered with rocks and boulders. The view resembled nothing so much as a flat section of desert. In fact, the winning
25 entry in a contest at J.P.L. for the photograph most accurately predicting what Mars would look like was a snapshot taken from a particularly arid section of the Mojave Desert.

The scientists were soon ready to turn their
30 attention from visible life to microorganisms. The twin Viking landers carried out experiments designed to detect organic compounds. Researchers thought it possible that life had developed on early Mars just as it is thought to have developed on
35 Earth, through the gradual chemical evolution of complex organic molecules. To detect biological activity, Martian soil samples were treated with various nutrients that would produce characteristic by-products if life forms were active in the soil.
40 The results from all three experiments were inconclusive. The fourth experiment heated a soil sample to look for signs of organic material but found none—an unexpected result because organic compounds were thought to have been present due
45 to the steady bombardment of the Martian surface by meteorites.

The absence of organic materials, some scientists speculated, was the result of intense ultraviolet radiation penetrating the atmosphere
50 of Mars and destroying organic compounds in the soil. Although Mars' atmosphere was at one time rich in carbon dioxide and thus thick enough to protect its surface from the harmful rays of the sun, the carbon dioxide had gradually left the
55 atmosphere and been converted into rocks. This means that even if life had gotten a start on early Mars, it could not have survived the exposure to ultraviolet radiation that occurred when the atmosphere thinned. Mars never developed a
60 protective layer of ozone as Earth did.

Despite the disappointing Viking results, there are those who still keep open the possibility of life on Mars. They point out that the Viking data cannot be considered the final word on Martian life
65 because the two landers sampled only limited—and

uninteresting—sites. The Viking landing sites were not chosen for what they might tell of the planet's biology. They were chosen primarily because they appeared to be safe for landing a spacecraft. The
70 landing sites were on parts of the Martian plains that appeared relatively featureless according to orbital photographs.

The type of terrain that these researchers suggest may be a possible hiding place for active
75 life has an Earthly parallel: the ice-free region of southern Victoria Land, Antarctica, where the temperatures in some dry valleys average below zero. Organisms known as endoliths, a form of blue-green algae that has adapted to this harsh
80 environment, were found living inside certain translucent, porous rocks in these Antarctic valleys. The argument based on this discovery is that if life did exist on early Mars, it is possible that it escaped worsening conditions by similarly seeking refuge
85 in rocks. Skeptics object, however, that Mars in its present state is simply too dry, even compared with Antarctic valleys, to sustain any life whatsoever.

Should Mars eventually prove barren of life, as some suspect, then this finding would have
90 a significant impact on the current view of the chemical origins of life. It could be much more difficult to get life started on a planet than scientists thought before the Viking landings.

The possibility exists, of course, that our
95 definition of what constitutes life may not hold true throughout the universe. It has long been speculated that our current belief that all life must contain carbon, oxygen, calcium, chlorine, potassium, and phosphorous simply because this holds true on our
100 planet might be too narrow a view. In 2010, NASA scientists believed they had discovered a bacterium that used arsenic in place of phosphorous, though these exciting findings later proved to be incorrect. The possibility remains, however, that future
105 astrobiologists exploring the Martian surface from 140 million miles away might be able to make use of a more advanced definition of what we call "life."

You need to know this:

- ACT Reading passages are preceded by short blurbs that tell you about the author and source of the passage.
- There are three categories of key words that reveal an author's purpose and point of view and that unlock the passage's structure:
  - **opinion and emphasis**—words that signal that the author finds a detail noteworthy (e.g., *especially, crucial, important, above all*) or has an opinion about it (e.g., *fortunately, disappointing, I suggest, it seems likely*)
  - **connection and contrast**—words that suggest that a subsequent detail continues the same point (e.g., *moreover, in addition, also, further*) or that indicate a change in direction or point of difference (e.g., *but, yet, despite, on the other hand*)
    - In some passages, these key words may show steps in a process or developments over time (e.g., *traditionally, in the past, recently, today, first, second, finally, earlier, since*)
  - **evidence and example**—words that indicate an argument (the use of evidence to support a conclusion), either the author's or someone else's (e.g., *thus, therefore, because*), or that introduce an example to clarify or support another point (e.g., *for example, this shows, to illustrate*)
- ACT experts read strategically, jotting down brief, accurate, and useful margin notes next to each paragraph.
- Expert test takers summarize the passage as a whole by paying attention to its big picture:
  - **Main Idea**—the author's primary conclusion or overall takeaway
  - **Purpose**—the author's reason for writing the passage
    - Express this as a verb (e.g., *to explain, to evaluate, to argue, to refute*)

> ### WHY READ THE PASSAGE BEFORE READING THE QUESTIONS?
>
> Each ACT Reading passage is accompanied by 10 questions. These questions will ask about both the passage as a whole and specific paragraphs, details, or arguments within the passage. ACT experts use deliberate reading strategies to answer all of the questions quickly and accurately with as little rereading as possible.

You need to do this:

> ### ACT READING PASSAGE STRATEGY
>
> Step 1. Extract everything you can from the pre-passage blurb
>
> Step 2. Read each paragraph actively
>
> Step 3. Summarize the passage's big picture

Extract everything you can from the pre-passage blurb

Quickly prepare for the passage by unpacking the pre-passage blurb.

- What do the title and date of the original book or article tell you about the author and her purpose for writing?
- What information can you glean from the source (nonfiction book, novel, academic journal, etc.)?
- Is there any other information that provides context for the passage?

Read each paragraph actively

Note key words (circling or underlining them may help) and use them to focus your reading on:

- the author's purpose and point of view,
- the relationships between ideas, and
- the illustrations or other support provided for passage claims.

Reading

WHY PAY ATTENTION TO KEY WORDS?

Key words indicate opinions and signal structure that make the difference between correct and incorrect answers on ACT questions. Consider this test-like question and two potential choices:

The passage makes clear that coffee beans that grow at high altitudes typically produce:

A. dark, mellow coffee when brewed.

B. light, acidic coffee when brewed.

To answer that based on an ACT passage, you will need to determine whether the author said:

Type X coffee beans grow at very high altitudes, *so* they produce a dark, mellow coffee when brewed.

That would make choice (A) correct. But if the author instead said:

Type X coffee beans grow at very high altitudes, *but* they produce a *surprisingly* dark, mellow coffee when brewed.

Then choice (B) would be correct. The facts in the statements did not change at all, but the correct answer to the ACT question would be different in each case because of the key words the author chose to include.

As you read, jot down brief, accurate margin notes that will help you research questions about specific details, examples, and paragraphs.

- These notes can be referred to as a passage map, designed to guide you as you research your answers.
- Paraphrase the text (put it into your own words) as you go.
- Ask, "What's the author's point and purpose?" for each paragraph.

WHY JOT DOWN NOTES NEXT TO EACH PARAGRAPH?

The ACT Reading Test is an open-book test. The answer is always in the passage. Margin notes help you zero in on the details and opinions you need to answer questions like these:

- As it is used in line 25, the word *dictate* most nearly means:
- The comparison between a gymnasium and an open market in paragraph 4 is meant to:
- The passage most strongly suggests that the Mayan people were the first to flourish in coastal Mexico because they:

Summarize the passage's big picture

At the end of the passage, pause for a few seconds to summarize the passage's big picture to prepare for Global questions. Ask yourself:

- "What is the main idea of the entire passage?"
- "Why did the author write it?"

WHY SUMMARIZE THE PASSAGE'S BIG PICTURE?

Summarizing the big picture prepares you to answer Global questions such as the following:

"Which of the following best states the main idea of the passage?"

Explanation

NATURAL SCIENCE: This passage is adapted from an essay about astrobiology.

Astrobiology, also known as exobiology, is a complex, multidisciplinary science dedicated to studying the possibility of life outside the confines of Earth. Humanity has speculated for centuries
5 about whether or not we are alone in the universe, but with the advent of space exploration in the 1950s and 1960s, for the first time in human history there was the possibility of actually exploring the surface of alien planets. Scientists
10 and engineers worked together to build what they called landers, spacecraft capable not only of landing on other planets, but also of exploring and photographing them.

When the first of the two Viking landers touched
15 down on Martian soil on July 20, 1976, and began to send camera images back to Earth, the scientists at the Jet Propulsion Laboratory could not suppress a certain nervous anticipation. Like people who hold a ticket to a lottery, they had a one-in-a-million chance
20 of winning. The first photographs that arrived, however, did not contain any evidence of life. They revealed merely a barren landscape littered with rocks and boulders. The view resembled nothing so much as a flat section of desert. In fact, the winning
25 entry in a contest at J.P.L. for the photograph most accurately predicting what Mars would look like was a snapshot taken from a particularly arid section of the Mojave Desert.

The scientists were soon ready to turn their
30 attention from visible life to microorganisms. The twin Viking landers carried out experiments designed to detect organic compounds. Researchers thought it possible that life had developed on early Mars just as it is thought to have developed on
35 Earth, through the gradual chemical evolution of complex organic molecules. To detect biological activity, Martian soil samples were treated with various nutrients that would produce characteristic by-products if life forms were active in the soil.
40 The results from all three experiments were inconclusive. The fourth experiment heated a soil sample to look for signs of organic material but

ANALYSIS

Pre-passage blurb: In the pre-passage blurb, we learn the topic of the essay: astrobiology.

astrobiology: finding non-Earth life **¶1** The author defines astrobiology and provides a brief explanation for why it is a field of study.

Mars landing no signs of life **¶2** The author changes tone in the second paragraph, prompting excitement, only to shift back into a more neutral voice for the second half of the paragraph as she describes the disappointing results of the Viking landers in 1976.

inconclusive tests for micro-organisms **¶3** This paragraph transitions from what was expected out of the initial landing to what happened next, describing the next set of efforts undertaken to better study life beyond Earth, this time with a focus on microorganisms. Unfortunately, the results from these experiments were inconclusive.

found none—an unexpected result because organic compounds were thought to have been present due
45 to the steady bombardment of the Martian surface by meteorites.

The absence of organic materials, some scientists speculated, was the result of intense ultraviolet radiation penetrating the atmosphere
50 of Mars and destroying organic compounds in the soil. Although Mars' atmosphere was at one time rich in carbon dioxide and thus thick enough to protect its surface from the harmful rays of the sun, the carbon dioxide had gradually left the
55 atmosphere and been converted into rocks. This means that even if life had gotten a start on early Mars, it could not have survived the exposure to ultraviolet radiation that occurred when the atmosphere thinned. Mars never developed a
60 protective layer of ozone as Earth did.

Despite the disappointing Viking results, there are those who still keep open the possibility of life on Mars. They point out that the Viking data cannot be considered the final word on Martian life
65 because the two landers sampled only limited—and uninteresting—sites. The Viking landing sites were not chosen for what they might tell of the planet's biology. They were chosen primarily because they appeared to be safe for landing a spacecraft. The
70 landing sites were on parts of the Martian plains that appeared relatively featureless according to orbital photographs.

The type of terrain that these researchers suggest may be a possible hiding place for active
75 life has an Earthly parallel: the ice-free region of southern Victoria Land, Antarctica, where the temperatures in some dry valleys average below zero. Organisms known as endoliths, a form of blue-green algae that has adapted to this harsh
80 environment, were found living inside certain translucent, porous rocks in these Antarctic valleys. The argument based on this discovery is that if life did exist on early Mars, it is possible that it escaped worsening conditions by similarly seeking refuge
85 in rocks. Skeptics object, however, that Mars in its present state is simply too dry, even compared with Antarctic valleys, to sustain any life whatsoever.

no organic material b/c UV?

¶4 There is some speculation around why organic materials are absent; some scientists believe it was the result of intense UV light.

may be life elsewhere, testing locations limited

¶5 Scientists haven't given up; more research is needed, and they have suggestions about how this research can be better conducted.

how life could exist in rocks

¶6 Although Earth and Mars are very different planets, there is one place in Antarctica that might allow us to study the development of life in very dry places without leaving the planet; there are skeptics, though.

Should Mars eventually prove barren of life, as some suspect, then this finding would have
90 a significant impact on the current view of the chemical origins of life. It could be much more difficult to get life started on a planet than scientists thought before the Viking landings.

The possibility exists, of course, that our
95 definition of what constitutes life may not hold true throughout the universe. It has long been speculated that our current belief that all life must contain carbon, oxygen, calcium, chlorine, potassium, and phosphorous simply because this holds true on our
100 planet might be too narrow a view. In 2010, NASA scientists believed they had discovered a bacterium that used arsenic in place of phosphorous, though these exciting findings later proved to be incorrect. The possibility remains, however, that future
105 astrobiologists exploring the Martian surface from 140 million miles away might be able to make use of a more advanced definition of what we call "life."

impact if no life

definition of life may change

¶7 If Mars does prove to be completely free of life, this finding could be just as impactful on our collective scientific knowledge.

¶8 Our very definition of life may be incorrect. There is still much more to learn in the field of astrobiology!

BIG PICTURE SUMMARY

Main idea: Despite initial tests for Martian life yielding inconclusive results, the continued search for possible life-forms could yield valuable information.

Author's purpose: To inform the reader about both a brief history of and the predicted future of astrobiology discoveries

---

Now, try another passage on your own. Use the ACT Reading strategies and tactics you've been learning to read and map this passage as quickly and accurately as you can.

Try on Your Own

Directions: Actively read and map the following passage by:

1. circling or underlining key words from the opinion and emphasis, connection and contrast, or evidence and example categories mentioned earlier in the lesson

2. jotting down brief, accurate margin notes that reflect good paraphrases of each paragraph

3. summing up the big picture

When you're done, compare your work to that of an expert in the explanations found at the end of the chapter.

HUMANITIES: This passage is adapted from an article about modern architecture.

Fallingwater, a small country house constructed in 1936, stands as perhaps the greatest residential building achievement of the American architect Frank Lloyd Wright. In designing the dwelling
5 for the Pittsburgh millionaire Edgar J. Kaufmann, Wright was confronted with an unusually challenging site beside a waterfall deep in a Pennsylvania ravine. However, Wright viewed this difficult location not as an obstacle but as a unique
10 opportunity to put his architectural ideas into concrete form.

In the early 1930s, Edgar J. Kaufmann's son, Edgar J. Kaufmann Jr., studied with Wright as an apprentice at Wright's Taliesin Studio in Spring
15 Green, Wisconsin. At the time, architecture critics deemed Wright's style anachronistic and assumed that his career was coming to an end. Kaufmann Jr., on the other hand, greatly admired Wright's work and was delighted to introduce his parents
20 to the esteemed architect. Shortly thereafter, the Kaufmanns asked Wright to design Fallingwater.

The site Kaufmann chose for his country getaway was originally the location of a cabin in Mill Run, Pennsylvania, that he offered as a vacation
25 retreat for the numerous employees he oversaw at Kaufmann's Department Store, located in downtown Pittsburgh. When the Great Depression struck, Kaufmann's employees could no longer afford the cost of traveling more than 60 miles to Mill Run,
30 and Kaufmann decided that the land, a wooded area nestled along the banks of a mountain stream called Bear Run, was an ideal location for a vacation home. Kaufmann had assumed that the home would stand

at the bottom of a nearby waterfall, where it would
35 provide a perfect venue from which to appreciate the view. However, Wright had other ideas. When Wright showed Kaufmann his plans, Kaufmann initially balked, but Wright convinced him that incorporating the falls into the design of the house
40 was far preferable. In the end, Wright was able to turn Fallingwater into an artistic link between untamed nature and domestic tranquility—and a masterpiece in his brilliant career.

Edgar J. Kaufmann's original plan to build his
45 house on the ample flat land at the bottom of the waterfall would indisputably have proven less challenging. Wright's more daring response to the site required builders to construct the house on a small stone precipice atop the falls. Wright
50 further proposed extending the living room of the house out over the rushing water and making use of modern building techniques so that no vertical supports would be needed to hold up the room. Wright brilliantly utilized the "cantilever"
55 technique, in which steel rods are laid inside a shelf of concrete, eliminating the need for external supports. Unfortunately, however, the builders did not employ an adequate amount of reinforcing steel to support the first floor. Kaufmann had hired
60 consulting engineers to review Wright's design prior to Fallingwater's construction, but Wright dismissed the engineers' claims that the main floor girders needed additional support. Over time, the first floor cantilever began to sag, and in 2002, a technique
65 called post-tensioning was used to permanently repair the gradual collapse.

Despite Wright's miscalculation, Fallingwater, as a whole, is an impressive structure. Rather than allowing the environment to determine the

70 placement and shape of the house, Wright sought to construct a home that intentionally confronted and interacted with the landscape. Each bedroom has its own terrace, and cornerless windows open outward so that window panes do not obstruct

75 the spectacular view. In addition, Fallingwater contains a great many traditional and natural building materials. The home's 5,300-square foot expanse includes custom-designed black walnut wood furniture and walls and floors constructed

80 of locally sourced sandstone. The boulders that provide the foundation for the house also extend up through the floor and form part of the fireplace. A staircase in the living room extends down to an enclosed bathing pool at the top of

85 the waterfall. To Wright, the ideal dwelling in this spot was not simply a modern extravaganza or a direct extension of natural surroundings; rather, it was a little of both.

Architecture enthusiasts have taken a wide

90 range of approaches to understanding this unique building. Some have asserted that the house exalts the artist's triumph over untamed nature.

Others have compared Wright's building to a cave, providing a psychological and physical safe

95 haven from a harsh, violent world. The members of the American Institute of Architects named Fallingwater the "best all-time work of American architecture," and the Western Pennsylvania Conservancy, which has owned and preserved

100 Fallingwater since 1963, hails the building as an inspiration.

Edgar Kaufmann Jr. may have summed up the innovation and awe of Fallingwater best when he said, "Wright understood that people were

105 creatures of nature; hence, an architecture which conformed to nature would conform to what was basic in people. . . . Sociability and privacy are both available, as are the comforts of home and the adventures of the seasons." This, then, is Frank

110 Lloyd Wright's achievement in Fallingwater: a home that connects the human and the natural for the invigoration and exaltation of both.

How Much Have You Learned?

Directions: Take five minutes to actively read the following passage by:

1. noting the key words
2. jotting down margin notes next to each paragraph
3. summarizing the big picture

When you're done, compare your work to the explanations at the end of the chapter.

SOCIAL SCIENCE: This passage is adapted from an article about how humans develop language.

The influential theory of universal grammar (UG) postulates that all humans have an innate, genetic understanding of certain grammatical "rules," which are universal across all languages and
5 absolutely not affected by environment. The idea of such a universal grammar has a long history, starting with Roger Bacon's thirteenth-century book *Overview of Grammar* and continuing through the Renaissance with attempts to construct an
10 ideal language. In the eighteenth century, the first edition of the Encyclopedia Britannica included a section dedicated to universal grammar. In modern times, however, the linguistic theory of universal grammar is most closely associated with Noam
15 Chomsky, who did much to codify and popularize it in the 1950s–1970s. According to Chomsky, we are all born with a knowledge of "deep structure," basic linguistic constructions that allow us, if not to understand all languages, at least to understand
20 how they are put together. From there, we have only to learn how the parameters are set in our particular language in order to create an unlimited number of "correct" utterances.

For example, he suggests that structure
25 dependency—a rule that says that sentences are defined by phrase structure, not linear structure— is inherent to all languages, with minor variations. Thus, the meaning of a sentence is really dependent on the meaning of its phrases, rather than each
30 individual word. In addition, the head parameter rule stipulates that each phrase contains a "head" (main) word, and all languages have the head word in essentially the same position within the phrase. Chomsky's famous sentence "Colorless green ideas

35 sleep furiously" exemplifies this theory of universal grammar—while the sentence itself is meaningless, it is easily recognizable as a grammatical sentence that fits a basic but higher level of organization. "Furiously sleep ideas green colorless," on the other
40 hand, is obviously not a grammatical sentence, and it is difficult to discern any kind of meaning in it. For other evidence to support this theory, Chomsky points to our relative ease in translating one language to another; again, while we may
45 not necessarily recognize individual words in an unfamiliar language, we can certainly recognize and engage with sentences that are grammatical.

This evidence is still fairly theoretical, receiving play mostly in the linguistic sphere rather than in
50 the biological sciences. Most of those researching the theory seem more concerned with attempting to draw universal parallels across languages than with searching for biological evidence of such phenomena. We might ask: Where exactly are these
55 universal grammar constraints located in our genetic code? How and when are they altered by natural evolutionary processes—or do they remain relatively unaltered and non-mutated from generation to generation? As both languages and human beings
60 evolve over time, does UG also evolve or stay relatively stable?

Even within the linguistic sphere, Chomsky's theory has drawn criticism. Some scientists suggest that by ignoring the role of environment
65 in language development, Chomsky completely discredits the possibly important effect our surroundings could have on language development. Still other researchers say that universal grammar is not nearly as ordered and absolute as Chomsky
70 and other linguists make it out to be—that merely

identifying similarities in different languages does not prove that a universal grammar underlies them. They suggest that since the universal grammar theory is not falsifiable, it is in fact pseudoscientific
75 rather than scientific, the result of our flawed human tendency to impose order where there is none.

More recent researchers have begun to advocate that, rather than focusing on explaining linguistic
80 similarities among various languages, we instead acknowledge the evolutionary roots of language and look specifically for neurobiological explanations. Claiming that the humanistic exploration of universal grammar is too abstract, they recommend that we
85 instead view language (and grammar) as a function of the brain. Some progress has been made in studying the neurobiology of language; for instance, scientists have identified specific regions of the brain that handle language. However, these findings are simple
90 and preliminary, offering little insight into the vast intricacy of human language use.

Neither linguistics nor biology alone is sufficient to understand the foundations of language. Language is unbelievably complex:
95 even a single word can offer several definitions and associations. Thus, any single connection between, say, two languages causes those myriad associations to become oversimplified and sterile. For example, simply pointing out that the subject
100 of a sentence is in the same position in Turkish and English as an illustration of UG merely acknowledges that single linguistic association, while failing to consider any social circumstances that may cause the mind to modify that grammar.
105 In short, say scientists, not until we create a better marriage between biology and linguistics—and a better understanding of the human brain—can we even begin to address the complexities of human language development.

Reflect

Directions: Take a few minutes to recall what you've learned and what you've been practicing in this chapter. Consider the following questions, jot down your best answer for each one, and then compare your reflections to the expert responses on the following page. Use your level of confidence to determine what to do next.

1. Why do ACT experts note keywords as they read?

    _____

2. What are the three categories of keywords? Provide some examples from each category.

    1. _____

        - Examples:
            - _____
            - _____
            - _____

    2. _____

        - Examples:
            - _____
            - _____
            - _____

    3. _____

        - Examples:
            - _____
            - _____
            - _____

3. Why do ACT experts jot down margin notes next to the text?

    _____

4. What are the elements of a strong big picture summary?

    _____

Responses

1. Why do ACT experts note keywords as they read?

Keywords indicate what the author finds important, express his point of view about the subject and details of the passage, and signal key points in the passage structure. Keywords are the pieces of text that help test takers see which parts of the passage are likely to be mentioned in questions and help the test taker to distinguish between correct and incorrect answer choices about those parts of the passage.

2. What are the three categories of keywords? Provide some examples from each category.

  1. *Opinion and emphasis*
     - Examples:
       - *indeed*
       - *quite*
       - *masterfully*
       - *inadequate*
  2. *Connection and contrast*
     - Examples:
       - *furthermore*
       - *plus*
       - *however*
       - *on the contrary*
  3. *Evidence and example*
     - Examples:
       - *consequently*
       - *since*
       - *for instance*
       - *such as*

3. Why do ACT experts jot down margin notes next to the text?

Margin notes help the test taker research questions that ask about details, examples, and arguments mentioned in the passage by providing a "map" to their location in the text. Margin notes can also help students answer questions about the passage structure and the purpose of a specific paragraph.

4. What are the elements of a strong big picture summary?

A strong big picture summary prepares a test taker to answer any question about the main idea of the passage or the author's primary or overall purpose in writing it. After reading the passage, ACT experts pause to ask, "What's the main point of the passage?" and "Why did the author write it?"

Next Steps

If you answered most questions correctly in the "How Much Have You Learned" section, and if your responses to the Reflect questions were similar to those of an expert, then consider strategic reading and passage mapping an area of strength and move on to the next chapter. Come back to this topic periodically to prevent yourself from getting rusty.

If you don't yet feel confident, review the material in "Reading Passage Strategies" and then try the questions you missed again. As always, be sure to review the explanations closely. Then go online (**kaptest.com/login**) to use your Qbank for more practice. If you haven't already registered your book, do so at *kaptest.com/moreonline*.

GO ONLINE

kaptest.com/login

Reading

Reading

Answers and Explanations

ACT Reading Strategies: Key Words, Margin Notes, and the Big Picture Summary

HUMANITIES: This passage is adapted from an article about modern architecture.

Fallingwater, a small country house constructed in 1936, stands as perhaps the greatest residential building achievement of the American architect Frank Lloyd Wright. In designing the dwelling

5   for the Pittsburgh millionaire Edgar J. Kaufmann, Wright was confronted with an unusually challenging site beside a waterfall deep in a Pennsylvania ravine. However, Wright viewed this difficult location not as an obstacle but as a unique

10 opportunity to put his architectural ideas into concrete form.

In the early 1930s, Edgar J. Kaufmann's son, Edgar J. Kaufmann Jr., studied with Wright as an apprentice at Wright's Taliesin Studio in Spring

15 Green, Wisconsin. At the time, architecture critics deemed Wright's style anachronistic and assumed that his career was coming to an end. Kaufmann Jr., on the other hand, greatly admired Wright's work and was delighted to introduce his parents

20 to the esteemed architect. Shortly thereafter, the Kaufmanns asked Wright to design Fallingwater.

The site Kaufmann chose for his country getaway was originally the location of a cabin in Mill Run, Pennsylvania, that he offered as a vacation

25 retreat for the numerous employees he oversaw at Kaufmann's Department Store, located in downtown Pittsburgh. When the Great Depression struck, Kaufmann's employees could no longer afford the cost of traveling more than 60 miles to Mill Run,

30 and Kaufmann decided that the land, a wooded area nestled along the banks of a mountain stream called Bear Run, was an ideal location for a vacation home. Kaufmann had assumed that the home would stand at the bottom of a nearby waterfall, where it would

35 provide a perfect venue from which to appreciate the view. However, Wright had other ideas. When Wright showed Kaufmann his plans, Kaufmann initially balked, but Wright convinced him that incorporating the falls into the design of the house

Margin notes:

Fallingwater: architectural achievement by FLW

how FLW came to design Fallingwater

location; below vs. on falls

ANALYSIS

Pre-passage blurb: The blurb tells us that the topic of this passage is modern architecture.

¶1 This paragraph introduces you to both Fallingwater and Frank Lloyd Wright. Fallingwater is significant not because of its difficult location but because of how Wright used it as an opportunity to showcase his unique architectural ideas.

¶2 Despite the opinion of critics that his career was coming to an end, Wright was commissioned to build Fallingwater after the Kaufmann family was introduced to him by their son.

¶3 Kaufmann chose an ideal location for his vacation home: the bottom of a waterfall. Wright was able to convince him to build the home around the falls, which linked both nature and domestic life.

40 was far preferable. In the end, Wright was able
to turn Fallingwater into an artistic link between
untamed nature and domestic tranquility—and a
masterpiece in his brilliant career.

Edgar J. Kaufmann's original plan to build his
45 house on the ample flat land at the bottom of
the waterfall would indisputably have proven less
challenging. Wright's more daring response to
the site required builders to construct the house
on a small stone precipice atop the falls. Wright
50 further proposed extending the living room of
the house out over the rushing water and making
use of modern building techniques so that no
vertical supports would be needed to hold up the
room. Wright brilliantly utilized the "cantilever"
55 technique, in which steel rods are laid inside a
shelf of concrete, eliminating the need for external
supports. Unfortunately, however, the builders did
not employ an adequate amount of reinforcing steel
to support the first floor. Kaufmann had hired
60 consulting engineers to review Wright's design prior
to Fallingwater's construction, but Wright dismissed
the engineers' claims that the main floor girders
needed additional support. Over time, the first floor
cantilever began to sag, and in 2002, a technique
65 called post-tensioning was used to permanently
repair the gradual collapse.

challenges

¶4 Kaufmann had a safer plan to build his home at the bottom of the falls, but Wright was more daring. He utilized a technique that allowed the living room to extend over the falls. Although this design was brilliant (even though it ignored the engineers' recommendation for more support), it did need repairs in 2002.

Despite Wright's miscalculation, Fallingwater,
as a whole, is an impressive structure. Rather
than allowing the environment to determine the
70 placement and shape of the house, Wright sought
to construct a home that intentionally confronted
and interacted with the landscape. Each bedroom
has its own terrace, and cornerless windows open
outward so that window panes do not obstruct
75 the spectacular view. In addition, Fallingwater
contains a great many traditional and natural
building materials. The home's 5,300-square foot
expanse includes custom-designed black walnut
wood furniture and walls and floors constructed
80 of locally sourced sandstone. The boulders
that provide the foundation for the house also
extend up through the floor and form part of the
fireplace. A staircase in the living room extends
down to an enclosed bathing pool at the top of

*house
interacts
w/ nature*

¶5 This paragraph lists several examples of how Wright was able to turn Fallingwater into a masterpiece that combined modern design with nature.

85 the waterfall. To Wright, the ideal dwelling in this
spot was not simply a modern extravaganza or a
direct extension of natural surroundings; rather, it
was a little of both.

   Architecture enthusiasts have taken a wide
90 range of approaches to understanding this unique
building. Some have asserted that the house
exalts the artist's triumph over untamed nature.
Others have compared Wright's building to a
cave, providing a psychological and physical safe
95 haven from a harsh, violent world. The members
of the American Institute of Architects named
Fallingwater the "best all-time work of American
architecture," and the Western Pennsylvania
Conservancy, which has owned and preserved
100 Fallingwater since 1963, hails the building as
an inspiration.

critical
responses

¶6 Paragraph 6 gives you insight into the opinion of other architects, which was overwhelmingly positive.

   Edgar Kaufmann Jr. may have summed up the
innovation and awe of Fallingwater best when
he said, "Wright understood that people were
105 creatures of nature; hence, an architecture which
conformed to nature would conform to what was
basic in people. . . . Sociability and privacy are
both available, as are the comforts of home and
the adventures of the seasons." This, then, is Frank
110 Lloyd Wright's achievement in Fallingwater: a home
that connects the human and the natural for the
invigoration and exaltation of both.

connects
human and
nature

¶7 The conclusion to the passage sums up by revealing Kaufmann's thoughts on Fallingwater: a home that connects humans with nature for the benefit of both.

BIG PICTURE SUMMARY

Main idea: Fallingwater, an unusual and impressive building, was an architectural achievement by Frank Lloyd Wright.

Author's purpose: To inform the reader about the history of a unique piece of architecture

---

As with the other passages in this chapter, don't worry about whether you used the exact language found in the expert's passage map and big picture summary. Instead, focus on how the expert used the skills and strategies outlined here to prepare herself to tackle the question set with speed and confidence.

How Much Have You Learned?

The influential theory of universal grammar (UG) postulates that all humans have an innate, genetic understanding of certain grammatical "rules," which are universal across all languages and
5 absolutely not affected by environment. The idea of such a universal grammar has a long history, starting with Roger Bacon's thirteenth-century book *Overview of Grammar* and continuing through the Renaissance with attempts to construct an
10 ideal language. In the eighteenth century, the first edition of the Encyclopedia Britannica included a section dedicated to universal grammar. In modern times, however, the linguistic theory of universal grammar is most closely associated with Noam
15 Chomsky, who did much to codify and popularize it in the 1950s–1970s. According to Chomsky, we are all born with a knowledge of "deep structure," basic linguistic constructions that allow us, if not to understand all languages, at least to understand
20 how they are put together. From there, we have only to learn how the parameters are set in our particular language in order to create an unlimited number of "correct" utterances.

For example, he suggests that structure
25 dependency—a rule that says that sentences are defined by phrase structure, not linear structure— is inherent to all languages, with minor variations. Thus, the meaning of a sentence is really dependent on the meaning of its phrases, rather than each
30 individual word. In addition, the head parameter rule stipulates that each phrase contains a "head" (main) word, and all languages have the head word in essentially the same position within the phrase. Chomsky's famous sentence "Colorless green ideas
35 sleep furiously" exemplifies this theory of universal grammar—while the sentence itself is meaningless, it is easily recognizable as a grammatical sentence that fits a basic but higher level of organization. "Furiously sleep ideas green colorless," on the other
40 hand, is obviously not a grammatical sentence, and it is difficult to discern any kind of meaning in it. For other evidence to support this theory,

ANALYSIS

Pre-passage blurb: The blurb tells you that the article is about how humans develop language.

theory of UG through history

¶1 The theory of UG has been prevalent throughout history. It states that all humans have an innate understanding of universal grammar rules. These rules are not affected by environment and are universal across all languages.

ex. of rules that support UG

¶2 This paragraph gives two specific examples of rules that support Chomsky's theory of UG. The structure dependency rule says that sentences are defined by phrases, and the head parameter rule states that each phrase has a main word that is in the same position across languages. Chomsky also points to the ease by which we can translate from one language to another as further evidence to support his theory.

Chomsky points to our relative ease in translating one language to another; again, while we may
45 not necessarily recognize individual words in an unfamiliar language, we can certainly recognize and engage with sentences that are grammatical.

This evidence is still fairly theoretical, receiving play mostly in the linguistic sphere rather than in
50 the biological sciences. Most of those researching the theory seem more concerned with attempting to draw universal parallels across languages than with searching for biological evidence of such phenomena. We might ask: Where exactly are these
55 universal grammar constraints located in our genetic code? How and when are they altered by natural evolutionary processes—or do they remain relatively unaltered and non-mutated from generation to generation? As both languages and human beings
60 evolve over time, does UG also evolve or stay relatively stable?

Even within the linguistic sphere, Chomsky's theory has drawn criticism. Some scientists suggest that by ignoring the role of environment
65 in language development, Chomsky completely discredits the possibly important effect our surroundings could have on language development. Still other researchers say that universal grammar is not nearly as ordered and absolute as Chomsky and other linguists make it out to be—that merely
70 identifying similarities in different languages does not prove that a universal grammar underlies them. They suggest that since the universal grammar theory is not falsifiable, it is in fact pseudoscientific
75 rather than scientific, the result of our flawed human tendency to impose order where there is none.

More recent researchers have begun to advocate that, rather than focusing on explaining linguistic
80 similarities among various languages, we instead acknowledge the evolutionary roots of language and look specifically for neurobiological explanations. Claiming that the humanistic exploration of universal grammar is too abstract, they recommend that we
85 instead view language (and grammar) as a function of the brain. Some progress has been made in studying the neurobiology of language; for instance, scientists

ev.= theoretical, biological ?

¶3 This paragraph tells you that the theory of UG is prominent mostly in the area of linguistics and not in biology. There are genetic questions relating to the theory: is UG evolving or stable over time?

criticism

¶4 Paragraph 4 gives you insight into what critics think. Some say Chomsky's theory ignores the influence environment could have on language. Others say that similarities and differences among languages does not mean that a universal theory ties them together. There is a question as to whether the theory is science at all.

lang. and brain

¶5 Recently, researchers have looked for neurobiological explanations for language. So far, this brain research has offered little insight into the intricacies of human language.

have identified specific regions of the brain that handle language. However, these findings are simple
90 and preliminary, offering little insight into the vast intricacy of human language use.

   Neither linguistics nor biology alone is sufficient to understand the foundations of language. Language is unbelievably complex:
95 even a single word can offer several definitions and associations. Thus, any single connection between, say, two languages causes those myriad associations to become oversimplified and sterile. For example, simply pointing out that the subject
100 of a sentence is in the same position in Turkish and English as an illustration of UG merely acknowledges that single linguistic association, while failing to consider any social circumstances that may cause the mind to modify that grammar.
105 In short, say scientists, not until we create a better marriage between biology and linguistics—and a better understanding of the human brain—can we even begin to address the complexities of human language development.

biology &
linguistics
both needed

¶6 In this concluding paragraph, you learn that it is necessary to better merge biology and linguistics to understand the complexities of human language; anything less would be an oversimplification of a complex process.

BIG PICTURE SUMMARY

Main idea: Chomsky's theory of innate linguistic structure is popular among linguists but does not address biological influences on language development.

Author's purpose: To inform the reader about the limitations and possibilities of universal grammar

---

CHAPTER 17

Identifying Question Types

LEARNING OBJECTIVES

After completing this chapter, you will be able to:

- Unpack ACT Reading question stems by
  - distinguishing among the 5 ACT Reading question types
  - determining if the correct answer is best found by researching the passage text or by consulting your big picture summary

---

Vocab-in-Context: 3/36 SmartPoints® (Medium yield)

Function: 6/36 SmartPoints® (High yield)

Inference: 10/36 SmartPoints® (Very high yield)

Detail: 13/36 SmartPoints® (Very high yield)

Global: 4/36 SmartPoints® (Medium yield)

How Much Do You Know?

Directions: In this chapter, you'll learn to unpack ACT Reading question stems (step 1 of the ACT Reading Question Method). Unpacking a question stem means pinpointing your task (as identified by the question type) and noting where the answer will be found (a specific reference within the passage text or in your big picture summary). For your reference as you complete this quiz, here are the ACT Reading question types:

- Global—asks about big picture ideas, including both main idea and tone
- Detail—asks about explicitly stated points
- Inference—asks about points that are unstated but strongly suggested based on two or more details from the passage
- Function—asks why or how the author wrote specific parts of the text; also includes questions about figurative language or rhetorical questions and other questions related to the way the author crafts the sentence
- Vocab-in-Context—asks for the intended meaning of a word within the context of the sentence

For each of the following question stems, identify the question type, cite the language in the stem that helped you identify that type, and indicate where you would begin to research this question: either your big picture summary or a specific part of the text.

Note that this chapter will not include actual passages; for more information about reading passages strategically, review chapter 16, and for more information about passages and question sets as a whole, review chapters 15 and 18–21.

Example

The author most strongly suggests that public transportation options in rural locations:

Question type: *Inference*

Identifying language: *"most strongly suggests"*

Research where? *passage, where author discusses public transportation in rural areas*

1. Which of the following statements best expresses the main idea of the passage?

   Question type:
   Identifying language:
   Research where?

2. According to the passage, the author's grandfather's birth happened:

   Question type:
   Identifying language:
   Research where?

3. The final sentence of the second paragraph (line 30) most directly serves to emphasize that the exiles:

   Question type:
   Identifying language:
   Research where?

4. Why did the narrator's grandfather and other recent immigrants say "*ya amerikanets*"?

   Question type:
   Identifying language:
   Research where?

5.   According to the third paragraph, what made settling in America a difficult time for the narrator's grandfather?

     Question type:

     Identifying language:

     Research where?

6.   What "advantage" did the narrator's grandfather most likely find in telling people about his relationship with Russia?

     Question type:

     Identifying language:

     Research where?

7.   In the seventh paragraph, the passage states that the speaker's grandfather traveled to Russia because:

     Question type:

     Identifying language:

     Research where?

8.   In lines 96–99, the speaker describes the typical view people have of real estate agents primarily in order to:

     Question type:

     Identifying language:

     Research where?

9.   As it is used in line 104, the word *realization* most nearly means:

     Question type:

     Identifying language:

     Research where?

10. Based on the passage, why was the speaker's grandfather attracted to real estate as a profession?

     Question type:

     Identifying language:

     Research where?

Reading

K   487

Check Your Work

1. Which of the following statements best expresses the main idea of the passage?

   Question type: Global

   Identifying language: "main idea"

   Research where? big picture summary

2. According to the passage, the author's grandfather's birth happened:

   Question type: Detail

   Identifying language: "According to the passage"

   Research where? passage, where author discusses grandfather's birth (first paragraph)

3. The final sentence of the second paragraph (line 30) most directly serves to emphasize that the exiles:

   Question type: Function

   Identifying language: "most directly serves to emphasize"

   Research where? passage map, second paragraph

4. Why did the narrator's grandfather and other recent immigrants say *"ya amerikanets"*?

   Question type: Detail

   Identifying language: "Why did [people] say [phrase]?"

   Research where? passage, the line numbers and paragraph where the narrator's grandfather and other immigrants say this

5. According to the third paragraph, what made settling in America a difficult time for the narrator's grandfather?

   Question type: Detail

   Identifying language: "According to the third paragraph"

   Research where? passage, third paragraph

6. What "advantage" did the narrator's grandfather most likely find in telling people about his relationship with Russia?

   Question type: Inference

   Identifying language: "most likely"

   Research where? passage, line numbers and paragraph where the grandfather is telling people about his relationship with Russia

7. In the seventh paragraph, the passage states that the speaker's grandfather traveled to Russia because:

   Question type: Detail

   Identifying language: "the passage states"

   Research where? passage, seventh paragraph

8. In lines 96–99, the speaker describes the typical view of real estate agents primarily in order to:

   Question type: Function

   Identifying language: "The speaker describes . . . in order to"

   Research where? passage, lines 96–99

9. As it is used in line 104, the word *realization* most nearly means:

   Question type: Vocab-in-Context

   Identifying language: "the word . . . most nearly means"

   Research where? passage, line 104

10. Based on the passage, why was the speaker's grandfather attracted to real estate as a profession?

    Question type: Global

    Identifying language: "Based on the passage"

    Research where? passage map and big picture summary

How to Unpack ACT Reading Question Stems

LEARNING OBJECTIVES

After this lesson, you will be able to:

* Unpack ACT Reading question stems by
  * distinguishing among 5 ACT Reading question types
  * determining if the correct answer is best found by researching the passage text or by consulting your big picture summary

To unpack question stems like these:

1. One of the main points of the second paragraph (lines 14–28) is that:

2. The passage suggests that an important difference between Mars and Earth is that, unlike Earth, Mars:

3. According to the passage, which of the following describes the atmosphere of Mars?

4. The passage suggests that Mars is void of organic compounds because:

5. The passage states that the Viking landing sites were chosen because of their:

6. As it is used in line 88, the word *barren* most nearly means:

7. The researchers' argument that life may exist in Martian rocks rests on the idea that:

8. The author mentions blue-green algae in the sixth paragraph primarily in order to:

9. It can be inferred from the passage that the possibility mentioned in line 94 refers to:

10. In the final paragraph, which of the following is listed as a compound that is necessary for life?

You need to know this:

There are 5 question types, each of which defines a specific task:

* **Global**—asks about big picture ideas, including both main idea and tone
  * Which of the following best states the main idea of the passage?
  * Which of the following best describes the author's attitude toward the Bureau of Indian Affairs relocation program described in lines 54–64?
  * Which of the following statements best captures why the Bell Project exemplified Wilma Mankiller's vision of the Cherokee?
* **Detail**—asks about explicitly stated points
  * According to the passage, what makes a tropical beach a specialized area?
  * According to the passage, Wilma Mankiller included so much Cherokee history in her autobiography because:
  * The passage states that among the Cherokee tribe's accomplishments in the mid- to late 1800s was:
* **Inference**—asks about points that are unstated but strongly suggested based on two or more details from the passage
  * The passage most strongly suggests that the Mayan people were the first to flourish in coastal Mexico because they:

- When Mankiller states, "we found the strength to do what had been done before," she's most clearly referring to:
- As depicted in the passage, the attitude of the Bureau of Indian Affairs in carrying out the relocation program can best be described as:

- **Function**—asks why or how the author wrote specific parts of the text; also includes questions about figurative language or rhetorical questions and other questions related to the way the author crafts the sentence

  - The comparison between a gymnasium and an open market in paragraph 4 is meant to:
  - The author mentions the forced relocation of the Cherokee in lines 24–27 in order to:
  - The author introduces the San Francisco Indian Center in lines 66–69 in order to:

- **Vocab-in-Context**—asks for the intended meaning of a word within the context of the sentence

  - As it is used in line 25, the word *dictate* most nearly means:
  - As it is used in line 72, the phrase *charged with* most nearly means:

There are specific types of clues in ACT Reading question stems that can help you answer questions more accurately and efficiently:

- **Line numbers**—Mentions of "line 53" or "lines 37–40," often in parentheses, tend to stand out and give you a clear place to start your research.
- **Paragraph numbers**—A reference to "paragraph 5," "the third paragraph," or "the last two paragraphs" is not as precise as a line reference but will still give you an idea of where to look. Start with your margin notes for the paragraph.
- **Quoted text** (often accompanied by line numbers)—Check the context of the quoted term or phrase to see what the author meant by it in the passage.
- **Proper nouns**—Names like "Professor James," "World War II," and "Baltimore" will likely stand out in question stems due to the capitalization. If a particular proper noun is discussed in only part of the passage, it narrows the range of text you have to research.
- **Specific content clues**—Sometimes a question stem will repeat terminology used in part of the passage, like "federalism" or "action potentials." Use your passage map to direct your research to the right part of the passage.
- **Whole passage clues**—If a question lacks specific content clues but refers to the passage as a whole or to the author in general, you are likely dealing with a Global question or an open-ended Inference question, which should lead you to your big picture summary rather than to rereading parts of the text.

You need to do this:

ACT READING QUESTION METHOD
Step 1. Unpack the question stem
Step 2. Research the answer
Step 3. Predict the answer
Step 4. Find the one correct answer

Step 1. Unpack ACT Reading question stems by:

- Identifying the question type and anticipating how it will need to be answered.
- Noting research clues that indicate how best to research the correct answer.

You will complete Steps 2, 3, and 4 in chapter 18.

Why distinguish question types in ACT Reading?

Unpacking the question stem puts you in control. You'll know exactly what the question is asking, where to find the correct answer, and what form the correct answer will take.

- Global: The correct answer must take the entire passage into account. A choice that reflects only part of the passage is incorrect.
- Detail: The correct answer must be stated in the passage explicitly. A choice that is not directly stated in the passage is incorrect.
- Inference: The correct answer will be a conclusion that can be drawn from the passage. A choice that draws too strong of a conclusion from the evidence available in the passage is incorrect.
- Function: The correct answer will say why a certain detail is included. Look up the detail, then ask yourself what the author was trying to accomplish by putting it there.
- Vocab-in-Context: The correct answer will give the meaning of a word as it is used in the context of the passage. Choices that give common meanings of the word are often incorrect.

Correct answers to Reading questions are never random or vague. They are tailored to the precise language of the stem, so being able to distinguish the question types will save you time and eliminate confusion during the test.

Explanations

1. This is a Global question. The identifying language in the question stem is "the main point." You can locate support for the correct answer in your big picture summary and passage map notes.

2. This is an Inference question. The identifying language in the question stem is "The passage suggests." You can locate support for the correct answer in the passage, using your passage map notes to help guide you to the answer more efficiently.

3. This is a Detail question. The identifying language in the question stem is "According to the passage." You can locate the correct answer in the passage, using your passage map notes to guide you to the correct paragraph more efficiently.

4. This is an Inference question. The identifying language in the question stem is "The passage suggests." You can locate support for the correct answer in the passage, using your passage map notes to guide you to the correct paragraph more efficiently.

5. This is a Detail question. The identifying language in the question stem is "The passage states." You can locate the correct answer in the passage, using your passage map notes to guide you to the correct paragraph more efficiently.

6. This is a Vocab-in-Context question. The identifying language in the question stem is "as it is used in line #" and "most nearly means." You can locate support for the correct answer by reading the entire sentence that includes the word and more, if needed.

7. This is an Inference question. The identifying language in the question stem is not as clear, but the more open-ended phrasing is a clue that it might be Inference rather than Detail. You can locate support for the correct answer in the passage, using your passage map to figure out where the researchers talked about life in Martian rocks.

8. This is a Function question. The identifying language in the question stem is "The author mentions . . . in order to." You can locate support for the correct answer by going back to the cited example and rereading the entire paragraph.

9. This is an Inference question. The identifying language in the question stem is the word *inferred*. You can locate support for the correct answer in the passage by going to line 94, rereading the sentence, and reviewing your big picture summary for a reminder of the passage as a whole if needed.

10. This is a Detail question. The identifying language in the question stem is that the question asks for something *listed* in the paragraph. You can locate the correct answer by going back to the final paragraph and figuring out what is listed as a necessary component for life.

Try on Your Own

Directions: Analyze each of the following question stems by:

1.   identifying the word or phrase that describes your task

2.   naming the question type

3.   noting how best to research the correct answer (research the text or consult the big picture summary)

Answers are found at the end of the chapter.

1.   Which of the following statements best expresses the main idea of the passage?

    Question type:
    Identifying language:
    Research where?

2.   Based on the passage, architecture critics regarded Frank Lloyd Wright's career prior to Fallingwater's construction (lines 12–17) as:

    Question type:
    Identifying language:
    Research where?

3.   It can be reasonably inferred that the site chosen for Fallingwater was:

    Question type:
    Identifying language:
    Research where?

4.   The passage indicates that Edgar J. Kaufmann's original plans for the site were:

    Question type:
    Identifying language:
    Research where?

5.   The author's use of the phrases "black walnut wood" and "locally sourced sandstone" (lines 78–80) most nearly serves to emphasize which of the following points?

    Question type:
    Identifying language:
    Research where?

6.   According to the passage, a cantilever is designed to include:

    Question type:
    Identifying language:
    Research where?

7.   It can reasonably be inferred that the miscalculation the author mentions in line 67 refers to:

    Question type:
    Identifying language:
    Research where?

8.   One of the main purposes of the information in lines 72–86 is to:

    Question type:
    Identifying language:
    Research where?

9.   Architecture enthusiasts' comparisons of Fallingwater to a cave (lines 93–95) most strongly suggest that the house provides a sense of:

    Question type:
    Identifying language:
    Research where?

10.   As it is used in line 112, the phrase *invigoration and exaltation* most nearly means:

    Question type:
    Identifying language:
    Research where?

For any question types that you misidentified, return to the definitions and question stem examples before taking the final assessment in this chapter.

How Much Have You Learned?

Directions: For practice identifying reading question types, analyze each of the following question stems by:

1. naming the question type,

2. identifying the word or phrase that describes your task, and

3. noting how best to research the correct answer (research the text or consult the big picture summary).

Answers are found at the end of the chapter.

1. The passage as a whole can best be described as:

   Question type:
   Identifying language:
   Research where?

2. Based on the passage, how do Renaissance efforts to design a language relate to Chomsky's theory of universal grammar?

   Question type:
   Identifying language:
   Research where?

3. In the first paragraph, Chomsky claimed that an "innate, genetic understanding":

   Question type:
   Identifying language:
   Research where?

4. According to the passage, universal grammar's structure dependency rule states that:

   Question type:
   Identifying language:
   Research where?

5. The author includes the quotes "Colorless green ideas sleep furiously" and "Furiously sleep ideas green colorless" primarily in order to:

   Question type:
   Identifying language:
   Research where?

6. The questions in paragraph 3 primarily serve to:

   Question type:
   Identifying language:
   Research where?

7. The passage suggests that the researchers mentioned in line 73 believe which of the following?

   Question type:
   Identifying language:
   Research where?

8. One of the main purposes of the fifth paragraph is to:

   Question type:
   Identifying language:
   Research where?

9. As it is used in line 98, the word *sterile* most nearly means:

   Question type:
   Identifying language:
   Research where?

10. As it is used in lines 105–106, the phrase *a better marriage* most nearly means:

    Question type:
    Identifying language:
    Research where?

Reflect

Directions: Take a few minutes to recall what you've learned and what you've been practicing in this chapter. Consider the following questions, jot down your best answer for each one, and then compare your reflections to the expert responses on the following page. Use your level of confidence to determine what to do next.

1. Why is it important to always unpack the question stem before proceeding?

    _____

    _____

    _____

2. Can you name the 5 ACT Reading question types and cite words or phrases that identify each one?

    1. _____

        • Identifying language: _____

        _____

    2. _____

        • Identifying language: _____

        _____

    3. _____

        • Identifying language: _____

        _____

    4. _____

        • Identifying language: _____

        _____

    5. _____

        • Identifying language: _____

        _____

3. How will you approach ACT Reading question stems differently as you continue to practice and improve your performance in the Reading section? What are the main differences you see between ACT Reading questions and those you're used to from tests in school?

    _____

    _____

    _____

Responses

1. Why is it important to always unpack the question stem before proceeding?

Knowing the ACT Reading question types makes you a more strategic and efficient reader because the test maker uses the same question types on every test. Fully analyzing each question stem helps you research the text more effectively, predict the correct answer in a way that fits the question stem, and avoid wrong answers made from misreading the question.

2. Can you name the 5 ACT Reading question types and cite words or phrases that identify each one? (*answers in no particular order*)

   1. Global
      - Identifying language: *the author's attitude, main idea*
   2. Detail
      - Identifying language: *according to [line/paragraph/passage], states that, claims*
   3. Inference
      - Identifying language: *most strongly suggests, most strongly implies*
   4. Function
      - Identifying language: *the primary function of, in order to*
   5. Vocab-in-Context
      - Identifying language: *as used in line [number], the word most nearly means*

3. How will you approach ACT Reading question stems differently as you continue to practice and improve your performance in the Reading section? What are the main differences you see between ACT Reading questions and those you're used to from tests in school?

There is no one-size-fits-all answer here. Reflect on your own strengths and weaknesses as you consider how to best improve your performance in the ACT Reading section. Depending on the kinds of classes and teachers you've had in high school, the skills rewarded on ACT Reading questions may be more or less familiar, but almost every test taker needs to be aware of her own instincts as a reader, and needs to break certain reading habits, to master this section of the test. The more you give yourself an honest self-assessment, the better prepared you'll be to handle all of the ACT Reading question types confidently.

Next Steps

If you answered most questions correctly in the "How Much Have You Learned" section, and if your responses to the Reflect questions were similar to those of an expert, then consider identifying Reading question types an area of strength and move on to the next chapter. Come back to this topic periodically to prevent yourself from getting rusty.

If you don't yet feel confident, review the material in "How to Unpack ACT Reading Question Stems" and then try the questions you missed again. As always, be sure to review the explanations closely. Then go online (**kaptest.com/login**) to watch video lessons about how to handle each ACT Reading question type and use your Qbank for more practice. If you haven't already registered your book, do so at *kaptest.com/moreonline*.

GO ONLINE

kaptest.com/login

Answers and Explanations

How to Unpack ACT Reading Question Stems

1. Which of the following statements best expresses the main idea of the passage?

   Question type: Global
   Identifying language: "main idea"
   Research where? big picture summary

2. Based on the passage, architecture critics regarded Frank Lloyd Wright's career prior to Fallingwater's construction (lines 12–17) as:

   Question type: Detail
   Identifying language: "Based on the passage"
   Research where? lines 12–17

3. It can be reasonably inferred that the site chosen for Fallingwater was:

   Question type: Inference
   Identifying language: "It can be reasonably inferred"
   Research where? the paragraph that talks about Fallingwater's location

4. The passage indicates that Edgar J. Kaufmann's original plans for the site were:

   Question type: Inference
   Identifying language: *indicates*
   Research where? Likely near the beginning of the passage; use your passage map to identify the correct location to review

5. The author's use of the phrases "black walnut wood" and "locally sourced sandstone" (lines 78–80) most nearly serves to emphasize which of the following points?

   Question type: Function
   Identifying language: "most nearly serves to emphasize"
   Research where? around the cited lines

6. According to the passage, a cantilever is designed to include:

   Question type: Detail
   Identifying language: "According to the passage"
   Research where? the paragraph that discusses how Fallingwater was built

7. It can reasonably be inferred that the miscalculation the author mentions in line 67 refers to:

   Question type: Inference
   Identifying language: "It can reasonably be inferred"
   Research where? line 67 and the surrounding lines

8. One of the main purposes of the information in lines 72–86 is to:

   Question type: Function
   Identifying language: "one of the main purposes"
   Research where? the cited lines and the passage map to determine how the cited lines fit within the whole

9. Architecture enthusiasts' comparisons of Fallingwater to a cave (lines 93–95) most strongly suggest that the house provides a sense of:

   Question type: Inference
   Identifying language: "most strongly suggests"
   Research where? the cited lines

10. As it is used in line 112, the phrase *invigoration and exaltation* most nearly means:

    Question type: Vocab-in-Context
    Identifying language: "as it is used in line # . . . most nearly means"
    Research where? at least the entire sentence that includes the cited phrase

How Much Have You Learned?

1. The passage as a whole can best be described as:

   Question type: Global
   Identifying language: "passage as a whole"
   Research where? big picture summary

2. Based on the passage, how do Renaissance efforts to design a language relate to Chomsky's theory of universal grammar?

   Question type: Inference
   Identifying language: "Based on the passage"
   Research where? passage, where author discusses Renaissance efforts to design a language

3. In the first paragraph, Chomsky claimed that an "innate, genetic understanding":

   Question type: Detail
   Identifying language: "Chomsky claimed"
   Research where? passage, paragraph 1

4. According to the passage, universal grammar's structure dependency rule states that:

   Question type: Detail
   Identifying language: "According to the passage"
   Research where? passage, where author discusses structure dependency rule

5. The author includes the quotes "Colorless green ideas sleep furiously" and "Furiously sleep ideas green colorless" primarily in order to:

   Question type: Function
   Identifying language: "author includes . . . in order to"
   Research where? passage, where author references the quotes "Colorless green ideas sleep furiously" and "Furiously sleep ideas green colorless"

6. The questions in paragraph 3 primarily serve to:

   Question type: Function
   Identifying language: "serve to"
   Research where? passage, paragraph 3

7. The passage suggests that the researchers mentioned in line 73 believe which of the following?

   Question type: Inference
   Identifying language: "passage suggests"
   Research where? passage, around line 73

8. One of the main purposes of the fifth paragraph is to:

   Question type: Function
   Identifying language: "main purposes"
   Research where? passage, paragraph 5

9. As it is used in line 98, the word *sterile* most nearly means:

   Question type: Vocab-in-Context
   Identifying language: "most nearly means"
   Research where? passage, line 98

10. As it is used in lines 105–106, the phrase *a better marriage* most nearly means:

    Question type: Vocab-in-Context
    Identifying language: "most nearly means"
    Research where? passage, lines 105–106

CHAPTER 18

Answering Reading Questions

LEARNING OBJECTIVES

After completing this chapter, you will be able to:

- Research the answer in the passage text or your big picture summary
- Predict the correct answer
- Identify the one correct answer choice

Vocab-in-Context: 3/36 SmartPoints® (Medium yield)

Function: 6/36 SmartPoints® (High yield)

Inference: 10/36 SmartPoints® (Very high yield)

Detail: 13/36 SmartPoints® (Very high yield)

Global: 4/36 SmartPoints® (Medium yield)

How Much Do You Know?

Directions: In this chapter, you'll learn how best to research, predict, and find the correct answers to ACT Reading questions. For this quiz, first take a couple of minutes to refresh your memory of the passage. Then, for each question:

1. research the answer in the passage text or from your big picture summary,

2. predict the correct answer in your own words, and

3. identify the one correct answer.

HUMANITIES: This passage explores the relationship between the immigrant experience and one person's career choice.

My grandfather was born in a turbulent time in Russia. His non-communist lineage made him unwelcome before he had left the womb. His father, an officer in the Russian army, was considered
5 an enemy of the communist Bolsheviks, so my grandfather lived less than a year in what was his native Moscow and spent most of his younger years moving across Asia. Despite this, he had pride in being Russian, associated with Russians throughout
10 his life, and would frequently quiz me on Russian history. This all in tribute to a country that ended up under hostile rule during the time his mother was pregnant with him.

As a child, exiled to Siberia, my grandfather
15 heard his father tell of the greatness that existed within the country that had forced the family into exile. It was known that, first with his parents, and later as an adult, my grandfather was going to have to seek a new place to call home.
20 Despite this foregone conclusion, Russia was still romanticized, and my grandfather learned to treat the country with reverence. This was in contrast to the sentiments found in other recently exiled Russians, who would not simply lament the actions
25 taken by the country but disparage all eight million square miles. In my family's search for a place to settle, attempting to forge a consistent identity was nearly impossible, as no one knew whether the next location would hold for a month, let alone a year.
30 All hoped for an unattainable "new Moscow."

The first long-term refuge was found, ironically, in China, which would have its own communist revolution. After several years of relative stability, this revolution precipitated the move to the
35 United States. Upon arrival in San Francisco, my grandfather, along with my grandmother and their young son, my father, found other Russian immigrants who were also new to the country. "*Ya amerikanets,*" people would say, and despite the fact
40 that they were recent immigrants who associated primarily with those of shared ethnicity and circumstance, they would play the role they desired and repeat "*ya amerikanets*"—"I am American." They would share many stories about their native
45 land, but did not repeat "*ya russkiy,*" because being Russian went without saying. While it was clear that this would be the last country my grandfather would reside in and that he wished to become more American, it was perhaps the most confusing
50 of times. It was less a problem of acclimating to an adopted setting and more of dealing with a permanent setting at all. The only consistency throughout the first thirty years of my grandfather's life was the knowledge that every "home" was
55 temporary, and now this was no longer the case. I often wonder if his successful career in the real estate business had anything to do with what must have been a rare transformation of circumstance.

Not only was my grandfather interested in real
60 estate, he was ardent about the importance of ownership, a naturally discordant view to that of the then Soviet Union. Thus, selling homes became a purpose in addition to an occupation.

Part of his success in real estate was owed to
65 strategic compromise. Considering American sentiments regarding Russia during the Cold War, there were times that he was sure he lost certain house sales due to his last name and accent.

However, to those willing to listen, he found
70 advantages to informing people that he was an
exiled Russian who ardently disagreed with the
communist government. He would also point out
his pride in being a new American and allow a
potential buyer to degrade Russia without blinking.

75   Fortunately, the 1950s were a time of settling
across the country, and this made real estate a
very lucrative profession. It wasn't just this that
attracted my grandfather, though; he also saw it as
an opportunity to give tiny parts of the country to
80 other people—returning the favor, in a way.

        Yet, it always seemed that something vital
still rested in the opposite hemisphere. Once
communism fell, he began returning to Russia
yearly. He and my grandmother never showed the
85 family pictures from Russia the way they would
from the various cruise ships they traveled on; it
could be deduced that returning to Russia was a
journey of personal necessity for him rather than
pleasure, and the encounter elucidated his existence
90 in a way that being solely American could not. In
selling real estate, my grandfather had worked to
make this unnecessary. I believe that he wished for
people to keep those houses and pass them down to
later generations, giving the space a sort of familial
95 permanence rather than a fleeting stay.

        For most, the thought of real estate agents
conjures up images of smiling advertisements
on benches and buses and the skill of selling
something so important. Many are wary of
100 salespeople in general, questioning the practice
of convincing people something is in their best
interest when the salesperson stands to personally
benefit. My grandfather did financially benefit from
sales, but there was more to it: his realization of the
105 American dream only made him want to be a part
of others reaching for the same thing, whether their
native home was around the block or thousands of
miles away.

1. Which of the following statements best expresses
    the main idea of the passage?

    A. Immigrants would often rather live in their
        native land.

    B. American-born people tend not to understand
        how displacement affects immigrants.

    C. Immigrants who acclimate well to America
        may still have indelible ties to their native land.

    D. Immigrants are sometimes surprised by the
        stability offered to them in America.

2. According to the passage, the author's grandfather's
    birth happened:

    F. during the communist revolution.

    G. under communist rule.

    H. prior to the communist revolution.

    J. after the fall of communism.

3. The final sentence of the second paragraph (line 30)
    most directly serves to emphasize that the exiles:

    A. wished for a counter-revolution led by
        opponents to communism.

    B. yearned for a home that they had lost.

    C. longed to rebuild and revitalize Moscow.

    D. preferred to settle near other Russians.

4. Why did the narrator's grandfather and other recent
    immigrants say "*ya amerikanets*"?

    F. They wanted to become American.

    G. They were worried about anti-Russian
        sentiment.

    H. It reinforced the immigrant community.

    J. It distanced them from their origins.

5. According to the third paragraph, what made settling in America difficult for the narrator's grandfather?

    A. San Francisco was different from any place he'd been before.

    B. He had to adjust to the idea of having a permanent home.

    C. He did not speak the language when he first arrived.

    D. He knew he would never be able to live in Russia again.

6. What "advantage" did the narrator's grandfather most likely find in telling people about his relationship with Russia?

    F. It gave him an edge over competitors because it was a gimmick they could not match.

    G. It made potential customers more inclined to buy from him because they felt pity for him.

    H. It gave him an edge over competitors because customers viewed him as more honest.

    J. It made potential customers more inclined to buy from him because he catered to their worldview.

7. In the seventh paragraph, the passage states that the speaker's grandfather traveled to Russia because:

    A. it was an enjoyable vacation.

    B. the communist government fell.

    C. he felt a personal need to go.

    D. the cruise ships stopped there.

8. The speaker describes the typical view people have of real estate agents in (lines 96–99) primarily in order to:

    F. express discomfort with the profession.

    G. undermine the validity of this view.

    H. set up a contrast with his grandfather.

    J. make a personal connection with readers.

9. As it is used in line 104, the word *realization* most nearly means:

    A. the fruition of a desire.

    B. full understanding of an idea.

    C. a sudden epiphany.

    D. profit from a transaction.

10. Based on the passage, why was the speaker's grandfather attracted to real estate as a profession?

    F. It was extremely lucrative at the time he joined the profession.

    G. The profession would not have been available to him in Russia.

    H. It was among the better professional opportunities open to immigrants.

    J. He wanted to give to others what America had given to him.

Check Your Work

Passage Map Notes:

¶1: grandfather, chaotic childhood

¶2: still loves Russia

¶3: moves to US, becomes real estate agent

¶4: real estate is his vocation

¶5: allows people to insult Russia

¶6: wants to give back

¶7: visits Russia every year

¶8: wants to give people a home

BIG PICTURE SUMMARY

Main idea: A Russian immigrant attempts to make a life and find a purpose in his new homeland through real estate.

Author's purpose: To reminisce about his grandfather's life experiences, memories, and impact

1. C

Difficulty: High

Category: Global

Getting to the Answer: Since this question asks for the main idea, it is a Global question. Refer to your passage notes in order to answer it. The passage makes it clear throughout that both Russia and America are extremely important to the identity of the speaker's grandfather. The correct answer is (C).

Choice A does not fit the passage, since the author's grandfather is clearly pleased to be American. The passage does not discuss how American-born people view displacement, so B is out of scope. Choice D, while discussed in the passage, is far too narrowly focused to be the main idea.

2. G

Difficulty: Medium

Category: Detail

Getting to the Answer: The clue "According to the passage" shows that this is a Detail question. The last sentence in the first paragraph (lines 11–13) states that the country came under new rule while the grandfather's mother was pregnant with him. Therefore, you can predict that he was born after the revolution and under communist rule. Choice (G) is correct. Choices F, H, and J contradict that statement.

3. B

Difficulty: Medium

Category: Function

Getting to the Answer: The phrase "most directly serves to emphasize" in the question stem identifies this as a Function question. For context, read the surrounding lines in addition to the one cited. The passage states that, in searching for a place to settle, the exiles hoped for a place like the one they left. However, the author calls this *unattainable*. Predict that this line emphasizes the exiles' homesickness and pain. Choice (B) is correct.

Choice A is out of scope; the passage never discusses a counter-revolution. Choice C contradicts the passage; the "new Moscow" that the author cites refers not to a new version of the old city but to a new city that is like the one they left. Finally, choice D is incorrect because settling near other Russians is not *unattainable*.

4. F

Difficulty: Medium

Category: Detail

Getting to the Answer: Sometimes you will see questions, like this one, for which the question type is difficult to determine based on the wording alone. Here, it might be either Detail or Inference, depending on whether the passage directly tells you why the phrase was used. Either way, you will need to research in the passage. According to the passage, "*ya amerikanets*" means "I am American," and the immigrants said it in order to "play the role" they wanted. You can predict that they aspired to be American, which matches (F).

While the passage does state that the author's grandfather was the victim of some anti-Russian sentiments, this is not mentioned until the fifth paragraph. This makes choice G outside the scope of this question. The passage never mentions reinforcing the community, so H is incorrect. Finally, J contradicts the passage, which says that "being Russian went without saying."

5. B

Difficulty: Low

Category: Detail

Getting to the Answer: The clue "According to the third paragraph" shows that this is a Detail question. Lines 46–55 state that this period was confusing because the grandfather had never settled anywhere permanently. Predict that the narrator's grandfather had to accustom himself to staying in one place. Choice (B) is correct.

While A and D may be true, a new, non-Russian place was not what caused the difficulty, according to the passage. It is not clear in the passage whether the grandfather spoke English upon arrival, so C is incorrect.

6. J

Difficulty: Medium

Category: Inference

Getting to the Answer: The phrase "most likely" in this question stem is a clue that it is an Inference question. Since the stem does not provide a line or paragraph number, use your passage notes to locate the relevant text in paragraph 5. Here, the passage states that the grandfather lost sales because of anti-Russian bias from some customers, but he gained standing with others by telling them that he was an anti-communist exile and allowing them to insult Russia. You can predict that indulging his customers' bias allowed him to make more sales. Choice (J) is correct.

The passage does not compare him with competitors in any way, so F and H are out of scope. There is no evidence in the passage that customers pitied him, so G is also incorrect.

7. C

Difficulty: Medium

Category: Detail

Getting to the Answer: The phrase "the passage states" shows that this is a Detail question. Paragraph 7 calls the trip "a journey of personal necessity." Predict that the speaker's grandfather felt compelled to go. The correct answer is (C).

Choice A is the exact opposite of what the passage says. The fall of communism in Russia allowed him to go, but is not the reason he decided to go, so B is incorrect. Finally, choice D is a distortion; while the passage mentions trips on cruise ships, it suggests they were separate from the trips to Russia.

8. H

Difficulty: Medium

Category: Function

Getting to the Answer: The wording "The speaker describes . . . in order to" indicates that this is a Function question. After describing a typical view of real estate agents in the final paragraph, the speaker immediately goes on to say that the grandfather does not fit this depiction. You can predict that the description is necessary background information to show the contrast with the narrator's grandfather. This matches (H).

Choice F is a distortion; while the speaker acknowledges that some people feel discomfort with salespeople, that is not the purpose of the description. Choice G is extreme; the speaker merely wants to say that the grandfather is not like this. Choice J is incorrect because the speaker goes on to contradict the image described, so there is no personal connection with readers.

9. A

Difficulty: High

Category: Vocab-in-Context

Getting to the Answer: This question displays the wording characteristic of a Vocab-in-Context question: "the word . . . most nearly means." The sentence indicated discusses the "realization of the American dream" and the desire to help others trying to do the same, so you can predict that in this context *realization* means achievement or gain. Choice (A) is correct.

Choices B and C both describe the most common meanings of the word, which are rarely correct for this type of question. Choice D refers to a transaction, which does not fit with the discussion of the American dream.

10. J

Difficulty: High

Category: Global

Getting to the Answer: This question includes the phrase "Based on the passage," which can indicate an Inference question. However, it asks for the grandfather's professional motivations, which are discussed through much of the passage—and even parts of the passage that do not directly discuss them provide information relevant to understanding them. Thus, this is a Global question. The passage makes clear that having a home and continuity in America was important to the grandfather, as was offering these benefits to others. Choice (J) is therefore correct.

Choice F is a misused detail; although the profession was lucrative, the speaker says that money was not the grandfather's primary motivation. Similarly, while metaphorically thumbing his nose at the Soviet Union may have been a perk of the job (since ownership conflicted with the Soviet Union's views), there is no evidence that the grandfather was motivated to become a realtor specifically because it was impossible in Russia. Thus, G is also incorrect. Finally, H introduces ideas not mentioned in the passage at all, so it is out of scope.

How to Answer ACT Reading Questions

LEARNING OBJECTIVES

After this lesson, you will be able to:

- Research the answer in the passage text or your big picture summary
- Predict the correct answer
- Identify the one correct answer choice

To answer questions like these:

NATURAL SCIENCE: This passage is adapted from an essay about astrobiology.

Astrobiology, also known as exobiology, is a complex, multidisciplinary science dedicated to studying the possibility of life outside the confines of Earth. Humanity has speculated for centuries
5 about whether or not we are alone in the universe, but with the advent of space exploration in the 1950s and 1960s, for the first time in human history there was the possibility of actually exploring the surface of alien planets. Scientists
10 and engineers worked together to build what they called landers, spacecraft capable not only of landing on other planets, but also of exploring and photographing them.

When the first of the two Viking landers touched
15 down on Martian soil on July 20, 1976, and began to send camera images back to Earth, the scientists at the Jet Propulsion Laboratory could not suppress a certain nervous anticipation. Like people who hold a ticket to a lottery, they had a one-in-a-million chance
20 of winning. The first photographs that arrived, however, did not contain any evidence of life. They revealed merely a barren landscape littered with rocks and boulders. The view resembled nothing so much as a flat section of desert. In fact, the winning
25 entry in a contest at J.P.L. for the photograph most accurately predicting what Mars would look like was a snapshot taken from a particularly arid section of the Mojave Desert.

The scientists were soon ready to turn their
30 attention from visible life to microorganisms. The twin Viking landers carried out experiments designed to detect organic compounds. Researchers

thought it possible that life had developed on early Mars just as it is thought to have developed on
35 Earth, through the gradual chemical evolution of complex organic molecules. To detect biological activity, Martian soil samples were treated with various nutrients that would produce characteristic by-products if life forms were active in the soil.
40 The results from all three experiments were inconclusive. The fourth experiment heated a soil sample to look for signs of organic material but found none—an unexpected result because organic compounds were thought to have been present due
45 to the steady bombardment of the Martian surface by meteorites.

The absence of organic materials, some scientists speculated, was the result of intense ultraviolet radiation penetrating the atmosphere
50 of Mars and destroying organic compounds in the soil. Although Mars' atmosphere was at one time rich in carbon dioxide and thus thick enough to protect its surface from the harmful rays of the sun, the carbon dioxide had gradually left the
55 atmosphere and been converted into rocks. This means that even if life had gotten a start on early Mars, it could not have survived the exposure to ultraviolet radiation that occurred when the atmosphere thinned. Mars never developed a
60 protective layer of ozone as Earth did.

Despite the disappointing Viking results, there are those who still keep open the possibility of life on Mars. They point out that the Viking data cannot be considered the final word on Martian life
65 because the two landers sampled only limited—and uninteresting—sites. The Viking landing sites were not chosen for what they might tell of the planet's

biology. They were chosen primarily because they appeared to be safe for landing a spacecraft. The
70 landing sites were on parts of the Martian plains that appeared relatively featureless according to orbital photographs.

The type of terrain that these researchers suggest may be a possible hiding place for active
75 life has an Earthly parallel: the ice-free region of southern Victoria Land, Antarctica, where the temperatures in some dry valleys average below zero. Organisms known as endoliths, a form of blue-green algae that has adapted to this harsh
80 environment, were found living inside certain translucent, porous rocks in these Antarctic valleys. The argument based on this discovery is that if life did exist on early Mars, it is possible that it escaped worsening conditions by similarly seeking refuge
85 in rocks. Skeptics object, however, that Mars in its present state is simply too dry, even compared with Antarctic valleys, to sustain any life whatsoever.

Should Mars eventually prove barren of life, as some suspect, then this finding would have
90 a significant impact on the current view of the chemical origins of life. It could be much more difficult to get life started on a planet than scientists thought before the Viking landings.

The possibility exists, of course, that our
95 definition of what constitutes life may not hold true throughout the universe. It has long been speculated that our current belief that all life must contain carbon, oxygen, calcium, chlorine, potassium, and phosphorous simply because this holds true on our
100 planet might be too narrow a view. In 2010, NASA scientists believed they had discovered a bacterium that used arsenic in place of phosphorous, though these exciting findings later proved to be incorrect. The possibility remains, however, that future
105 astrobiologists exploring the Martian surface from 140 million miles away might be able to make use of a more advanced definition of what we call "life."

1. One of the main points of the second paragraph (lines 14–28) is that:

    A. scientists were disappointed by the inconclusive results of their experiments.

    B. theories about how life developed on Earth were shown to be flawed.

    C. there was no experimental confirmation that life existed on Mars.

    D. meteorite bombardment of the Martian surface is less constant than scientists predicted.

2. The passage suggests that an important difference between Mars and Earth is that, unlike Earth, Mars:

    F. accumulated organic compounds in its soil.

    G. lies in the path of harmful rays of ultraviolet radiation.

    H. once possessed an atmosphere rich in carbon dioxide.

    J. could not sustain any life that developed.

3. According to the passage, which of the following describes the atmosphere of Mars?

    A. Rich in carbon dioxide

    B. Lacks a protective ozone layer

    C. Contains rocks converted from organic compounds

    D. Not susceptible to ultraviolet radiation

4. The passage suggests that Mars is void of organic compounds because:

    F. the lack of an ozone layer did not allow life to proliferate on Mars.

    G. they were destroyed by constant meteorite bombardment.

    H. carbon dioxide left the atmosphere and was converted to rocks.

    J. endoliths were found living in hidden areas.

5. The passage states that the Viking landing sites were chosen because of their:

    A. scientific value.

    B. safety.

    C. biology.

    D. diversity.

6. As it is used in line 88, the word *barren* most nearly means:

    F. full of rocks.

    G. abundantly productive.

    H. with a reddish hue.

    J. void of life.

7. The researchers' argument that life may exist in Martian rocks rests on the idea that:

    A. organisms usually adopt identical survival strategies in similar environments.

    B. life developed in the form of blue-green algae on Mars.

    C. life could have evolved in the same way on two different planets.

    D. organisms that survived in Antarctica could survive on Mars.

8. The author mentions blue-green algae in the sixth paragraph primarily in order to:

    F. give an example of a translucent organism that existed on Earth and Mars.

    G. draw a similarity between survival mechanisms of terrestrial and, potentially, Martian organisms.

    H. show how Martian organisms escaped harsh environments by seeking out shelter in rocks.

    J. draw a parallel between the harsh conditions in Martian valleys and Antarctic valleys.

9. It can be inferred from the passage that the possibility mentioned in line 94 refers to:

    A. a chance for scientists to prove our current definition of life definitively correct.

    B. the opportunity to open up new possibilities for what we call life.

    C. a deeper understanding of bacteria that survive on arsenic.

    D. the development of new technology that would allow scientists to study foreign atmospheres directly.

10. In the final paragraph, which of the following is listed as a compound that is necessary for life?

    F. Arsenic

    G. Sodium

    H. Potassium

    J. Magnesium

You need to know this:

Use clues to direct your research to a specific portion of the passage or to your big picture summary.

- **Line numbers**—Reread the indicated text and possibly the lines before and after; look for key words indicating why the referenced text has been included or how it's used.
- **Paragraph numbers**—Consult your margin notes to see the paragraph's purpose and scope before rereading the text. Sometimes your passage map alone is enough to find an answer.
- **Quoted text**—Go back to the passage to read the entire quote if the stem or answer choices use ellipses (. . .). Then check the surrounding context of the quoted term or phrase to see what the author meant by it in the passage.
- **Proper nouns**—Use your passage map or look for capital letters in the text to find the term, and then check the context to see why the author included it in the passage; note whether the author had a positive, negative, or neutral evaluation of it.

- **Specific content clues**—Use your margin notes to help you search the passage for terms or ideas mentioned in the question stem; these clues will usually refer to something the author offered an opinion about or emphasized.
- **Whole passage clues**—Begin by reviewing your big picture summary, and only go back to the passage if you can't find the information you need. If you do get stuck, the first and last paragraphs are typically the best places to go for global takeaways.

Predicting what you're looking for in the correct answer saves time and reduces confusion as you read each choice.

ACT Reading questions always have one correct answer and three incorrect choices.

- The correct answer will match what the passage says in a way that responds to the task set out in the question stem.
- Incorrect choices often fall into one of five categories. Not every incorrect choice matches one of these types exactly, but learning to spot them can help you eliminate some incorrect answers more quickly.

  - **Out of scope**—contains a statement that is too broad, too narrow, or beyond the purview of the passage
  - **Extreme**—contains language that is too strong (all, never, every, none) to be supported by the passage
  - **Distortion**—based on details or ideas from the passage, but distorts or misstates what the author says or implies
  - **Opposite**—directly contradicts what the correct answer must say
  - **Misused detail**—accurately states something from the passage, but in a manner that incorrectly answers the question

You need to do this:

ACT READING QUESTION METHOD

Step 1. Unpack the question stem

Step 2. Research the answer

Step 3. Predict the answer

Step 4. Find the one correct answer

Step 1. Unpack the question stem.

- This step is covered in chapter 17. Make sure you have completed that lesson before continuing through this one.

Step 2. Research the answer.

- When clues point to a specific part of the passage (line or paragraph numbers, quotations, content discussed only in particular paragraphs), begin by rereading the specified text and immediate context.
  - If the immediate context does not provide enough information to answer the question, gradually expand outward, rereading sentences that come before and after.
- With whole passage clues or questions that seem to lack clear content clues, begin by reviewing your big picture summary.
- If you can't figure out where to research the question and your big picture summary doesn't help either, consider using process of elimination, skipping the question and coming back to it later, or just making a guess.

Step 3. Predict or characterize what the correct answer will say or suggest.

- Don't worry about phrasing your prediction as a complete sentence or repeating exactly the language used in the passage. Just try to answer the question in your own words based on your research.
- If you struggle to predict, use your active reading of the passage to characterize the correct answer, setting expectations about characteristics it must possess.
  - For example, if the author has a negative view of a topic in the question, expect a correct answer with negative language and eliminate choices that suggest a positive or neutral view.

Step 4. Find the one correct answer.

- Identify the choice that matches your prediction, if possible.
  - Don't expect a word-for-word match, but look for a correspondence of ideas. For example, if you predict that the function of a detail is to "provide support for the main idea," an answer choice that says it "supplies evidence for the author's thesis" would likely be correct.
- If there is no clear match, use process of elimination.
  - Eliminate any choice that contradicts your prediction or that clearly falls into one of the five incorrect choice categories.
  - Choose the only answer remaining, or guess among those you were unable to eliminate.

Explanations

Passage Map Notes:

¶1: astrobiology: finding non-Earth life

¶2: Mars landing no signs of life

¶3: inconclusive tests for microorganisms

¶4: no organic material b/c UV?

¶5: may be life elsewhere, testing locations limited

¶6: how life could exist in rocks

¶7: impact if no life

¶8: definition of life may change

BIG PICTURE SUMMARY

Main idea: Despite initial tests for Martian life yielding inconclusive results, the continued search for possible lifeforms could yield valuable information.

Author's purpose: To inform the reader about both a brief history of and the predicted future of astrobiology discoveries

Question	Explanation
1. One of the main points of the second paragraph (lines 14–28) is that: A. scientists were disappointed by the inconclusive results of their experiments. B. theories about how life developed on Earth were shown to be flawed. C. there was no experimental confirmation that life existed on Mars. D. meteorite bombardment of the Martian surface is less constant than scientists predicted.	**1. C** **Difficulty:** Medium **Category:** Global **Getting to the Answer:** A question asking for "The main point" of a passage or paragraph is a Global question. Use your passage notes to answer these questions. Your notes should indicate that paragraph 2 discusses four experiments carried out by the Viking landers. These experiments were designed to detect signs of life but were inconclusive. Look for a match for this general prediction. The correct answer is (C). Choice A is a distortion; while it is reasonable to think that the scientists would be disappointed by the results, this is not mentioned in this paragraph. Choice B is out of scope; no such conclusions are suggested about Earth. Choice D both contradicts information in the passage—which describes the bombardment as steady—and isn't part of this paragraph, so it is also incorrect.

Question	Explanation
2. The passage suggests that an important difference between Mars and Earth is that, unlike Earth, Mars: F. accumulated organic compounds in its soil. G. lies in the path of harmful rays of ultraviolet radiation. H. once possessed an atmosphere rich in carbon dioxide. J. could not sustain any life that developed.	**2. J** **Difficulty:** High **Category:** Inference **Getting to the Answer:** The clue "The passage suggests" indicates that this is an Inference question, but the question stem does not point to any one paragraph definitively. When you receive limited help from the question stem, use your passage notes to help you confirm or rule out choices. Eliminate F because, according to paragraph 2, no organic compounds were found in Martian soil. Choice G is incorrect because the question asks for a difference between Earth and Mars. Both Earth and Mars lie in the path of ultraviolet radiation; the crucial distinction is that Earth is shielded by ozone. Choice H is also a distortion because the passage does not mention the amount of carbon dioxide in Earth's atmosphere. In paragraph 4, the passage tells us that even if life had begun on Mars, it could not have survived. The correct answer, then, is (J).
3. According to the passage, which of the following describes the atmosphere of Mars? A. Rich in carbon dioxide B. Lacks a protective ozone layer C. Contains rocks converted from organic compounds D. Not susceptible to ultraviolet radiation	**3. B** **Difficulty:** Low **Category:** Detail **Getting to the Answer:** You can recognize this as a Detail question because of the phrase "According to the passage." Check your passage notes and go back to the fourth paragraph to form your prediction. Paragraph 4 says that the Martian atmosphere did not develop a protective ozone layer. Choice (B) is correct. Choices A, C, and D all contradict information in paragraph 4.

Question	Explanation
4. The passage suggests that Mars is void of organic compounds because: F. the lack of an ozone layer did not allow life to proliferate on Mars. G. they were destroyed by constant meteorite bombardment. H. carbon dioxide left the atmosphere and was converted to rocks. J. endoliths were found living in hidden areas.	**4. F** **Difficulty:** Medium **Category:** Inference **Getting to the Answer:** You can tell this is an Inference question because of the phrase "the passage suggests." Paragraph 4 gives details about why Mars lacks organic compounds. Ultraviolet radiation penetrated the atmosphere and destroyed organic compounds in the soil; this occurred because Mars did not develop a protective ozone layer. Put these pieces together to get answer choice (F). Choice G distorts what the passage says; meteorite bombardment was not mentioned in relation to the destruction of organic compounds. Choice H is another distortion because, while true, this is not why Mars is void of organic compounds. Choice J is a misused detail; endoliths are mentioned in reference to Antarctic valleys on Earth, not Mars.
5. The passage states that the Viking landing sites were chosen because of their: A. scientific value. B. safety. C. biology. D. diversity.	**5. B** **Difficulty:** Low **Category:** Detail **Getting to the Answer:** The wording "The passage states" identifies this as a Detail question. While the question stem does not contain a line reference, the answer to a Detail question will be stated directly in the passage. Your notes should help direct you to paragraph 5. In lines 68–69, the passage says, "They were chosen primarily because they appeared to be safe for landing a spacecraft." This matches (B) exactly. None of the other choices match this statement.

Question	Explanation

6. As it is used in line 88, the word *barren* most nearly means:
 	
   F.   full of rocks.
   G. abundantly productive.
   H. with a reddish hue.
   J.   void of life.
	6. J
	Difficulty: Medium
	Category: Vocab-in-Context
	
	Getting to the Answer: This question has the distinctive phrasing of a Vocab-in-Context question, including "As it is used" and "most nearly means." Use the context of the passage to help answer this question. Pretend that the word *barren* is a blank, read around the cited line for clues, and make a prediction. The clues from the passage include: "did not contain any evidence of life." A good prediction for this word is "empty." Choice (J) is correct.
	
	Be careful with F! Even though the passage mentions that the area is littered with rocks, *barren* refers to the fact that there was no evidence of life. Choice G is opposite of what the passage suggests, and H references ideas from elsewhere in the passage.

7. The researchers' argument that life may exist in Martian rocks rests on the idea that:
 	
   A. organisms usually adopt identical survival strategies in similar environments.
   B. life developed in the form of blue-green algae on Mars.
   C. life could have evolved in the same way on two different planets.
   D. organisms that survived in Antarctica could survive on Mars.
	7. C
	Difficulty: High
	Category: Inference
	
	Getting to the Answer: With generally worded Inference questions, skim your notes to help you find the location of the relevant details in the passage. Martian rocks are discussed in paragraph 5: the author states that some scientists hypothesize that life on Mars may have "escaped worsening conditions by . . . seeking refuge in rocks" (lines 83–85), as happened on Earth. Predict that a way in which organisms may adapt to harsh conditions is similar on Earth and on Mars. Choice (C) is correct.
	
	Choice A is a distortion of the facts in the passage. This passage only discusses potential similarities between harsh environments on Earth and Mars, not in any other locations, and the author's statement that Mars is much drier than even the driest part of Antarctica proves that the two environments are not actually similar, only that they have some potential similarities. Additionally, the only organism discussed is blue-green algae. Choice B is incorrect because blue-green algae developed on Earth, not Mars. Choice D is incorrect because it suggests that the same organisms that survive in Antarctica could also survive on Mars, but there is no evidence to support that and, indeed, the lack of evidence of life on Mars is irrefutable evidence against D.

Reading

Question	Explanation
8. The author mentions blue-green algae in the sixth paragraph primarily in order to:	**8. G**

8. The author mentions blue-green algae in the sixth paragraph primarily in order to:

F. give an example of a translucent organism that existed on Earth and Mars.

G. draw a similarity between survival mechanisms of terrestrial and, potentially, Martian organisms.

H. show how Martian organisms escaped harsh environments by seeking out shelter in rocks.

J. draw a parallel between the harsh conditions in Martian valleys and Antarctic valleys.

8. G

Difficulty: Medium

Category: Function

Getting to the Answer: "The author mentions . . . in order to" is a clue that this is a Function question. Paragraph 6 discusses a terrestrial organism that has adapted to harsh conditions: blue-green algae. The passage further states that this argument is based on the idea that an organism on Mars could have escaped harsh conditions by seeking refuge in rocks, like the blue-green algae have done on Earth. The author discusses how blue-green algae have survived and how it could be possible for Martian organisms to adapt and survive in a similar way. Choice (G) is correct.

Choice F is a distortion; the rocks were translucent, not the blue-green algae. Choice H also twists the facts in the passage, which merely suggests that this is a possibility, not a certainty. Finally, choice J is out of scope; Martian valleys are not mentioned.

9. It can be inferred from the passage that the possibility mentioned in line 94 refers to:

A. a chance for scientists to prove our current definition of life definitively correct.

B. the opportunity to open up new possibilities for what we call life.

C. a deeper understanding of bacteria that survive on arsenic.

D. the development of new technology that would allow scientists to study foreign atmospheres directly.

9. B

Difficulty: Medium

Category: Inference

Getting to the Answer: The word "inferred" in the question is a clear indicator that this is an Inference question! The final paragraph of this passage includes speculation about what could happen in the future regarding human understanding of life. The correct answer will reflect the idea that something might happen (not that it will or has already happened). Choice (B) is correct.

Choice A is too definitive for something that *could* happen. Choice C is a distortion; scientists have not found bacteria that survive on arsenic. Choice D is out of scope, as technology to study foreign atmospheres directly is not mentioned.

Reading

Question	Explanation

10. In the final paragraph, which of the following is listed as a compound that is necessary for life?

    F.   Arsenic

    G.   Sodium

    H.   Potassium

    J.   Magnesium

10. H

Difficulty: Low

Category: Detail

Getting to the Answer: This question asks for something listed in the final paragraph, so it is a Detail question. When answering a question like this, take a moment to go back to the passage to research your answer. Here, you should eliminate all answer choices that are not listed as compounds that are necessary for life. The last paragraph does not mention G or J at all, so they are not correct. Choice F is incorrect because, while arsenic is mentioned in the final paragraph, it is not among the compounds that are believed to be necessary for life. Potassium, (H), is part of the list and is correct.

Try on Your Own

Directions: Put the expert question strategies to work on the following passage. First, take a few minutes to refresh your memory of the passage below, which you first saw in chapter 16. Then, for each question:

1.   Identify the question type

2.   Note where/how you will research the answer

3.   Jot down your prediction of the correct answer

4.   Find the one correct answer

Answers are found at the end of the chapter.

HUMANITIES: This passage is adapted from an article about modern architecture.

Fallingwater, a small country house constructed in 1936, stands as perhaps the greatest residential building achievement of the American architect Frank Lloyd Wright. In designing the dwelling
5   for the Pittsburgh millionaire Edgar J. Kaufmann, Wright was confronted with an unusually challenging site beside a waterfall deep in a Pennsylvania ravine. However, Wright viewed this difficult location not as an obstacle but as a unique
10   opportunity to put his architectural ideas into concrete form.

In the early 1930s, Edgar J. Kaufmann's son, Edgar J. Kaufmann Jr., studied with Wright as an apprentice at Wright's Taliesin Studio in Spring
15   Green, Wisconsin. At the time, architecture critics deemed Wright's style anachronistic and assumed that his career was coming to an end. Kaufmann Jr., on the other hand, greatly admired Wright's work and was delighted to introduce his parents
20   to the esteemed architect. Shortly thereafter, the Kaufmanns asked Wright to design Fallingwater.

The site Kaufmann chose for his country getaway was originally the location of a cabin in Mill Run, Pennsylvania, that he offered as a vacation
25   retreat for the numerous employees he oversaw at Kaufmann's Department Store, located in downtown Pittsburgh. When the Great Depression struck, Kaufmann's employees could no longer afford the cost of traveling more than 60 miles to Mill Run,
30   and Kaufmann decided that the land, a wooded area nestled along the banks of a mountain stream called Bear Run, was an ideal location for a vacation home.

Kaufmann had assumed that the home would stand at the bottom of a nearby waterfall, where it would
35   provide a perfect venue from which to appreciate the view. However, Wright had other ideas. When Wright showed Kaufmann his plans, Kaufmann initially balked, but Wright convinced him that incorporating the falls into the design of the house
40   was far preferable. In the end, Wright was able to turn Fallingwater into an artistic link between untamed nature and domestic tranquility—and a masterpiece in his brilliant career.

Edgar J. Kaufmann's original plan to build his
45   house on the ample flat land at the bottom of the waterfall would indisputably have proven less challenging. Wright's more daring response to the site required builders to construct the house on a small stone precipice atop the falls. Wright
50   further proposed extending the living room of the house out over the rushing water and making use of modern building techniques so that no vertical supports would be needed to hold up the room. Wright brilliantly utilized the "cantilever"
55   technique, in which steel rods are laid inside a shelf of concrete, eliminating the need for external supports. Unfortunately, however, the builders did not employ an adequate amount of reinforcing steel to support the first floor. Kaufmann had hired
60   consulting engineers to review Wright's design prior to Fallingwater's construction, but Wright dismissed the engineers' claims that the main floor girders needed additional support. Over time, the first floor cantilever began to sag, and in 2002, a technique
65   called post-tensioning was used to permanently repair the gradual collapse.

Despite Wright's miscalculation, Fallingwater, as a whole, is an impressive structure. Rather than allowing the environment to determine the
70 placement and shape of the house, Wright sought to construct a home that intentionally confronted and interacted with the landscape. Each bedroom has its own terrace, and cornerless windows open outward so that window panes do not obstruct
75 the spectacular view. In addition, Fallingwater contains a great many traditional and natural building materials. The home's 5,300-square foot expanse includes custom-designed black walnut wood furniture and walls and floors constructed
80 of locally sourced sandstone. The boulders that provide the foundation for the house also extend up through the floor and form part of the fireplace. A staircase in the living room extends down to an enclosed bathing pool at the top of
85 the waterfall. To Wright, the ideal dwelling in this spot was not simply a modern extravaganza or a direct extension of natural surroundings; rather, it was a little of both.

Architecture enthusiasts have taken a wide
90 range of approaches to understanding this unique building. Some have asserted that the house exalts the artist's triumph over untamed nature. Others have compared Wright's building to a cave, providing a psychological and physical safe
95 haven from a harsh, violent world. The members of the American Institute of Architects named Fallingwater the "best all-time work of American architecture," and the Western Pennsylvania Conservancy, which has owned and preserved
100 Fallingwater since 1963, hails the building as an inspiration.

Edgar Kaufmann Jr. may have summed up the innovation and awe of Fallingwater best when he said, "Wright understood that people were
105 creatures of nature; hence, an architecture which conformed to nature would conform to what was basic in people. . . . Sociability and privacy are both available, as are the comforts of home and the adventures of the seasons." This, then, is Frank
110 Lloyd Wright's achievement in Fallingwater: a home that connects the human and the natural for the invigoration and exaltation of both.

1. Which of the following statements best expresses the main idea of the passage?

    A. Fallingwater's designs were heavily influenced by its owner's wealth, social position, and political opinions.

    B. Fallingwater proved to be only as durable as construction techniques available at the time would allow.

    C. Wright designed Kaufmann's home to be both impressive and in harmony with its natural surroundings.

    D. Wright proved that humans can triumph over the natural, untamed landscape and claim it as their own.

2. Based on the passage, architecture critics regarded Frank Lloyd Wright's career prior to Fallingwater's construction (lines 15–17) as:

    F. antiquated but likely to rebound.

    G. out of date and declining.

    H. admirable and well-regarded.

    J. requiring additional support.

3. It can be reasonably inferred that the site chosen for Fallingwater was:

    A. the location of a cabin that Kaufmann banned his employees from using after they failed to properly care for the property.

    B. unlikely to have been selected if Kaufmann's employees had continued to use it as a refuge from the urban atmosphere of Pittsburgh.

    C. postponed for several years due to the difficulty of constructing a house on a small stone precipice atop the falls.

    D. strategically chosen based on the location of the waterfall in proximity to wildlife such as white-tailed deer.

4. The passage indicates that Edgar J. Kaufmann's original plans for the site were:

   F. straightforward and conventional.

   G. daring and bold.

   H. idealistic and whimsical.

   J. socially outlandish and culturally unorthodox.

5. The author's use of the phrases "black walnut wood" and "locally sourced sandstone" (lines 78–80) most nearly serves to emphasize which of the following points?

   A. Black walnut trees should be used sparingly to prevent deforestation.

   B. Sandstone is a preferable building material because of its stability.

   C. Fallingwater features multiple types of organic building materials.

   D. Natural elements are essential to creating a cave-like environment.

6. According to the passage, a cantilever is designed to include:

   F. vertical supports that hold up a room.

   G. concrete-encased steel rods.

   H. reinforcing steel to support the first floor.

   J. post-tensioning to correct sagging.

7. It can reasonably be inferred that the miscalculation the author mentions in line 67 refers to:

   A. an issue that might have been prevented if Wright had heeded engineers' warnings.

   B. a suboptimal structure plagued by gravitational forces that led to a complete collapse.

   C. cornerless windows that open outward to offer an unobstructed view of the landscape.

   D. a staircase that extends down to an enclosed bathing pool at the top of the waterfall.

8. One of the main purposes of the information in lines 72–85 is to:

   F. argue that Fallingwater would not have suffered from gradual collapse if it had been built during a time of advanced engineering.

   G. describe the intricacies of Wright's "cantilever" technique and its subsequent consequences.

   H. explain specific ways in which Fallingwater and the surrounding natural beauty enhance one another.

   J. show how architecture enthusiasts have generated a myriad of theories regarding the significance of Fallingwater.

9. Architecture enthusiasts' comparisons of Fallingwater to a cave (lines 93–95) most strongly suggest that the house provides a sense of:

   A. familial warmth accompanied by a sense of belonging.

   B. murkiness that is exacerbated by the dampness of the structure.

   C. inescapable claustrophobia that could lead one to panic.

   D. security and safety that is both literal and emotional.

10. As it is used in line 112, the phrase "invigoration and exaltation" most nearly means:

    F. robustness and jubilation.

    G. renewing and superiority.

    H. briskness and blessing.

    J. inspiration and glorification.

Reading

How Much Have You Learned?

Directions: For practice answering Reading questions, review the passage from chapter 16 and the question stems from chapter 17. Use your notes from those chapters to help you make predictions and answer the questions. Be sure to study the explanations, even for questions you got correct. They can be found at the end of this chapter.

SOCIAL SCIENCE: This passage is adapted from an article about how humans develop language.

The influential theory of universal grammar (UG) postulates that all humans have an innate, genetic understanding of certain grammatical "rules," which are universal across all languages and
5 absolutely not affected by environment. The idea of such a universal grammar has a long history, starting with Roger Bacon's thirteenth-century book *Overview of Grammar* and continuing through the Renaissance with attempts to construct an
10 ideal language. In the eighteenth century, the first edition of the Encyclopedia Britannica included a section dedicated to universal grammar. In modern times, however, the linguistic theory of universal grammar is most closely associated with Noam
15 Chomsky, who did much to codify and popularize it in the 1950s–1970s. According to Chomsky, we are all born with a knowledge of "deep structure," basic linguistic constructions that allow us, if not to understand all languages, at least to understand
20 how they are put together. From there, we have only to learn how the parameters are set in our particular language in order to create an unlimited number of "correct" utterances.

For example, he suggests that structure
25 dependency—a rule that says that sentences are defined by phrase structure, not linear structure— is inherent to all languages, with minor variations. Thus, the meaning of a sentence is really dependent on the meaning of its phrases, rather than each
30 individual word. In addition, the head parameter rule stipulates that each phrase contains a "head" (main) word, and all languages have the head word in essentially the same position within the phrase. Chomsky's famous sentence "Colorless green ideas
35 sleep furiously" exemplifies this theory of universal grammar—while the sentence itself is meaningless, it is easily recognizable as a grammatical sentence that fits a basic but higher level of organization.

"Furiously sleep ideas green colorless," on the other
40 hand, is obviously not a grammatical sentence, and it is difficult to discern any kind of meaning in it. For other evidence to support this theory, Chomsky points to our relative ease in translating one language to another; again, while we may
45 not necessarily recognize individual words in an unfamiliar language, we can certainly recognize and engage with sentences that are grammatical.

This evidence is still fairly theoretical, receiving play mostly in the linguistic sphere rather than in
50 the biological sciences. Most of those researching the theory seem more concerned with attempting to draw universal parallels across languages than with searching for biological evidence of such phenomena. We might ask: Where exactly are these
55 universal grammar constraints located in our genetic code? How and when are they altered by natural evolutionary processes—or do they remain relatively unaltered and non-mutated from generation to generation? As both languages and human beings
60 evolve over time, does UG also evolve or stay relatively stable?

Even within the linguistic sphere, Chomsky's theory has drawn criticism. Some scientists suggest that by ignoring the role of environment
65 in language development, Chomsky completely discredits the possibly important effect our surroundings could have on language development. Still other researchers say that universal grammar is not nearly as ordered and absolute as Chomsky
70 and other linguists make it out to be—that merely identifying similarities in different languages does not prove that a universal grammar underlies them. They suggest that since the universal grammar theory is not falsifiable, it is in fact pseudoscientific
75 rather than scientific, the result of our flawed human tendency to impose order where there is none.

More recent researchers have begun to advocate that, rather than focusing on explaining linguistic
80   similarities among various languages, we instead acknowledge the evolutionary roots of language and look specifically for neurobiological explanations. Claiming that the humanistic exploration of universal grammar is too abstract, they recommend that we
85   instead view language (and grammar) as a function of the brain. Some progress has been made in studying the neurobiology of language; for instance, scientists have identified specific regions of the brain that handle language. However, these findings are simple
90   and preliminary, offering little insight into the vast intricacy of human language use.

Neither linguistics nor biology alone is sufficient to understand the foundations of language. Language is unbelievably complex:
95   even a single word can offer several definitions and associations. Thus, any single connection between, say, two languages causes those myriad associations to become oversimplified and sterile. For example, simply pointing out that the subject
100   of a sentence is in the same position in Turkish and English as an illustration of UG merely acknowledges that single linguistic association, while failing to consider any social circumstances that may cause the mind to modify that grammar.
105   In short, say scientists, not until we create a better marriage between biology and linguistics—and a better understanding of the human brain—can we even begin to address the complexities of human language development.

1.   The passage as a whole can best be described as:

A.   an argument against the validity of an outdated theory.

B.   a description of how scientific understanding of a topic has evolved historically.

C.   an examination of a well-known theory and how it might be improved.

D.   a defense of the contributions of a theory in spite of its imperfections.

2.   Based on the passage, how do Renaissance efforts to design a language relate to Chomsky's theory of universal grammar?

F.   Renaissance linguists based their undertaking on Chomsky's theory.

G.   Both believed in the possibility of perfecting language.

H.   Chomsky's theory was inspired in part by that constructed language.

J.   They share underlying assumptions about human language.

3.   In the first paragraph, Chomsky claimed that an "innate, genetic understanding":

A.   allows humans to understand all language.

B.   allows humans to understand all language structure.

C.   allows humans to easily speak in multiple languages.

D.   explains that grammar is a natural function of the human brain.

Reading

4. According to the passage, universal grammar's structure dependency rule states that:

    F. the linear arrangement of words defines the meaning of sentences.

    G. a sentence's grammatical structure is dependent upon its meaning.

    H. a sentence's meaning relies on the meaning of the phrases that compose it.

    J. head words are the most critical to understanding the meaning of sentences.

5. The author includes the quotes "Colorless green ideas sleep furiously" and "Furiously sleep ideas green colorless" primarily in order to:

    A. support the idea that humans can recognize grammatical and ungrammatical structures regardless of content.

    B. show the importance of word order in determining whether a statement is grammatical or not.

    C. identify the correct position of the head word in two different phrase structures.

    D. demonstrate why it is easy to translate from one language to another even when dealing with unfamiliar vocabulary.

6. The questions in paragraph 3 primarily serve to:

    F. demonstrate that biology is a better lens for examining language.

    G. suggest potential theoretical weaknesses of universal grammar.

    H. list topics universal grammar seeks to elucidate.

    J. dismiss the possibility of an evolutionary basis for language.

7. The passage suggests that the researchers mentioned in line 68 believe which of the following?

    A. Identifying similarities across all known languages is the only way to prove universal grammar correct.

    B. Universal grammar is not chaotic enough to be a scientific theory.

    C. For a theory to be truly scientific, it must be possible to prove it wrong.

    D. Pseudoscience is a major problem in the field of linguistics.

8. One of the main purposes of the fifth paragraph is to:

    F. introduce the idea of examining language through neurobiology.

    G. describe the evolutionary development of language.

    H. outline the strides made in studying how the brain produces language.

    J. identify criticisms of the theory of universal grammar.

9. As it is used in line 98, the word *sterile* most nearly means:

    A. cold and sanitary.

    B. formal and meaningless.

    C. frigid and barren.

    D. dry and musty.

10. As it is used in lines 105–106, the phrase *a better marriage* most nearly means:

    F. a more equitable partnership.

    G. a more effective synthesis.

    H. stronger communication.

    J. a permanent relationship.

Reflect

Directions: Take a few minutes to recall what you've learned and what you've been practicing in this chapter. Consider the following questions, jot down your best answer for each one, and then compare your reflections to the expert responses on the following page. Use your level of confidence to determine what to do next.

1. Why do ACT experts research and predict the correct answer to Reading questions before reading the answer choices?

    _____

    _____

    _____

2. What are the types of research clues contained in ACT Reading question stems?

    _____

    _____

    _____

3. What are the five common wrong answer types associated with ACT Reading questions?

    - _____

    - _____

    - _____

    - _____

    - _____

4. How will you approach the process of answering ACT Reading questions more strategically going forward? Are there any specific habits you will practice to make your approach to ACT Reading more effective and efficient?

    _____

    _____

    _____

Responses

1. Why do ACT experts research and predict the correct answer to Reading questions before reading the answer choices?

Expert test takers know that the correct answer to each ACT Reading question is based on the text of the passage. They research to avoid answering based on memory or on a whim. Predicting the correct answer before reading the choices increases accuracy and speed by helping the test taker avoid rereading, confusion, and comparing answer choices to one another.

2. What are the types of research clues contained in ACT Reading question stems?

Line numbers, paragraph numbers, quoted text, proper nouns, specific content clues, and whole passage clues.

3. What are the five common wrong answer types associated with ACT Reading questions?

-   *Out of scope*
-   *Extreme*
-   *Distortion*
-   *Opposite*
-   *Misused detail*

4. How will you approach the process of answering ACT Reading questions more strategically going forward? Are there any specific habits you will practice to make your approach to ACT Reading more effective and efficient?

There is no one-size-fits-all answer here. Reflect on your own habits in answering ACT Reading questions and give yourself an honest assessment of your strengths and weaknesses. Consider the strategies you've seen experts use in this chapter, and put them to work in your own practice to increase your accuracy, speed, and confidence.

Next Steps

If you answered most questions correctly in the "How Much Have You Learned" section, and if your responses to the Reflect questions were similar to those of an expert, then consider answering Reading questions an area of strength and move on to the next chapter. Come back to this topic periodically to prevent yourself from getting rusty.

If you don't yet feel confident, review the material in "How to Answer ACT Reading Questions" and then try the questions you missed again. As always, be sure to review the explanations closely. Then go online (**kaptest.com/login**) to use your Qbank for more practice. If you haven't already registered your book, do so at *kaptest.com/moreonline*.

GO ONLINE

kaptest.com/login

Answers and Explanations

How to Answer ACT Reading Questions

¶1: Fallingwater: architectural achievement by FLW

¶2: how FLW came to design Fallingwater

¶3: location; below vs. on falls

¶4: challenges

¶5: house interacts w/nature

¶6: critical responses

¶7: connects human and nature

BIG PICTURE SUMMARY

Main idea: Fallingwater, an unusual and impressive building, was an architectural achievement by Frank Lloyd Wright.

Author's purpose: To inform the reader about the history of a unique piece of architecture

---

1.   C
Difficulty: Low

Category: Global

Getting to the Answer: This is a Global question because it is asking for the main idea of the passage. Use your passage notes to answer this question. Your notes should indicate that paragraph 1 introduces Fallingwater as one of Wright's greatest achievements and paragraph 7 concludes that Fallingwater interconnects humans and nature. Predict that Fallingwater is amazing and reflects nature, which matches (C).

The passage offers no evidence that Kaufmann's money, social status, or political beliefs influenced Wright's designs; A is incorrect. Choice B is out of scope; durability refers to a specific aspect of Fallingwater's construction, but Global questions are concerned with the passage as a whole. In addition, it was Wright's dismissal of the engineers' recommendation to provide additional support for the main floor girders that led to durability issues, not the limitations of the available construction techniques. Choice D is a distortion; Wright wanted the house to be an "extension of natural surroundings," not a triumph over them.

2.   G
Difficulty: Medium

Category: Detail

Getting to the Answer: The phrase "Based on the passage" indicates that this is a Detail question. Paragraph 2 discusses Wright's career before Kaufman asked him to design Fallingwater. Lines 15–17 state that "architecture critics deemed Wright's style anachronistic and assumed that his career was coming to an end." *Anachronistic* refers to something that is not in its correct time period, so predict that critics thought that Wright's designs were too old to be relevant and that his career was deteriorating. Choice (G) is correct.

The critics did think that Wright's technique was antiquated, but they did not think it was likely to rebound; F is incorrect. Choices H and J are misused details. Edgar J. Kaufmann Jr., not the critics, admired Wright and held him in high regard, and Fallingwater's main floor girders, not Wright, required additional support.

3.   B
Difficulty: Medium

Category: Inference

Getting to the Answer: The clue "It can be reasonably inferred" shows that this is an Inference question. Lines 23–27 state that the site was "originally the location of a cabin that he offered as a vacation retreat for the numerous employees he oversaw at Kaufmann's Department Store located in downtown Pittsburgh." However, "When the Great Depression struck, Kaufmann's employees could no longer afford the cost of traveling more than 60 miles to Mill Run" (lines 27–29). Since Kaufmann decided to build a new home only after his employees ceased traveling to the cabin, it can be inferred that if his employees had not stopped using the cabin, Kaufmann may not have decided to build a new home. Choice (B) is correct.

Choices A and D are out of scope; the passage does not mention how well (or poorly) Kaufmann's employees cared for the property or what type of wildlife exists near the waterfall. Choice C is a distortion; it took some convincing for Kaufmann to agree to build Fallingwater at the top of the waterfall, but the passage does not state that construction was postponed.

4. F

Difficulty: Medium

Category: Inference

Getting to the Answer: This is an Inference question because the question stem includes the word *indicates*. The correct answer to an Inference question will always be directly supported by the text. Your passage notes should point you to the fourth paragraph. The author writes that Kaufmann had originally planned to put the house on a flat site near the bottom of the waterfall, but Wright convinced him to accept a more daring location right over the waterfall. Predict that Kaufmann's original plans were not daring but traditional; the correct answer is (F).

Choices G and H are the opposite of your prediction; Wright's design, not Kaufmann's plan, was daring, bold, idealistic, and whimsical. Choice J is out of scope; the passage never indicates how the plans were considered within a social or cultural context.

5. C

Difficulty: Medium

Category: Function

Getting to the Answer: The phrase "most nearly serves to emphasize" indicates that this is a Function question. For more context, read the surrounding lines in addition to the one cited. The passage states that "Fallingwater contains a great many traditional and natural building materials" (lines 75–77). Predict that the phrases emphasize the natural materials that Wright used. Choice (C) is correct.

Choices A and B are out of scope; the passage does not mention deforestation or the stability of sandstone. The author doesn't mention the idea of a cave until the next paragraph, so D is incorrect.

6. G

Difficulty: Low

Category: Detail

Getting to the Answer: "According to the passage" indicates that this is a Detail question. Lines 55–56 state that "steel rods are laid inside a shelf of concrete," which matches (G).

Choice F is opposite because a cantilever eliminates the need for vertical supports. Choices H and J are misused details. Wright disregarded the engineers' recommendation to include additional reinforcing steel to support the first floor, and post-tensioning wasn't used until 2002, well after the initial design.

7. A

Difficulty: High

Category: Inference

Getting to the Answer: This is an Inference question because it asks for what "can reasonably be inferred." The line reference provided is at the very beginning of paragraph 5, and it refers to the miscalculation discussed in the previous paragraph. Your passage notes should indicate that paragraph 4 is about Wright's decision to use the "cantilever" technique. Lines 57–59 state that "the builders did not employ an adequate amount of reinforcing steel to support the first floor." Furthermore, "Wright dismissed the engineers' claims that the main floor girders needed additional support. Over time, the first floor cantilever began to sag, and in 2002, a technique called post-tensioning was used to permanently repair the gradual collapse" (lines 62–66). This information indicates that if Wright had listened to the engineers and included additional reinforcing steel, the cantilever may not have started to sag. Choice (A) is correct.

Choice B is extreme; the passage says that the collapse was gradual, not complete. Choices C and D are misused details; both answer choices are mentioned in the passage, but they are notable features that demonstrate how Fallingwater's design embraces nature, not examples of miscalculations.

8. H

Difficulty: Medium

Category: Function

Getting to the Answer: The phrase "One of the main purposes" shows that this is a Function question. Use your passage notes to review the main purpose of the paragraph that contains the sentences indicated by the question stem. Your notes should show that paragraph 5 discusses the ways in which Fallingwater intertwines impressive architecture with natural beauty. Predict that lines 72–85 provide details about this connection; (H) is correct.

Choice F is out of scope because the passage does not discuss whether Fallingwater would have proven more durable if it had been built during a period of more advanced engineering. Choices G and J are incorrect because they reflect the purposes of the fourth and sixth paragraphs, respectively, not the fifth paragraph.

9. D

Difficulty: Medium

Category: Inference

Getting to the Answer: When an Inference question asks for a characterization of an opinion, be sure to keep in mind whose opinion it is. Here, it is the architecture enthusiasts' notions of a cave that are important. According to the cited sentence, architecture enthusiasts compared Fallingwater to a cave because the house provided "a psychological and physical safe haven from a harsh, violent world" (lines 94–95). The critics' use of cave imagery suggests a feeling of safety, which matches (D).

Choices A, B, and C are distortions of what the architecture enthusiasts alluded to in their characterization. Eliminate these choices because the passage does not provide support for a sense of familial warmth, murkiness, or claustrophobia.

10. J

Difficulty: High

Category: Vocab-in-Context

Getting to the Answer: This question includes wording characteristic of a Vocab-in-Context question: "the phrase . . . most nearly means." The sentence indicated is the final sentence in a paragraph that begins with the statement "Edgar Kaufmann Jr. may have summed up the innovation and awe of Fallingwater best," so you can predict that in this context *invigoration and exaltation* means "innovation and awe." Choice (J) is correct.

Choice F includes definitions of *vigor* and *exultation*, which sound similar to *invigoration* and *exaltation* but have different meanings. Choices G and H are distortions; they represent other possible definitions of these words, but they do not make sense when plugged back into the sentence.

How Much Have You Learned?

¶1: theory of UG through history

¶2: ex. of rules that support UG

¶3: ev.=theoretical, biological?

¶4: criticism

¶5: lang. and brain

¶6: biology & linguistics both needed

BIG PICTURE SUMMARY

Main idea: Chomsky's theory of innate linguistic structure is popular among linguists but does not address biological influences on language development.

Author's purpose: To inform the reader about the limitations and possibilities of universal grammar

1. C

Difficulty: Medium

Category: Global

Getting to the Answer: The phrasing "The passage as a whole" shows that this is a Global question. Consult your notes for an overview. The passage is fairly neutral; it describes universal grammar and then discusses criticisms of the theory and how to resolve them. The correct answer is (C).

Choice A is extreme; the passage does not argue that universal grammar is invalid or outdated, only that it has flaws. The passage is not focused on the history of universal grammar, despite a brief outline in the first paragraph, so B is incorrect as well. Choice D is a distortion; the passage does not defend universal grammar.

2.   J

Difficulty: High

Category: Inference

Getting to the Answer: The clue words "Based on the passage" identify this as an Inference question. The first paragraph states that universal grammar proposes that all humans have an inherent understanding of universal language principles. It then goes on to say, "The idea of such a universal grammar has a long history," including Renaissance linguists attempting to design an ideal language. You can predict that universal grammar and Renaissance linguists had similar beliefs about humans' innate understanding of grammar. This matches (J).

Choice F is incorrect because Chomsky's work came after that of the Renaissance linguists. Choice G is a distortion; while the Renaissance linguists believed this, there is no evidence that Chomsky did. Choice H is out of scope; the passage gives no information about what inspired Chomsky's theory.

3.   B

Difficulty: Medium

Category: Detail

Getting to the Answer: The clue words "Chomsky claimed" in the question stem show that the answer must have been directly stated in the passage. Thus, this is a Detail question. Go back to the first paragraph to find out what Chomsky said. According to Chomsky, we can innately perceive how languages "are put together." Predict that the correct answer should have something to do with how humans can intuitively understand the deep structure of languages. Answer choice (B) is correct.

Choices A and C are extreme; while humans can grasp the structure of all languages, they cannot necessarily understand or speak all languages. Choice D is mentioned in the passage, but it is given as a possible direction for future research. There is no evidence that Chomsky himself is concerned with human biology.

4.   H

Difficulty: Low

Category: Detail

Getting to the Answer: This question stem includes the phrase "According to the passage," showing that it is a Detail question. The passage discusses the structure dependency rule in the second paragraph; predict that a sentence's structure and meaning depend on its phrases. Choice (H) is correct.

Choice F is opposite; the passage says that neither linear structure nor individual words define sentence meanings. Choice G is also opposite; meaning depends on structure, not vice versa. Finally, the passage does not discuss how head words relate to meaning, so J is incorrect.

5.   A

Difficulty: Medium

Category: Function

Getting to the Answer: The wording "the author includes . . . in order to" marks this as a Function question. Research the context of these quotes to determine why the author included them. In the passage, they are offered as examples of unmistakably grammatical and ungrammatical sentences. Choice (A) is correct.

Choice B is a distortion; although the word order changes, the passage explicitly states that grammar is defined by phrases, not linear structure. Choice C is incorrect because the passage does not identify any head words. Choice D is incorrect because the example sentences are not translated.

6.   G

Difficulty: Medium

Category: Function

Getting to the Answer: The phrase "primarily serve to" indicates that this is a Function question. Go back to paragraph 3 to determine the purpose of the cited questions. The first part of the paragraph contrasts the purely linguistic investigations of universal grammar with its lack of biological inquiry. Since the cited questions all relate to the biological implications of the theory, you can predict that they are included to point out possible oversights in universal grammar. Choice (G) is correct.

Choice F is extreme; the author is merely suggesting that biology should be considered, not that it is better. Choice H is opposite; the point of the questions is that universal grammar has not addressed these topics. Finally, the author is not dismissing any theory here, so J is incorrect.

7. C

Difficulty: Medium

Category: Inference

Getting to the Answer: The clue word *suggests* indicates that this is an Inference question. The researchers from the cited line have multiple opinions listed in the passage, which makes a precise prediction difficult here. Instead, read lines 62–77 to get a general idea of what they think, and then go through the answer choices one by one, eliminating until you find a match.

Choice A is incorrect because the researchers do not offer a way to prove universal grammar correct. Choice B is a distortion; while the researches do say universal grammar is too ordered, they do not suggest that increased chaos would make it more scientific. However, they do say that being impossible to disprove makes universal grammar pseudoscientific; therefore, you can infer that they believe a legitimately scientific theory must be possible to disprove. Choice (C) is correct.

Once you have found an answer that fits the passage, you can move on without checking any remaining choices. However, if you are unsure, you can check all four. Choice D is out of scope; the passage does not discuss whether pseudoscience is a major problem in linguistic studies.

8. F

Difficulty: Medium

Category: Function

Getting to the Answer: The phrase "One of the main purposes" shows that this is a Function question. Consult your notes to determine the function of the fifth paragraph and predict that it discusses neurobiological investigations of language. The correct answer is (F).

Choice G is out of scope; the passage does not explain how language evolved. Choices H and J are misused details; although the paragraph mentions some discoveries and one criticism, neither is one of its overall purposes.

9. B

Difficulty: Medium

Category: Vocab-in-Context

Getting to the Answer: This question has the characteristic phrasing of a Vocab-in-Context question: "the word . . . most nearly means." Read the sentence that includes the cited line to get a feel for how this word is being used. The passage states that language is incredibly complex, so focusing too much on any one connection between words leads to an understanding that is rigid and lacking in nuance. Choice (B) is correct.

Choice A matches a common definition of *sterile*, but remember that the test rarely asks for the usual meanings of word. Choices C and D both reflect physical descriptions, but the context of this sentence is metaphorical.

10. G

Difficulty: Medium

Category: Vocab-in-Context

Getting to the Answer: This question has the distinctive wording of a vocab-in-context question: "the phrase . . . most nearly means." Read the sentence that includes the cited line to determine what this phrase means in context. The passage suggests that both linguistics and biology, working together, are needed to understand language. Predict that the phrase means "improved integration." The correct answer is (G).

Choice F is incorrect because the passage does not suggest that the current relationship between the disciplines is unfair. Choice H is incorrect because the disciplines need to integrate, not just communicate. Choice J is incorrect because the passage does not suggest a permanent relationship.

CHAPTER 19

Literature Passages

LEARNING OBJECTIVES

After completing this chapter, you will be able to:

- Draw inferences about characters' motivations and relationships
- Identify the tone of a literature passage

How Much Do You Know?

Directions: In this chapter, you'll learn to apply the ACT Reading Method efficiently and effectively to literature passages. Take 9 minutes to actively read this passage and answer the 10 accompanying questions. Pay close attention to the relationships between characters as you read. When you're finished, compare your work to the explanations on the following pages.

LITERARY NARRATIVE: This passage is adapted from a short essay within a memoir.

The liminal state of being somewhere entirely new, entirely alien: is there any feeling like it? Heavy with potential, exciting, but always, just beneath the surface, there is the fluttery-heart
5 feeling of fear of the unknown. There was supposed to be a shopping center, and in it a department store, for all those things that somehow, between being taken from the cabinets and drawers of the past and arriving in cardboard boxes to the present,
10 managed to disappear. But how to find it?

Now, I suppose, it is as simple as plugging information into a phone, but this was before the days of such ubiquitous magic. Imagine, if you can, not having satellites and geocached location
15 data, the word "googol" still referring only to a number. There were maps, but I had no map. There were people, but they were strangers, all of them strangers, and the fluttery dread was enough to prevent my asking them for help.

20 But there was also something quixotic about it all—a quest! An adventure! Standing on the front steps of this house where the bed was against the wrong wall, and the hot water took so much longer to gush from the tap, and the backyard smelled of
25 fresh-cut grass rather than the turned earth of my old garden. This had been the right decision. Surely, it must have been. The warm air, the breeze, the smell of fried food from the restaurant at the end of the street, with its OPEN "24/7" sign and dirty
30 windows. The restaurant owners, and all those who lived in the tall, narrow houses around me—they had made a home here. I could do the same.

So, shoulders set and deep breath taken, I set off to see the unknown vanquished, turning right,
35 reciting to myself the vague directions from the landlord: take a right, look for the bridge with the red railing, and then it's on the left, just past

Crane Street, you can't miss it. (I probably could, I remember thinking at the time. I was, and am,
40 quite talented at missing things, to be completely honest.) My determination was a thin, delicate veneer that I pretended was armor-strong as my familiar old boots began their journey down a new sidewalk (new to me only, though, judging by
45 the cracks and the stubborn late blooms pushing through them; the tree roots forcing concrete into tiny, craggy mountains).

And there was something, too, to realizing that one day, and probably sooner than now seemed
50 possible, I would sigh to think of having to walk this way, bored of it all, wondering if I could get by without trash bags or coffee filters or lemon juice for one more day. I wouldn't even notice anymore the blue mailbox of the house two doors
55 down from mine, nor the crooked little pine tree across the street, nor the way the street sign at the intersection was bent in the middle. I wouldn't need to look at that sign anymore to know the road that I was crossing. (That street was Hawthorn, by
60 the way, and my own street was Oak, despite the aforementioned pine. There were oaks as well, as I recall, though they might have been something else; my knowledge of trees generally extends to "conifer" versus "deciduous" and no further.)

65 I would walk one day, then, with my head down, but with much less hesitation, no more wondering if I'd gone too far without noticing the bridge with the red railing or Crane Street, because I'd know where the bridge was, and Crane Street, and
70 everything else in this sprawling maze of a city. I'd know which buses to take, which stores had better prices than the one where I was going, which restaurants had the best desserts, which houses had a cat who liked to sit on the porch and watch
75 me pass.

And how mundane it would all be! How easy, how *dull*. There was dread in that, too, when I realized. Because there was beauty in the unfamiliar, though it was fragile, easy as an eggshell
80 to shatter into a million pieces when one stopped noticing it and no longer felt the need to be so cautious. This quest of mine was one to savor for as long as it lasted.

And there, as promised, was the bridge with
85 the red railing, and the creek beneath was rocky and quick, shimmering, and beyond it, the boxy-brick, pocked-and-pitted walls of what must be my destination. Just a generic shopping center, like so many hundreds of others. But still, who knew what
90 awaited me inside? More unknown magic: perhaps a book of spells, or a genie's lamp, or a gateway to a new world. There was only one way to find out. And I had made it this far—I would make it to the end.

1. The narrator's attitude in the passage as a whole can best be described as:

   A. desperate, but tentatively hopeful.

   B. uncertain, but ultimately upbeat.

   C. excited, but initially dour.

   D. cynical, but nonetheless determined.

2. The narrator describes what she is seeing as she travels in lines 53–59 primarily in order to:

   F. share with the reader more information to help paint a mental picture of the new place in which the narrator lives.

   G. contrast these details with the place where the narrator lived before she moved and describe what is different about the two places.

   H. compare what she sees to what she remembers from several other places she has lived.

   J. give examples of things that the narrator will no longer notice when the same trip becomes tedious and dull.

3. As it is used in the first paragraph, the word *alien* most nearly means something that is:

   A. sinister and threatening.

   B. unfamiliar and strange.

   C. out-of-place but exciting.

   D. unwelcoming but peaceful.

4. The narrator uses the phrase "I set off to see the unknown vanquished" in the fourth paragraph in order to:

   F. continue the mental theme of seeing the trip to the store as a fantastical quest.

   G. show the difficulty of overcoming fear of the unknown when in a new place.

   H. describe the way in which the narrator chose to travel to her new home.

   J. convey to the reader the dangers of not knowing where you're going.

5. It can reasonably be inferred from the passage that the narrator is writing about a time period:

   A. in the present day.

   B. in the distant past.

   C. in the near future.

   D. in the recent past.

6. In lines 78–82, the narrator compares finding beauty in the unknown to an eggshell primarily in order to emphasize:

   F. how much stronger she will be when she knows her surroundings better.

   G. how difficult it is to know one's own strength when faced with being in a new place.

   H. how delicate her current viewpoint is compared to how she will feel later.

   J. how mentally fragile she is feeling after she has come to a new place to live.

Reading

7. According to the passage, the narrator was given directions to the shopping center by:

    A.   her landlord.

    B.   restaurant owners.

    C.   her real estate agent.

    D.   the neighbors.

8. In line 70, the narrator describes the new city in which she lives as a "sprawling maze" primarily in order to emphasize:

    F.   the lack of planning that went into the city.

    G.   the difference between her old home and her new one.

    H.   her own dislike of using a map to find the shopping center.

    J.   her current lack of knowledge of the city.

9. What do the narrator's fanciful ideas regarding what she may find at the shopping center (lines 89–92) suggest about her?

    A.   She truly believes she will find something magical inside the shopping center.

    B.   She wants to prolong the sense of adventure after completing her initial "quest."

    C.   She is not certain of what types of items the shopping center might sell.

    D.   She is fighting the potential for shopping trips to become mundane and tedious.

10. In lines 4–5, the narrator employs which of the following literary devices in order to describe what she will know about the city in future?

    F.   Personification

    G.   Symbolism

    H.   Alliteration

    J.   Metaphor

Check Your Work

Passage Map Notes:

¶1: narrator just moved, excited & nervous

¶2: needs store, lacks tools to find it

¶3–4: changing feelings about new home and "quest" – excitement, uncertainty, determination

¶5–6: narr. will be familiar and bored in future

¶7: narr. wants to keep sense of adventure

¶8: finds store, thinks about future adventures

BIG PICTURE SUMMARY

Main idea: The narrator is recounting how it feels to navigate a new location for the first time.

Author's purpose: To describe her current feelings and anticipate how those feelings might change in the future

---

1.   B

Difficulty: Medium

Category: Global

Getting to the Answer: The clue words "passage as a whole" indicate this is a Global question. Consult your notes to refresh your memory on the whole passage and ask yourself how you might describe the narrator's attitude: while the narrator questions her decision to move to a new area, she ultimately chooses to try to see exploring her new environment as an enjoyable adventure. This matches (B).

The other answer choices all contain one part that is too extreme. While *tentatively hopeful* might accurately describe the narrator's attitude, *desperate* is too strong a word for how she feels, so A is incorrect. In C, while the narrator is indeed *excited*, there is nothing *dour*, or gloomy, about her attitude at the beginning of the passage. And finally, in D, the narrator could be said to be *nonetheless determined*, but her attitude is not *cynical*.

2.   J

Difficulty: Low

Category: Function

Getting to the Answer: "Primarily in order to" in the question stem tells you this is a Function question. Review these lines in the passage. The narrator uses all the details of what she is seeing in her new neighborhood as a contrast to what will happen in the future, when she no longer notices those things because the familiar trip to the store will have lost its luster. This matches (J).

In F, while the narrator is in fact helping paint a mental picture of the new area, that is not why those details are included. Choice G might be a tempting choice if you did not refer back to the passage—the narrator does compare the house she lives in now to where she lived before, but that comparison was earlier in the passage. Multiple past residences are not discussed in the passage, making H incorrect.

3.   B

Difficulty: Medium

Category: Vocab-in-Context

Getting to the Answer: The phrase "most nearly means" indicates this is a Vocab-in-Context question. Refer back to the first paragraph to see how the narrator uses the word *alien*. It appears in the first line, alongside being in a place that is "entirely new." Predict that *alien* relates to that, referring to a place in which the narrator is not yet entirely comfortable. This matches (B), which is the correct answer.

While the narrator is not yet comfortable with her new location, nothing implies that she finds it either sinister or threatening; A is too extreme and thus incorrect. Choice C might be tempting, but while it describes the narrator's overall feeling over the course of the passage, it isn't what is meant by the word *alien* specifically; C is incorrect. Choice D is out of scope; nothing is said about the narrator's new location being unwelcoming or peaceful.

4. F

Difficulty: Medium

Category: Function

Getting to the Answer: Since the question asks how a particular phrase is used, this is a Function question. Ask yourself how that particular phrase functions in relation to the rest of the passage. The narrator is trying to see her trip as "a quest! An adventure!" and you could predict that this phrase continues to use the kind of language you might associate with such a viewpoint. This matches (F), which is the correct answer.

While the narrator does discuss the fear of being in a new place, she is not referring to that fear when using the phrase quoted, making G incorrect. The narrator is describing going to the department store, not her home, which means H is out. Finally, the narrator does not discuss any true dangers at all (if anything, she seems to realize her fears are unfounded) which means you can eliminate J.

5. D

Difficulty: Low

Category: Inference

Getting to the Answer: The question asks what "can reasonably be inferred," making this an Inference question. Look at your passage notes to get a feel for when the narrator might be writing, and eliminate answer choices as you go. In the second paragraph, the narrator discusses cell phones that can be used to look up where something is located not yet existing, which eliminates A. Throughout the passage, the narrator is looking for a shopping center, a relatively modern invention, which eliminates B. There is nothing at all in the passage implying it might be set in the near future, so C is out. This leaves (D); based on the passage, it does appear likely the narrator is writing of a time in the recent past, so (D) is correct.

6. H

Difficulty: Medium

Category: Function

Getting to the Answer: Here, you are asked why the narrator makes a particular comparison, making this a Function question. Why does the narrator compare her current feeling to an eggshell? Review the lines in question. Predict that the narrator is emphasizing how easy that feeling is to crush with the passing of time. Now review the answer choices: the match to the prediction is (H).

Choices F, G, and J are all out of scope. They may or may not be true of the narrator, but none of them are why the narrator compared finding beauty in the unknown to an eggshell.

7. A

Difficulty: Low

Category: Detail

Getting to the Answer: "According to the passage" indicates that this is a Detail question. Refer back to the paragraph in which the narrator discusses being given directions. The landlord gave her the directions—this matches (A). The narrator does not mention speaking to the restaurant owners, a real estate agent, or her neighbors, eliminating B, C, and D.

8. J

Difficulty: Medium

Category: Function

Getting to the Answer: "Primarily in order to emphasize" tells you this is a Function question. It wants to know why the narrator describes the city the way she did. Refer back to the line as well as the lines immediately around it. Predict that the narrator is emphasizing how little she knows now about the city compared to what she will know once it has grown familiar to her. This matches (J)—she calls the city a "sprawling maze" because it is currently unfamiliar.

Nothing is said about whether or not the city was planned, so F is incorrect. While the narrator does discuss differences between her old home and her new home, this isn't why she called the city a "sprawling maze," making G incorrect. Finally, while the narrator mentions maps, all she says is that she has none, not that she dislikes using them, so H is incorrect.

9. B

Difficulty: Medium

Category: Inference

Getting to the Answer: "What can be inferred" indicates that this is an Inference question. Refer back to the final paragraph, and predict that the narrator means that she will continue to imagine herself on an adventure despite having found what she was looking for originally (the shopping center). Choice (B) matches the prediction and is the correct answer.

There is nothing to indicate that the narrator truly believes she will find magical items in the shopping center, eliminating A. She may or may not be certain of what the shopping center sells, but this isn't why she mentions finding magical things inside, eliminating C. And while she does believe going shopping in this new place will eventually become boring, she does not reference magical items in relation to that, eliminating D.

10. H

Difficulty: High

Category: Function

Getting to the Answer: This is a rare question type, but don't let it trip you up! Tackle it just as you would any other question in the reading section. Because it asks you what the narrator is doing with a particular literary device, this is a Function question. Refer back to the referenced paragraph. The narrator uses alliteration, the occurrence of the same letter or sound at the beginning of closely connected words, in the phrase "fluttery-heart feeling of fear," so (H) is correct. The referenced lines do not contain personification, symbolism, or metaphor, eliminating F, G, and J.

How to Read ACT Literature Passages

LEARNING OBJECTIVES

After this lesson, you will be able to:

- Draw inferences about characters' motivations and relationships
- Identify the tone of a literature passage

Exactly one passage in each ACT Reading section is a literature passage: an excerpt from a novel or short story. The ACT literature passage will be labeled **PROSE FICTION** or **LITERARY NARRATIVE**, and it will always be the first passage in the Reading Test. That doesn't mean you have to tackle it first, though. Some test takers may find fiction more engaging and feel comfortable reading dialogue and interpreting an author's descriptions of characters and settings. Others may find their strengths lie in more concrete, nonfiction passages on science and social studies. Don't make a snap judgment based on how you feel now, though. Practice all of the passage types to give yourself an honest, informed assessment. You'll find more tips and strategies on how best to approach the section in the chapter on ACT Reading section management.

To read passages and answer questions like these:

PROSE FICTION: This passage is adapted from a collection of short stories.

She had a little ball she liked to bounce, until one day she didn't. One minute it was there, the next—it wasn't. Even at six years old, she knew bouncy balls didn't just . . . just *disappear*. But
5   it was only her, and the empty hallway, and no bouncy ball.

She crawled around looking for it, even though it hadn't fallen, because it had vanished in mid-air. But it was nowhere. It hadn't slipped into one of the
10 floor vents (it was too big, anyway), it hadn't rolled under a door. It was just gone.

She didn't tell anyone about it; she knew they wouldn't believe her. "You always lose things. Stop being so *careless*." The same things they said when
15 she really had misplaced one of her school-books, or her hairbrush, or half of a pair of socks. But this was different.

And it wasn't the only time it happened.

Things around her had a perplexing, marvelous
20 habit of disappearing. Never when anyone was around, and never when she might have predicted it. Sometimes those mysteriously-purloined items came back, though. Like the doorknob. It once

vanished as she was turning it, only to reappear
25 as she backed away, startled, her hand still outstretched and curved around something that was no longer there. She remembered the feeling in the moment, a vertiginous swoop of discomfort. But a few seconds later, there it was again. She
30 wasn't just seeing things—she'd felt it go, the cold metal against her palm, and then nothing. Or there was the time she put her pencil down on her desk and when she reached for it again, it wasn't there. Instead, she found it later, on the middle of her bed.

35 She grew up, as children will do, and got used to the experience. Nothing important ever disappeared permanently, thankfully—or at least, not in *that* way. She *wished* sometimes she could blame her odd, thieving ghost for her missing homework.

40 And was it a ghost? Or something else? There was no way to know. It never bothered anyone else in the house—not her mother, or father, or her little sister, or even the various pets they had over the years. As she grew older, she sometimes
45 asked for things back, and usually, they would eventually show up, though in odd places. Once, she demanded her favorite hair clip back, and it appeared on top of her head. "Oh, *very funny*."

But it was friendly, for the most part. It didn't
50 pinch, or rattle the cupboards menacingly, or make things go bump in the night. It merely took things.

Perhaps, she reasoned, it was the ghostly equivalent of a magpie. She read up about ghosts, and apparently, what hers did was not all that unusual.
55 Sometimes, she read aloud, in case her ghost was also curious about others of its kind and what they did. "But no pulling the covers off my bed at night, ghost. That's just creepy."

She wondered if it had a name. She simply
60 thought of it as her ghost, no greater eponymity required. It followed her away from home, to college, where it thieved the thumbtacks from her cork board and pens from the cup on her desk. It followed her to her first apartment, taking spoons
65 and refrigerator magnets and, once, the charger for her phone. She demanded that one back, too. She found it behind a bookcase in the spare bedroom, a room she did not use unless she had visitors. There were no visitors at the time.

70 It never left wherever she was living. She could go to work, and anything that disappeared was her own fault, or at best the fault of her coworker who seemed to believe the snacks and drinks in the fridge were intended to be shared by anyone too penny-pinching
75 to bother to bring their own. She could go out with friends, and not have to worry about disappearing French fries. It was a home ghost.

Eventually, she married and had children, and they, like others, were not bothered by the
80 ghost, though her children teased her about her inability to keep track of things; what had been exasperating to her parents was a joke to the kids. But she knew the ghost approved of them, because one day, her six-year-old daughter came running to
85 find her, grinning with excitement and delight:

"Mommy, look! It just appeared out of nowhere! Like *magic*!"

A bouncy ball.

1. The point of view from which the passage is told is best described as that of:

   A. a first-person narrator who tells a story that continues throughout her life.
   B. a first-person narrator who offers insights into the thoughts of other characters as she chronicles the events in her life.
   C. a limited third-person narrator who relates events from the perspective of the main character.
   D. an omniscient third-person narrator who relates the thoughts and actions of the characters.

2. According to the passage, the first time an object disappeared, the girl:

   F. thought she had lost or misplaced it.
   G. found it later in an unexpected place.
   H. was afraid to tell her parents.
   J. saw it vanish before her eyes.

3. The narrator mentions the episode with the doorknob primarily in order to:

   A. illustrate that the girl is not hallucinating.
   B. support the idea that the ghost is friendly.
   C. demonstrate that any objects that disappear are later returned.
   D. question whether the objects are actually disappearing.

4. The use of italics on the words "very funny" in line 48 is most likely intended to convey a tone of:

   F. hilarity.
   G. impatience.
   H. sarcasm.
   J. importance.

5. According to the passage, when the girl first starts to notice items disappearing, she feels:

   A. concerned.

   B. delighted.

   C. frightened.

   D. worried.

6. Which of the following statements best captures the reason the girl reads aloud from books about ghosts?

   F. Reading aloud makes the girl more confident and calms her fears.

   G. The girl wants to help the ghost learn about other ghosts.

   H. The girl hopes her parents will overhear her and learn about the ghost.

   J. The girl is learning to read, and she is interested in ghosts.

7. The narrator describes the main character as responsible when objects disappear from:

   A. her childhood bedroom.

   B. her college apartment.

   C. her workplace.

   D. her home as an adult.

8. The statement "There were no visitors at the time" (lines 68–69) primarily serves to suggest that:

   F. the ghost put the phone charger behind the bookcase.

   G. the phone charger had disappeared much earlier than the girl thought.

   H. earlier visitors may have borrowed the phone charger.

   J. the ghost would not return the charger.

9. According to the passage, the frequent disappearance of objects caused the girl's parents to:

   A. demand the objects be returned.

   B. scold her for carelessness.

   C. spend money to replace the missing objects.

   D. become annoyed.

10. It can reasonably be inferred from the passage that the girl believes that the ghost approves of her children because:

   F. the children were never bothered by the ghost.

   G. the ghost returned the first object taken from the girl.

   H. the children thought the ghost was a joke.

   J. objects stopped disappearing once the children were born.

You need to know this:

The ACT does not generally test symbolism, but it does test your ability to draw inferences about characters' relationships and attitudes and to recognize how the author creates a specific tone or effect.

Unpack the Pre-Passage "Blurb" Effectively

Be sure to read the little blurb that precedes an ACT Reading passage; this can be especially helpful on literature passages. The blurb will always give you the author's name, the title of the book or short story from which the passage was adapted, and the original publication date. When necessary, it may provide information about the main characters and setting.

Author. If you happen to know the author, great, but don't expect to. If the name rings a bell that helps you identify the time frame or setting of the passage, take advantage of that, but otherwise, let it go. No questions will ask about the author's identity or biographical information.

Title. A book's title may help you identify its genre—tragedy, romance, coming-of-age stories, etc. It may also give you clues about the setting or theme of the passage.

Publication date. The ACT has used literature passages drawn from various time periods over the last 200 years or so. Obviously, language use and references will be different in passages from the 1850s than in those from the 1950s, and you can use that information to provide context about social conditions and historical events, or even about unusual vocabulary.

Characters and setting. When the test adds any information beyond author, title, and date, pay close attention. The people writing the test questions felt this information was essential for test takers to know, and it will always give you a head start in interpreting the passage and anticipating where the story is likely to go. Knowing, for example, that the main character is an adolescent or a mother, or knowing that a story takes place in a coal-mining town or an aristocratic palace, will change your understanding of the passage from the outset.

Tune In to the Narrator's "Voice"

Within the first few lines, you will be able to distinguish a passage written in first person (the narrator as the main character, knowing only what that character knows) from one written in third person (the narrator is separate from the characters). Keeping this in mind as you read will help you spot the purpose of each paragraph and will help you later with Inference questions ("With which of the following would the narrator/character most likely agree?").

In addition, take note of language that indicates the narrator's or a character's point of view. In a standard science or social studies passage, opinion and emphasis key words help you keep track of an author's ideas about a topic. In literature passages, the author may put these ideas in the mind or the mouth of a character or in the way a scene or object is described. Take note of the passage's tone (e.g., joyful, nostalgic, anxious, angry, hopeful, ironic, satirical, etc.), especially if an event or conversation brings about a change in tone. Typically, one or more of the questions will reward your attention to the passage's tone and characters' points of view.

Track What Happens and the Main Character's Reaction or Response

In a standard ACT Reading passage on science or social studies, you can use an author's purpose to anticipate where the passage will go. When the author says there is a debate over a recent theory, you expect the next couple of paragraphs to lay out one side and then the other. If the author introduces a new idea, there will probably be an example to illustrate it. Literature passages unfold a little differently, but if you are reading actively, you can still anticipate and track the development of the story. Use what you know about a character to anticipate the action and to interpret the character's reactions. If an older worker who is concerned about having enough money for retirement has a conversation with her boss, you can understand what she's after, even if she is using language that talks around the subject.

If a studious young man absorbed in a book is interrupted by a boisterous group of revelers, you can expect some annoyance or judgment in his reaction, even if he doesn't say anything to the newcomers. Keeping track of these things will help you jot down good paragraph summaries, just as you would in nonfiction passages.

When a character's reaction or response to an event surprises you, consider whether this signals a change in the tone of the passage or indicates that you've glossed over or misunderstood something about the character or situation. In either case, it's always valuable to track not only the plot but also the character's reactions to and interpretations of what is happening.

Use What You Already Know About ACT Reading Strategies and Question Types

While literature passages have a distinct look and feel, the questions that accompany them are of the same types as those that follow standard science and social studies passages. Thus, while the best test takers apply a few unique reading strategies tailored to literature, their overall approach remains similar to what they use for all passages. In every case, ACT experts read actively to prepare themselves for the question set. To do that, they read for the big picture, for the author's (or in this case, narrator's or characters') opinions and point of view, and for the passage's structure by noting the purpose and main idea of each paragraph.

For the most part, the questions that accompany literature passages are worded similarly to those for science or social studies passages. However, in literature passages, you may also see questions asking:

- for the passage's theme (which corresponds to its main idea)
- about a shift in the narrator's focus
- how the author creates a certain effect
- what is going on in a character's mind

As long as you read actively for tone and characters' motivations, you'll be ready for questions like these.

You need to do this:

- Use the pre-passage blurb to identify all that you can about:
  - The author's identity
  - The time frame and location
  - The passage's main character or characters
- Quickly recognize whether the passage is in first person or third person.
- Focus on the main character's defining characteristics: demographics (such as age, social position, occupation, race, and gender) and mental traits (attitudes, opinions, desires, and conflicts).
- Anticipate the character's responses to events or interactions with other characters.
- Note the purpose of each paragraph as you read.

Explanations

Passage Map Notes:

¶1–2: girl, 6 yrs old, ball disappears

¶3: doesn't tell anyone

¶4–6: objects really disappear, not seeing things

¶7–9: ghost? description

¶10: "house" ghost

¶11–13: adult, ghost still with her

BIG PICTURE SUMMARY

Main idea: The author shares instances when a "house ghost" has taken and replaced items over the years.

Author's purpose: To describe the author's interactions with a ghost over time

---

1.   C

Difficulty: Medium

Category: Global

Getting to the Answer: There will be several types of questions on the ACT that will test your knowledge of basic literary concepts. This passage has a narrator who describes the events and tells the story from the point of view of the girl, so (C) is correct.

A good clue that the passage does not have a first-person narrator is the lack of the word "I" in the text. A first-person narrator tells the story from his or her own perspective. Eliminate A and B. An omniscient narrator knows everything, but this narrator questions whether there's really a ghost, or something else; an omniscient narrator would know the answer to that question. Eliminate D as well.

2.   J

Difficulty: Medium

Category: Detail

Getting to the Answer: The phrase "According to the passage" tells you that this is a Detail question. The first time an object disappears is mentioned in the first two paragraphs, so return there and read carefully. Line 8 states, "it had vanished in mid-air," which matches (J), the correct answer.

Choice F is a subtle distortion of information in the passage. Although the girl looked for the ball, she knew that it hadn't fallen and was too big to fall into a floor vent. At the end of the text, the girl's daughter finds the ball, so G is incorrect. Choice H is also incorrect. The girl chooses not to tell her parents, but she is never described as being afraid to do so.

3.   A

Difficulty: High

Category: Function

Getting to the Answer: "The author mentions . . . in order to" is a clue that this is a Function question. The doorknob anecdote appears in the fifth paragraph. The sample passage map notes tell you that section is explaining that the girl is not just seeing things disappear, but that the objects actually do vanish. The doorknob story emphasizes that by noting that the girl was able to feel the object until it disappeared. This story brings in the sense of touch to show that the girl's eyes are not deceiving her. This matches (A), the correct answer.

Choices B is a misused detail; the ghost is friendly, but that is not why the author describes the incident with the doorknob. Choice C is extreme; the passage only says that some objects are returned, not all of them. Choice D is an opposite choice. The anecdote is supporting, not questioning, the fact that the objects are actually disappearing.

4. H

Difficulty: Medium

Category: Function

Getting to the Answer: The phrase "intended to convey" demonstrates that this is a Function question. Italics are used to emphasize the words, so imagine the girl's tone when she says them. Her favorite hair clip has disappeared, and when it returns, it's on top of her head . . . where it will be used, but not in that way. It's as if her ghost is teasing her, so she teases right back. Choice (H), *sarcasm*, is the best match.

Choice F, *hilarity*, is too literal. If the girl were amused, she would have laughed or smiled, but this is not mentioned in the text. Similarly, G and J do not have any support in the passage and are incorrect. There is no evidence that the girl has lost patience or that she thinks this is an important event.

5. B

Difficulty: Medium

Category: Detail

Getting to the Answer: Because this question includes the phrase "According to the passage," you can identify it as a Detail question. Whenever you are asked about an emotion, there will be a key word in the passage that will support the correct choice. The context clue in the question tells you to identify the girl's feelings when she first starts to notice objects disappearing, so return to the beginning of the passage and scan for a key word. The first sentence of the fifth paragraph describes the disappearances as "perplexing and marvelous," so the girl may be confused by them, but she also enjoys them. Choice (B) is correct.

Choices A, C, and D all have negative connotations not supported by the passage and so are incorrect.

6. G

Difficulty: Medium

Category: Detail

Getting to the Answer: This question includes few clues as to question type; it might be either Detail or Inference, depending on whether the passage states the reason or you need to infer it. Your first step to answering it, however, is the same: find the part of the passage that discusses the girl reading aloud

and research there. The passage map directs you to the middle of the passage, paragraphs 7–9, for the description of the ghost. Reading aloud, the detail mentioned in the question, is found in the eighth paragraph, when the girl reads aloud "in case her ghost was also curious about others of its kind." This matches (G), the correct answer.

None of the other choices are mentioned in the passage, so they are all incorrect.

7. C

Difficulty: Medium

Category: Detail

Getting to the Answer: The clue word "describes" shows this is a Detail question. The passage map indicates that the tenth paragraph describes the ghost as a "house" ghost. The second sentence of that paragraph states that when things go missing at the girl's workplace it is either her fault or the fault of one of her coworkers. Choice (C) is correct.

The incorrect choices are all the opposite of what's in the passage. These are all places where objects have disappeared because of the ghost.

8. F

Difficulty: Medium

Category: Function

Getting to the Answer: The wording "The statement . . . serves to" marks this as a Function question. The lines cited in the question appear in the ninth paragraph, where the sample passage map indicates there is a discussion of characteristics of the ghost. Review the paragraph. The anecdote about the missing phone charger is described, the girl requests the return of the charger, and she later finds it in the guest room. The narrator states "there were no visitors at the time" to emphasize that the disappearance and reappearance of the charger was due to the ghost, not anyone else. Choice (F) is correct.

Choices G and H are not mentioned in the text, and so are incorrect. Choice J contradicts the passage; the ghost did return the charger in this case.

9. D

Difficulty: High

Category: Detail

Getting to the Answer: You can identify this as a Detail question because of the clue "According to the passage." The girl's parents are mentioned twice in the passage: once in the third paragraph and once in the last paragraph. In the third paragraph, her parents chide her for being careless, but the text states they are doing so "when she really had misplaced" one of her things, not because the ghost had made some object disappear. Eliminate B. In the last paragraph, the girl's parents are described as "exasperated," and this matches (D), the correct answer. Choices A and C are not mentioned in the passage, so they are incorrect.

10. G

Difficulty: Medium

Category: Inference

Getting to the Answer: The girl's children are only mentioned in the final paragraphs, so review that section to identify why the girl believes her ghost approves of her children. That context clue is mentioned in line 83, followed by an anecdote of the girl's own six-year-old daughter "magically" finding the same ball that was the first object of the girl's to disappear. The implication is that the ghost showed its approval of the child by returning the ball. Choice (G) is correct.

Choice F is a misused detail; it accurately describes the relationship of the ghost and the children, but it is not mentioned as the sign of the ghost's approval and is thus incorrect. Choice H is a subtle distortion of information in the passage. The children thought the disappearing objects were lost by their mother; her "carelessness" was the joke, not the ghost. Choice J contradicts the passage; it is clear that disappearances continued after the narrator's children were born.

Reading

Try on Your Own

Directions: Actively read this literature passage and answer the questions. Remember to note the tone of the story as you read and pay close attention to characters' attitudes and relationships.

Answers are found at the end of the chapter.

LITERARY NARRATIVE: This passage is excerpted from a series of short biographical stories.

There was a smoothness to the rhythm of her days. She was an old, old woman, and her name was Betty, and each of her days was just like the last. First thing, the careful way she had to move, when
5 it was early and everything about her seemed to have turned stiff and cold in the night. Easing into it, sitting up, joints slowly remembering how to do their creaky old job, but not happy about it—no, not happy about it at all.

10 She made coffee with a percolator, filling it from the sink, knowing just how long it would take. Her son had gotten her one of those coffee machines with the little plastic cups the year before, for her birthday, but she just couldn't take to using it. It
15 was alien. She no longer knew how to deal with alien. So she put it away in the cabinet, where it wouldn't take up all her counter space, and got it out when her son visited, so he wouldn't know she didn't appreciate his thoughtfulness, and he was
20 the one who filled it up, him or his wife or his daughter, who drank coffee at only thirteen. But for Betty herself, the percolator.

She drank her coffee slowly, with honey and milk in it. Sometimes she sat on the porch, when the
25 weather was nice, and watched the sun rise over the old crackerbox houses, houses older even than she was. But more often she sat at her worn kitchen table, still linoleum-surfaced, aluminum-legged, perhaps not the style anyone would choose in the
30 now, but things had been different in the then. She made breakfast with her second cup of coffee: a slice of toast, sometimes with jam, others with more of the honey. She did have a sweet tooth, did Betty. And she knew her doctor wouldn't like that second
35 cup of coffee (and probably not the first, either), but she had lived long enough for such indulgences.

Besides, if she didn't tell him, who was going to? Nobody, that was who.

After breakfast, she dressed: another slow
40 process. Rolling up her stockings, her fingers shaky as they buttoned up her dress. Then she saw to her hair, combing it, all that fluffy white where once there had been smooth chestnut brown. Makeup, as her mother had taught her to do it, not too much,
45 just enough to bring some color to her cheeks.

Most days, after she was dressed it was time for her stories on the TV. That was the rest of her morning, one show giving way to the next, the usual commercials for Metamucil and heart
50 medicine and walk-in bathtubs. They knew who was watching those shows. She supposed there were people who studied that kind of thing, who was watching what and when. So it was this stuff during the weekdays, and ads for cars in the evenings, and
55 sugary breakfast cereals and McDonalds toys on Saturday mornings. Although her granddaughter didn't watch much TV—she was always on her phone, watching stuff that way.

(Betty also had a cell phone, and like the coffee
60 machine it was a gift from her son, and like the coffee machine it mostly sat unused. It wasn't one of the fancy ones like her granddaughter had, just a little black box that flipped open, but still, she didn't see the point. She had a perfectly good phone
65 on the wall in the kitchen, and one by her recliner in the living room, and that was good enough.)

For lunch she might have a sandwich, sometimes a bowl of soup if the day was cold or rainy. And with her lunch a glass of milk, because she had
70 heard that it was good for older women to get plenty of calcium, it helped prevent that bone disease where they broke too easily. She read magazines with her lunch, or worked in her crossword puzzle book—she picked one up a few
75 times a month from the market. She was good at

them, though by now, there were some clues she
knew they used over and over, and she wished
they'd come up with new ones instead.

80 After lunch, it was time for chores. She liked to
sweep; it reminded her of doing it in her father's
store, hardly as tall then as the broom handle.
He'd had a tobacco shop, back when everyone and
their dog seemed to smoke, and she remembered
the lovely smell of it, all those jars of smoky-sweet
85 brown-and-red shreds of tobacco. She'd swept and
danced and pretended she was a princess forced
into penury, like in the movies. Now, she dusted,
and mopped when she needed to see a little shine to
the floors, and washed up her dishes from breakfast
90 and lunch, leaving them to dry in the sun from the
little window above the sink.

In the evening, she watched the news while she
ate dinner, though it sometimes made her sad to see
all the things people did to each other. It was
95 all just so terrible; it hadn't been like that when she
was a child. Sometimes, after, she watched a movie,
if there was anything good on. If not, she might
read a book; she did like those stories about people
living in villages in Ireland or Scotland, with their
100 sweet little romances and the exotic-sounding ways
of spelling words so you could hear their accents in
your head. And then the day was over—just like the
day before, and it was time to undo all that she had
done, return to her nightgown and slip beneath her
105 quilt, sleeping in the safe knowledge that tomorrow
would be just the same as today.

1. Betty's attitude toward technology throughout the
   passage could best be described as reluctance to:

   A. have any modern technology at all in her
      home.

   B. understand any modern technology purchased
      for her by others.

   C. use modern technology developed after she
      grew old.

   D. admit there is modern technology she doesn't
      understand.

2. Based on lines 46–56, it can be reasonably inferred
   that Betty believes the products in the commercials
   shown during the day:

   F. are marketed to older people like herself.

   G. are marketed to those who are retired.

   H. are things she should consider purchasing.

   J. are things her granddaughter would not want.

3. In the first paragraph, the author describes the
   way Betty moves slowly when she wakes up in the
   morning in order to:

   A. contrast it with the way she later moves when
      she is getting dressed and brushing her hair.

   B. reinforce with supporting details the idea
      that Betty is elderly, as was stated at the very
      beginning.

   C. provide the reader with additional informa-
      tion about what waking up is like for all older
      people.

   D. set up a parallel with the later descriptions of
      how Betty goes to bed again at the end of the
      night.

4. What can most reasonably be inferred based
   on the reference to "still linoleum-surfaced,
   aluminum-legged" in line 28?

   F. Betty's home has some furniture that could be
      considered an outdated style.

   G. Furniture that was made in the past was made
      to last longer than furniture made in the
      present.

   H. Betty's son will likely buy her a new kitchen
      table and chairs for her next birthday.

   J. Tables are no longer made with the surface
      and the legs being of two different types of
      material.

Reading

K 547

5. Which of the following statements most accurately describes Betty's attitude toward her doctor and his opinion on her drinking coffee?

   A. She feels some guilt for having the second cup of coffee, but not about having the first, even though he would approve of neither.

   B. She chooses not to think about it, because she knows she is not supposed to be drinking coffee at her age.

   C. She believes it is acceptable because her son bought her a coffee maker, even though she knows the doctor would not approve of it.

   D. Because he does not know she drinks it, she is dismissive of his potential disapproval of her drinking coffee.

6. One of the primary purposes of the sixth paragraph is to:

   F. emphasize the differences between Betty's life and her granddaughter's life.

   G. provide a factual example of why Betty would be better off without a cell phone.

   H. further reinforce Betty's dislike of technology she seems to consider superfluous.

   J. show that Betty believes technology should progress no further than it already has.

7. The author uses the word *safe* in the final paragraph to emphasize that:

   A. the area where Betty lives does not have crime problems.

   B. Betty finds comfort in following the same routine each day.

   C. Betty knows nothing bad will happen while she's asleep.

   D. going to bed is easier for Betty than getting up in the morning.

8. Chronologically, which of the following events happened first?

   F. Betty receiving the coffee maker as a gift from her son.

   G. Betty helping to sweep out her father's tobacco shop.

   H. Betty putting her makeup on the way that her mother taught her.

   J. Betty sitting outside on the porch on days when the weather is nice.

9. Based on the information in lines 79–91, what can most reasonably be inferred about Betty's memories of childhood?

   A. She has fond memories of childhood, but she might view them with somewhat rose-colored glasses.

   B. She does not like to reflect on her childhood because she had to work too young and the world is even less kind now.

   C. She looks back on her childhood as a time when nothing ever went wrong and the world was a safer, better place.

   D. She does not remember her childhood well, but she believes the world is a better place now than then.

10. In the first paragraph, the word *rhythm* most nearly means:

   F. ups and downs.

   G. a series of sounds.

   H. a poetic feeling.

   J. recurring events.

How Much Have You Learned?

Directions: For test-like practice, give yourself 9 minutes to complete this question set. Be sure to study the explanations, even for questions you got correct. They can be found at the end of this chapter.

LITERARY NARRATIVE: This passage is adapted from an essay about family pets.

I have wondered, sometimes, about how my cats view their world. Do they have any means to appreciate the warm air that blows from the vents, the bowl of food that is always full, the blanket left
5 on the bay window for them to curl up in as they watch life outside? They are always comfortable, but they have known no other life. Do they understand that it could be very different?

I knew a cat once named Reginald. (Reginald, of
10 all things to name a cat!) Reginald had known the harshness of life. He should have been a mean old thing, with his torn-up ears, fur patchy and matted, scars on the pale skin beneath, his tail crooked from a break that had healed badly. Ugly as sin,
15 was Reginald; big and orange-furred. And he would have had every right to trust no one and no thing, because just looking at him, you could tell that very few ones or things had ever treated him well until he found his way to our neighborhood.

20 But I've never met a sweeter cat. He would come looking for a little love, purring up a storm, and he'd happily take a bowl of food, though he never wanted to come inside. He was an outdoorsman; it was where he had always been. Everyone in the
25 neighborhood knew Reginald. I don't know who named him, but we all knew that was his name. He was a collective cat. Where he came from, I don't know either, but he was already old when he showed up. A cat like Reginald seemed the type who was
30 born old, old and weary, but happy for any taste of affection.

I had three cats of my own at the time, and they were fat old things, spoiled rotten. They'd see Reginald out the window sometimes and hiss
35 and spit and puff up, but Reginald paid them no mind. He knew his place in the world. And I guess he was smart enough to understand that glass stood between him and them, and there was

nothing they could do about it, no matter how
40 much they postured. He'd sit outside to wash his uneven orange fur, taking pride in what he had, keeping himself clean as well as he could.

Some of the children in the neighborhood liked to pretend he was as mean as he looked, and it
45 almost seemed like he could understand them— they'd run and shriek and hide, and he'd come after them, not getting too close, just looking at them with his big golden eyes, and they'd run again, laughing and shouting at one another to *be careful,*
50 *be careful, there he is!* He'd do it as long as they continued. They weren't *really* scared; the same children would be out the next day with a slice of ham or turkey, feeding it to him bit by bit as he purred and purred and purred.

55 In winter, I would leave my garage door cracked, so he had somewhere to go, and I wasn't the only one. As I said, he wasn't interested in coming inside, but a place out of the cold, with an old blanket or towels to lay on, seemed to be acceptable
60 to him. On snowy days, I'd warm up a can of food for him, and he accepted that too. Meanwhile, my own pudgy beasts batted at the snow through the windows, and I wondered how quickly they'd retreat if they were to feel the actual bite of it.

65 Reginald disappeared late in the spring five or six years after he first appeared in our neighborhood. Someone said that cats went off by themselves to die. There was a field that disappeared into the woods, and people swore they
70 had seen him heading that way, slow and arthritic by then. I don't know if that's true, but if there was any cat who would have wanted to die with dignity, on his own terms, it was Reginald. I hope that whatever happened to him, it was painless.
75 He deserved at least that much blessing in his difficult life.

My own cats have vet care, howling through it, fighting me about going into their carriers. Reginald probably never saw a vet in his life. I
80 don't know how old he was. No one did. My cats have every amenity provided them and certainly expect to continue to be catered to. Reginald asked for nothing, but we gave him what we could. He was an old fighter, that one. He had earned a little
85 pampering.

But I sometimes find myself wondering how different my own cats would be, if they had been through what Reginald did: would they still know how to be affectionate? Would they be like
90 Reginald, purring and head-butting, appreciative of every scrap? Do they understand that things could be very different for them?

I suspect they don't, but I do. When I fill their food bowls, or scoop out their litter box, or
95 wash their blankets, I think of Reginald, even now, when many years have passed since he disappeared. I make sure their every whim is satisfied, because they might have been in Reginald's place, and it breaks my heart to think of them going through
100 what he went through. But I also like to think that, spoiled as they are in their present life, they might, like Reginald, still know how to appreciate a little human kindness. They might play games with kids, unconcerned about their status as the designated
105 monster. They might accept a place to sleep in the garage on cold nights. I hope someone would give them those things, if I could not.

And I also hope that wherever Reginald is now, he's okay. I hope he's warm, and dry, and well-fed. I
110 hope his ears and his fur are whole. I hope there are games to play.

I hope he is at peace.

1. The passage as a whole might be characterized as the author's:

A. attempt to come to terms with the hardship of life for stray animals.

B. explanation of how and why her cats are different from Reginald.

C. reminiscence about a friendly neighborhood stray and her own cats.

D. exploration of human nature when a neighborhood cares for a cat.

2. The author seems to believe that Reginald viewed his place in the world:

F. with affable acceptance; he took what was offered to him and appreciated it, but saw no need to ask for more.

G. with begrudging amiability; he knew that what he needed was only offered as long as he acted in an expected way.

H. with necessary wariness; he was aware that the people around him might turn on him as it seemed had happened in the past.

J. with unnecessary greed; rather than choose to live with one person, he wanted to take from the whole neighborhood.

3. In the passage, the primary purpose of lines 32–36 is to:

A. provide an explanation for why the author's cats are different from Reginald.

B. juxtapose Reginald and the author's cats.

C. explore the similarities between the author's cats and Reginald.

D. attempt to explain why Reginald behaved as he did when he saw the author's cats.

4. In the second-to-last paragraph, it is reasonable to conclude that one of the reasons the author cares for her cats as she does is because:

    F. she worries that she won't be able to take care of them in the future.

    G. she is required to take good care of them since she owns them.

    H. she feels some sense of guilt that she couldn't do more for Reginald.

    J. she thinks that they would not be able to care for themselves like Reginald.

5. As it is used in line 75, *blessing* most nearly means:

    A. a small gift.

    B. a source of protection.

    C. a peaceful prayer.

    D. an act of acceptance.

6. The author physically describes Reginald in lines 11–15 primarily in order to:

    F. establish why Reginald behaved as he did.

    G. contrast Reginald's appearance with his demeanor.

    H. show that Reginald had lived a hard life.

    J. indicate that Reginald's appearance was deserved.

7. The author calls Reginald an "outdoorsman" in line 23 in order to:

    A. reinforce his behavior outside as opposed to inside.

    B. anthropomorphize Reginald's choice to stay outside.

    C. identify why Reginald became a cat for the neighborhood.

    D. provide a reason why Reginald was not allowed inside the house.

8. The passage as a whole strongly suggests that Reginald:

    F. was able to appreciate whatever was offered to him.

    G. had often gotten into fights as a younger cat.

    H. was able to understand the rules of the games children played.

    J. had always understood he was not a house cat.

9. Within the context of the passage, the primary purpose of lines 51–54 is to:

    A. show that Reginald's outward appearance ultimately matched his demeanor.

    B. provide evidence that Reginald could sometimes be a friendly cat around children.

    C. show that children can behave differently in different circumstances.

    D. provide evidence that the children were just pretending that Reginald was monstrous.

10. Based on the passage, how did Reginald's personality affect his later life?

    F. He was begrudgingly cared for by people who felt sorry for him.

    G. He became reluctantly affectionate as he learned to trust people.

    H. He was readily helped out by people in the neighborhood.

    J. He was a favorite of neighborhood children but not adults.

Reading

Reflect

Directions: Take a few minutes to recall what you've learned and what you've been practicing in this chapter. Consider the following questions, jot down your best answer for each one, and then compare your reflections to the expert responses on the following page. Use your level of confidence to determine what to do next.

1. What are ACT Reading literature passages? How do expert test takers adjust their active reading to tackle literature passages most effectively?

    _____

    _____

    _____

2. How are the questions that accompany literature passages different than those accompanying standard science and social studies passages?

    _____

    _____

    _____

3. How confident do you feel with literature passages? What can you do in practice to improve your performance and gain even more confidence with these types of passages?

    _____

    _____

    _____

Responses

1. What are ACT Reading literature passages? How do expert test takers adjust their active reading to tackle literature passages most effectively?

On each ACT test, one reading stimulus is taken from a work of fiction, such as a novel or short story. Expert test takers actively read literature passages by paying attention to what happens to the main character and how he or she responds to these events.

2. How are the questions that accompany literature passages different than those accompanying standard science and social studies passages?

For the most part, questions accompanying literature passages are similar to those from standard nonfiction passages, but in literature, you may see:

1. *Global questions that focus on a change in the passage's tone*

2. *Inference questions that ask what the passage's narrator (as opposed to its author) would agree with*

3. *Function questions that ask how or why a character (as opposed to the author) used a detail or reference from the text*

3. How confident do you feel with literature passages? What can you do in practice to improve your performance and gain even more confidence with these types of passages?

There is no one-size-fits-all answer for this question. Give yourself honest self-assessment. If you feel that literature passages are a strength, that's great! Continue to practice them so that you'll be able to rack up the points associated with these passages on test day. If you feel less confident about literature passages, review the strategies in this chapter, and try to consistently apply the expert approaches outlined here whenever you practice passages in this format.

Next Steps

If you answered most questions correctly in the "How Much Have You Learned" section, and if your responses to the Reflect questions were similar to those of an expert, then consider Literature passages an area of strength and move on to the next chapter. Come back to this topic periodically to prevent yourself from getting rusty.

If you don't yet feel confident, review the instructional text in this chapter, especially the sections on characters' responses and points of view. Then try the questions you missed again. As always, be sure to review the explanations closely. Then go online (**kaptest.com/login**) to use your Qbank for more practice. If you haven't already registered your book, do so at *kaptest.com/moreonline*.

GO ONLINE

kaptest.com/login

Reading

Answers and Explanations

How to Read ACT Literature Passages

Passage Map Notes:

¶1: Betty: old woman waking up

¶2: B prefers old coffee machine, not new; son wants to help

¶3–5: morning routine; B likes her way, but aware of others'

¶6: B sees no use for cell phone

¶7: lunch

¶8: cleaning, childhood memories

¶9: end of day, next day will be same

BIG PICTURE SUMMARY

Main idea: Betty is an older woman with a routine who generally feels times were better before technology and other "new" things took over.

Author's purpose: To recount a typical day in Betty's life

1. C

Difficulty: Medium

Category: Global

Getting to the Answer: The phrase "throughout the passage" indicates this is a Global question (albeit one that also asks you to infer something). Because it is difficult to make a prediction about the correct answer in broad cases like this one, review your passage notes before looking at the answer choices. Knock them out one by one:

Choice A is too extreme. The passage says Betty allows modern technology in her home, she just doesn't necessarily use all of it. Choice B is a distortion. While the passage says that Betty is reluctant to use the coffee maker and the cell phone her son purchased for her, it doesn't say she won't use them because they were purchased by him.

Now look at (C). In the second paragraph, it says, "She now no longer knew how to deal with alien." However, she can turn on a TV, implying that she was able to learn how to use technology earlier in life—this is a change for her. Choice (C) is a reasonable inference based on the passage as a whole, and is correct. Choice D is incorrect because the passage does not include anything to support or refute Betty's willingness to admit when she's struggling to understand modern technology.

2. F

Difficulty: Low

Category: Inference

Getting to the Answer: The clue words "it can be reasonably inferred" indicate that this is an Inference question. Review the referenced lines and those immediately around them. Based on the paragraph, you might predict that Betty believes the target market for those things shown on daytime TV commercials are older people who might be more likely to have health or mobility issues. This matches (F).

Choice G is too extreme; there is nothing to indicate Betty believes people who are retired are the marketing demographic of the commercials. Choices H and J are out of scope; there is no way to know whether Betty has considered buying any of the things advertised or whether her granddaughter would want them.

3. B

Difficulty: Medium

Category: Function

Getting to the Answer: "Describes . . . in order to" should stand out as a clue that this is a Function question. Review your passage notes. Predict that the correct answer will show that Betty's waking-up process is slow because she's so very old. Choice (B) is correct.

Choice A can be eliminated because the two situations are not set up in contrast to one another. Choice C is too extreme; while this is true of Betty, you can't say for sure that the same is true of all older people. Choice D has the same problem as A. While both waking up and returning to bed are described, they are not presented as parallels to one another.

4.   F

Difficulty: Low

Category: Inference

Getting to the Answer: The word *inferred* in the question makes it pretty straightforward to identify the question type: it's Inference! Look back to the referenced lines. Predict that the correct answer will address the fact that tables with linoleum surfaces and aluminum legs are no longer popular. Choice (F) is correct.

There is no information in the passage to support the other answer choices. Just because Betty has an old table does not mean all furniture from the past was made to last longer, so G is out. While Betty's son might get her a new table and chairs, there's nothing to indicate it is likely, so you can eliminate H. Finally, while the passage says Betty's table is made of two different materials that seem to no longer be a popular choice, that does not prevent modern tables from being made of two different materials, as J says.

5.   D

Difficulty: Low

Category: Inference

Getting to the Answer: "Most accurately describes" indicates that this is an Inference question. Refer to your notes to find out where the doctor is mentioned: in the third paragraph. Predict that the correct answer will indicate that Betty considered what the doctor might say, but then decided it didn't matter because she wasn't going to tell him and neither was anyone else. That matches (D).

Choice A might be tempting if you consider that she thinks about what her doctor would say at the same point in the passage where the second cup is mentioned, but there is no indication that she feels guilty while having that second cup. Choice B is not supported by the passage, because clearly she is thinking of it. Finally, C is not supported because no link is made between the coffee maker her son got her and her attitude toward the doctor.

6.   H

Difficulty: High

Category: Function

Getting to the Answer: The phrase "One of the primary purposes" should serve as a clue that this is a Function question. The question wants to know why a particular paragraph was included in the passage. Review your notes on the sixth paragraph and predict that the paragraph was included to show another example of something, like the coffee maker described earlier, that Betty considers unnecessary in her life because she already has something that serves the same purpose. Choice (H) is correct.

Be careful of the incorrect choices on this one, though! They might all be tempting in different ways. The paragraph does highlight a difference between Betty's life and that of her granddaughter: they have different types of cell phones. That's not the reason why the paragraph was included, however, so F is out. For G, while Betty herself seems to believe there's no reason to have a cell phone, this would not be considered a factual reason—it's just her opinion. Finally, in J, while Betty doesn't see the need to change her own technology, there is nothing to indicate she opposes it progressing for the rest of the world.

7.   B

Difficulty: Low

Category: Function

Getting to the Answer: "The author uses" indicates this is a Function question. Refer back to the final paragraph. The word *safe* comes before *knowledge*—the knowledge that tomorrow will be the same as the day Betty has just experienced. Predict that the word is used to emphasize that she likes each day being the same. This matches (B).

Both A and C are out of scope; nothing is said in the passage about crime or about what Betty thinks will happen while she's asleep. And while D is implied to be true, that isn't the reason why the author uses the word *safe*.

Reading

8.   G

Difficulty: Medium

Category: Detail

Getting to the Answer: Since this question asks about particular events, it is a Detail question. Review your notes to make sure you remember the order in which things occurred in Betty's life. There's no way to predict, so review the answer choices and figure out which came first.

Choice F happened while Betty was an adult, but we don't know exactly when. Choice (G) came before F (as it happened during Betty's childhood), so F must be incorrect. Choice H happened in the passage, so it came after both F and (G) and must therefore be incorrect. J does not happen at any particular time in the passage, but definitely happened after the author's childhood, so (G) is the correct choice.

9.   A

Difficulty: Medium

Category: Inference

Getting to the Answer: The clue words "what can reasonably be inferred" tell you this is an Inference question. Review the lines listed to make your prediction: Betty seems to have enjoyed helping out in her father's shop, and she believes, based on the news, that things are different now than they were when she was young, though no evidence is given to support this. Choice (A) is correct.

There is nothing in the passage to support the idea that Betty feels she was forced to work too young; if anything, as mentioned above, she seems to have enjoyed the work. So, B is incorrect. In C, while she does seem to believe the world was a safer and better place when she was young, there's nothing in the passage to indicate nothing ever went wrong for her then. Finally, in D, nothing in the passage supports the idea that she doesn't remember her childhood well.

10.   J

Difficulty: Low

Category: Vocab-in-Context

Getting to the Answer: "Most nearly means" should tell you this is a Vocab-in-Context question. How is the word *rhythm* used in this passage? In the first paragraph, the *rhythm* is each day being like the last. This matches (J). While F, G, and H might also be described as a rhythm, they don't fit in with the way the word is used in the context of the passage.

How Much Have You Learned?

Passage Map Notes:

¶1: narrator's cats comfortable, narr. wonders if they know it

¶2: Reginald: stray cat who had hard life

¶3: R sweet anyway, neighborhood cares for him

¶4: narr. cats vs. R

¶5: children play w/ R

¶6: winter care

¶7: R disappears; narr. hopes he had easy death

¶8–10: narr. compares own cats' lives to R's life, hopes they would still be happy

¶11–12: narr. hopes for happy afterlife for R

BIG PICTURE SUMMARY

Main idea: Reginald is a beloved neighborhood cat whose life is very different from the narrator's own pets.

Author's purpose: To compare the life experiences of a friendly neighborhood cat with the lives of the narrator's house cats

1.   C

Difficulty: Medium

Category: Global

Getting to the Answer: "The passage as a whole" indicates that this is a Global question. Review your notes and predict that the correct answer will be something that includes the author discussing both Reginald and the author's cats. That matches (C).

While the author does consider how hard it is for stray cats, as well as how her cats are different from Reginald, neither A nor B encompasses the passage as a whole. Finally, while the author does say that Reginald was cared for by the neighborhood, there is no exploration of human nature, knocking out D.

2.   F

Difficulty: Medium

Category: Inference

Getting to the Answer: The clue words "seems to believe" signal that this is an Inference question. Review your notes: the author seems to believe Reginald was content with his way of life. Choice (F) is the best match for this.

There is nothing to indicate that Reginald was *begrudging*, or that he was acting as he did in order to gain something for himself, which eliminates G. He seems to have been the opposite of wary, which eliminates H. And he wasn't greedy, he was just, as the author says, "an outdoorsman" who preferred not to choose one place to call home, which eliminates J.

3.   B

Difficulty: Low

Category: Function

Getting to the Answer: "Primary purpose" serves as a clue that this is a Function question. Refer back to those lines in the passage. Predict that the author describes her own cats to show how different they were from Reginald. This matches (B).

While the author is writing about how different her cats are from Reginald, she doesn't explain why in the referenced lines, which eliminates A. The author is highlighting differences, not similarities, which eliminates C. Finally, you can eliminate D because while the author does go on to describe how Reginald behaved when her cats were posturing and offers a potential explanation why, she is not yet discussing that explanation in the referenced lines.

4. H

Difficulty: Medium

Category: Inference

Getting to the Answer: The words "reasonable to conclude" should clue you in that this is an Inference question. The author says that "it breaks my heart to think of them going through what he went through," so predict that the correct answer is related to that. The best match for the prediction is (H).

While the author does mention in that paragraph the possibility of not being able to care for her cats, she doesn't say that she expects this to happen, as in F. There is nothing in the passage to indicate she feels it is an obligation to care for them, as in G. Finally, while she worries that they would potentially struggle to care for themselves, this is not the reason why she cares for them, as in J.

5. A

Difficulty: Low

Category: Vocab-in-Context

Getting to the Answer: The phrase "most nearly means" indicates that this is a Vocab-in-Context question. Refer back to the line in question. The author is discussing a painless death for Reginald, so predict that *blessing* is used to mean something like "favor." This matches (A).

While B, C, and D are all acceptable definitions of *blessing*, none of them match the way in which the author of the passage uses the word.

6. G

Difficulty: Low

Category: Function

Getting to the Answer: "Primarily in order to" indicates this is a Function question. Refer back to the referenced lines and those around them. Predict that the author describes Reginald's appearance in order to contrast it with his friendly personality. This matches (G).

Choice F is a distortion; rather than his appearance matching his behavior, Reginald's appearance was in contrast to how he behaved. In H, while Reginald's appearance does indicate he had not lived an easy life, this isn't *why* the author described his appearance. Choice J is not supported by the passage at all; the author, if anything, seems to believe that Reginald deserved better than what he had gotten from life.

7. B

Difficulty: Medium

Category: Function

Getting to the Answer: "In order to" signals that this is a Function question. Why does the author describe Reginald as an *outdoorsman*? This is a word that would normally be used to describe a person, but it is in this case used to describe a cat. This matches (B).

Choice A is not supported because the passage says nothing about Reginald's behavior when inside as opposed to outside. While Reginald is described as a neighborhood cat, this is not why the author uses the term *outdoorsman*, eliminating choice C. And in choice D, the author never indicates that Reginald would not have been welcomed into the house, just that he chose to remain outdoors.

8. F

Difficulty: Medium

Category: Global

Getting to the Answer: The clue words "passage as a whole" indicate this is a Global question. It is often difficult to make specific predictions about Global questions, so go choice by choice, eliminating as you go.

Choice (F) is supported by the passage: the author mentions several times how much Reginald seemed to appreciate anything that was given to him. Choice G might or might not be true; though the author discusses Reginald having scars, she does not provide evidence that he got into fights. Choice H is too extreme. While the author says Reginald seemed to play a monster for the children, there is nothing to indicate he understood the games they played generally. Choice J, like G, might or might not be true. The author says nothing about Reginald's ability to understand he was not a house cat.

9. D

Difficulty: Low

Category: Function

Getting to the Answer: The clue words "the primary purpose" indicate this is a Function question. Refer back to the lines referenced in the passage. Predict that the correct answer will indicate that the children did not truly believe they needed to run away from Reginald. This matches (D), the correct answer.

The author makes it clear that Reginald's appearance did not match his demeanor, eliminating A. The idea that Reginald was only sometimes friendly around children is not supported by the passage, eliminating B. And the author did not discuss the children's behavior in order to show that it changes in different circumstances, eliminating C.

10. H

Difficulty: Low

Category: Inference

Getting to the Answer: The phrase "based on the passage" indicates this is an Inference question. Refer to your notes to get an idea of how Reginald's personality impacted his life, and predict that his affectionate nature meant he became a cat everyone in the neighborhood helped care for. This matches (H), the correct answer.

There is nothing to indicate people "begrudgingly" cared for him out of sympathy, which eliminates F. Similarly, nothing in the passage supports the idea that he became affectionate only reluctantly, eliminating G. Finally, while the passage supports that Reginald was popular with the neighborhood children, nothing indicates that he wasn't also popular with the adults (the passage author seems to be an adult), eliminating J.

CHAPTER 20

Paired Passages

LEARNING OBJECTIVES

After completing this chapter, you will be able to:

- Apply unique strategies to effectively read ACT Reading paired passages in preparation for their question sets

- Identify the variations on common ACT Reading questions as they are used in paired passages

---

How Much Do You Know?

Directions: In this chapter, you'll learn to apply the ACT Reading Method to paired passages. Take 9 minutes to read the following paired passages and answer the 10 accompanying questions. When you're finished, compare your work to that of an ACT expert on the following pages. Identify ways in which the expert reads these paired passages differently than she would an independent passage.

HUMANITIES: Passage A is adapted from an online article about the difficulty women have historically had being successfully published using their own names. Passage B is adapted from an essay about the history of anonymous works.

Passage A

In 1913, modernist author Virginia Woolf wrote an essay for the *Times Literary Supplement*, originally published anonymously. In this essay, she discusses a particular phenomenon suffered by
5 female writers of the past: a lack of respect within their lifetimes for their talents. She frames this essay around Jane Austen, who was, during Woolf's lifetime, in the midst of a resurgence of popularity.

It is difficult to imagine two writers more
10 different from one another than Woolf, who lived from 1886 to 1941, and Austen, who died in 1817, more than half a century before Woolf was born; Woolf's labyrinthine, stream-of-consciousness style and arduous prose stands in sharp contrast
15 to Austen's witty social commentaries masked as lighthearted novels. In the essay, while Woolf clearly respects Austen as a writer, she does criticize what she perceives as timidity in Austen's writing. Woolf refers at one point to Austen removing a
20 hedge from one of her novels when she found out they didn't grow where the story is set, "rather than run the risk of inventing one which could not exist." Austen, Woolf believed, was too afraid to test boundaries.

25 But consider this belief in light of another essay by Woolf. In 1929's "A Room of One's Own," she discusses a proverbial sister of William Shakespeare, equal in genius and equal in desire to make her living as a playwright but prevented from doing
30 so because she is a woman. Until the nineteenth century, Woolf says, it was almost impossible for a woman to become a successful writer. This was because, "unless her parents were exceptionally

rich or very noble" and gave their blessing, she was
35 unlikely to have the opportunities necessary to develop her craft.

This second essay potentially sheds light on Austen and her writing style. In "A Room of One's Own," Woolf discusses how limited life must have
40 been for women in the past. Jane Austen, who began her professional writing career in 1811 and died in 1817, never married, and while she was educated, it would have been a far more limited education than a wealthy man would have received
45 at the same time. She was forced to publish her works anonymously, even when they proved popular. As Woolf herself famously wrote, "I would venture to guess that Anon . . . was often a woman."

Should it come as a surprise, then, under the
50 conditions of Austen's upbringing and career, that she was rather rigid and conservative in the way she told her stories? It was hard enough for her to be published at all. She did not have the wealth or the increased freedoms of Woolf, writing a
55 century later. Whether Woolf is right or wrong in her criticism of Austen as a timid writer, it is surly easily understood why, based on Woolf's own 1929 essay, Austen chose to write as she did.

Passage B

In 1967, Roland Barthes, a French literary critic,
60 wrote an essay entitled "La mort de l'auteur," "The Death of the Author." In the essay, Barthes makes the argument that authors and their works should be considered entirely separately from one another: a text should be interpreted on its own terms, rather
65 than through a lens of biographical scrutiny.

But what of the other form of "death of the author": the infamous Anonymous, authors who published with no credit given to them for their craft? Books now considered to be classics that were

70 originally published anonymously include Mary
Shelley's *Frankenstein* and the works of Jane Austen.
And who is Mary Ann Evans? Likely, few would
immediately recognize her name, but many would
be able to come up with at least one work written by
75 George Eliot. This was Evans' pen name, employed
because she wanted her works to be taken seriously
rather than dismissed as the light romances that
were then believed to be the sole purview of female
writers. When the Brontë sisters sought publication,
80 they too did so under anonymity; Charlotte, Emily,
and Anne Brontë became in print the masculine-
sounding Currer, Ellis, and Acton Bell.

Now certainly, authorial anonymity is not
limited to women. While many women published
85 anonymous works because use of their own names
might result in dismissal of the seriousness of their
work or even outright rejection from publishers,
some men, including such well-known figures
as Edgar Allan Poe, Thomas Paine, Alexander
90 Hamilton, and James Madison, published
anonymously at various points in their careers to
avoid the risk of personal consequences or concerns.
It is even true that women could, in rare, lucky
circumstances, find success under their own
95 names: Ann Radcliffe, for instance, was one of the
most successful authors of the late 1700s, writing
wildly popular Gothic fiction.

Regardless of Radcliffe's unusual success,
however, it is clear that many women who
100 sought a career in writing in the Georgian and
Victorian eras felt the need to disguise who
they truly were, or were compelled to do so by
publishers afraid of public reception. "Death
of the author," in these cases, often meant that
105 women in writing only had their true identities,
and the associated respect they might earn from
their talent, revealed after their own quite literal
deaths.

1. In Passage A, Woolf's choice to publish her 1913
essay anonymously while criticizing Austen as a
timid writer could best be described as:

   A. hypocritical; Austen had a choice and still
   chose anonymity, while Woolf did not.

   B. ironic; Woolf was criticizing behavior that
   could be called very similar to her own.

   C. symbolic; Woolf likely chose anonymity as
   a point of solidarity with women in Austen's
   time.

   D. modernistic; Woolf used her own novel-
   writing techniques to showcase Austen's.

2. Which of the following statements best explains
why the author chose, in lines 40–47 of Passage A,
to showcase particular aspects of Austen's personal
life and education?

   F. The author is attempting to convey why Austen might have written in a manner that could
   be called "timid."

   G. The author uses details to evoke feelings of
   sympathy in the reader in order to make
   them appreciate Austen's work as superior to
   Woolf's.

   H. The author is trying to make Austen appear to
   be a better writer than she might seem merely
   from her "rigid and conservative" novels.

   J. The author provides details in order to later
   compare and contrast Austen's life with
   Woolf's.

3. As it is used in line 14, the word *sharp* most nearly
means:

   A. raised and pitchy.

   B. razor-like and dangerous.

   C. abrupt and unexpected.

   D. notable and different.

4. In the second paragraph of Passage B, the author mentions other reasons some authors have chosen to publish anonymously primarily in order to:

   F. establish the notion that women have never chosen to publish anonymously, but some men have chosen to do so.

   G. set up a contrast between the common reasons men and women were published anonymously in the past.

   H. entertain the idea that while both men and women have published anonymously, more men do it than women.

   J. showcase the possibility that there are better reasons to choose to publish anonymously than public reaction.

5. In Passage B, it can most reasonably be inferred that Ann Radcliffe's success as an author might best be attributed to:

   A. being a female author at a time when those were rare.

   B. having her real name attached to her works.

   C. writing in a genre that was then very popular.

   D. publishing under a pen name everyone at the time recognized.

6. Based on the information in the first paragraph of Passage B, it can be most reasonably inferred that Roland Barthes believed:

   F. women were not given enough credit for their writing talent in past centuries.

   G. knowing the details of a writer's life is not necessary for literary criticism.

   H. only after an author dies can someone truly criticize their written works.

   J. men and women often published anonymously for different reasons.

7. The purpose of the information in lines 72–82 of Passage B is to:

   A. provide additional information on why women might be forced to publish anonymously.

   B. offer a contrast between women who publish as Anonymous and those who use pen names.

   C. set up a comparison between women and men who publish anonymously.

   D. show that in some cases women adopted male pen names in order to be more commercially successful writers.

8. Using Barthes' definition of "death of the author" in Passage B, what is one potential drawback to employing Barthes' philosophy to criticize Jane Austen, as Woolf did in Passage A?

   F. It would mean failing to recognize that Austen was likely influenced by the circumstances of her life in her writing.

   G. It would insist upon looking at Austen through a different lens than the one that Woolf chose to employ.

   H. It would require accepting Woolf's premise even if this might be unfair to women writers of the 18th and 19th centuries.

   J. There would be no danger, because "death of the author" would mean that Woolf's criticism is entirely unfounded.

9. Compared to Passage A, Passage B provides more detailed information regarding reasons why:

    A. men in the past might publish anonymously for the same reasons women often did.

    B. women in the past were often forced to publish anonymously.

    C. Jane Austen chose to remain an anonymous author during her lifetime.

    D. women in the past often chose masculine-sounding pen names.

10. In 1818, Jane Austen's *Northanger Abbey* was published. It parodied Gothic fiction like that of Ann Radcliffe. In light of the passages, it can most reasonably be inferred that this work:

    F. is one example of the "resurgence of popularity" (line 8) that Austen enjoyed before her death in 1817.

    G. was published with Austen's name attached since it was published posthumously.

    H. is further evidence that Gothic fiction was very popular during Austen's lifetime.

    J. is further evidence that women might choose to publish anonymously if writing subversively.

Check Your Work

Passage Map Notes:

Passage A:

¶1: VW essay about disrespected female writers and JA

¶2: contrasts between VW & JA, VW criticism of JA

¶3: 2nd VW essay: hard for past female writers

¶4–5: 2nd essay relates to JA

Passage B:

¶6: RB: "death of the author" – separate writer & text

¶7: author: "death of the author" – female writers stuck w/ anonymity

¶8: men sometimes anon, but not b/c had to be

¶9: female writers only get credit after death

BIG PICTURE SUMMARY

Passage A:

Main idea: The limited social approval of female writers may explain why Jane Austen did not take many risks in her writing.

Author's purpose: To defend Jane Austen against Woolf's earlier criticism using Woolf's argument in "A Room of One's Own"

Passage B:

Main idea: Many female authors wrote under male pseudonyms because they would not have been taken seriously otherwise.

Author's purpose: To explain why some authors, especially female authors, published anonymously

1.　B

Difficulty: High

Category: Inference

Getting to the Answer: The phrase "could best be described as" gives you the clues necessary to identify this as an Inference question. Predict that the correct answer will recognize that Woolf was also being a "timid" writer in choosing anonymity even as she criticized the same in Austen. This matches (B).

While Woolf's behavior might be called hypocritical, as in A, the second part flips the situation: it was Woolf who had a choice, not Austen. In C, there is no evidence given for symbolism in Woolf's essay or in her choice to remain anonymous when it was published. Finally, in D, while Woolf's novel-writing techniques are discussed, the passage does not say she used those particular techniques in showcasing Austen's.

2.　F

Difficulty: Medium

Category: Function

Getting to the Answer: The phrase "why the author chose . . . to showcase" indicates this is a Function question. Refer back to that part of the passage to refresh your memory. Predict that the correct answer will show that these details were included to support the idea that it was very difficult for women who wrote in Austen's time, which might help explain the style that Woolf criticizes. This matches (F).

In G, while the author could be said to be attempting to evoke sympathy, she is not trying to make one writer appear superior to the other. Nor does the author attempt to prove that Austen is a better writer than her novels make her appear, which eliminates H. Finally, in J, while the author does point out some of the differences for women in Austen's time and in Woolf's in the passage, that was not why the author included the details referenced in the question.

3.   D

Difficulty: Low

Category: Vocab-in-Context

Getting to the Answer: "Most nearly means" tells you that this is a Vocab-in-Context question. Refer back to the line referenced. *Sharp* here refers to contrast—the author of the passage is discussing how different Woolf and Austen's writing is from one another. This matches (D), which is correct.

Note, however, that all the incorrect answer choices are acceptable definitions of *sharp*. Always make sure it is clear in your mind how the author is using a word with multiple definitions before you start looking at the answer choices!

4.   G

Difficulty: Medium

Category: Function

Getting to the Answer: Use the clue words "primarily in order to" to establish that this is a Function question. Refer back to the paragraph referenced, and read paragraph 3 for additional context. Predict that the correct answer will show that the author of the passage was acknowledging that men were also published anonymously, but it was by choice, whereas women were either forced into anonymity by publishers or chose it in order for their work to be taken seriously. Choice (G) matches this prediction, and is correct.

Choice F is too extreme. There is nothing to indicate that women have never made the choice to publish anonymously. Choice H is out of scope; the passage does not discuss whether more men or women publish anonymously. Finally, J is a distortion. The author's intent is to create a contrast between reasons to publish anonymously, not to prove that reasons other than public reaction are preferable.

5.   C

Difficulty: Low

Category: Inference

Getting to the Answer: The phrase "most reasonably be inferred" indicates that this is an Inference question. Refer to the third paragraph of Passage B, where Radcliffe is discussed. Predict that the correct answer will show that Radcliffe's success can be attributed to her writing popular Gothic fiction. This matches (C), which is correct.

Choices A and B are both distortions; female authors *were* rare at the time, and Radcliffe's choice to have her real name attached to her works was unusual, but her success came despite those things, not because of them. Choice D is simply factually incorrect, based on the information in the passage: Radcliffe was the rare exception, a successful female writer in the 1700s despite not using a pen name or publishing anonymously.

6.   G

Difficulty: Low

Category: Inference

Getting to the Answer: The phrase "most reasonably inferred" offers you clues to identify this as an Inference question. Refer back to the first paragraph to refresh your memory on Barthes' beliefs. Predict that the correct answer will show that Barthes believed an author's work and their biography should be kept separate. This matches (G).

While A is part of the passage, it is not something Barthes necessarily believed. For H, Barthes was referring to "death" in a metaphorical sense, not a literal one. And J, like F, is in the passage, but the information in the passage does not suggest that Barthes believed this.

7. D

Difficulty: Medium

Category: Function

Getting to the Answer: "The purpose of the information" tells you that this is a Function question. The author initially discusses women who published anonymously, but in the lines referenced, goes on to list some who adopted masculine-sounding pen names instead. Predict the correct answer will reflect this. The correct answer, then, is (D).

Choice A is incorrect because the lines referenced do not discuss why women might be forced to publish anonymously. It specifically mentions that in these cases, women chose to use male-sounding pen names. Choice B is incorrect because no contrast was given between the two groups. Choice C is incorrect because the information was not given in order to set up a comparison.

8. F

Difficulty: High

Category: Inference

Getting to the Answer: The phrase "what is one potential drawback" tells you this is an Inference question. "Death of the author," according to Passage B, means separating an author's life from their works. Passage A, however, argues that Woolf actually fails to take into account how Austen's life might have influenced her writing. By employing "death of the author," then, Austen might receive unfair criticism, like Woolf's. This matches (F).

While the author of Passage B mentions a "lens," as in G, there is nothing to support that Barthes' idea would "insist upon" looking at Austen differently than Woolf does. In H, while it might be argued that Woolf is unsympathetic to Austen, overall, she was sympathetic to the challenges of women writing in the past. Finally, in J, the premise of "death of the author" is more akin to Woolf's criticism, rather than standing in opposition to it.

9. B

Difficulty: Low

Category: Detail

Getting to the Answer: The phrase "provides more detailed information" signals that this is a Detail question. It is difficult to make a prediction based on such a broad question, so review each answer choice, knocking out incorrect answers as you go.

While Passage B does discuss men publishing anonymously, this is not discussed at all in Passage A, so it cannot be discussed in a *more detailed* way if another way isn't even present in the other passage. Choice A is incorrect. Choice (B) is supported by the passages: while Passage A mentions that Austen was forced into anonymous publication, Passage B gives information on some of the potential reasons why. So (B) is correct. Choice C is not supported at all by Passage A, which specifically mentions that Austen was forced to publish anonymously, not that she chose to do so. Choice D, like A, is discussed in Passage B but is not mentioned at all in Passage A, so Passage B cannot be said to offer more detailed information.

10. H

Difficulty: Medium

Category: Inference

Getting to the Answer: The clue words "most reasonably be inferred" indicate that this is an Inference question. In Passage B, Radcliffe is discussed as a rare example of a successful female author who wrote under her own name. She was successful because the genre she was writing in was very popular. Predict that Austen's writing a parody of that genre is further evidence of its popularity. This matches (H).

Choice F is a distortion; there was a "resurgence of popularity" during Woolf's lifetime, which was well after Austen died. While both passages say Austen was published anonymously, no information is given about when her name began to be associated with her works; G is incorrect. There is also no mention in either passage of women writing subversively, so J is also incorrect.

How To Read ACT Paired Passages

> ### LEARNING OBJECTIVES
>
> After this lesson, you will be able to:
>
> - Apply unique strategies to effectively read ACT Reading paired passages in preparation for their question sets
> - Identify the variations on common ACT Reading questions as they are used in paired passages

What are paired passages?

In every ACT Reading section, one of the four stimuli is a pair of shorter passages instead of a single longer passage. Occasionally, all four passages on an ACT Reading Test will be independent passages, but you should be prepared to encounter a paired passage set on test day.

The two passages could be in any of the four genres, and within a specific genre, they will share the same topic—often with each one having its own take on the subject matter. The combined length of the paired passages is approximately the length of most single passages, so you don't have much, if any, extra reading to do.

In this chapter, you'll learn how ACT experts actively read paired passages a little differently than they read single passages, and you'll see how the test uses variations of standard ACT Reading questions to test your comprehension of both passages.

To read passages and answer questions like these:

NATURAL SCIENCE: Passage A is adapted from a magazine article about recent technological efforts in conservation. Passage B is adapted from an online article about the success of using artificial intelligence to stop poachers.

Passage A

Conservationists are struggling to address the decimation of a growing number of plant and animal species due to environmental and human-made circumstances. Protecting the Earth's
5 biodiversity requires a better understanding of the behavior of animals in their natural habitats and the factors leading to their decline; this is one aspect of conservation where technology can lend a hand. Artificial intelligence, commonly referred
10 to as AI, has proved to be an important resource in the fight to protect species that already are, or might soon qualify as, endangered. The ability of AI to rapidly process large quantities of data makes it ideal for analyzing the decades of extensive
15 tracking information researchers have gathered. More importantly, AI may reveal patterns that might not be readily discernible solely through human analysis.

The cheetah population in sub-Saharan Africa
20 is a specific example of a species that has faced severe threats on several fronts. From 1900 to 2015, cheetahs saw an estimated 93% decline in population. This same time period also saw a 76% reduction in land that was formerly classified
25 as cheetah habitat. Additionally, smuggling and common misperceptions about the dangers of cheetahs to livestock exacerbated the population decline. Initially, as conservationists began to realize the need to protect cheetahs in their native
30 habitat, they focused on centuries-old tracking techniques. More recently, however, researchers have recognized how effective AI can be in conservation efforts.

Starting in 2001, the WildTrack team of
35 researchers worked with statistical analysis software
development companies JMP and SAS to create
the Footprint Identification Technique, or FIT.
Conservationists collected several high-quality
digital images—footprints in the sand, snow, mud,
40 and other natural substrates—and uploaded these
images into the JMP software. The researchers then
selected landmark points to form a basic outline of
each footprint. AI extrapolates more details from
the footprint, which is then assigned as a unique
45 identifier for that specific cheetah. This non-
invasive "digital tag" is then used in combination
with GPS to precisely track individual cheetahs in
their natural habitat.

This same technology can be used to identify
50 and track a variety of endangered or vulnerable
species (the WildTrack team has developed
algorithms for more than 15 species). Progressive
learning algorithms, which allow the AI to use
mathematical models to identify species, sex, and
55 age-class, become more accurate as the amount of
established data grows. Conservation experts can
use the collected data to predict the movements of
isolated populations, track births and deaths within
the population, and determine the best locations
60 for reintroducing species to their native habitat.
With so much work still to be done to protect the
Earth's endangered species, conservationists are
embracing the power of AI and looking for even
more sophisticated applications the future.

Passage B

65 For years, wildlife reserves and the animals
who live there have been under attack. Poaching,
the illegal hunting and capturing of wild animals,
is the leading human cause of the severe decline
in numbers of certain species. Many poachers use
70 technology to aid them in their illegal activity. For
example, some poachers track elephants and rhinos
using GPS and night-vision goggles and kill them
for their tusks and horns. Conservation officials are
working to counter these attacks by applying AI-
75 modeling; the sheer size of most wildlife reserves
requires a technologically-advanced approach to
most effectively protect the animals from poachers.

The Protection Assistant for Wildlife Security
(PAWS) program employs machine learning and
80 behavior modeling to aid wildlife reserve patrols.
By combining data about previous poaching
activity and patrol routes, the system can predict
where future poaching will likely take place and
design continuously changing patrol routes using
85 game-theory modeling. The constant variations of
the routes prevent poachers from picking up on
patterns, which in turn increases the chance of
catching poachers in the act. PAWS manages to
seamlessly blend machine learning with human
90 knowledge: the algorithm provides a few different
routes, and patrollers can choose the best one based
on their years of experience working to prevent
poaching.

Another aspect of the patrols that benefits from
95 technology is route optimization that accounts
for the terrain. While a substantial quantity of
data, gathered over years of conservation work,
exists about the most trafficked routes of animals
frequently targeted by poachers, past patrol routes
100 often involved climbs or descents that greatly
limited the amount of land secured by regular
patrols. Now AI can calculate the best routes
for both the human patrollers and the drones
in order to maximize the patrolled area. During
105 an eight-month trial of the program at Uganda's
Queen Elizabeth National Park, rangers found
approximately 10 times as many poachers in
areas designated as high-probability versus low-
probability by the algorithm.

110 Those taking the lead in the efforts to end
poaching for good sincerely hope that the
AI-enhanced patrol routes will serve as a significant
deterrent for poachers. As AI systems continue to
find more effective solutions through data analysis,
115 conservation experts feel confident that, with the
help of technology, they can win the battle against
poachers.

1. According to Passage A, AI is a valuable conservation resource because:

    A. it allows conservation officials to thwart attacks by poachers.

    B. it can allow researchers to uncover norms that human analysis might miss.

    C. it can calculate patrol routes for human and drone patrollers.

    D. it is the best way for researchers to protect endangered species.

2. The author of Passage A most likely mentions the statistics referenced in lines 21–25 in order to show:

    F. how AI has helped the cheetah population recover.

    G. how soon cheetahs will become extinct.

    H. how AI has helped prevent cheetahs from being attacked by poachers.

    J. how serious the threat facing the cheetah population is.

3. In Passage A, it can most reasonably be inferred that the decline in cheetah populations is due largely to:

    A. poachers attacking the cheetahs at an unprecedented rate.

    B. loss of land in natural cheetah habitats.

    C. tracking cheetahs using the Footprint Identification Technique.

    D. famine and drought, resulting in a lack of food for cheetah populations.

4. Passage A most strongly suggests that the Footprint Identification Technique:

    F. could be used to help other vulnerable species.

    G. will be used to save all species from extinction.

    H. will combine machine learning and human expertise.

    J. could be used to calculate future algorithms to track poachers.

5. As it is used in line 74, the word *counter* most nearly means:

    A. to oppose.

    B. to promote.

    C. to ignore.

    D. to tally.

6. According to Passage B, which of the following techniques does PAWS utilize to aid conservation officials in protecting animals from poachers?

    F. It uses centuries-old tracking techniques to find poachers.

    G. It uses an algorithm to provide only the best route to track poachers.

    H. It combines human knowledge with computer learning to give patrollers options.

    J. It uses a non-invasive digital tag to track animals.

7. It can most reasonably be inferred that the author of Passage B uses the phrase "win the battle" (line 116) to refer to the hope that wildlife reserves will eventually be:

    A. ignored by both poachers and conservation officials alike.

    B. emptied of wild animals after being overrun by poachers.

    C. completely protected with the help of AI.

    D. managed in a way that balances the needs of all groups.

8. Passage A and Passage B are similar in that they both support the use of AI to:

   F. limit the negative effect poachers are having on certain wildlife populations.

   G. preserve the natural habitats of species that are experiencing population decline.

   H. eliminate the need for human intervention in the protection of wildlife.

   J. protect wildlife species from the threats causing population decline.

9. Compared to the author of Passage A, the author of Passage B provides more information about:

   A. using AI to track species in their native habitats.

   B. using AI-enhanced technology against poachers.

   C. using machine learning to aid in conservation education.

   D. using AI to calculate large quantities of data.

10. It can be reasonably inferred that after learning about AI capabilities such as the Footprint Identification Technique, the conservationists described in Passage B would likely:

   F. utilize these capabilities to aid in catching poachers.

   G. dismiss these capabilities as unnecessary.

   H. praise these capabilities as revolutionary.

   J. question the ethical nature of these capabilities.

You need to know this:

Paired passages always address the same topic but will likely have different purposes and may reflect different opinions. Common relationships between the passages include:

- (Passage A) An excerpt from a piece of literature; and (Passage B) a related essay by the same author
- (Passage A) A history of an issue and/or a person, and (Passage B) a commentary on or evaluation of the same issue or person
- (Passage A) A report on an event or conflict, and (Passage B) a report on a different-but-related event or conflict
- (Passage A) Commentary on an issue as reflected through one context, and (Passage B) commentary on the same issue reflected through a different context

The authors of paired passages may disagree with each other but do not have to.

When paired passages refer to the same detail, each author may have a different reason for including the detail and a different point of view toward it.

The question set accompanying paired passages addresses the passages in order: roughly, the first third of the questions are about Passage A, the next third are about Passage B, and the final third are about the relationships between the two passages.

The questions that address single passages are just like those from standard science and social science passages.

Some questions that address the relationships between the passages are variations on standard ACT Reading question types.

You need to do this:

Unpack the blurb to discover all that you can about each passage and author; anticipate the possible relationships between the passages.

Manage your active reading and the question set strategically:

- Actively read Passage A as you would a standard passage—note key words, jot down the purpose of each paragraph, and summarize the big picture.
- Answer the questions associated exclusively with Passage A (roughly, the first third of the question set).
- Actively read Passage B as you would a standard passage—note key words, jot down the purpose of each paragraph, and summarize the big picture.
- Answer the questions associated exclusively with Passage B (roughly, the next third in the question set).
- Answer the questions that ask about both passages in relationship to each other (the final third in the question set).

Research, predict, and answer questions exclusively addressing one of the passages as you would any standard ACT Reading question.

- To predict and answer Global questions comparing or contrasting both passages, consider your big picture summaries.
- To research, predict, and answer Inference questions comparing or contrasting both passages:
  - Locate the piece of text at issue in the question stem.
  - Consider the other author's likely reaction to or opinion of that piece of text. Locate the piece of text that supplies the other author's likely response.

Explanations

Passage Map Notes:

Passage A:

¶1: AI helpful for conservation

¶2: cheetah conservation situation

¶3: FIT: AI used to track cheetah footprints

¶4: FIT helpful for other species also

Passage B:

¶5: using AI to counter poachers

¶6: PAWS: AI helps suggest varied patrol routes

¶7: AI considers terrain, plans patrols for max effectiveness

¶8: conservationists hopeful

BIG PICTURE SUMMARY

Passage A:

Main idea: AI technology helps environmentalists preserve endangered animal species by gathering data about their movements.

Author's purpose: To describe how AI technology aids in tracking endangered animals

Passage B:

Main idea: AI technology makes anti-poaching wildlife patrols more effective by generating unpredictable patrol routes using game theory and by optimizing patrol routes for the given terrain.

Author's purpose: To describe how AI technology can assist environmentalists in countering poachers

---

1. B

Difficulty: Medium

Category: Detail

Getting to the Answer: The phrase "according to Passage A" shows that this is a Detail question, so it is important to check the passage for support. The end of the first paragraph tells us that AI can process large quantities of data, but, more importantly, it may reveal patterns that human analysis may miss. This matches (B) nicely.

Choices A and C reference information from Passage B. Choice D is extreme; beware of words like "best" or "worst." The passage talks about the benefits of AI but never states that it is the best way to protect endangered species.

2. J

Difficulty: Medium

Category: Function

Getting to the Answer: The wording "the author . . . in order to" tells us that this is a Function question. Paragraph 2 begins by stating that the cheetah population has faced severe threats. It tells us that from 1900–2015, the cheetah population saw a 93% decline in population and a 76% reduction in habitat. These statistics, then, serve to demonstrate the severity of the threat to the cheetah population. Choice (J) is correct.

Choice F is the opposite of what the statistics show; the cheetah population is in decline, not recovery. Choice G is extreme, as the passage never states that the cheetah will become extinct. Choice H refers to information from Passage B.

3.   B

Difficulty: Medium

Category: Inference

Getting to the Answer: "It can most reasonably be inferred" is a phrase that indicates an Inference question. The correct answer will require you to link together facts in the passage to form a conclusion. The passage tells you that the cheetah population is in decline due to several factors, but, at the same time that the 93% population decline occurred, there was a 76% loss of cheetah habitat—a significant statistic. You can conclude, then, that the decline is largely due to the loss of land, which matches (B).

Choice A refers to information in Passage B. Choice C does as well, and it is a misused detail; the Footprint Identification Technique was used to help the cheetah population, not hurt it. Choice D is out of scope; drought and famine were not discussed in this passage.

4.   F

Difficulty: Medium

Category: Inference

Getting to the Answer: Inference questions often contain the phrase "most strongly suggests." Paragraph 3 explains the Footprint Identification Technique, and paragraph 4 begins by referencing "the same technology," which can be used to track a variety of species. You can conclude that this technology can be used to help other species, choice (F).

Choice G is extreme; beware of words like "all." Choices H and J refer to information from Passage B.

5.   A

Difficulty: Medium

Category: Vocab-in-Context

Getting to the Answer: This question, like all Vocab-in-Context questions, asks you to identify what a word "most nearly means." Reread the sentence for context and predict a new word by pretending that "counter" is a blank in the sentence. A good prediction here would be something similar to "go against" the attacks by poachers. Choice (A) matches.

Choice B is the opposite of what the passage suggests. Choice C is incorrect because conservation officials do not want to ignore the attacks of poachers. Choice D refers to the action of counting, which also does not describe conservationists' intentions towards poachers.

6.   H

Difficulty: Medium

Category: Detail

Getting to the Answer: This question begins with, "According to Passage B," which indicates that it is a Detail question. Your strategy here should be to go back to the passage where PAWS is mentioned to get the correct answer. Paragraph 2 states that the system blends machine learning with human knowledge that patrollers can use to track poachers. This matches (H).

Choices F and J are misused details; they refer to cheetah-tracking methods discussed in Passage A. Choice G is extreme, as the passage states that the algorithm provides patrollers with options, not just the best route.

7. C

Difficulty: Medium

Category: Inference

Getting to the Answer: Inference questions require you to use facts in the passage to determine something that is not stated directly. Here you are tasked with figuring out what the unstated hope is. Refer to the final paragraph of Passage B to help you predict that the hope is that AI will help conservationists win the fight against poachers. This matches (C).

Answer choice A is the opposite of what you are looking for, as it contradicts the information in the passage. B also contradicts what the passage states; this passage is about preservation, not poachers overrunning natural habitats. D might be tempting, but it distorts the facts; conservationists are not interested in protecting the needs of poachers.

8. J

Difficulty: Medium

Category: Global

Getting to the Answer: This question is Global in nature because it asks about a similarity between the two passages. Both passages deal with AI being used in wildlife conservation efforts. This matches (J).

Choice F refers to Passage B only. Choice G refers to Passage A. Answer choice H is out of scope; this passage does not discuss AI replacing humans.

9. B

Difficulty: Medium

Category: Global

Getting to the Answer: Read this question carefully. It asks what the author "provides more information about," but it is difficult to determine the scope of the question, so it might be either Global or Detail. However, since an open-ended question like this is difficult to predict an answer for whether it is a Global or a Detail question, your approach will be the same: work through the choices one by one to find the correct answer. Note that the question is focused on Passage B, so you can immediately eliminate any choice not mentioned in Passage B. Choice A refers to the Footprint Identification Technique mentioned in Passage A; eliminate it. Choice (B) is correct; Passage A does not discuss poachers, whereas techniques to address poaching are the main idea of Passage B.

You can move on after finding the correct answer, but if you want to, check the others: neither passage discusses education, so C is incorrect. Choice D refers to information mentioned in Passage A, not Passage B.

10. F

Difficulty: High

Category: Inference

Getting to the Answer: This question uses the phrase "it can be reasonably inferred" to ask us what one group might do with new information. The facts presented in each passage will help. The conservationists described by the author of Passage B are focused on stopping poachers. The Footprint Identification Technique is currently used to track cheetahs, but it can be used to track other species. It is reasonable to conclude that the conservationists described in Passage B would use this technique to help track poachers, so (F) is correct.

Choice G is the opposite of the correct answer; both authors deem it necessary to help wildlife. Choice H is extreme; while the author of Passage B would likely see the positive side of using the Footprint Identification Technique, the words *praise* and *revolutionary* do not match the tone of the passage. Choice J is out of scope, as ethics are not mentioned.

Try on Your Own

Directions: Take as much time as you need on these questions. Work carefully and methodically. There will be an opportunity for timed practice at the end of the chapter.

SOCIAL STUDIES: Passage A was adapted from a speech given by a prominent city planner. Passage B was adapted from a speech given by a community organizer promoting the inclusion of a new community center in a Chicago suburb.

Passage A

The North American suburb is an architectural and civic phenomenon that arose in response to the need to "get away" from the city and all the noise, pollution, and stress that went along with it.
5   Suburban communities, however, were not sufficient by themselves to support a full life. The people who lived in them needed to work, shop, and socialize, and most of the active part of their lives remained fixed in urban centers. Therefore, suburbs were
10   clustered around their parent cities, with all the suburban inhabitants commuting daily to the city center for work and play.

All of this seems perfectly logical and inevitable. The suburb should be the perfect
15   halfway point between city and country—away from the noise, congestion, and pollution, but not so far away that there's no access to culture, to income, to all the exciting benefits of urban life. In reality, though, few suburbs have actually
20   approached this ideal. Some critics have charged that, as suburbs have grown to the size of sprawling towns themselves, they are revealed as communities somehow devoid of community necessities. They lack local stores, community
25   centers, and places for kids to hang out; instead, they offer parking lots, chain stores, and strip malls.

The structure of the modern suburb, while offering a respite from city pollution, has created
30   health and environmental risks of its own. Because of the separation of living and commercial spaces imposed by many suburban zoning laws, nearly every activity, aside from visiting adjacent houses or the occasional neighborhood park, requires
35   an automobile trip. All of this driving creates pollution. Of course, America has had a long love affair with the car, and any city planner who thinks

he can single-handedly change that is in for a rude surprise. Surely, though, we must begin to balance
40   the appeal and freedom of the car with ecological and civic responsibility.

This does not mean, however, that we need to abandon suburbs altogether, as some have suggested. Instead, we need to more knowingly
45   pursue that ideal of the best of city and country. Suburbs could be fascinating and beautiful places; we need only exercise our power to determine the nature of the places in which we live.

Passage B

"America doesn't need any more!" is a common
50   refrain for those who see suburbs merely as a means to line construction companies' pockets without contributing much to the value and diversity of American culture. I, however, see the problem of suburbs as one of degree rather than
55   kind. I haven't given up yet on the possibility of infusing the suburbs with public spaces that we can be proud of, that are rewarding to the human spirit. What can be done to bring diversity and character into these respites from the hustle and
60   bustle of the city?

A crucial starting point is reshaping the narrative of what the suburbs are intended to be a respite from. As young people form family units and those families grow, naturally they desire more
65   space. In most major cities the desire for more space comes at a significant premium, one which all too often middle-income families are unable to afford. The suburbs have the potential to serve as a happy medium: an affordable neighborhood with space for
70   families to grow, all of the more robust amenities of a major city in close proximity, and a pace of life less frenetic than traditionally expected in the city.

For these public spaces to truly be representative, more is needed. We need community engagement
75   that will help us explore our identity, discover what we value, and determine what makes us

different from the surrounding areas. In turn, this will allow us to celebrate the character of our unique community in our public spaces. I, for
80 one, do believe that the developers that we work with are invested in our community beyond just their financial bottom line. The proposed projects each reflect thoughtful attempts to appeal to our entire community; now, we have an opportunity to
85 determine which one resonates the most with us.

   The suburbs still have the potential to deliver on the core principles that led to their development. Space to spread out need not mean distancing ourselves from our neighbors. The cities do not
90 hold a monopoly on character; we are the architects of the character of our community, and that is what America needs more of: community architects, ready to go to work.

1. In Passage A, the discussion in the final paragraph implies that the author:

   A. blames poor city planning for the existence of the suburb.

   B. thinks today's suburbs are actually fascinating and beautiful.

   C. believes most people take too little interest in their surroundings

   D. is optimistic about the possibilities of the American suburb.

2. Passage A most strongly suggests that "many suburban zoning laws" (line 32):

   F. ban parks from suburban neighborhoods.

   G. make it difficult to sustain successful business.

   H. contribute to adverse environmental effects.

   J. address environmental concerns at the cost of cultural diversity.

3. According to the third paragraph of Passage A, city planners need to consider:

   A. accepting suburban residents' reluctance to give up driving.

   B. minimizing every boundary between residential and retail space.

   C. placing more local stores and kids' hangouts across the street from houses.

   D. moving the local parks to safer and more accessible neighborhoods.

4. The main purpose of Passage A is to:

   F. bemoan the detrimental effect suburbs have had on individual quality of life.

   G. discourage the suburb dweller's dependence on the automobile.

   H. encourage a different, more effective vision of the place of suburbs in communities.

   J. call for a return to the type of suburb that prevailed before World War II.

5. As it is used in line 66 in Passage B, the word *premium* most nearly refers to a living space that is:

    A. a prize that might be won.

    B. part of an insurance policy.

    C. a high price.

    D. higher quality.

6. In Passage B, lines 68–72 function as examples of reasons why:

    F. suburbs have the potential to be comparable to or even potentially preferable to city living.

    G. diversity might naturally come to suburban living spaces.

    H. suburban living is inherently superior to urban living in all situations.

    J. families usually choose to move from urban areas to suburban areas as they have children.

7. Based on the first paragraph of Passage B, it can reasonably be inferred that the author of the passage believes:

    A. more needs to be done to make urban living spaces affordable to families as they grow.

    B. construction companies charge too much for projects that do not serve communities.

    C. suburban communities are currently harmful to the spirits of people living there.

    D. many who decry suburbs are basing their beliefs on things that are possible to change.

8. The authors of both Passage A and Passage B would most likely agree with which of the following statements?

    F. Urban spaces should be seen as less desirable places to live for the majority of the population.

    G. While suburban spaces have not always lived up to their potential, there are ways to continue to improve them.

    H. Research would probably show that living in an urban area is more affordable for most families.

    J. Nobody who currently lives in a suburban area feels the sense of community that urban areas provide.

9. Compared to the author of Passage B, the author of Passage A discusses in more detail:

    A. specific criticisms of suburban spaces.

    B. reasons why suburban living is more affordable.

    C. specific ways to improve suburban living.

    D. the need for more diversity in suburban spaces.

10. How would the author of Passage A likely respond to Passage B's assertion that "developers that we work with are invested in our community beyond just their financial bottom line"?

    F. The author of Passage A is likely to agree with it because suburban areas are designed to be affordable.

    G. The author of Passage A is likely to agree with it because developers are now supporting local stores and community centers.

    H. The author of Passage A is likely to disagree with it because suburbs currently seem to be designed without community in mind.

    J. The author of Passage A is likely to disagree with it because suburban areas are rarely profitable for anyone.

How Much Have You Learned?

Directions: For test-like practice, give yourself 9 minutes to complete this question set. Be sure to study the explanations, even for questions you got correct. They can be found at the end of this chapter.

LITERARY NARRATIVE: Passage A is adapted from the essay "The Language Barrier or Silence" by Joseph Fellows. Passage B is adapted from the essay "The First and Last Time" by Randy Benson.

Passage A by Joseph Fellows

I hadn't slept the night before I left, nor could I even doze on the plane. Piqued and red-eyed is not how I had envisioned my first day abroad. I had also hoped to have a little bit of the German language
5   under my belt before mingling with locals.

Unfortunately, the absurdly unpredictable nature of the *der/die/das* articles frustrated me so much that I never really got past the general salutations and simple, commonly used phrases. I was therefore
10 stubbornly determined to get as much mileage out of *danke* and *bitte* as I could. Every German person in Tegel Airport must have thought me incredibly gracious but dimwitted. I tried saying *freut mich, Sie kennenzulernen* (nice to meet you) to the cab
15 driver that I hailed, and after three tries, each receiving a quizzical stare in return, I gave up and simply told him my destination in English. I then squeezed myself into the tiny Peugeot; evidently, SUVs are not fashionable in Europe.

20 The bed-and-breakfast I had booked was nice—very quaint, but obviously a tourist spot. The owner was a scowling old woman who said little and waddled around, pointing and grunting, rightfully assuming I was linguistically stunted.
25 Thoroughly intimidated by the locals and their language, I decided to take a walk through historic Berlin in hopes of bonding with the nature and architecture, rather than the people. I was immediately glad that I did. Despite being
30 exhausted and surly, I found myself awestruck and humbled by the ubiquitous artistry of the city.

Despite knowing little about World War II and having been born forty years after, I was profoundly affected by my first view of the Kaiser Wilhelm
35 Gedächtniskirche (Memorial Church), with its crushed steeple and bomb-ravaged stone walls, existing in jarring juxtaposition to the surrounding modern architecture.

Further east near the Berlin Zoo, I found
40 a lovely park along the murky water of the Landwehrkanal, and eventually, I came to a massive traffic circle. In the midst of this automotive maelstrom of Berlin rush hour stood the magnificent Siegessäule (Victory Column).
45 The immaculate craftsmanship against the verdant horizon and cerulean sky—there are no words in any language to describe it. So I sat on a stone bench, smiled contentedly, and said nothing.

Passage B by Randy Benson

My room was gray and windowless, with a
50 cement floor painted blood-red. The mattress had no sheets, but I was too disoriented to care. Bad way to start the semester. Why had I decided to follow Greg here anyway?

After we stored our bags in a locker at Termini,
55 Greg marched me to a trattorìa where we feasted on pasta, fish, veal, salad, cheese, and fruit. After the meal, Greg took me on a bistro-and-basilica tour. "C'mon, Paisan'. I'm gonna show you how to do Rome right."

60 After two churches and two restaurants, I said to Greg, "I understand loving the food here. But what's your thing with churches?"

Greg looked at me like I had a trinity of heads. "I know you're not really that clueless, Paisan'. Quit
65 being such a middle-class American sophomore and ask me a real question, like 'Gee, Greg, that bone church we just went through makes me wonder whatever would possess a herd of Capuchin monks to make artistic masterpieces out of their own
70 skeletal remains.'"

Actually, the thought of the bone church made the hunk of Fontinella cheese I'd just wolfed down

twist in my stomach. "No. I don't wanna talk about the bones. I wanna know why you're dragging me
75 through churches. Is it just a scenic way to pace ourselves between bistros?"

"You mean to tell me, Paisan', that you really got nothing out of St. Peter's?"

I wasn't going to admit it to Greg, but St. Peter's
80 really was kind of awesome. Made my jaw drop, actually.

"Eh. It's a big church. Who cares?"

"You should, Paisan'. This is Rome, man. The Republic. The Empire. The Church. In a place
85 like this, I shouldn't have to agitate you into an outburst of culture. Up 'til now, everything about life has numbed you. This place is gonna wake up your soul." At this, he pushed another hunk of Fontinella at me, and I had no confidence that it
90 would sit any better than the last after one more church full of bones.

After seven more churches and three more bistros, we finally ground to a halt at the Cafe Montespiné. The locals gawked at the Americani
95 and engaged Greg in conversations that mixed French, Greek, Italian, and Martian. We dragged ourselves out of Montespiné at 4:30 in the morning, with half of our newfound friends still acting like the night was just starting.

100 Which is why I woke up this morning, bleary-eyed, in the previous night's clothes, my head heavy as a crushed Italian moon-rock breakfast roll. Maybe not the best way to start the semester. But I have to admit—it was quite a start.

1. The narrator includes the interaction with the cab driver (lines 13–17) primarily in order to:

   A. explain how the narrator got from the airport to the bed-and-breakfast.

   B. provide an example of the narrator's aggravation with the German language.

   C. show the affinity that the narrator has for the German language.

   D. explain how to greet someone unfamiliar in German.

2. In the third paragraph of Passage A (lines 20–31), the narrator's decision to go for a walk is prompted by:

   F. his insecurity that had developed as a result of his frustration with the German language.

   G. his anger toward the owner of the bed-and-breakfast.

   H. his eagerness to sightsee and experience the culture of the city.

   J. his stubborn determination to succeed at speaking the German language.

3. The narrator states that "there are no words" (line 46) to describe the view at the Siegessäule because the narrator:

   A. can't speak German well enough to translate the description thoroughly.

   B. is too frustrated with the German language to take the time to depict the scene's beauty.

   C. feels that any explanation of the beauty of the scene could not do it justice.

   D. chose to sit quietly on the stone bench rather than say anything.

4. In Passage B, the narrator's descriptions of Greg suggest that the narrator sees Greg as:

    F. too daring and bold to be a traveling companion in the future.

    G. compelling enough to follow and see what happens next.

    H. too numb to experience any pleasure in Rome.

    J. a fanatic driven by passion for churches.

5. In Passage B, the narrator uses line 79 ("I wasn't going to admit it to Greg") in order to:

    A. illustrate the narrator's unwillingness to follow Greg's scheme.

    B. argue that admiration of Roman churches is a more private matter.

    C. call attention to the jaw-dropping nature of St. Peter's.

    D. suggest the favorable influence that Greg's tour is having on the narrator.

6. In the last paragraph of Passage B (lines 100–104), the narrator summarizes his:

    F. transition from sleep to regret for staying out the previous night.

    G. transition from sleep to a celebratory embrace of new life circumstances.

    H. recognition of the previous night as a unique way to begin the stay in Rome.

    J. return to a reality made much happier by the absence of Greg.

7. Compared to Passage B's narrator, Passage A's narrator spends more time discussing:

    A. the history of the city he is visiting.

    B. his interactions with the local people.

    C. the various religious landmarks he encounters.

    D. his inability to speak the foreign language fluently.

8. Which of the following statements best describes the difference in the tone of the two passages?

    F. Passage A is impersonal and historical, whereas Passage B is thoughtfully nostalgic.

    G. Passage A is animated and comical, whereas Passage B is serious and introspective.

    H. Both passages begin with a sense of trepidation but end with an air of equability and calm.

    J. Both passages begin humorously and end on a note of introspection.

9. Both Passage A and Passage B highlight the narrators':

    A. individual reactions to novel surroundings and non-native languages.

    B. emotional shortcomings in response to stressful stimuli.

    C. determination to impress others with recently honed language skills.

    D. decisions to return home after unsuccessful attempts to acclimate.

10. Which of the following best describes the narrators' reactions to the architecture in the cities they visited?

    F. Passage A's narrator appreciates the architecture, whereas Passage B's narrator is indifferent.

    G. Passage A's narrator does not notice the architecture, whereas Passage B's narrator is wholly captivated by it.

    H. Passage A's narrator and Passage B's narrator both begin by appreciating the architecture and then grow tired of it.

    J. Passage A's narrator finds peace by looking at the architecture, whereas Passage B's narrator has a more complicated response to it.

Reflect

Directions: Take a few minutes to recall what you've learned and what you've been practicing in this chapter. Consider the following questions, jot down your best answer for each one, and then compare your reflections to the expert responses on the following page. Use your level of confidence to determine what to do next.

1. What are ACT Reading paired passages? How do expert test takers adjust their active reading to tackle paired passages most effectively?

   _____

   _____

   _____

2. How are the question sets that accompany paired passages different from those accompanying standard independent passages?

   _____

   _____

   _____

3. How confident do you feel with paired passages? What can you do in practice to improve your performance and gain even more confidence with this type of passage?

   _____

   _____

   _____

Responses

1. What are ACT Reading paired passages? How do expert test takers adjust their active reading to tackle paired passages most effectively?

On each ACT test, one Reading stimulus is a pair of shorter passages instead of a single, long passage. Expert test takers actively read each passage and answer the questions exclusively associated with each. Then, experts compare and contrast the passages' big pictures and details and answer questions associated with both.

2. How are the question sets that accompany paired passages different from those accompanying standard single passages?

Roughly, the first third of the question set exclusively addresses Passage A; the next third exclusively addresses Passage B; and the final third addresses comparisons and contrasts between the passages. The compare/contrast-both-passage question stems are uniquely worded to reward students who accurately summarize the big picture of each passage and who can determine how one author would likely respond to something argued or proposed by the other author.

3. How confident do you feel with paired passages? What can you do in practice to improve your performance and gain even more confidence with this type of passage?

There is no one-size-fits-all answer for this question. Give yourself honest self-assessment. If you feel that paired passages are a strength, congratulations! Continue to practice them so that you'll be able to rack up the points associated with these passages on test day. If you feel less confident about the paired passage format, review the strategies in this chapter and try to consistently apply the expert approaches outlined here whenever you practice passages in this format.

Next Steps

If you answered most questions correctly in the "How Much Have You Learned" section, and if your responses to the Reflect questions were similar to those of an expert, then consider paired passages an area of strength and move on to the next chapter. Come back to this topic periodically to prevent yourself from getting rusty.

If you don't yet feel confident, review the material in "How to Read ACT Paired Passages," then try the questions you missed again. As always, be sure to review the explanations closely. Then go online (**kaptest.com/login**) to use your Qbank for more practice. If you haven't already registered your book, do so at *kaptest.com/moreonline*.

GO ONLINE

kaptest.com/login

Answers and Explanations

How To Read ACT Paired Passages

Passage Map Notes:

Passage A:

¶1: suburb origins

¶2: ideal vs. actual

¶3: necessity of cars leads to pollution

¶4: need to improve suburbs

Passage B:

¶5: we can & should improve suburbs

¶6: what suburbs ought to be

¶7: community engagement → uniqueness → improvement

¶8: author sees potential, calls on audience

BIG PICTURE SUMMARY

Passage A:

Main idea: Suburbs often lack the necessities of everyday life and their reliance upon cars creates pollution.

Author's purpose: To describe the ways in which suburbs are less than perfect and suggest that they could be improved

Passage B:

Main idea: Suburbs can be made to have character with thoughtful planning.

Author's purpose: To argue that suburbs have the potential to allow residents more than they would have in cities without sacrificing community identity

---

1. D

Difficulty: Low

Category: Inference

Getting to the Answer: The clue word *implies* shows that this is an Inference question. Do not rely on your memory; go back to the last paragraph of Passage A and research what was said. The author claims that we do not "need to abandon suburbs altogether" and that "suburbs could be fascinating and beautiful places." Choice (D) matches these sentiments and is thus correct.

Choice A is incorrect because the author never casts *blame*. Choice B may be tempting, but it goes beyond what is actually stated in the text. The author says that suburbs have the potential to be beautiful, not that they already are. Finally, choice C is incorrect because the passage never discusses people taking interest in their surroundings.

2. H

Difficulty: High

Category: Inference

Getting to the Answer: The word *suggests* identifies this as an Inference question. Read a little bit before and a little bit after the cited line. This research will help shape your prediction. Here, the reference to "suburban zoning laws" is used to show the separation between living and commercial spaces in the suburbs, causing almost everything to require an automobile trip. Finally, the author says that "all of this driving comes at the cost of pollution." This matches answer choice (H).

Choice F contradicts the passage; in lines 32–35, the author describes how one of the few places that a suburbanite can actually walk to is a neighborhood park. If suburban zoning laws banned parks from neighborhoods, even this would be impossible. Choices G and J are out of scope, since *successful businesses* and *cultural diversity* are not mentioned anywhere in this passage.

3.   A

Difficulty: Low

Category: Detail

Getting to the Answer: The phrase *According to* is a clue that this is a Detail question. It directs you to the third paragraph, so go back and do some research. The author says that Americans love their cars and that "any city planner who thinks he can single-handedly change that is in for a rude surprise." Predict that the correct answer must therefore have something to do with how people love driving. Choice (A) is correct.

Choice B is extreme; the author does not advocate minimizing *every* boundary. Choice C is a misused detail; while the author suggests that more local stores and places for young people are needed, they are not the focus of this paragraph. Finally, D is incorrect because there is no mention of "safer and more accessible neighborhoods" in this paragraph.

4.   H

Difficulty: Medium

Category: Global

Getting to the Answer: You can tell this is a Global question because it asks for "The main purpose" of the passage. When answering Global questions, look back at your notes for each paragraph, think of the big picture, and do not be distracted by details. The passage begins by explaining how suburbs naturally developed out of cities and then moves into a discussion of some of the negative aspects of suburban living. However, the passage ends on a note of optimism, with the author claiming that "we need to more knowingly pursue that ideal of the best of city and country." Predict that the correct answer should say something about how the suburbs are by and large a sensible idea but could be better still. Choice (H) is correct.

Choice F is too extreme; since the author concludes optimistically, he is not *bemoaning* the effects of suburbs throughout the whole passage. Choice G is too narrow to be the answer to a Global question; automobiles are mentioned in the fourth paragraph only. Finally, choice J is out of scope; the passage never discusses suburbs before World War II.

5.   C

Difficulty: Low

Category: Vocab-in-Context

Getting to the Answer: "As it is used" should serve as a clue that this is a Vocab-in-Context question. Refer back to the second paragraph of Passage B, where a larger living space in the city is described as something many families will be "unable to afford." Predict that *premium* in this case means "expensive." This matches (C).

The other answer choices are all acceptable meanings for the word *premium*, but none of them match the way that the word is used within the context of the passage.

6.   F

Difficulty: High

Category: Function

Getting to the Answer: The keyword *function* tells you that this is, yes, a Function question! Refer back to the lines in question, which are immediately preceded by "The suburbs have the potential to serve as a happy medium." Predict that the correct answer will reflect this. This matches (F), which is the correct answer.

While the author does encourage increased diversity in suburban areas, he is not specifically addressing this need in the lines referenced, eliminating G. Choice H is too extreme; while the author does encourage suburban living, he implies it could be roughly equal to living in an urban environment, not automatically better. Choice J is too extreme. The author is giving reasons why suburbs might be appealing to growing families, but does not say anything about whether or not families *usually* choose to move to suburbs as a result.

7.   D

Difficulty: Medium

Category: Inference

Getting to the Answer: The clue words "can reasonably be inferred" indicate this is an Inference question. The question asks for something the author might believe, so it is difficult to make a specific prediction. Instead, look at each answer choice, eliminating them one by one.

For A, while the author does discuss the higher cost of living in urban areas, that is not part of this paragraph; eliminate it. Choice B is a distortion; the passage suggests that other people believe this, not that the author does. Choice C is extreme; while the author does say that suburbs could be more rewarding, the paragraph does not imply that they are actively harmful. Finally, (D) is supported by the passage—the author discusses how some believe that suburban areas are just a way for construction companies to make money, but the author believes they do not have to be that way. (D) is correct.

8.   G

Difficulty: Medium

Category: Inference

Getting to the Answer: The key words "most likely agree" signal that this is an Inference question. It asks for a statement with which both authors would most likely agree, so review your notes on both passages. This is too broad a question to make a prediction, so eliminate answer choices one by one until you find one that fits.

Choice F is too broad: both authors discuss some of the advantages that come from urban living. Choice (G) would be supported by both authors: they both discuss some of the problems in suburbs, but believe these can be fixed with better planning and effort. You can stop at this point, but if you did look at H or J: H is not supported by the author of Passage B, who specifically discusses the higher cost of living in urban areas for families needing more space. Choice J is too extreme to be supported by the author of Passage A, who does criticize the lack of community in suburban areas, but never says that absolutely nobody in a suburban area feels a sense of community.

9.   A

Difficulty: Low

Category: Detail

Getting to the Answer: As the word *detail* is mentioned, this is, of course, a Detail question. Review your notes on both passages. What does Passage A focus on that Passage B does not? Passage A focuses more on what people specifically complain about regarding suburbs, so predict that the correct answer will reflect this. And it does—choice (A) matches the prediction, and is correct.

Affordability, as in B, and a need for diversity, as in D, are actually things discussed in Passage B. Neither passage discusses specific ways to improve suburbs, though both say they believe it is possible, which means you can eliminate C.

10.   H

Difficulty: High

Category: Inference

Getting to the Answer: Asking how the author would "likely respond" signals that this is an Inference question. Predict that while the two authors agree that suburban areas are a good idea theoretically, the author of Passage A would be unlikely to agree that current developers are invested in the community, as the author of Passage B suggests here, because all the evidence in suburbs as they currently exist points to the contrary. This matches (H).

The author of Passage A does not discuss affordability at all, so you have no frame of reference as to whether he would agree that current developers are designing affordable locations or not, which eliminates F. Though Passage A does cite lack of local stores and community centers as a criticism some have made of suburbs, there is nothing to support the idea that developers are focusing more on building them now, which eliminates G. Similarly, the author of Passage A does not discuss the profitability of suburbs, which eliminates J.

How Much Have You Learned?

Passage Map Notes

Passage A:

¶1: Horrible flight; trouble speaking German

¶2: More language trouble

¶3: Intimidated but goes for walk

¶4: Beautiful Berlin has impressive architecture

¶5: Content with trip in silence

Passage B:

¶6: Bare room, disoriented

¶7: Greg (G) takes lead, Paisan' = Narrator (N)

¶8: Why churches?

¶9: Bone churches

¶10: N doesn't understand

¶11–13: N impressed by St. Peter's / acts unimpressed

¶14: G enthusiastic about Rome

¶15: Late night with locals

¶16: N has rough morning but interesting experience

BIG PICTURE SUMMARY

Passage A:

Main idea: The narrator is feeling frustrated with the language of a foreign country, but finds pleasure in the aesthetics of his new surroundings.

Author's purpose: To relate a story about feeling out of place in a foreign environment

Passage B:

Main idea: Despite initial reservations, the narrator has an intense first night studying abroad after following Greg.

Author's purpose: To recount his first night in a new foreign city while studying abroad

1. B

Difficulty: High

Category: Function

Getting to the Answer: The wording "The narrator includes . . . in order to" identifies this as a Function question. Every part of a passage contributes to the purpose of the larger section. According to the sample passage map for Passage A, the interaction between the narrator and the cab driver shows the narrator having language troubles, which is a theme throughout the passage. Choice (B) is correct.

Although A and D describe features of paragraph 1, they do not reflect the reason the narrator included the interaction. It's clear that the narrator does NOT have an affinity, or natural talent, for the German language, so C is incorrect.

2. F

Difficulty: Medium

Category: Detail

Getting to the Answer: This question stem provides few clues as to question type; it might be either Detail or Inference, depending on whether the passage states directly what prompted the narrator's walk. However, your first step to answering it will be the same regardless: find the appropriate section of the passage and research the answer. In the third paragraph, the narrator mentions being "Thoroughly intimidated by the locals and their language" when describing his decision to go for a walk. Choice (F) is correct.

Although the narrator pointed out that the owner was *scowling*, there is no evidence that he is actually angry with her, so G is incorrect. The narrator did express his desire to "bond with nature and architecture," but "the culture of a city" includes the people in it as well, so H is incorrect. Choice J might be tempting because of the narrator's self-professed stubborn determination in line 10, but that detail is not connected to the narrator's reason for taking a walk.

3.   C

Difficulty: Medium

Category: Inference

Getting to the Answer: Although this question does not contain typical clue words, you can conclude that it is an Inference question because it asks about something the narrator has already said that will not be stated outright. Like other Inference questions, however, it will be supported by specific details that are in the passage. Immediately after the cited line, the narrator says he smiled contentedly, so he must mean "there are no words" in a positive way. Only (C) matches this positive tone, and it is therefore correct.

Choice A is a misused detail; even though the narrator couldn't describe the scene well in German, he would choose not to even in English. The tone of the final paragraph is one of contentment, which suggests that the narrator is no longer frustrated with his inability to speak German, so B is incorrect. Choice D merely repeats that the narrator sat quietly, without explaining why.

4.   G

Difficulty: Medium

Category: Inference

Getting to the Answer: The clue word *suggest* marks this as an Inference question. For an Inference question that asks about a relationship, use the information provided about that relationship to form a prediction. The narrator expresses mixed feelings about going along with Greg. In the first paragraph, the narrator conveys some ambivalence when he wonders, "Why had I decided to follow Greg here anyway?" (lines 52–53). However, the narrator follows Greg all day and half the night, and he admits to enjoying St. Peter's. Choice (G) is correct. The narrator is compelled by Greg's behavior and tour-guide tendencies, and he thereby remains curious enough to stay with Greg through the entire night's tour.

When a character has mixed feelings, watch out for answer choices that are too extreme, such as F. Choice H is the opposite of how the narrator sees Greg; Greg seems to enjoy Rome immensely. It more closely resembles how Greg describes the narrator. Choice J is not supported by the passage; although Greg does want to tour historical churches, nothing about his stated reasons for doing so suggests fanaticism.

5.   D

Difficulty: Medium

Category: Function

Getting to the Answer: The phrasing "the narrator uses . . . in order to" shows that this is a Function question. It asks about the purpose of a particular part of Passage B in relation to the whole. In short, why does the narrator reveal that he is unwilling to admit to Greg an admiration of St. Peter's? The function of a part of a literary narrative passage often has to do with the characters' feelings, values, and relationships. The fact that the narrator isn't going to admit his enjoyment to Greg shows that the narrator is enjoying himself in spite of his protests, so (D) is correct.

When answering Function questions, watch out for answer choices that describe the passage without revealing the cited text's function within the passage. Because the narrator is willing to follow Greg all day, A is incorrect. While the narrator's attitude may call attention to St. Peter's, the point of the passage is not to praise St. Peter's; it is to describe two characters and their interaction. Thus, C is incorrect. Choice B is out of scope because nothing in the text indicates that the narrator sees admiration of churches as a private matter.

6.   H

Difficulty: Medium

Category: Detail

Getting to the Answer: The words *author summarizes* show this question is asking about something the passage states directly, so it is a Detail question. Use your passage map notes for the final paragraph as a prediction. The sample passage map states that the narrator had a rough morning but viewed the previous day as an interesting experience. Only (H) accurately expresses that the previous night was an interesting experience without adding an extreme emotion.

Choices F, G, and J do not align with the narrator's tone: F is too negative, whereas G and J are too positive.

7. D

Difficulty: Medium

Category: Global

Getting to the Answer: When asked to compare two passages as a whole, use the main focus of each passage to form a prediction. Passage A focuses on the narrator's frustrations with the language barrier in Berlin, whereas Passage B describes a whirlwind tour through Rome. While the narrator of Passage B mentions "conversations that mixed French, Greek, Italian, and Martian" (lines 95–96), language is not a major theme in Passage B as it is in Passage A. The correct answer is (D).

Although both narrators mention some historical facts, interactions with locals, and the names of religious landmarks they've encountered, these topics are presented as supporting details in both texts rather than central points of each passage as a whole. Choices A, B, and C are incorrect.

8. H

Difficulty: High

Category: Global

Getting to the Answer: The tone of a passage includes the narrator's attitudes toward the subject matter. Pay attention to shifts in attitude. Both narrators are anxious at the start of their respective passages, but both come to appreciate their individual experiences in a foreign country. Thus, (H) is correct.

Choice F is a distortion; Passage A has a more polished quality, but that does not mean it is impersonal or historical. Nothing about Passage B makes it more nostalgic, or sentimental, than Passage A. Choice G mixes up the passages; Passage A is more serious and introspective than Passage B, while Passage B is more animated and comical. Choice J is a distortion; while Passage B is humorous in the beginning, Passage A has a more serious tone.

9. A

Difficulty: Medium

Category: Global

Getting to the Answer: The question stem asks for what both passages prominently feature. Each passage describes the experience of visiting a foreign country from the personal perspective of the narrator, which matches (A).

Choice B is extreme; both narrators feel frustration, but the passages do not portray that emotion as a shortcoming. Passage A's narrator does discuss speaking a foreign language, but he admits that he was not fluent, and Passage B does not mention the narrator speaking Italian at all, so C is incorrect. The narrators do not mention returning home, so D is out of scope.

10. J

Difficulty: High

Category: Inference

Getting to the Answer: Since you are asked to describe feelings that are not directly stated, this is an Inference question. When asked to compare two passages in this way, use your passage maps to form a prediction. According to the map for Passage A, the narrator is impressed by Berlin's architecture and feels content. According to the map for Passage B, its narrator questions why he and his companion are visiting so many churches, and he hides his appreciation for St. Peter's. Choice (J) is correct because it describes Narrator A's contentment and Narrator B's more complicated response.

Choice F is incorrect because Narrator B is secretly in awe of St. Peter's, which shows that he is not indifferent. Choice G is incorrect because Narrator A does notice the architecture and Narrator B is not entirely captivated by it. Choice H is incorrect because Narrator A does not grow tired of the architecture.

CHAPTER 21

ACT Reading: Timing and Section Management Strategies

LEARNING OBJECTIVE

After completing this chapter, you will be able to:

- Recognize at a glance which passages in a section are likely to be easiest for you

---

Timing

You have 35 minutes to complete 4 passages with 10 questions each, so you need to complete each passage and accompanying questions in an average of 9 minutes to finish on time. (Note that passages are not all the same length or difficulty, so some will take longer than others.) After 17 minutes, you should be about halfway done with the Reading questions. When the proctor informs you that there are 5 minutes remaining, you should ideally be working on the fourth set of questions.

Note that this is a brisk pace. Reading for structure can help, as can triaging questions and skipping those that you can see at a glance will be time-consuming. Your real task is not actually to attempt all the questions in 35 minutes but to get as many points from the section as you can.

Section Management

You may want to triage entire passages on the Reading section, not just questions. Some test takers have a hard time with literature or natural science, while others struggle more with humanities or social science passages; if you have distinct preferences about subject matter, you might consider leaving a particular passage type for last. For example, the Reading Test always opens with the literature passage. If that's the passage you feel least confident about, it makes sense to skip it and do it last. (Just be careful with your bubbling.)

Remember that you probably won't spend the same amount of time on each question. Every question counts for the same number of points, so be sure to complete the questions you find easiest to answer first. Approached correctly, Vocab-in-Context and Detail questions should be quick: use the question stem and your passage map notes to quickly research the information in the passage that will help you make a strong prediction and choose the one correct answer.

Finally, moving efficiently through this section is important, but that does not mean that you should skip over any text. Reading all of the text in the passage is essential to answering questions efficiently and accurately.

When considering the structure of the entire test, keep in mind that you will have a break right before this section. If you start to feel tired, remember that you are more than halfway done with the test. If you start reading the same sentence over and over, put your pencil down, close your eyes, and take three slow, deep breaths. The more focused you can remain, the easier it will be for you to determine each correct answer.

There is a half-length Reading section in the "How Much Have You Learned?" section that comes next. Use it to practice timing: skip questions you find too time-consuming, return to them if you have time, and keep an eye on the clock. When you are finished, check your work—and reflect on how well you managed the pacing.

As mentioned in chapter 15, there is one exception to the "read the passage first" rule: when you have only five minutes remaining in the Reading Test and at least one passage left to start. In this case, skip the passage and look for the questions that could be researched quickly. Vocab-in-Context questions, for example, can usually be answered using only the full sentence containing the word or phrase, and Detail questions might provide line references to tell you exactly where to look. Finally, remember not to leave anything blank; when you have one minute left, do a final answer grid check to confirm you didn't miss anything.

How Much Have You Learned?

Directions: Use this question set to practice effective question triage. Skip those questions that you feel will take too long; come back to them if you have time. Try to get as many questions correct as you can in 18 minutes. As always, be sure to study the explanations, even for questions you got right. They can be found at the end of this chapter.

LITERARY NARRATIVE: This passage is adapted from a short story about summertime in the author's hometown.

Ivan Pavlov was a physiologist who researched learned behaviors and the ways in which repeat exposure to specific stimuli can result in behaviors that occur without intention.

At the sound of the whistle, Pavlovian, we'd all push up from the sides of the pool. (We never used the ladders or the steps in the shallow end. It was a point of pride to have the strength to
5 push up from the sides.) For the next 20 minutes, we had to be out, all the kids; let the adults have some time without us splashing and screaming and generally creating pandemonium. We all went to the same place, compelled, drawn like flies: the
10 snack bar. Jiang first, because he was the oldest, his legs were longer. He was bossy, sometimes. Aisha came next, pretending like she didn't even care anymore, even though we all knew she did, or she would have stayed by the side of the pool, on one
15 of those lounge chairs that had the long vinyl slats that always stuck to your skin. Then Faiyaz and Neerav, who only we could tell apart besides their parents. Wolf—he was Wolfgang, named for his grandfather, but he hated the name—was usually
20 last, because he was never in the same hurry the rest of us always seemed to be in. It didn't matter, because there were a thousand kids, all in clumps, pushing and shouting, as if the bored teenage girl doling out ice cream was going to suddenly decide
25 to close up shop.

We pushed and shouted, too. Pushing and shouting just seemed to be part of what you were supposed to do, and so we did it. Neerav sometimes seemed to be shouting just for the enjoyment of
30 adding his voice to the cacophonous mess. The bored teenage girl probably took a lot of aspirin. When we finally got our turn at the counter, we all got the same thing, ignoring the bags of chips and

the M&Ms and the cans of soda. Each and every
35 time, all of us in it together: ice cream. We were there to buy ice cream.

It wasn't even *good* ice cream—the stuff we had in our freezers at home was better by far. But we were all dropped off at the pool to spend our
40 summer mornings, and ice cream was our shared snack of choice. Little bits of memory come back with the scent of chlorine or hot pavement, even now: Wolf counting quarters because he never remembered to bring much money; the rest of us
45 had crumpled dollar bills we kept rolled up in our towels. The way the paper peeled off the top of the ice cream, the little stick to push it up. The ice cream was usually on the stale side, freezer-burnt. But it was the best-tasting ice cream in all the
50 world, because we could buy it ourselves. Kids don't have a whole lot of power, but we bought ice cream from the bored teenage girl at the snack bar by our own choice.

We'd go back to the lounge chairs to eat, sitting
55 there watching the kids still waiting to get theirs, or the adults who swam laps, smooth and steady. Wolf would be covered in ice cream before the end of it, his face and arms sticky and streaked orange; for some reason he could never keep it from dripping.
60 We'd be back in the water soon enough anyway, and it would all wash away again. Aisha ate hers slowly, while Faiyaz and Neerav competed to see who could finish first. Jiang sat on the edge of one of the round metal tables, one long leg swinging,
65 staring off at nothing in particular.

Long, slow summer days. It was too hot to run except for ice cream, when we were out of the water. Sometimes, we played with the other kids at the pool—Marco Polo, the normal sort of thing—but
70 more often, it was just us. We were together, and that was enough.

At some point, we must have begun to outgrow
it. Did Jiang give up ice cream at the pool first,
or Aisha? Aisha seems more likely. There came a
75 day when we were too old to care. By then we had
money, allowances we earned doing chores at home.
We saved up for less ephemeral things—books, or
clothes, or Neerav's endless supply of comic books.
But we couldn't say when, precisely, it happened,
80 though we must have been aware of it at the time.

We all still talk on the phone now, and of course
we can go out together anytime we like, but summer
days at the neighborhood pool seem to have gone
the same way as the sticky orange ice cream—just
85 not around anymore. The world changed, it seems,
between the time of our childhood summers and
now, and the disappearance of those pools, of the
snack bars and adult swim time, was part of that
change. Or maybe we just no longer notice them,
90 because there's no one to blow the whistle, nowhere
to run for ice cream?

1. The passage as a whole is characterized by the
    author's sense of:

    A. cynicism, in light of her changed perception of
        the world as an adult.

    B. nostalgia, looking back on what seem to be
        fond memories of childhood.

    C. heartlessness, considering her jaded memories
        of the past.

    D. wonder, as seen in her knowledge that ice
        cream tasted better as a child.

2. The final paragraph most strongly implies that the
    author is:

    F. an adult.

    G. a child.

    H. an elderly person.

    J. a college student.

3. The author uses the word *Pavlovian* in line 1 pri-
    marily in order to describe:

    A. the way that the whistle sounded to the kids in
        the pool.

    B. the reaction of the kids to the whistle when
        pushing out of the pool.

    C. the pandemonium created by all the kids being
        in the pool together.

    D. the rush of the kids all running to the snack bar.

4. In the context of the passage, the primary function of
    lines 77–78 is to give an example of something that:

    F. stands in contrast to going to the pool.

    G. was a worse use of money than ice cream.

    H. stands in contrast to buying ice cream.

    J. was a better use of money than going to the pool.

5. The author describes the taste of the ice cream in
    lines 47–48 primarily in order to:

    A. contrast with the later assertion that it was the
        best-tasting ice cream in the world.

    B. show that buying the ice cream was actually a
        waste of everyone's money.

    C. offer an explanation as to why everyone even-
        tually quit buying the ice cream.

    D. indicate why everyone chose ice cream over
        M&Ms or bags of chips.

6. The author in lines 10–14 most strongly implies that:

    F. she remembered that Jiang always liked the ice
        cream more than Aisha did.

    G. ice cream consumption is only for kids who
        are spending the day at the pool.

    H. deciding not to go to the pool and eat ice
        cream is a normal part of growing up.

    J. Aisha wants to appear to be more mature than
        the other kids at the pool.

7. As it is used in line 30, *mess* most nearly means:

    A. a dirty area.

    B. a difficult situation.

    C. a disordered state.

    D. a place to eat.

8. According to the final paragraph, the author of the passage believes that:

    F. community pools were built for children, not adults.

    G. adults were not allowed at the snack bar at the pool.

    H. there are not as many community pools now.

    J. childhood friends should always keep in touch.

9. One of the main purposes of the information in lines 5–8 is to explain:

    A. what the kids chose to get to eat.

    B. when it was time to go to the snack bar.

    C. why the kids were all forced to leave the pool at once.

    D. how the kids chose to always get ice cream.

10. The author mentions "the scent of chlorine or hot pavement" in the third paragraph primarily in order to:

    F. indicate what stood out most strongly to her while at she and her friends were at the pool.

    G. show that pools smelled the same way in the past that they do in the present.

    H. imply that smells of chlorine and hot pavement are often associated with one another.

    J. share particular smells that still remind her of the times that she and her friends ate ice cream at the pool.

HUMANITIES: This passage was adapted from an article about land art in a small art newspaper.

Humans have always bent their imaginations to aesthetically reshape the world around them. However, a particular problem for early artists seems to have been finding ways to make artwork
5 last. It was not an easy task to create artwork with natural and often perishable materials. Despite these difficulties, countless examples of ancient art fill museums throughout the world, from the cave drawings in Lascaux to Egyptian hieroglyphics to
10 Greek sculpture. However, a modern movement called land art, which embraces this difficulty, has gained recognition around the world. Land art is defined as art that either naturally deteriorates or is deliberately dismantled after it is constructed.

15 Land or earth art was first developed during the mid-1960s as a backlash in the art community against the increasing commercialization of art and seclusion of art from the natural world. Artists like Alan Sonfist sought to incorporate nature in
20 their work as well as return to the fundamental principles upon which they believed art was based. The pioneers of land art rejected museums and art galleries as the rightful settings for creative work. They sought to remove the "plastic" influences and
25 what they viewed as the corrosive influence on pure aesthetics. Thus, land art began with a mission to create three-dimensional works set in and wrought from the natural world.

The dawn of the movement coincided with
30 an emerging ecological movement. Land artists typically prefer the rural to the urban, sometimes searching for a spiritual connection with the earth. Land artworks from the movement's inception recall much older land works like Stonehenge, the
35 Nazca Lines of Peru, or the Great Pyramids of Giza. Constructed in remote locations such as the deserts of the American West, they experiment with perceptions of light, space, and even the passage of time. In so doing, they evoke the spirituality of far
40 more ancient works.

Above all, land artists utilize simple materials. Unlike other minimalist artists, land artists use only natural media such as rocks, soil, sand, wood,
water, and even plant matter in the creation of
45 their masterpieces. Land art icon Robert Smithson constructed his work *Spiral Jetty* using nothing more than stones, mud, algae, and water. Created in the Great Salt Lake in 1970 during a severe drought, *Spiral Jetty* was a 1,500-meter spiral of
50 rocks that projected from the lake shore and was allowed to deteriorate without intervention. The Jetty was covered by the lake within a few years and remained underwater until 2004 when, to the delight of contemporary artists, another drought
55 revealed the 30-year-old sculpture.

Another feature of land art is its massive scale, which typically prevents it from being displayed in any museum or gallery. Since land art makes extensive use of landscape, entire vistas can be
60 said to be part of a work. The sheer size of land art thus requires collaboration between artists and engineers, as well as the employment of laborers and volunteers, in order to complete a project. For example, Australian artist Andrew Rogers's piece
65 *Rhythms of Life* was constructed in twelve different sites around the world, making the work the largest piece of aesthetic art to date—a feat reminiscent of Christo and Jeanne-Claude's 1991 *Umbrellas* project, which placed massive blue and yellow umbrellas in
70 selected stretches of the Japanese countryside and the California mountains. Christo, however, denies the label of "land artist," claiming that his and his wife's work does not share the common principles of land art, since it neither rejects gallery art nor
75 eschews the use of synthetic building materials.

Despite the artists' ideological differences, Christo and Jeanne-Claude's work does share other similarities to the work of land artists in that both are intentionally short-lived. Land art is extensively
80 photographed during exhibition but afterward exists only on film or in memory. Some critics and art lovers decry limiting public access to a work of art by deliberately creating it to be temporary. Because creating land art often requires substantial
85 funding, allowing the finished product to fall into ruin or even purposefully dismantling it is considered by critics of the movement to be a waste of resources. Land artists counter such indictments

by pointing out that they only borrow the elements
90 of nature to produce their work, and once a piece
has been exhibited, they feel justified in returning
the materials to their rightful owner. Moreover, they
assert that the very ephemeral nature of their works
is an integral part of those works. Land artworks
95 that capture the imagination can live on in memory
and appear even greater to the public consciousness
than they really were. As Christo once stated,
"Do you know that I don't have any artworks that
exist? They all go away when they're finished . . .
100 giving my works an almost legendary character. I
think it takes much greater courage to create things
to be gone than to create things that will remain."

The same could be said of the land art movement
itself. Because of their massive scale, land artworks
105 are costly to produce. Land artists frequently rely on
wealthy private patrons, foundations, or government
grants in order to create their masterpieces. With
economic downturns came a loss of funding, and in
recent years the movement has faded. Or, perhaps, it
110 has transformed—as all movements must once they
have done their work to change and inspire others.

11. According to the passage, why did ancient artists
have a difficult time creating lasting artworks?

   A. Such works were not popular among land
   artists of the time.

   B. The media available to ancient artists were
   prone to decay.

   C. Patrons refused to pay the necessary expense
   for such work.

   D. The elements of nature succumbed to man-
   made endeavors.

12. According to the passage, which of the following is
true of the land art movement's inception?

   F. The movement originated with the creation of
   Spiral Jetty by Robert Smithson.

   G. The movement began as a backlash against the
   creation of permanent artworks.

   H. The movement was primarily motivated by a
   desire to use natural materials in art.

   J. The movement was a negative reaction to
   attributes of modern art during the 1960s.

13. The passage most strongly suggests that some ancient land works were concerned with:

   A. the natural world.

   B. the rural/urban divide.

   C. time and space.

   D. permanence.

14. It can be inferred from the fourth paragraph that
one distinction between minimalist artists and land
artists is that minimalist artists:

   F. create works that are extremely small.

   G. prefer exotic components over ordinary ones.

   H. are uninterested in spiritual aspects of art.

   J. make use of synthetic materials in their work.

15. As it is used in line 45, the word *icon* most nearly
means:

   A. religious idol.

   B. small graphic symbol.

   C. revered person.

   D. representative image.

Reading

16. The author mentions *Rhythms of Life* in line 65 primarily in order to:

    F. provide an example of how large land artworks can be.

    G. compare *Rhythms of Life* to the *Umbrellas* project.

    H. emphasize the diminutive scale of land artworks.

    J. describe the largest work of aesthetic art in human history.

17. One of the main purposes of the sixth paragraph is to:

    A. examine the implications of creating artworks that exist for a brief period of time.

    B. refute criticism of land art and the work of Christo and Jeanne-Claude.

    C. analyze the difference between land art and Christo and Jeanne-Claude's work.

    D. provide examples of legendary pieces of land art.

18. The author quotes Christo in lines 98–102 primarily in order to:

    F. argue that none of the preeminent works of modern art still exist.

    G. demonstrate that when Christo and Jeanne-Claude dismantle their artwork, they exhibit a courage entirely lacking in land artists.

    H. show that the destruction of a piece of artwork can enhance that work's reputation in the minds of critics and admirers.

    J. provide information about how artists care very little about wasting natural resources when they allow their artwork to be destroyed.

19. According to the passage, what happens to the building materials of land artwork after it is taken apart?

    A. They are recycled.

    B. They revert to nature.

    C. They pass to a new owner.

    D. They are used in future art.

20. The author's attitude toward the passage's main topic can best be described as:

    F. critical and dismissive.

    G. skeptical and disappointed.

    H. passionate and dedicated.

    J. interested and supportive.

Answers and Explanations

Passage Map Notes:

¶1: kids at pool getting snacks, friends introduced

¶2: always rowdy, get the same thing

¶3: narrator looks back as adult: memories, reflection

¶4: how friends ate differently

¶5: how things used to be

¶6–7: narr. reflects: outgrew it, sense of loss

BIG PICTURE SUMMARY

Main idea: The narrator reminisces about her summer days at the pool and reflects on how life has changed since her childhood.

Author's purpose: To evoke a sense of nostalgia

---

1. B

Difficulty: Low

Category: Global

Getting to the Answer: "The passage as a whole" signals that this is a Global question. Review your notes and predict that the author is looking back on a happy time in her life. This matches (B).

A and C can be eliminated because there is no cynicism nor heartlessness displayed by the author. D is not supported by the passage; though the author says that the ice cream she bought at the pool tasted good, she never says that ice cream as a whole tasted better when she was a child.

2. F

Difficulty: Low

Category: Inference

Getting to the Answer: The phrase "most strongly implies" tells you that this is an Inference question. In the final paragraph, the author mentions "between the time of our childhood summers and now"—predict that they have grown up since the time she is writing about. This matches (F).

This same phrase eliminates G because the author discusses childhood as being in the past. Choices H and J are not supported by the passage; the author may or may not be either elderly or a college student.

3. B

Difficulty: High

Category: Function

Getting to the Answer: The clue words "primarily in order to describe" indicate that this is a Function question. Refer to the line in question, and predict that *Pavlovian* is used here to describe how the kids all leave the pool when the whistle sounds. That matches (B).

A is incorrect because it is the kids' reaction that is described as *Pavlovian*, not the sound of the whistle itself. Neither the pandemonium nor the snack bar are referenced as *Pavlovian*, eliminating C and D.

4. H

Difficulty: Medium

Category: Function

Getting to the Answer: The phrase "primary function" lets you identify this as a Function question. Review the cited lines and predict that the correct answer will identify that books, clothes, and comic books were bought instead of ice cream. This matches (H).

Choices F and J can be eliminated because the author is contrasting what she and the others bought later to ice cream; there is no indication in the passage of whether they had to pay to use the pool at all. Choice G may or may not be true; while the author says this is what everyone later chose to spend their money on, she doesn't say that those things are a worse use of money than ice cream. (If anything, she implies that they were a better use because they lasted longer!)

5.   A

Difficulty: Low

Category: Function

Getting to the Answer: The clue words "primarily in order to" tell you that this is a Function question. Refer back to the lines referenced and predict that the author describes the ice cream as "on the stale side, freezer-burnt" to show that it really wasn't all that good. Nonetheless, it was "the best-tasting ice cream in all the world" because the kids bought it themselves. This matches (A).

Choice B might be tempting since the author does go on to say that the kids eventually chose to spend their money on other things, but this isn't the reason why the narrator describes the taste of the ice cream. Choice C is incorrect because, while the taste is described earlier in a relatively negative fashion, there is nothing to indicate that this is why the kids eventually quit buying it. Finally, D is not supported by the passage, since the ice cream is not described as being superior to either M&Ms or bags of chips.

6.   J

Difficulty: High

Category: Inference

Getting to the Answer: "Most strongly implies" indicates that this is an Inference question. Refer back to the lines in question and review what's stated about Aisha: "Jiang . . . was the oldest . . . Aisha came next, pretending like she didn't even care anymore, even though we all knew she did, or she would have stayed by the side of the pool." The author's assertion that Aisha pretended not to care and was *more likely* to be the first one to outgrow it supports a prediction that Aisha tries to act older than her age. This matches (J).

Although the author describes the way the ice cream is consumed, there's nothing to support the statement that Jiang liked the ice cream *more* than Aisha, so F is incorrect. Choice G is extreme; although the ice cream seems like an essential part of the pool-day experience, the author explicitly states that not only was there ice cream at home, it was better than the ice cream at the pool. Although the author talks about outgrowing it, there is no evidence that the author believes one outgrows pools and ice cream entirely, especially given her observation of adults at the pool while she was there as a child.

7.   C

Difficulty: Medium

Category: Vocab-in-Context

Getting to the Answer: The phrase "most nearly means" tells you that this is a Vocab-in-Context question. Refer back to the line in question, and predict that *mess* here means something like "unruly." The best match for this is (C).

While A, B, and D are all other definitions of *mess*, none of them matches the way the word is used within the passage.

8.   H

Difficulty: Medium

Category: Inference

Getting to the Answer: "According to the final paragraph" indicates that this could be either a Detail or an Inference question, depending on the information in the correct choice. Refer to your notes for the final paragraph, but realize it is hard to make a firm prediction from such a broad question. Instead, check each answer choice, eliminating them out one by one until you find the choice supported by the paragraph in question.

While the author does describe going to the community pool as a child, there is nothing to support the idea that she thinks such pools are just for children, which eliminates F. There is also nothing to support the idea that she thinks snack bars are just for children, which eliminates G. The author states that "The world changed, it seems, between the time of our childhood summers and now, and the disappearance of those pools, the snack bars and adult swim time, was part of that change." She does follow this by saying, "maybe we just no longer notice them," but this is presented as speculation, not counter-evidence, so (H) is correct. (If you're curious, note that J is too extreme—while the author says that she has kept up with the childhood friends from the passage, she never says that all childhood friends should stay in touch.)

9. C

Difficulty: Low

Category: Function

Getting to the Answer: The phrase "purposes of the information" means that this is a Function question. Refer back to the paragraph and predict that the referenced lines tell you why the kids all got out of the pool. This matches (C).

Nothing in the referenced lines gives any information about what foods the kids chose to get, eliminating A and D. While it is true that this was the time when the kids went to the snack bar, that wasn't what the referenced lines explained.

10. J

Difficulty: Medium

Category: Function

Getting to the Answer: "Primarily in order to" tells you that this is a Function question. Look back to the third paragraph to remind yourself why the author mentioned the chlorine and hot pavement. Predict that the correct answer will show that these smells bring up memories of eating ice cream at the pool. This matches (J).

Choice F may or may not be true; just because those particular smells bring back memories doesn't mean they stood out most strongly when she was a child. Nothing is said about how pools smell now versus then, nor about an association between chlorine and hot pavement, which eliminates G and H.

Passage Map Notes:

¶1: land art embraces impermanent art

¶2: reacted against contemporary art

¶3: connection to natural world

¶4: use natural materials

¶5: massive scale

¶6: impermanence; critics vs. artists

¶7: movement faded/changed

BIG PICTURE SUMMARY

Main idea: Land art is a modern art style and movement based on art that is designed to be impermanent and steeped in nature.

Author's purpose: To inform the reader about the land art movement

11. B

Difficulty: Low

Category: Detail

Getting to the Answer: The phrase "According to the passage" indicates that this is a Detail question. The first paragraph describes materials available to ancient artists as "perishable" (line 6). Choice (B) matches this prediction.

Choice A is a misused detail; the passage describes land art as a contemporary movement. Choice C is also a misused detail; there is no mention of patrons for ancient art, only modern works. Finally, choice D is a distortion; while the passage does describe ancient media as perishable, it does not suggest that "man-made endeavors" themselves caused the natural materials to deteriorate.

12. J

Difficulty: Medium

Category: Detail

Getting to the Answer: "According to the passage" is a clue that this is a Detail question. The second paragraph discusses the influences that led to the land art movement as a "backlash . . . against the increasing commercialization of art and seclusion of art from the natural world" (lines 16–18). Predict that land art opposed these trends. Choice (J) matches this prediction and is correct.

Choice F is a misused detail; the passage never states that *Spiral Jetty* was the first land artwork. Choice G is a distortion; the first paragraph discusses the impermanence of land art, but the author never suggests that land art was a direct reaction against permanent art. Choice H is extreme; the passage does discuss the use of natural materials in land art but never suggests that land art originated specifically from a desire to use such materials.

13. C

Difficulty: Medium

Category: Inference

Getting to the Answer: The phrase "most strongly suggests" shows that this is an Inference question. In paragraph 3, the passage states that land art works evoke ancient works through their interest in light, space, and time. Predict that ancient art will share these same concerns. This matches choice (C).

Choice A is a concern of land art, but not one that the passage connects to ancient land works. Choice B is out of scope; while the passage states that land artists prefer rural to urban, it does not mention the divide between them. Finally, choice D is a misused detail; the passage discusses the problem of permanence for ancient artists but not for ancient land works.

14. J

Difficulty: Medium

Category: Inference

Getting to the Answer: The clue word *inferred* shows that this is an Inference question. The fourth paragraph contrasts minimalists with land artists by stating that land artists prefer to use natural materials. You can infer that minimalists at least sometimes use non-natural materials to create art. The correct answer is (J).

Choice F is out of scope; the passage does not discuss the typical size of minimalist works. Choice G is a distortion; although the passage states that land artists prefer simple materials, the phrasing "other minimalist artists" suggests that minimalists may prefer them as well. The contrast is between natural and synthetic, not simple and exotic. Similarly, while the passage states that some land artists were concerned with spiritual aspects of nature, the passage does not discuss this with regard to minimalists, so H is incorrect.

15. C

Difficulty: Medium

Category: Vocab-in-Context

Getting to the Answer: This stem has the characteristic wording of a Vocab-in-Context question. Read the sentence to determine how the word is being used in the passage. Here, *icon* refers to a specific, important artist. Choice (C) matches this prediction.

Choices A, B, and D all represent other meanings of the word *icon*. The sentence uses the phrase "Land art icon" to describe a person (Robert Smithson), and it is not logical to describe a person as either a "land art small graphic symbol" or a "land art representative image," so B and D are incorrect. While a person can be described as a religious idol, the sentence and paragraph do not contain any support for the idea that Robert Smithson is a religious idol, so A is incorrect.

16. F

Difficulty: Medium

Category: Function

Getting to the Answer: The phrasing "author mentions . . . in order to" indicates this is a Function question. Consider the cited line and surrounding sentences in the context of the paragraph as a whole. The purpose of the paragraph is to discuss the massive scale of land art works, and the cited line begins with "For example." Thus, you can predict that the author mentions *Rhythms of Life* as an example supporting the paragraph's main idea. Choice (F) is correct.

Choice G is a misused detail; the two works are compared, but that is not the author's main purpose for including this detail. Choice H is opposite; the passage describes *Rhythms of Life* as massive, not diminutive. Choice J is a misused detail; the passage does state that this work is the largest to date, but that is not the author's purpose for mentioning *Rhythms of Life*.

17. A

Difficulty: Medium

Category: Function

Getting to the Answer: The phrase "main purposes" is a clue that this is a Function question. Review your notes to determine what the author wants to communicate in the sixth paragraph. This paragraph describes the consequences of creating short-lived artwork, so (A) is correct.

Choice B is out of scope; the author does address criticism, just not for the entire paragraph. Choice C is out of scope; this comparison is made, but that is not one of the primary purposes of the whole paragraph. Finally, choice D is out of scope; the author does not provide any examples in this paragraph.

18. H

Difficulty: High

Category: Function

Getting to the Answer: The wording "author quotes . . . in order to" identifies this as a Function question. Examine the context in the paragraph to determine the author's purpose. The author quotes Christo, who uses words like *legendary* and *courage*, to support the explanation of artists' reasons for allowing their work to be destroyed. You can predict that this quote reinforces

the idea that impermanence can raise the stature of art. Choice (H) captures this sentiment.

Choice F is extreme; the passage never states that no successful artworks still exist. Choice G is opposite; the paragraph cites similarities between land artists and Christo and Jeanne-Claude, not differences. Choice J is a distortion of the information in the passage; critics say that land artists waste resources, but land artists argue that they only borrow materials. It's possible that some land artists do waste resources, but the cited Christo quote does not support the idea that artists in general care very little about waste.

19. B

Difficulty: Medium

Category: Detail

Getting to the Answer: The phrase "According to the passage" shows that this is a Detail question. Lines 88–92 state that the materials from land art are taken from nature and returned to nature. Choice (B) is correct.

Choice A is out of scope; the passage does not discuss recycling. Choice C is opposite; the passage describes nature as the rightful owner of the materials, so the materials are returned to a previous owner, not passed to a new one. Choice D is out of scope; the passage does not describe the reuse of land art materials.

20. J

Difficulty: Medium

Category: Global

Getting to the Answer: The clues "author's attitude" and "main topic" indicate this is a Global question; consult your notes to determine the author's view of land art. The passage is mostly descriptive in tone, but it does present land art as unusual and interesting. Moreover, the author's positive view of the movement comes through in some places: in the sixth paragraph, the author defends land art, and in the final paragraph, the author refers to land art inspiring others. Choice (J) is therefore correct.

Choice F is opposite; the passage does not dismiss land art but explores it thoroughly. While it mentions some criticisms of the movement, it immediately offers counters to these criticisms. Choice G is also opposite; the author is interested in and enthusiastic about land art, not skeptical or dismissive. Choice H is extreme; while the tone is generally positive, "passionate and dedicated" goes too far.

ACT Science

CHAPTER 22

The Method for ACT Science

LEARNING OBJECTIVE

After completing this chapter, you will be able to:

- Effectively and efficiently apply the ACT Science Method

How to Do ACT Science

The ACT Science Test is a test of your scientific reasoning ability, not a test of your knowledge of scientific content. While you do need to have knowledge of basic scientific concepts and terminology to answer some of the questions, you do NOT need to understand advanced concepts or memorize equations.

If you've completed high-school-level courses covering topics in biology, chemistry, earth/space science, and physics, then you should already know everything you'll need to know for test day. In fact, you can still do quite well on the ACT Science Test even if you've never studied or you're still taking classes on some of these subjects.

If you run across a question that requires background knowledge you don't have, eliminate as many answer choices as possible and then make an educated guess from the remaining choices. Most importantly, you should avoid wasting time by focusing your attention on the vast majority of questions that don't require outside knowledge.

In this chapter, we'll give you an overview of how to tackle Science passages and questions. The other chapters in this unit will help you improve your approach for the six ACT Science question types.

To see the ACT Science Method in action, try the passage and questions that follow on your own. Then, compare your approach to our recommendations for how to approach ACT Science. Finally, reflect on how you can become a more efficient test taker.

Passage I

Researchers compared the characteristics of grassland prescribed fires during the growing and dormant season to three experimental small-scale fire approaches. In all experiments, thermocouples 10 cm above the soil were used to determine time-temperature profiles.

Experiment 1

Two dormant-season and two growing-season prescribed burns, ignited via a ring-fire technique, were performed within a tallgrass prairie. The average fuel loads for the dormant-season and growing-season fires were 5,036 kg ha-1 and 5,545 kg ha-1, respectively. The results are shown in Figure 1.

Experiment 2

Four 2 m × 2 m aluminum sheets were used to form a burn box around *in situ* vegetation of a prairie similar in composition to the prairie burned in Experiment 1. A propane torch was used to ignite the fire, and additional timothy hay was added to adjust the fuel load to 3,000 kg ha-1. The experiment was repeated 4 times. The average results are shown in Figure 2.

Experiment 3

Grass species were grown in 15-cm plastic pots. The pots were placed below a metal burn table that was 1.2 m × 2.4 m with five 16.5-cm diameter circles. A drip torch was used to ignite the fire, and timothy hay was added at a rate of 3,000 kg ha-1. The experiment was repeated 4 times. The average results are shown in Figure 2.

Experiment 4

A propane prong composed of a pipe, tube, and propane tank was shaped into a U with two 30-cm arms with holes (as shown in the diagram). Five pots, like those in Experiment 3, were each burned for 60 sec between the prongs inside a closed structure with ventilation. The average results are shown in Figure 2.

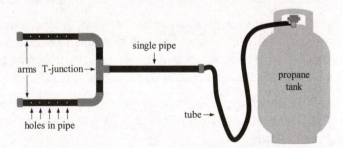

Adapted from Katherin Kral, *et al.*, "Simulating Grassland Prescribed Fires Using Experimental Approaches." © 2015 by Fire Ecology.

Diagram

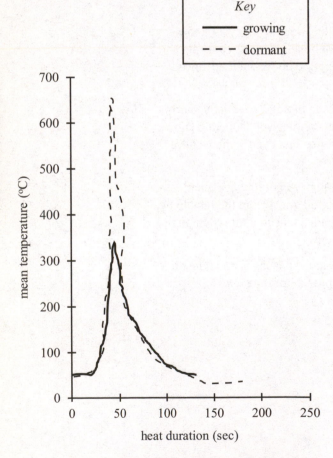

This data is from *Fire Ecology*, Vol. 11, Iss. 3, December 2015, pp. 34-44.

Figure 1

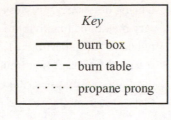

Key
—— burn box
- - - burn table
· · · · · propane prong

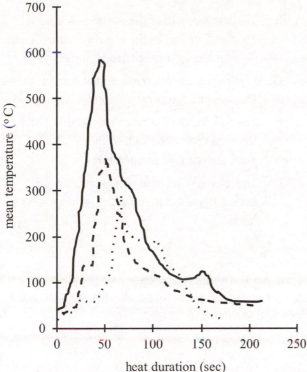

This data is from *Fire Ecology*, Vol. 11, Iss. 3, December 2015, pp. 34-44.

Figure 2

1. Experiment 2 differed from Experiment 3 in which of the following ways?

   A. In Experiment 2, timothy hay was added to adjust the fuel load, whereas in Experiment 3, greenhouse-grown plants were added to adjust the fuel load.

   B. In Experiment 2, natural habitat plants were burned, whereas in Experiment 3, greenhouse-grown plants were burned.

   C. A propane torch was used to ignite the fire in Experiment 2, whereas a ring-fire technique was used to ignite the fire in Experiment 3.

   D. The average fuel load in Experiment 2 was 5,036 kg ha^{-1}, whereas the average fuel load in Experiment 3 was 3,000 kg ha^{-1}.

2. Bends in a pipe and variations in pipe diameter create pressure differentials that cause fluids to undergo mixing. According to the diagram, where would mixing of air and propane most likely occur to support combustion?

   F. Arms

   G. T-junction

   H. Single pipe

   J. Tube

3. The researchers had predicted that the burn-box approach would best simulate the temperature profile of growing-season prescribed fires. Are the results of the study consistent with this prediction?

   A. Yes; the maximum mean temperatures for both growing-season and burn-box fires was around 350°C.

   B. Yes; the maximum mean temperatures for both growing-season and burn-box fires was around 650°C.

   C. No; the maximum mean temperature for growing-season fires was 650°C, whereas the maximum mean temperature for burn box was 350°C.

   D. No; the maximum mean temperature for growing-season fires was 350°C, whereas the maximum mean temperature for burn box was 650°C.

4. Suppose the maximum mean temperature and heat duration of an additional trial were 300°C and 175 sec, respectively. The time-temperature profile for this trial would most likely have been for a:

   F. dormant-season prescribed fire.

   G. burn-box fire.

   H. burn-table fire.

   J. propane-prong fire.

5. The scientists further calculated heat dosage, the product of heat duration and temperature, to predict plant mortality. Based on the results, which of the following fires had the highest heat dosage?

    A. Growing-season

    B. Burn-box

    C. Burn-table

    D. Propane-prong

6. During dormancy, grasses enter a state of temporary metabolic inactivity to conserve water and nutrients. In Experiment 1, what is the most likely reason the average maximum temperature for the dormant-season prescribed fire was almost twice that of the growing-season prescribed fire?

    F. The temperature of the dormant season is greater than that of the growing season, so the dormant-season fires burned hotter.

    G. More wind during the dormant season spread the fires at a faster rate.

    H. The fuel for the dormant-season fires had lower moisture content, so they produced hotter maximum temperatures.

    J. The average fuel load was greater for the dormant-season than for the growing-season fires.

Many test takers will see a diagram like the one in Experiment 4 and panic. Others will waste a great deal of time looking at all the data without a clear goal. You want to avoid both those outcomes. Before diving into how to tackle *this* passage, it's important first to understand the passage *types* you'll see in ACT Science, as the passage type will dictate your approach.

Passage Types

Passages in ACT Science fall into three passage types:

- Data Representation
- Research Summaries
- Conflicting Viewpoints

While the passage order varies, you can always expect to see three Research Summaries passages, two Data Representation passages, and one Conflicting Viewpoints passage. Regardless of type, passages in the ACT Science Test are taken from a variety of natural science subjects. These include topics in:

- Earth and Space Science—astronomy, geology, meteorology, etc.
- Biology—botany, genetics, zoology, etc.
- Chemistry—acids/bases, kinetics/equilibria, organic chemistry, etc.
- Physics—electromagnetism, mechanics, thermodynamics, etc.

While the text of Science passages is considerably shorter than what is found in the English and Reading tests, most Science passages are accompanied by graphs, tables, and/or diagrams, which you will have to interpret and analyze.

The ACT Science Method

Your first step for any ACT Science passage will be to **identify the passage type**. Recall that there are three types of passages; let the passage type guide your approach to the question set:

- Data Representation passages tend to be light on text but heavy on data presented in graphs or tables.
- Research Summaries passages tend to contain more text, consisting largely of descriptions of multiple experimental procedures, and often feature their own graphs or tables filled with results.
- Conflicting Viewpoints passages contain accounts of two or more competing theories/hypotheses on a particular phenomenon, typically featuring more text and fewer figures than the other two passage types.

Your next step is based on the type of passage. You need to **analyze the passage and figures strategically**, and this analysis will be different for each passage type. Chapter 23 will focus on the question types most common in Data Representation passages, chapter 24 will focus on the question types most common in Research Summaries passages, and chapter 25 will focus on the question types most common in Conflicting Viewpoints passages. However, it's important to note that question types are not exclusive to one passage type.

After you have analyzed the passage, you will **examine each question stem**. The specific information an individual question wants you to consider will be unique to your ACT exam, but the way in which the questions ask for that information—and the approaches required to answer them—fall into consistent patterns, or question types. The six question types fall into three categories:

- Data
  - Interpreting Data
  - Using Data
- Experiments
  - Experimental Design
  - Synthesizing Data
- Thinking Like a Scientist
  - Applying Core Knowledge
  - Supporting Hypotheses

Chapters 23–25 will provide additional information about how to more efficiently and effectively examine question stems. While each question type will be unique in the skills and approach required, it's important on *every question* to identify information in the question stem and answer choices like variables, units, or figure headings to help you hone in on the specific parts of the passage that apply to the question (for example, "mass," "kg," or "Figure 1").

Now that you've analyzed the passage and the question stem, you're ready to **predict and answer**:

- Locate the corresponding data in the passage and circle the parts of the figure or text that directly relate to the question.
- Based on what you discover in the passage, formulate a prediction about what the correct answer should say.
- Match your prediction to the correct answer choice.

Chapters 23–25 will provide additional information about how improve predictions based on passage and question type.

Here's what we did:

> ### ACT SCIENCE METHOD
>
> Step 1. Identify the passage type
>
> Step 2. Analyze the passage and figures strategically
>
> Step 3. Examine the question stem
>
> Step 4. Predict and answer

Take a look at a strategic approach to Passage I. Look for at least one way per question that your original approach could have been faster and more confident.

Identify the passage type

The passage provided at the start of this section has clearly labeled headers for Experiments 1 through 4, indicating that it is a Research Summaries passage.

Analyze the passage and figures strategically

Central idea: The first paragraph indicates the experiments are comparing the burn characteristics of prescribed fires to grasslands during dormant and growing seasons to three smaller-scale experimental approaches. Note: *when* the experimenters measure the burn (growing vs. dormant season) and the burn method used are factors under their control; thus, they are independent variables. The paragraph also mentions that experimenters will be collecting time-temperature profiles; therefore, time and temperature are both dependent variables, as they will change depending on the burn type and season.

Experiment 1 and Figure 1: The details within the text are likely irrelevant to the majority of the questions. The figure, however, provides lots of key info in a quick glance:

- The *x*-axis is heat duration; the *y*-axis is mean temperature
- Dormant-season burns are several hundred degrees hotter and last ~40–50 seconds longer than growing-season burns

Experiments 2–4 and Figure 2: Skim the details within the text about the methods of each experiment quickly; these can easily be returned to if there is a specific question about them. Instead, focus your attention on Figure 2, which shows:

- The same axes and variables that were in Figure 1
- In both max temperature and duration, burn box > burn table > propane prong

Diagram: Don't spend time on this now. There will likely be a question on the experimental apparatus of Experiment 4 since the diagram is included, but wait to see what the question is first.

Examine the question stem, predict, and answer

Question	Explanation
1. Experiment 2 differed from Experiment 3 in which of the following ways? A. In Experiment 2, timothy hay was added to adjust the fuel load, whereas in Experiment 3, greenhouse-grown plants were added to adjust the fuel load. B. In Experiment 2, natural habitat plants were burned, whereas in Experiment 3, greenhouse-grown plants were burned. C. A propane torch was used to ignite the fire in Experiment 2, whereas a ring-fire technique was used to ignite the fire in Experiment 3. D. The average fuel load in Experiment 2 was 5,036 kg ha^{-1}, whereas the average fuel load in Experiment 3 was 3,000 kg ha^{-1}.	Methodology questions are not common, but they can come up from time to time. Step 2 in the ACT Science Method recommends skimming the text of the experiments during your first pass; now is the time to return to that text with the specific question in mind: "What's different between Experiments 2 and 3?" A quick return to the text reveals that Experiment 2 used "*in situ* vegetation," whereas in Experiment 3, "grass species were grown in 15-cm plastic pots." The correct answer won't necessarily be an exact match to the language of the passage; rather, it may use synonyms to some of the key terms. Notice how (B) correctly matches the described difference without mirroring the passage word for word. Both experiments added timothy hay to adjust the fuel load, eliminating A. While C correctly notes a propane torch was used in Experiment 2, a drip torch was used in Experiment 3, not a ring-fire technique. Lastly, D is incorrect because the average fuel load in both experiments was 3,000 kg ha^{-1}.
2. Bends in a pipe and variations in pipe diameter create pressure differentials that cause fluids to undergo mixing. According to the diagram, where would mixing of air and propane most likely occur to support combustion? F. Arms G. T-junction H. Single pipe J. Tube	The key to answering this question comes from the question stem itself, which can become clearer if you paraphrase what the question is stating: combustion takes place where air and propane mixes, which happens when there are bends in a pipe and variations in pipe diameter. Examine the diagram with this in mind, and note that this best describes a T-junction where the two wider arms combine with the single pipe at 90° angles. This prediction matches (G).

Science

Question	Explanation
3. The researchers had predicted that the burn-box approach would best simulate the temperature profile of growing-season prescribed fires. Are the results of the study consistent with this prediction? A. Yes; the maximum mean temperatures for both growing-season and burn-box fires was around 350°C. B. Yes; the maximum mean temperatures for both growing-season and burn-box fires was around 650°C. C. No; the maximum mean temperature for growing-season fires was 650°C, whereas the maximum mean temperature for burn box was 350°C. D. No; the maximum mean temperature for growing-season fires was 350°C, whereas the maximum mean temperature for burn box was 650°C.	When asking if the results are consistent with the prediction, the question is really saying that you need to compare the growing-season fire to the burn-box fire. To compare their results, you will need to examine both Figure 1 and Figure 2 for the maximum mean temperature of each. Growing-season fires had a max temp of 350°C, whereas the burn box had a max temp of 600°C, matching (D). Note: the difference between their max temps makes the results not consistent with the prediction.
4. Suppose the maximum mean temperature and heat duration of an additional trial were 300°C and 175 sec, respectively. The time-temperature profile for this trial would most likely have been for a: F. dormant-season prescribed fire. G. burn-box fire. H. burn-table fire. J. propane-prong fire.	Paraphrase the question, including the new information provided in it: which burn profile is most similar to the temperature (300°C) and time (175 sec) of the new trial? These parameters match the profile of the propane-prong fire from Figure 2, making (J) correct.

Question	Explanation
5. The scientists further calculated heat dosage, the product of heat duration and temperature, to predict plant mortality. Based on the results, which of the following fires had the highest heat dosage?	Heat dosage is a new concept, but it is simply heat duration × temperature, the two variables from Figures 1 and 2. The question stem thus indicates that you'll need to compare the heat durations and temperatures of four of the fires.
A. Growing-season	From Figure 2, note that the burn box > the burn table > the propane prong in both duration and max temperature, so the burn box must also have a greater heat dosage than either the burn table or the propane prong.
B. Burn-box	
C. Burn-table	
D. Propane-prong	
	To determine whether the growing-season burn or the burn box has the higher heat dosage, their respective data must be compared from Figures 1 and 2. Growing-season burns had a max temp of ~350°C and duration of ~130 seconds; the burn box had a max temp of ~600°C and duration of ~210 seconds. Again, without performing any calculations, you can predict that the burn box will have the greater heat dosage since it has both higher temp and duration.
	Lastly, match the prediction with the correct answer choice, (B).
6. During dormancy, grasses enter a state of temporary metabolic inactivity to conserve water and nutrients. In Experiment 1, what is the most likely reason the average maximum temperature for the dormant-season prescribed fire was almost twice that of the growing-season prescribed fire?	The question is asking you to infer *why* dormant-season fires burn twice as hot as growing-season fires. This may seem like a difficult question at first, and you may be tempted to go back and pore over the passage for helpful details. Resist that time-wasting approach and focus on the new information provided: dormant grasses are metabolically inactive due to *fewer nutrients* and *less water*. The only answer choice to highlight one of these differences is (H) by explaining that the hotter temperatures were due to "lower moisture content."
F. The temperature of the dormant season is greater than that of the growing season, so the dormant-season fires burned hotter.	
G. More wind during the dormant season spread the fires at a faster rate.	
H. The fuel for the dormant-season fires had lower moisture content, so they produced hotter maximum temperatures.	
J. The average fuel load was greater for the dormant-season than for the growing-season fires.	

In the next section, you'll see another ACT Science passage. Try to apply the ACT Science Method presented in this lesson to read and answer the questions as quickly and confidently as possible.

How Much Have You Learned?

Directions: Take as much time as you need on these questions. Work carefully and methodically. There will be opportunities for timed practice in future chapters.

Passage II

A snowmobile's total braking distance, D, is the distance a snowmobile travels from the moment a driver first sees a "stop" signal until the snowmobile comes to a complete stop.

Students used 2 methods to calculate D using equations from physics. Method 1 calculated D using S and T and assuming a driver reaction time of 0.8 sec. S is the distance traveled after a driver sees a "stop" signal but before a driver begins the braking process; T is the average distance traveled after the brakes are applied. Method 2 maintains that D is simply the initial speed in ft/sec multiplied by 2 sec, based on the hypothesis that D is the distance the snowmobile would have traveled over 2 sec if the brakes had not been applied. Table 1 shows the results of both methods given various initial speeds, and Figure 1 graphs D from both methods versus initial speed.

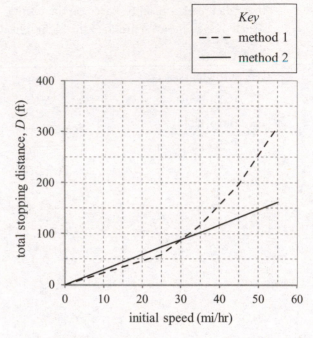

Figure 1

Table 1					
Initial speed (mi/hr)	Initial speed (ft/sec)	Method 1			Method 2
		S(ft)	T(ft)	D(ft)	D(ft)
25	37	29	28	57	73
35	51	41	75	116	102
45	66	53	144	197	132
55	81	65	245	310	162

1. Based on Table 1, what is the approximate value of D according to Method 1 when the initial speed is 58 ft/sec ?

   A. 70 ft

   B. 150 ft

   C. 250 ft

   D. 320 ft

2. According to Figure 1, at approximately which of the following initial speeds is the value of D from Method 1 equal to that from Method 2 ?

   F. 20 mi/hr

   G. 30 mi/hr

   H. 40 mi/hr

   J. 50 mi/hr

3. Suppose that a snowmobile was traveling at an initial speed of 75 mi/hr. Its D, according to Method 2, would most likely have been:

   A. less than 100 ft.

   B. between 100 and 200 ft.

   C. between 200 and 300 ft.

   D. greater than 300 ft.

4. Based on the results of the study, the S for an initial speed of 25 mi/hr, compared to S for an initial speed of 55 mi/hr, is approximately:

   F. $\frac{1}{4}$ as large.

   G. $\frac{1}{2}$ as large.

   H. 2 times as large.

   J. 4 times as large.

5. The average distance traveled after the brakes are applied (T) plotted against the distance traveled after a driver sees a stop sign (S) for Method 1 is best represented by which of the following graphs?

   A.

   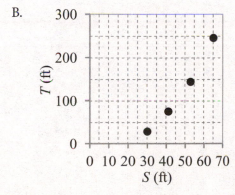

   B.

   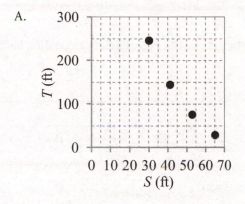

   C.

   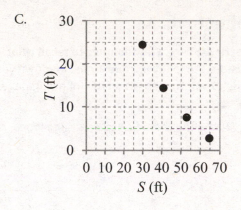

   D.

   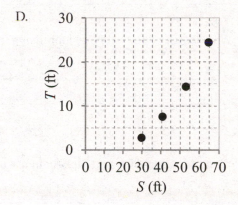

6. Which of the following describes a difference between Method 1 and Method 2? In Method 1:

   F. speeds were measured in mi/hr, but in Method 2, speeds were measured in ft/sec.

   G. distance was calculated based on a reaction speed of 0.8 sec, but in Method 2, distance was calculated based on a reaction speed of 2.0 sec.

   H. distance was calculated from the sum of two factors, but in Method 2, distance was calculated as the product of two factors.

   J. multiple trials were conducted at each speed, but in Method 2, only one trial was conducted at each speed.

Reflect

Directions: Take a few minutes to recall what you've learned and what you've been practicing in this chapter. Consider the following questions, jot down your best answer for each one, and then compare your reflections to the expert responses on the following page. Use your level of confidence to determine what to do next.

1. Name the three Science passage types.

    _____

    _____

    _____

2. Why do ACT experts start by identifying the passage type before analyzing the passage and figures?

    _____

    _____

    _____

3. What does an ACT expert look for in the question stem of an ACT Science question?

    _____

    _____

    _____

4. Why do expert test takers predict or characterize the correct answer to each ACT Science question before assessing the answer choices?

    _____

    _____

    _____

5. What will you do differently on future passages and their questions?

    _____

    _____

    _____

Responses

1. Name the three Science passage types.

The three Science passage types are Data Representation, Research Summaries, and Conflicting Viewpoints.

2. Why do ACT experts start by identifying the passage type before analyzing the passage and figures?

The approach you take to analyzing the text and figures depends on the type of passage you have, which is why taking the time to identify the passage type before reading is so crucial.

3. What does an ACT expert look for in the question stem of an ACT Science question?

Each question stem indicates the type of question and contains clues as to whether the answer will come from researching the passage text or from a particular figure or table. Many question stems have specific clues (for example, asking for a comparison of particular experimental methods) that tell us precisely where to research.

4. Why do expert test takers predict or characterize the correct answer to each ACT Science question before assessing the answer choices?

Predicting or characterizing the correct answer allows us to evaluate each answer choice one time and to avoid rereading for every answer choice. Wrong answers often distort what the passage said or misuse details from the passage; they might mix methodologies between experiments or what was said with each hypothesis. Thus, it's best to have your own prediction of what the correct answer must say before diving into the choices.

5. What will you do differently on future passages and their questions?

There is no one correct answer to this question as you bring your own strengths and opportunities to the Science Test. Start by becoming more familiar with the ACT Science Method and the expert analysis and explanations in Part V. As you review, keep track of your mistakes and repeat lessons that are related to these areas of opportunity. Practice makes permanent!

Some test takers are overwhelmed by the unfamiliarity of the passage topics; if that's you, remember that Applying Core Knowledge questions are worth only 2/36 Science SmartPoints while the other question types are all worth at least 6/36. That means the points you can earn using your core science knowledge are minuscule compared to those you can earn by approaching this section systematically and strategically. It also means that your answer to this reflection question should almost certainly NOT include "memorize more science facts."

Next Steps

If you answered most questions correctly in the "How Much Have You Learned?" section, and if your responses to the Reflect questions were similar to those of an expert, then consider the ACT Science Method an area of strength and move on to the next chapter. Come back to this topic periodically to prevent yourself from getting rusty.

If you don't yet feel confident, review the material in "How to Do ACT Science" and then try the questions you missed again. As always, be sure to review the explanations closely. Then go online (**kaptest.com/login**) to watch a video about the Kaplan Method for ACT Science and use your Qbank for more practice. If you haven't already registered your book, do so at kaptest.com/moreonline.

GO ONLINE

kaptest.com/login

Science

Answers and Explanations

How Much Have You Learned?

1. B

Difficulty: Low

Category: Using Data

Getting to the Answer: The initial speed given in the question is in ft/sec (column 2) and not mi/hr (column 1). Fifty-eight ft/sec is not listed in Table 1, so you need to interpolate, or read between known data points: 51 ft/sec and 66 ft/sec. At 51 ft/sec, D from Method 1 is 116 ft, and at 66 ft/sec, D from Method 1 is 197 ft. Therefore, D at 58 ft/sec should fall between 116 and 197 ft. The only choice within that range is 150 ft, so (B) is correct.

Watch out for choice D, which gives a value that you might estimate if you looked at the mi/hr column instead of the ft/sec column.

2. G

Difficulty: Low

Category: Interpreting Data

Getting to the Answer: The value of D from Method 1 is equal to that from Method 2 where the two lines intersect on Figure 1. Draw a line down from where the two lines cross to the x-axis to find the corresponding initial speed of approximately 30 mi/hr. The correct choice is (G).

3. C

Difficulty: Low

Category: Using Data

Getting to the Answer: Since 75 mi/hr is beyond the range of the presented data, you need to extrapolate. Either continue the straight line that represents Method 2 to 75 mi/hr on Figure 1 or use Table 1 to estimate D. The straight line from Figure 1, if extended, gives a D of about 225 ft. Looking at Table 1, you can see that each 10 mi/hr increase in initial speed increases D by about 30 ft. Hence, an initial speed of 75 mi/hr would have a D that's about 60 ft greater than the D at 55 mi/hr: 60 ft + 162 ft = 222 ft. Either way, the answer lies between 200 and 300 ft, so the correct choice is (C). Choice D would be the result if you were looking at Method 1 instead of Method 2.

4. G

Difficulty: Low

Category: Using Data

Getting to the Answer: According to Table 1, S for an initial speed of 25 mi/hr is 29 ft, and S for an initial speed of 55 mi/hr is 65 ft. Since 29 is less than 65, eliminate H and J (which would indicate that 29 is larger than 65). Twenty-nine is a bit less than half of 65, so (G) is correct.

5. B

Difficulty: Medium

Category: Synthesizing Data

Getting to the Answer: According to Table 1, as the values for S increase, the values for T also increase. Hence, the relationship is direct. Eliminate choices A and C, which show an inverse relationship. Check values from Table 1 on the remaining two graphs. According to the table, for S = 29, T = 28. Choice (B) plots the data as given in the table, so the correct answer is (B).

Choice D has the appropriate shape, but the vertical axis is incorrect (it runs from 0 to 30 ft, rather than 0 to 300 ft).

6. H

Difficulty: Medium

Category: Experimental Design

Getting to the Answer: According to the passage, Method 1 calculates distance using S and T. In Table 1, the sum of S and T is D. Method 2 is calculated by taking "the initial speed in ft/sec multiplied by 2 sec." Thus, choice (H) is correct.

Both Method 1 and Method 2 had initial speeds given in both mi/hr and ft/sec, so F is incorrect. While the reaction speed rate of Method 1 was 0.8 sec, Method 1 was not calculated based on this or any specified reaction rate, so G is incorrect. Choice J is also incorrect because both methods were used to obtain calculations from the same four speeds.

CHAPTER 23

Data

LEARNING OBJECTIVES

After completing this chapter, you will be able to:

- Identify Data Representation passages
- List strategies for dealing with complex data representations
- Identify a value from a table or a graph
- Identify a trend in the data
- Describe a relationship between variables
- Perform basic calculations using data
- Infer values not directly provided using interpolation, extrapolation, and lines of best fit
- Draw conclusions about data based on new information

Interpreting Data: 7/36 SmartPoints® (Very high yield)

Using Data: 9/36 SmartPoints® (Very high yield)

How Much Do You Know?

Directions: Try out the questions below. Show your work so that you can compare your solutions to the ones found on the next page. The "Category" heading in the explanation for each question gives the title of the lesson that covers how to solve it. If you answered the question(s) for a given lesson correctly, and if your scratchwork looks like ours, you may be able to move quickly through that lesson. If you answered incorrectly or used a different approach, you may want to take your time on that lesson.

Passage I

The extent to which a solute will dissolve in a given solvent is dependent on several factors, including conditions of temperature and pressure and the electrochemical natures of the solute and solvent.

Students measured the solubilities in distilled water of several pairs of common sodium (Na) and potassium (K) salts at various temperatures. The pairs were NaCl and KCl, $NaNO_3$ and KNO_3, and $NaClO_3$ and $KClO_3$. All measurements were conducted at 1 atmosphere of pressure. After pooling and averaging all the data, the students plotted solubility curves to produce Figure 1.

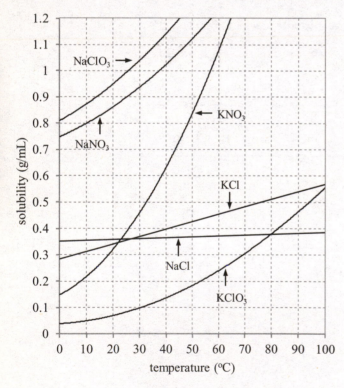

Figure 1

1. For the given salts, what is the relationship, if any, between solubility and temperature?

   A. As the temperature increases, the solubility increases.

   B. As the temperature increases, the solubility decreases.

   C. As the temperature increases, the solubility remains the same.

   D. Solubility and temperature are unrelated.

2. Based on Figure 1, which solute exhibits the *greatest* variation in solubility between 0°C and 60°C ?

   F. KNO_3

   G. NaCl

   H. KCl

   J. $KClO_3$

3. According to Figure 1, for which of the following salts would it be possible to dissolve more than 0.65 g/mL at 55°C ?

   A. Any of the Na salts

   B. Any of the K salts

   C. Either of the NO_3 salts

   D. Either of the ClO_3 salts

4. According to the data, how many more grams of KNO_3 in 1 L of distilled water are dissolved at 50°C and normal atmospheric pressure than of $KClO_3$ under the same conditions?

   F. 0.18 g

   G. 0.66 g

   H. 180 g

   J. 660 g

5. Based on Figure 1, what is the order of the given solutes from least solubility to greatest solubility, at 90°C ?

   A. $KClO_3$, KCl, NaCl

   B. NaCl, $KClO_3$, KCl

   C. KCl, $KClO_3$, NaCl

   D. $KClO_3$, KCl, NaCl

6. Based on Figure 1, if the temperature of KCl had been increased to 135°C, the solubility would most likely have been:

   F. 0.38 mg/mL

   G. 0.56 mg/mL

   H. 0.65 mg/mL

   J. 0.95 mg/mL

7. Consider the statement "When a solution is cooled, the amount of solute dissolved in excess of the lower solubility will precipitate out." If a 100-mL solution into which 0.3 g/mL of $KClO_3$ has been dissolved is cooled from 70°C to 30°C, approximately how many grams of $KClO_3$ would precipitate out?

   A. 0.2 g

   B.   2 g

   C.   20 g

   D.   40 g

Check Your Work

1. A

Difficulty: Low

Category: Interpreting Data

Getting to the Answer: When you're looking for the relationship between two variables in a line graph, check to see if they go up or down together, if one remains constant as the other changes, or if one goes down as the other goes up. All six lines rise from left to right across the graph, indicating that solubility goes up as temperature goes up. Choice (A) is correct.

2. F

Difficulty: Low

Category: Interpreting Data

Getting to the Answer: Unless the question stem specifically tells you to make guesses about what might happen beyond the range of a figure, consider only the given data when answering questions. The question stem limits you to the range between 0°C and 60°C. The phrase "exhibits the greatest variation in solubility" means "has the biggest change in solubility." KNO_3 starts very low (about 0.15 g/mL at 0°C) and comes close to 1.1 g/mL at 60°C, so it shows the greatest increase in solubility over the specified range. The solutes in G, H, and J have much smaller changes in solubility over the given temperature range. The correct answer is (F).

3. C

Difficulty: Medium

Category: Interpreting Data

Getting to the Answer: When a question gives you a specific range of values for the x- or y-axis, make sure you focus your attention within that range. To find the solubility of the different salts at 55°C, draw a vertical line up from the x-axis. To find solubilities greater than 0.65 g/mL, draw a horizontal line across the graph from the y-axis. Only three of the solubility curves ever rise above 0.65 g/mL: those for $NaClO_3$, $NaNO_3$, and KNO_3. None of the answer choices include all three of those salts, but (C) lists two of the three, so (C) is the correct answer.

The other three answer choices contain at least one salt with a solubility below 0.65 g/mL at 55°C.

4. J

Difficulty: High

Category: Using Data

Getting to the Answer: The question stem tells you where in the figure you'll find your answer. This question asks about a solution at 50°C, so start there. Trace the vertical line up from the x-axis at 50°C until it crosses the curve for KNO_3. Find the solubility of KNO_3 by drawing a horizontal line from the point of intersection to the y-axis. The solubility is about 0.84 g/mL. For $KClO_3$, repeat the process to find that the solubility is about 0.18 g/mL. The difference is 0.84 − 0.18 = 0.66 g/mL. Note, however, that the volume given in the question stem is not 1 mL, but 1 L (or 1,000 mL), so you'll need to multiply the difference by 1,000: 0.66 g/mL × 1,000 mL = 660 g. Choice (J) is correct.

Choice G is a trap that you might fall into if you forget to check your units. Choices F and H are incorrect because they represent the amount of $KClO_3$ dissolved in 1 mL and in 1 L, respectively.

5. G

Difficulty: Medium

Category: Interpreting Data

Getting to the Answer: To determine solubility at 90°C, draw a vertical line up 90°C on the x-axis. At 90°C, NaCl has a solubility of ~0.38 g/mL, $KClO_3$ has a solubility of ~0.47 g/mL and KCl has a solubility of ~0.54 g/mL. The correct answer is therefore (G).

Answer choice H reverses the order and lists from greatest to least.

6. C

Difficulty: Medium

Category: Using Data

Getting to the Answer: To determine a value beyond the given graph, extend the line of KCl. At 100°C, the solubility of KCl is ~0.56 mg/mL; since it increases as temperature increases, eliminate A and B. For every 35° increase in temperature, the solubility of KCl increases 0.1 mg/mL. Therefore, the expected solubility at 135°C would be 0.1 mg/mL greater than the solubility at 100°C, or ~0.66 mg/mL. Thus, (C) is correct.

7. C

Difficulty: High

Category: Using Data

Getting to the Answer: To determine the mass that will precipitate out, first determine the mass of solute dissolved at the higher temperature. At 70°C, $KClO_3$ has a solubility of 0.3 g/mL, so 100 mL $\times$ 0.3 g/mL = 30 g $KClO_3$. At 30°C, $KClO_3$ has a solubility of 0.1 g/mL, so 100 mL $\times$ 0.1 g/mL = 10 g $KClO_3$. The difference is 30 g − 10 g = 20 g, so (C) is correct.

Choice A incorrectly calculates the difference in solubility per 1-mL solution, not for a 100-mL solution.

Data Representation Passages

To read passages and answer questions like these:

Passage II

To investigate the suitability of magnesium alloys for bone repair, four identical ingots were prepared of alloys A, B, C, and D, respectively. Five mechanical properties—grain size (µm), yield tensile strength (MPa), ultimate tensile strength (MPa), yield compressive strength (MPa), and ultimate compressive strength (MPa)—of each ingot were tested, with the results shown in Table 1. The ingots were then immersed in simulated body fluid for a period of 15 days, and the pH level was tested at the same time each day. The results are shown in Figure 1.

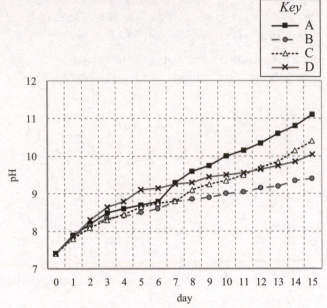

This data is from *Crystals*, Vol. 8, No. 7, June 2018, p. 271.

Figure 1

Table 1				
Average grain size (µm)	Yield tensile strength (MPa)	Ultimate tensile strength (MPa)	Yield compressive strength (MPa)	Ultimate compressive strength (MPa)
A	3.2	262.67	298.17	256.7	361.32
B	2.5	246	293.26	296.49	342.62
C	2	301.33	334.61	315.69	359.78
D	1.5	315.33	315.33	279.16	354.45

1. For each of the alloys measured in Table 1, as the grain size of the ingot increased, the ultimate compressive strength:

    A. increased only.

    B. decreased only.

    C. varied, but with no general trend.

    D. remained the same.

2. Suppose the duration of the study had been extended and additional measurements were taken on the following days. Based on Figure 1, on day 16, the pH of Ingot D would most likely have been:

    F. <10.

    G. between 10 and 10.5.

    H. between 10.5 and 11.

    J. >11.

You need to know this:

Two of the six passages you will see on test day will be Data Representation passages. In order to identify Data Representation passages as part of step 1, look for these typical characteristics:

- More figures than the other two passage types and a short 1–2 paragraph passage
- Multiple charts, tables, graphs, and diagrams

The majority of questions in Data Representation passages are either Interpreting Data questions or Using Data questions that can usually be answered based on the data in the figures.

Rarely, a question in a Data Representation set will be categorized as an Experiments question type (Experimental Design or Synthesizing Data) that might require support from the short passage. It is more common for the questions about a Research Summaries passage to include an Interpreting Data or a Using Data question. Review the "Research Summaries and Experimental Design Questions" lesson in chapter 24 for more information on how to strategically approach Research Summaries.

You need to do this:

Identifying the variables and units of each figure before moving straight to the questions. The "Interpreting Data Questions" and "Using Data Questions" lessons in this chapter describe the data interpretation skills needed to answer most ACT Science Data questions:

- Identifying features of figures (headings, units, axis labels, etc.)
- Determining how the value of one variable changes as the value of another changes
- Identifying mathematical relationships among data (linear, exponential, etc.)
- Reading values from figures with two or three variables
- Interpolating and extrapolating from data points
- Translating information into a table, graph, or diagram
- Analyzing given information when presented with new information

When presented with a complex figure:

- Focus on the variables, units, axes, and legend (if applicable) during your initial review and block out the rest
- When returning to the figure after reading a question, check the figure key or table headings to ensure you are referring to the correct variable(s)
- Circle relevant points to avoid distractions when comparing data from multiple curves in a graph or multiple rows/columns in a table

Explanation

Identify

The small section of introductory text followed only by a table and a figure indicate that this is a Data Representation passage.

Analyze

Skip the text in this Data Representation passage and move straight to the figures. You can go back for more information if needed.

Table 1: The rows indicate that four samples (A–D) are being tested; the columns indicate that five measurements (grain size, yield tensile strength, ultimate tensile strength, yield compressive strength, and ultimate compressive strength) are being taken.

Figure 1: The x-axis is time in days. The y-axis is pH. Note that for all four samples, pH increases as the number of days increases (positive correlation).

Examine, predict, and answer

Question	Explanation
1. For each of the alloys measured in Table 1, as the grain size of the ingot increased, the ultimate compressive strength: A. increased only. B. decreased only. C. varied, but with no general trend. D. remained the same.	**Answer: C** **Difficulty:** Low **Category:** Interpreting Data **Getting to the Answer:** This question asks if there's a correlation between grain size and ultimate compressive strength. Fortunately, the grain sizes are listed in the table in descending order, so to find the trend as they increase, examine what happens to the ultimate compressive strength starting at the bottom row, Ingot D, and moving to the top row, Ingot A. From Ingot D to Ingot C, there's an increase, but there's a decrease from Ingot C to Ingot B, and then there's another increase from Ingot B to Ingot A. Thus, there is no general trend, which means that (C) is correct. Choices A and B are incorrect because the ultimate compressive strength both increased and decreased as grain size increased; similarly, D is incorrect because the compressive strength did not remain the same as grain size increased.
2. Suppose the duration of the study had been extended and additional measurements were taken on the following days. Based on Figure 1, on day 16, the pH of Ingot D would most likely have been: F. <10. G. between 10 and 10.5. H. between 10.5 and 11. J. >11.	**Answer: G** **Difficulty:** Medium **Category:** Using Data **Getting to the Answer:** In order to find out what the pH level of Ingot D would likely have been on day 16, inspect the line representing that ingot in Figure 1 to see the trend in the last few days of the study. On day 13, the pH of Ingot D was approximately 9.6. On day 14, it had increased to around 9.8, and on day 15, it was approximately 10. Thus, if it continues this trend, on day 16, the pH level would have been approximately 10.2, making (G) the correct answer.

Try on Your Own

Directions: Take as much time as you need on the remaining questions in this set. Work carefully and methodically. There will be an opportunity for timed practice at the end of the chapter.

Answers are found at the end of the chapter.

3. According to Table 1, the yield compressive strength of Ingot C was closest to which of the following values?

   A. 296 MPa

   B. 316 MPa

   C. 343 MPa

   D. 360 MPa

4. Ultimate tensile strength is a measure of the maximum amount of force a material can withstand before breaking. Suppose the researchers exerted a force of 295 MPa on an unlabeled ingot, under which stress the ingot shattered. The unlabeled ingot was most likely composed of the same alloy as:

   F. Ingot A.

   G. Ingot B.

   H. Ingot C.

   J. Ingot D.

5. A *biocompatible* material is one capable of being implanted into the body without causing any harm to the surrounding tissues. Suppose that a pH above 9 is potentially harmful to human bone and tissue growth. According to Figure 1, Ingot A would be biocompatible for:

   A. 5 days.

   B. 6 days.

   C. 7 days.

   D. 8 days.

Science

Interpreting Data Questions

To answer a question like this:

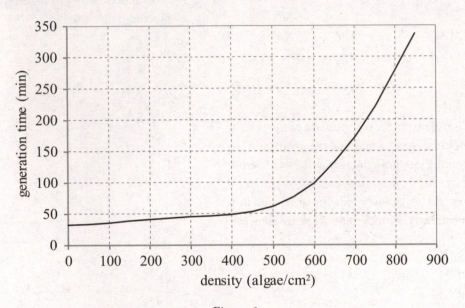

Figure 1

Based on Figure 1, if a colony of *Dactylococcopsis salina*, a type of algae, covered a pond floor with a density of 400 algae per square centimeter, approximately how long would its generation time most likely be?

A.   20 min

B.   50 min

C.   100 min

D.   200 min

You need to know this:

When you read from a graph or table, don't make an uninformed guess about the value. Instead, use your pencil to track what you are looking for:

- In a graph, find the value of a data point by tracing or drawing a line up from the *x*-axis and over to the *y*-axis or vice versa
- In a table, circle data to keep your eyes from reading the wrong row or column

You can use your answer grid as a straightedge to help determine values, but be careful not to write on it unintentionally.

Data in tables may not always be in ascending or descending order.

- When the data is not in order, use your pencil and the margin space to reorder the data for one variable from least to greatest or greatest to least.
- Then, reorder the other variable and match the data of the other variable to the reordered data to identify the trend(s).

Some Interpreting Data questions will ask you to determine a trend in the data; that is, how one variable changes in response to another.

Sometimes these data will form a linear relationship.

- A linear relationship is one where a specific change in the independent variable will cause the dependent variable to change by the same amount each time.
- When plotted on a graph, the data form a straight line.
- The variables may be directly or inversely related.

Other times, data will form an exponential relationship.

- An exponential relationship is one where a specific change in the independent variable will cause the dependent variable to change by the same percent each time.
- When plotted on a graph, the data forms a nonlinear relationship, the exact shape of which depends on the power of the exponent.
- Exponential relationships also can be direct or inverse.

You need to do this:

- Determine the type of relationship(s), if any, formed by the data
  - If the dependent variable changes at a constant rate as the independent variable is changed, the relationship is linear.
  - If the dependent variable changes at an exponential rate as the independent variable is changed, the relationship is exponential.
- Identify whether the relationship between variables is direct or inverse or note that there is not a clear relationship between variables.
  - If, as one variable increases, the other also increases (or, as one variable decreases, the other decreases), the relationship is direct (positive slope).
  - If, as one variable increases, the other decreases, or vice versa, the relationship is inverse (negative slope).
  - If, as one variable doubles, the other quadruples, then the relationship is direct.
  - If, instead, as one variable doubles, the other is quartered, then the relationship is inverse.

Explanation

Identify

This question may appear to be missing a passage, but all ACT Science questions are associated with a passage; the fact that the question can be answered using only Figure I is an indication that this question is likely associated with a Data Representation passage.

Analyze

Identify the key information in the figure:

Figure 1: axes are algae density vs. generation time; units are algae/cm^2 and min, respectively; there is an exponential, direct relationship

Examine, predict, and answer

The question stem directly references Figure 1 and asks for the generation time that would be associated with a density of 400 algae/cm^2.

Using Figure 1, look to where the graph intersects with the *x*-value of 400. The *y*-value that corresponds with this time is 50. Thus, an algae with a density of 400 algae/cm^2 would have a generation time of 50 min. Now, look at the answer choices and see that this is a match for (B).

Drills

If Interpreting Data questions give you trouble, study the information above and try out these drill questions before completing the Try on Your Own questions below.

a.   Identify the trend in Figure A:

b.   Identify the trend in Figure B:

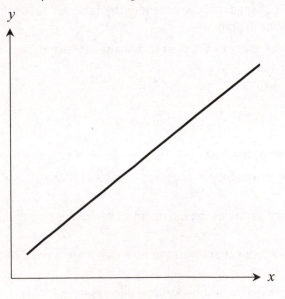

Figure A

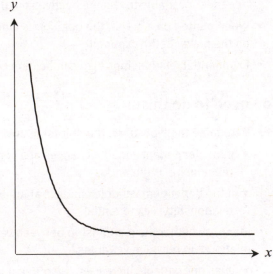

Figure B

c. Identify the relationship between A and B in Figure C:

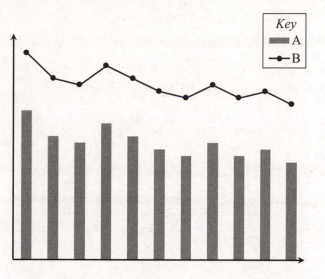

Figure C

d. Identify the relationship between minutes walking and energy consumed in Table D:

Table D	
Time walking (min)	**Energy used (Cal)**
2	10
4	20
6	30
8	40
10	50

e. Identify the relationship between pH and $[H^+]$ in Table E:

Table E	
pH	**$[H^+]$ (µmol/L)**
3	1,000
4	100
5	10
6	1
7	0.1
8	0.01

Try on Your Own

Directions: Take as much time as you need on these questions. Work carefully and methodically. There will be an opportunity for timed practice at the end of the chapter.

Answers are found at the end of the chapter.

Passage III

Gravitational acceleration, g, is the acceleration of an object due to gravity. The conventional standard value of g at the Earth's surface is exactly 9.80665 m/sec^2. Scientists wished to study variations in g at various latitudes, altitudes, and depths. They measured the gravitational acceleration of a 5-kg block in a vacuum as a function of (north) latitude at sea level and of altitude at 15°N latitude. The results are plotted in Figure 1.

To calculate gravitational acceleration as a function of depth in the Earth's interior, they used $g(d) = 2.8 \times 10^{-7}(R - d)\rho$, where R is the Earth's radius of 6,371 km, d is the Earth's depth, and ρ is the density at depth d (see Figure 2).

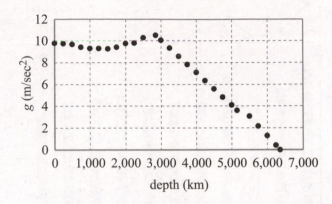

Figure 2

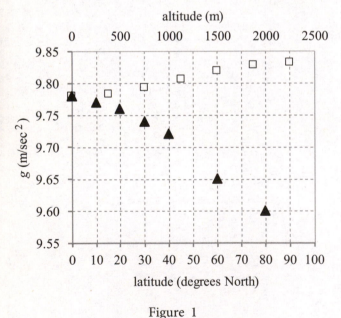

Figure 1

1. According to Figure 1, at approximately what latitude is the gravitational acceleration at 9.81 m/s^2 at sea level?

    A. 0°N
    B. 20°N
    C. 50°N
    D. 90°N

2. According to Figure 1, as altitude increases, gravitational acceleration:

    F. increases only.
    G. decreases only.
    H. increases and then decreases.
    J. decreases and then increases.

Drill answers from previous page:

a. linear, positive

b. exponential, negative

c. direct

d. direct

e. inverse

3. Based on Figure 1, the gravitational acceleration when a block is at an altitude of 500 meters above sea level is approximately:

   A. 9.60 m/s^2.

   B. 9.65 m/s^2.

   C. 9.76 m/s^2.

   D. 9.80 m/s^2.

5. The core of the Earth is between 2,900-6,371 kilometers deep. According to Figure 2, as core depth increases, gravitational acceleration:

   A. increases only.

   B. decreases only.

   C. increases and then decreases.

   D. decreases and then increases.

4. At the center of the Earth, $d = R$. Based on Figure 2, what is the acceleration due to gravity, in meters per second squared, at the Earth's center?

   F. 0

   G. 4.9

   H. 9.8

   J. 10.3

6. Assume the Earth is a sphere; the radius of the Earth's interior layers is measured from the Earth's center, whereas the depth of the interior layers is measured from the surface. Based on Figure 2 and the passage, at approximately what radius is the gravitational acceleration 4 m/s^2?

   F. 1,300 km

   G. 2,000 km

   H. 5,100 km

   J. 6,300 km

Using Data Questions

To answer a question like this:

The utilization and replenishment of Earth's carbon supply is a cyclic process involving all living matter. This cycle is shown in the following diagram.

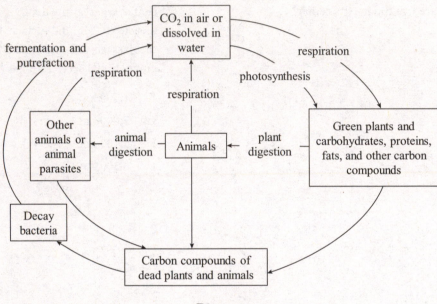

Diagram

Consider the carbon cycle illustrated in the diagram. What effect would a sudden drop in the amount of Earth's decay bacteria have on the amount of carbon dioxide in the atmosphere?

A. The CO_2 level would drop to a life-threatening level since bacteria are the sole source of CO_2.

B. The CO_2 level would rise because bacteria usually consume CO_2.

C. The CO_2 level would decrease but not completely drop because bacteria are not the only source of CO_2.

D. The CO_2 level would increase slightly due to an imbalance in the carbon cycle.

You need to know this:

The ACT Science section does NOT allow for the use of a calculator. This means any calculations required by these questions are readily solvable in your head or with paper and pencil.

Keeping track of the units in the passage and the figures as well as in the question stem and the choices requires close attention and careful scratchwork. Calculations could involve numbers presented in scientific notation.

Some Using Data questions will ask you to solve for a value that isn't given directly in the table or figure and may require **interpolation**, **extrapolation**, or determination of a **line of best fit**.

- Interpolation means estimating a value between known data points.
- Extrapolation means estimating a value outside the known range.
- A line of best fit is the line that most closely matches the pattern in the data.

Other Using Data questions will ask you to draw a conclusion about the information presented based on data and a new scenario.

You need to do this:

- When questions ask you to extrapolate or predict the value of a data point that is beyond the range of the presented data, assume the data trend continues on the table or graph. For instance, if the trend of the data in a graph is increasing linearly, assume it will continue to increase linearly.
- For data in a scatterplot, a general trend can be determined by looking at the line of best fit. This line should pass through the center of the data points and may pass through some of the points, none of the points, or all of the points.
- Questions that ask you to draw new conclusions often include key terms like "suppose" or "consider" in their question stems.

Explanation

Identify

This question may appear to be missing a passage, but all ACT Science questions are associated with a passage; the fact that the question can be answered using only the diagram is an indication that this question is likely associated with a Data Representation passage.

Analyze

Identify the key information in the diagram:

- **Diagram:** don't get bogged down in the details before getting to the associated question; the big picture is that carbon cycles between the air/water and plants/animals/bacteria through various forms of ingestion and respiration.

Examine, predict, and answer

The question stem directly refers you to the diagram and asks you to determine the impact that decreasing the number of decay bacteria would have on the amount of carbon dioxide in the atmosphere.

Predict the expected effect on carbon dioxide:

- The arrow from "Decay bacteria" to "CO_2 in air or dissolved in water" indicates that these bacteria produce CO_2 through fermentation and putrefaction.

- Thus, decreasing the amount of decay bacteria will reduce the amount of CO_2 in the air/water.

- However, animals and animal parasites also produce CO_2 through respiration, so a decrease in the decay bacteria would not completely deplete CO_2 levels.

Choice (C) is correct.

Drills

If Using Data questions give you trouble, study the information above and try out these drill questions before completing the Try on Your Own questions below. Drill answers can be found on the bottom of page 729.

a. Based on Figure A, what is the approximate amount of dissolved oxygen, in milligrams per liter, at a water temperature of 5°C ?

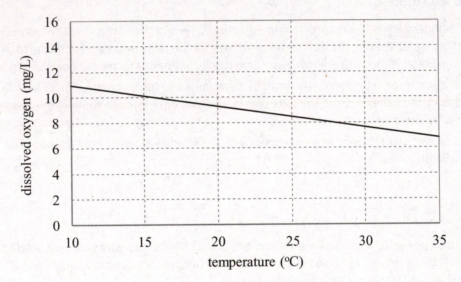

Figure A

b. According to Figure B, the temperature at which the rate of oxygen consumption is 4 mL/g h is approximately how many times greater than the temperature at which carbon dioxide production is at the same rate?

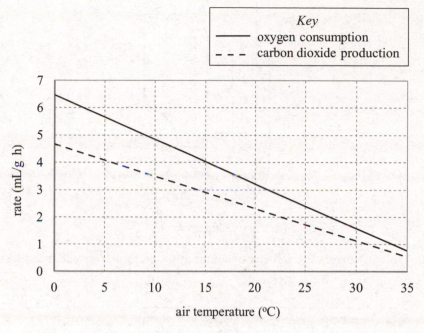

Figure B

c. According to Figure C, what is the approximate mean surface temperature, in degrees Fahrenheit, at a distance of 250 million miles from the sun?

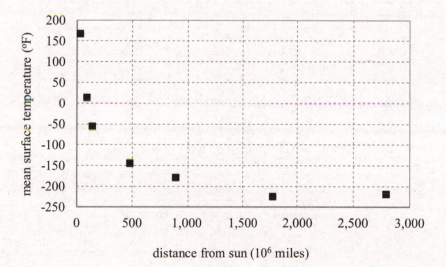

distance from sun (10^6 miles)

Figure C

d.   Based on the diagram, if the gas pressure is increased, will *h* increase, stay the same, or decrease?

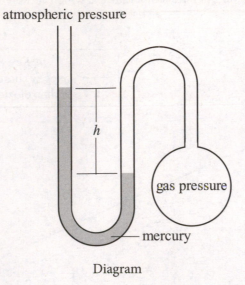

atmospheric pressure

h

gas pressure

mercury

Diagram

e.   According to Table E, what is the velocity of sound in water, in meters per second, at a density of 990 kg/m³ ?

Table E	
Density (kg/m³)	Velocity of sound in water (m/s)
1,000	1,447
998	1,482
996	1,509
992	1,529
988	1,543
983	1,552

f.   Based on Table F, what is the force, in Newtons, for a mass of 290 g ?

Table F	
Mass (g)	Force (N)
70	0.15
110	0.65
150	1.15
190	1.65
230	2.15
270	2.65

Try on Your Own

Directions: Take as much time as you need on these questions. Work carefully and methodically. There will be an opportunity for timed practice at the end of the chapter.

Answers are found at the end of the chapter.

Passage IV

A solution is a mixture composed of a solute (usually solid or gas) dissolved in a solvent (usually liquid). Solutions that can conduct an electrical current are called electrolytes. A study was conducted to examine the conditions that affect solute conductivity.

Various solutes were dissolved in 100 ml of water at 25°C in quantities of 10 mg and 30 mg. Table 1 shows the conductivity of each solution measured in millisiemens per centimeter (mS/cm). Figure 1 shows the conductivity of each solution at various temperatures (C).

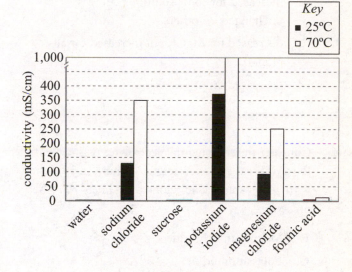

Figure 1

Table 1		
Solute	Conductivity measurement (mS/cm) of 10 mg	Conductivity measurement (mS/cm) of 30 mg
Water (H_2O)	0.0	0.0
Sodium chloride (NaCl)	73.6	129.7
Sucrose ($C_{12}H_{22}O_{11}$)	0.0	0.0
Potassium iodide (KI)	119.2	371.8
Magnesium chloride ($MgCl_2$)	102.8	93.3
Formic acid (HCOOH)	3.6	4.8

1. Based on the results, which of the following solutions of NaCl should conduct the most electricity?

   A. 10 g in 100 mL of H_2O at 10°C
   B. 20 g in 100 mL of H_2O at 20°C
   C. 20 g in 100 mL of H_2O at 70°C
   D. 30 g in 100 mL of H_2O at 80°C

2. Suppose that when a solute reaches saturation, the conductivity of the solution decreases. Which of the following solutes most likely has a saturation point of 20 mg per 100 ml H_2O ?

   F. NaCl
   G. KI
   H. $MgCl_2$
   J. HCOOH

Drill answers from previous page:

a. 12

b. 15 ÷ 5 = 3

c. –100

d. increases

e. between 1,529 and 1,543

f. 2.9

3. Consider the data presented in Figure 1. As the temperature of the electrolytic solutions was increased, the conductivity:

    A. increased only.

    B. increased for some solutions but was unchanged for others.

    C. decreased for $MgCl_2$ but increased for all others.

    D. decreased only.

4. Consider the statement, "Electrolytes dissociate into ions, whereas non-electrolytes do not." In a solution with which solute would ions most likely NOT be present?

    F. Magnesium chloride

    G. Potassium iodide

    H. Sucrose

    J. Sodium chloride

5. Consider the statement, "Strong electrolytes are good conductors of electricity; weak electrolytes are poor conductors of electricity." According to the results of the study, which of the following is most likely to be a poor electrolyte?

    A. H_2O

    B. NaCl

    C. KI

    D. HCOOH

6. Suppose a solution of potassium iodide (KI) was created using 20 mg of solute at 25°C. According to Table 1, the conductivity of this solution would most likely be:

    F. less than 119 mS/cm.

    G. between 119 mS/cm and 371.8 mS/cm.

    H. between 371.8 mS/cm and 1,000.9 mS/cm.

    J. greater than 1,000.9 mS/cm.

Science

How Much Have You Learned?

Directions: For test-like practice, give yourself 6 minutes to complete this question set. Be sure to study the explanations, even for questions you got correct. They can be found at the end of this chapter.

Passage V

When a spring of L cm in length having a spring constant k is hung vertically with a mass of m attached, the downward force of gravity (g) displaces the spring x cm to its equilibrium position. Pulling further than x cm downward and then releasing will cause the spring to oscillate up and down. The time it takes to complete one cycle is called "period of oscillation (T)."

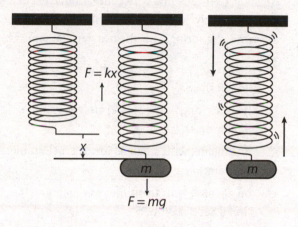

Diagram

To examine the effect of gravity on displacement, x was calculated for a spring for different m on the surface of Earth, Titan (Saturn's largest moon), and Jupiter (see Figure 1). For the same spring on Earth, Figure 2 shows T plotted against m.

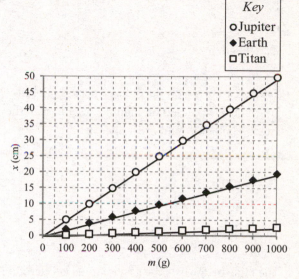

Figure 1

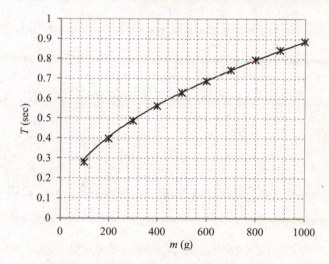

Figure 2

Science

1. Based on Figure 1, what is the expected displacement of the spring on Earth's surface with a block of 0.8 kg attached?

   A. 1 cm
   B. 10 cm
   C. 15 cm
   D. 40 cm

2. Suppose a spring on Earth has a period of oscillation of 1 sec. Based on Figure 2, the mass of the attached block would most likely be:

   F. 5 g.
   G. 20 g.
   H. 400 g.
   J. 1,300 g.

3. The table below lists the gravitational acceleration (in m/sec^2) for four different astronomical bodies. Based on Figure 1, would the displacement for a given mass on Earth be greater or less than the displacement for that same mass on Mercury?

Planet or moon	Gravitational acceleration at surface (m/sec^2)
Jupiter	24.9
Earth	9.8
Mercury	3.7
Titan	1.4

   A. Greater than; as gravitational acceleration increases, displacement increases.
   B. Greater than; as gravitational acceleration increases, displacement decreases.
   C. Less than; as gravitational acceleration increases, displacement increases.
   D. Less than; as gravitational acceleration increases, displacement decreases.

4. Suppose the spring in Figure 1 has a displacement of 10 cm on Jupiter's surface. For the spring to have the same displacement on Earth's surface, m would have to be approximately:

   F. 2.5 times greater than that on Jupiter's surface.
   G. 2.5 times less than that on Jupiter's surface.
   H. 250 times greater than that on Jupiter's surface.
   J. 250 times less than that on Jupiter's surface.

5. Consider the relationship between m, g, x, and k in Figure 1. If two springs having the same spring constant k are attached with different masses m and $2m$ respectively, in order for displacement x to be the same, the spring with the heavier mass must be:

   A. half as long as the spring attached to the lighter mass.
   B. twice as long as the spring attached to the lighter mass.
   C. on a planet with a half as much gravitational acceleration.
   D. on a planet with two times as much gravitational acceleration.

6. The *frequency* of motion for a mass on a spring is defined as the number of oscillations per unit of time. Based on Figure 2, the spring with the highest frequency would have an attached mass of:

   F. 100 g.
   G. 200 g.
   H. 1,000 g.
   J. 1,200 g.

Reflect

Directions: Take a few minutes to recall what you've learned and what you've been practicing in this chapter. Consider the following questions, jot down your best answer for each one, and then compare your reflections to the expert responses on the following page. Use your level of confidence to determine what to do next.

1. When presented with a complex figure that has no clear trends, what key features will an ACT expert focus on?

   _____

   _____

   _____

2. When might an ACT expert find it useful to make marks or circles on a figure or table?

   _____

   _____

   _____

3. What does an ACT expert do when data in a table aren't presented in ascending or descending order?

   _____

   _____

   _____

4. Why is it that both linear and exponential relationships can be either direct or inverse?

   _____

   _____

   _____

5. When drawing a line of best fit, does it need to pass through all the data points?

   _____

   _____

   _____

6. How will you approach Data Representation passages differently as you continue to practice and improve your performance in the ACT Science section?

   _____

   _____

   _____

Responses

1. When presented with a complex figure that has no clear trends, what key features will an ACT expert focus on?

In figures that are overwhelming at first glance or contain no clear pattern, it is best to revert to focusing on the variables, units, axes, and any legends that are present and save any analysis of the data for when you're answering a specific question.

2. When might an ACT expert find it useful to make marks or circles on a figure or table?

ACT experts often find it useful to circle relevant points to avoid distractions, especially when comparing data from multiple curves in a graph or multiple rows/columns in a table.

3. What does an ACT expert do when data in a table aren't presented in ascending or descending order?

Use your pencil to rewrite the data to order one variable from least to greatest or vice versa. Then, match the data of the other variable to the reordered data to identify the trend.

4. Why is it that both linear and exponential relationships can be either direct or inverse?

Direct and inverse refer to the direction of the effect that changing the independent variable has on the dependent variable, while linear and exponential refer to whether a specific change in the independent variable will cause the dependent variable to change by the same amount each time (linear) or by the same percent each time (exponential). These concepts overlap, as a positive increase in the independent variable could cause the dependent variable to change by a positive amount (direct, linear), a positive percent (direct, exponential), a negative amount (inverse, linear), or a negative percent (inverse, exponential).

5. When drawing a line of best fit, does it need to pass through all the data points?

The line of best fit is the line that most closely matches the pattern in the data. This line should pass through the center of the data points and may pass through some of the points, none of the points, or all of the points.

6. How will you approach Data Representation passages differently as you continue to practice and improve your performance in the ACT Science section?

There is no one-size-fits-all answer here. Reflect on your own habits in interpreting data presented in tables and figures as well as answering ACT Science questions and give yourself an honest assessment of your strengths and weaknesses. Consider the strategies you've seen experts use in this chapter, and put them to work in your own practice to increase your accuracy, speed, and confidence.

Next Steps

If you answered most questions correctly in the "How Much Have You Learned?" section, and if your responses to the Reflect questions were similar to those of an expert, then consider Data Representation passages an area of strength and move on to the next chapter. Come back to this topic periodically to prevent yourself from getting rusty.

If you don't yet feel confident, review the material in this chapter, then try the questions you missed again. As always, be sure to review the explanations closely. Then go online (**kaptest.com/login**) to use your Qbank for more practice. If you haven't already registered your book, do so at *kaptest.com/moreonline*.

GO ONLINE

kaptest.com/login

Answers and Explanations

Data Representation Passages

1. Review the Explanation portion of the Data Representation Passages lesson.

2. Review the Explanation portion of the Data Representation Passages lesson.

3. B

Difficulty: Low

Category: Interpreting Data

Getting to the Answer: Find the row in Table 1 for Ingot C, then look for the column representing yield compressive strength. Doing so shows this strength to be 315.69, which means that (B) is correct.

4. G

Difficulty: Low

Category: Using Data

Getting to the Answer: If a force of 295 MPa broke an ingot, that must mean that the ingot's ultimate tensile strength was less than 295 MPa. This type of strength is detailed in the fourth column of Table 1. The only ingot with an ultimate tensile strength less than 295 MPa was Ingot B; therefore, (G) is correct.

5. B

Difficulty: Medium

Category: Interpreting Data

Getting to the Answer: Find the line for Ingot A in Figure 1 and see how long it stayed below a pH level of 9. On day 6, the pH level was around 8.75, which would mean it was still biocompatible. On day 7, the pH level jumped to 9.25, which would mean that it was no longer biocompatible. Choice (B) is correct because Ingot A would be biocompatible for 6 days.

Interpreting Data Questions

1. C

Difficulty: Low

Category: Interpreting Data

Getting to the Answer: On Figure 1, draw a horizontal line from 9.81 m/s^2 over to the data for latitude and draw a vertical line from the point of intersection down to the x-axis to determine the degrees of latitude. At 9.81 m/s^2, the latitude falls somewhere between 40°N and 60°N. The only answer choice in that range is (C).

2. G

Difficulty: Low

Category: Interpreting Data

Getting to the Answer: To determine the relationship between two variables on a graph, check the trend of the data. Do the variables go up or down together, does one stay constant as the other changes, does one go down as the other goes up, or is there a more complex pattern? According to Figure 1, as altitude increases, gravitational acceleration always decreases, so the correct answer is (G).

3. C

Difficulty: Low

Category: Interpreting Data

Getting to the Answer: Pay attention to which data points go with which axis—altitude is on the top x-axis. The question asks for gravitational acceleration at 500 m above sea level. On Figure 1, locate 500 m on the top x-axis and trace the vertical line down to the data point that represents altitude (represented by a solid triangle). Then from that point, draw a horizontal line to the y-axis to determine the gravitational acceleration. The gravitational acceleration is 9.76 m/s^2, as in (C).

4. F

Difficulty: Medium

Category: Interpreting Data

Getting to the Answer: According to the stimulus, R, the Earth's radius, is equal to 6,371 km. Look at Figure 2 to see what the gravitational acceleration would be at that depth; at that point on the graph, the curve reaches the *x*-axis. This means that the acceleration due to gravity at the center of the Earth is 0, and (F) is correct.

5. B

Difficulty: Medium

Category: Interpreting Data

Getting to the Answer: Find 2,900 km and 637 km in Figure 2 and determine the trend between those points. At just before 3,000 km, or approximately 2,900 km, the curve starts trending downward, and it keeps going down until it hits 0 at 6,371 km. Since the data trends downward between these two points, (B) is correct.

6. F

Difficulty: Hard

Category: Interpreting Data

Getting to the Answer: First, use Figure 2 to determine at what depth the gravitational acceleration is 4 m/s^2: at a depth of approximately 5,000 km. Next, subtract this depth from the radius of the Earth (6,371 km, according to the passage) to see how far this point is from the Earth's center: approximately 1,300 km. Choice (F) is correct.

Calculation and Inference Questions

1. D

Difficulty: Medium

Category: Using Data

Getting to the Answer: This question requires you to extrapolate from the results in Table 1 and Figure 1. You know from comparing the NaCl values that the conductivity is higher for 30.0 g of NaCl than for 10.0 g. You also know from comparing values in Figure 1 that higher temperatures result in higher conductivity measurements. Thus, to find the NaCl solution that conducts the most electricity (in other words, the one with the highest conductivity), you should look for the choice with the most solute and the highest temperature. Choice (D) is thus correct.

2. H

Difficulty: Medium

Category: Using Data

Getting to the Answer: To determine which solute reached saturation at 20 mg per 100 ml, you need to determine which solution exhibited a decrease in conductivity when the level of solute was increased from 10 mg per 100 ml to 30 mg per 100 ml. Compare the values in Table 1. The only solute whose conductivity decreased is $MgCl_2$, so the correct answer is (H).

3. A

Difficulty: Medium

Category: Using Data

Getting to the Answer: The passage describes an electrolytic solution as one that conducts electric current; thus, only the solutions with a conductivity greater than 0 (NaCl, KI, $MgCl_2$ and HCOOH) should be considered. For each of the four electrolytes, the conductivity at 70°C was greater than at 30°C. The correct answer is (A).

Choice B incorrectly describes a trend for non-electrolyte solutions. Conductivity of $MgCl_2$ decreased (choice C) when more solute was added, not when the temperature was increased.

4. H

Difficulty: Medium

Category: Using Data

Getting to the Answer: The passage describes an electrolyte as a solution that conducts electric current. The information in the question stem indicates that non-electrolytes do not dissociate into ions; therefore, ions would not be present in a non-electrolyte solution. Sucrose had a conductivity of zero and is thus a non-electrolyte. The correct answer is (H).

5. D

Difficulty: Medium

Category: Using Data

Getting to the Answer: According to the passage, an electrolyte can conduct electric current, so H_2O (choice A) can be eliminated. Of the remaining electrolytes, NaCl and KI are both good conductors of electricity; their conductivity measurements are more than 10 times larger than HCOOH at any given concentration or temperature. The weak electrolyte is therefore HCOOH. Choice (D) is correct.

6. G

Difficulty: Low

Category: Using Data

Getting to the Answer: In order to find the most likely conductivity of a solute concentration that lies between two known concentrations, first identify the conductivity of the known concentrations. The conductivity of the new concentration is most likely to fall between these known values. According to Table 1, a 10 g KI solution had a conductivity of 119 mS/cm, and a 30 g KI solution had a conductivity of 371.8 mS/cm. Therefore, a 20 g KI solution will have a conductivity in between those values. Choice (G) is correct.

Choice H describes the conductivity of a KI solution with 30 g that has been heated above 25°C but less than 70°C.

How Much Have You Learned?

1. C

Difficulty: Low

Category: Interpreting Data

Getting to the Answer: Trace the vertical line in Figure 1 up from 800 g, which equals 0.8 kg, on the x-axis to the diamond-marked line that represents Earth. Then from the point of intersection, draw a horizontal line to the y-axis to determine the expected displacement. The displacement is approximately 15 cm, so (C) is the correct answer.

Choice A would be the displacement for a spring on Titan, and D would be the displacement for a spring on Jupiter.

2. J

Difficulty: Medium

Category: Using Data

Getting to the Answer: Use your pencil to extend the lines in graphs when required. This question directs you to Figure 2. What are the patterns in that data? For Earth, mass (m) increases as the period of oscillation (T) increases. When you extend the data curve following that trend, it's clear that the mass must be greater than 1,000 g. Only one answer, choice (J), has a mass that fits, so (J) is correct.

3. A

Difficulty: Medium

Category: Using Data

Getting to the Answer: To determine the relationship between g and x, you have to combine the information from Figure 1 with the table provided in the question stem, which lists g for each planet or moon. For any given m greater than 0 in Figure 1, the spring's displacement is the highest for Jupiter, in the middle for Earth, and the lowest for Titan. According to the table, Jupiter has the highest gravitational acceleration at 24.9 m/sec^2, followed by Earth at 9.8 m/sec^2, followed by Titan at 1.4 m/sec^2. Thus, as gravitational acceleration increases, the spring's displacement increases. Because Earth has a greater gravitational acceleration than Mercury, the displacement on Earth would be greater than on Mercury. The correct answer is (A).

4. F

Difficulty: Medium

Category: Using Data

Getting to the Answer: Approach questions methodically and you'll eliminate careless mistakes. According to Figure 1, a spring will have a displacement of 10 cm on Jupiter's surface when a mass (m) of 200 g is attached. What m would give the same spring on Earth a displacement of 10 cm? Trace the horizontal line that corresponds to 10 cm until it intersects the diamond-marked line that represents data for Earth. The intersection occurs around an m of 500 g. 500 g divided by 200 g is 2.5. Thus, to give the same displacement on Earth, m would have to be 2.5 times greater than the m for Jupiter. The correct answer is (F).

Watch out for G, which suggests that m would be 2.5 times *less*.

5. C

Difficulty: High

Category: Using Data

Getting to the Answer: The equations in Figure 1 provide the relationships between the variables m, g, x, and k: $F = mg$ and $F = kx$. Therefore, $mg = kx$. Since the spring constant and displacement are the same for each of the two springs, kx is the same value for both springs. Therefore, if mass is doubled in one spring, the gravitational acceleration must be halved in order for the equation to continue equaling kx. Answer (C) is correct.

Choices A and B are incorrect because the length of the spring is not shown to be a factor in the diagram.

6. F

Difficulty: Medium

Category: Interpreting Data

Getting to the Answer: According to the passage, the "time it takes to complete one cycle is called 'period of oscillation (T).'" Since frequency is defined as the number of oscillations per unit of time, the shorter the period of oscillation, the more oscillations are able to be completed, and thus, the higher the frequency. The fastest period of oscillation in Figure 2 is 0.29 secs and occurs when the attached mass is 100 g. Therefore, the correct choice is (F).

CHAPTER 24

Experiments

Experimental Design: 6/36 SmartPoints® (High yield)

Synthesizing Data: 6/36 SmartPoints® (High yield)

How Much Do You Know?

Directions: Try out the questions below. Show your work so that you can compare your solutions to the ones found on the next page. The "Category" heading in the explanation for each question gives the title of the lesson that covers how to solve it. If you answered the question(s) for a given lesson correctly, and if your scratchwork looks like ours, you may be able to move quickly through that lesson. If you answered incorrectly or used a different approach, you may want to take your time on that lesson.

Passage I

As part of an ecological impact study, two experiments examined the factors affecting the rate of algae growth produced under various conditions. Experimenters utilized a man-made reservoir known as Lake Eight that has two basins of equal size connected by a strait.

Experiment 1

The two basins of Lake Eight were separated by an impermeable partition (see Diagram). Basin A was fertilized with phosphorus, carbon, and nitrogen, whereas Basin B received only carbon and nitrogen. The researchers also varied the temperature of different regions within each basin. Two months after fertilization, the number of algal blooms per square meter of water surface area was measured, yielding the data in Table 1.

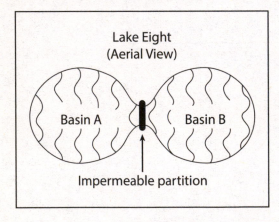

Diagram

	Table 1		
Basin	Additives	Temperature (°C)	Algal blooms per square meter
Basin A	phosphorus, carbon, and nitrogen	10	0.18
		25	0.48
		35	0.56
Basin B	carbon and nitrogen	10	0.04
		25	0.07
		35	0.08

Experiment 2

One year later, Experiment 1 was repeated, except that sodium bicarbonate ($NaHCO_3$) was added in place of phosphorus. The results are shown in Table 2.

	Table 2		
Basin	Additives	Temperature (°C)	Algal blooms per square meter
Basin A	sodium bicarbonate, carbon, and nitrogen	10	0.26
		25	0.56
		35	0.78
Basin B	carbon and nitrogen	10	0.04
		25	0.07
		35	0.08

1. Which factor was varied in Experiment 1 ?

   A. Basin surface area

   B. Algae growth rate

   C. Algal blooms per square meter

   D. Water temperature

2. Experiment 1 differed from Experiment 2 in that Experiment 2:

   F. did not fertilize Basin B with phosphorus.

   G. did not fertilize Basin A with phosphorus.

   H. did not fertilize Basin A with sodium bicarbonate.

   J. fertilized Basin B with carbon and nitrogen only.

HINT: For Q3, remember that Research Summaries passages like this one will include mostly Experiments questions, but sometimes the question set will include one or more Data questions. To learn about answering questions like this one, review the "Using Data Questions" lesson in chapter 23.

---

3. Suppose that extensive algal blooms cause pollution problems and that detergents are a major source of phosphorus in fresh water. To reduce the pollution associated with algal blooms, it would be most useful to:

   A. increase the amount of detergent present in fresh water.

   B. decrease the amount of detergent present in fresh water.

   C. replace the phosphorus in detergents with sodium bicarbonate.

   D. balance the phosphorus added to detergents with equal amounts of sodium bicarbonate.

4. Based on the results of Experiments 1 and 2, which of the following bodies of water is likely to produce the greatest number of algal blooms per square meter?

   F. A 45°C pond fertilized with sodium bicarbonate

   G. A 5°C pond fertilized with sodium bicarbonate

   H. A 45°C pond fertilized with phosphorus

   J. A 5°C pond fertilized with a mixture that is equal parts phosphorus and sodium bicarbonate

5. The experimenters chose to modify the fertilizers added to Basin A between the two experiments without changing those added to Basin B. Which of the following statements gives the most likely reason the experimenters made that choice? The experimenters:

   A. wanted to use the same control for both experiments.

   B. wanted to test variations in the amount of fertilizer used.

   C. wanted to confirm the results from Experiment 1.

   D. did not have another fertilizer to test.

6. Suppose that Basin A had not been fertilized with carbon and nitrogen in Experiment 2. At the conclusion of their two years of testing, the experimenters would NOT have been able to:

   F. measure the effect of sodium bicarbonate on algae growth.

   G. measure the effect of phosphorus on algae growth.

   H. measure the effect of carbon and nitrogen alone on algae growth.

   J. measure the effect of temperature on algae growth.

Check Your Work

1. D

Difficulty: Low

Category: Experimental Design

Getting to the Answer: Understanding the scientific method will help you score points on questions like these. An independent variable is one that is altered directly by the researchers. The description of Experiment 1 states that the researchers "varied the temperatures," so (D) is correct.

Choice A is incorrect because the surface area of each basin is constant. Choice B is incorrect because the rate of algal growth was not directly manipulated by the researchers, although it certainly had an impact on their results. Choice C is incorrect because the number of algal blooms was the dependent variable: the one the researchers measured, not the one they varied.

2. G

Difficulty: Medium

Category: Experimental Design

Getting to the Answer: In the description of Experiment 2, the only difference between it and Experiment 1 is said to be that sodium bicarbonate was used in place of phosphorus. In Experiment 1, the phosphorus was added to Basin A, so the difference between the two experiments is whether phosphorus or sodium bicarbonate was used in Basin A. Thus, (G) is correct.

Choice F is incorrect because neither experiment used phosphorus in Basin B. Experiment 2 is the experiment in which sodium bicarbonate was used in Basin B, so H is incorrect. Basin B was fertilized with only carbon and nitrogen in both experiments, so J is incorrect.

3. B

Difficulty: Medium

Category: Using Data

Getting to the Answer: You're looking for a choice that would decrease algal bloom density. Decreasing the amount of detergent would decrease the amount of phosphorus in the water, which would in turn reduce algal blooms (based on the results of Experiment 1) and the associated pollution. Choice (B), then, is correct.

Based on the results of Experiment 1, A would likely increase algal blooms; and based on the results of Experiment 2, C would also probably increase the growth of algal blooms. Choice D might also increase the growth, though the combination of phosphorus and sodium bicarbonate was not directly studied in the experiments from the passage.

4. F

Difficulty: Low

Category: Synthesizing Data

Getting to the Answer: First, identify the trends that exist in the data; then you can extrapolate those trends to evaluate the choices and determine which body of water would have the most algal blooms. As temperatures increased in both experiments, algal blooms increased, so the correct answer will be one of the choices with a higher temperature; eliminate G and J. In Experiment 2, at every temperature, sodium bicarbonate produced more algal blooms than phosphorus did at the same temperatures in Experiment 1. Thus, (F) is correct.

It should be noted that J is incorrect because the effects of using both phosphorus and sodium bicarbonate were not studied, so no conclusions can be made about how it would affect algal blooms.

5. A

Difficulty: High

Category: Experimental Design

Getting to the Answer: What role did Basin B play in Experiment 1? It acted as the control, or the baseline case, which allowed researchers to isolate the effects of phosphorus on algal bloom density. In Experiment 2, the experimenters wanted to be able to isolate the effect of adding sodium bicarbonate instead of phosphorus. Therefore, they used the same fertilizers in Basin B to allow for the same kind of comparison as in the first experiment. The correct answer is (A).

The passage does not mention how much fertilizer is used, so B is incorrect. Choice C might be tempting because the results of Experiment 2 for Basin B are the same as those of Experiment 1 for Basin B, but this is not the main reason the experimenters repeated the conditions. Choice D is incorrect since it is never suggested in the passage.

6. F

Difficulty: Low

Category: Experimental Design

Getting to the Answer: Note that the question is asking what the experiments would have been able to measure at the conclusion of their *two* years of study, meaning that this includes the results of both Experiment 1 and Experiment 2. If Basin A was not fertilized with carbon and nitrogen, then no algae growth would occur, and the effect of the added fertilizer ingredient, sodium bicarbonate, could not be measured. Thus, (F) is correct. The remaining choices were all answered by Experiment 1 and Basin B of Experiment 2.

Research Summaries and Experimental Design Questions

To read passages and answer questions like these:

Passage II

The Brazilian tree frog (*Hyla faber*) exchanges gases through both its skin and its lungs. The exchange rate depends on the temperature of the frogs' environment. A pair of experiments was performed to investigate this dependence.

Experiment 1

Fifty frogs were placed in a controlled atmosphere that, with the exception of temperature, was designed to simulate the frogs' native habitat. The temperature was varied from 5°C to 25°C, and equilibrium was attained before each successive temperature change. The amount of oxygen absorbed by the frogs' lungs and skin per hour was measured, and the results for all the frogs were averaged. These results are shown in Table 1.

Table 1		
Temperature (°C)	Moles O_2 absorbed/hr	
	Skin	Lungs
5	15.4	8.3
10	22.7	35.1
15	43.6	64.9
20	42.1	73.5
25	40.4	78.7

Experiment 2

The same frogs were placed under the same conditions as in Experiment 1. For this experiment, the amount of carbon dioxide eliminated through the frogs' skin and lungs was measured. The results were averaged and are shown below in Table 2.

Table 2		
Temperature (°C)	Moles CO_2 eliminated/hr	
	Skin	Lungs
5	18.9	2.1
10	43.8	12.7
15	79.2	21.3
20	91.6	21.9
25	96.5	21.4

1. Which of the following factors did the researchers intentionally vary?

    A. The number of frogs studied

    B. The humidity of the frogs' simulated habitat

    C. The temperature of the frogs' simulated habitat

    D. The amount of oxygen in the frogs' simulated habitat

2.   Which of the following statements about gas
      exchange in *Hyla faber* is consistent with the results
      of Experiments 1 and 2? The Brazilian tree frog:

      F.   exchanges oxygen and carbon dioxide
           primarily through the skin.

      G.   absorbs oxygen primarily in the lungs but
           eliminates carbon dioxide primarily through
           the skin.

      H.   absorbs more oxygen in the lungs than carbon
           dioxide eliminated through the skin.

      J.   exchanges oxygen and carbon dioxide through
           both the skin and lungs equally.

3.   Which of the following statements describes a
      difference between Experiments 1 and 2?
      In Experiment 2:

      A.   a different species of tree frog was used.

      B.   a broader range of temperatures was studied.

      C.   only oxygen absorption through the skin was
           measured.

      D.   carbon-dioxide elimination was measured.

4.   Why was the study designed so that the frogs
      were placed in a controlled atmosphere designed
      to simulate their native habitat? These conditions
      ensured that the researchers could:

      F.   manipulate some variables but leave other
           elements as they were naturally.

      G.   prevent the predation of frogs by their natural
           predators.

      H.   control the frogs' food supply.

      J.   control the frogs' oxygen intake.

5.   Which of the following best explains why the
      researchers allowed the temperature in the
      simulated habitat to achieve equilibrium before
      each temperature change? The researchers wanted
      to allow:

      A.   time for additional oxygen to be removed from
           the habitat.

      B.   time for the frogs to adjust their gas exchange
           rate to the new temperature.

      C.   time for the researchers to increase or decrease
           carbon dioxide levels in the habitat.

      D.   time for the habitat's humidity level to adjust
           with the new temperature.

6. The amount of oxygen absorbed through the skin at various temperatures is best represented by which of the following graphs?

F.

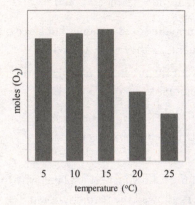

G.

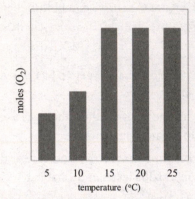

H.

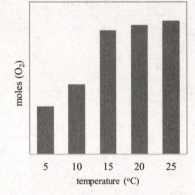

J.

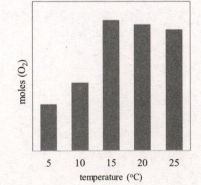

Science

You need to know this:

Experimental Design questions most often appear as part of a Research Summaries passage question set.

Research Summaries

Three of the six passages you will see on test day will be Research Summaries. In order to identify a Research Summaries passage as part of step 1, look for these typical characteristics:

- an introductory paragraph or two providing background information about a scientific phenomenon and/or some additional details on an experimental setup
- a series of experiments, differentiated with helpful labels like "Study 1" and "Experiment 2"
- details about each experiment, typically focusing on method
- at least one graph or table with experimental results

Research Summaries passages can feature the question types discussed in chapter 23 that are about the results of the experiments. However, these passages will focus on questions related to experimental design and the scientific method.

Experimental Design Questions

Approximately 20%–30% of the questions in the ACT Science Test fall into this category, and they appear more often within Research Summaries passages than with any other passage type. These questions involve:

- evaluating experimental tools and procedures
- interpreting experimental design by identifying variables and controls
- analyzing experimental designs and results
- predicting results of additional trials or experiments
- identifying the expected impact of modifying an experiment's design

The scientific method is a well-known process for conducting scientific research, but the specific steps and terminology used to describe the method can vary. For the ACT Science Test, you might find it helpful to think of the scientific method as the following set of steps:

1. Ask a question based on observations and initial research.

    Observation and Research: All scientific investigation begins by noticing a phenomenon that is interesting and posing a question about it.

2. Formulate a hypothesis that answers the question.

    Hypothesis: Based on initial observations and research, scientists form hypotheses. A hypothesis is an attempt to explain a particular observation and often indicates the independent and dependent variables.

3. Design an experiment to test the hypothesis.

    Experimental Design: A good experimental design will isolate the effect of one or more independent variables (manipulated quantities) on one or more dependent variables (measured quantities).

    Independent Variable: The variable being manipulated by the experimenters, typically the basis of the groups in the experiment

    Dependent Variable: The variable being measured by the experimenters, typically the "results" of the study

4. Conduct the experiment and record data.

    Control: A control group serves as a baseline within an experiment that allows for effective comparison. A control group is a group that does not receive any treatment or manipulation by the independent variable.

5. Analyze the data and draw conclusions.

   Analysis and Conclusion: Once data is obtained, scientists will look at that data and interpret it. Using trends in the results, scientists can conclude whether or not their hypothesis is supported.

6. Communicate the results.

   Publish: As a final step, scientists will often publish their results to share them with the scientific community.

Experimental Design questions will require you to:

- recognize and define hypotheses, variables, and control group
- describe and apply information from one or more experiments in terms of the scientific method

You need to do this:

When working through step 2, analyzing the passage and figures strategically, for Research Summaries passages in particular, you should NOT spend time trying to understand or analyze everything, and you should NOT be intimidated by technical terminology. You *should*:

- examine the introductory text for the central idea and purpose of the experiments
- move quickly though the text of the experiments and their methods, only pausing to underline key words
- locate variables in the figures and, if applicable, identify whether the variables are independent or dependent
- locate units of measurement
- identify noticeable trends

Again, do NOT spend time trying to understand or analyze everything; you will return to examine the text and figures in more detail when questions reference them.

As you complete step 2 for Research Summaries, identify these mentally or in the margins:

- the hypothesis for each experiment: What is the researcher attempting to prove or disprove?
- the independent variable(s) for each experiment: What is the researcher manipulating?
- the dependent variable(s) for each experiment: What is the researcher measuring?
- the control group for each experiment: What will the researcher use as a baseline for the final results?

Some Experimental Design questions will test your ability to determine:

- the purpose of an experiment: What is the researcher testing?
- the methods of an experiment: look to the experimental design. What group is serving as the control and what group is being tested/treated?
- the results of an experiment: What form did the researcher use to share the results? What do the results mean in terms of a real-world situation?

Identifying the hypotheses, variables, and control group make it easier to determine the purpose of an experiment, evaluate its methods, and interpret its results, so considering all six steps of the scientific method while analyzing the passage and figures will help you work through Research Summaries more efficiently and effectively.

Explanation

Identify

Passage II includes a short introductory paragraph followed by sections with clearly labeled headings of Experiment 1 and Experiment 2, so this is a Research Summaries passage.

Analyze

Central idea: The first paragraph indicates there will be two experiments examining the relationship between the tree frog's gas exchange through its skin/lungs and atmospheric temperature.

Experiment 1 and Table 1: Quickly skim the methodology described in the text and describe the important information in the table:

- Oxygen absorption in the skin and lungs (dependent variables) is being measured at five different temperatures: 5, 10, 15, 20, and 25°C (independent variable)
- Trend in skin absorption: increases dramatically from 5 to 15, decreases slightly from 15 to 25
- Trend in lung absorption: increases dramatically from 5 to 15, then continues to increase from 15 to 25

Experiment 2 and Table 2: Again, skim the text and describe the important information in the table:

- Same table setup and independent variable, except carbon dioxide elimination (dependent variable) is being measured instead of oxygen absorption
- Trend in skin elimination: increases dramatically from 5 to 15, then continues to increase from 15 to 25
- Trend in lung elimination: increases dramatically from 5 to 15, then is fairly constant from 15 to 25

Examine, predict, and answer

Question	Explanation
1. Which of the following factors did the researchers intentionally vary? A. The number of frogs studied B. The humidity of the frogs' simulated habitat C. The temperature of the frogs' simulated habitat D. The amount of oxygen in the frogs' simulated habitat	**1. C** **Difficulty:** Low **Category:** Experimental Design **Getting to the Answer:** The phrase *intentionally vary* indicates that this question is asking for the independent variable. The passage explains that, for both experiments, "temperature was varied from 5°C to 25°C," so choice (C) is correct. Choice A is incorrect because the passage states that the number of frogs studied was constant (50 total). Choice B is incorrect because the passage does not mention humidity. Watch out for D, which is a common trap for these kinds of questions. The amount of oxygen that the frogs *absorbed* (not the amount in the habitat) varied according to temperature, but that was the dependent variable in Experiment 1, not the independent variable.

Question	Explanation
2. Which of the following statements about gas exchange in *Hyla faber* is consistent with the results of Experiments 1 and 2? The Brazilian tree frog: F. exchanges oxygen and carbon dioxide primarily through the skin. G. absorbs oxygen primarily in the lungs but eliminates carbon dioxide primarily through the skin. H. absorbs more oxygen in the lungs than carbon dioxide eliminated through the skin. J. exchanges oxygen and carbon dioxide through both the skin and lungs equally.	2. **G** **Difficulty:** Medium **Category:** Synthesizing Data **Getting to the Answer:** This question requires synthesizing data in both Tables 1 and 2 and is asking about the primary location of gas exchange. Table 1 indicates that the frogs absorb more oxygen in the lungs than in the skin, except at the lowest temperature. Choice F is therefore incorrect. Table 2 indicates that the frogs eliminate carbon dioxide primarily through the skin, as the moles eliminated through the skin are always higher than the moles eliminated by the lungs. The findings are therefore consistent with (G). The amount of carbon dioxide eliminated through the skin is greater than the amount of oxygen absorbed at any given temperature, so H is incorrect. The gas exchange rates are not equal, so J is incorrect.
3. Which of the following statements describes a difference between Experiments 1 and 2? In Experiment 2: A. a different species of tree frog was used. B. a broader range of temperatures was studied. C. only oxygen absorption through the skin was measured. D. carbon-dioxide elimination was measured.	3. **D** **Difficulty:** Low **Category:** Experimental Design **Getting to the Answer:** According to the description of Experiment 2, the frogs studied and the conditions of the habitat were the same as in Experiment 1. The only difference was that "the amount of carbon dioxide eliminated through the skin and lungs was measured" instead of the amount of oxygen absorbed. Choice (D) is thus correct.

Question	Explanation

Question

4. Why was the study designed so that the frogs were placed in a controlled atmosphere designed to simulate their native habitat? These conditions ensured that the researchers could:

    F. manipulate some variables but leave other elements as they were naturally.

    G. prevent the predation of frogs by their natural predators.

    H. control the frogs' food supply.

    J. control the frogs' oxygen intake.

Explanation

4. F

Difficulty: Low

Category: Experimental Design

Getting to the Answer: According to the introduction of the passage, the researchers wanted to investigate the dependence of gas exchange on temperature in the Brazilian tree frog. If the researchers had constructed an artificial environment that greatly differed from the frogs' natural habitat, then it would be impossible to tell whether temperature alone was responsible for changes in oxygen absorption and carbon dioxide elimination, or whether there was some other environmental difference or combination of differences that caused these changes. Making sure that the only differences are those that occur in the independent variable ensures more accurate results. Choice (F) is correct.

Choices G and H are incorrect because predators and food supply are factors outside the scope of the experiment that are unrelated to the variables in question. Choice J is incorrect because oxygen intake was not directly controlled by the experimenters; rather, it was one of the dependent variables that was measured.

Question	Explanation
5. Which of the following best explains why the researchers allowed the temperature in the simulated habitat to achieve equilibrium before each temperature change? The researchers wanted to allow: A. time for additional oxygen to be removed from the habitat. B. time for the frogs to adjust their gas exchange rate to the new temperature. C. time for the researchers to increase or decrease carbon dioxide levels in the habitat. D. time for the habitat's humidity level to adjust with the new temperature.	**5. B** **Difficulty:** Medium **Category:** Experimental Design **Getting to the Answer:** According to the first paragraph of the passage, the researchers were interested in investigating the dependence of the frogs' gas exchange rate on the temperature of their environment. The description of the first experiment also indicates that the researchers simulated the frogs' native habitat "with the exception of temperature." Thus, the researchers did not remove oxygen from the habitat or modify its carbon dioxide levels, meaning A and C can be eliminated. Similarly, there is no suggestion in the passage that the humidity level changed, so D is also incorrect. This leaves only (B). And indeed, to achieve their stated purpose, the researchers had to allow the frogs' rate of gas exchange to adjust to each new temperature. Otherwise, the data they collected would not actually demonstrate a connection between the independent variable and the dependent variable. Choice (B) is correct.

Question	Explanation

6. The amount of oxygen absorbed through the skin at various temperatures is best represented by which of the following graphs?

F.

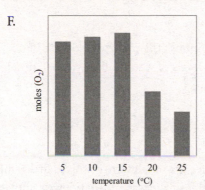

G.

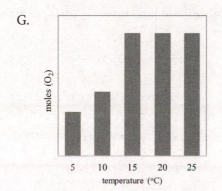

H.

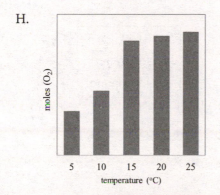

J.

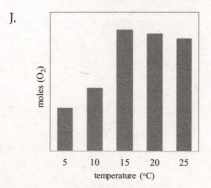

6.   J

Difficulty: Low

Category: Synthesizing Data

Getting to the Answer: Because the answer choices do not have scales on their *y*-axes, you should compare the data table to the answer choice graphs by identifying the trend of the data. Moles of oxygen absorbed through the skin are lowest at 5°C, increase to a peak at 15°C , and then slightly decrease at 25°C . That matches (J).

Choice F also shows an increase followed by a decrease. However, the values for 20°C and 25°C are lower than the values at 5°C and 10°C; this is inconsistent with the data table, so this graph is incorrect.

Drills

If Experimental Design questions give you trouble, study the information above and try out these drill questions before completing the Try on Your Own questions below.

a.   What is the independent variable in Experiment A?

Experiment A

Cotton cultivars were grown in 25 plots under greenhouse conditions. The plots were divided into five sections, and each section was irrigated daily with different levels of water salinity for 20 minutes. Growth was measured every 10 days over a 2-month period.

b.   What is the dependent variable in Experiment B?

Experiment B

Four different batches of iodized salt were sampled. For each sample, 40 g of salt were dissolved in 200 mL of water along with 2–5 drops of starch solution in a beaker. Sodium thiosulfate was added dropwise until the purple color disappeared. The equivalent volume was used to calculate the iodine content in parts per million.

c.   What is the control in Experiment C?

Experiment C

Petroleum-tolerant and non-petroleum-tolerant fungal isolates were cultured in flasks enriched with crude oil at room temperature for 10 days. The researchers varied the amount of crude oil in each flask and monitored the degree of turbidity over a 10-day period to measure the capacity of hydrocarbon degradation by the fungi.

d.   What is/are the independent variable(s) in Figure D?

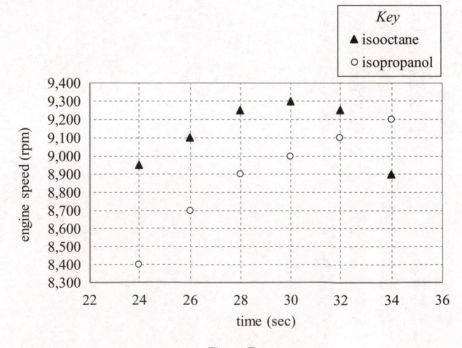

Figure D

e.   What is/are the dependent variable(s) in Table E?

Table E		
Tree species	Ambient temperature (°C)	Shade temperature (°C)
A. chinensis	38.9	32.5
F. benjamina	38.5	33.8
L. floribunda	38.7	34.3
M. indica	38.3	32.9
P. africanum	38.0	33.7

Try on Your Own

Directions: Take as much time as you need on these questions. Work carefully and methodically. There will be an opportunity for timed practice at the end of the chapter.

Answers are found at the end of the chapter.

Passage III

When a pure hydrocarbon-based fuel combusts under ideal circumstances, a reaction that produces carbon dioxide, water, and heat occurs:

$$CH_4 + 2O_2 \rightarrow CO_2 + H_2O + heat$$

When gasoline, a hydrocarbon-based fuel, is combusted in vehicle engines, the reaction often produces other by-products released in the vehicle exhaust, including carbon monoxide, nitric acid, sulfuric acid, soot, and/or smoke. This contamination can occur through the refinement process of gasoline itself or from the atmosphere in which a reaction occurs.

Students conducted a series of experiments to learn more about the conditions that affect vehicle emissions.

Experiment 1

Students connected a collection bag to the exhaust pipe of three of their school buses. The buses' engines were started, and the exhausts were captured by collection bags. A syringe was then used to extract a 5-mL sample of each exhaust. The exhaust was injected into a gas chromatograph, which separates mixtures of gases into their individual components. Students compared the exhaust to mixtures of known hydrocarbon concentration samples to determine what percentage of the sample (by volume) was composed of unburned hydrocarbons.

Each bus was started on a 70°F day, and samples of the exhausts were collected and extracted at 30-second intervals for 3 minutes. The buses were then allowed to idle for 15 minutes and samples were again collected. The results are reproduced in Table 1.

Table 1			
Time after starting (min)	Percentage of hydrocarbons in the exhaust		
	Bus 1 1994 Model X	Bus 2 1992 Model X	Bus 3 2006 Model X
0.5	10.3	9.0	5.4
1	11.2	9.8	4.9
1.5	12.0	13.2	6.0
2	10.5	22.9	4.9
2.5	9.6	21.0	4.5
3	9.5	20.1	4.2
18	5.6	6.3	1.8
18.5	5.6	6.3	1.8

Science

Experiment 2

The students hypothesized that temperature would also affect the efficiency of the combustion reaction. The buses were tested again at different external temperatures after being allowed to idle for 15 minutes, using the same procedure as Experiment 1. The results are reproduced in Figure 1.

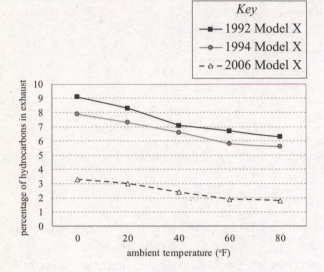

Key
- ■ 1992 Model X
- ● 1994 Model X
- -△- 2006 Model X

Figure 1

1. Which of the following factors did the students vary in Experiment 1 ?

   A. The time of day at which the samples were taken

   B. The instruments used to collect the exhaust samples

   C. The age of the buses tested

   D. The amount of exhaust used in the gas chromatograph

2. Consider that many states require buses to undergo emissions testing to ensure that peak hydrocarbon levels remain below a required threshold in order to pass an annual inspection. Based on the results of the students' experiments, approximately how long after starting should the exhaust be tested during the inspection process?

   F. Less than 75 seconds

   G. Between 75 and 150 seconds

   H. Between 150 and 240 seconds

   J. More than 15 minutes

3. Which of the following best explains why the students collected exhaust samples in a collection bag?

   A. To keep air and other gases from contaminating the exhaust samples

   B. To allow outside air and gases to mix with the exhaust samples equally

   C. To capture only the hydrocarbons in the exhaust

   D. To filter out sediments from the exhaust

4. How many temperatures were tested in Experiment 1, and how many temperatures were tested in Experiment 2?

	Experiment 1	Experiment 2
F.	1	1
G.	1	5
H.	5	5
J.	7	5

Drill answers from previous page:

a. levels of water salinity

b. iodine content

c. non-petroleum-tolerant fungal cultures

d. fuel type and time

e. shade temperature

5. Which of the following statements best describes why Experiment 2 was designed so that the buses idled for 15 minutes prior to the exhaust measurements being taken?

   A. More exhaust is needed for analysis at warmer temperatures, so the buses needed to run for a longer period of time.

   B. The percentage of hydrocarbon emissions for each bus fluctuated immediately after startup, so any change could be attributed solely to the age of the bus.

   C. After idling, the percentage of hydrocarbon emissions for each bus stabilized, so any change could be attributed solely to temperature.

   D. It took longer for the buses to start in cold weather.

6. The students hypothesized that a sample taken from their school buses' exhaust after a period of idling would contain more hydrocarbons than one taken after the engines had been turned off and restarted. Do the results of Experiment 1 support this hypothesis?

   F. Yes; the highest percentage of hydrocarbons was found in the exhaust of the bus after idling.

   G. Yes; the lowest percentage of hydrocarbons was found in the exhaust of the bus after idling.

   H. No; the highest percentage of hydrocarbons was found in the exhaust of the bus shortly after restarting.

   J. No; the lowest percentage of hydrocarbons was found in the exhaust of the bus shortly after restarting.

Synthesizing Data Questions

To answer a question like this:

The half-life of a radioactive isotope is the amount of time necessary for one-half of the initial number of its nuclei to decay. The decay curves of two radioactive thorium isotopes (^{231}Th and ^{234}Th) are graphed below as functions of the ratio of N, the number of nuclei remaining after a given time period, to N_0, the initial number of nuclei. The results are recorded in Figure 1 and Figure 2, respectively.

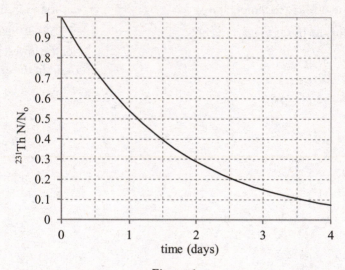

Figure 1

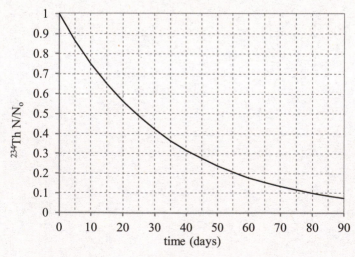

Figure 2

According to Figures 1 and 2, the half-life of ^{234}Th is approximately how many times longer than the half-life of ^{231}Th ?

A. 1

B. 12

C. 24

D. 48

You need to know this:

Synthesizing Data questions require you to—you guessed it—synthesize information from multiple figures (tables, graphs, and diagrams only) or multiple formats (text from the passage or question stem and one or more figures).

- Synthesizing information means combining or piecing together a number of elements into a coherent whole.
- Synthesizing Data questions appear more commonly in connection with Research Summaries than Data Interpretation passages.
- These questions are usually a little more complicated than other Data or Experiments questions, and answering them will usually require more steps.

For Research Summaries, the steps you take to answer individual Synthesizing Data questions will likely overlap with the steps you take to answer the other questions about the passage. Identifying the steps of the scientific method when reading this type of passage will help you answer the accompanying Synthesizing Data questions more efficiently.

Some Synthesizing Data questions will ask you to combine information from multiple figures. Others will ask you to synthesize written information and one or more figures.

You need to do this:

When examining the question stem, step 3, determine which text and/or figures will be needed to answer the question. Look for clues like a reference to a particular figure or a hypothetical situation presented in the question stem.

These questions can be asked in many different ways. You may need to:

- use information from one figure to look up information from another figure
- perform basic mathematical operations, such as adding, subtracting, multiplying, or dividing
- apply patterns in the data to new variables in order to predict how they will behave
- apply or manipulate information from multiple figures in some other way

After completing step 3, remember to repeat step 2 (strategically analyzing the figures) using the clues from the question stem to focus your second analysis and locate the information needed to answer the question. Use this information to make a prediction before choosing an answer.

When asked to identify the correct figure that matches the presented data:

- check the trend of the data: is it increasing, decreasing, or constant?
- match the shape of the trend to the answer choices: is it linear, exponential, or something else?
- check specific values at one or more given points to confirm the correct answer

Science

Explanation

Examine the text, figures, and question stem for key information:

- **Intro:** the *half-life* of an isotope is defined as the amount of time needed for one-half of the initial number of nuclei to decay
- **Figures 1/2:** the decay curves of two radioactive thorium isotopes (^{231}Th and ^{234}Th, respectively)
- **Question stem:** the half-life of each isotope needs to be determined to see by what factor they differ

Predict and answer:

- To figure out the half-life of ^{231}Th, look at the first graph (when half of the nuclei have decayed, the N/N_0 ratio will be ½ or 0.5).
- Draw a horizontal line across the graph from 0.5 on the *y*-axis and, where that line intersects the curve, draw a vertical line down to the *x*-axis.
- This line intersects the *x*-axis slightly above 1.0, which means the amount of time it takes for half of the nuclei to decay is about 1 day.
- Repeat the process to determine the half-life for ^{234}Th (its half-life is about 24 days).
- Determine that the half-life of ^{234}Th is approximately 24 times the half-life of ^{231}Th.

Choice (C) is correct.

Science

Try on Your Own

Directions: Take as much time as you need on these questions. Work carefully and methodically. There will be an opportunity for timed practice at the end of the chapter.

Answers are found at the end of the chapter.

Passage V

During anaerobic fermentation, the conversion of pyruvate to acetic acid and CO_2 is catalyzed by the enzyme pyruvate decarboxylase (PDC). PDC is prone to *point mutations* (the replacement of one nucleotide with another) at specific locations in its gene sequence. These mutations can have wide-ranging impacts on the enzyme's function.

Study 1

Table 1 lists nucleotide sequences for the wild-type PDC gene along with three different mutant variants. Table 2 provides the amino acids coded for by each three-nucleotide codon.

Table 1		
	Codon	
Enzyme	Location 1	Location 2
Wild-type	CAA	GAT
Mutant 1	CAA	AAT
Mutant 2	GAA	GAT
Mutant 3	CAA	GAC

Table 2	
Codon	Amino Acid
AAT	Asparagine
CAA	Glutamine
GAA	Glutamic Acid
GAC	Aspartic Acid
GAT	Aspartic Acid

Study 2

To determine the efficiency of the enzyme and its mutated forms, researchers ran several trials using the wild-type of the enzyme as well as three mutant types. Each was reacted with 1.5 mL of 0.08 M pyruvate, and decarboxylation of pyruvate was measured in number of molecules converted over time. Results are shown in Figure 1.

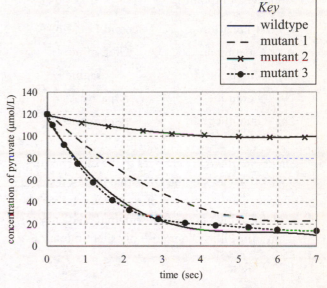

This data is from *Natural Science*, Vol. 4, No. 11, October 2012, pp. 881–893.

Figure 1

1. According to Tables 1 and 2, which enzyme contains a molecule of glutamic acid?

   A. Wild-type
   B. Mutant 1
   C. Mutant 2
   D. Mutant 3

2. Suppose that after introducing an unlabeled enzyme to a quantity of pyruvate, the researchers measure the concentration at 2 seconds to be 60 μ mol/L. Which of the following is most likely the nucleotide sequence of the unlabeled enzyme?

    F. CAA GAT

    G. CAA AAT

    H. CAA GAC

    J. GAA GAT

3. Based on Tables 1 and 2, what is the amino-acid sequence of Mutant 1?

	First Location	Second Location
A.	Asparagine	Glutamine
B.	Glutamine	Asparagine
C.	Glutamine	Aspartic Acid
D.	Glutamic Acid	Asparagine

4. *Silent mutations* are changes to the sequence of nucleotide bases in the DNA that do not result in a change of amino acid or affect the function of the protein. Which of the following mutated enzymes, if any, most likely contains only silent mutations?

    F. Mutant 1

    G. Mutant 2

    H. Mutant 3

    J. None of the mutated enzymes

5. The researchers had predicted that the nucleotide sequence in the first location was more directly responsible for the decarboxylation activity of the enzyme than the sequence in the second location. Are the results of the study consistent with this hypothesis?

    A. Yes; Mutant 2 shows the least enzymatic activity.

    B. Yes; Mutant 2 shows the most enzymatic activity.

    C. No; both the wild-type and Mutant 3 show similar enzymatic activity.

    D. No; Mutants 1 and 3 show less enzymatic activity than Mutant 2.

How Much Have You Learned?

Directions: For test-like practice, give yourself 7 minutes to complete this question set. Be sure to study the explanations, even for questions you got correct. They can be found at the end of this chapter.

Passage VI

Crop output can be stunted in areas with longer winters, persistent cloudy weather, or smog. Even in optimal growth conditions, production efficiency is less than optimal because lower leaves on tightly packed plants receive less light than those closer to the top. As a result, there is an interest in using artificial light to increase production.

Experiment 1

Researchers grew 100 tomato plants in a greenhouse under several conditions. To simulate cloudy weather, they used a shade cloth that blocked out some of the incoming light. Forty plants were placed under the shade cloth for 4 out of every 10 days. Another 40 were placed under the same cloth for 6 out of 10 days. Within each of these groups, half of the plants were grown with white LED lights illuminating the lower two-thirds of the leaves, while half were not. The final 20 plants were grown uncovered as a control group. After two months, plant growth and tomato yield were compared for all groups. Results are shown in Figure 1.

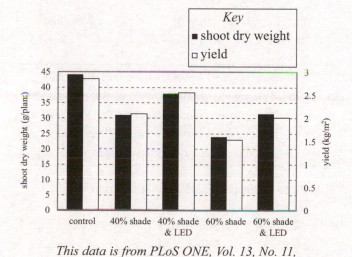

This data is from PLoS ONE, Vol. 13, No. 11, November 2018.

Figure 1

Experiment 2

To determine the optimal lighting conditions for growth, researchers repeated the procedure in Experiment 1 for 40% shade and an LED, this time using fluorescent light bulbs and several varieties of LED bulbs: white, blue, green, and two varieties of red—far-red (FR) and high-light (HL). The results are shown in Figure 2.

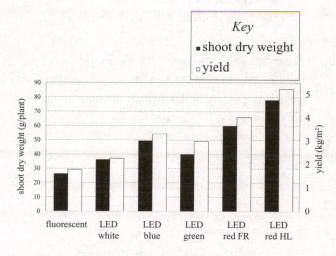

Figure 2

1. Which of the following variables remained constant throughout both experiments?

    A. Light coverage

    B. Light source

    C. Plant species

    D. Dry weight

2. The researchers conducting the study chose to grow 20 of the tomato plants in a greenhouse outside of the shade cloth in Experiment 1. Which of the following statements gives the most likely reason for this decision? The researchers wanted:

F. to determine if fluorescent lighting was more optimal for tomato yield.

G. to ensure that at least one group of tomato plants would survive.

H. to simulate the cloudy conditions tomato plants experience in areas with long winters.

J. to compare the results of those grown under the shade cloth to those that weren't.

3. According to the results of the study, did the addition of LED lights increase or decrease the crop yield of the plants under a shade cover, and did the use of colored LED lighting increase or decrease the crop yield compared to white LED lighting?

LED Under Shade Cover	Colored LED Lighting
A. Increase	Increase
B. Increase	Decrease
C. Decrease	Increase
D. Decrease	Decrease

4. The colors of visible light vary depending on their wavelengths; lights on the red end of the visible-light spectrum contain longer wavelengths than those on the violet end of the spectrum. Do the results of Experiment 2 support the hypothesis that increasing the wavelength of an LED light source leads to increased growth?

F. Yes; the highest growth was observed in the plants exposed to red LED light.

G. Yes; plants exposed to red LED light grew more than plants exposed to blue LED light.

H. No; the lowest growth was observed in plants exposed to blue LED light.

J. No; there is no correlation between wavelength and growth.

HINT: Research Summaries passages like this one will include mostly Experiments questions, but sometimes the question set will include one or more Data questions. To learn about answering questions like Q5, review the "Using Data Questions" lesson in chapter 23.

5. Suppose that an additional trial in Experiment 1 had been performed using 60% shade cover and fluorescent bulbs on the lower two-thirds of leaves. The approximate dry weight would most likely have been:

A. less than 20 g/plant.

B. between 20 g/plant and 30 g/plant.

C. between 30 g/plant and 40 g/plant.

D. greater than 40 g/plant.

6. Suppose the researchers wanted to determine whether percent shade impacts the effect of colored LED bulbs on growth. Which of the following experiments should be performed?

F. Repeat Experiment 1, except use a fluorescent light bulb instead of a white LED light.

G. Repeat Experiment 1, except use 80% shade instead of 60% shade.

H. Repeat Experiment 2, except use black light instead of white.

J. Repeat Experiment 2, except use 60% shade instead of 40% shade.

HINT: Applying Core Knowledge questions will require background knowledge unrelated to the passage type, so be prepared to see them appear throughout Part V. To review strategies for questions like Q7, review the "Applying Core Knowledge Questions" lesson in chapter 25.

7. Plant pigments absorb light at different wavelengths, using solar energy to convert carbon dioxide into carbohydrates through a process called photosynthesis. Which of the following molecules is produced as a direct result of photosynthesis?

A. Fructose

B. Galactose

C. Glucose

D. Sucrose

Reflect

Directions: Take a few minutes to recall what you've learned and what you've been practicing in this chapter. Consider the following questions, jot down your best answer for each one, and then compare your reflections to the expert responses on the following page. Use your level of confidence to determine what to do next.

1. When presented with a Research Summaries passage, how much should the ACT expert try to understand in depth before moving on to the questions?

2. How does an ACT expert use scientific method concepts when answering ACT Science questions?

3. How would not having a control group impact the results of a study?

4. What key features does an ACT expert focus on when asked to synthesize multiple figures or formats?

5. How will you approach Research Summaries passages differently as you continue to practice and improve your performance in the ACT Science section?

Science

Responses

1. When presented with a Research Summaries passage, how much should the ACT expert try to understand in depth before moving on to the questions?

Not much! Move quickly though the text of the experiments and their methods, only pausing to underline key words. Do not be intimated by technical terminology, as it will have little impact on answering questions.

2. How does an ACT expert use scientific method concepts when answering ACT Science questions?

An ACT expert uses scientific method concepts to find the key components (hypotheses, independent and dependent variables, and controls) of each experiment, making it easier to recognize the purpose of an experiment, understand its methods, and interpret its results.

3. How would not having a control group impact the results of a study?

A control group is a group that does not receive any treatment or manipulation by the independent variable. Without a control group, a manipulation to the independent variable has no baseline within the experiment that allows for effective comparison. In other words, no conclusions can be drawn about the impact of the independent variable on the dependent variable.

4. What key features does an ACT expert focus on when asked to synthesize multiple figures or formats?

When synthesizing information from multiple figures or formats, an ACT expert focuses on the trend of the data (positive, negative, or constant) and the shape in the trend (linear, exponential, or something else). An ACT expert also makes sure to check specific values at a given point.

5. How will you approach Research Summaries passages differently as you continue to practice and improve your performance in the ACT Science section?

There is no one-size-fits-all answer here. Reflect on your own habits in identifying the key features of experiments and interpreting their results and give yourself an honest assessment of your strengths and weaknesses. Consider the strategies you've seen experts use in this chapter, and put them to work in your own practice to increase your accuracy, speed, and confidence.

Next Steps

If you answered most questions correctly in the "How Much Have You Learned?" section, and if your responses to the Reflect questions were similar to those of an expert, then consider Research Summaries passages an area of strength and move on to the next chapter. Come back to this topic periodically to prevent yourself from getting rusty.

If you don't yet feel confident, review the material in this chapter, then try the questions you missed again. As always, be sure to review the explanations closely. Then go online (**kaptest.com/login**) to use your Qbank for more practice. If you haven't already registered your book, do so at *kaptest.com/moreonline.*

GO ONLINE

kaptest.com/login

Answers and Explanations

Research Summaries and Experimental Design Questions

1. C

Difficulty: Low

Category: Experimental Design

Getting to the Answer: This question is asking for an independent variable from Experiment 1. In that experiment, students took exhaust samples at intervals of 30 seconds from buses of the same model that were built in different years. So, time after starting and age of bus are the two independent variables. Only (C) mentions either of these variables, so it is correct.

Choice A may be tempting because it mentions time, but it does so incorrectly: the exhaust samples were collected at 30-second intervals, but the time of day at which they were collected wasn't mentioned. Choice B is incorrect because the same method of collection was used for each sample with each bus. Choice D is incorrect because you are told that 5 mL of each exhaust sample were injected into the gas chromatograph.

2. G

Difficulty: Low

Category: Using Data

Getting to the Answer: The goal is to test emissions when hydrocarbons are at their peak, so check Table 1 and Table 2 and determine the time at which each bus emits the highest percentage of hydrocarbons. Bus 1 emits peak hydrocarbons (12%) at 90 seconds, Bus 2 at 120 seconds (22.9%), and Bus 3 at 90 seconds (6%). This matches (G).

3. A

Difficulty: Medium

Category: Experimental Design

Getting to the Answer: The students were collecting exhaust samples to determine what percentage of the exhaust was composed of hydrocarbons, so they'd want to keep each exhaust sample as pure as possible. A bag attached to the tailpipe would collect the exhaust before it mixed with, and was diluted by, the outside air. Therefore, (A) is correct.

Choice B goes against the students' purpose. They wanted to compare the percentages of hydrocarbons in the exhaust, but adding air and other gases would make their results unreliable. Choice C is incorrect because you know that the collection bag captures all of the exhaust, not only hydrocarbons. Choice D is incorrect because you are given no reason to assume the bag filters anything from the exhaust.

4. G

Difficulty: Medium

Category: Experimental Design

Getting to the Answer: According to the description, in the first experiment, all of the testing was done on a 70°F day, which means there was only one temperature tested in that experiment. Thus, you can eliminate H and J, which both claim more than one temperature was tested in Experiment 1. The point of Experiment 2 was to test the effect of temperature on engine efficiency. It's helpful to notice, however, that you don't need to actually count the number of temperatures that were tested. Of the remaining choices, F and (G), only (G) correctly indicates that multiple temperatures were tested in Experiment 2. Therefore (G) is correct.

5. C

Difficulty: High

Category: Experimental Design

Getting to the Answer: To see the effect of idling, take a look at Table 1 to see what happened to the results after the buses idled. For each bus, the results after idling were identical to those before idling, which indicates that the percentage of hydrocarbons in the emissions stabilizes after the engine has been running for a while. This is likely why they let the engines idle in the second experiment, so (C) is correct.

Choice A is incorrect because there's no indication that more exhaust is needed at higher temperatures; furthermore, since the students collected samples in Experiment 2 in the same manner as in Experiment 1, the same amount was collected in each sample. Choice B may be tempting, as the hydrocarbon levels in the exhaust did fluctuate after the engines started up; however, it doesn't explain how idling for 15 minutes would solve the issue of the age of the bus affecting the results. Choice D is irrelevant; while it may be true that engines take longer to start in cold weather, no measurements were taken until the engines actually started.

6. H

Difficulty: Low

Category: Synthesizing Data

Getting to the Answer: Look at Table 1 to see the levels of hydrocarbons in the exhaust after an engine start and after idling. For all three buses, the hydrocarbon levels were highest in the few minutes after start and lowest after a period of idling. This disproves the hypothesis that there would be more hydrocarbons after idling, so (H) is correct.

Choices F and G can both be eliminated because they state that the results supported the hypothesis. Even though J states that the hypothesis was not supported, it misstates the facts that support that result, so it is incorrect.

Synthesizing Data Questions

1. C

Difficulty: Low

Category: Synthesizing Data

Getting to the Answer: First, look at Table 2 to determine which codon codes for glutamic acid. The only one that does is GAA. Now, use Table 1 to determine which of the enzyme types contains a GAA sequence at one of the two locations. Only Mutant 2 does, so (C) is correct.

2. G

Difficulty: Medium

Category: Synthesizing Data

Getting to the Answer: First, look at the graph to see which type of enzyme resulted in a concentration of $60\ \mu$ mol/L of pyruvate after 2 seconds; a line drawn up from 2 seconds on the x-axis intersects with the curve for Mutant 1 at $60\ \mu$ mol/L. Next, look at Table 1 to get the nucleotide sequence of Mutant 1: it has CAA at the first position and AAT at the second. Choice (G) is correct.

3. B

Difficulty: Medium

Category: Synthesizing Data

Getting to the Answer: According to Table 1, Mutant 1 has a CAA codon at the first position and an AAT codon at the second position. According to Table 2, CAA codes for glutamine and AAT codes for asparagine. Therefore, (B) is correct.

4. H

Difficulty: Medium

Category: Synthesizing Data

Getting to the Answer: None of the given data relates to the function of PDC, so in determining whether any of the mutant variations of PDC are the result of silent mutations, you only need to consider whether the mutant strains code for the same amino acids in the two locations. A quick scan of Table 1 shows that none of the mutant variants have the same codons as the wild-type. However, according to Table 2, there's one pair of codons that code for the same amino acid; GAC and GAT both code for aspartic acid. Looking back at Table 1, Mutant 3 has the same codon in the first position as does the wild-type, and at the second position, Mutant 3 has GAC while the wild-type has GAT. Thus, Mutant 3 is the only mutant strain that codes for the same amino acids as the wild-type, which means it's the one most likely to be a silent mutation. Choice (H) is correct.

5. A

Difficulty: Hard

Category: Synthesizing Data

Getting to the Answer: To see if there's a correlation between decarboxylation activity and the nucleotide sequence at the first location, first look at Figure 1, which shows the decarboxylation rates of the various enzymes. There are three enzymes (wild-type, Mutant 1, and Mutant 3) that show very similar trends in decarboxylation activity, while Mutant 2 has a much lower rate. Looking at Table 1, Mutant 2 has GAA at the first position, while the other three enzymes all have CAA. Since the three types with similar decarboxylation rates have the same nucleotide sequence at the first location and the enzyme with a much lower rate has a different nucleotide sequence, that's consistent with the hypothesis that the sequence at the first location is more responsible for decarboxylation activity, and (A) is correct.

Choice B is incorrect because it comes to the right conclusion for the wrong reason: Mutant 2 has the least decarboxylation activity, not the most. Choice C uses a correct fact—that Mutants 1 and 3 show similar levels of activity—to support the wrong conclusion. Choice D both comes to the wrong conclusions and misstates the facts: Mutants 1 and 3 have higher levels of enzymatic activity, not lower.

How Much Have You Learned?

1. C

Difficulty: Low

Category: Experimental Design

Getting to the Answer: Evaluate the choices one by one to find the one that was constant in both experiments. In Experiment 1, only some plants were exposed to artificial light, so this was an independent variable and A can be eliminated. Choice B is incorrect because the light sources were intentionally varied as an independent variable in Experiment 2. In both experiments, only tomato plants were used to test

the hypothesis, so (C) is correct. The dry weight was measured in both experiments as a dependent variable, so D is incorrect.

2. J

Difficulty: Low

Category: Experimental Design

Getting to the Answer: In the description of Experiment 1, it's stated that 80 of the tomato plants were grown under a shade cloth, while the other 20 were grown as a control group. This means that they were grown to compare the results of plants grown with a cloth to those without; (J) is correct.

Choice F may have been tempting. Some of the plants under the cloth were lit artificially, so in part, the control group was intended to measure the effects of artificial light. However, in Experiment 1, only LED lights, not fluorescent lights, were used, so F can be eliminated. Choice G is incorrect because there's no indication that the researchers wanted only one group to survive. Choice H is incorrect because it's the plants under the cloth that were meant to simulate growth under shady conditions, not the plants outside of the cloth.

3. A

Difficulty: Low

Category: Synthesizing Data

Getting to the Answer: Figure 2 compares crop yield to the type of lighting used. All LED lighting resulted in a higher crop yield than fluorescent lighting, and the yields from colored LED lights were higher than the yield from white LED lighting. Thus, (A) is correct.

Science

4. J

Difficulty: Hard

Category: Synthesizing Data

Getting to the Answer: In Figure 2, the colors are already arranged in order of increasing wavelength; the colors towards the red end of the spectrum are on the right, while those towards the violet end are on the left. If there were a correlation between increased wavelengths, the four bars representing colored light (blue, green, red FR, red HL) would increase in height from left to right, but they do not. In fact, as the light changed from blue to green, the light wavelength increased but the dry weight decreased. Thus, the answer is (J).

While it is true that the plants with the highest yield were those exposed to red light, this fact on its own is not enough to indicate a correlation, so F is incorrect. Choice G is incorrect for similar reasons; plants with red light did grow more than plants with blue light, but plants with green light break the trend. Choice H comes to the correct conclusion based on an incorrect fact; the plants with the lowest growth were those exposed to green light.

5. B

Difficulty: Low

Category: Using Data

Getting to the Answer: Look at Figure 2 to get an idea of the relationship between the dry weight of plants grown under 40% shade cover and white LED and fluorescent bulbs. In that experiment, plants grown under fluorescent bulbs appear to have approximately three-quarters of the yield and dry weight as those grown under white LED light. Thus, if a new trial in Experiment 1 had been done with 60% shade and fluorescent bulbs, the plants getting the fluorescent light would have had approximately three-quarters of the dry weight that the plants grown in 60% shade under white LEDs had. That dry weight was approximately 32 g/plant, so under fluorescent bulbs, the dry weight would likely be roughly 24 g/plant. That means (B) is correct.

6. J

Difficulty: Medium

Category: Experimental Design

Getting to the Answer: Experiment 2 examines the effect of different colored LED bulbs on growth. Eliminate F and G. To determine the effect of percent shade, the researchers should repeat Experiment 2 using a different percent shade. Choice (J) is correct. Using a black light instead of white would test another color LED but not a different percent shade.

7. C

Difficulty: Medium

Category: Applying Core Knowledge

Getting to the Answer: This question is testing your knowledge of photosynthesis. Glucose is produced in plants as a result of photosynthesis, so (C) is correct.

The three incorrect choices are all types of sugar molecules, but they are not produced during photosynthesis.

CHAPTER 25

Thinking Like a Scientist

LEARNING OBJECTIVES

After completing this chapter, you will be able to:

- Identify Conflicting Viewpoints passages
- Identify the central claim of each viewpoint
- Determine how various viewpoints are connected (or not)
- Determine which hypothesis is supported given the data
- Determine how data and information from the passage or question stem relates to a particular viewpoint
- Apply knowledge of core science concepts in earth and space science, biology, chemistry, and physics to interpret data

Supporting Hypotheses: 6/36 SmartPoints® (High yield)

Applying Core Knowledge: 2/36 SmartPoints® (Very low yield)

How Much Do You Know?

Directions: Try out the questions below. Show your work so that you can compare your solutions to the ones found on the next page. The "Category" heading in the explanation for each question gives the title of the lesson that covers how to solve it. If you answered the question(s) for a given lesson correctly, and if your scratchwork looks like ours, you may be able to move quickly through that lesson. If you answered incorrectly or used a different approach, you may want to take your time on that lesson.

Passage I

The Himalayan blackberry, *Rubus armeniacus*, is a thorny shrub native to Eurasia. However, while not native to the state of Washington, it spreads aggressively and forms impenetrable thickets that negatively impact the local ecosystem. Thus, it is considered invasive. Consider these three hypotheses regarding how to control the spread of *R. armeniacus*.

Hypothesis 1

Without competition, the Himalayan blackberry will quickly dominate a landscape and alter the soil to suit its own propagation. The decomposition of blackberry leaf litter at the end of autumn replenishes soil nitrogen, which the blackberry canes use to grow in the spring. One way to control the spread of the invasive canes is to deplete the source of soil nitrogen by removing the leaf litter, which also improves soil conditions for native species.

Hypothesis 2

Blackberry leaves have high concentrations of 2-heptanol, a compound that decreases herbivory of the leaves by native Washington species. Without this predation, the blackberry is able to expand unchecked. Goats, however, will eat the blackberry bushes down to the soil and trample the residual canes. Clear plastic soil covers can then be applied to kill the root crown and prevent seed germination.

Hypothesis 3

The Himalayan blackberry releases thousands of seeds per square meter and is thus able to crowd out native species through rapid reproduction. Harvesting blackberries will reduce seed banks and prevent birds and pollinators from spreading the species. Fewer blackberry seedlings will mean more room for native trees to germinate and grow, which will eventually generate so much shade that blackberries will be unable to survive.

1. Which hypothesis, if any, asserts that the control of available soil nutrients will help to stop the spread of the Himalayan blackberry?

   A. Hypothesis 1
   B. Hypothesis 2
   C. Hypothesis 3
   D. None of the hypotheses

2. Which hypothesis, if any, asserts that consuming the fruit of the Himalayan blackberry is necessary in order to control its spread?

   F. Hypothesis 1
   G. Hypothesis 2
   H. Hypothesis 3
   J. None of the hypotheses

3. Blackberry seeds have an impermeable seed coat that allows them to germinate after ingestion and after several years in the soil. A supporter of which of the hypotheses would be likely to claim that to ensure invasive Himalayan blackberries are eradicated, steps must be taken to reduce the spread of viable seeds?

   A. Hypothesis 3 only
   B. Hypotheses 1 and 2 only
   C. Hypotheses 1 and 3 only
   D. Hypotheses 2 and 3 only

4. In order to grow, Himalayan blackberries must capture light energy from the sun and convert it into a form of chemical energy usable by its cells. In which of the following organelles does this process occur?

F. Cell wall

G. Chloroplast

H. Mitochondria

J. Nucleus

5. Which of the following statements about the relationship between Himalayan blackberries and native species is consistent with all 3 hypotheses?

A. Encouraging the growth of native species is necessary to reduce the spread of Himalayan blackberries.

B. Germination rates of Himalayan blackberries outpace germination rates of native species.

C. The spread of the Himalayan blackberry disrupts the native ecosystem in places it is found.

D. The pollination and spread of native species is threatened when herbivores preferentially consume blackberry leaves.

6. Consider the statement, "The chemical composition of Himalayan blackberry leaves contributes to the species' ability to displace native species." Supporters of which of the hypotheses would be likely to agree with this statement?

F. Hypothesis 1 only

G. Hypothesis 2 only

H. Hypotheses 1 and 2 only

J. Hypotheses 2 and 3 only

Check Your Work

1. A

Difficulty: Low

Category: Supporting Hypotheses

Getting to the Answer: Each hypothesis posits a different method of controlling the spread of the Himalayan blackberry. Hypothesis 1 states that removing leaf litter will deplete nitrogen levels in the soil, thus depriving blackberries of an essential nutrient. Choice (A) is the correct answer.

Hypothesis 2 focuses on using goats to eat the bushes and soil covers to kill the roots; it has nothing to do with soil nutrients, so B is incorrect. Hypothesis 3 states that harvesting blackberries will reduce the number of seeds available to grow into new plants. Again, there's nothing about soil nutrients, so C can be eliminated. Choice D claims that there's no hypothesis involving soil nutrients; this is incorrect since Hypothesis 1 mentions them.

2. J

Difficulty: Medium

Category: Supporting Hypotheses

Getting to the Answer: Pay careful attention to what the question is asking, which is whether any of the hypotheses claim that the fruit NEEDS to be eaten to control the spread of the blackberry. Hypothesis 1 doesn't mention the fruit at all; it only states that removing the leaf litter will stop the spread. Eliminate F. Hypothesis 2 asserts that the spread of this blackberry bush can be controlled by having goats eat the bushes. This may make G tempting, but remember that the question asks whether consumption of the fruit is necessary. Hypothesis 2 only asserts that consumption of the bush is necessary; perhaps the goats eat the bushes when there is no fruit. Eliminate G. Choice H may also be tempting, since it claims that harvesting the fruit will stop the spread of the plant. However, nothing in the hypothesis requires the fruit to be consumed once it is harvested, so H is also incorrect. The correct answer is (J).

3. D

Difficulty: Hard

Category: Supporting Hypotheses

Getting to the Answer: Hypothesis 1 does not rely on controlling the spread of seeds; rather, it focuses on making the soil conditions unfavorable for the Himalayan blackberry. So, a supporter of that theory wouldn't think the spread of seeds needs to be reduced, since any seeds that do survive wouldn't be able to grow well in the new soil conditions. Thus, eliminate B and C. Hypothesis 2 asserts that goats will stop the spread of the bush by eating the plants; however, note that it also says that steps need to be taken to prevent seed germination. A supporter of this theory would, then, think something needs to be done to control the spread of seeds. The only remaining choice featuring Hypothesis 2 is (D), so it must be correct. Hypothesis 3 is also included in (D); this is because it also claims that stopping the spread of seeds should be part of the plan. Choice A is incorrect because it does not include Hypothesis 2.

4. G

Difficulty: Hard

Category: Applying Core Knowledge

Getting to the Answer: The question stem describes converting sunlight into usable energy; this process is known as photosynthesis. Since chloroplasts are the organelles in which photosynthesis is carried out by chlorophyll, (G) is the correct answer.

Cell walls provide structure to the cell and to the plant itself, but they are not directly involved in photosynthesis, so F can be eliminated. Mitochondria are often described as "the powerhouse of the cell" and are involved in energy production; however, they don't convert sunlight to energy, so H is incorrect. Choice J can be eliminated because the nucleus is where most of a cell's DNA is stored.

5.   C

Difficulty: Medium

Category: Supporting Hypotheses

Getting to the Answer: Each hypothesis opens with facts about how the Himalayan blackberry disrupts the native ecosystem and then explains a method to counter that disruption. Thus, (C) would be consistent with each of the hypotheses and is the correct answer.

Hypotheses 1 and 3 both mention that implementation would result in better conditions for native plants. Hypothesis 2, however, does not, so A is incorrect. Choice B can be eliminated because only Hypothesis 3 mentions the rapid reproduction of the Himalayan blackberry. Choice D is incorrect because only Hypothesis 2 mentions predation by herbivores. Even then, D gets that relationship wrong: it's not that herbivores eat blackberries over local plants, it's that blackberries repel herbivores, allowing their spread.

6.   H

Difficulty: Hard

Category: Supporting Hypotheses

Getting to the Answer: Quickly summarize each hypothesis to evaluate whether it claims that the chemical composition of the Himalayan blackberry provides it an advantage over local plants. Hypothesis 1 claims that leaf litter from the blackberry contributes nitrogen to the soil, which contributes to further blackberry growth. Thus, it's consistent with the statement in the stem. Hypothesis 2 states that a chemical compound in the leaves of the blackberry discourages predation by herbivores, which contributes to the spread of the blackberry. So, this hypothesis is also consistent. At this point, you can confidently pick (H), as it's the only choice that includes both of these hypotheses. For the record, though, Hypothesis 3 is not included in the correct choice because it does not mention the chemical composition of the blackberry as a cause of its rapid spread.

Applying Core Knowledge Questions

LEARNING OBJECTIVE

After this lesson, you will be able to:

- Apply knowledge of core science concepts in earth and space science, biology, chemistry, and physics to interpret data

To answer a question like this:

Human activity has increased the amount of carbon dioxide in the atmosphere; when this atmospheric carbon dioxide dissolves into the oceans, it leads to ocean acidification. Which of the following represents the change in pH of the Earth's oceans due to ocean acidification?

A. Decreases

B. Remains the same

C. Increases

D. The information given is insufficient to determine the change in pH.

You need to know this:

Advanced knowledge in Earth/space sciences, biology, chemistry, and physics is not required for ACT Science questions, but general background knowledge and a grasp of science terms in these domains may be needed to correctly answer some of the questions.

Earth and space science:

- Geology (soil, crust, mantle)
- Astronomy (star, constellation, planet, galaxy)
- Meteorology (greenhouse gases, atmosphere, climate)

Biology:

- Cell components and processes (nucleus, mitochondria, ribosomes, chloroplasts, lysosome, ATP, mitosis, meiosis, respiration, photosynthesis)
- Macromolecules (carbohydrates, lipids, proteins, DNA, RNA)
- Genetics (alleles, traits, inheritance, mutations)
- Bacterial growth

Chemistry:

- Chemical reactions (formula, reactants, products, moles)
- Atomic structure and interaction of charges (proton, electron, neutron)
- States of matter (solid, liquid, gas) and phase transitions (freezing/melting and boiling point of water)
- Properties of molecules (atomic structure, molar mass)
- pH scale (acid, base, neutral)

Physics:

- Gravity (mass *vs.* weight)
- Normal and frictional forces (and their typical directions)
- Kinetic and potential energy
- Kinematics (velocity, acceleration)
- Circuits (current, voltage, resistor, capacitor)
- Waves (period, amplitude)
- Density

You need to do this:

Review the basic concepts listed above for Earth/space sciences, biology, chemistry, and physics. Familiarize yourself with the terms and their definitions, but remember that any knowledge more detailed than that will be provided by the passage and questions.

Explanation

Identify

Without additional information, such as a figure, it's difficult to identify the passage type. However, for Applying Core Knowledge questions, your approach to Steps 2–4 will not change based on the passage type.

Analyze

The process of answering Applying Core Knowledge questions does not usually include any passage analysis because the answers to these questions are usually based on some combination of information from the question stem and your background knowledge.

Examine, predict, and answer

Question stem: The question is asking about the change in pH that has resulted from acidification.

- You need to draw from your general knowledge that acids have low pH (below 7) and bases have high pH (above 7).
- Since the ocean is becoming more acidic from the increased amounts of carbon dioxide being dissolved by the ocean, the pH of the ocean is decreasing.

Choice (A) is correct.

Try on Your Own

Directions: Take as much time as you need on these questions. Work carefully and methodically. There will be an opportunity for timed practice at the end of the chapter.

Answers are found at the end of the chapter.

Passage II

Most natural substances can occur in any of three phases (states of matter): solid, liquid, or gas. A phase diagram indicates what phase (or phases) a substance can be found in at varying temperatures and pressures. The molecular structure of a substance determines the conditions under which it will experience a phase change, such as freezing or boiling. Solid lines in a phase diagram represent these phase changes, when two phases exist in equilibrium as the substance transitions from one phase to another. Figure 1 presents a phase diagram for water (H_2O), while Figure 2 presents a phase diagram for carbon dioxide (CO_2).

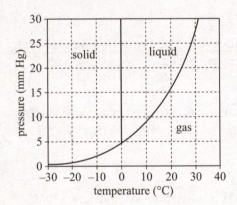

Figure 1

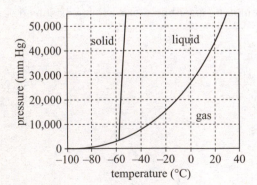

Figure 2

1. Based on Figure 2, CO_2 exists in the liquid phase between which of the following temperatures?

    A. $-100°C$ to $-57°C$

    B. $-57°C$ to $31°C$

    C. $31°C$ to $57°C$

    D. $57°C$ to $100°C$

2. According to Figures 1 and 2, H_2O and CO_2 exist in which phase(s) at 13°C and 28 mm Hg and 28,000 mm Hg, respectively?

H_2O	CO_2
F. solid	liquid
G. liquid	liquid
H. gas	gas
J. liquid	gas

3. When a substance undergoes a phase change, the behavior of the particles of that substance also change. Which of the following statements best describes the behavior of a liquid molecule?

   A. Liquid molecules are tightly packed with regular molecular arrangements.

   B. Liquid molecules move freely at high speeds.

   C. Liquid molecules are not easily compressible.

   D. Liquid molecules assume the entire shape and volume of their container.

4. Based on the data, the freezing point of CO_2 at 70,000 mm Hg is approximately:

   F. −100°C

   G. −50°C

   H. −30°C

   J. 0°C

5. Based on Figure 1, at a pressure greater than 5 mm Hg, H_2O can directly transition between which states of matter as the temperature decreases?

   A. From solid to liquid

   B. From solid to gas

   C. From liquid to gas

   D. From liquid to solid

6. Compared to the temperature at which CO_2 melts, the temperature at which H_2O melts is:

   F. lower.

   G. equal.

   H. higher.

   J. higher at some pressures and lower at other pressures.

7. The *triple point* is the temperature and pressure at which all three phases of a substance exist in equilibrium. According to Figure 2, the triple point of CO_2 is at approximately what temperature and pressure?

	temperature	pressure
A.	−55°C	4,000 mm Hg
B.	0°C	5 mm Hg
C.	5°C	0 mm Hg
D.	4,000°C	−55 mm Hg

Science

Conflicting Viewpoints Passages and Supporting Hypotheses Questions

To answer a question like this:

Several plans have been proposed to get rid of space debris. Consider the following two proposals.

Proposal 1

Capture mechanisms such as nets, harpoons, and robotic arms can be used to pick up uncooperative debris that threaten other spacecraft in orbit. Orbiting at an altitude between 800 and 1,000 kilometers, large satellite hunters would use their own propulsion to steer the catch into the atmosphere, where it would burn up.

Proposal 2

Electrodynamic tethers, which generate magnetic drag, can be used to slow down the speed of space debris so that it falls closer to Earth and then burns up. Since the tethers generate thrust from the interaction with Earth's electromagnetic field, they do not need an additional power source.

Which proposal, if any, would align with the claim that space debris falling out of Earth's orbit down to Earth will burn up?

A. Proposal 1 only

B. Proposal 2 only

C. Both Proposals 1 and 2

D. Neither Proposal 1 nor 2

You need to know this:

Supporting Hypotheses questions most often appear as part of a Conflicting Viewpoints passage question set.

Conflicting Viewpoints

One of the six passages you will see on test day will be a Conflicting Viewpoints passage. In order to identify a Conflicting Viewpoints passage as part of step 1, look for these typical characteristics:

- multiple theories or hypotheses about a particular phenomenon
- an introductory paragraph(s) that defines key terms and provides background information about the phenomenon
- individually labeled viewpoints (often a "scientist" or "student") with a 1–2 paragraph theory to explain the phenomenon

Sometimes, a Conflicting Viewpoints passage will include one or more figures that illustrate the phenomenon or the theories.

The majority of questions in Conflicting Viewpoints passages require you to evaluate hypotheses. These passages will often include at least one other question type, such as an Applying Core Knowledge question.

A key skill associated with Conflicting Viewpoints passages is the ability to **identify central claims or implications of each viewpoint**.

- The central claims are the main points that sum up the theory; they are explicitly stated in the passage, whereas implications are what can be inferred from the theory.
- Questions about a theory's claims are typically straightforward because they ask about only one viewpoint, usually by referring to details of that viewpoint that are spelled out explicitly in the passage.
- To avoid trap answers, predict an answer before reading the answer choices.

Supporting Hypotheses Questions

Supporting Hypotheses questions may involve:

- Finding basic information and identifying key assumptions in theories
- Identifying strengths and weaknesses of theories
- Identifying similarities and differences among theories
- Determining which theories are supported or weakened by new information
- Determining which hypothesis, prediction, or conclusion is consistent or inconsistent with a theory or other piece of information from the passage

Some Supporting Hypotheses questions will ask you to **determine how the viewpoints are connected (or not)**. In other words, you should be comfortable noting the similarities and differences in two viewpoints.

- To find the answer, use clues in the question stem to go back to the relevant part of the passage.
- A question might ask you to identify points of agreement or disagreement among theories.
- Details mentioned in the introductory paragraph(s) or explicitly stated in multiple theories should generally be regarded as points of agreement, while details included in one theory but not in the other(s) should be treated as points of disagreement.

Other Supporting Hypotheses questions will ask you to **determine which hypothesis is supported by data**, while others will ask **how a particular viewpoint is affected by data or text from the passage**.

- A question may ask you to identify evidence, hypotheses, conclusions, or predictions that are *consistent* (or, less often, *inconsistent*) with a particular viewpoint or another piece of passage information.
- You may be asked either to determine whether new information in the question stem *strengthens*/*weakens* one or more of the viewpoints or to identify a piece of strengthening/weakening evidence among the answer choices.
- Information that strengthens a theory makes the theory more likely to be true, while information that weakens a theory makes it less likely to be true.
- The information does not have to prove a viewpoint true in order to strengthen it, nor does it have to prove it false to weaken it.

You need to do this:

After you have identified a Conflicting Viewpoints passage, use step 2 (analyze the passage and figures strategically) to consider each viewpoint or hypothesis individually and note, either mentally or in the margins, how the viewpoint relates to the phenomenon or issue. You should:

- examine the introductory text for the phenomenon or issue in question
- move quickly through the remaining text to identify the point of view presented by each hypothesis or scientist, paying particular attention to any similarities and differences between them
- locate units, labels, and variables in the figures, if applicable

You will be asked to consider how new information presented in the question stem relates to the given theories or hypotheses, so be sure you have a clear understanding of how the hypotheses differ from each other so that you do not confuse them.

Explanation

Identify

The introduction mentions *several plans* and there are two headings labeled *Proposal*; these clues indicate that this is a Conflicting Viewpoints passage.

Analyze

Summarize the key features of both proposals:

- **Proposal 1:** space debris would be captured with nets, harpoons, and robotic arms, then propulsion systems steer it into the atmosphere to burn up
- **Proposal 2:** electromagnetic tethers would be used to slow space debris to the point that it falls closer to Earth and burns up

Examine, predict, and answer

Summarize the information presented in the question stem: examination of each proposal as it relates to the claim will be required.

- The claim states that space debris falling out of Earth's orbit down to Earth will burn up.
- In Proposal 1, the language of *steer the catch into the atmosphere* is analogous to Proposal 2's phrase *slow down the speed of space debris so that it falls closer to Earth*, which both state will make it burn.
- Proposal 2 specifically states the debris will fall closer to Earth and burn.
- Thus, both proposals support the claim.

Choice (C) is correct.

This Conflicting Viewpoints passage only had one question, so it made sense to analyze both proposals at once. For test-like question sets, remember to divide and conquer the hypotheses.

Drills

If Evaluating Models questions give you trouble, study the information above and try out these drill questions before completing the Try on Your Own questions below. Drill answers can be found on the bottom of page 785.

a. What is the central claim of Hypothesis A?

Hypothesis A

Increasing water temperature accelerates development of eel larvae by promoting larval yolk utilization and expression of targeted genes relating to development.

b. What is the central claim of Hypothesis B?

Hypothesis B

Increased disease prevalence and transmission rates occur at warmer water temperatures, so eel larvae mortality is directly linked to increased temperature.

c. What is the point of disagreement between Hypotheses A and B?

d. Is Hypothesis A or B supported by Table C?

Table C		
Water temperature (°C)	Eel larvae length (mm)	Eel larvae weight (g)
14	50	0.134
18	57	0.139
22	65	0.144
26	69	0.146

e.   Is Figure D consistent with Hypothesis B?

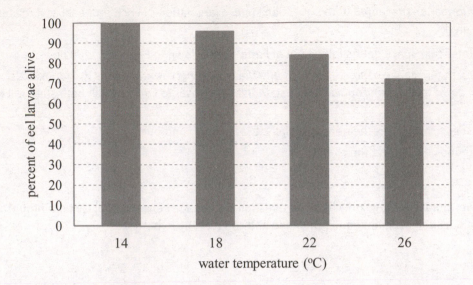

Figure D

Try on Your Own

Directions: Take as much time as you need on these questions. Work carefully and methodically. There will be an opportunity for timed practice at the end of the chapter.

Answers are found at the end of the chapter.

Passage IV

Sweet wormwood, *Artemisia annua* L., contains many commercially useful and therapeutic compounds that can be extracted with a variety of methods. Fifty-gram plant samples were subjected to four different extraction methods in order to determine how the method used affected the amount of each compound in the oil extracted. Sample A consisted of dried plant material vacuum-sealed in a rigid chamber, Sample B of dried plant material subjected to steam distillation, Sample C of dried plant material subjected to hydrodistillation, and Sample D of plant material extracted using petroleum ether as a solvent. Table 1 lists the various compounds collected in micrograms (µg) per 100 mL of oil.

Table 1				
Compound	A	B	C	D
β-myrcene	17.1	3.7	4.2	0.9
1,8-cineole	8.5	5.3	5.4	0.3
Artemisia ketone	46.4	30.2	28.3	16.5
Artemisia alcohol	2.5	3.1	2.2	2.8
Camphor	13.2	24	16.9	20
β-caryophyllene	0.1	3.1	3.9	1.2
Monoterpene hydrocarbons (MH)	24.9	5.1	5	0.9
Oxygenated monoterpenes (MO)	70.6	69.9	60.9	42.6
Sesquiterpene hydrocarbons (SH)	0.5	13.3	13	2.6
Oxygenated diterpenes (DO)	0.6	2.2	4.6	2.3

Consider the following hypotheses that explain the varying amounts of compound obtained from each sample.

Hypothesis 1

Exposure to heat during both steam distillation and hydrodistillation leads to the loss of compounds that can be destroyed by heat.

Hypothesis 2

Exposure to heat during both steam distillation and hydrodistillation leads to an increase in compounds as more oil is able to be extracted from the plant.

Hypothesis 3

One step in the petroleum ether extraction process involves evaporation of the solvent, and some of the volatile plant compounds evaporate along with the solvent.

1. Consider the amount of β-myrcene extracted from a 50-g sample of sweet wormwood. The results obtained from the extraction processes support which of the hypotheses?

   A. Hypothesis 1 only
   B. Hypothesis 2 only
   C. Hypotheses 1 and 3 only
   D. Hypotheses 2 and 3 only

2. Consider the amount of camphor extracted from a 50-g sample of sweet wormwood. The results obtained from the extraction processes support which of the hypotheses?

   F. Hypothesis 1
   G. Hypothesis 2
   H. Hypothesis 3
   J. None of the hypotheses

Science

Drill answers from previous page:

a. Increasing water temperature increases growth rate of eel larvae.

b. Increasing water temperature increases mortality of eel larvae.

c. The effect increasing water temperature has on eels

d. Hypothesis A; at higher water temperatures, eel larvae are longer and heavier

e. Yes; at higher water temperatures, number of eel larvae alive is lower

3. Based on Hypothesis 1, which of the following figures depicts the amount of compounds present in the dried plant material before steam distillation and the amount extracted in the oil after?

    (Note: In each figure, "a" represents "before extraction," and "A" represents "after extraction")

A.

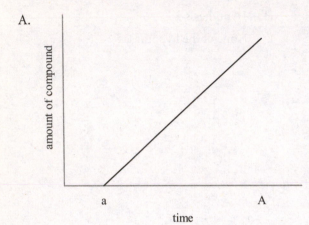

C.

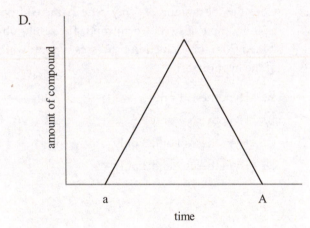

B.

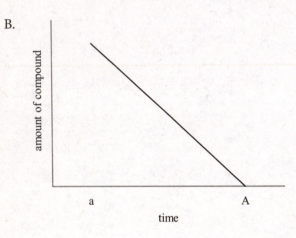

D.

4. Which hypothesis, if any, asserts that heat-sensitive compounds of sweet wormwood can be lost during the hydrodistillation process?

   F. Hypothesis 1

   G. Hypothesis 2

   H. Hypothesis 3

   J. None of the hypotheses

5. Which of the following statements about compound extraction in *Artemisia annua* L. is consistent with all 3 hypotheses?

   A. The proportion of heat-sensitive compounds extracted does not change when using a vacuum chamber.

   B. The chemical composition of the extracted compounds varies depending upon the extraction method.

   C. The extraction method alters the quantity of compounds extracted.

   D. The proportion of volatile compounds extracted will increase when exposed to heat.

6. Hydrosols are aromatic waters containing extracted compounds that form when the vapor created during steam or hydro-distillation condenses. A supporter of which Hypothesis, 1 or 2, would be likely to claim that an herbal hydrosol will contain more aromatic compounds per unit of measurement than dry plant material?

   F. Hypothesis 1 only

   G. Hypothesis 2 only

   H. Both Hypotheses 1 and 2

   J. Neither Hypotheses 1 nor 2

Passage V

Zika virus (ZIKV) is spread by *Aedes* spp. mosquitoes. First discovered in Africa in the 1940s, ZIKV spread into Southeast Asia in the 1960s and caused explosive outbreaks in Pacific and Indian Ocean Islands in the 2000s. This led to the 2015–2016 epidemic, which caused over 500,000 cases in the Americas. Consider the following four hypotheses proposing what changes fueled the ZIKV epidemic.

Hypothesis 1

Climate change causes increased year-round temperatures, which led to a warmer environment that better supported overwinter egg survival of *Aedes* spp. mosquitoes and extended the length of ZIKV transmission, which occurs between 18°C−34°C. Natural disasters, which contaminate water and increase the number of mosquito breeding sites, promoted transmission.

Hypothesis 2

Increased deforestation and urbanization created areas with higher human population densities, which are more suitable for the propagation of *Aedes* spp. mosquitoes and thereby led to higher rates of ZIKV incidence. Additionally, intercontinental air travel and human movement between socioeconomically distinct regions expanded the infection risk of ZIKV.

Hypothesis 3

Aggressive and unregulated use of insecticides caused widespread resistance to develop in *Aedes* spp. mosquitoes. Additionally, ZIKV persisted in animal reservoirs, which were a source for recolonization. Land use changes led to increased contact between humans and infected animals that thrive near industrialized cities, increasing ZIKV transmission.

Hypothesis 4

Economic recession created a new group of people at risk for ZIKV infection due to poor living conditions, including inadequate infrastructure for sanitary living conditions and insufficient access to readily available clean water. This resulted in increased water storage in household containers, which accounted for more than 50% of mosquito breeding sites and thus increased human exposure to ZIKV.

7. Which of the hypotheses assert that unclean drinking water leads to higher rates of ZIKV incidence?

   A. Hypothesis 2 only
   B. Hypothesis 4 only
   C. Hypotheses 1 and 4
   D. Hypotheses 1, 2, and 4

8. Consider the statement "The growth of cities resulting from industrialization increased ZIKV exposure and infection in humans." Supporters of which of the hypotheses would be likely to agree with this claim?

   F. Hypotheses 2 and 3 only
   G. Hypotheses 2 and 4 only
   H. Hypotheses 3 and 4 only
   J. Hypotheses 2, 3, and 4 only

9. The table below lists the annual temperature range (in degrees Celsius) of 4 regions.

Region	Annual Temperature Range (°C)
Region 1	−4–20
Region 2	20–35
Region 3	30–40
Region 4	40–50

   Based on Hypothesis 1, the climate of which region would promote ZIKV transmission?

   A. Region 1
   B. Region 2
   C. Region 3
   D. Region 4

10. Based on Hypothesis 2, which of the following would have the highest risk for ZIKV transmission?

    F. ½ million people in 100 square kilometers
    G. 1 million people in 100 square kilometers
    H. 1 million people in 200 square kilometers
    J. 2 million people in 600 square kilometers

11. Which of the following statements about *Aedes* spp. mosquito propagation is consistent with Hypothesis 3?

    A. Water-storage containers provide breeding sites for *Aedes* spp. mosquito propagation.
    B. Urbanized areas are more suitable for the propagation of *Aedes* spp. mosquitoes.
    C. Increased year-round temperatures promote the propagation of the *Aedes* spp. mosquitoes.
    D. Insecticide resistance in *Aedes* spp. mosquitoes leads to increased propagation.

12. Suppose a sylvatic cycle (the transmission of a virus between wild hosts and vectors) between monkeys and *Aedes* spp. mosquitoes has been identified. A supporter of which hypothesis, if any, would likely claim that the establishment of sylvatic ZIKV makes elimination of ZIKV practically impossible?

    F. Hypothesis 1
    G. Hypothesis 2
    H. Hypothesis 3
    J. Hypothesis 4

How Much Have You Learned?

Directions: For test-like practice, give yourself 6 minutes to complete this question set. Be sure to study the explanations, even for questions you got right. They can be found at the end of this chapter.

Passage VI

Natural processes like tectonic deformation and Earth tides contribute to stress build-up on faults (curved fractures in the rocks of the Earth's crust). Earthquakes occur when the stress built up within the rocks is released as the rocks crack and slip past each other. Researchers propose that human activities may also modulate seismicity (the frequency of earthquakes). Three postulates are presented.

Postulate 1

Earthquakes are induced by surface-mass addition, such as water impoundment behind dams. Increased seismic activity is correlated with water depth in such reservoirs. Approximately 6% of reservoirs with volumes exceeding 0.1 km^3 are reported to be seismogenic (capable of generating earthquakes). A large surface load increases the shear and normal stresses and causes fluid to migrate into fault zones and increase pore pressure, which results in perturbations on faults.

Postulate 2

Extraction of mass from the Earth's subsurface via mining induces earthquakes. For instance, groundwater extraction artificially lowers the water table. This depletion of groundwater reduces normal stress that prevents slip on faults. Extraction of coal and gas is similarly linked to seismicity. Mining excavations cause stress perturbations in surrounding rocks that can exceed the strength of competent rock and cause earthquakes.

Postulate 3

Introduction of mass into the subsurface via injection induces seismicity. Disposal of waste and underground storage of gas and hydrogen into rock increases the pore pressure, which encourages rock failure. Higher frequency of earthquakes is correlated with greater volume injected. Likewise, hydraulic fracturing, or fracking, activates faults. Fracking pumps high-pressure fluid into fractured rock to create porosity for extraction of gas and oil. The combination of fluid injection and pressure depletion produces earthquakes, releasing the stress.

1. Which of the postulates assert that fluid in rock increases pore pressure?

    A. Postulates 1 and 2 only
    B. Postulates 2 and 3 only
    C. Postulates 1 and 3 only
    D. Postulates 1, 2, and 3

2. Which of the following statements is supported by Postulate 1?

    F. Tall buildings, which increase the stress on the ground at their bases, can influence seismicity.
    G. Quarrying, which removes mass from the Earth's surface, can induce earthquakes.
    H. Substantial coastal land loss due to erosion can alter stresses at 2-km depth and trigger earthquakes.
    J. Underground nuclear tests that displace faults can generate several hundred small earthquakes.

3. Suppose that the removal of mass from the Earth's crust reduces the normal stress that prevents slip on faults. Which of the following would exert an opposite force to mitigate pressure reduction?

    A. Mass addition
    B. Mining
    C. Fracking
    D. Groundwater extraction

4. The following table lists the density of 4 fluids.

Fluid	Density (kg/m³)
hydrocarbon	500
hydrogen	0.1
natural gas	0.5
water	1,000

Suppose that 1,000 kg of a fluid are injected into the Earth's subsurface. Based on Postulate 3, the injection of which fluid would most likely induce earthquakes?

F. Hydrocarbon

G. Hydrogen

H. Natural gas

J. Water

5. Which of the following statements about earthquakes is consistent with all three postulates?

A. Pre-existing tectonic stress is not sufficient to trigger large earthquakes.

B. Earthquakes occur in response to perturbations on faults to release tectonic stress.

C. Induced earthquakes release more stress on faults than that which is artificially loaded on them.

D. Earthquakes occur only in previously seismically inactive regions.

6. Based on Postulate 1, which of the following reservoir dimensions would be most likely to be seismogenic?

F. 0.1 km × 0.1 km × 6 km

G. 0.1 km × 0.2 km × 4 km

H. 0.1 km × 0.3 km × 4 km

J. 0.2 km × 0.1 km × 5 km

7. Suppose that excavation of tunnels for road and railway transport has been linked to earthquakes. A supporter of which of the postulates would be likely to claim, "The earthquakes resulted from an unfavorable juxtaposition of rocks, in which the rocks unable to support the large stress gradient created by the excavation activated the fault zone"?

A. Postulate 2 only

B. Postulate 3 only

C. Postulates 2 and 3 only

D. Postulates 1, 2, and 3

Science

Reflect

Directions: Take a few minutes to recall what you've learned and what you've been practicing in this chapter. Consider the following questions, jot down your best answer for each one, and then compare your reflections to the expert responses on the following page. Use your level of confidence to determine what to do next.

1.   When presented with a Conflicting Viewpoints passage, what approach does an ACT expert use to go through the multiple theories and their associated questions?

_____

_____

_____

2.   Will two theories in a Conflicting Viewpoints passage always draw opposite conclusions about the data?

_____

_____

_____

3.   Will an ACT Science question potentially require an outside piece of knowledge you don't know to be able to correctly answer it?

_____

_____

_____

4.   What key features does an ACT expert look for when asked to identify an answer choice that would weaken a given theory?

_____

_____

_____

5.   How will you approach Conflicting Viewpoints passages differently as you continue to practice and improve your performance in the ACT Science section?

_____

_____

_____

Science

Responses

1. When presented with a Conflicting Viewpoints passage, what approach does an ACT expert use to go through the multiple theories and their associated questions?

First, read the introductory paragraph(s) and the first viewpoint, then search for questions that ask only about the first viewpoint and answer them. Next, read the second viewpoint, then search for questions that ask only about the second viewpoint and answer them; if there are additional viewpoints, repeat this process with each of them. Finally, answer questions that ask about multiple viewpoints and any other remaining questions.

2. Will two theories in a Conflicting Viewpoints passage always draw opposite conclusions about the data?

Of course not! Despite the name of the passage type, two theories don't necessarily have to disagree about the presented data. In fact, the data presented may support one, both, or neither of theories. There may also be more than two theories presented in a passage.

3. Will an ACT Science question potentially require an outside piece of knowledge you don't know to be able to correctly answer it?

While this is a possibility, it's important again to stress that if you've taken your high-school science courses, then these questions will be few and far between. If this happens to you on test day, do your best to eliminate any answer choices you can and make an educated guess. Most importantly, don't waste time on it; move on the massive chunk of questions that don't require outside knowledge.

4. What key features does an ACT expert look for when asked to identify an answer choice that would weaken a given theory?

Information that weakens a theory makes it less likely to be true. An answer choice does not need to definitively prove the theory false to weaken it. Rather, it just needs to detract from the theory's claims by differing with one of its statements or assumptions.

5. How will you approach Conflicting Viewpoints passages differently as you continue to practice and improve your performance in the ACT Science section?

There is no one-size-fits-all answer here. Reflect on your own habits in identifying the central claims of a theory and whether it is supported by the given data or a new piece of information, and give yourself an honest assessment of your strengths and weaknesses. Consider the strategies you've seen experts use in this chapter, and put them to work in your own practice to increase your accuracy, speed, and confidence.

Next Steps

If you answered most questions correctly in the "How Much Have You Learned?" section, and if your responses to the Reflect questions were similar to those of an expert, then consider Conflicting Viewpoints passages an area of strength and move on to the next chapter. Come back to this topic periodically to prevent yourself from getting rusty.

If you don't yet feel confident, review the material in this chapter and then try the questions you missed again. As always, be sure to review the explanations closely. Then go online (**kaptest.com/login**) to use your Qbank for more practice. If you haven't already registered your book, do so at *kaptest.com/moreonline*.

GO ONLINE

kaptest.com/login

Answers and Explanations

Applying Core Knowledge Questions

1. B
Difficulty: Low

Category: Interpreting Data

Getting to the Answer: In Figure 2, carbon dioxide becomes a liquid around −57°C, when the pressure is about 4,000 mm Hg, and remains a liquid up to about 31°C, at pressures over 50,000 mm Hg. The correct answer is (B).

2. J
Difficulty: Medium

Category: Interpreting Data

Getting to the Answer: First, determine the phase of water at 13°C and 28 mm Hg. According to Figure 1, at 13°C and 28 mm Hg, H_2O exists as a liquid. Eliminate F and H. Next, determine the phase of carbon dioxide at 13°C and 28,000 mm Hg. According to Figure 2, CO_2 exists as a gas at that temperature and pressure. Thus, the correct answer is (J).

3. C
Difficulty: Low

Category: Applying Core Knowledge

Getting to the Answer: Liquids are characterized by closely packed, free-flowing molecules. There is little space between liquid molecules, so liquids are not easily compressible. The correct answer is (C).

Choice A describes a characteristic of a solid. Choice B describes a characteristic of a gas. While liquids do assume the shape of whichever part of a container their volume occupies, liquid molecules do not assume the *entire* shape and volume of a container. That is a characteristic of a gas, so D is incorrect.

4. G
Difficulty: Medium

Category: Applying Core Knowledge

Getting to the Answer: The freezing point is the point at which liquid transitions to solid at a given pressure. In Figure 2, 70,000 mm Hg is beyond the range of the graph. Extend the y-axis to 70,000 mm Hg and continue the solid-liquid boundary line (its slope suggests that, for every increase of 10,000 mm Hg in pressure, there is a temperature increase of a degree or two in the freezing point). Because the freezing point at a pressure of 50,000 mm Hg is just under −50°C, you can expect that the freezing point at 70,000 mm Hg would be only a few degrees higher than that, or roughly −50°C, as in (G).

5. D
Difficulty: Medium

Category: Interpreting Data

Getting to the Answer: On Figure 1, look at the area above 5 mm Hg and ignore the area below. Above 5 mm Hg, as temperature decreases, water transitions from gas directly to liquid and then from liquid directly to solid. Since the transition from gas to liquid is not an option, the correct answer is (D), from liquid to solid.

6. H
Difficulty: Medium

Category: Synthesizing Data

Getting to the Answer: A substance melts when it transitions from solid to liquid. The solid-liquid boundary for H_2O falls along 0°C, while the solid-liquid boundary for CO_2 falls between about −57°C and −51°C. Because −51°C is less than 0°C, H_2O always melts at a higher temperature than CO_2. The correct answer is (H).

7. A
Difficulty: Medium

Category: Interpreting Data

Getting to the Answer: The triple point is the temperature and pressure at which the three phases of a substance exist in equilibrium. In Figure 2, the triple point is where the solid-liquid, liquid-gas, and solid-gas boundary lines meet. The temperature and pressure at this point are approximately −55°C and 4,000 mm Hg, respectively. The correct answer is (A).

Conflicting Viewpoints Passages and Supporting Hypotheses Questions

1. C

Difficulty: Medium

Category: Supporting Hypotheses

Getting to the Answer: Consider how the data for β-myrcene relate to each hypothesis. Hypothesis 1 says that steam distillation and hydrodistillation reduce the levels of certain compounds, and Samples B and C, respectively, were the samples subject to those methods. Samples B and C do contain lower levels of β-myrcene than does Sample A, which is consistent with Hypothesis 1. Thus, you can eliminate B and D, which both leave out Hypothesis 1. The only difference between the remaining choices is that one includes Hypothesis 3 and one does not. This means that you can skip Hypothesis 2 and evaluate Hypothesis 3. This hypothesis says that in samples subject to petroleum ether extraction, as sample D was, some compounds will be lost as the ether evaporates. This is consistent with Sample D, so (C) is correct.

2. G

Difficulty: Medium

Category: Supporting Hypotheses

Getting to the Answer: According to Table 1, the levels of camphor in samples B and C, which were subject to steam distillation and hydrodistillation, respectively, were greater than the level of camphor in sample A. This is consistent with Hypothesis 2, which states that these kinds of distillation can increase the levels of certain compounds in the extracted oil. Choice (G) is correct.

3. B

Difficulty: Low

Category: Synthesizing Data

Getting to the Answer: The lines of each of these graphs represent the change in the amount of compounds in the plant matter before steam distillation and the amount of compounds in the extracted oil. According to Hypothesis 1, steam distillation leads to the loss of certain compounds, so the correct choice will have a graph with a line that slopes downward. Only (B) has such a line, so it is correct.

4. F

Difficulty: Low

Category: Supporting Hypotheses

Getting to the Answer: Only the first two hypotheses mention hydrodistillation, so you can eliminate H. Of Hypotheses 1 and 2, the first claims that hydrodistillation decreases the amounts of some compounds, while the second claims that hydrodistillation increases the concentration of certain compounds in extracted oils. Since you're looking for a hypothesis about compounds lost during distillation, (F) must be the correct answer.

5. C

Difficulty: Medium

Category: Supporting Hypotheses

Getting to the Answer: This is an open-ended question; since you can't predict an answer, move through the choices one by one. Choice A is incorrect because none of the hypotheses make any claims about the effects of using a vacuum chamber. Be careful with B; while the levels of compounds change with each extraction method, none of the hypotheses claim that the chemical composition of the compounds changes depending on the extraction method. Choice (C) is correct; each hypothesis claims that the extraction method will affect the amount of compounds in the extracted oil. Choice D is incorrect because it is only consistent with Hypothesis 2 and is actually contradicted by Hypothesis 1.

6. G

Difficulty: Hard

Category: Supporting Hypotheses

Getting to the Answer: Hypotheses 1 and 2 both deal with the effects of steam and hydrodistillation. Hypothesis 1 claims that these methods decrease the amounts of certain compounds, while Hypothesis 2 claims that the methods increase the levels of certain compounds. Thus, only a supporter of Hypothesis 2 would claim that hydrosols have a higher proportion of certain compounds, and (G) is correct.

7.   C

Difficulty: Medium

Category: Supporting Hypotheses

Getting to the Answer: Before you evaluate the choices in a question like this, scan the answer choices quickly; here, you'll notice that Hypothesis 3 is not present in any of the choices, so there's no need to consider it. Hypothesis 1 specifically mentions contaminated water, so it must be included in the correct answer; eliminate A and B. Hypothesis 2 focuses on urbanization and increased travel by humans; since there's no mention of unclean water, it won't show up in the correct choice. The only choice that includes Hypothesis 1 and not Hypothesis 2 is (C), so it must be correct.

There's no need to evaluate Hypotheses 3 and 4, but if you do, you'll see that Hypothesis 3 focuses on pesticide resistance and animal transmission, not water, but Hypothesis 4 does mention lack of access to clean water, which is why it's included in the correct answer.

8.   F

Difficulty: Hard

Category: Supporting Hypotheses

Getting to the Answer: A quick scan of the choices shows that Hypothesis 1 doesn't show up in any of the choices, so there's no need to consider it as you approach this question. Hypothesis 2 asserts that "urbanization," or the growth of cities, is one of the causes of increased ZIKV exposure, so supporters of that hypothesis would likely agree with the statement in the question stem. Thus, eliminate H, as it does not include Hypothesis 2. Hypothesis 3 mentions that conditions in industrialized cities increase the risk of ZIKV exposure, so it also must be in the correct choice; eliminate G. Hypothesis 4 asserts that poor living conditions contribute to the spread of ZIKV, but it doesn't say whether these are in urbanized areas. Thus, Hypothesis 4 should not be in the correct answer, and (F) is correct.

9.   B

Difficulty: Medium

Category: Synthesizing Data

Getting to the Answer: Hypothesis 2 claims that climate change and increased temperatures have increased the risk of ZIKV exposure. Be careful, though; don't just pick the region with the warmest temperatures.

The hypothesis also mentions a specific temperature range: 18°C−34°C. Region 2 aligns most closely with this range of temperatures, so (B) is correct.

10.   G

Difficulty: Hard

Category: Applying Core Knowledge

Getting to the Answer: Hypothesis 2 asserts that areas with higher population densities are at an increased risk of ZIKV transmission, so you need to be able to compare the population densities of the regions in the choices. The region in (G) has more people in the same area as the region in F, so F can be eliminated right away. The region in H has the same number of people as that in (G), but in a larger area, so eliminate H as well. The region in J has twice as many people as the region in (G), but in six times the area, so J must have a smaller population density. (G) is correct.

11.   D

Difficulty: Medium

Category: Supporting Hypotheses

Getting to the Answer: This asks for something that's consistent with Hypothesis 3, so see what it says about ZIKV: that insecticide resistance in mosquitoes leads to increased levels of ZIKV transmission. That's consistent with (D), which is the correct answer.

Choice A is consistent with Hypothesis 4, which asserts that water storage containers can provide breeding sites for mosquitoes. Choice B is consistent with Hypothesis 2, which states that urbanized areas are more suitable for mosquitoes. Increased year-round temperatures as a cause of ZIKV is a part of Hypothesis 1, so C is incorrect.

12.   H

Difficulty: Hard

Category: Supporting Hypotheses

Getting to the Answer: You'll need to determine which hypothesis is consistent with a claim that transmission of ZIKV between monkeys and mosquitoes makes ZIKV nearly impossible to eliminate. Of the four hypotheses, only Hypothesis 3 deals with infected animals. It claims that the virus can persist in "animal reservoirs," such as the monkeys mentioned in the question stem. Thus, (H) is correct.

How Much Have You Learned?

1. C

Difficulty: Medium

Category: Supporting Hypotheses

Getting to the Answer: Examine the postulates to see which ones are consistent with the claim in the question stem. Postulate 1 asserts that surface load causes fluid to enter fault zones and increase pore pressure, so it needs to be included in the correct answer. Eliminate B. Postulate 2 doesn't mention pore pressure at all, so it can't be part of the correct answer. The only choice remaining that includes Postulate 1 and not Postulate 2 is (C), so it must be correct.

There's no need to consider Postulate 3 to get to the answer, but it's included because it does assert that hydrogen, a fluid, increases the pore pressure of rock.

2. F

Difficulty: Hard

Category: Supporting Hypotheses

Getting to the Answer: Postulate 1 asserts that earthquakes can be caused by the stresses induced by the addition of mass to the surface. This supports (F), which says that the increased stress due to the weight of a building influences seismicity.

Choice G is consistent with Postulate 2, which claims that the removal of underground mass can cause earthquakes. None of the postulates deal with the effects of erosion or nuclear tests on earthquakes, so H and J are incorrect.

3. A

Difficulty: Medium

Category: Applying Core Knowledge

Getting to the Answer: The normal force is an upward force; the removal of mass from the crust would cause stress from the force to be unbalanced, so a downward force would be needed to counteract that effect. Adding mass would create more of a downward force, so (A) is correct.

Choices B and D are incorrect because both mining and groundwater extraction would result in more mass being removed, which would exacerbate the problem. Choice C is incorrect because fracking stresses rock by injecting fluid; this would not provide an upward force to mitigate the problem.

4. G

Difficulty: Hard

Category: Synthesizing Data

Getting to the Answer: Postulate 3 asserts that injecting fluids into subsurface rock induces earthquakes by increasing pore pressure; the greater the volume injected, the more likely an earthquake is. Since $density = \frac{mass}{volume}$, then $volume = \frac{mass}{density}$. Before you plug any numbers into this formula to figure out which fluid has the greatest volume, think critically about it first. Mass will be constant for all four fluids, so the greatest volume will be from the gas with the lowest density. That's hydrogen, which means (G) is correct.

5. B

Difficulty: Medium

Category: Supporting Hypotheses

Getting to the Answer: This is an open-ended question; it would be hard to predict something consistent with all three postulates, so evaluate the choices one by one. Even though each postulate describes how new stresses can induce earthquakes, it's possible that pre-existing stresses can also trigger earthquakes, so A is incorrect. Choice (B) is correct because even though each postulate describes a different cause of earthquakes, each one focuses on some kind of perturbation or disturbance near a fault that triggers the earthquake. Choice C can be eliminated because none of the postulates compare the relative strengths of earthquakes and the stress loaded onto faults. Finally, D can be eliminated because none of the postulates claim that these induced earthquakes are the only types of quakes possible.

6. H

Difficulty: Hard

Category: Applying Core Knowledge

Getting to the Answer: According to Postulate 1, reservoirs can cause earthquakes due to the increased stress from their mass, with larger reservoirs more likely to cause seismic perturbations. Thus, you'll need to calculate the volume of each of these reservoirs to see which one is largest. You can't use a calculator, but some critical thinking can help streamline the calculations. First, each one has 0.1 as one of the dimensions, so that will have no effect on the comparison. Multiply the other 2 numbers together to see which of those products is biggest: $0.1 \times 6 = 0.6$, $0.2 \times 4 = 0.8$, $0.3 \times 4 = 1.2$, and $0.2 \times 5 = 1$. Of those, 1.2 is biggest, so (H) is correct.

7. A

Difficulty: Hard

Category: Applying Core Knowledge

Getting to the Answer: The claim being made is that tunnel excavation led to the remaining rocks being unable to support the resulting stress. This is in line with Postulate 2, which makes the same claim in regard to mining excavations. Postulates 1 and 3 make no claims about what happens during excavation, however. Postulate 1 asserts that earthquakes can be caused by extra mass on the surface, while Postulate 3 claims earthquakes are caused by fluid injected into subsurface rocks. Thus, (A) is correct, as only Postulate 2 is consistent with this claim.

CHAPTER 26

ACT Science: Timing and Section Management Strategies

LEARNING OBJECTIVE

After completing this chapter, you will be able to:

- Triage the ACT Science section by making quick decisions about which questions to do and which to skip

Timing

You have 35 minutes to complete 6 passages with 6–8 questions each, so you need to complete each passage and accompanying questions in less than 6 minutes. (Note that passages and question sets are not all the same length or difficulty, so some will take longer than others. After 17 minutes, you should have completed about three passages and question sets.

This is a brisk pace, but working through the Data Representation passages quickly will save you some extra time for Research Summaries and Conflicting Viewpoints passages. In addition, plan to triage questions and skip those that you can see at a glance will be time-consuming or difficult. Your real task is not actually to attempt all the questions in 35 minutes but to get as many points from the section as you can.

Section Management

Mark up the passages. ACT Science questions may seem to come in many varieties, but they are ultimately predictable. With enough practice and the right strategies (like those provided in chapters 23, 24, and 25), you can learn what questions to expect as you read through a passage. By marking up the passage as recommended in these chapters, you can prepare yourself to answer its questions more quickly.

Focus on getting the points. Remember: the goal is to answer as many Science questions correctly as possible. There are no points awarded simply for making your way through a tough passage or getting that one particular high-difficulty question correct. That doesn't mean you should rush through the passages as quickly as possible—that can actually cost you time when you find yourself having to reread more while working on questions—or skip every high-difficulty question, but it does mean that you should approach every passage and question set strategically using the recommendations in chapters 23, 24, and 25. In addition, know when to stop working on a question and make a strategic guess so you can spend your time getting points elsewhere.

Don't be afraid to guess. When you encounter an especially tough question that you think would take you too long to answer, it's better to make a random guess, even if you can't eliminate any choices, than to leave it blank and expect to come back later. You have a 0% chance of getting a Science question right if you leave it blank but a 25% chance of getting it right with a blind guess.

Eliminate answers that contradict the passage. If you can't figure out what to predict, narrow down the possibilities by ruling out definite wrong answers. If an answer choice comes into conflict with scientific information from the text or with data from the passage's graphs and tables, it is almost certainly incorrect. In addition, you can sometimes eliminate answer choices that contradict a key piece of information from the question stem itself. In other cases, you can use common sense and basic logic to rule out choices that are implausible. Using process of elimination like this will either reveal the one answer that must be correct or at least increase your odds of guessing correctly among the remaining options.

Don't overthink it. Remember that the actual core knowledge on the ACT Science Test is relatively basic. Most data relationships will be relatively simple linear ones, either direct or inverse—don't strain your brain looking for something more complex when you don't need to. In addition, you'll never need to remember advanced scientific concepts or equations, and you won't need to perform elaborate calculations. If it seems like answering a question will require advanced knowledge or a complex calculation, you're most likely overthinking it.

Don't worry if you find yourself guessing on a lot of questions because you can miss quite a few questions on the Science Test and still get a great score. The median ACT test taker gets only about half of the Science questions correct!

There are three Science passage sets in the "How Much Have You Learned?" section that comes next. Use these passages to practice timing: skip questions you find too time-consuming, return to them if you have time, and keep an eye on the clock. On tougher questions, eliminate choices when you can and guess when you need to. When you are finished, check your work—and reflect on how well you managed the timing.

Keep practicing these timing strategies when you take full-length tests, both in your book and online.

How Much Have You Learned?

Directions: For test-like practice, give yourself 18 minutes to complete this question set. Be sure to study the explanations, even for questions you got right. They can be found at the end of this chapter.

Passage I

Many proteins undergo denaturation upon heating. A denatured protein is unfolded and can no longer perform its normal biological functions. Denaturation usually occurs over a temperature range. Some proteins can fold back (renature) into their original conformation when the temperature is decreased. A series of experiments was performed to determine the denaturation and renaturation behavior of 3 different proteins.

Experiment 1

Fifteen separate 15-mL samples of each of the proteins ribonuclease (RNase), carboxypeptidase (Case), and hexokinase (Hase) were heated slowly from 20°C to 160°C and cooled slowly back to 20°C. After every 5°C increase in temperature, 0.002 mL of each sample was removed and chemically analyzed to determine the temperature at which denaturation occurred. After every 5°C decrease in temperature, 0.002 mL of each sample was removed and analyzed to determine the temperature at which renaturation occurred. The results of the experiment are shown in Table 1.

Table 1			
Protein	Approximate molecular weight (amu)	Denaturation temperature range (°C)	Renaturation temperature range (°C)
RNase	13,700	135–145	110–135
Case	35,000	150–155	60–140
Hase	100,000	85–95	–

Experiment 2

Solubility is also a measure of protein denaturation. A protein can be considered fully denatured when its solubility drops to zero. Each 0.002 mL sample of ribonuclease, carboxypeptidase, and hexokinase was

dissolved in 10 mL of ethyl alcohol, and its solubility was measured. The solubility measurements were taken in 5°C increments as the samples were heated from 20°C to 160°C and again as they were cooled from 160°C to 20°C. The results are shown in Figure 1 and Figure 2.

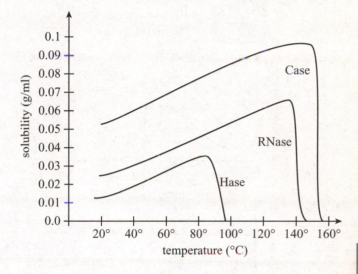

Figure 1

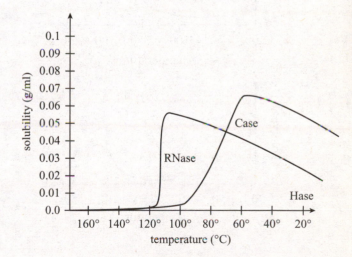

Figure 2

1. Suppose that protein RNase was heated from 40°C to 150°C and then cooled back to 40°C. Which of the following plots would its solubility curve most likely resemble?

    A.
    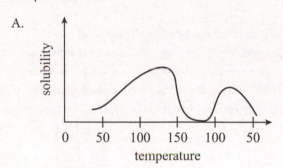

    B.
    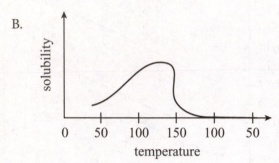

    C.
    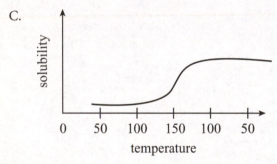

    D.
    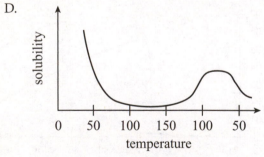

2. According to Figure 1, what would most likely be the solubility of Case in 10 mL of ethyl alcohol at 0°C ?

    F. 0.055 g/mL
    G. 0.045 g/mL
    H. 0.015 g/mL
    J. 0.000 g/mL

3. According to Table 1, within which temperature range, if any, did protein Hase renature?

    A. 85–95°C
    B. 60–140°C
    C. 110–135°C
    D. Hase did not renature.

4. Based on Table 1 and Figure 1, the maximum of the solubility curves for each of the three proteins corresponds to:

    F. denaturation molecular weight.
    G. renaturation molecular weight.
    H. denaturation temperature range.
    J. renaturation temperature range.

5. A student hypothesized that a higher molecular weight yields a higher average denaturation temperature. Are the results of Experiment 1 consistent with this hypothesis?

    A. Yes, because RNase had the highest molecular weight and highest average denaturation temperature.
    B. Yes, because Case had the highest molecular weight and the highest average denaturation temperature.
    C. No, because higher molecular weights actually correspond to lower average denaturation temperatures.
    D. No, because there is no correlation between molecular weight and average denaturation temperature.

6. Which of the following statements best explains why peak solubility of Case was lower after going through the process of denaturation and renaturation?

    F. Part of the renatured protein formed a precipitate.

    G. The samples before denaturation and after renaturation were taken from different parts of the solution.

    H. Only a fraction of denatured protein renatured back into its native, active form.

    J. There were contaminants in the samples that lowered solubility.

7. Suppose a fourth protein, ovalbumin, denatures between 115°C and 130°C and renatures between 70°C and 100°C. If the procedures of Experiment 2 were repeated with ovalbumin, its solubility curve would most likely peak at about:

    A. 85°C.

    B. 95°C.

    C. 105°C.

    D. 115°C.

Passage II

The rings of Saturn, the sixth planet from the sun, are less than a kilometer thick and composed of particles containing ice, rock debris, and dust. The origin of Saturn's rings, however, is not fully understood. Three hypotheses on ring origin are discussed.

Hypothesis 1

Saturn's rings were formed from collision-generated debris. Large objects such as asteroid-type bodies and/or moons passed very close to Saturn and experienced strong tidal forces, which caused collisions between the objects. When these large bodies collided, smaller fragments formed, which in turn collided and created debris. The pushing and pulling from the gravity of Saturn and its moons caused the debris to scatter and orbit, thus creating Saturn's rings.

Hypothesis 2

The particles that make up Saturn's rings were supplied by water-rich plumes venting from satellites in the south polar region of Saturn. During geological activity of the satellites, cryovolcanoes shot geyser-like jets of water vapor, molecular hydrogen, sodium chloride crystals, and ice particles up 500 km into space. Some fell back as snow, while the rest escaped and formed Saturn's rings. Over 100 geysers have been identified.

Hypothesis 3

The rings of Saturn were formed from the particles of the protoplanetary cloud around Saturn. Gravity kept dust and debris left over from the formation of Saturn in orbit. After the appearance of the magnetic field of Saturn, orbits of ice-carbon superconductive particles moved from the protoplanetary cloud to the magnetic equator plane, where magnetic energy was at a minimum. The rings resulted from the electromagnetic interaction of the particles with the planetary magnetic field.

8. Which hypothesis, if any, asserts that the materials of Saturn's rings are relics of the earliest days of Saturn's formation?

    F. Hypothesis 1

    G. Hypothesis 2

    H. Hypothesis 3

    J. None of the hypotheses

9. Assume all the outer planets, those outside the asteroid belt, have rings. Supporters of which of the hypotheses would be likely to agree with the statement, "Rings form around outer planets because the sun's heat cannot destroy superconductivity outside the asteroid belt"?

    A. Hypothesis 2 only

    B. Hypothesis 3 only

    C. Hypotheses 2 and 3

    D. Hypotheses 1, 2, and 3

10. Suppose around 200 million years ago, a moon passing too close to Saturn was ripped apart. A supporter of which of the hypotheses would be likely to claim that the moon got trapped in Saturn's gravitational pull, which tore it to shreds and circularized the orbits of the debris?

    F. Hypothesis 1 only

    G. Hypothesis 3 only

    H. Hypotheses 1 and 3 only

    J. Hypotheses 1, 2, and 3

11. As described by Hypothesis 2, which of the following is the most likely force that caused the water vapor erupted by geysers to fall back as snow?

    A. Air resistance

    B. Spring

    C. Gravitational

    D. Centrifugal

12. Which of the following statements about Saturn's rings is consistent with all 3 hypotheses?

    F. Fragments from collisions make up the rings.

    G. The rings are composed of ice particles, rock debris, and dust.

    H. The gravity of Saturn caused snow crystals to orbit and thereby form rings.

    J. The rings are a plane of solid ice and rock that is less than a kilometer thick.

13. By convention, the direction of a magnetic field goes outward from the north pole toward the south pole. Based on Hypothesis 3, which of the following figures best depicts the magnetic field around Saturn?

    A.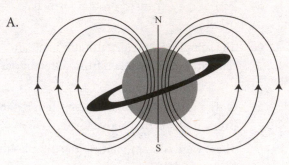

    B.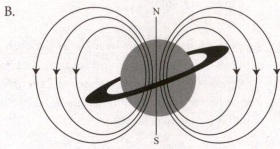

    C.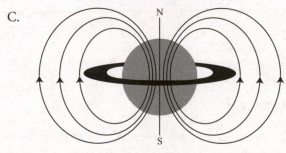

    D.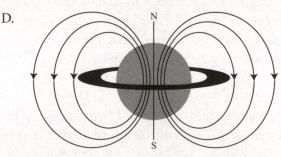

Passage III

Landfill leachate poses a threat to groundwater used for drinking, irrigation, animal feed, and industry. To assess the extent of pollution of a landfill site on the nearby water supply, 19 wells were sampled and analyzed for physicochemical properties. Wells 1, 2, and 3 were upstream of the landfill, while the remaining 10 wells were downstream. Table 1 and Table 2 show the pH, electrical conductivity (EC), and chemical oxygen demand (COD) of the groundwater in the wells during a period of low tide and high tide, respectively. Table 3 shows the landfill's impact on the level of pollution.

Table 1			
Low Tide			
Well	pH	EC (ms/cm)	COD (mg/L)
1	7.0	1.3	0
2	7.4	0.5	0
3	7.7	0.6	0
4	6.8	10.1	275
5	7.5	8.9	234
6	7.7	1.8	43
7	7.3	2.4	67
8	6.8	6.5	83
9	7.2	3.4	70
10	7.2	1.4	65
11	7.2	4.6	54
12	7.0	6.1	113
13	7.4	2.3	37

Table 2			
High Tide			
Well	pH	EC (ms/cm)	COD (mg/L)
1	6.7	1.1	0
2	6.8	0.5	0
3	6.6	0.6	0
4	6.7	11.6	290
5	7.5	8.0	324
6	6.9	1.5	56
7	6.5	5.9	89
8	6.3	6.1	112
9	6.7	3.6	74
10	6.9	1.3	82
11	7.2	4.3	66
12	7.0	6.2	154
13	7.2	1.9	53

Table 3		
Pollution level	EC (ms/cm)	COD (mg/L)
None	<1.4	0
Minimal	1.4–6.5	0
Moderate	1.4–6.5	>0 to <200
Extreme	>6.5	>200

14. According to the results of the study, what is the level of pollution for Well 13?

F. None
G. Hardly any
H. Moderate
J. Extreme

15. Based on Tables 1 and 2, the average EC, in ms/cm, for the control group data is closest to which of the following?

A. 0.6
B. 0.8
C. 2.4
D. 3.0

16. The level of *water mineralization* is proportional to the value of the water's electrical conductivity (EC). According to Table 1, which of the following wells has the strongest water mineralization?

    F. Well 4
    G. Well 6
    H. Well 11
    J. Well 12

17. Consider this statement: "The wells downstream of the landfill had greater chemical oxygen demand levels during high tide than during low tide." Do the data in the tables support this prediction?

    A. Yes; for Wells 1–3, the values for COD were higher during high tide than during low tide.
    B. Yes; for Wells 4–13, the values for COD were higher during high tide than during low tide.
    C. No; for Wells 1–3, the values for COD were lower during high tide than during low tide.
    D. No; for Wells 4–13, the values for COD were lower during high tide than during low tide.

18. The pH data for Wells 6–9 in Tables 1 and 2 is best represented by which of the following graphs?

    F.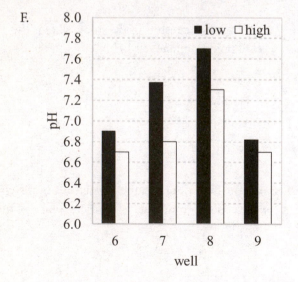

G.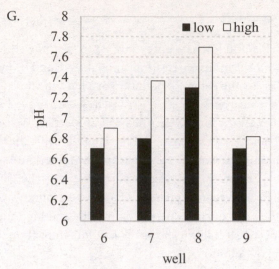

H.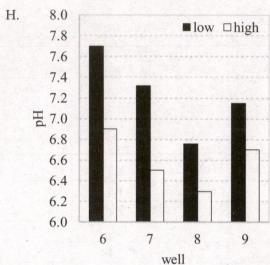

J.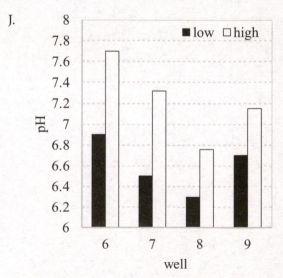

19. Suppose the scientists sampled another well for which the values are in the following table.

pH	EC (ms/cm)	COD (mg/L)
7.7	0.5	0

Based on Tables 1 and 2, when and where was the well most likely sampled?

A. Low tide, upstream

B. Low tide, downstream

C. High tide, upstream

D. High tide, downstream

Answers and Explanations

How Much Have You Learned?

1. A

Difficulty: Low

Category: Synthesizing Data

Getting to the Answer: This question is asking you to combine parts of the graphs in Figures 1 and 2 into a single graph. Notice that Figure 1 shows the solubility of RNase increasing until it hits a peak at about 135°C, after which it rapidly drops off. Figure 2 shows RNase with no solubility at higher temperatures, but with a rapid increase just before a relatively smaller peak at about 115°C, followed by a more gradual decline as the temperature cools. Thus, the correct graph should look like two hills separated by a valley, with the larger peak coming first. This corresponds to the graph in (A), the correct answer.

Choice B is incorrect because it shows only the first peak, but not the second one as RNase renatures. Choice C is incorrect because it shows a single increase followed by a plateau, which corresponds to nothing in Figures 1 or 2. Choice D is incorrect because it doesn't capture the rise in solubility of the first peak and has it at too low of a temperature, even though it captures the second peak accurately.

2. G

Difficulty: Low

Category: Using Data

Getting to the Answer: Extend the curve representing Case until it intersects the 0°C line (the *y*-axis). The value at that intersection should be a bit less than 0.05 g/mL. Thus, the correct answer is (G).

Choice F can't be correct, because it is higher than the solubility at 20°C, and solubility clearly drops with decreasing temperature. Choices H and J would be too low.

3. D

Difficulty: Low

Category: Interpreting Data

Getting to the Answer: According to Table 1, no renaturation temperature range is listed for Hase, so you can infer Hase did not renature upon cooling after heating. The correct answer is (D).

Choice A corresponds to Hase's denaturation temperature range, and B and C correspond to the renaturation temperatures of Case and RNase, respectively.

4. H

Difficulty: Medium

Category: Synthesizing Data

Getting to the Answer: Solubility curves are found in Figure 1, where solubility is a function of temperature, so you can eliminate F and G (also, nothing in the passage suggests that molecular weight changes during denaturation or renaturation). Piecing together Table 1 with Figure 1, you can see that maximum solubility falls within the denaturation temperature range, so the correct answer is (H).

5. D

Difficulty: Medium

Category: Supporting Hypotheses

Getting to the Answer: Molecular weight and denaturation temperature can both be found in Table 1. The average denaturation temperature would fall in the middle of the denaturation temperature range. First, rank the proteins from highest to lowest molecular weight: Hase is highest, Case is in the middle, and RNase is lowest. Then match the denaturation temperature ranges to the reordered proteins: Hase is 80–95°C, Case is 150–155°C, and RNase is 135–145°C. Case has the highest temperatures in its denaturation range, but its molecular weight falls in the middle, so there is no correlation and the hypothesis is not supported. The correct answer is (D).

Choices A and B both incorrectly state that there is a correlation. Choice C is incorrect because it suggests an inverse relationship that is not supported by the data.

6. H

Difficulty: High

Category: Applying Core Knowledge

Getting to the Answer: What would best explain why the peak solubility is lower after Case denatures and then renatures? The passage states that "some proteins can fold back (renature) into their original conformation when the temperature is decreased," which suggests that not all of the molecules of a particular protein will necessarily renature after denaturing. The correct answer is (H). Choices F, G, and J are not supported by the passage.

7. D

Difficulty: High

Category: Using Data

Getting to the Answer: This question requires you to predict the results of repeating Experiment 2 with a new protein. You are given its denaturation and renaturation ranges and are asked to figure out where its solubility would peak. For the original experiments, the ranges appear in Table 1, and peak solubility can be found in Figure 1. Each protein's solubility peaks at the lower end of its denaturation range. So, you should expect that the solubility of ovalbumin will peak at the lower bound of its range at 115°C. Thus, the correct answer is (D).

8. H

Difficulty: Medium

Category: Supporting Hypotheses

Getting to the Answer: Hypotheses 1 and 2 assert that the rings were created by collision debris and plumes of various materials, respectively, but neither makes any reference as to when the rings were created. Eliminate F and G. Hypothesis 3 asserts that the rings were formed from remnants of Saturn's protoplanetary cloud; this is the material from which Saturn itself was formed, so (H) is correct.

9. B

Difficulty: Medium

Category: Supporting Hypotheses

Getting to the Answer: Someone making a statement such as the one in the question stem thinks that superconductivity played a role in the formation of planetary rings. Hypothesis 3 is the only one that even mentions superconductivity; it asserts that the rings resulted from interaction between superconductive particles and the planetary magnetic field. Thus, (B) is correct.

10. F

Difficulty: Medium

Category: Supporting Hypotheses

Getting to the Answer: The scenario posited in the question stem results in a circular ring of debris around Saturn after a moon was ripped apart by Saturn's gravity. This is consistent with Hypothesis 1, which asserts that the rings were formed from moons or asteroids destroyed by tidal forces or by collisions. It is not consistent, however, with either of the other hypotheses. Hypothesis 2 claims the rings were caused by plumes ejected from Saturn's moons, while Hypothesis 3 claims they were formed by the remnants of the protoplanetary cloud. Thus, (F) is correct.

11. C

Difficulty: Low

Category: Applying Core Knowledge

Getting to the Answer: To answer this question, you'll need a force that would pull something back towards the surface of a moon. That's gravity, which makes (C) correct.

Choice A is incorrect because air resistance is a force that works in the opposite direction of an object as it moves through air; it wouldn't pull the water vapor back towards the surface. Spring force is the force needed to extend (or compress) a spring a particular distance; since no springs are involved in the ring-creation process, B is incorrect. Centrifugal force is an inertial force that appears to push a body outwards against the axis of rotation. Since the vapor is moving toward the planet, D is incorrect.

12. G

Difficulty: Medium

Category: Supporting Hypotheses

Getting to the Answer: It's hard to predict a statement that would be consistent with all 3 hypotheses, so evaluate the choices one by one. Choice F is incorrect because it is only consistent with Hypothesis 1; Hypotheses 2 and 3 claim that the particles come from hydrovolcanoes and protoplanetary remnants, respectively. The passage does state that the rings are made of ice, dust, and rock; the hypotheses only differ in how the rings were formed, not what they're made out of. Thus, (G) is correct. Choice H is consistent only with Hypothesis 2, so it's wrong. Choice J is incorrect because the rings are not a solid plane; they're composed of particles.

13. D

Difficulty: Medium

Category: Synthesizing Data

Getting to the Answer: According to the question stem, the magnetic field originates at the north pole and moves to the south pole. Choices A and C have the field moving out of the south pole toward the north, so eliminate them. The right answer must also be consistent with Hypothesis 3, which says the rings formed at the magnetic equator. The magnetic equator is halfway between the poles and perpendicular to them; only (D) has the rings placed correctly, so it is correct.

14. H

Difficulty: Low

Category: Synthesizing Data

Getting to the Answer: First, you'll need to look at Tables 1 and 2 to find the EC and COD for Well 13 at low and high tides. The EC ranges from 2.3 at low tide to 1.9 at high tide, and the COD ranges from 37 at low tide to 53 at high tide. All of these figures fit into the moderate range for both EC (1.4 to 6.5) and COD (0 to 200), so (H) is correct.

15. B

Difficulty: Medium

Category: Using Data

Getting to the Answer: First, look at the passage to determine which wells are the control group. Wells 1, 2, and 3 are upstream of the landfill and thus won't be contaminated by it, so they're the controls. To find the average EC, you'll need to add up the low- and high-tide values and divide by 6, the number of terms. According to Tables 1 and 2, the low-tide EC values for Wells 1, 2, and 3 are 1.3, 0.5, and 0.6, and the high-tide EC values are 1.1, 0.5, and 0.6. Since you can't use a calculator, don't waste time doing exact calculations; approximate wherever you can. Round the two 0.6 values down to 0.5; now you have four 0.5 values to add up, which is equal to 2. Round down 1.1 to 1, and now the total is 3. The final value is 1.3, so the total of the EC values is 4.3. To find the average, you'd divide this by 6. Again, though, you don't need to calculate this exactly; $\frac{4.3}{6}$ would be equal to a bit more than $\frac{2}{3}$ (which is approximately equal to 0.67), and the only choice that fits is (B), 0.8.

Choice A may be tempting because it is close to the approximated value of the average. However, remember that the estimate was that the answer would be higher than $\frac{2}{3}$, and you even rounded some numbers down to get that estimate, so the answer can't be lower than 0.67.

16. F

Difficulty: Medium

Category: Interpreting Data

Getting to the Answer: If water mineralization is proportional to EC, then the well with the highest EC will have the strongest water mineralization. The question directs you to Table 1, so look there to see which of the 4 wells in the choices has the highest EC: Well 4, at 10.1. The answer is (F).

17. B

Difficulty: Hard

Category: Synthesizing Data

Getting to the Answer: For this question, you'll need to compare COD values at low tide versus high tide for the wells downstream of the landfill, which, according to the passage, are Wells 4–13. For each of those wells, the COD value in the 4th column is higher at high tide (Table 2) than at low tide (Table 1). This supports the prediction, so (B) is correct.

Choice A is incorrect, even though it comes to the right conclusion, because it bases that conclusion on data for Wells 1–3, which are upstream, not downstream. Choices C and D are incorrect because both come to the wrong conclusion based on incorrect interpretations of the data.

18. H

Difficulty: Hard

Category: Synthesizing Data

Getting to the Answer: First, scan the graphs in the answer choices to see what kind of trends you should look for in the data. All graphs show all low-tide pH values as higher than their corresponding high-tide values or vice versa. That means you can look at the data for just one well and eliminate half of the answer choices based on whether the high-tide pH is higher or lower than the low-tide value. Looking at Well 6, at low tide the pH is 7.7 and at high tide it's 6.9. So, you can eliminate G and J, each of which says the high tide values would be higher. Finally, to see which of the two remaining answers is correct, see which one portrays the values for Well 6 correctly. Choice (H) does so, so it's correct.

19. A

Difficulty: High

Category: Using Data

Getting to the Answer: The value of COD for the additional well sample is 0 mg/L. Based on Tables 1 and 2, COD is only 0 mg/L for Wells 1–3, which are located upstream from the landfill. Note that the EC value of 0.5 ms/cm also matches those for Wells 1–3. Eliminate B and D. Notice the pH values in Table 1 for low tide are greater than 7, while those in Table 2 for high tide are less than 7. The pH of the additional well is 7.7, which would match the pH of the wells for low tide. Choice (A) is correct.

PART 6

ACT Writing

CHAPTER 27

The Method for the ACT Writing Test

LEARNING OBJECTIVES

After completing this chapter, you will be able to:

- Make an informed decision about whether or not you will write the essay for the ACT Writing Test

- Describe the format, structure, and timing of the ACT Writing Test

- Organize supporting points in an essay outline

- State what the graders are looking for

Should I Write the ACT Writing Test?

Is the ACT Writing Test Optional?

The first thing most students point out about the ACT Writing Test is exactly this: it's optional. This is true, and whether or not you choose to write it will depend on a number of factors.

That said, there are colleges and universities that either recommend writing the ACT Writing Test or outright require it. An updated list of those schools can be found at the ACT website.

Why Is There An ACT Writing Test?

Every college student is surrounded by opinions, in and out of class. Many are expressed by friends, fellow students, and professors around them. Others appear in books, articles, essays, documentary films, TV news shows, and other media.

Some opinions are casual (for example, "coleslaw is yucky") and can be left at that. Other opinions, however, have wide-ranging consequences and need support. The process of backing up opinions ("conclusions") with support ("evidence") is called **argumentation** and will be at the heart of much if not most of your college work. A key role of higher education is to prepare people for careers in which evidence-based decision-making is central to success, and thus schools must emphasize reading arguments in a critical way.

Here's the bottom line: **constructing arguments and dissecting others' arguments are skills that all college students should master.** Students who develop these skills do so in part by answering the following questions:

- How should people decide what they believe?
- How can people get others to accept their beliefs?
- What does and does not constitute proper evidence?
- What are the most common types of evidence, and how can each be used effectively?

The ACT Writing Test provides you with an opportunity to show colleges and universities that you already have a handle on those questions. The ACT Writing Test asks you to analyze multiple perspectives on a complex issue. You need to not only be able to argue in favor of and support one perspective, but you must also discuss how your perspective relates to at least one other perspective. Learning how to consider multiple points of view on one topic is key to mastering the Writing Test.

Should I complete the ACT Writing Test?

Whether or not you choose to write the ACT Writing Test will depend on these factors:

- **Do any of the colleges you are planning to apply to require the ACT Writing Test?** If yes, you must write it.

- **Do any of the colleges you are planning to apply to recommend the Writing Test?** If yes, try to determine how heavily these schools' admissions boards weigh the Writing Test scores and act accordingly.

- **How much time do you have to prepare before test day?** The ACT Writing Test is not as time-consuming to master as the essay for some other exams, but the amount of time you would need to prepare will depend on your current writing performance. If you are pressed for time, you may consider not writing the Writing Test and using the time you have to prepare for the four required tests that affect your ACT composite score. On the other hand, if you have a lot of time between now and test day, preparing for and earning a high score on the Writing Test might give you an advantage in the admissions process and will open up more schools for your consideration.

Writing

Writing Test Essentials

> **LEARNING OBJECTIVE**
>
> After this lesson, you will be able to:
>
> ● Describe the format, structure, and timing of the ACT Writing Test

What is the format of the prompt?

The writing prompt will present a specific, complex issue and three perspectives on it. You are asked to ana-lyze those multiple perspectives and to arrive at a point of view on the issue. Then you must state your point of view clearly, support it with clear and relevant examples, and compare it to at least one other perspective; this perspective does not have to be one of the three provided in the prompt.

Although a different issue will be presented on each ACT Writing Test, the Writing Test directions, prompt format, and Essay Task will always be the same. This means that, by becoming familiar with the expectations ahead of time, you can save yourself valuable time on test day. When other students will be busy wading through the directions and figuring out what to do, you will be able to jump right into reading through the issues and perspectives. The predictable format also means that with preparation and practice, you can achieve success on the ACT Writing Test. You can visit the ACT website to review the exact language you will see on the test.

The most helpful part of the Writing Test prompt is the first sentence in the Essay Task, which will clearly and succinctly tell you to write an essay evaluating multiple perspectives on [*insert topic here*]. Start here to es-tablish a clear goal before you read the issue context or the three perspectives.

What essay structure will work best?

Here's a structure that is an excellent basis for the ACT Writing Test assignment. If you understand and practice it, you'll get a head start on the 40 minutes right out of the box. The details of this structure will be discussed later in this chapter:

¶1—Introduce the topic stated in the Essay Task and state your thesis.

¶2—Connect your thesis to your first example/reason that supports your thesis; provide a short description of that example or reason; include specific, relevant information and maintain focus on using this paragraph to support your thesis.

Time valve: If you are running out of time, don't write a second body paragraph about your thesis. Instead, take the time to write/finish a thorough body paragraph about a second perspective and craft a clear conclu-sion paragraph.

¶3—Connect your thesis to your second example/reason that supports your thesis; provide a short descrip-tion of that example or reason; include specific, relevant information and maintain focus on using this para-graph to support your thesis.

¶4—Explain how your thesis compares and contrasts with Perspectives One, Two, and/or Three (or an outside perspective).

¶5—Summarize your thesis.

Memorize this structure and use it on your practice essays. If you know the form of your essay beforehand, you just have to fill in the content on test day.

How is the ACT Writing Test timed?

The Writing Test is 40 minutes long and includes one prompt. You will use that time to read the prompt and then plan, write, and proofread your response.

With only 40 minutes for the Writing Test, efficient use of time is critical. Divide your time as follows:

- 8 minutes: Read the prompt and plan your essay.
- 30 minutes: Produce (write) your essay, sticking to the plan.
- 2 minutes: Proofread and correct any errors.

On the Writing Test, you won't be able to guess on the last few questions when you're running out of time. Thus, it is important to time yourself carefully to avoid losing focus and coherence toward the end. If you do start running out of time, don't try to squeeze in an extra body paragraph. Instead, take the time to write a thorough final body paragraph and a clear conclusion paragraph. The conclusion is a necessary component of your essay, and its exclusion will cost you more than a strong body paragraph will gain you.

Even when you're rushed, leave yourself one to two minutes to proofread for errors that affect clarity. It's human nature to make errors while writing, and it's important to give yourself a chance to fix any extreme mistakes before time is up.

How is the ACT Writing Test scored?

Your essay will be scored according to four domains: Ideas and Analysis, Development and Support, Organization, and Language Use and Conventions. Two trained readers score your essay on a scale of 1–6 for each of the four Writing Test domains; those scores are added to arrive at your four Writing domain scores (each from 2 to 12). You will also receive an overall Writing Test score ranging from 2 to 12, which is determined by a rounded average of the four domain scores. Essays can receive a zero if they are entirely off-topic, left blank, illegible, or written in a language other than English. If there's a difference of more than 1 point between the two readers' scores (for example, one reader gives the essay a 3 and the other a 5), your essay will be read by a third reader.

Statistically speaking, there will be few essays that score 12 out of 12 for all four Writing Test domains. If each grader gives your essay a 4 or 5 for each of the four domains (making your subscores 8–10), that will place you within the upper range of those taking the exam.

Writing

Dissecting the Prompt

> **LEARNING OBJECTIVE**
>
> After this lesson, you will be able to:
>
> - Organize supporting points in an essay outline

The Prompt and The Plan: 8 minutes

What should I read first?

The Essay Task. The first sentence in the task will tell you what your focus should be for the next 40 minutes, so seek it out first and reference it whenever you feel yourself getting off-topic. Skip the Directions box if you have spent the time familiarizing yourself with those directions already. Read the issue background ("American History Curriculum") and the three perspectives.

What am I trying to get out of the prompt and perspectives?

Focus on identifying at least two points of view related to the topic in the Essay Task. You will need to pick a perspective to support as well as at least one other perspective to discuss in relation to your own.

The perspective you choose to support does not have to match your personal opinion. You should choose a perspective for which you have at least two strong pieces of support.

Directions

The essay is used to evaluate your writing skills. You will have **40 minutes** to review the prompt and plan and write an essay in English. Before you begin, read everything in this test booklet carefully to make sure you understand the task.

Your essay will be judged based on the evidence it provides of your ability to do the following:

- Assert your own perspective on a complex issue and evaluate the relationship between your perspective and at least one other perspective
- Use reasoning and evidence to refine and justify your ideas
- Present your ideas in an organized way
- Convey your ideas effectively using standard written English

Write your essay on the lined essay pages in the answer booklet. All writing on those lined pages will be scored. Use the unlined pages in this test booklet to plan your essay. Your work on these unlined pages will not be scored.

Put your pencil down as soon as time is called.

DO NOT OPEN THIS BOOKLET UNTIL TOLD TO DO SO.

American History Curriculum

Educators and curriculum designers continuously debate the best way to teach American history to high-school students. Whether students are reading historical interpretations or primary source documents, teachers often put the most emphasis on memorizing important names and dates. Although history is generally regarded as a compilation of facts, should high-school students be expected to learn more about history than general information regarding famous people and events? Given the richness of American history, it is worthwhile to explore best practices in presenting the story of the United States to students.

Read and carefully consider these perspectives. Each suggests a particular way of thinking about the most effective way to teach American history to high-school students.

Perspective One	Perspective Two	Perspective Three
It is important to focus on a nation's prominent historical leaders when studying history. Leaders are representative of the nation as a whole, so studying historical figures provides a full perspective.	History is about how society has changed over time, so the most effective way to study it is to examine the rise and fall of broad social shifts.	To learn the story of America, students need to know what happened, when, and who influenced those events. Learning about important events is the most effective way to study history.

Essay Task

Write a clear, well-reasoned essay evaluating multiple perspectives on the most effective way to teach American history to high-school students. In your essay, be sure to:

- assert your own perspective on the issue and evaluate the relationship between your perspective and at least one other perspective
- use reasoning and evidence to refine and justify your ideas
- present your ideas in an organized way
- convey your ideas effectively using standard written English

Your perspective may be fully, somewhat, or not at all in agreement with one or more of the three perspectives in the prompt.

Your test booklet will include pages for planning your essay that provide both prewriting questions and space for notes. It is helpful to review these prewriting questions ahead of time. Since you will already be familiar with the Essay Task from the first page, don't spend too much time reading the Planning Your Essay questions on test day. Instead, after carefully reading the essay prompt, you're ready to start outlining. Keep in mind that anything you write on these pages will not be scored.

Planning Your Essay

These pages will not be scored.

Use the space below to brainstorm and plan your essay. Consider the following as you think about the prompt:

- Strengths and weaknesses of the three perspectives in the prompt
  - What observations do they offer, and what do they overlook?
  - Why are they persuasive or why are they not persuasive?
- Your own background and identity
  - What is your perspective on this issue, and what are its strengths and weaknesses?
  - What evidence will you use in your essay?

It's our recommendation that you plan on an introduction, a conclusion—we'll get to those—and three body paragraphs. We further recommend that you address three or more perspectives in your essay.

You can make do with only two (and, thus, two body paragraphs). But if you carefully examine the published ACT essays that the test makers have identified as superior, you will notice that most if not all of them come up with three. And if you practice this a few times, you'll get better and better at it.

You will decide what kind of outline is appropriate for this particular assignment based on what makes you feel most comfortable and capable as you practice the essay. It's unlikely that you'd create a "sentence outline," in which each Roman numeral, capitalized, and lowercase point is written as a complete sentence: who would have the time? You will likely find it simpler to create a topic outline. Here, for instance, is a possible template:

¶1—Introduce the topic stated in the Essay Task and state your thesis.

¶2—Connect your thesis to your first example/reason that supports your thesis; provide a short description of that example or reason; include specific, relevant information and maintain focus on using this paragraph to support your thesis.

¶3—Connect your thesis to your second example/reason that supports your thesis; provide a short description of that example or reason; include specific, relevant information and maintain focus on using this paragraph to support your thesis.

¶4—Explain how your thesis compares and contrasts with Perspectives One, Two, and/or Three (or an outside perspective).

¶5—Summarize your thesis.

Others might like to go the "idea map" route—jotting down points they want to make, and then connecting those thoughts with arrows that they can follow as they write.

Experiment with more than one method. Go with the one you feel you have the best grasp of. Again, if you would like to read through the exact wording you will see on test day, visit the test maker's website and download the *Preparing for the ACT* guide.

What the Graders Want

After reviewing the grading criteria for the ACT Writing Test, consider how the sample response demonstrates the elements of a successful essay.

Grading Criteria

To minimize subjectivity in the essay grading process, the ACT has developed a standardized set of criteria for graders to use when evaluating essays. Graders are trained to understand the criteria in specific ways so as to reduce the possibility of personal bias or wild subjectivity. By carefully studying many graded essays and graders' comments, we have been able to zero in on what the graders seem to favor, as well as what they tend to disdain. Here's a handy set of charts that will help you understand what graders are looking for so that you can write a successful essay:

Ideas and Analysis

Graders Tend to Favor:	Graders Tend to Disdain:
thoughtful analysis of multiple perspectives	focusing on only one perspective (usually your own)
insightful context into the issue	little to no discussion, only restatement of the issue and/or perspectives
discussion of the issue's complexities and various perspectives' assumptions	discussions that are only somewhat, if at all, related to the issue and perspectives in the prompt

Development and Support

Graders Tend to Favor:	Graders Tend to Disdain:
development of ideas throughout the essay	developing only one paragraph or idea in your essay
development of ideas within each paragraph	restating ideas or only mentioning the facts without any analysis
support throughout the essay	limited to no support

Organization

Graders Tend to Favor:	Graders Tend to Disdain:
clear, precise transitions	transitions rarely used or used inconsistently
organization around a clear purpose	each paragraph seemingly having a different goal
logical progression of ideas throughout the essay	unclear grouping of ideas
logical progression of ideas throughout a paragraph	bouncing from idea to idea within a paragraph

Language Use

Graders Tend to Favor:	Graders Tend to Disdain:
skillful word choice	repetitive, basic, or unreasonably advanced word use
clear and correct sentence structure	grammatically incorrect sentences that do not convey a complete thought—or convey too many!
consistent style and tone	style and tone shifts from casual to formal and everything in between

Sample Student Response

A good understanding of American history is an important part of a well-rounded education. History enables us to understand how and why our culture and political systems came about. Just as scientific discoveries build one upon the other, our knowledge of social systems improves when we understand their foundations through the study of history. Because of this importance, teachers look for the best way to teach history. Three of these methods include focusing on the lives of important leaders, concentrating on the welfare of the society as a whole, and focusing on the important events and dates. Since simple memorization of dates and events does not lead to a deeper understanding of the development of our culture or social systems, history should be taught by examining the development of the entire population, as shaped by the lives and decisions of important leaders.

The best comprehension of history comes through examining the development or progress of the entire population. While great changes are inspired or instigated by great leaders, these changes must be perpetuated by the population as a whole if they are to be effective. My grandparents and teachers have told me that, when they were growing up, there were "White Only" restrooms and water fountains. Even as recently as 50 years ago, some Americans were subjected to open discrimination, despite the Emancipation Proclamation and the efforts of Abraham Lincoln. What is most important for Americans to understand through the study of history is how our society and culture have developed since Lincoln's bold decision. We have moved from enslaving persons of African descent, through enshrining discrimination in law, to electing Barack Obama, a president of African descent, twice by the votes of a majority of the population. Understanding the dynamics and developments that led to this remarkable turnaround are the most important aspects of history, and support the idea that the optimal teaching of history is done through analysis of the welfare of the entire population of a nation, as shaped by the decisions of its leaders.

Especially in American history, where most of the important leaders were democratically elected by a majority of the population, major historical characters could be considered as representative of the nation as a whole, because voters are unlikely to choose candidates with values and backgrounds much different from their own. However, this view overlooks the very exceptionality built into the electoral process. In order to persuade the majority of people to vote for him, a candidate must possess attributes or talents that distinguish him, and make him preferable to his opponent. The example of Abraham Lincoln is illustrative. While Lincoln came from a humble background, similar to that of many rural Americans of his time, his penetrating thinking and persuasive oratory set him apart and were not characteristic of the population as a whole. Lincoln's personal history is an important backdrop to the decisions he made that shaped US history; however, what is most necessary for Americans to understand and appreciate are the changes he brought to the entire nation through his leadership of the North during the Civil War, and through his Emancipation Proclamation. This is why it is necessary to supplement the study of the lives of national leaders with the understanding of how their decisions affected the population as a whole.

The study of history enables us to understand how societies progress, and to use the knowledge of the past to make better decisions in the present. The least valuable understanding of history comes through memorization of dates and events. Although some argue that knowledge of dates and events is necessary for us to learn from the past, if a person could recite the precise date of the signing of the Emancipation Proclamation, or the dates of Barack Obama's inaugurations, that knowledge would be insufficient to describe or explain the effects of those events. A general knowledge of the approximate time of major events is enough to analyze their impact, and again, their impact is best measured by evaluating the development or progress of the population of the nation as a whole.

The most effective way to learn from history is to study how leaders' decisions of the past have impacted society as a whole. In order to make the best decisions, we must have some metric to evaluate the success of the choices made in the past, both the decisions of society's influential leaders and society's acceptance of those decisions. The welfare of the society as a whole is an excellent measure, and should be the focus of teaching history.

Next Steps

Try the Writing Test prompts in the "How Much Have You Learned" section of this chapter. Reach out to a teacher or tutor for more information about getting scores and feedback for your practice essays. Come back to this topic periodically between now and test day to prevent yourself from getting rusty.

How Much Have You Learned?

Directions: There are two prompts available to you in this section. You may choose to complete both at your own speed, both using test-like timing, or some combination in between. Be sure to study the sample student responses; they can be found at the end of this chapter.

Planning Your Essay

These pages will not be scored.

Use the space below to brainstorm and plan your essay. Consider the following as you think about the prompt:

- Strengths and weaknesses of the three perspectives in the prompt
  - What observations do they offer, and what do they overlook?
  - Why are they persuasive or why are they not persuasive?
- Your own background and identity
  - What is your perspective on this issue, and what are its strengths and weaknesses?
  - What evidence will you use in your essay?

Prompt 1

College Tuition

As the cost of college continues to rise, some states are creating programs that provide free or reduced tuition for students who are accepted into community colleges and state universities. While these programs require considerable amounts of taxpayer money, proponents argue that a more educated population benefits the entire nation. Should states continue to fund these programs despite the exorbitant cost? Considering that affording college costs is a major factor in students' decision to pursue higher education, it is prudent for politicians and educators to explore this issue.

Read and carefully consider these perspectives. Each suggests a particular way of thinking about alleviating the burden of college tuition for students.

Perspective One	Perspective Two	Perspective Three
Studies show that attending college, while expensive, is worth the investment. As long as students have access to low-interest loans they can pay off post-graduation, states have no obligation to help students pay for college.	Money currently funding reduced or free tuition should instead be spent on programs helping college graduates secure employment. Guaranteed jobs will provide incentive to graduate, and repaying student loans teaches responsibility and fiscal planning.	In-state college tuition should be free or greatly reduced for all students who receive acceptance letters. Providing affordable education will help more students complete college, which betters society as a whole.

Writing

Essay Task

Write a clear, well-reasoned essay about alleviating the burden of college tuition for students. In your essay, be sure to:

- assert your own perspective on the issue and evaluate the relationship between your perspective and at least one other perspective
- use reasoning and evidence to refine and justify your ideas
- present your ideas in an organized way
- convey your ideas effectively using standard written English

Your perspective may be fully, somewhat, or not at all in agreement with one or more of the three perspectives in the prompt.

Planning Your Essay

Your work on these prewriting pages will not be scored.

Use the space below to brainstorm and plan your essay. Consider the following as you think about the prompt:

- Strengths and weaknesses of the three perspectives in the prompt
  - What observations do they offer, and what do they overlook?
  - Why are they persuasive or why are they not persuasive?
- Your own background and identity
  - What is your perspective on this issue, and what are its strengths and weaknesses?
  - What evidence will you use in your essay?

Prompt 2

Education Technology

Education technology (ed tech) companies gather data about the elementary through high school students who use their products. Some worry that this student data may be sold to outside companies or used to profile students. However, student data is extremely valuable in helping both for-profit and not-for-profit companies develop effective educational software. While schools have a responsibility to protect students, some argue that all ed tech companies should be allowed to buy student data to develop better educational products, even if the data is used for commercial purposes. As ed tech continues to evolve, it is important to develop policies that both protect and benefit students.

Read and carefully consider these perspectives. Each suggests a particular way of thinking about sharing student data.

Perspective One	**Perspective Two**	**Perspective Three**
Information gathered about minors should be wholly protected. It is better to protect students from possible harm than to risk their information being misused, even with the goal of fostering innovation.	There is a clear distinction between educational initiatives and for-profit strategies. Student data should be available exclusively to not-for-profit ed tech developers who provide software at little or no cost to users.	Because of the proliferation of both software and student tech use, it is inevitable that ed tech companies will have access to student data. Therefore, the use of this data should be regulated.

Essay Task

Write a clear, well-reasoned essay evaluating multiple perspectives on sharing student data. In your essay, be sure to:

- assert your own perspective on the issue and evaluate the relationship between your perspective and at least one other perspective
- use reasoning and evidence to refine and justify your ideas
- present your ideas in an organized way
- convey your ideas effectively using standard written English

Your perspective may be fully, somewhat, or not at all in agreement with one or more of the three perspectives in the prompt.

Planning Your Essay

Your work on these prewriting pages will not be scored.

Use the space below to brainstorm and plan your essay. Consider the following as you think about the prompt:

- Strengths and weaknesses of the three perspectives in the prompt
  - What observations do they offer, and what do they overlook?
  - Why are they persuasive or why are they not persuasive?
- Your own background and identity
  - What is your perspective on this issue, and what are its strengths and weaknesses?
  - What evidence will you use in your essay?

Writing

Answers and Explanations

How Much Have You Learned?

Prompt 1

College Tuition

Score of 6

The costs of a college education are rising rapidly and have made a college degree prohibitively expensive for many students. To alleviate this problem, three approaches have been suggested. The first would provide low-interest loans to students and remove any responsibility from the states to provide reduced tuition; the second would provide funding for employment programs to enable graduates to find work so they could repay their tuition loans; and the last would offer reduced tuition to in-state students as part of the state's responsibility to improve the welfare of society as a whole. Because state colleges and universities receive substantial funding from state taxes, and because these state taxes are paid by residents of the state, state colleges and universities should offer substantial tuition discounts to in-state students.

One important reason why the state has a responsibility to provide discounted tuition to residents is that the discount is paid by residents themselves in the form of taxes. Some might consider such discounts to be undeserved handouts, but that viewpoint couldn't be further from the truth. The very source of funding for state colleges and universities is the citizens of the state itself. Because state residents (or their parents) have paid state taxes for years to support their local colleges, they should be eligible for reduced tuition. Given the high burden posed by paying for a college education, it is only just that students receive the benefit of their tax dollars in relieving this burden.

States should provide reduced tuition to their residents as an extension of the social contract. The founding fathers of our country insisted on the provision of education to every citizen and demanded that states offer free public education. In today's world, a high-school diploma is no longer sufficient for many jobs. The increasing complexity of technology, and our dependence on it, demands more highly trained workers in engineering, computer science, management sciences, economics, and social systems. As demands on our nation's workers increase, the level of education supported by the state must also increase. Providing a lower-cost tuition to in-state students is not only fair because of the support residents have provided these schools through their taxes, but also because a well-educated population will improve the welfare of the citizens of the state as a whole. Businesses will be more willing to open factories and operations in states where well-educated employees are available. Technology companies are known to "cluster" in areas like Northern California; Austin, Texas; and the North Carolina Triangle, where major state-sponsored colleges generate qualified graduates. More businesses mean more taxes to generate funds for the state, as well as more support services such as restaurants, retail operations, and personal services that provide even more employment opportunities for the state's residents. Because residents of the state have provided the funds that have supported local colleges and universities, and because a better-educated population will lead to improvements in the general welfare of the entire state, local residents should be offered reduced tuition to state schools.

Some might argue that the funds dedicated to state colleges should be used for employment programs so graduates are able to find work and pay off their loans, thus learning about responsible financial planning. This view would create an entire new tier of administrators between graduates and their potential employers. The money that could be used for lower tuition would instead be dedicated to paying the salaries of the advisors and administrators who would be assisting the graduates. It would be a much more efficient use of the state's resources to simply provide lower tuition to in-state students. In addition, the value of this plan in generating financial responsibility and fiscal planning skills is overstated. Tuition, while substantial, is only one part of the costs of a college education. Students will still learn financial responsibility and fiscal planning as they pay for books, equipment, housing, transportation, food, and other living expenses. Providing an employment-assistance service to college graduates is not a wise use of taxpayers' funds dedicated to education.

As states and students struggle with the rising costs of education, states must recognize the value of a well-educated population, invest in their residents, and use the money raised by state taxes to provide reduced tuition to in-state students. Ultimately, other schemes such as low-cost loans or employment-assistance services divert the money residents have paid to fund education to banks, administrators, and program managers. These funds are more efficiently and appropriately used to directly support residents through low-cost tuition to state colleges and universities. Offering tuition reduction more directly benefits the taxpayers, and it benefits the community as well by encouraging economic growth.

Score of 5

College costs are rising quickly, even much faster than the overall cost of living. Because the high costs are making it impossible for many qualified students to attend college, some have proposed that states offer support to students to enable accepted students to attend state colleges and universities. Three forms of this support have been proposed: low-cost student loans, employment assistance for graduates, and lower-cost tuition to state residents. Because an educated population benefits the state as a whole, and because funds to support state colleges and universities are generated by taxes paid by state residents, states should assist qualified students with tuition assistance.

An educated population benefits everyone, but these benefits cannot be fully realized unless tuition discounts are implemented. For most non-technical degrees, the tuition costs alone for college can come to more than $50,000. For scientific and technical degrees, like engineering and medicine, the costs are much higher because these degree programs take longer to complete. My sister graduated 5 years ago with a degree in elementary education, and college loans of $70,000. Her starting salary was under $30,000. Even with a lower interest rate than she's paying, it would take her many years to pay off her loans. During this time, she won't be able to buy a house, a new car, or have much discretionary spending. My sister teaches fourth grade in a public school. She's an example of a hard-working person whose education is contributing to the welfare of society as a whole. If she could buy a home or hire a housekeeper once a month, these types of modest expenditures would contribute to strengthening the local economy. Low-cost student loans as a solution to the problem of higher tuition are short-sighted. They may seem to relieve the burden on the students, but they actually prevent dedicated graduates from contributing to local economies for extended periods of time.

Furthermore, the funds that support public education are the result of taxpayers' contributions to the government. State residents should receive the most direct benefit from the use of these taxes, and one impactful way to use this money would be to relieve the burden of college tuition by reducing tuition for in-state residents. These residents (or their parents) have already contributed to the funds that would be used in this way, and the benefit is clear. This use of state funds would enable students to graduate with much more manageable tuition loans, thus allowing them to make fuller economic contributions back into the system from which they received the benefit of a reduced tuition.

While some argue that schools should divert their funds to employment services rather than tuition discounts, there are many problems with this apparent solution. Offering employment services to students assumes that graduates are not able to find work to pay off their loans. But for the students who are contributing the most to the welfare of society, like my sister, this is not the case. Almost every municipality is looking for more excellent teachers, nurses, doctors, police officers, computer programmers, and other well-educated professionals. Locating suitable employment is not the problem; the problem is the large amount of debt graduates accumulate through their college careers. Even if jobs were hard to find, this plan doesn't guarantee graduates a position. What if the state located a position far away from a graduate's family? Or found a position that paid substantially below the average market rate for that job? Would the student have to accept whatever position the state identified? The faulty assumptions behind this plan make it a poor choice.

The best solution to rising tuition is for states to offer qualified resident students tuition discounts. While it may seem to be the most expensive option, that is a short-term view. In the long run, it may even generate enough money to pay for itself through the improved business climate. If major companies relocated to the state because of the excellent, qualified workforce created by the reduced tuition program, the tax revenues generated by that company could not only defray many tuition subsidies, but also contribute to the state's general revenue. To improve their business environment, and thus, improve the overall welfare of the community, states should enable their qualified students to attend local colleges and universities. The best way to defray the ever-rising costs of tuition is for the states to offer tuition discounts to these students that are funded by taxes. Low-cost loans and job-placement programs are insufficient to provide qualified students the assistance they need and deserve, and the funds have already been paid by residents in the form of taxes.

Score of 4

The cost of going to college is so high, it's keeping many good students from attending, so it's been suggested that states should come up with some ways to assist student in funding their high education. To address the question of whether states should assist students or not, three views have been presented. Some say the states have no obligation to help because students will be able to repay their student loans once they start working. Others say that the states should start and support job placement services that enable graduates to find work quickly; others believe the states should assist students with tuition discounts. I think the best approach is for states to offer their students reduced tuition to state colleges and universities because the money used to support state schools is raised from taxes paid by the residents, and this will enable state residents to become better educated, improving the society as a whole.

I think the best solution is for the states to use taxes to provide lower-cost tuition for graduates. My parents have paid property taxes here my whole life, and we pay sales tax on everything we buy. Part of those taxes should be used to support the state colleges and universities. My sister graduated from college 5 years ago and has been teaching fourth grade ever since. But she says that after paying for her rent, car, food, and insurance she only has enough left over to make the minimum payment on her student loans. She says it's going to take her another 12 years to finish paying her student loans. States should use the money raised by our taxes to help its residents.

Educated people help improve our communities, which is another reason the state should help reduce tuition. My sister is helping the state by working in a public school educating children. It is the responsibility of the state to assist its residents. Because my sister's job helps her students and so makes our state a better place to live, the state should've helped her graduate without the burden of a large debt from student loans. The state has a responsibility to help our best and brightest improve our communities, and reducing student tuition is a major way the state can help achieve that goal.

Some believe that states should use some of the money they raise for schools for setting up job placement services that will enable their college graduates to find work quickly, but in my opinion, this will not be very helpful. My sister was able to find a job quickly, but still struggles to pay off her loans, so this idea wouldn't help her at all. For many people, the problem isn't finding a job, but in the large amount of money they've had to borrow to finish college. These loans become a great burden over time, and reducing tuition would help more than employment services.

College tuition goes up every year. It's important for states to assist their residents because more educated people make the state a better place to live. Those who say the state has no responsibility to help ignore the benefits that come to the society as a whole from a more educated population. Those who say the state should assist college students by providing an employment service after graduation are assuming that the graduates can't find work, and this is not always the case. States should assist their residents with lower tuitions funded by state taxes.

Score of 3

Going to college is very, very expensive. Because the cost of tuition can prevent some students from going college, three views have been presented to assist them. These are: first, for states to offer low-cost loans, second, for states to provide services that will assist graduates to secure employment so they can repay their loans, and finally, for states to offer tuition discounts to residents. I think that states should give us lower tuition.

Because our parents have paid taxes, and the out-of-state students haven't, I think that it's only fair that we get lower tuitions. That way, any student who is accepted will be able to attend college. I live in Florida and the television ads are always saying that the state lottery contributes a lot of money to education, so some of that money can be used for lower tuition.

If you get a student loan, you have to pay it back and it's easy to end up with huge student loans, so I don't think low-cost student loans are a good idea. The state should do more to help us because we are going to live and work here and make the state a better place. If we're improving the community by getting a good education, the state should help us to do this. Just as the state builds roads to help us get around, and hospitals to take of us when we're sick, and pays police and firemen to keep us safe, the state should help us get a good education. These are all things that make our communities better places to live.

Having a job service for college graduates shouldn't be needed. If you can't get a job, why would you go to college? For the state to find you a job after college seems unnecessary. And that doesn't do anything about the high cost of college. States should be doing something to help make college less expensive so more of us can go.

Because educating it's citizens makes the state a better place to live, just like having good roads, good hospitals and good public services, the states should provide free or reduced tuition for all students who receive acceptance letters. Low-cost student loans and job-placement services are not enough help.

Score of 2

I'm hoping to go to college, but I don't know . . . it's very expensive and my family is already paying for my brother's college. My parents say that I'll have to come up with some way to help them. Just like my brother, he works in the dorm and over the summer he works with a landscape company. There are 3 ideas to help students like me go to college, their can be low-cost loans from the state or the state can help people find jobs or the state can give students free tuition. My parents say some states give the students that live there a discount on tuitions, and I think that's a very good idea. After all, we live here and will work here, and so it's good for the state if we have college degrees. People with college degrees can become engineers or computer programmers, and if you don't have a degree, you can't. We need more engineers and programmers because so many things run on computers.

If there are a lot of people with college degrees in our state, then that's good for the state. More people will want to come here to live, and that means more people will be buying houses, cars and food etc here. That will create more jobs for other people like salesperson and store clerks, and that will help the state. I don't think low-cost loans or job programs will be that helpful.

Score of 1

I think paying for college will be hard, because it's so expensive. I think it would be a good thing for the state to provide lower tuition because if I go to college, I'll be able to get a good job, get married and raise a family. I won't be able to take care of my family as well without a college degree. If I do go to college, I want to make sure my kids have a good life. I don't want to owe a lot of money. It's too hard to pay back. So, it would be good if tuition cost less.

Prompt 2

Education Technology

Score of 6

With the explosion in information technology, many companies are developing applications to enhance students' learning. Some of these companies are profit-based and some are non-profit, entering this endeavor to benefit students and society, not themselves. Because the personal data of technology users is marketable, three perspectives have arisen about the usage of the students' personal information. Some believe this data should never be shared, because it is collected from persons below the legal age of consent. Others believe that the data can be shared, but only among not-for-profit developers who will use the data for further non-profit projects. Finally, some believe that use of this technology, with real-time feedback, implies that the user understands and agrees that the information they provide will be freely available to anyone, for any purpose. Because disclosure of personal information can have serious consequences, and because the students using this software cannot legally consent to a contract, personal information obtained from educational technology should never be shared without consent from the students' parents or guardians.

Even though the information collected by ed tech software has the potential to be utilized to further aid student learning through new applications, this potential benefit is not great enough to permit the sharing of students' personal data in light of its great risks. One doesn't have to look very far to find examples of harm caused by personal information obtained improperly from the internet. My uncle's identity was stolen from his PayPal account, and, while the money that was stolen was replaced, he had to close all his bank accounts and change all his credit cards. Recently, the major company Sony was hacked and their company e-mails were posted on the internet. Educational technology companies should keep the welfare of their student users foremost and not share information obtained through the use of their software. Perhaps I might want to try to take a difficult course online, and then fail it because either the course was too hard, or because I wasn't able to learn it well from the technology. If that information were shared and published on the internet, it might negatively affect my college applications, even though I was just taking an extra class to try to improve myself. Because of the potential harm caused by abuse of personal information, educational technology companies should not share their students' information freely.

In addition to the risks posed by the sharing of student data, such sharing should only be done when one has obtained express consent—and such consent is not usually obtained by ed tech companies. Some believe that students using educational technology understand and agree that, because they're using a real-time application with continuous data sharing, their information can be shared indiscriminately with any organization, for any purpose. This perspective is severely flawed in two ways: it assumes that students would think about and agree to this sharing, and it permits the obtaining of permission for this sharing (however indirectly) from students who are below the legal age of consent. Because most websites offer some privacy protection—for example, any shopping, credit card, or banking site is protected—technology users tend to assume their data is protected. Even Facebook and Google, which rely on users sharing information, encourage their subscribers to limit those who can observe or contribute to their accounts. Students are far more likely to assume their data on educational websites is similarly protected, rather than to think that they are agreeing to limitless distribution of their information. Even if students actually agreed to this sharing, if they are under the age of 18, they're not able to legally consent to this activity. Therefore, educational technology companies should not distribute student information.

Some would argue that the information generated by students' activity on the educational software provides valuable information to improve the technology and should be shared with non-profit entities working to improve educational outcomes. While this may seem to be an acceptable compromise, this view assumes that the sensitive personal data obtained from students will never be stolen or misused. Again, from current events, we know that employees can steal data, as did Edward Snowden, and that even sophisticated systems such as PayPal and Sony can be hacked. If non-profit educational technology companies want to share data, they could strip off all personal identifiers and share information such as number of users, average scores, average time spent, etc. as long as there were no way to trace any information back to the individual student. This could further the goal of developing educational technology while preserving the privacy of students. Without protecting the identities of individual students, this data should not be shared, even with not-for-profit entities.

If educational technology companies want to use the personal information of their subscribers to further improve their products without putting students at risk, they have two options. First, they could disclose their proposed usages and obtain permission from the parents or legal guardians of their users. Second, they could strip off any information that could personally identify the students and use that information in any way they choose. The tremendous success of Khan Academy, a free non-profit educational website that only collects an email address from its users, indicates that these technologies can be developed and improved rapidly without risking the harm to students that could be generated from data sharing. Through the examples of my uncle's identity theft, the hacking of Sony, and Edward Snowden, it is clear that there are many potential problems facing students if their personal information is shared. These risks exist whether they are used to generate profits or for altruistic purposes. Student information obtained from educational websites should not be distributed to other entities without the permission of the student's parents or guardians.

Score of 5

Educational technology companies are generating extensive data through the use of their programs. Non-profit companies want to use this information to improve their offerings more quickly, and for-profit companies want to defray some of the costs of developing these products through the sale of their users' information. Some people believe that any data collected from students under the age of 18 should be completely protected, others believe that that data may be shared among non-profit companies, and others believe that the data may be shared with anyone, because the students are using a real-time system and thus have no expectation of privacy. Because of all the problems that may arise if information is used inappropriately, and because products can be improved without sharing data, student data obtained from educational technology should not be shared.

Those who say student data should be completely protected are correct, because of the many problems that can arise if data is misused. E-mail bullying has caused many students to suffer. If students' scores were ever stolen from an educational website, and published, it could lead to similar trauma. We know from experience that personal information obtained by a company is not safe from hackers. Student data should be completely protected because of these risks.

Many non-profit educational technology companies want to share student data among themselves to share ideas and more quickly improve their products, but this sharing is not necessary to improve their products. After all, Khan Academy is a very successful educational technology program that has risen up very quickly on its own. From one man producing YouTube videos for his niece, Khan Academy is rapidly growing to fulfill its goal of providing a free education to anyone in the world. Their success indicates that data sharing is not necessary to produce excellent educational technology.

Some people think that sharing student data should be an expected outcome of using educational technology. However, students use educational technology to learn; they don't expect to be targeted by advertisers as a result of their search for knowledge or self-improvement. To assume that students know that their information will be shared, just because they're using a real-time application, doesn't make any sense. When we buy something from the internet, our important identity and financial data are protected. Yes, we may later see an advertisement or a recommendation for another product, but even though the sale was made in real-time, our personal information is protected. Users of educational technology sites would expect no less.

Because so many serious problems can arise from the misuse of personal information, data from students under the age of 18 on educational websites should be completely protected. To allow non-profit companies to use it still exposes innocent students to harmful consequences. To allow any company to use it is not only wrong, but unnecessary. Since the protection of minors should be our highest priority and effective education technology can be created without it, student data from ed tech companies should never be shared.

Score of 4

Educational technology companies are considering sharing the data they collect. Some think any data sharing is wrong, because most of the students who generate that data are under the age of 18. Some think that it's acceptable to share data among non-profit companies to improve their products, while some believe that the data can be shared with anyone for any reason. Data shouldn't be shared because of the dangers that may arise when students' data is shared.

The safest route is for educational technology companies to never share their student data. Any time data is shared, there's a risk that it will be stolen and misused. My mom had to get a new Target credit card last year after one of their employees stole a lot of credit card numbers. Perhaps an employee of an educational technology company might do the same thing, and my test scores or home address could be posted on the internet. It's not worth taking that chance. When I'm using an educational website, I expect my information will remain private.

Sharing students' data might not even be legal. People under 18 are considered minors and are not able to consent to their information being used. These products do not ask for consent from parents, so using the data they collect would be wrong. Students are using these sites to improve themselves and to learn. To take that opportunity to use their personal information just to make more money is taking advantage of them. Educational websites should never sell or make money from their students.

Non-profit educational technology companies are trying to help people learn and improve, so some argue that they should be allowed to share student data to modify and improve their products more quickly—but again, any data sharing brings risks. The more people have access to data, the more likely it is that there may be someone who would steal or misuse it. The risks of the harm that may come about from sharing the information are greater than the benefits that may arise.

Student data is personal and private, and it's important for companies to recognize that. Even nonprofit companies should protect students' information and privacy. The risk of damage that may occur if personal information is misused is greater than any advantage that might come from sharing that data, and sharing it might not be legal anyway.

Score of 3

Three perspectives have been offered in regards to ed tech companies sharing the data they collect from elementary and high school students. Some people believe students data should be wholly protected, some people believe it can be shared as long as it's just being used to make the programs better, and some think that everyone should be able to use the data however they like. I agree that students data should be wholly protected because a lot of times, when your information is on the internet, it can cause problems.

My mom is always checking my computer to make sure I don't use the internet wrong. She doesn't let me put our address in my Facebook, even if I just want my friends to be able to come over. She says that somehow crooks could find out where we live. If my school was giving my address out, she'd be upset.

I bet the companies would want to share students information to be able to make their programs better, but it's not worth the risk. Why should I have to worry about bad stuff happeneing to me just because I use some companies website?

And of course companies want to make more money, but I don't want them to make money by making my life more dangerous. That's not fair. Why should they make money off my information? I'm just doing what I have to for my classes.

So the only right thing is for companies to protect student information. This way, students can learn more, and still be safe.

Score of 2

There's three perspectives on sharing student information. First, it should be wholly protected. Second, it should be exclusively available to not-for-profit tech developers. Third, it can be used by anyone. I think it should be protected.

I use the Khan Academy website a lot, and really like it. It enables me to review tough subjects that were covered in my classes and to get in some extra math practice. All I needed to do to use Khan Academy was provide an email account. I used my "trash" email account because I didn't want a lot of extra spam coming to my regular email. But to my surprise, I didn't get any spam from them. I'm more likely to use their site now that I know my information is safe, and that they are not using my email to send me a lot of unwanted advertisements. If I thought they might give my information to other companies, I wouldn't sign up.

Score of 1

I don't want anyone, from any company to have my personal information. I don't want people to know where I live or what I'm doing. I certainly don't want anyone to know my grades if I don't tell them. Privacy is important, and just because I'm trying to learn on the internet, and not in a classroom, I shouldn't have to give up my privacy.

PART 7

Countdown to Test Day

CHAPTER 28

Countdown to Test Day

The Week Before the Test

- Focus your additional practice on the question types and/or subject areas in which you usually score highest. Now is the time to sharpen your best skills, not cram new information.

- Make sure you are registered for the test. Remember, Kaplan cannot register you. If you missed the registration deadlines, you can request waitlist status on the test maker's website, **www.act.org**.

- Confirm the location of your test site. Never been there before? Make a practice run to make sure you know exactly how long it will take to get from your home to your test site. Build in extra time in case you hit traffic or construction on the morning of the test.

- Get a great night's sleep the two days before the test.

The Day Before the Test

- Review the methods and strategies you learned in this book.

- Put new batteries in your calculator.

- Pack your backpack or bag for test day with the following items:

  - Photo ID

  - Registration slip or printout

  - Directions to your test site location

  - Five or more sharpened no. 2 pencils (no mechanical pencils)

  - Pencil sharpener

  - Eraser

  - Calculator

  - Extra batteries

  - Non-prohibited timepiece

  - Tissues

  - Prepackaged snacks, like granola bars

  - Bottled water, juice, or sports drink

  - Sweatshirt, sweater, or jacket

The Night Before the Test

- No studying!
- Do something relaxing that will take your mind off the test, such as watching a movie or playing video games with friends.
- Set your alarm to wake up early enough so that you won't feel rushed.
- Go to bed early, but not too much earlier than you usually do. You want to fall asleep quickly, not spend hours tossing and turning.

The Morning of the Test

- Dress comfortably and in layers. You need to be prepared for any temperature.
- Eat a filling breakfast, but don't stray far from your usual routine. If you normally aren't a breakfast eater, don't eat a huge meal, but make sure you have something substantial.
- Read something over breakfast. You need to warm up your brain so you don't go into the test cold. Read a few pages of a newspaper, magazine, or novel.
- Get to your test site early. There is likely to be some confusion about where to go and how to sign in, so allow yourself plenty of time, even if you are taking the test at your own school.
- Leave your cell phone at home or in your car's glovebox. Many test sites do not allow them in the building.
- While you're waiting to sign in or be seated, read more of what you read over breakfast to stay in reading mode.

During the Test

- Be calm and confident. You're ready for this!
- Remember that while the ACT is an almost three-hour marathon (or $3\frac{1}{2}$ hours if you opt to do the Writing Test), it is also a series of shorter sections. Focus on the section you're working on at that moment; don't think about previous or upcoming sections.
- Use the methods and strategies you have learned in this book as often as you can. Allow yourself to fall into the good habits you built during your practice.
- Don't linger too long on any one question. Mark it and come back to it later.
- Can't figure out an answer? Try to eliminate some choices and take a strategic guess. Remember, there is no penalty for an incorrect answer, so even if you can't eliminate any choices, you should take a guess.
- There will be plenty of questions you CAN answer, so spend your time on those first!
- Maintain good posture throughout the test. It will help you stay alert.
- If you find yourself losing concentration, getting frustrated, or stressing about the time, stop for 30 seconds. Close your eyes, put your pencil down, take a few deep breaths, and relax your shoulders. You'll be much more productive after taking a few moments to relax.
- Use your breaks effectively. During the five-minute breaks, go to the restroom, eat your snacks, and get your energy up for the next section.

After the Test

- Congratulate yourself! Then, reward yourself by doing something fun. You've earned it!
- If you got sick during the test or if something else happened that might have negatively affected your score, you can cancel your scores by the Wednesday following your test date. Request a score cancellation form from your test proctor, or visit the test maker's website for more information.
- Your scores will be available online approximately three to four weeks after your test and will be mailed to you in approximately six weeks.

PART 8

Practice Test

GO ONLINE

Please log in to your online resources to access an online webgrid that will score your in-book test and create a performance summary.

How to Score Your Practice Test

The ACT is scored differently from most tests that you take at school. Your ACT score on a test section is not reported as the total number of questions you answered correctly, nor does it directly represent the percentage of questions you answered correctly. Instead, the test makers add up all of your correct answers in a section to get what's called your raw score. They then use a conversion chart, or scale, that matches up a particular raw score with what's called a scaled score. The scaled score is the number that gets reported as your score for that ACT subject test.

You gain one point for every question you answer correctly. You lose no points for answering a question incorrectly OR for leaving a question blank. This means you should ALWAYS answer EVERY question on the ACT—even if you have to guess.

Score Tracker

1. **Figure out your raw score for each subject test.** Refer to the answer key to determine how many questions you answered correctly. Enter the results below:

RAW SCORES

English: ☐

Math: ☐

Reading: ☐

Science: ☐

2. **Covert your raw scores to scaled scores for each subject test.** Locate your raw score for each subject test in the following table. The score in the far left column indicates your estimated scaled score if this were an actual ACT. Enter your scaled scores in the boxes that follow the table.

SCALE SCORE	RAW SCORES				SCALE SCORE
	Test 1 English	Test 2 Mathematics	Test 3 Reading	Test 4 Science	
36	74–75	59–60	40	40	36
35	71–73	57–58	38–39	–	35
34	70	55–56	37	39	34
33	69	54	36	38	33
32	68	53	34–35	–	32
31	67	51–52	33	37	31
30	66	49–50	32	36	30
29	64–65	47–48	31	–	29
28	63	45–46	30	35	28
27	61–62	42–44	–	34	27
26	59–60	39–41	29	32–33	26
25	56–58	37–38	28	31	25
24	53–55	34–36	26–27	29–30	24
23	50–52	32–33	25	26–28	23
22	47–49	31	23–24	24–25	22
21	44–46	29–30	22	22–23	21
20	41–43	27–28	20–21	20–21	20
19	39–40	25–26	19	18–19	19
18	37–38	22–24	18	17	18
17	35–36	19–21	16–17	15–16	17
16	32–34	16–18	15	14	16
15	29–31	13–15	14	13	15
14	26–28	10–12	12–13	11–12	14
13	24–25	8–9	11	10	13
12	22–23	7	10	9	12
11	19–21	5–6	8–9	8	11
10	16–18	4	7	7	10
9	13–15	–	6	6	9
8	11–12	3	5	5	8
7	9–10	–	–	4	7
6	7–8	2	4	3	6
5	6	–	3	–	5
4	4–5	1	2	2	4
3	3	–	–	1	3
2	2	–	1	–	2
1	0–1	0	0	0	1

SCALED SCORES

English:

Math:

Reading:

Science:

3. **Calculate your estimated Composite score.** Simply add together your scaled scores for each subject test and divide by four.

ACT Practice Test
ANSWER SHEET

ENGLISH TEST

1. A B C D	11. A B C D	21. A B C D	31. A B C D	41. A B C D	51. A B C D	61. A B C D	71. A B C D
2. F G H J	12. F G H J	22. F G H J	32. F G H J	42. F G H J	52. F G H J	62. F G H J	72. F G H J
3. A B C D	13. A B C D	23. A B C D	33. A B C D	43. A B C D	53. A B C D	63. A B C D	73. A B C D
4. F G H J	14. F G H J	24. F G H J	34. F G H J	44. F G H J	54. F G H J	64. F G H J	74. F G H J
5. A B C D	15. A B C D	25. A B C D	35. A B C D	45. A B C D	55. A B C D	65. A B C D	75. A B C D
6. F G H J	16. F G H J	26. F G H J	36. F G H J	46. F G H J	56. F G H J	66. F G H J	
7. A B C D	17. A B C D	27. A B C D	37. A B C D	47. A B C D	57. A B C D	67. A B C D	
8. F G H J	18. F G H J	28. F G H J	38. F G H J	48. F G H J	58. F G H J	68. F G H J	
9. A B C D	19. A B C D	29. A B C D	39. A B C D	49. A B C D	59. A B C D	69. A B C D	
10. F G H J	20. F G H J	30. F G H J	40. F G H J	50. F G H J	60. F G H J	70. F G H J	

MATHEMATICS TEST

1. A B C D E	11. A B C D E	21. A B C D E	31. A B C D E	41. A B C D E	51. A B C D E
2. F G H J K	12. F G H J K	22. F G H J K	32. F G H J K	42. F G H J K	52. F G H J K
3. A B C D E	13. A B C D E	23. A B C D E	33. A B C D E	43. A B C D E	53. A B C D E
4. F G H J K	14. F G H J K	24. F G H J K	34. F G H J K	44. F G H J K	54. F G H J K
5. A B C D E	15. A B C D E	25. A B C D E	35. A B C D E	45. A B C D E	55. A B C D E
6. F G H J K	16. F G H J K	26. F G H J K	36. F G H J K	46. F G H J K	56. F G H J K
7. A B C D E	17. A B C D E	27. A B C D E	37. A B C D E	47. A B C D E	57. A B C D E
8. F G H J K	18. F G H J K	28. F G H J K	38. F G H J K	48. F G H J K	58. F G H J K
9. A B C D E	19. A B C D E	29. A B C D E	39. A B C D E	49. A B C D E	59. A B C D E
10. F G H J K	20. F G H J K	30. F G H J K	40. F G H J K	50. F G H J K	60. F G H J K

READING TEST

1. A B C D	6. F G H J	11. A B C D	16. F G H J	21. A B C D	26. F G H J	31. A B C D	36. F G H J
2. F G H J	7. A B C D	12. F G H J	17. A B C D	22. F G H J	27. A B C D	32. F G H J	37. A B C D
3. A B C D	8. F G H J	13. A B C D	18. F G H J	23. A B C D	28. F G H J	33. A B C D	38. F G H J
4. F G H J	9. A B C D	14. F G H J	19. A B C D	24. F G H J	29. A B C D	34. F G H J	39. A B C D
5. A B C D	10. F G H J	15. A B C D	20. F G H J	25. A B C D	30. F G H J	35. A B C D	40. F G H J

SCIENCE TEST

1. A B C D	6. F G H J	11. A B C D	16. F G H J	21. A B C D	26. F G H J	31. A B C D	36. F G H J
2. F G H J	7. A B C D	12. F G H J	17. A B C D	22. F G H J	27. A B C D	32. F G H J	37. A B C D
3. A B C D	8. F G H J	13. A B C D	18. F G H J	23. A B C D	28. F G H J	33. A B C D	38. F G H J
4. F G H J	9. A B C D	14. F G H J	19. A B C D	24. F G H J	29. A B C D	34. F G H J	39. A B C D
5. A B C D	10. F G H J	15. A B C D	20. F G H J	25. A B C D	30. F G H J	35. A B C D	40. F G H J

English Test

45 Minutes—75 Questions

Directions: Each passage has certain words and phrases that are underlined and numbered. The questions in the right column will provide alternatives for the underlined segments. Most questions require you to choose the answer that makes the sentence grammatically correct, concise, and relevant. If the word or phrase in the passage is already the correct, concise, and relevant choice, select Choice A, NO CHANGE. Some questions will ask a question about the underlined segment. When a question is presented, choose the best answer.

Some questions will ask about part or all of the passage. These questions do not refer to a specific underlined segment. Instead, these questions will accompany a number in a box.

For each question, choose your answer and fill in the corresponding bubble on your answer sheet. Read the passage once before you answer the questions. You will often need to read several sentences beyond the underlined portion to be able to choose the correct answer. Be sure to read enough to answer each question.

Passage I

My Old-Fashioned Father

My father, though he is only in his early 50s, is stuck in his old-fashioned ways. He has a general mistrust of any innovation or technology that he can't immediately

1.
A. NO CHANGE
B. ways he has a
C. ways having a
D. ways, and still has a

grasp and he always tells us, that if something isn't broken, then you shouldn't fix it.

2.
F. NO CHANGE
G. tells us, that,
H. tells us that,
J. tells us that

He has run a small grocery store in town, and if you were to look at a snapshot of his back office taken when he opened the store in 1975, you would

3.
A. NO CHANGE
B. was running
C. runs
D. ran

GO ON TO THE NEXT PAGE

see that not much has changed since. He is the most
<u>see that not much has changed since.</u> He is the most
$_4$
disorganized person I know and still uses a pencil

and paper to keep track of his <u>inventory.</u> His small office
$_5$
is about to burst with all the various documents, notes,

and receipts he has accumulated over the <u>years, his filing</u>
$_6$
<u>cabinets</u> have long since been filled up. The centerpiece
$_6$
of all the clutter is his ancient typewriter, which isn't
even electric. In the past few years, Father's search
for replacement typewriter ribbons has become an
increasingly difficult task, because they are no longer
being produced. He is perpetually tracking down the
few remaining places that still have these antiquated
ribbons in their dusty inventories. When people ask him
why he doesn't upgrade his equipment, he tells them,
"Electric typewriters won't work in a blackout. All I
need is a candle and some paper, and I'm fine." Little
does Father <u>know, however, is that</u> the "upgrade" people
$_7$
are speaking of is not to an electric typewriter but to a
computer.

4. F. NO CHANGE
    G. not be likely to see very much that has changed since.
    H. be able to see right away that not very much has changed since.
    J. not change very much.

5. Assuming that all are true, which of the following additions to the word "inventory" is most relevant in context?

    A. inventory of canned and dry goods.
    B. inventory, refusing to consider a more current method.
    C. inventory, which he writes down by hand.
    D. inventory of goods on the shelves and in the storeroom.

6. F. NO CHANGE
    G. years; his filing cabinets
    H. years, and besides that, his filing cabinets
    J. years and since his filing cabinets

7. A. NO CHANGE
    B. know, besides, that
    C. know, however, that
    D. know, beyond that,

GO ON TO THE NEXT PAGE ⟹

[1] Hoping to bring Father out of the Dark Ages, <u>my sister, and I</u> bought him a brand-new computer
8
for his fiftieth birthday. [2] We offered to help him to transfer all of his records onto it and to teach him

how to use it. [3] <u>Eagerly,</u> we told him about all the
9
new spreadsheet programs that would help simplify

his recordkeeping and organize his <u>accounts; and</u>
10
emphasized the advantage of not having to completely retype any document when he found a typo. [4] Rather than offering us a look of joy for the life-changing gift we had presented him, however, he again brought up the blackout scenario. [5] To Father, this is a concrete argument, although our town hasn't had a blackout in five years, and that one only lasted an hour or two. ⑪ ⑫

My father's state-of-the-art computer now serves as a very expensive bulletin board for the hundreds of

8. F. NO CHANGE
    G. me and my sister
    H. my sister and I
    J. my sister and I,

9. A. NO CHANGE
    B. On the other hand,
    C. In addition
    D. Rather,

10. F. NO CHANGE
     G. accounts and
     H. accounts and,
     J. accounts, we

11. The purpose of including this fact about the town's blackout history is to:

    A. make the father appear delusional.
    B. suggest that the father's reasons not to update his technology are ill-founded.
    C. add an interesting detail to set the scene.
    D. foreshadow an event that occurs later in the story.

12. The author wants to include the following statement in this paragraph:

    We expected it to save him a lot of time and effort.

    The most logical placement for this sentence would be:

    F. before Sentence 1.
    G. after Sentence 1.
    H. after Sentence 4.
    J. after Sentence 5.

GO ON TO THE NEXT PAGE

adhesive notes he uses to keep himself organized. <u>Sooner</u>
₁₃
<u>than later,</u> we fully expect it will completely disappear
13
under the mounting files and papers in the back office.

<u>In the depths of that disorganized office, the computer</u>
14
<u>will join the cell phone my mom gave him a few years</u>
14
<u>ago.</u> Interestingly enough, every once in a while, that
14
completely forgotten cell phone will ring from under the

heavy clutter of the past. [15]

13. A. NO CHANGE
    B. Sooner rather than later,
    C. Sooner or later,
    D. As soon as later,

14. F. NO CHANGE
    G. Deep in the disorganization of that office's, the computer will join the cell phone my mom gave him a few years back.
    H. In the disorganized depths of the office, the computer will soon be joined by the cell phone my mom gave him a few years ago.
    J. The computer will join the cell phone my mom gave him a few years back in the disorganized depths of that office.

15. Which of the following would provide the most appropriate conclusion for the passage?

    A. It's hard to say what else might be lost in there.
    B. We tell my father it's a reminder that he can't hide from the future forever.
    C. We have no idea who might be calling.
    D. Maybe one day I will try to find it and answer it.

GO ON TO THE NEXT PAGE

Passage II

Breaking Baseball's Color Barrier

A quick perusal of any modern major league baseball team will reveal a roster of players of multiple ethnicities <u>from the farthest</u> reaches of the globe. Second
16
only to soccer, baseball has evolved into a global sport

and <u>a symbol among races for equality.</u>
17
Its diversity today presents a stark contrast to the state of the sport just sixty years ago. As late as the 1940s, there existed an unwritten rule in baseball that prevented all but white players <u>to participate</u> in
18
the major leagues. This rule was known as the "color barrier" or "color line." The color line in baseball actually predated the birth of the major leagues. Prior to the official formation of any league of professional baseball teams, there existed an organization of amateur baseball clubs known as the National Association of Baseball Players, <u>which was the precursor to today's</u>
19
<u>National League.</u> On December 11, 1868, the governing
19
body of this association had unanimously adopted a

16. F. NO CHANGE
    G. from the most far
    H. from the most farthest
    J. from farther

17. A. NO CHANGE
    B. among races for equality a symbol.
    C. a symbol for equality among races.
    D. for equality among races a symbol.

18. F. NO CHANGE
    G. to be able to participate
    H. from participating
    J. to participation

19. Is the underlined portion relevant here?

    A. Yes, because it helps familiarize the reader with the range of baseball associations that once existed.

    B. Yes, because it helps clarify the development the author traces.

    C. No, because the names of the organizations are not important.

    D. No, because it is inconsistent with the style of the essay to provide specific historical data.

rule that effectively barred any team that had, any
20
"colored persons" on its roster. However, when baseball
20

20. F.   NO CHANGE
    G.   had any, "colored persons"
    H.   had any "colored persons"
    J.   had any "colored persons,"

started to organize into leagues by professional teams
21
in the early 1880s, the National Association of Baseball

Players' decree no longer had any weight, especially in

21. A.   NO CHANGE
    B.   of
    C.   from
    D.   about

the newly formed American Association. For a brief
22
period in those early years, a few African Americans
22
played side by side with white players on major league
22
diamonds.
22

    [1] Most baseball historians believe that the first

African American to play in the major leagues was

22. The writer is considering deleting the underlined portion. Should the writer make this deletion?

    F.   Yes, because the information is not relevant to the topic of the paragraph.

    G.   Yes, because the information contradicts the first sentence of the paragraph.

    H.   No, because the information shows that white players did not object to integration.

    J.   No, because the statement provides a smooth transition to the specific information about early African American players in the next paragraph.

Moses "Fleet" Walker. [2] Walker was a catcher for the
23
Toledo Blue Stockings of the American Association

between 1884 and 1889. [3] During that time, a few

23. A.   NO CHANGE
    B.   Walker, being a catcher
    C.   Walker, a catcher
    D.   Walker who was a catcher

other African Americans, including Walker's brother
24

24. F.   NO CHANGE
    G.   that included
    H.   who would include
    J.   including among them

GO ON TO THE NEXT PAGE

Weldy, <u>would be joining him</u> on the Blue Stockings.
                    25
[4] Unfortunately, this respite from segregation did not last for very long; as Jim Crow laws took their hold on the nation, many of the most popular white ballplayers started to refuse to take the field with their African American teammates. [5] By the 1890s, the color barrier had fully returned to baseball, where it would endure for more than half a century. [26]

Jackie Robinson would become the first African American to cross the color line <u>at the time when</u>
                                                27
he debuted for the Brooklyn Dodgers in 1947. For Robinson's landmark achievements on and off the

diamond, he will <u>forever be recognized as</u> a hero of the
                        28

25. A. NO CHANGE
    B. joined him
    C. were to join him
    D. will join him

26. Upon reviewing this paragraph, the author discovers that he has neglected to include the following information:

    A handful of African Americans played for other teams as well.

    This sentence would be most logically placed after:

    F. Sentence 1.
    G. Sentence 2.
    H. Sentence 3.
    J. Sentence 4.

27. A. NO CHANGE
    B. when
    C. while
    D. when the time came that

28. F. NO CHANGE
    G. one day be recognized
    H. forever recognize
    J. be admired by a lot of people for being

civil rights movement and a sports icon. His response to
                                            _____
                                                 29
the prejudices of American society during the 1940s and
1950s opened the door for the multi-racial and multi-
national face of modern baseball, and fans of the sport
worldwide will be forever in his debt.

29. Which choice best maintains the essay's posi-
    tive tone while emphasizing the unique role that
    Robinson played?

    A. NO CHANGE
    B. The path that he blazed through
    C. The stance he took against
    D. His collaboration in the face of

Question 30 asks about the essay as a whole.

---

30. Suppose the writer had been assigned to develop
    a brief essay on the history of baseball. Would this
    essay successfully fulfill that goal?

    F. Yes, because it covers events in baseball over a
        period of more than a century.
    G. Yes, because it mentions key figures in baseball
        history.
    H. No, because people played baseball before
        1868.
    J. No, because the focus of this essay is on one
        particular aspect of baseball history.

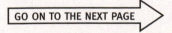
GO ON TO THE NEXT PAGE

Passage III

The Bear Mountain Bridge

When the gleaming Bear Mountain Bridge officially opened to traffic on Thanksgiving Day in <u>1924</u>, it
₃₁
was known as the Harriman Bridge, after Edward H. Harriman, a wealthy philanthropist and patriarch of the family most influential in the bridge's construction.

Before <u>they were</u> constructed, there were no bridges
₃₂
spanning the Hudson River south of Albany. By the early 1920s, the ferry services used to transport people back and forth across the river had become woefully inadequate. In February of 1922, in an effort to alleviate some of the burden on the ferries and create a permanent link across the Hudson, the New York State Legislature <u>had authorized</u> a group of private investors,
₃₃
led by Mary Harriman, to build a bridge. The group, known as the Bear Mountain Hudson Bridge Company (BMHBC),

was allotted thirty years to <u>build, construct, and</u>
₃₄
<u>maintain</u> the structure, at which time the span would be
₃₄
handed over to New York State.

The BMHBC invested almost $4,500,000 into the suspension bridge and hired the world-renowned design team <u>of Howard Baird and George Hodge</u>
₃₅

31. A. NO CHANGE
    B. 1924; it
    C. 1924. It
    D. 1924 and it

32. F. NO CHANGE
    G. the bridges were
    H. it was
    J. it were

33. A. NO CHANGE
    B. authorized
    C. was authorized
    D. would authorize

34. F. NO CHANGE
    G. build and construct and maintain
    H. construct and maintain
    J. construct, and maintain

35. A. NO CHANGE
    B. of Howard Baird, and George Hodge
    C. of Howard Baird and, George Hodge
    D. of, Howard Baird and George Hodge

as architects. [36] Baird and Hodge enlisted the help of
John A. Roebling and Sons,

who were instrumental in the steel work of the
37
Brooklyn Bridge and would later work on the Golden
Gate and George Washington Bridges.

Amazingly, the bridge took only twenty months and
eleven days to complete, and not one life was lost. [38]

It was a technological marvel and would stand as a
model for the suspension bridges of the future. At the
time of the Harriman Bridge's completion, it was, at
2,257 feet, the longest single-span steel suspension

bridge in the world. Therefore, the two main cables used
39
in the suspension were 18 inches in diameter, and each
contained 7,752 individual steel wires wrapped in 37
thick strands. If completely unraveled, the single wires

in both cables would be 7,377 miles longer. The bridge
40
links Bear Mountain on the western bank of the Hudson

36. The purpose of including the cost of the bridge is to:

F. provide a piece of information critical to the point of the essay.
G. insert a necessary transition between the second and third paragraphs.
H. add a detail contributing to the reader's understanding of the magnitude of the project.
J. provide an explanation of how the group raised money to invest in the bridge.

37. A. NO CHANGE
B. who was
C. a company
D. a company that had been

38. If the writer were to delete the preceding sentence, the essay would primarily lose:

F. information about how long the project had been expected to take.
G. a warning about the dangers of large-scale construction projects.
H. crucial information about the duration of the project.
J. a necessary transition between Paragraphs 3 and 4.

39. A. NO CHANGE
B. Nonetheless, the
C. At the same time, the
D. The

40. F. NO CHANGE
G. long.
H. in total length.
J. lengthy.

GO ON TO THE NEXT PAGE

to Anthony's Nose on the eastern <u>side, it lies</u> so precisely
₄₁
on an east-west plane that one can check a compass by
it. It carries Routes 6 and 202 across the Hudson and is
the point of river crossing for the Appalachian Trail.

In an attempt to recoup some of its investment after
the bridge <u>opened, the BMHBC charged</u> an exorbitant
₄₂
toll of eighty cents per crossing. Even with the high
toll, however, it operated at a loss for thirteen of its first
sixteen years. Finally it was acquired, more than ten
years earlier than planned, by the New York State Bridge
Authority. The bridge was renamed the Bear Mountain
Bridge. <u>Moreover,</u> the Bear Mountain Bridge sees
₄₃

<u>more than</u> six million vehicles cross its concrete decks
₄₄
each year.

41. A. NO CHANGE
     B. side, lies
     C. side, lying
     D. side; and it lies

42. F. NO CHANGE
     G. opened the BMHBC charged
     H. opened: the BMHBC charged
     J. opened; the BMHBC charged

43. A. NO CHANGE
     B. In contrast,
     C. Besides that fact,
     D. Today,

44. F. NO CHANGE
     G. over
     H. even more than
     J. a higher amount than

Question 45 asks about the essay as a whole.

45. Suppose the author had been assigned to write
     a brief history of bridge building in the United
     States. Would this essay successfully fulfill that
     requirement?

     A. Yes, because it provides information on the
         entire process from the initial funding through
         the opening of the bridge.

     B. Yes, because Bear Mountain Bridge is histori-
         cally significant.

     C. No, because it focuses on only one bridge.

     D. No, because the essay is primarily concerned
         with the financial aspects of building and
         maintaining the bridge.

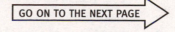
GO ON TO THE NEXT PAGE

Passage IV

The Dream of the American West

As the sun <u>was slowly rising</u> over the Atlantic Ocean
46
and painted New York harbor a spectacular fiery orange,
I started my old Toyota's engine. At this early hour,
there was still some semblance of the night's tranquility
left on the city sidewalks, but I knew that, as the minutes
ticked by, <u>the streets would flood with humanity.</u>
47

I smiled <u>with</u> the thought that soon all the wonderful
48
chaos of New York City would be disappearing behind

me as I <u>embarked on my trip to the other side of</u> the
49
country.

<u>As the morning sun climbed into the sky,</u>
50

46. F.   NO CHANGE
     G.   rising slowly
     H.   rose slowly
     J.   continued to rise

47. The author wants to contrast the statement about
     the quiet of the night streets with a related detail
     about the daytime activity. Assuming that all of the
     choices are true, which of the following best accom-
     plishes that goal?

     A.   NO CHANGE
     B.   some people might appear.
     C.   everything would be different.
     D.   the tranquility would be unbroken.

48. F.   NO CHANGE
     G.   along with
     H.   at
     J.   all because of

49. A.   NO CHANGE
     B.   embarked on this journey across
     C.   traveled to the other side of
     D.   traveled across

50. Which of the following alternatives to the under-
     lined portion would NOT be acceptable?

     F.   At sunrise,
     G.   Watching the morning sun climb into the sky,
     H.   The morning sun climbed into the sky,
     J.   As the sun rose,

GO ON TO THE NEXT PAGE ⇒

I shuddered with excitement <u>to think that my final stop</u> [51] <u>would be in California, where the sun itself ends its</u> [51] <u>journey across America.</u> [51] Like the sun, however, I still had quite a journey before me.

I had been planning this road trip across the United States for as long as I could remember. In my life, I had been fortunate enough to see some of the most beautiful countries in the world. However, it had always bothered

me that although I'd stood in the shadow of the <u>Eiffel</u> [52] <u>Tower, marveled in the desert heat at the Pyramids</u> [52] <u>of Giza,</u> [52] I'd never seen any of the wonders of my own country, except those found in my hometown of New York City. All of that was about to change.

<u>As I left the city, the tall buildings began to give way</u> [53] <u>to smaller ones, then to transform into the quaint rows</u> [53] <u>of houses that clustered the crowded suburbs.</u> [53] Trees and grass, then the yellow-green of cornfields and the golden

wash of wheat were slowly <u>replacing the familiar mazes</u> [54] <u>of cement and steel.</u> [54] My world no longer stretched

51. The writer is considering revising this sentence by deleting the underlined portion. If she did so, the paragraph would primarily lose:

A. information about the reasons for the writer's trip.
B. information about the writer's destination.
C. a description of the writer's planned route.
D. a comparison between the sunrise in New York and the sunset in California.

52. F. NO CHANGE
G. Eiffel Tower and had marveled in the desert heat at the Pyramids of Giza,
H. Eiffel Tower and marveled in the desert heat at the Pyramids of Giza
J. Eiffel Tower, and had marveled, in the desert heat, at the Pyramids of Giza

53. Given that all are true, which of the following provides the most effective transition between the third paragraph and the description of the Midwest in the fourth paragraph?

A. NO CHANGE
B. In fact, there were changes on the horizon almost immediately.
C. My excitement hadn't diminished.
D. I realized that people who lived in other areas might feel the same way about visiting New York.

54. Assuming that all are true, which of the following provides information most relevant to the main focus of the paragraph?

F. NO CHANGE
G. appearing before me.
H. racing past my window.
J. becoming monotonous.

vertically toward <u>the sky, it now spread</u> horizontally
towards eternity. For two days, I pushed through the
wind-whipped farmlands of Mid-America, hypnotized
by the beauty of the undulating yet unbroken lines. At
night, the breeze from my car would stir the wheat fields
to dance beneath the moon, and the silos hid in the
shadows, quietly imposing their <u>simply</u> serenity upon
everything.

Then, as the <u>night's shadows</u> gave way to light,
there seemed to be a great force rising to meet the

<u>sun as it made its reappearance.</u>

<u>Still,</u> I had no idea

what I was looking at. Then, there was no <u>mistaking it.</u>
The unbroken lines of Mid-America had given way to
the jagged and majestic heights of the Rockies and the
gateway to the American West.

55. A. NO CHANGE
    B. the sky but it now spread
    C. the sky; it now spread
    D. the sky spreading

56. F. NO CHANGE
    G. simple
    H. simplest
    J. simpler

57. A. NO CHANGE
    B. nights shadows
    C. shadows from the night
    D. night shadow

58. F. NO CHANGE
    G. sun as it reappeared.
    H. reappearing sun.
    J. sun as it was also rising.

59. A. NO CHANGE
    B. Even so,
    C. At first,
    D. Eventually,

60. F. NO CHANGE
    G. mistake to be made.
    H. chance to mistake it.
    J. having made a mistake.

GO ON TO THE NEXT PAGE ⟹

Passage V

Traveling at the Speed of Sound

The term "supersonic" refers to anything that travels faster than the speed of sound. When the last of the supersonic Concorde passenger planes made its final trip across the Atlantic in November of 2003, an interesting chapter in history was finally closed. The fleet of supersonic Concorde SSTs, or

"Supersonic Transports," they were jointly operated by Air France and British Airways, had been making the intercontinental trip across the Atlantic for almost thirty years. These amazing machines cruised at Mach 2, more than twice the speed of sound. They flew to a height almost twice that of standard passenger airplanes. The Concorde routinely made the trip from New York to London in less than three hours and was much more expensive than normal transatlantic

flights. Furthermore, the majority of the passengers who traveled on the Concorde were celebrities or the extremely wealthy, it also attracted ordinary people who simply wanted to know how it felt to travel faster than the speed of sound. Some would save money for years just to gain that knowledge.

What is the speed of sound? Many people are surprised to learn that there is no fixed answer to this question. The speed that sound travels through a

---

61. A. NO CHANGE
    B. November, of 2003 an interesting
    C. November of 2003 an interesting
    D. November of 2003; an interesting

62. F. NO CHANGE
    G. those were
    H. which were
    J. which being

63. A. NO CHANGE
    B. at an altitude
    C. toward an altitude
    D. very high

64. F. NO CHANGE
    G. Despite,
    H. Though,
    J. Along with,

65. A. NO CHANGE
    B. to which
    C. at which
    D. where

GO ON TO THE NEXT PAGE

given medium depends on a number of factors. To understand the speed of sound, we must first understand what a "sound" really is. 66

The standard dictionary definition of sound is "a vibration or disturbance transmitted, like waves through water, through a material medium such as a gas." Our

66. The purpose of this paragraph, as it relates to the surrounding paragraphs, is primarily to:

F. provide an example of the main idea before continuing discussion of that idea.

G. transition from a discussion of certain aircraft to the science behind them.

H. present a counterargument to the main thesis before refuting that counterargument.

J. transition from the general topic of aircraft to a story about specific airplanes.

ears are able to pick up those sound waves and <u>convert</u> them into what we hear. This means that the speed at

67. Which of the following alternatives to the underlined portion would be the LEAST acceptable?

A. change

B. translate

C. alter

D. transform

which sound travels through gas <u>directly depends on what gas it is traveling through, and the temperature and pressure of the gas.</u> When discussing aircraft breaking the speed of sound, that gas medium, of course, is air.

68. F. NO CHANGE

G. depends directly on the type, temperature, and pressure of the gas it is traveling through.

H. directly depends on what gas it is, and also on the temperature and pressure of that gas.

J. depends directly on the type, temperature, and pressure of the gas.

As air temperature and pressure decrease <u>with altitude,</u> so does the speed of sound. An airplane flying at the speed of sound at sea level is traveling roughly at 761 mph;

69. A. NO CHANGE

B. with height

C. with a drop in altitude

D. at higher altitudes

<u>however</u> when that same plane climbs to 20,000 feet, the speed of sound is only about 707 mph. This is why the Concorde's cruising altitude was so much higher than

70. F. NO CHANGE

G. however,

H. and so,

J. even so

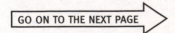
GO ON TO THE NEXT PAGE

that of a regular passenger aircraft; <u>planes can reach</u>
71
<u>supersonic speeds more easily at higher altitudes.</u>
71

In the years since the Concorde <u>has been</u>
72
decommissioned, only fighter pilots and astronauts

have been able to experience the sensation of breaking

"the sound barrier." <u>But that is all about to change very</u>
73
<u>soon.</u> Newer and faster supersonic passenger planes are
73
being developed that will be technologically superior

to the Concorde and much cheaper to operate. <u>Now,</u>
74
supersonic passenger travel will be available not only to

the rich and famous, <u>but also be for</u> the masses, so they,
75
too, can experience life at supersonic speeds.

71. Given that all are true, which of the following provides the most logical conclusion for this sentence?

A.   NO CHANGE

B.   they're much faster.

C.   they use much more fuel than regular aircraft.

D.   they're rarely visible because they fly above the cloud cover.

72. F.   NO CHANGE

G.   came to be

H.   was

J.   had been

73. A.   NO CHANGE

B.   Soon, however, that is about to change.

C.   Soon, however, that will change.

D.   That is about to change soon.

74. F.   NO CHANGE

G.   Nearby,

H.   Soon,

J.   Upcoming,

75. A.   NO CHANGE

B.   but also be available to

C.   but also to

D.   but for

IF YOU FINISH BEFORE TIME IS CALLED, YOU MAY CHECK YOUR WORK ON THIS SECTION ONLY. DO NOT TURN TO ANY OTHER SECTION IN THE TEST.   **STOP**

Practice Test

K   779

Mathematics Test

60 Minutes—60 Questions

Directions: Choose the correct solution to each question and fill in the corresponding bubble on your answer sheet.

Do not continue to spend time on questions if you get stuck. Solve as many questions as you can before returning to any if time permits.

You may use a calculator on this test for any question you choose. However, some questions may be better solved without a calculator.

Note: Unless otherwise stated, you can assume:

1. Figures are NOT necessarily drawn to scale.

2. Geometric figures are two dimensional.

3. The term *line* indicates a straight line.

4. The term *average* indicates arithmetic mean.

1. The eighth grade girls' basketball team played a total of 13 games this season. If they scored a total of 364 points, what was the mean (average) score per game?

   A. 13
   B. 16
   C. 20
   D. 28
   E. 32

2. When $4\frac{3}{7}$ is written as an improper fraction in simplest form, what is the numerator of the fraction?

   F. 12
   G. 21
   H. 27
   J. 28
   K. 31

3. If $4x + 18 = 38$, then $x = ?$

   A. 3
   B. 4.5
   C. 5
   D. 12
   E. 20

4. John weighs 1.5 times as much as Ellen. If John weighs 144 pounds, how many pounds does Ellen weigh?

   F. 84
   G. 96
   H. 104
   J. 164
   K. 216

GO ON TO THE NEXT PAGE

5. What positive number when divided by its reciprocal gives a result of $\frac{9}{16}$?

    A. $\frac{3}{16}$

    B. $\frac{3}{4}$

    C. $\frac{4}{3}$

    D. $\frac{16}{9}$

    E. $\frac{16}{3}$

6. If $\sqrt[3]{x} = \frac{1}{4}$, then $x = $?

    F. $\frac{1}{256}$

    G. $\frac{1}{64}$

    H. $\frac{1}{12}$

    J. $\frac{1}{\sqrt[3]{4}}$

    K. 64

7. If $x^2 + 14 = 63$, then x could be which of the following?

    A. 4.5

    B. 7

    C. 14

    D. 24.5

    E. 49

8. Two vectors are given by $v_1 = \langle 7, -3 \rangle$ and $v_2 = \langle a, b \rangle$. If $v_1 + v_2 = \langle 5, 5 \rangle$, then what is the value of a ?

    F. -2

    G. 2

    H. 5

    J. 8

    K. 12

9. Based on past graduations, a university estimates that 6% of the graduating class will not attend the graduation ceremony. Based on this estimate, if there are 1,250 graduates, how many will not attend the ceremony?

    A. 75

    B. 140

    C. 220

    D. 350

    E. 425

10. $5.2^3 + 6.8^2 = $?

    F. 46.240

    G. 94.872

    H. 120.534

    J. 140.608

    K. 186.848

11. Lexi uses her debit card to make a purchase totaling $40. When she records the debit in her checkbook register, she accidentally adds $40 to her balance rather than subtracting it, which results in an inaccurate total. Because of her error, Lexi's checkbook register shows:

    A. $80 less than it should.

    B. $40 less than it should.

    C. $20 more than it should.

    D. $40 more than it should.

    E. $80 more than it should.

12. $3^3 \div 9 + (6^2 - 12) \div 4 = $?

    F. 3

    G. 6.75

    H. 9

    J. 12

    K. 15

13. If bananas cost $0.24 and oranges cost $0.38, what is the total cost of x bananas and y oranges?

   A. $(x + y)(\$0.24 + \$0.38)$

   B. $\$0.24x + \$0.38y$

   C. $\$0.62(x + y)$

   D. $\dfrac{\$0.24}{x} + \dfrac{\$0.38}{y}$

   E. $\$0.38x + \$0.24y$

14. In the following figure, all of the small triangles are the same size. What percent of the entire figure is shaded?

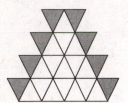

   F.   8

   G.   24

   H. $33\dfrac{1}{3}$

   J.   50

   K. $66\dfrac{2}{3}$

15. In a high school senior class, the ratio of girls to boys is 5:3. If there are a total of 168 students in the senior class, how many girls are there?

   A.   63

   B.   100

   C.   105

   D.   147

   E.   152

16. On her first three geometry tests, Sarah scored an 89, a 93, and an 84. If there are four tests total and Sarah needs at least a 90 average for the four, what is the lowest score she can receive on the final test?

   F.   86

   G.   90

   H.   92

   J.   94

   K.   96

17. What is the solution set of $3x - 11 \geq 22$?

   A. $x \geq -11$

   B. $x < -3$

   C. $x \geq 0$

   D. $x > 3$

   E. $x \geq 11$

18. Dillon is going to randomly pick a domino from a pile of dominoes that are all facing downward. Of the dominoes in the pile, 48 have an even number of dots on them. He randomly picks a single domino. If the probability that he picks a domino with an even number of dots is $\dfrac{3}{4}$, how many dominoes are in the pile?

   F.   36

   G.   48

   H.   56

   J.   64

   K.   72

19. What is the value of $3x - 8y$ when $x = 4$ and $y = -\dfrac{1}{2}$?

   A. -4

   B.   8

   C.   12

   D.   16

   E.   28

GO ON TO THE NEXT PAGE ⟹

20. Court reporters type every word spoken during trials and hearings so that there is a written record of what transpired. Suppose a certain court reporter can type 3.75 words per second, and a trial transcript contains 25 pages with an average of 675 words per page. If this court reporter typed the transcript at his typical rate, how long was he actively typing?

    F.   1 hour, 15 minutes

    G.   1 hour, 40 minutes

    H.   2 hours, 10 minutes

    J.   2 hours, 30 minutes

    K.   3 hours

21. In the following figure, lines *m* and *l* are parallel and the measure of ∠*a is* 68°. What is the measure of ∠*f*?

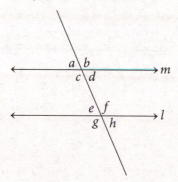

    A.   22°

    B.   68°

    C.   80°

    D.   112°

    E.   292°

22. On a map, the scale is the ratio of the distance shown on the map to the actual distance. A geography teacher has a map on her wall with a scale of 1 inch:100 miles. She uses the school's copier to shrink the large wall map down to the size of a piece of paper to hand out to each of her students. To do this, she makes the map $\frac{1}{4}$ of its original size. Suppose on the students' maps, the distance between two cities is 2.5 inches. How many actual miles apart are those cities?

    F.   25

    G.   250

    H.   800

    J.   1,000

    K.   1,200

23. A piece of letter-sized paper is $8\frac{1}{2}$ inches wide and 11 inches long. Suppose you want to cut strips of paper that are $\frac{5}{8}$ of an inch wide and 11 inches long. What is the maximum number of strips of paper you could make from 1 piece of letter-sized paper?

    A.   5

    B.   6

    C.   12

    D.   13

    E.   14

24. In the following figure, $\overline{MN}$ and $\overline{PQ}$ are parallel. Point A lies on $\overline{MN}$, and points B and C lie on $\overline{PQ}$. If $AB = AC$ and $\angle MAB$ has a measure of $55°$, what is the measure of $\angle ACB$?

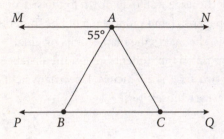

F. $35°$

G. $55°$

H. $65°$

J. $80°$

K. $125°$

25. What is the slope of the line that passes through the points $(-10,0)$ and $(0,-6)$?

A. $-\dfrac{5}{3}$

B. $-\dfrac{3}{5}$

C. $\dfrac{3}{5}$

D. $\dfrac{5}{3}$

E. 0

26. For all x, $(x+4)(x-4) + (2x+2)(x-2) = ?$

F. $x^2 - 2x - 20$

G. $3x^2 - 12$

H. $3x^2 - 2x - 20$

J. $3x^2 + 2x - 20$

K. $3x^2 + 2x + 20$

27. What is the length of a line segment with endpoints $(3,-6)$ and $(-2,6)$?

A.   1

B.   5

C.   10

D.   13

E.   15

28. If 60% of h is 80, what is 30% of h ?

F.   30

G.   40

H.   50

J.   60

K.   70

29. Set A contains 7 consecutive even integers. If the average of Set A's integers is 46, which of the following is the smallest integer of Set A ?

A.   36

B.   38

C.   40

D.   42

E.   44

30. Which of the following statements describes the total of the first n terms of the arithmetic sequence below?

$$1, 3, 5, 7, 9, \ldots$$

F.   The total is always equal to 25 regardless of n.

G.   The total is always equal to $2n$.

H.   The total is always equal to $3n$.

J.   The total is always equal to n^2.

K.   There is no consistent pattern for the total.

GO ON TO THE NEXT PAGE

31. Which of the following matrices is equal to the matrix product $\begin{bmatrix} -2 & 0 \\ 1 & -3 \end{bmatrix} \cdot \begin{bmatrix} 2 \\ 2 \end{bmatrix}$?

A. $\begin{bmatrix} -4 & 0 \\ 2 & -6 \end{bmatrix}$

B. $\begin{bmatrix} -4 & 2 \\ 2 & -6 \end{bmatrix}$

C. $\begin{bmatrix} 0 & 0 \\ 0 & 0 \end{bmatrix}$

D. $\begin{bmatrix} -4 \\ -4 \end{bmatrix}$

E. $\begin{bmatrix} -4 \\ -6 \end{bmatrix}$

32. A playground is $(x + 7)$ units long and $(x + 3)$ units wide. If a square of side length x is sectioned off from the playground to make a sandpit, which of the following could be the remaining area of the playground?

F. $x^2 + 10x + 21$

G. $10x + 21$

H. $2x + 10$

J. $21x$

K. 21

33. Assume m and n are nonzero integers such that $m > 0$ and $n < 0$. Which of the following *must* be negative?

A. $-n^m$

B. $-mn$

C. m^n

D. $-n - m$

E. $n - m$

34. The point $(-3, -2)$ is the midpoint of the line segment in the standard (x, y) coordinate plane with endpoints $(1, 9)$ and (m, n). Which of the following is (m, n) ?

F. $(-7, -13)$

G. $(-2, 7)$

H. $(-1, 3.5)$

J. $(2, 5.5)$

K. $(5, 20)$

35. If $f(x) = 16x^2 - 20x$, what is the value of $f(3)$?

A. -12

B. 36

C. 84

D. 144

E. 372

36. What is the length of side $\overline{AC}$ in triangle ABC graphed on the following coordinate plane?

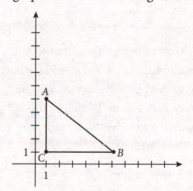

F. 3

G. 4

H. 5

J. 6

K. 7

GO ON TO THE NEXT PAGE

37. If $f(x) = \frac{1}{3}x + 13$ and $g(x) = 3x^2 + 6x + 12$, which expression represents $f(g(x))$?

   A. $x^2 + 12x + 4$

   B. $\frac{x^2}{3} + 2x + 194$

   C. $x^2 + 2x + 17$

   D. $x^2 + 2x + 25$

   E. $x^2 + 2x + 54$

38. What is the equation of a line that is perpendicular to the line $y = \frac{2}{3}x + 5$ and contains the point $(4, -3)$?

   F. $y = \frac{2}{3}x + 4$

   G. $y = -\frac{2}{3}x + 3$

   H. $y = -\frac{3}{2}x + 3$

   J. $y = -\frac{3}{2}x - 9$

   K. $y = -\frac{3}{2}x + 9$

39. The formula for converting a Fahrenheit temperature reading to Celsius is $C = \frac{5}{9}(F - 32)$, where C is the reading in degrees Celsius and F is the reading in degrees Fahrenheit. Which of the following is the Fahrenheit equivalent to a reading of $95°$ Celsius?

   A. $35°F$

   B. $53°F$

   C. $63°F$

   D. $203°F$

   E. $207°F$

40. When 3 times x is increased by 5, the result is less than 11. Which of the following is a graph of the real numbers x for which the previous statement is true?

   F.
   G.
   H.
   J.
   K.

41. In the following triangle, what is the value of $\cos R$?

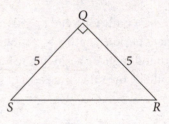

   A. $\dfrac{\sqrt{2}}{6}$

   B. $\dfrac{\sqrt{2}}{5}$

   C. $\dfrac{\sqrt{2}}{2}$

   D. $2\sqrt{2}$

   E. $5\sqrt{2}$

GO ON TO THE NEXT PAGE

42. Marvin has two saltwater fish tanks in his home. One has tangs and angelfish in a ratio of 5 to 2. The second tank has tangs and puffers in a ratio of 2 to 3. Marvin wants to put a tank in his office with angelfish and puffers using the same ratio he has at home to make it easier to buy food for them in bulk. What ratio of angelfish to puffers should he use?

   F.   2:3

   G.   2:5

   H.   5:2

   J.   5:7

   K.   4:15

43. The volume of a sphere is given by the formula $V = \frac{4}{3}\pi r^3$, where r is the radius of the sphere. What is the volume, in cubic inches, of a sphere that has a diameter of 6 inches?

   A. 3π

   B. 9π

   C. 27π

   D. 36π

   E. 288π

44. For all $x \neq -1$, which of the following is equivalent to $\frac{x^2 - 5x - 6}{x + 1} + x + 1$?

   F. $x - 5$

   G. $2x - 5$

   H. $x^2 - 5x - 6$

   J. $\frac{2x - 5}{x + 1}$

   K. $\frac{x^2 - 4x - 5}{x + 1}$

45. Which of the following expressions is the greatest monomial factor of $60a^3b + 45a^2b^2$?

   A. $15a^2b$

   B. $15a^3b^2$

   C. $15a^5b^3$

   D. $180a^3b^2$

   E. $180a^5b^3$

Use the following information to answer questions 46 and 47.

The population of fish in a certain pond from 1985 to 1995 is shown in the graph below.

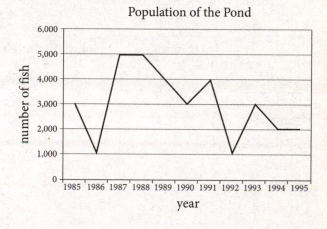

Population of the Pond

46. Which of the following best describes the percent change in the population from 1985 to 1995 ?

   F.   33.33% increase

   G.   33.33% decrease

   H.   50% decrease

   J.   333.33% increase

   K.   333.33% decrease

47. Which of the following years contains the median population for the data?

    A. 1986

    B. 1989

    C. 1990

    D. 1991

    E. 1995

48. The table below shows the results of a study identifying the number of males and females with and without college degrees who were unemployed or employed at the time of the study. If one person from the study is chosen at random, what is the probability that that person is an employed person with a college degree?

	Unemployed	Employed	Totals
Female, degree	12	188	200
Female, no degree	44	156	200
Male, degree	23	177	200
Male, no degree	41	159	200
Totals	120	680	800

    F. $\dfrac{73}{160}$

    G. $\dfrac{10}{17}$

    H. $\dfrac{73}{136}$

    J. $\dfrac{17}{20}$

    K. $\dfrac{73}{80}$

49. Which of the following expressions gives the number of distinct permutations of the letters in GEOMETRY ?

    A. $8!(2!)$

    B. $8!$

    C. $\dfrac{8!}{2!}$

    D. $\dfrac{8!}{6!}$

    E. $\dfrac{8!}{(6!)(2!)}$

50. The graph below represents the solution set to which inequality, assuming each grid line represents 1 unit?

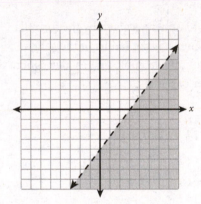

    F. $y < -\dfrac{4}{3}x - 4$

    G. $y > -\dfrac{3}{4}x - 4$

    H. $y < \dfrac{3}{4}x - 4$

    J. $y < \dfrac{4}{3}x - 4$

    K. $y > \dfrac{4}{3}x - 4$

51. A function h is defined by $h(x,y,z) = 4xy^2 - yz^3$. What is the value of $h(2,-1,3)$?

    A. -35

    B. -19

    C. -1

    D. 19

    E. 35

GO ON TO THE NEXT PAGE

52. The radius of a circle is increased so that the radius of the new circle is triple that of the original circle. How many times larger is the area of the new circle than that of the original circle?

    F. $\dfrac{1}{3}$

    G. 3

    H. 6

    J. 6π

    K. 9

53. The function $f(x) = 0.5 \sin(2x)$ is graphed below over the domain $[0, 2\pi]$. What is the period of the function?

    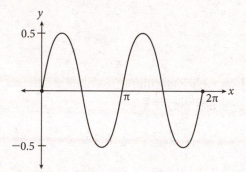

    A. $\dfrac{\pi}{4}$

    B. $\dfrac{\pi}{2}$

    C. π

    D. 2π

    E. 4π

54. For what value of x is the equation $\sqrt[3]{4x - 12} + 25 = 27$ true?

    F. -5

    G. -1

    H. -2.5

    J. 5

    K. 6.5

55. The chord shown in the figure is 8 units long. If the chord is 3 units from the center of the circle, what is the area of the circle?

    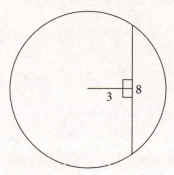

    A. 9π

    B. 16π

    C. 18π

    D. 25π

    E. 28π

56. If $f(x) = 3^{3x + 3}$ and $g(x) = 27^{\left(\frac{2}{3}x - \frac{1}{3}\right)}$, for what value of x, if any, does the graph of $f(x)$ intersect the graph of $g(x)$?

    F. -4

    G. $-\dfrac{7}{4}$

    H. $-\dfrac{10}{7}$

    J. 2

    K. The graphs do not intersect.

57. What value of x satisfies the equation $\log_3(5x - 40) - \log_3 5 = 2$?

    A. 17

    B. 9

    C. 1

    D. -9

    E. -17

58. A finite arithmetic sequence has five terms. The first term is 4. What is the difference between the mean and the median of the five terms?

    F. 0
    G. 1
    H. 2
    J. 4
    K. 5

59. In the following triangle, if cos $\angle BAC = 0.6$ and the hypotenuse of the triangle is 15, what is the length of side BC ?

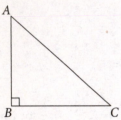

    A. 3
    B. 5
    C. 10
    D. 12
    E. 15

60. The table below shows several points that lie on the graph of a parabola. Based on the data in the table, what is the value of y when $x = -4$?

x	y
−2	3
0	−3
2	−5
4	−3
6	3
8	13

    F. −13
    G. −5
    H. 5
    J. 13
    K. Cannot be determined from the given information

IF YOU FINISH BEFORE TIME IS CALLED, YOU MAY CHECK YOUR WORK ON THIS SECTION ONLY. DO NOT TURN TO ANY OTHER SECTION IN THE TEST.   STOP

Reading Test

35 Minutes—40 Questions

Directions: The Reading Test includes multiple passages. Each passage includes multiple questions. After reading each passage, choose the best answer and fill in the corresponding bubble on your answer sheet. You may review the passages as often as necessary.

Passage I

PROSE FICTION: This passage is adapted from *The Age of Innocence*, by Edith Wharton (1920).

It was generally agreed in New York that the Countess Olenska had "lost her looks."

She had appeared there first, in Newland Archer's boyhood, as a brilliantly pretty little girl
5 of nine or ten, of whom people said that she "ought to be painted." Her parents had been continental wanderers, and after a roaming babyhood she had lost them both, and been taken in charge by her aunt, Medora Manson, also a wanderer, who was
10 herself returning to New York to "settle down."

Poor Medora, repeatedly widowed, was always coming home to settle down (each time in a less expensive house), and bringing with her a new husband or an adopted child, but after a few
15 months she invariably parted from her husband or quarrelled with her ward, and, having got rid of her house at a loss, set out again on her wanderings. As her mother had been a Rushworth, and her last unhappy marriage had linked her to one of
20 the crazy Chiverses, New York looked indulgently on her eccentricities, but when she returned with her little orphaned niece, whose parents had been popular in spite of their regrettable taste for travel, people thought it a pity that the pretty child should
25 be in such hands.

Everyone was disposed to be kind to little Ellen Mingott, though her dusky red cheeks and tight curls gave her an air of gaiety that seemed unsuitable in a child who should still have been in
30 black for her parents. It was one of the misguided Medora's many peculiarities to flout the unalterable rules that regulated American mourning, and when she stepped from the steamer her family was scandalized to see that the crepe veil she wore for
35 her own brother was seven inches shorter than those of her sisters-in-law, while little Ellen wore a crimson dress and amber beads.

But New York had so long resigned itself to Medora that only a few old ladies shook their
40 heads over Ellen's gaudy clothes, while her other relations fell under the charm of her high spirits. She was a fearless and familiar little thing, who asked disconcerting questions, made precocious comments, and possessed outlandish arts, such
45 as dancing a Spanish shawl dance and singing Neapolitan love-songs to a guitar. Under the direction of her aunt, the little girl received an expensive but incoherent education, which included "drawing from the model," a thing never dreamed
50 of before, and playing the piano in quintets with professional musicians.

Of course no good could come of this, and when, a few years later, poor Chivers finally died, his widow again pulled up stakes and departed
55 with Ellen, who had grown into a tall bony girl with conspicuous eyes. For some time no more was heard of them; then news came of Ellen's marriage to an immensely rich Polish nobleman of legendary fame. She disappeared, and when a few years later
60 Medora again came back to New York, subdued, impoverished, mourning a third husband, and in quest of a still smaller house, people wondered that her rich niece had not been able to do something for her. Then came the news that Ellen's own
65 marriage had ended in disaster, and that she was herself returning home to seek rest and oblivion among her kinsfolk.

These things passed through Newland Archer's mind a week later as he watched the Countess
70 Olenska enter the van der Luyden drawing room on the evening of the momentous dinner. In the

middle of the room she paused, looking about her
with a grave mouth and smiling eyes, and in that
instant, Newland Archer rejected the general verdict
75 on her looks. It was true that her early radiance
was gone. The red cheeks had paled; she was thin,
worn, a little older-looking than her age, which
must have been nearly thirty. But there was about
her the mysterious authority of beauty, a sureness
80 in the carriage of the head, the movement of the
eyes, which, without being in the least theatrical,
struck him as highly trained and full of a conscious
power. At the same time she was simpler in manner
than most of the ladies present, and many people
85 (as he heard afterward) were disappointed that her
appearance was not more "stylish"—for stylishness
was what New York most valued. It was, perhaps,
Archer reflected, because her early vivacity had
disappeared; because she was so quiet—quiet in
90 her movements, her voice, and the tones of her
voice. New York had expected something a good
deal more resonant in a young woman with such a
history.

1. The author describes which of the following practices as undesirable to New York society?

   A. Playing the piano
   B. Performing Spanish shawl dances
   C. Traveling
   D. Adopting children

2. With which of the following would the author
   most likely agree regarding New York society as it
   pertains to Medora?

   F. It is rigid and unaccepting of different
      behavior.
   G. It is usually whimsical, with few solid rules.
   H. It is often based on unrealistic expectations.
   J. It is snobbish but occasionally accepting of less
      common behavior.

3. It is most reasonable to infer that, after the death of
   Medora's third husband, Ellen did not help her aunt
   primarily because:

   A. Ellen was no longer wealthy, since her own
      marriage had failed.
   B. Medora had become embittered because she
      hadn't heard from Ellen for so long.
   C. Ellen resented the incoherent education she
      received from her aunt.
   D. receiving help from her niece would interfere
      with Medora's desire to be eccentric.

4. Based on the characterization of Newland Archer in
   the last paragraph, he can best be described as:

   F. reflective and nonjudgmental.
   G. likable but withdrawn.
   H. disinterested but fair.
   J. stylish and gregarious.

5. In her descriptions of Medora, the author intends
   to give the impression that Medora is:

   A. eccentric and peripatetic.
   B. impoverished and resentful.
   C. kind and loyal.
   D. precocious and pretty.

6. As it is used in line 31, the word *flout* most nearly
   means:

   F. eliminate.
   G. exemplify.
   H. disregard.
   J. float.

GO ON TO THE NEXT PAGE ⟹

7. What does the narrator suggest is a central characteristic of Medora Manson?

    A. Arrogance

    B. Immodesty

    C. Nonconformity

    D. Orthodoxy

8. Which of the following characters learns to do something otherwise unheard of by New York society?

    F. Ellen Mingott

    G. Newland Archer

    H. Medora Manson

    J. Count Olenska

9. The author includes reference to Medora's mother and Medora's marriage to "one of the crazy Chiverses" (lines 19–20) in order to indicate that:

    A. she had an unhappy childhood.

    B. her eccentricities were not surprising.

    C. she was the perfect person to raise Ellen.

    D. she was a wanderer.

10. One can reasonably infer from the passage that on the occasion of the dinner, Newland and Ellen:

    F. had not seen each other for some time.

    G. were interested in becoming romantically involved.

    H. were both disappointed with New York society.

    J. had just met, but were immediately attracted to each other.

Passage II

SOCIAL SCIENCE: This passage discusses challenges facing Florida's two largest economic sectors due to climate change.

Every state in the U.S. relies on at least one or two industries to drive its economic growth. Boasting a top-five economy among the 50 states, Florida thrives on its tourism industry and
5 agricultural production. Recent climate change reports are a cause for concern for the policymakers who want to keep the state on its current upward economic trajectory. How serious are the threats that the state faces, and can anything be done to
10 stave off the effects of climate change before they irreparably damage the Floridian economy?

The National Climate Assessment, a government-mandated report released every four years, references South Florida frequently as a locale
15 that is likely to experience the worsening effects of climate change sooner rather than later. In September 2017, for example, Hurricane Irma wreaked havoc on large swaths of the Florida coastline when it made landfall in the Florida
20 Keys; economists put the price tag for Irma at $50 billion, making it the costliest hurricane in Florida's history. It is estimated that if Irma had made a more direct hit on Miami, Florida's second-most popular tourist destination, the damage would have
25 been closer to $200 billion. Many scientists feel that rising sea levels are making areas like Miami and Orlando increasingly vulnerable to such catastrophic weather events.

Another top tourist attraction in Florida, the
30 Everglades, is already experiencing a reduction in size due to a combination of rising sea levels and serious weather events. Large sections of the Everglades are less than three feet above sea level, and soon many of the low-lying regions will be
35 completely submerged. This does not bode well for the over one million visitors who make the trek to the national park each year nor for the more than $20 million in revenue that the Everglades National Park generates annually. In addition, the sea level
40 rise causes salt water to push further inland and upstream, which endangers not only tourism but also the drinking water of several communities.

On a peninsula like Florida, it seems ironic that a lack of water could become an issue, but an Environmental Protection Agency report published in 2016 pointed to a lack of irrigation due to warmer temperatures as a potential downside of a longer growing season. Florida relies on groundwater pumped from permeable underground aquifers, and Florida farms consume nearly half of the state's public water supply. Citrus fruits require substantial amounts of irrigation to maintain crop size; a 2003 agriculture study found that a 20% reduction in irrigation resulted in significant losses for citrus crops. The citrus fruit industry in Florida is a $10 billion industry, so any negative trends have a direct impact on Florida's overall economic health.

Climate change has an impact on the produce side of Florida's agriculture as well as the livestock side; although it makes up a smaller portion of Florida's $120 billion in agricultural revenue than the citrus industry, the livestock industry exports cattle, calves, milk, poultry, and eggs both nationally and internationally. One problem that arises with livestock as a result of warmer temperatures is a reduction in productivity because of metabolic disruption caused by heat stress. The livestock industry also relies on the extensive perennial grasslands of the region, which have degraded in quality because of the greater frequency of severe weather events. Additionally, the combination of temperature and rainfall increases have led to greater instances of livestock diseases like the West Nile virus; the increase in humidity leads directly to larger mosquito populations.

With so many challenges facing their state, Floridians are taking a proactive approach to combating some of the consequences of climate change. In Miami, lawmakers are considering some rather unconventional recommendations. For example, a group of Harvard students presented Miami Beach leaders with two unique options to help adapt to rising seas: concrete cisterns strategically placed on roofs throughout the city to capture rainwater, and "sacrificial floors" designed to absorb excess water before it reaches the inhabited floors. Researchers are encouraging the South Florida Water Management District to change their timetable for increasing freshwater flow to the Everglades to maintain the level of freshwater higher than sea level. Farmers are investing in micro-surface and subsurface drip irrigation systems to reduce the overall volume of water needed to maintain their crops and making the move to mixed crop-livestock farms, as studies have shown this farming style to be mutually beneficial to both crops and livestock.

While a complete reversal of the consequences of climate change seems improbable, Floridians can be encouraged by the fact that leaders in their state are taking some pragmatic steps to cope with the changes. Furthermore, as those policymakers look to protect the sectors that have long served as the foundation of Florida's economy, there is also a push to continue to diversify. International trade—Florida is already one of the largest export states—seems an ideal sector to expand with the increasingly globalized nature of economic systems. Despite the challenges, Florida is preparing to weather the storm of climate change as it has weathered so many storms before.

11. The primary purpose of the passage is to:

   A. describe how climate change has harmed Florida's land and industries.

   B. discuss the threats climate change poses to Florida and how to address them.

   C. argue for the implementation of unorthodox means of combating climate change.

   D. explain the varied ways in which climate change can impact people's lives.

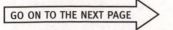
GO ON TO THE NEXT PAGE

12. According to the passage, what makes Hurricane Irma significant?

    F. It cost Florida nearly $200 billion in lost revenue and infrastructure repair.

    G. It was the first hurricane to hit Florida that was significantly exacerbated by climate change.

    H. It demonstrated to scientists how damaging rising sea levels could be.

    J. It caused more economic damage to Florida than any other hurricane.

13. The second paragraph implies that South Florida:

    A. is a major source of tourism revenue for the state.

    B. is likely to be entirely submerged by rising sea levels.

    C. is more vulnerable to extreme weather than North Florida.

    D. is central to agricultural production in Florida.

14. The passage makes clear that the main threat climate change poses to the Everglades is:

    F. contamination; salt water pushed inland will poison fresh water sources.

    G. submersion; rising sea levels will put lands at low elevations under water.

    H. habitat destruction; extreme weather will degrade the park's lush vegetation.

    J. isolation; changes to the landscape will cut the park off from visitors.

15. The author references the 2016 Environmental Protection Agency report (lines 45–48) and the 2003 study (lines 53–55) primarily in order to:

    A. provide specific numerical evidence for the cost of climate change.

    B. counter an argument that contradicts the author's point.

    C. open a discussion about their long-term implications for Florida.

    D. add support for the paragraph's claims from authoritative sources.

16. The passage states that compared to the citrus industry, the livestock industry in Florida:

    F. consumes more water.

    G. creates less pollution.

    H. exports more products.

    J. generates less income.

17. According to the passage, how might climate change negatively impact the livestock industry in Florida?

    A. Decreased crop yields would mean less food for the animals.

    B. Higher temperatures would put a strain on the animals' bodies.

    C. Animals exposed to poor weather would be more likely to become ill.

    D. Water shortages would cause the animals to become dehydrated.

18. Which of the following best describes the purpose of the sixth paragraph?

    F. It outlines suggested infrastructure adaptations to be applied throughout Florida.

    G. It summarizes the primary challenges facing Florida's economy due to climate change.

    H. It explains some of the ways Floridians are planning to address problems caused by climate change.

    J. It examines how to best direct water supplies in order to compensate for imbalances in rainfall.

19. According to the passage, how is the agriculture industry preparing to address problems caused by climate change?

    A. Farmers are replacing microsurface and subsurface drip irrigation with more efficient systems.

    B. Industry associations are working to expand underground aquifers.

    C. Farms are integrating crops and livestock to improve production of both.

    D. Farmers are stepping up vaccinations of livestock to combat the spread of disease.

20. The detail "Florida is already one of the largest export states" (lines 107–108) most nearly serves to:

    F. identify one of the main drivers of Florida's economic expansion.

    G. compare Florida's trade balance to that of other states.

    H. explain why expanding Florida's international trade is likely to be effective.

    J. emphasize the benefits of diversifying Florida's economy.

Passage III

HUMANITIES: One of the most enjoyable ways to analyze culture is through music. By analyzing musical styles and lyrics, one can explore quintessential characteristics of particular cultures. Passage A explores the relationship between the central and southern areas of the Appalachian mountain range and country music. Passage B contrasts bluegrass and country music and culture.

Passage A

Country music has its roots in the southern portions of the United States, specifically in the remote and undeveloped backcountry of the central and southern areas of the Appalachian mountain
5 range. Recognized as a distinct cultural region since the late nineteenth century, the area became home to European settlements in the eighteenth century, primarily led by Ulster Scots from Ireland. Early inhabitants have been characterized as
10 fiercely independent, to the point of rudeness and inhospitality. It was in this area that the region's truly indigenous music, now known as country music, was born.

Rooted in spirituals as well as folk music,
15 cowboy songs, and traditional Celtic melodies, country music originated in the 1920s. The motifs are generally ballads and dance tunes, simple in form and accompanied mostly by guitar, banjo, and violin. Though today there are many genres of
20 country music, all have their roots in this mélange of sources.

The term "country" has replaced the original pejorative term "hillbilly." Hillbillies referred to Appalachian inhabitants who were considered poor,
25 uneducated, isolated, and wary; the name change reflects a more accepting characterization of these mountain dwellers.

Hank Williams put country music on the map nationally, and is credited with the movement of
30 country music from the South to more national prominence. Other early innovators include the Carter family, Ernest Tubb, Woody Guthrie, Loretta Lynn, and Bill Monroe, father of bluegrass music. More recently, Faith Hill, Reba McEntire, and
35 Shania Twain have carried on the tradition.

What might be considered the "home base" of country music is in Nashville, Tennessee, and the

GO ON TO THE NEXT PAGE ➡

legendary music hall, the Grand Ole Opry. Founded
in 1925 by George D. Hay, it had its genesis in the
40 pioneer radio station WSM's program *Barn Dance*.
Country singers are considered to have reached
the pinnacle of the profession if they are asked to
become members of the Opry. While noted country
music performers and acts take the stage at the Opry
45 numerous times, Elvis Presley performed there only
once, in 1954. His act was so poorly received that it
was suggested he return to his job as a truck driver.

The offshoots and relatives of country music
highlight the complexity of this genre. In a move
50 away from its mountain origins, and turning a
focus to the West, honky-tonk music became
popular in the early twentieth century. Its name is
a reference to its roots in honky-tonk bars, where
the music was played. Additionally, Western swing
55 emerged as one of the first genres to blend country
and jazz musical styles, which required a great deal
of skill and creativity. Some of the most talented
and sophisticated musicians performing in any
genre were musicians who played in bluegrass string
60 bands, another relative of country music.

Country music has always been an expression of
American identity. Its sound, lyrics, and performers
are purely American, and though the music now
has an international audience, it remains American
65 in its heart and soul.

Passage B

A style of music closely related to country is the
similarly indigenous music known as bluegrass,
which originated in the Appalachian highland
regions extending westwards to the Ozark
70 Mountains in southern Missouri and northern
Arkansas. Derived from the music brought over
by European settlers of the region, bluegrass is
a mixture of Scottish, Welsh, Irish, and English
melodic forms, infused, over time, with African-
75 American influences. Indeed, many bluegrass songs,
such as "Barbara Allen" and "House Carpenter,"
preserve their European roots, maintaining the
traditional musical style and narratives almost
intact. Story-telling ballads, often laments, are
80 common themes. Given the predominance of
coal mining in the Appalachian region, it is not
surprising that ballads relating to mining tragedies
are also common.

Unlike country music, in which musicians
85 commonly play the same melodies together,
bluegrass highlights one player at a time, with the
others providing accompaniment. This tradition of
each musician taking turns with solos, and often
improvising, can also be seen in jazz ensembles.
90 Traditional bluegrass music is typically played
on instruments such as banjo, guitar, mandolin,
bass, harmonica, and Dobro (resonator guitar).
Even household objects, including washboards and
spoons, have, from time to time, been drafted for
95 use as instruments. Vocals also differ from country
music in that, rather than featuring a single voice,
bluegrass incorporates baritone and tenor harmonies.

Initially included under the catch-all phrase "folk
music," and later referred to as "hillbilly," bluegrass
100 did not come into his own category until the late
1950s, and appeared first in the comprehensive guide,
Music Index, in 1965. Presumably it was named after
Bill Monroe's Blue Grass band, the seminal bluegrass
band. A rapid, almost frenetic pace, characterizes
105 bluegrass tempos. Even today, decades after their
most active performing era, The Foggy Mountain
Boys members Lester Flatt, a bluegrass guitarist and
mandolinist, and Earl Scruggs, known for his three-
finger banjo picking style, are widely considered the
110 foremost artists on their instruments.

Partially because of its pace and complexity,
bluegrass has often been recorded for movie
soundtracks. "Dueling Banjos," played in the movie
Deliverance, exemplifies the skill required by the
115 feverish tempo of the genre. The soundtrack for *O
Brother, Where Art Thou?* incorporates bluegrass and
its musical cousins folk, country, gospel, and blues.
Bluegrass festivals are held throughout the country
and as far away as the Czech Republic. Interactive,
120 often inviting audience participation, they feature
performers such as Dolly Parton and Alison Krauss.

Central to bluegrass music are the themes of the
working class—miners, railroad workers, farmers.
The phrase "high, lonesome sound" was coined to
125 represent the bluegrass undertones of intensity and
cheerlessness, symbolizing the hard-scrabble life of
the American worker. As with so much of a nation's
traditional music, and for better or worse, bluegrass
music reflects America.

GO ON TO THE NEXT PAGE

21. According to the passage, country music originated from all of the following EXCEPT:

    A. Celtic melodies.

    B. spirituals.

    C. jazz.

    D. cowboy songs.

22. Which of the following would be the most logical place to hear the best of country music?

    F. Honky-tonk bars

    G. Ireland

    H. The Appalachian backcountry

    J. The Grand Ole Opry

23. As it is used in line 23, the word *pejorative* most nearly means:

    A. traditional.

    B. accurate.

    C. disparaging.

    D. mountain dwelling.

24. If a song were a lament with Welsh and African-American derivation, the author of Passage B would classify it as:

    F. bluegrass.

    G. country.

    H. jazz.

    J. hillbilly.

25. According to the passage, the instruments played in bluegrass music are:

    A. both typical and unusual.

    B. derived from African-American influences.

    C. made famous by the piece "Dueling Banjos."

    D. restricted to those used in the Ozarks.

26. In addition to highlighting one player at a time, bluegrass music differs from country music in that it often:

    F. features harmonies sung by bass and tenor voices.

    G. features a single voice.

    H. is characterized by musicians commonly playing the same melodies together.

    J. is played on instruments such as the banjo and guitar.

27. It can be inferred that laments and high, lonesome sounds both reflect:

    A. the influence of Irish music.

    B. the challenges of American life.

    C. songs sung by Shania Twain.

    D. hillbilly music.

28. As it is used in the introductory information, "quintessential" most nearly means:

    F. old-fashioned.

    G. representative.

    H. charming.

    J. unconventional.

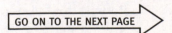
GO ON TO THE NEXT PAGE

29. Passage A states that there were "talented and sophisticated" (line 57–58) musicians playing bluegrass music. Which sentence in Passage B suggests this claim?

   A. "Central to bluegrass music are the themes of the working class—miners, railroad workers, farmers."

   B. "Partially because of its pace and complexity, bluegrass has often been recorded for movie soundtracks."

   C. "Lester Flatt, a bluegrass guitarist and mandolinist, and Earl Scruggs, known for his three-finger banjo picking style, are widely considered the foremost artists on their instruments."

   D. "A style of music closely related to country is the similarly indigenous music known as bluegrass …"

30. It can be inferred that both authors would agree that:

   F. country and bluegrass music are popular genres.

   G. both genres—country and bluegrass—are showcased at the Grand Ole Opry.

   H. music genres can evolve.

   J. country and bluegrass music are gaining in acceptance.

Passage IV

NATURAL SCIENCE: This passage is adapted from an article about the history of artificial satellites.

When the researchers at California Polytechnic university (CalPoly) and Stanford University determined the specifications of the CubeSat design back in 1999, they likely did not realize the full
5 potential of the miniature satellites. NASA's Mars Cube One (MarCO) mission has provided strong evidence that CubeSats offer many advantages for deep space exploration. The ability to build a large portion of the CubeSat with off-the-
10 shelf components means that future missions can be more cost-effective. The low cost of the satellites may also allow for more radical scientific experiments to be performed in space.

Experimental radio and antenna designs were
15 an important part of the mission. The MarCO-A and MarCO-B satellites, affectionately referred to as "Eve" and "WALL-E" by the engineering team, had softball-sized UHF and X-band radios mounted to the main unit. These allowed the satellites, which
20 were launched into space at the same time as the InSight lander, to send back photos of the landing in under eight minutes. By contrast, the lander itself took over an hour to transmit its successful landing. The same radio and antenna technology
25 also allowed for more efficient monitoring of the landing process. With only a 40% success rate as of 2017, Mars landings remain notoriously difficult. The data recorded by the MarCO satellites will help future missions.

30   Even beyond the completion of the Mars mission, engineers like Joel Krajewski, project manager for MarCO, hope to use the data sent back by the satellites to test how long technological systems can withstand the harships of space. Both units
35 will continue to relay system data until they cease to function. The successful survival of the two modified satellites could lead to the possibility of longer explorations much deeper into the outer reaches of the universe.

40   In order to increase the success of the mission, the MarCO team fitted the satellites with some specific modifications. The cameras that MarCO-B

used to take stills of the planet as the satellite approached Mars represent a significantly more
45 economical approach. The consumer-grade cameras highlight the potential for greatly reducing the costs associated with deep space missions. Soon after receipt, images of the Red Planet, along with its moons Phobos and Deimos, were proudly
50 displayed on the NASA website. An elated Cody Colley, mission manager from JPL, happily reported, "WALL-E sent some great postcards from Mars!" It is of note that the entire MarCO project checked in at $18.5 million. Compared
55 to the price tag associated with building and sending a more traditional satellite into space, which can easily reach $100 million, CubeSats represent an unprecedented breakthrough in the financial burden of space exploration.

60   Cost reductions also mean that it is increasingly possible for science experiments that stood little chance of being greenlighted in the past to make it into deep space via a CubeSat. Several projects already exist in near-Earth orbit, including a 2009
65 study on antibacterial effectiveness in zero-g, a QuakeSat in 2003 to measure for Extremely Low Frequency (ELF) signals that some scientists believe occur before earthquakes, and the 2015 LightSail 1 mission to test propulsion systems.
70 The ability to travel greater distances into space in an economical manner will no doubt encourage researchers to propose more novel experiments for future missions.

    The possibility of linked networks of CubeSats
75 in deep space offers another intriguing proposition. The QB50 project involved the cooperation of over 30 international universities to send CubeSats into near-earth orbit to study temporal and spatial characteristics of the lower thermosphere.
80 Benefits of linked networks include increased flexibility to distribute tasks among the satellites and reduced probability of single-point failure. This kind of redundancy against failure, along with the ability to adapt in real-time, is even more
85 helpful in deep space where the satellites face an incredibly challenging environment.

    Since its inception in 1958, NASA has encouraged its researchers, scientists, and

engineers to push the limits of existing technology.
90 In building on the work of teams at CalPoly and Stanford, the engineers at NASA have proven that cost-effective CubeSat technology has the potential to exponentially increase scientific experimentation in deep space. As the MarCO team continues to
95 collect data from "Eve" and "WALL-E," the lessons learned will no doubt set a new standard for the vast array of deep space CubeSats to come.

31. Which of the following best describes the author's attitude towards the passage's main topic?

   A. Cautious optimism

   B. Dispassionate concern

   C. Disillusioned frustration

   D. Enthusiastic anticipation

32. According to the passage, the CubeSat was first designed by:

   F. Joel Krajewski

   G. Cody Colley

   H. CalPoly and Stanford researchers

   J. NASA scientists and engineers

33. As it is used in line 12, the word *radical* most nearly means:

   A. militarized and aggressive.

   B. ideologically extreme.

   C. primitive and organic.

   D. profoundly innovative.

GO ON TO THE NEXT PAGE ⟶

34. According to the passage, why was the MarCO satellites' experimental communication technology notable?

    F. It transmitted landing data over seven times faster than the previous technology.

    G. It took barely an hour to transmit landing data back to NASA.

    H. Its off-the-shelf components made it much less expensive than other radios.

    J. The radios were unusually space-efficient, being the size of softballs.

35. It can be inferred from the second paragraph that compared to the InSight lander, the MarCO satellites:

    A. take higher-resolution photos from greater distances.

    B. demonstrate greater efficiency by utilizing miniaturized technology.

    C. provided more helpful information to improve future Mars landings.

    D. are able to land more effectively in difficult Martian conditions.

36. The fourth paragraph primarily serves to:

    F. argue for using consumer-grade components wherever possible for future NASA projects.

    G. explain how innovative choices in technology led to significant cost reductions for the MarCO satellites.

    H. describe the many reasons why the MarCO project was less expensive than comparable satellite projects.

    J. praise the superiority of the images the MarCO satellites sent back from Mars.

37. Based on the passage, why did the scientists at NASA most likely post photos from the MarCO satellites on their website?

    A. They hoped to gain support for future missions.

    B. They wanted to prove that the new satellites were viable.

    C. They needed to satisfy public demands for information.

    D. They were pleased with the success of the mission.

38. Which of the following does the passage suggest about the experiments referenced in lines 64–69?

    F. Their creators had to wait a very long time for approval of their ideas.

    G. It is unlikely they would have been carried out using more traditional satellites.

    H. They required linked networks of satellites to effectively test different variables.

    J. They had to be conducted farther from Earth than most satellites go.

39. The passage states that the advantages of linked networks of satellites include:

   A. considerable reductions in cost from traditional satellites.

   B. increased adaptability and protection against breakdown.

   C. encouraging international cooperation due to shared ownership.

   D. the possibility of studying previously-inaccessible parts of the atmosphere.

40. The comparisons in lines 22–26 and lines 54–59 are examples of how the author:

   F. juxtaposes old and new in order to systematically dismantle old methods.

   G. references prestigious institutions to increase the passage's authority.

   H. uses specific statistics in order to support points made in the passage.

   J. employs positive language to convey zeal for the passage's subject.

Practice Test

IF YOU FINISH BEFORE TIME IS CALLED, YOU MAY CHECK YOUR WORK ON THIS SECTION ONLY. DO NOT TURN TO ANY OTHER SECTION IN THE TEST.   **STOP**

802 K

Science Test

35 Minutes—40 Questions

Directions: The Science Test includes multiple passages. Each passage includes multiple questions. After reading each passage, choose the best answer and fill in the corresponding bubble on your answer sheet. You may review the passages as often as necessary.

You may NOT use a calculator on this test.

Passage I

Soil, by volume, consists on average of 45% minerals, 25% water, 25% air, and 5% organic matter (including both living and nonliving organisms). Time and topography shape the composition of soil and cause it to develop into layers known as *horizons*. The soil horizons in a particular area are collectively known as the *soil profile*. The composition of soil varies in each horizon, as do the most common minerals, as can be seen in the soil profile depicted in the diagram. The diagram also shows the depth of each horizon and the overall density of the soil.

diagram

Table 1 lists the zinc and calcium contents (as percentages) in the minerals that compose soil.

Table 1		
Mineral	Zinc content (%)	Calcium content (%)
Feldspar	35–40	0–10
Hornblende	30–35	10–20

Table 1 (continued from previous column)		
Mineral	Zinc content (%)	Calcium content (%)
Quartz	25–30	20–30
Mica	20–25	30–40
Serpentine	15–20	40–50
Anorthite	10–15	50–60
Limestone	5–10	60–70
Shale	0–5	70–80

Table 2 shows the average percentage of minerals that compose granite and sandstone, two rock types that are commonly found in soil.

Table 2		
Mineral	Percentage of mineral in:	
	Sandstone	Granite
Feldspar	30	54
Hornblende	2	0
Quartz	50	33
Mica	10	10
Serpentine	0	0
Anorthite	0	0
Limestone	5	0
Shale	0	0
Augite	3	3

GO ON TO THE NEXT PAGE

1. An analysis of an unknown mineral found in soil revealed its zinc content to be 32% and its calcium content to be 12%. Based on the data in Table 1, geologists would most likely classify this mineral as:

   A. hornblende.
   B. anorthite.
   C. serpentine.
   D. mica.

2. Geologists digging down into the A horizon would most likely find which of the following minerals?

   F. Limestone
   G. Shale
   H. Serpentine
   J. Mica

3. Based on the data presented in the diagram and Table 1, which of the following statements best describes the relationship between the zinc content of a mineral and the depth below surface level at which it is dominant? As zinc content increases:

   A. depth increases.
   B. depth decreases.
   C. depth first increases, then decreases.
   D. depth first decreases, then increases.

4. If geologists were to drill 30 feet into the Earth, which of the following minerals would they most likely encounter?

   F. Quartz, mica, and limestone
   G. Feldspar, shale, and serpentine
   H. Feldspar, quartz, and anorthite
   J. Hornblende, limestone, and serpentine

5. If augite is most commonly found in soil in close proximity to the other minerals that make up granite, then augite would most likely be found at a depth of:

   A. less than 10 feet.
   B. between 10 feet and 30 feet.
   C. between 30 feet and 60 feet.
   D. greater than 60 feet.

6. Based on the passage, how is the percentage of zinc content related to the percentage of calcium content in the minerals that make up soil?

   F. The percentage of zinc content increases as the percentage of calcium content increases.
   G. The percentage of zinc content increases as the percentage of calcium content decreases.
   H. Both the percentage of zinc content and the percentage of calcium content remain constant.
   J. There is no discernible relationship between the percentage of zinc content and the percentage of calcium content.

Passage II

Students conducted the following studies to determine the melting points of several materials. They attempted to melt the materials by submerging them in a variety of aqueous solutions that were heated to their boiling points. They used the following equation to calculate the boiling points of these solutions:

$$\Delta T_b = K_b \times m \times i,$$

where

ΔT_b = increase in boiling point above pure solvent

$K_b = 0.512 \dfrac{°C \times kg}{mol}$

$m = \text{molality} = \dfrac{\text{mol solute}}{\text{kg solvent}}$

i = number of ions present per molecule of solute

GO ON TO THE NEXT PAGE ⟹

Study 1

In order to prepare various solutions of sodium chloride (NaCl), 100.00 g of H_2O were added to a beaker. A known quantity of NaCl was dissolved into the water, and the resulting boiling point of the solution was recorded. This procedure was repeated with different amounts of NaCl as shown in Table 1.

		Table 1	
Solution	Mass of H_2O (g)	Amount of NaCl (mol)	Boiling point (°C)
1	100.00	0	100.00
2	100.00	0.085	100.88
3	100.00	0.171	101.75
4	100.00	0.257	102.63
5	100.00	0.342	103.50

Study 2

In order to prepare various solutions of calcium chloride ($CaCl_2$), 100 g of H_2O were added to a beaker. A known quantity of $CaCl_2$ was dissolved into the water and the resulting boiling point of the solution was recorded. This procedure was repeated with different amounts of $CaCl_2$ as shown in Table 2.

		Table 2	
Solution	Mass of H_2O (g)	Amount of $CaCl_2$ (mol)	Boiling point (°C)
6	100.00	0.270	104.15
7	100.00	0.360	105.53
8	100.00	0.450	106.91
9	100.00	0.541	108.29
10	100.00	0.631	109.67

Study 3

Each solution from Studies 1 and 2 was brought to a boil. A small sample of a material was placed in each solution. If the material melted, a "Y" was marked in Table 3. If the material did not melt, an "N" was marked

in Table 3. This procedure was repeated for all eight materials.

	Table 3									
	Solution									
Material	1	2	3	4	5	6	7	8	9	10
1	Y	Y	Y	Y	Y	Y	Y	Y	Y	Y
2	N	Y	Y	Y	Y	Y	Y	Y	Y	Y
3	N	N	Y	Y	Y	Y	Y	Y	Y	Y
4	N	N	N	N	Y	Y	Y	Y	Y	Y
5	N	N	N	N	N	Y	Y	Y	Y	Y
6	N	N	N	N	N	N	N	Y	Y	Y
7	N	N	N	N	N	N	N	N	N	Y
8	N	N	N	N	N	N	N	N	N	N

7. Which of the following modifications to Solution 5 of Study 1 would result in an increase in its boiling point?

   I.   Increasing the K_b of the solution

   II. Increasing the amount of NaCl

   III. Replacing the NaCl with an equal amount of $CaCl_2$

   A. I only

   B. I and II only

   C. II and III only

   D. I, II, and III

8. In Study 1, what was the boiling point of the solution with 0.171 mols of NaCl ?

   F. 100°C

   G. 100.88°C

   H. 101.75°C

   J. 109.67°C

9. Based on the results of the studies from the passage, the boiling point of Material 5 is most likely:

    A. less than 102.63°C.

    B. between 102.63°C and 103.50°C.

    C. between 103.50°C and 104.15°C.

    D. greater than 104.15°C.

10. If a sixth solution had been prepared during Study 2 using 0.721 mol $CaCl_2$, its boiling point would most likely be closest to which of the following?

    F. 108.75°C

    G. 111.07°C

    H. 113.72°C

    J. 115.02°C

11. A ninth material was submerged in Solutions 1–6 as in Experiment 3. Which of the following is LEAST likely to be a plausible set of results for this material?

	Solution					
	1	2	3	4	5	6
A.	Y	Y	Y	Y	N	N
B.	Y	Y	Y	Y	Y	Y
C.	N	N	N	N	Y	Y
D.	N	N	N	N	N	N

    A. A

    B. B

    C. C

    D. D

12. Which of the following best explains why the students recorded data for their solutes in mol rather than g or kg ?

    F. The H_2O was already measured in kg.

    G. The units for mass are less accurate.

    H. The change in boiling point depends on molality.

    J. The melting points of the various materials do not depend on the masses of the materials.

13. Would the results of Studies 1–3 support the claim that Material 7 has a lower melting point than Material 8 ?

    A. Yes, because in Solution 10, Material 7 melted and Material 8 did not.

    B. Yes, because in Solution 10, Material 8 melted and Material 7 did not.

    C. No, because the melting point of Material 8 cannot be determined from the data.

    D. No, because the melting point of Material 7 cannot be determined from the data.

Passage III

Engineers designing a roadway needed to test the composition of the soil that would form the roadbed. In order to determine whether their two sampling systems (System A and System B) give sufficiently accurate soil composition measurements, they first conducted a study to compare the two systems.

Soil samples were taken with varying levels of *humidity* (concentration of water). The concentrations of the compounds that form the majority of soil were measured. The results for the sampling systems were compared with data on file with the US Geological Survey (USGS), which compiles extremely accurate data. The engineers' and USGS's results are presented in Table 1 below.

GO ON TO THE NEXT PAGE ⇒

Table 1					
	Level of humidity				
Concentration (mg/L) of:	10%	25%	45%	65%	80%
Nitrogen (N)					
USGS	105	236	598	781	904
System A	112	342	716	953	1,283
System B	196	408	857	1,296	1,682
Potassium oxide (K_2O)					
USGS	9.4	9.1	8.9	8.7	8.2
System A	9.4	9.0	8.7	8.5	8.0
System B	9.5	9.2	9.0	8.8	8.3
Calcium (Ca)					
USGS	39.8	24.7	11.4	5.0	44.8
System A	42.5	31.4	10.4	8.0	42.9
System B	37.1	23.2	11.6	11.1	45.1
Phosphorus oxide (P_2O_5)					
USGS	69.0	71.2	74.8	78.9	122.3
System A	67.9	69.9	72.2	76.7	123.1
System B	74.0	75.6	78.7	82.1	126.3
Zinc (Zn)					
USGS	0.41	0.52	0.64	0.74	0.70
System A	0.67	0.80	0.88	0.97	0.93
System B	0.38	0.48	0.62	0.77	0.73

Note: Each system concentration measurement is the average of 5 measurements.

14. The hypothesis that increasing humidity increases the concentration of a compound is supported by all of the following EXCEPT:

   F. nitrogen.

   G. potassium oxide.

   H. phosphorus oxide.

   J. zinc.

15. At a humidity level of 25%, it could be concluded that System B least accurately measures the concentration of which of the following compounds, relative to the data on file with the USGS?

   A. N

   B. Ca

   C. K_2O

   D. P_2O_5

16. The engineers hypothesized that the concentration of potassium oxide (K_2O) decreases as the level of humidity increases. This hypothesis is supported by:

   F. the data from the USGS only.

   G. the System A measurements only.

   H. the data from the USGS and the System B measurements only.

   J. the data from the USGS, the System A measurements, and the System B measurements.

17. Do the results in Table 1 support the conclusion that System B is more accurate than System A for measuring the concentration of zinc?

   A. No, because the zinc measurements from System A are consistently higher than the zinc measurements from System B.

   B. No, because the zinc measurements from System A are closer to the data provided by the USGS than the zinc measurements from System B.

   C. Yes, because the zinc measurements from System B are consistently lower than the zinc measurements from System A.

   D. Yes, because the zinc measurements from System B are closer to the data provided by the USGS than the zinc measurements from System A.

18. The relationship between humidity level and calcium concentration, as measured by System B, is best represented by which of the following graphs?

F.

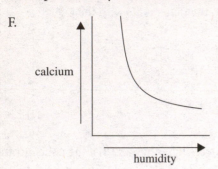

G.

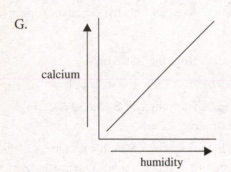

H.

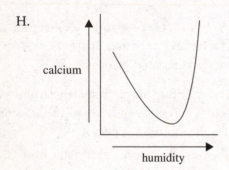

J.

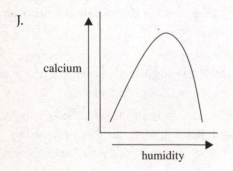

19. After conducting their comparisons, the engineers used System B to test a soil sample at the future road site. They measured the concentrations, in mg/L, of selected compounds in the sample and found that they were: potassium oxide = 9.1, calcium = 17.3, and zinc = 0.57. Based on the data in Table 1, the engineers should predict that the level of humidity is approximately:

A. 16%.

B. 37%.

C. 49%.

D. 57%.

Passage IV

Diabetes is a metabolic disorder that causes hyperglycemia (higher-than-normal blood glucose levels). The most common form is type 2 diabetes, which occurs when the body does not produce enough insulin or has a lowered level of response to insulin (insulin resistance). Insulin is a hormone produced in the pancreas that helps regulate blood glucose levels by stimulating cells to absorb and metabolize glucose. Typically occurring in adults, type 2 diabetes has developed in an increasing number of individuals over 45 years old. Three scientists offered hypotheses to explain the cause of type 2 diabetes.

Scientist 1

Studies have shown that the consumption of sugar-sweetened drinks in excess is associated with an increased risk of type 2 diabetes. Thus, the cause of type 2 diabetes is an overconsumption of sugar. When sugar intake is high, the insulin in the body is unable to normalize the increased blood glucose levels. In a study of individuals 18–25 years old who consumed more than the daily recommended amount of sugar, although their insulin levels were normal, their blood glucose levels were significantly elevated. When these individuals received small injections of supplemental insulin once a day, their blood sugar did not return to normal levels.

GO ON TO THE NEXT PAGE

Scientist 2

Type 2 diabetes primarily occurs as a result of obesity and lack of exercise. Experimental data have shown that diets high in fat but not high in sugar are associated with an increased risk of type 2 diabetes. In a study of healthy young men, those put on a high-fat diet had twice the blood glucose levels compared to those put on a high-carbohydrate diet. Excess fat in the bloodstream breaks down into free radicals that impair insulin action, causing cells to become insulin resistant and blood glucose levels to rise. Studies have also shown that the lack of exercise causes 7% of type 2 diabetes cases. Regular exercise can boost the body's efficiency to regulate blood glucose levels.

Scientist 3

Type 2 diabetes is not caused by lifestyle or diet but inherited. Studies have shown an increased risk of type 2 diabetes in people with a parent or sibling who has type 2 diabetes. More than 36 genes that contribute to the risk of type 2 diabetes have been found. Individuals have about a 15%–20% chance of developing type 2 diabetes if one of their parents has it and a roughly 50% chance if both parents have it. The chance of siblings having type 2 diabetes is 25%–50%.

20. The liver helps to regulate the amounts of glucose, protein, and fat in the blood. About 80% of people with diabetes have buildup of fat in the liver. This information, if true, would strengthen the viewpoint of:

    F. Scientist 1 only.
    G. Scientist 2 only.
    H. both Scientist 1 and Scientist 2.
    J. neither Scientist 1 nor Scientist 2.

21. Scientists 1 and 2 would most likely agree that the occurrence of type 2 diabetes in an individual is associated with the patient's:

    A. lifestyle.
    B. diet.
    C. genetics.
    D. age.

22. According to the passage, adults who have had their pancreas removed should exhibit:

    F. increased blood insulin levels.
    G. decreased blood sugar levels.
    H. increased blood sugar levels.
    J. decreased body fat content.

23. Suppose that an individual had an 18% chance of developing type 2 diabetes. Based on the passage, Scientist 3 would most likely predict that this individual has:

    A. a high-sugar diet.
    B. a high-fat diet.
    C. one parent with type 2 diabetes.
    D. two parents with type 2 diabetes.

24. Suppose a 50-year-old patient developed type 2 diabetes. Which of the following statements is most consistent with the information in the passage?

    F. Scientist 1 would conclude that the patient consumes excess fat daily.
    G. Scientist 2 would conclude that the patient has a high-sugar diet.
    H. Scientist 3 would conclude that the patient fails to exercise.
    J. Scientist 3 would conclude that the patient had at least one parent with type 2 diabetes.

25. Which of the following discoveries, if accurate, would support the viewpoint of Scientist 1 ?

    A. High intake of sugar causes insulin resistance.
    B. High intake of fat causes impaired insulin action.
    C. Low intake of sugar causes increased insulin production.
    D. Low intake of sugar causes increased free radical production.

26. Which of the following arguments could Scientist 3 use as an effective counter to Scientist 2's claim that lack of exercise causes 7% of type 2 diabetes cases?

    F. The 7% that lacked exercise also have family histories of type 2 diabetes.

    G. More than 36 genes that contribute to the risk of type 2 diabetes have been found.

    H. The 7% that lacked exercise did not receive insulin injections.

    J. Scientist 2's hypothesis would suggest that more than 7% of type 2 diabetes cases should be due to lack of exercise.

Passage V

Human blood is composed of approximately 45% *formed elements*, including blood cells, and 50% plasma. The formed elements of blood are further broken down into red blood cells, white blood cells, and platelets. The mass of a particular blood sample is determined by the ratio of formed elements to plasma; the formed elements weigh approximately 1.10 grams per milliliter (g/mL) and plasma approximately 1.02 g/mL. This ratio varies according to an individual's diet, health, and genetic makeup.

The following studies were performed by a phlebotomist to determine the composition and mass of blood samples from three different individuals, each of whom was required to fast overnight before the samples were taken.

Study 1

A 10 mL blood sample was taken from each of the three patients. The densities of the blood samples were measured using the *oscillator technique*, which determines fluid densities by measuring sound velocity transmission.

Study 2

Each 10 mL blood sample was spun for 20 minutes in a centrifuge to force the heavier formed elements to separate from the plasma. The plasma was then siphoned off and its mass recorded.

Study 3

The formed elements left over from Study 2 were analyzed using the same centrifuge, except this time they were spun at a slower speed for 45 minutes so that the red blood cells, white blood cells, and platelets could separate out. The mass of each element was then recorded. The results of the three studies are shown in Table 1.

Table 1					
Patient	Plasma (g)	Red blood cells (g)	White blood cells (g)	Platelets (g)	Total density (g/mL)
A	4.54	2.75	1.09	1.32	1.056
B	4.54	2.70	1.08	1.35	1.054
C	4.64	2.65	1.08	1.34	1.050

27. The results of the studies indicate that the blood sample with the lowest density is the sample with the most:

    A. plasma.

    B. red blood cells.

    C. white blood cells.

    D. platelets.

28. Which of the following offers the most reasonable explanation for why the phlebotomist required each patient to fast overnight before taking blood samples?

    F. It is more difficult to withdraw blood from patients who have not fasted.

    G. Fasting causes large, temporary changes in the composition of blood.

    H. Fasting ensures that blood samples are not affected by temporary changes caused by consuming different foods.

    J. Blood from patients who have not fasted will not separate when spun in a centrifuge.

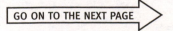
GO ON TO THE NEXT PAGE

29. Which of the following best explains why the amount of plasma, red blood cells, white blood cells, and platelets do not add up to 10.50 g in Patient C ?

    A. Some of the red blood cells might have remained in the plasma, yielding low red blood cell measurements.

    B. Some of the platelets might not have separated from the white blood cells, yielding high white blood cell counts.

    C. The centrifuge might have failed to fully separate the plasma from the formed elements.

    D. There are likely components other than plasma, red and white blood cells, and platelets in blood.

30. Based on the data collected from the studies, it is possible to determine that, as total blood density increases, the mass of red blood cells:

    F. increases only.

    G. increases, then decreases.

    H. decreases only.

    J. decreases, then increases.

31. Suppose that a 10 mL blood sample from a fourth individual contains approximately 5 mL of plasma and approximately 5 mL of formed elements. The mass of this blood sample would most likely be:

    A. less than 10.0 g.

    B. between 10.0 and 12.0 g.

    C. between 12.0 and 14.0 g.

    D. greater than 14.0 g.

32. The phlebotomist varied which of the following techniques between Study 2 and Study 3 ?

    F. The volume of blood taken from each patient

    G. The mass of blood taken from each patient

    H. The instrument used to separate the elements of the blood samples

    J. The amount of time the samples were left in the centrifuge

33. The patient with the greatest mass of red blood cells is:

    A. Patient A.

    B. Patient B.

    C. Patient C.

    D. not possible to determine from the information given.

Passage VI

A student performed experiments to determine the relationship between the amount of electrical current carried by a material and the physical dimensions and temperature of a sample of that material. Current is measured in amperes (A) and the resistance to the flow of current is measured in ohms (Ω). Current and resistance are related to voltage, measured in volts (V), by Ohm's law: $V = A \times \Omega$. (Note that Ohm's law can also be written as $V = I \times R$, where V is voltage, I is current, and R is resistance.)

Experiment 1

The student used several lengths of an iron rod with a 1 cm diameter. The rods were heated or cooled to the specified temperatures and used to complete the circuit shown in the diagram. The circuit contains a battery and an ammeter, which measures current in milliamperes (mA). The results are presented in Table 1.

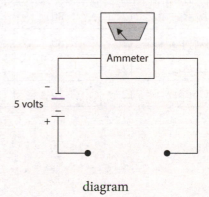

diagram

Table 1			
Trial	Length (cm)	Temperature (°C)	Current (mA)
1	16	80	20
2	16	20	40
3	12	80	27
4	12	20	53
5	10	80	32
6	10	20	64
7	8	80	40
8	8	20	80

Experiment 2

The student then repeated the experiment, this time using 1 cm diameter rods made from either iron or copper. The results are presented in Table 2.

Table 2				
Trial	Material	Length (cm)	Temperature (°C)	Current (mA)
9	Iron	16	80	20
10	Copper	16	80	100
11	Iron	16	20	40
12	Copper	16	20	200
13	Iron	12	80	27
14	Copper	12	80	135
15	Iron	12	20	53
16	Copper	12	20	265

34. Based on the experimental results, which of the following most accurately describes the relationships between current and rod length and between current and temperature?

   F. Current is directly related to length and inversely related to temperature.

   G. Current is inversely related to both length and temperature.

   H. Current is inversely related to length and directly related to temperature.

   J. Current is directly related to both length and temperature.

35. Based on the information from the passage, which of the following rods would have the highest value for resistance?

   A. A 12 cm iron rod at 20°C

   B. A 16 cm copper rod at 20°C

   C. A 16 cm iron rod at 80°C

   D. A 12 cm copper rod at 80°C

36. The *conductivity* of a material is a measure of how readily a length of the material allows the passage of an electric current. Conductivity is represented by σ, the Greek letter sigma, with standard units of siemens per meter (S/m). Siemens are equivalent to inverse ohms (that is, $1/\Omega$). Based on this information, which of the following equations accurately describes the relationship between conductivity and resistance?

   F. $\Omega = \dfrac{1}{\sigma}$

   G. $\sigma = \Omega \times m$

   H. $\sigma = \dfrac{1}{\Omega \times m}$

   J. $\Omega = \sigma \times m$

GO ON TO THE NEXT PAGE

37. If the rod used in Trial 4 of Experiment 1 were heated to a temperature of 50°C, the current it then conducts would most likely be:

    A. less than 27 mA.

    B. between 27 and 53 mA.

    C. between 53 and 80 mA.

    D. greater than 80 mA.

38. What would happen to the results of Experiment 2 if the student replaced the 5 V battery with a 10 V battery instead?

    F. The recorded current values would increase for both the copper and the iron rods.

    G. The recorded current values would increase for the copper rods but decrease for the iron rods.

    H. The recorded current values would decrease for the copper rods but increase for the iron rods.

    J. The recorded current values would decrease for both the copper and the iron rods.

39. Suppose the student took an iron rod of 8 cm and a copper rod of 8 cm, both with a 1 cm diameter, and attached them end to end, creating a composite rod with a length of 16 cm. Based on the results of Experiment 2, at a temperature of 20°C, this composite rod would most likely conduct a current of:

    A. less than 20 mA.

    B. between 20 and 40 mA.

    C. between 40 and 200 mA.

    D. greater than 200 mA.

40. Which of the following variables was NOT directly manipulated by the student in Experiment 2 ?

    F. Material

    G. Length

    H. Temperature

    J. Current

IF YOU FINISH BEFORE TIME IS CALLED, YOU MAY CHECK YOUR WORK ON THIS SECTION ONLY. DO NOT TURN TO ANY OTHER SECTION IN THE TEST.

STOP

Writing Test

40 Minutes

Directions

The essay is used to evaluate your writing skills. You will have **40 minutes** to review the prompt and plan and write an essay in English. Before you begin, read everything in this test booklet carefully to make sure you understand the task.

Your essay will be judged based on the evidence it provides of your ability to do the following:

- Assert your own perspective on a complex issue and evaluate the relationship between your perspective and at least one other perspective

- Use reasoning and evidence to refine and justify your ideas

- Present your ideas in an organized way

- Convey your ideas effectively using standard written English

Write your essay on the lined essay pages in the answer booklet. All writing on those lined pages will be scored. Use the unlined pages in this test booklet to plan your essay. Your work on these unlined pages will not be scored.

Put your pencil down as soon as time is called.

DO NOT OPEN THIS BOOKLET UNTIL TOLD TO DO SO.

GO ON TO THE NEXT PAGE ⟶

Scientific Research

A great deal of pure research, undertaken without specific goals but generally to further humankind's understanding of themselves and their world, is subsidized at least partly, if not fully, by the nation's government to help drive progress and promote outcomes that improve overall quality of life for citizens. Though pure research often involves considerable time, energy, and money without any assurances of positive outcomes, it can result in economic, medical, and technological benefits. However, it can also result in negative, harmful, and perhaps irreversible outcomes, in which case taxpayer dollars can be wasted and society put at risk. Should governments fund research when the outcome is unclear? Given that taxpayers prefer that their dollars be spent efficiently and effectively, it may be unwise to allocate significant funding to endeavors that may not benefit society as a whole.

Read and carefully consider these perspectives. Each discusses government funding of scientific research.

Perspective One	Perspective Two	Perspective Three
Governments should fund as much pure research as they can afford when the intent is to benefit the mass population. Without the government's money, many research projects would have to cease unless alternative funding is secured. Even research without clear, positive consequences should be pursued because the outcome may prove beneficial, and the research can always be paused or stopped entirely if negative repercussions begin to emerge.	Governments should be very cautious and limit efforts to fund research programs with unclear consequences. Rather, these programs should demonstrate their worth and intended results when seeking government money. Governments should evaluate the merit and benefit of each program on a case-by-case basis and fund only those projects that are designed to create—and will likely achieve—clear and acceptable outcomes.	Governments should partner with private contributors to fund research. Private contributors include companies doing research and development as well as nonprofit foundations. These partnerships will distance the government from taking responsibility for any unintended or undesired consequences and relieve the burden on the taxpayer for efforts that do not prove beneficial. Additionally, this approach incentivizes research teams to provide results-based research that can generate private funding, thus increasing the chance that the research will prove useful to multiple entities, including the government.

Essay Task

Write a clear, well-reasoned essay evaluating multiple perspectives on government funding of scientific research. In your essay, be sure to:

- Assert your own perspective on the issue and evaluate the relationship between your perspective and at least one other perspective
- Use reasoning and evidence to refine and justify your ideas
- Present your ideas in an organized way
- Convey your ideas effectively using standard written English

Your perspective may be fully, somewhat, or not at all in agreement with one or more of the three perspectives in the prompt.

GO ON TO THE NEXT PAGE →

Planning Your Essay

These pages are not scored.

Use the space below to brainstorm and plan your essay. Consider the following as you think about the prompt:

- Strengths and weaknesses of the three perspectives in the prompt
  - What observations do they offer, and what do they overlook?
  - Why are they persuasive or why are they not persuasive?
- Your own background and identity
  - What is your perspective on this issue, and what are its strengths and weaknesses?
  - What evidence will you use in your essay?

GO ON TO THE NEXT PAGE

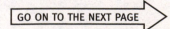

GO ON TO THE NEXT PAGE

Answer Key

English Test

1. A	16. F	31. A	46. H	61. A
2. J	17. C	32. H	47. A	62. H
3. C	18. H	33. B	48. H	63. B
4. F	19. B	34. H	49. D	64. H
5. B	20. H	35. A	50. H	65. C
6. G	21. B	36. H	51. B	66. G
7. C	22. J	37. D	52. G	67. C
8. H	23. A	38. J	53. A	68. J
9. A	24. F	39. D	54. F	69. D
10. G	25. B	40. G	55. C	70. G
11. B	26. H	41. C	56. G	71. A
12. G	27. B	42. F	57. A	72. H
13. C	28. F	43. D	58. H	73. C
14. F	29. B	44. F	59. C	74. H
15. B	30. J	45. C	60. F	75. C

Mathematics Test

1. D	13. B	25. B	37. C	49. C
2. K	14. H	26. H	38. H	50. J
3. C	15. C	27. D	39. D	51. E
4. G	16. J	28. G	40. J	52. K
5. B	17. E	29. C	41. C	53. C
6. G	18. J	30. J	42. K	54. J
7. B	19. D	31. D	43. D	55. D
8. F	20. F	32. G	44. G	56. F
9. A	21. D	33. E	45. A	57. A
10. K	22. J	34. F	46. G	58. F
11. E	23. D	35. C	47. C	59. D
12. H	24. G	36. G	48. F	60. J

Reading Test

1. C	11. B	21. C	31. D
2. J	12. J	22. J	32. H
3. A	13. A	23. C	33. D
4. F	14. G	24. F	34. F
5. A	15. D	25. A	35. C
6. H	16. J	26. F	36. G
7. C	17. B	27. B	37. D
8. F	18. H	28. G	38. G
9. B	19. C	29. C	39. B
10. F	20. H	30. H	40. H

Science Test

1. A	11. A	21. B	31. B
2. J	12. H	22. H	32. J
3. B	13. A	23. C	33. A
4. H	14. G	24. J	34. G
5. A	15. A	25. A	35. C
6. G	16. J	26. F	36. H
7. D	17. D	27. A	37. B
8. H	18. H	28. H	38. F
9. C	19. B	29. D	39. C
10. G	20. G	30. F	40. J

Answers and Explanations

English Test

My Old-Fashioned Father

1. A

Difficulty: Low

Category: Sentence Structure

Getting to the Answer: When a period appears in the underlined portion, check to see if each sentence is complete. Here, each sentence is complete and correct; therefore (A), NO CHANGE, is correct. Choice B creates a run-on sentence. Choices C and D create sentences that are awkward and overly wordy.

2. J

Difficulty: Medium

Category: Sentence Structure

Getting to the Answer: The ACT tests very specific punctuation rules. If punctuation is used in a way not covered by these rules, it will be incorrect. No commas are required in the underlined selection; (J) is correct. Choices F, G, and H all contain unnecessary commas.

3. C

Difficulty: Medium

Category: Sentence Structure

Getting to the Answer: When a verb is underlined, make sure it places the action properly in relation to the other events in the passage. This passage is written primarily in the present tense; *runs*, (C), is the best answer here. Choices A and B use verb tenses that do not make sense in context. The past tense verb in D is inconsistent with the rest of the passage.

4. F

Difficulty: Medium

Category: Conciseness

Getting to the Answer: Very rarely will a correct answer choice be significantly longer than the original selection. The underlined selection is grammatically and logically correct, so check the answer choices for a more concise version. You can eliminate G and H, both of which are wordier than the original. Choice J may be tempting

because it's shorter than the underlined selection, but it changes the meaning of the sentence; the back office, not the reader, is what hasn't changed. Choice (F) is correct.

5. B

Difficulty: Medium

Category: Development

Getting to the Answer: When an English Test question contains a question stem, read it carefully. More than one choice is likely to be both relevant and correct, but only one will satisfy the conditions of the stem. This paragraph deals with the author's father's refusal to give up his old-fashioned ways. Choice (B) is the most consistent choice. Choices A and D describe the items being inventoried, which is irrelevant to the point of the paragraph. Choice C is redundant; since we already know he uses paper and pencil to keep his inventory, it's understood that he's writing it by hand.

6. G

Difficulty: Medium

Category: Sentence Structure

Getting to the Answer: Commas cannot be used to combine independent clauses. Here, the comma connects two independent clauses. Choice (G) correctly replaces the comma with a semicolon. Choice H corrects the run-on error but is unnecessarily wordy. Choice J leaves the meaning of the second clause incomplete.

7. C

Difficulty: High

Category: Sentence Structure

Getting to the Answer: Beware of answer choices that make changes to parts of the selection that contain no errors; these choices will rarely be correct. As written, this sentence uses incorrect grammatical structure; the verb "is" is incorrect here, so you should eliminate A. Choice (C) eliminates it without introducing additional errors. Choices B and D correct the sentence's grammatical error, but neither uses the necessary contrast transition to relate this sentence to the one before it.

8.   H

Difficulty: Low

Category: Sentence Structure

Getting to the Answer: Commas are used in a series of three or more; they are incorrect in compounds. "My sister and I" is a compound; no comma is needed, so F is incorrect. Choice (H) corrects the error without adding any new ones. Choice G uses the incorrect pronoun case; because you wouldn't say "me bought him a brand-new computer," "me" is incorrect in the compound as well. Choice J incorrectly separates the sentence's subject and its predicate verb with a comma.

9.   A

Difficulty: High

Category: Organization

Getting to the Answer: When a transition word or phrase is underlined, make sure it properly relates the ideas it connects. The underlined word is the transition between the offer to help transfer records and the information about other ways the computer could be helpful. The second sentence is a continuation of the first, so you can eliminate B and D, both of which suggest a contrast. Choosing between (A) and C is a little more difficult, but remember that new errors may be introduced in answer choices. Choice C, *In addition*, would be acceptable if it were followed by a comma, but as written, it's incorrect. Choice (A) is correct.

10.   G

Difficulty: Medium

Category: Sentence Structure

Getting to the Answer: Semicolons can only combine independent clauses. Here, the second clause is not independent, so the semicolon is incorrect; eliminate F. Choice (G) correctly eliminates the semicolon. Choice H incorrectly places a comma after the conjunction. Choice J creates a run-on sentence.

11.   B

Difficulty: High

Category: Development

Getting to the Answer: When asked about the purpose of particular information, consider the purpose of the larger section. This paragraph describes the father's

resistance to technology, which stems in part from his desire to be able to work even in blackout conditions. The information about the town's history shows that blackout conditions seldom occur, making the father's reason a bad one. Choice (B) reflects this reasoning, and it is correct. Choice A is too extreme; the father's reason may be poor, but that does not make him delusional. Choices C and D do not relate to the purpose of the paragraph.

12.   G

Difficulty: Medium

Category: Organization

Getting to the Answer: When asked to add new information, read it into the passage at the points suggested to choose its most logical placement. There are three pronouns in this new sentence; clarity requires that it be placed somewhere that these pronouns have logical antecedents. Placing it after Sentence 1, as (G) suggests, gives each pronoun a clear antecedent: *we* is the author and his sister, *him* is their father, and *it* is the computer. Choice F puts the siblings' hopes about how a computer could help their father before the information that they bought him one. Choice H's placement makes the antecedent for *it* Father's *blackout scenario*, which doesn't make sense in context. Placing the new sentence where Choice J suggests gives the pronoun the antecedent *blackout*, which is also illogical.

13.   C

Difficulty: Medium

Category: Development

Getting to the Answer: Idiom questions often offer more than one idiomatically correct answer choice; use context to determine which is appropriate. "Sooner than later" is idiomatically incorrect, so you should eliminate A; these are comparison words, but nothing is compared here. Both B and (C) offer proper idioms, but (C) is the one that's appropriate here. Choice D is also incorrect idiomatic usage.

14.   F

Difficulty: Medium

Category: Development

Getting to the Answer: Remember to read for logic as well as for grammar and usage. The best version of this sentence is the way it is written; (F) is correct. Choice G redundantly uses the possessive *office's* where possession has already been indicated by *of*. Choice H misstates the information in the passage; the writer's father received the cell phone before the computer. Choice J incorrectly indicates that "the disorganized depths of that office" is where the writer's father received his cell phone, not where the cell phone ended up, which is opposite of the writer's intended meaning.

15. B

Difficulty: Low

Category: Organization

Getting to the Answer: When asked to add information, consider both the subject matter and the tone. This essay is about the author's father's resistance to technology. Choice (B) concludes the essay by referencing something stated at the beginning: that the writer's father tries to *hide* from the future. Choices A, C, and D, while relevant to the paragraph, do not provide strong conclusions to a passage about the father's aversion to technology.

Breaking Baseball's Color Barrier

16. F

Difficulty: Medium

Category: Agreement

Getting to the Answer: *More* or *–er* adjectives are used to compare two items; for more than two, use *most* or *–est*. This sentence is correct as written; (F), *farthest,* is appropriate when comparing all areas of the globe. Choice G uses *most far*, but *most* is only correct with adjectives that don't have *–est* forms. Choice H combines *most* with the *–est* suffix, which is never correct. Choice J uses *farther*, which indicates a comparison that is not present here.

17. C

Difficulty: Medium

Category: Sentence Structure

Getting to the Answer: The fact that the underlined portion contains multiple prepositions (*among* and *for*) is a clue to look for a misplaced modifier. It makes the most sense to describe equality as being *among races*, eliminating A and B. Choice D awkwardly places the noun after its modifying phrases, so (C) is correct.

18. H

Difficulty: Medium

Category: Agreement

Getting to the Answer: Most ACT idioms questions will hinge on preposition usage. "Prevented ... to participate" is idiomatically incorrect, so you can eliminate F. The proper idiom in this context is "prevented from participating," (H). Choices G and J are both idiomatically incorrect.

19. B

Difficulty: Medium

Category: Development

Getting to the Answer: When you're asked whether a piece of text is relevant, first determine the topic of the paragraph. This paragraph is about the evolution of the "*color line*" in baseball. Therefore, information that talks about the development of the industry and the shift in authority is relevant to the paragraph, so (B) is correct. Choice A is incorrect because, although the text does talk about previous associations, knowing that range doesn't further the purpose of the paragraph. Choices C and D can be eliminated, since they indicate that the information is irrelevant.

20. H

Difficulty: Medium

Category: Sentence Structure

Getting to the Answer: A verb should not be separated from its object by a comma. As written, this sentence places an incorrect comma between the verb *had* and its object; eliminate F. Choice (H) eliminates the comma without introducing any additional errors. Choices G and J both add incorrect commas.

21. B

Difficulty: Medium

Category: Agreement

Getting to the Answer: When a preposition is underlined, you're most likely being tested on idioms. Select the choice that sounds the most correct when read with the following noun phrase—in this case, *professional teams*. Because the leagues are made up of professional teams, (B) is correct here. Choices A, C, and D all suggest an incorrect relationship between the leagues and the teams.

22. J

Difficulty: Medium

Category: Development

Getting to the Answer: Determining whether the underlined text should be deleted will help you quickly eliminate two answer choices. If you eliminate the underlined selection, the passage skips abruptly from the decree losing its force to a discussion of specific African-American players. The underlined text introduces those players generally, as a result of the decree losing its impact, and therefore provides a necessary transition, as indicated in (J). Choices F and G can be eliminated, since they advocate deleting the selection. The reasoning in H is not supported by the passage.

23. A

Difficulty: Medium

Category: Sentence Structure

Getting to the Answer: Expect about 25% of your English Test questions to have no error. This sentence is correct as written, (A). Choices B, C, and D all create sentence fragments.

24. F

Difficulty: Medium

Category: Sentence Structure

Getting to the Answer: The phrase "including Walker's brother Weldy" is properly used here to modify "a few other African Americans"; no change is needed, so (F) is correct. Choice G is incorrect because no comma is used to introduce a clause beginning with *that*. Choices H and J make the sentence wordier unnecessarily.

25. B

Difficulty: Medium

Category: Agreement

Getting to the Answer: Use context to determine appropriate verb tense usage. The previous sentence says that Walker *was* a catcher; the introductory phrase in this sentence refers us to the same time period. Only (B) uses a consistent tense. Choices A, C, and D all refer to future actions.

26. H

Difficulty: Medium

Category: Organization

Getting to the Answer: Since NO CHANGE is not presented as an option, you'll need to find the most logical placement for the new sentence. *Other teams* must contrast with teams already mentioned, and the only place that happens is in Sentences 2 and 3. Sentence 2 talks about one player for the Blue Stockings and Sentence 3 mentions some additional players for the same team. Sentence 4 turns to the time when segregation returned, so the information about African Americans playing for other teams must come before that, between Sentences 3 and 4, (H).

27. B

Difficulty: Low

Category: Conciseness

Getting to the Answer: When you don't spot an error in grammar or usage, check for errors of style. "At the time when" is a longer way of saying "when"; (B) is correct here. Choice C uses *while*, which indicates a continuing period of time, but this sentence refers to a specific moment when Jackie Robinson crossed the color line. Choice D is even wordier than the original.

28. F

Difficulty: Medium

Category: Development

Getting to the Answer: Make sure your selection reflects the meaning of the sentence. The best version of this sentence is the way it is written, (F). Choice G changes the meaning of the sentence, implying that Robinson has yet to be recognized as a hero. Choice H also changes the sentence's meaning, indicating that Robinson is doing the recognizing rather than being recognized. Choice J is unnecessarily wordy.

29. B

Difficulty: High

Category: Development

Getting to the Answer: A question that asks about the essay's tone will likely include only answer choices that are grammatically correct. Be as picky as possible when determining which choice best fits the stated tone and emphasis. Choice A is too neutral, so it should be eliminated. Choice C does not emphasize the uniqueness of Robinson's role; eliminate it. Choice D mentions collaboration, which emphasizes teamwork rather than uniqueness, so it is also incorrect. Someone who blazes a path goes where no one has gone before. Thus, only (B) maintains a positive tone while showing that Robinson played a unique role.

30. J

Difficulty: Medium

Category: Development

Getting to the Answer: This question format appears frequently on the ACT; it's asking for the passage's main idea. This essay is about the color barrier in baseball; it would not fulfill an assignment to write about the history of baseball, so you can eliminate F and G. The fact that baseball was played before 1868, H, is not the reason this essay does not fulfill an assignment on baseball's history. Choice (J) correctly states the reasoning: the essay focuses only on one aspect of the game.

The Bear Mountain Bridge

31. A

Difficulty: Medium

Category: Sentence Structure

Getting to the Answer: An introductory phrase should be separated from the rest of the sentence by a comma. This introductory phrase is set off by a comma; the sentence is correct as written, (A). Choices B and C incorrectly treat the introductory phrase as an independent clause. Choice D incorrectly connects a dependent and an independent clause with the conjunction *and*.

32. H

Difficulty: Medium

Category: Agreement

Getting to the Answer: When a pronoun is underlined, check whether it matches its antecedent. The underlined portion refers to the bridge, so the correct answer will be singular; eliminate F and G. Choice J contains a subject-verb agreement error; the singular *it* requires the singular *was*. Choice (H) is correct.

33. B

Difficulty: Medium

Category: Agreement

Getting to the Answer: Make sure verb tenses make sense within the chronology of the passage. The past perfect is used in this sentence, but this tense is only correct when used to describe one past action completed before another. That is not the case here, so A is incorrect; (B) correctly replaces the verb with its past tense form. Choice C changes the meaning of the sentence (the legislature did the authorizing; it wasn't authorized by someone else) and creates a sentence that is grammatically incorrect. Choice D uses a conditional verb phrase, which is inappropriate in context.

34. H

Difficulty: Low

Category: Conciseness

Getting to the Answer: When the underlined selection contains a compound, check to see if the words mean the same thing. If so, the correct answer choice will eliminate one of them. *Build* and *construct* mean the same thing, so you can eliminate F and G right away. The only difference between (H) and J is a comma, which is incorrect in a compound; eliminate J.

35. A

Difficulty: Medium

Category: Sentence Structure

Getting to the Answer: Where the only difference among the answer choices is comma placement, remember your tested rules. This sentence needs NO CHANGE, (A). Choice B incorrectly places a comma between items in a compound. Choice C places a comma after the conjunction in a compound, which is also incorrect. Choice D incorrectly inserts a comma between a preposition and its object.

36. H

Difficulty: Medium

Category: Development

Getting to the Answer: Read the sentence without the material in question to determine what it adds to the paragraph and therefore why it was included. Looking at the paragraph as a whole, you can see that the author mentions the amount of money invested, the prominence of the architects, and the accomplishments of the firm the architects brought in to help. Removing one of these details detracts from that description; (H) is the best choice here. Choice F can be eliminated because this is not the only detail that supports the larger point; in and of itself, it's not critical. Removing this one phrase wouldn't impact the transition, as G suggests. Choice J is a trap. The segment in question does concern finances, but the text only mentions the amount of money invested, not how it was raised.

37. D

Difficulty: High

Category: Agreement

Getting to the Answer: On the ACT, "who" will only be correct when used to refer to people. Despite the fact that it's named after a person, "John A. Roebling and Sons" is the name of a company, so "who" isn't appropriate. That eliminates A and B. Choice C might be tempting because it's shorter than (D), but when C is read into the sentence, it creates a grammatical problem: "a company ... and would later" requires another verb. Choice (D) is correct.

38. J

Difficulty: Medium

Category: Development

Getting to the Answer: Consider context when you're asked about the role a piece of text plays. A question that asks what would be lost if text were deleted is really just asking for the function of that text. If you read the paragraphs before and after the sentence in question, you'll see that what is missing is a clear transition; (J) is correct. Choice F distorts the meaning of the sentence, which discusses how long the project actually took, not how long it was expected to take. Choice G is out of scope; danger is only mentioned in this one sentence and then only in terms of how few lives were lost constructing the bridge. Choice H overstates the significance of the detail regarding construction time.

39. D

Difficulty: Medium

Category: Organization

Getting to the Answer: When transition words are underlined, focus on the relationship between the sentences or clauses they combine. The preceding

sentence talks about the length of the bridge, and the sentence in which the underlined segment appears goes on to describe the cables in more detail. Since the second sentence isn't a result of the first sentence, you can eliminate A. Choice B inaccurately suggests an inconsistent or contradictory relationship between the sentences. Choice C is illogical; these are facts about the bridge, not events occurring simultaneously. The best choice here is no transition at all, as in (D).

40. G

Difficulty: Low

Category: Development

Getting to the Answer: When you're tested on Development: Precision, incorrect answer choices may have a related word that means something similar but doesn't make sense in context. They may also be wordy or passive. *Longer* means a comparison: one thing is longer *than* something else. Since this sentence doesn't offer a comparison, *longer* can't be correct. Eliminate F. Choices (G) and H are both grammatically correct in context, but H is unnecessarily wordy. *Lengthy*, in J, is not correct when used to describe a specific length.

41. C

Difficulty: Medium

Category: Sentence Structure

Getting to the Answer: When the underlined portion contains a comma, check for a run-on. Because the comma separates two independent clauses, A is incorrect. Choice B eliminates the subject of the second clause, so it is incorrect. Choice D incorrectly combines a semicolon and a FANBOYS conjunction. Choice (C) makes the second clause dependent and correctly separates the clauses with a comma. Choice (C) is correct.

42. F

Difficulty: Medium

Category: Sentence Structure

Getting to the Answer: Introductory phrases and clauses should be set off from the rest of the sentence by a comma. The comma here is used correctly, so no change is needed; (F) is correct. Choice G eliminates the comma, making the sentence difficult to understand. Both the colon in H and the semicolon in J would work only if the first clause were independent, which it is not.

43. D

Difficulty: Medium

Category: Organization

Getting to the Answer: When a transition word is underlined, check to see what ideas are being connected by the transition. The previous sentence mentions that the bridge was renamed, and the sentence beginning with the underlined portion switches to the present tense to describe the number of vehicles that cross the bridge daily. There is no logical contrast between these ideas, so B and C can be eliminated. Choice A indicates a continuation of the previous thought, but that does not fit the context; eliminate it. Choice (D) is correct because it transitions from the past-tense description in the previous sentence to the present-tense description of the bridge's daily activity.

44. F

Difficulty: Medium

Category: Agreement

Getting to the Answer: Use *over* for physical location and *more than* for numbers or amounts. This sentence is correct as written, (F). Choice G replaces *more than* with *over*, which, despite its common usage, is actually a preposition that indicates location, not amount. Choice H is unnecessarily wordy. Choice J is also wordy and uses *amount*, which is incorrect for a countable noun like *vehicles*.

45. C

Difficulty: Medium

Category: Development

Getting to the Answer: As you read ACT English passages, develop a sense of the topic or *big idea*, just like you do in Reading; this question format is very common on the ACT. This passage is about one specific bridge, so it would not satisfy the requirement set out in the question stem. You can therefore eliminate A and B right away. Now, turn to the reasoning. Choice D misstates the topic of the passage; (C) is correct.

The Dream of the American West

46. H

Difficulty: Medium

Category: Agreement

Getting to the Answer: Verbs in a compound should be in the same tense. The compound verb in this clause is "was ... rising ... and painted." Since the second verb is in the past tense, the first should be as well, so F is incorrect; (H) is correct. Choice G uses the gerund verb form without the necessary helping verb. Choice J is unnecessarily wordy.

47. A

Difficulty: Medium

Category: Development

Getting to the Answer: Read English Test question stems carefully. Often, all of the choices will be relevant and grammatically correct, but only one will fulfill the requirements of the stem. This question stem asks for a detail that shows a contrast between the quiet night streets and the daytime activity. The original text does this best. The verb in B does not convey the difference in the streets at these two times as well as *flood* in (A). Choice C is too general. Choice D does not provide the necessary contrast.

48. H

Difficulty: Medium

Category: Agreement

Getting to the Answer: Although all four answer choices form idioms that would be correct in some contexts, one smiles *at* someone or something; (H) is correct.

49. D

Difficulty: Medium

Category: Conciseness

Getting to the Answer: When you don't spot an error in grammar or usage, look for errors in style. Choice A is a wordy way of saying *traveled across*, (D). Choices B and C are unnecessarily wordy as well.

50. H

Difficulty: Low

Category: Sentence Structure

Getting to the Answer: Read question stems carefully. This one asks which answer choice would NOT be acceptable, which means that three of the choices will be correct in context. Choices F, G, and J are appropriate introductory clauses, but (H) is an independent clause, which makes the sentence a run-on.

51. B

Difficulty: Medium

Category: Development

Getting to the Answer: Use your Reading skills for questions like this one that ask for the function of a detail. The underlined portion tells you that the writer's journey will end in California. Choice (B) is correct. The underlined selection does not mention the reasons for the writer's trip, describe her route, or make any comparisons, so A, C, and D are incorrect.

52. G

Difficulty: Medium

Category: Sentence Structure

Getting to the Answer: Use commas in a list or series only if there are three or more items. Since the writer only mentions two places she has been, the first comma here is incorrect; eliminate F. Choice (G) corrects this without introducing any additional errors. Choice H eliminates the incorrect comma but removes the one at the end of the selection, which is needed to separate the introductory clause from the rest of the sentence. Choice J does not address the error.

53. A

Difficulty: Medium

Category: Organization

Getting to the Answer: To identify the most effective transition, you'll need to read both paragraphs. Paragraph 3 is about how the author has traveled to foreign countries but, within the United States, only knows New York City. Paragraph 4 describes her drive through the Midwest. The text as written takes the reader from New York City (tall buildings) to the less populated areas, leading to the description of the cornfields. Choice (A), NO CHANGE, is the best choice here. Choice B misstates the passage; the cornfields didn't appear *almost immediately*, but gradually. Choice C and D do not provide appropriate transitions between the paragraphs.

54. F

Difficulty: Medium

Category: Development

Getting to the Answer: When you're asked to identify the *most relevant* choice, use context clues. The paragraph is about the change the author experiences as she drives from New York across the country. That contrast is clear in the passage as written; (F) is the best choice here. Choices G and H do not relate to the paragraph's topic. Choice J is opposite; the writer describes many different settings, which is the opposite of *monotonous*.

55. C

Difficulty: Medium

Category: Sentence Structure

Getting to the Answer: There are a number of ways to correct a run-on sentence, but only one answer choice will do so without introducing any additional errors. Each of the clauses in this sentence is independent; (C) corrects the run-on by replacing the comma with a semicolon. Choice B omits the comma necessary with the coordinating conjunction *but*. Choice D loses the contrast between the clauses that is present in the original.

56. G

Difficulty: Medium

Category: Agreement

Getting to the Answer: When a single adverb is underlined, you are most likely being tested on idioms. Determine what is being modified. The underlined portion modifies the noun *serenity*, so it should be an adjective. Eliminate F. Choices H and J compare this serenity to other states of being, but there is no such comparison in the passage. Choice (G) is correct.

57. A

Difficulty: Medium

Category: Sentence Structure

Getting to the Answer: Only two apostrophe uses are tested on the ACT: possessive nouns and contractions. The noun here is possessive; the apostrophe is used correctly in (A). Choice B uses the plural *nights* instead of the possessive. Choice C is unnecessarily wordy and uses the idiomatically incorrect "shadows from the night." Choice D changes the meaning of the sentence.

58. H

Difficulty: Medium

Category: Conciseness

Getting to the Answer: If you don't spot a grammar or usage error, check for errors in style. As written, this sentence is unnecessarily wordy, so F is incorrect; (H) provides the best revision. Choices G and J are still unnecessarily wordy.

59. C

Difficulty: Medium

Category: Organization

Getting to the Answer: When a transition word or clause is underlined, determine the relationship between the ideas being connected. Look at the relationship between the sentences in this paragraph. The ideas are presented chronologically—that is, in the order in which they happened. Choice (C), *At first*, is the best transition into this series of events. Choices A and B imply contradiction or qualification, which is incorrect in context. Choice D implies that a lot went on prior to the writer's not having any idea what she was looking at, but this is presented as the first in a series of events.

60. F

Difficulty: High

Category: Conciseness

Getting to the Answer: The correct answer will rarely be longer than the original selection. This question requires no change, so (F) is correct. The pronoun's antecedent appears in the previous sentence ("what I was looking at") and the *-ing* verb form is used correctly. Choices G, H, and J are wordy; additionally, G introduces the passive voice unnecessarily.

Traveling at the Speed of Sound

61. A

Difficulty: Low

Category: Sentence Structure

Getting to the Answer: Commas are used to combine an independent and a dependent clause. This sentence is correct as written, (A), with the comma properly placed after the introductory clause. Choice B places the comma incorrectly; *of 2003* is part of the introductory clause. Choice C omits the necessary comma. Choice D incorrectly uses a semicolon between a dependent and an independent clause.

62. H

Difficulty: Medium

Category: Sentence Structure

Getting to the Answer: The underlined portion introduces nonessential information, so it should not form an independent clause. Choices F and G both make the clause an independent one; they should be eliminated. The passage is in the past tense, making the present tense verb in J incorrect. Choice (H) is correct.

63. B

Difficulty: Medium

Category: Development

Getting to the Answer: Development questions like this one require you to look at context; frequently, words will have similar meanings but be used differently. "Height" means "the distance from the top to the bottom of something"; "altitude" means "height above sea level." Since "altitude" is correct in this context, you can eliminate A. Choices (B) and C both use "altitude," but "at an altitude" is the correct idiom here; (B) is correct. Choice D creates a grammatically incorrect sentence.

64. H

Difficulty: High

Category: Organization

Getting to the Answer: When a transition word is underlined, check the logic of the transition as well as the grammar and punctuation. The sentence contrasts the famous and wealthy passengers with passengers who were ordinary people. Eliminate F and J because they do not express contrast. While G presents a contrast, it is grammatically incorrect. *Despite* creates a dependent clause requiring an *–ing* or *–ed* verb form, which is not present in the sentence. Choice (H) is correct, both logically and grammatically.

65. C

Difficulty: High

Category: Agreement

Getting to the Answer: Words like *that*, which are commonly misused in everyday speech, can make a question more challenging. Sound doesn't travel a speed, it travels *at* a speed; eliminate A. Only (C) makes the correction. Sound doesn't travel *to* a speed, as in B; *where*, D, will only be correct on the ACT when used to indicate location or direction.

66. G

Difficulty: Medium

Category: Development

Getting to the Answer: When asked about the purpose of a paragraph in relation to others, take a few seconds to summarize the paragraph in question, the one before it, and the one after it. The previous paragraph introduced the topic of supersonic aircraft. The paragraph in question transitions to questions of science, which are then discussed in the following paragraph. Choice (G) is correct. The paragraph does not provide an example or a counterargument, making F and H incorrect. The passage does not move from the general topic to a specific story, making J incorrect.

67. C

Difficulty: Medium

Category: Development

Getting to the Answer: Read English Test question stems carefully. This one asks for the LEAST acceptable alternative, which means that three of the choices will be correct in the sentence. All of the answer choices mean "change," so read each of them into the sentence. "Change them into," "translate them into," and "transform them into" are all appropriate usage, but "alter them into" is not because it changes the meaning. Choice (C) is correct here.

68. J

Difficulty: High

Category: Conciseness

Getting to the Answer: Look for constructions that repeat words unnecessarily; these will be incorrect on the ACT. The sentence tells you that the speed at which sound travels through gas depends on three things: what kind of gas it is, the temperature, and the pressure; "it is traveling through" is redundant, so F is incorrect. Choice (J) is the most concise answer, and it does not lose any of the meaning of the underlined selection. Choices G and H do not address the error.

69. D

Difficulty: High

Category: Development

Getting to the Answer: Don't choose the shortest answer if it fails to make the writer's meaning clear. "Air temperature and pressure decrease with altitude" isn't clear; "air temperature" and "pressure" themselves do not have altitude, and you're not told to what the altitude is referring, so A is incorrect. Choice (D) makes the writer's meaning clear; when altitudes are higher, the decrease in temperature and pressure occur. Choice B does not address the error and even compounds it by replacing "altitude" with "height." Choice C contradicts the facts in the passage; higher, not lower, altitudes have this effect.

70. G

Difficulty: Medium

Category: Sentence Structure

Getting to the Answer: Beware of answer choices that make unnecessary changes to the sentence. The information provided in the two clauses contrasts, so *however* is correct, but it requires a comma to separate it from the rest of the clause. Eliminate F. Choice (G) is correct. Choice H creates an inappropriate cause-and-effect relationship between the clauses. Choice J does not address the punctuation error.

71. A

Difficulty: Medium

Category: Organization

Getting to the Answer: When you're asked to choose the most logical conclusion, first determine the sentence's function within the paragraph. The first half of this sentence previews a reason that the Concorde cruises at a higher altitude than regular planes, and it ties that reason back to the contrast between the speed of sound at two different altitudes. You need, then, a conclusion to the sentence that both explains why the planes would fly higher and does so in light of the information about altitude in the preceding sentence. The best choice here is (A); the original version of the sentence is the most logical. Choice B doesn't provide a reason; it simply repeats information that has already been stated. Choice C is out of scope; fuel consumption isn't mentioned in the passage. Choice D is a result of the plane's higher altitude, not its cause.

72. H

Difficulty: High

Category: Agreement

Getting to the Answer: The use of *since* creates a specific marking point in the past and requires a verb that does the same. You need a simple past verb with *since*; (H) is correct. Choice F uses a tense that indicates an action that is ongoing, but the decommissioning of the Concorde has been completed. Choice G is unnecessarily wordy. The past perfect in J is only correct when used to indicate one past action completed prior to another stated past action, which is not the case here.

73. C

Difficulty: Medium

Category: Conciseness

Getting to the Answer: The phrases *about to* and *very soon* are redundant, making A, B, and D all incorrect. Furthermore, sentences beginning with coordinating (FANBOYS) conjunctions will not be correct on the ACT, which is an additional error in A. Only (C) correctly removes the redundancy.

74. H

Difficulty: Medium

Category: Organization

Getting to the Answer: When a transition word is underlined, check to see if it makes sense in the context. The sentence discusses upcoming advances to supersonic travel. Choice F places the advances in the present, which does not match the future tense *will* later in the sentence. Choice G is about location rather

than time, which does not fit the context. Choices (H) and J both refer to a future time, but only (H) makes sense in the context. The answer must be an adverb in order to describe when the advances will take place, but *Upcoming*, choice J, is an adjective. Choice (H) is therefore correct.

75. C

Difficulty: Medium

Category: Sentence Structure

Getting to the Answer: Here, the items combined by "not only ... but also" are "to the rich and famous" and "be for the masses." These items are correlated in the sentence, but they are not parallel in structure; eliminate A. Choices B and D do not address the error in parallel structure. Choice (C) corrects the error.

Mathematics Test

1. D

Difficulty: Low

Category: Statistics and Probability

Getting to the Answer: The basketball team scored 364 points in 13 games, so they scored an average of $\frac{364}{13} = 28$ points per game. Choice (D) is correct.

2. K

Difficulty: Low

Category: Number and Quantity

Getting to the Answer: To convert a mixed number to an improper fraction, you have two options:

Option 1: Rewrite the whole number part using the denominator of the fraction part, then add. Here, the result is $\frac{28}{7} + \frac{3}{7} = \frac{31}{7}$.

Option 2: Use the shortcut rule: multiply the whole number by the denominator of the fraction and add the numerator, then write the result over the original denominator. Here, you get $4 \times 7 + 3 = 28 + 3 = 31$ over 7, or $\frac{31}{7}$.

Using either method, you arrive at a numerator of 31, which is (K).

3. C

Difficulty: Low

Category: Algebra

Getting to the Answer: To solve for x, you need to isolate it on one side of the equation. To do this, subtract 18 from both sides, then divide by 4. The result is:

$$4x + 18 = 38$$
$$4x = 20$$
$$x = 5$$

Choice (C) is correct. Note that you could also Backsolve to answer this question, but the algebra is quicker.

4. G

Difficulty: Low

Category: Number and Quantity

Getting to the Answer: Because John weighs *more* than Ellen, begin by eliminating J and K, as doing so will reduce the chance of a miscalculation error. According to the question, John's 144 pounds represents 1.5 times Ellen's weight. Therefore, Ellen's weight must be $\frac{144}{1.5} = 96$ pounds. Choice (G) is correct.

If you're not sure whether to multiply or divide by 1.5, you could also set up an equation and solve it. Let $J =$ John's weight and $E =$ Ellen's weight. Translating from English to math gives:

$$J = 1.5E$$
$$144 = 1.5E$$
$$\frac{144}{1.5} = E$$
$$E = 96$$

5. B

Difficulty: Medium

Category: Number and Quantity

Getting to the Answer: To find the reciprocal of a number, swap the numerator and the denominator. You could use algebra to answer the question, but Backsolving is likely to be quicker. As usual, start with C: the reciprocal of $\frac{4}{3}$ is $\frac{3}{4}$ and $\frac{4}{3} \div \frac{3}{4} = \frac{4}{3} \times \frac{4}{3} = \frac{16}{9}$. This is too big (and it's the flip of what you're looking for), so try (B) next: the reciprocal of $\frac{3}{4}$ is $\frac{4}{3}$ and $\frac{3}{4} \div \frac{4}{3} = \frac{3}{4} \times \frac{3}{4} = \frac{9}{16}$. Choice (B) is correct.

6. G

Difficulty: Medium

Category: Algebra

Getting to the Answer: The inverse operation of cube rooting is cubing, so cube both sides of the equation to solve for x:

$$\sqrt[3]{x} = \frac{1}{4}$$
$$x = \left(\frac{1}{4}\right)^3 = \frac{1}{4} \times \frac{1}{4} \times \frac{1}{4} = \frac{1}{64}$$

That's (G).

7. B

Difficulty: Low

Category: Algebra

Getting to the Answer: Isolate the variable, then solve for x. To do this, subtract 14 from both sides, then take the square root:

$$x^2 + 14 = 63$$
$$x^2 = 49$$
$$x = \pm 7$$

Choice (B) matches the positive value of x.

8. F

Difficulty: Medium

Category: Number and Quantity

Getting to the Answer: Don't let the vector notation scare you. Adding vectors works exactly as you would expect: to add two vectors, add the corresponding components. The question only asks about the value of a, so focus on the first entries only: $7 + a = 5$, which gives $a = 5 - 7$, or -2. Choice (F) is correct.

9. A

Difficulty: Low

Category: Number and Quantity

Getting to the Answer: The quickest way to answer this question is to estimate. While you may or may not know 6% of 1,250 off the top of your head, 10% of 1,250 is 125. Because 6% < 10%, the correct answer must be less than 125. Only (A) works.

To solve this the more traditional way, multiply 1,250 by the decimal form of 6%: $1{,}250 \times 0.06 = 75$.

10. K

Difficulty: Low

Category: Number and Quantity

Getting to the Answer: When the choices are spaced far apart, estimation is generally the quickest way to the correct answer. To estimate, round 5.2 to 5 and 6.8 to 7. Because $5^3 + 7^2 = 125 + 49 = 174$, the correct answer will be close to 174. That would be (K).

11. E

Difficulty: Low

Category: Number and Quantity

Getting to the Answer: You certainly could reason this question out logically, but it's much easier to just pick a starting balance, make the error described in the question, and see which answer choice matches. Suppose Lexi starts with a balance of $100. If she accidentally adds $40 to this amount, the incorrect new balance is $140. If she had subtracted instead, the correct balance would have been $60. Thus, the incorrect balance is $140 - $60 = $80 more than is should be. Choice (E) is correct.

12. H

Difficulty: Medium

Category: Number and Quantity

Getting to the Answer: To answer this question, you'll need to follow the order of operations (PEMDAS).

First, evaluate the parentheses:
$$3^3 \div 9 + (6^2 - 12) \div 4$$
$$= 3^3 \div 9 + (36 - 12) \div 4$$
$$= 3^3 \div 9 + 24 \div 4$$

Next, simplify the exponent:
$$3^3 \div 9 + 24 \div 4 = 27 \div 9 + 24 \div 4$$

Then, take care of any multiplication and/or division, from left to right: $27 \div 9 + 24 \div 4 = 3 + 6$.

Finally, take care of any addition and/or subtraction, from left to right: $3 + 6 = 9$.

So (H) is correct.

13. B

Difficulty: Low

Category: Algebra

Getting to the Answer: Each banana costs $0.24, so the price of x bananas is $0.24x$. Similarly, each orange costs $0.38, so the price of y oranges is $0.38y$. Therefore, the total price of x bananas and y oranges is $0.24x + $0.38y$. That's (B).

14. H

Difficulty: Low

Category: Number and Quantity

Getting to the Answer: To find the percent shaded, divide the number of shaded triangles by the total number of triangles. There are 24 small triangles in all, and 8 of them are shaded: $\frac{8}{24} = \frac{1}{3} = 33\frac{1}{3}\%$. Choice (H) is correct.

15. C

Difficulty: Medium

Category: Number and Quantity

Getting to the Answer: The ratio of girls to boys is 5:3, so the ratio of girls to the total number of seniors is 5:(3 + 5), or 5:8. Call g the number of girls in the senior class. Set up a proportion and cross-multiply to solve for g:

$$\frac{5}{8} = \frac{g}{168}$$
$$8g = 840$$
$$g = 105$$

There are 105 girls in the senior class, which is (C).

16. J

Difficulty: Medium

Category: Statistics and Probability

Getting to the Answer: When a question about averages involves a missing value (here, the final test score), it often helps to think in terms of the sum instead. For Sarah's exam scores to average at least a 90, they must sum to at least $90 \times 4 = 360$. She already has an 89, a 93, and an 84, so she needs at least $360 - (89 + 93 + 84)$, which gives $360 - 266 = 94$ points on her final test. Choice (J) is correct.

17. E

Difficulty: Low

Category: Algebra

Getting to the Answer: Treat inequalities just as you would equations. The only exception is that if you multiply or divide by a negative number, you must flip the inequality symbol:

$$3x - 11 \geq 22$$
$$3x \geq 33$$
$$x \geq 11$$

This matches (E).

18. J

Difficulty: Medium

Category: Statistics and Probability

Getting to the Answer: Probability is the number of desired outcomes divided by the total number of possible outcomes. Here, you're given the probability $\left(\frac{3}{4}\right)$ and the number of desired outcomes (48). You're looking for the total number of possible outcomes (the number of dominos in the pile). Let d represent the number of dominos in the pile. Set up an equation using the definition of probability and the given information:

$$P(\text{even \# dots}) = \frac{\text{\# with even \# dots}}{\text{total \# dominos in pile}} = \frac{3}{4}$$
$$\frac{3}{4} = \frac{48}{d}$$
$$3d = 192$$
$$d = 64$$

Choice (J) is correct.

19. D

Difficulty: Low

Category: Algebra

Getting to the Answer: This is a straightforward substitution question, so just be careful of the negative signs. Plug in 4 for x and $-\frac{1}{2}$ for y and simplify:

$$3x - 8y$$
$$= 3(4) - 8\left(-\frac{1}{2}\right)$$
$$= 12 - (-4)$$
$$= 12 + 4$$
$$= 16$$

That's (D).

20. F

Difficulty: Medium

Category: Number and Quantity

Getting to the Answer: Whenever multiple rates are given, pay very careful attention to the units. As you read the question, decide how and when you will need to convert units. Use the factor-label method as needed. The answer choices are given in hours and minutes, so start by converting the given typing rate from words per second to words per minute:

$$\frac{3.75 \text{ words}}{1 \text{ second}} \times \frac{60 \text{ seconds}}{1 \text{ minute}} = \frac{225 \text{ words}}{1 \text{ minute}}$$

Next, find the number of words in the 25-page transcript:

$$\frac{675 \text{ words}}{1 \text{ page}} \times 25 \text{ pages} = 16{,}875 \text{ words}$$

Finally, let m be the number of minutes it takes the court reporter to type the whole transcript. Set up a proportion and solve for m:

$$\frac{225 \text{ words}}{1 \text{ minute}} = \frac{16{,}875 \text{ words}}{m \text{ minutes}}$$
$$225m = 16{,}875$$
$$m = 75$$

Because 75 minutes is not an answer choice, convert it to hours and minutes: 75 minutes = 1 hour, 15 minutes, making (F) the correct answer.

21. D

Difficulty: Low

Category: Geometry

Getting to the Answer: When two parallel lines are cut by a transversal, half of the angles will be acute and half will be obtuse. Each acute angle will have the same measure as every other acute angle. The same is true of every obtuse angle. Furthermore, the acute angles will be supplementary to the obtuse angles. Based on the information provided, $\angle a$ is an acute angle measuring 68°. Based on the figure, $\angle f$ is an obtuse angle, so $\angle a$ must be supplementary to $\angle f$. Therefore, the measure of $\angle f$ is $180° - 68° = 112°$. Choice (D) is correct.

22. J

Difficulty: Medium

Category: Number and Quantity

Getting to the Answer: If the student copy is $\frac{1}{4}$ the size of the wall map, then 2.5 inches on the student map would be $2.5 \times 4 = 10$ inches on the wall map. Now, set up a proportion to find the actual distance between the cities using the scale of the wall map:

$$\frac{1}{100} = \frac{10}{x}$$
$$x = 1{,}000$$

The correct answer is (J).

23. D

Difficulty: Medium

Category: Number and Quantity

Getting to the Answer: The piece of paper is $8\frac{1}{2}$ inches wide. To find the number of $\frac{5}{8}$-inch wide strips of paper you can cut, divide:

$$8\frac{1}{2} \div \frac{5}{8} = \frac{17}{2} \div \frac{5}{8}$$
$$= \frac{17}{2} \times \frac{8}{5}$$
$$= \frac{136}{10} = \frac{68}{5} = 13.6$$

Thus, you can make 13 strips of paper that are $\frac{5}{8}$ of an inch wide and 11 inches long, and you will have a small, thin strip of paper left over. Choice (D) is correct.

24. G

Difficulty: Medium

Category: Geometry

Getting to the Answer: This is a pair of parallel lines cut by a transversal, but this time, there's also a triangle thrown into the mix. Begin with segment $\overline{AB}$. This is a transversal, so $\angle MAB$ and $\angle ABC$ are alternate interior angles and $m\angle MAB = m\angle ABC = 55°$. Because triangle ABC is isosceles with $\overline{AB} = \overline{AC}$, $m\angle ACB$ is also 55° (base angles of an isosceles triangle have equal measures). Choice (G) is correct.

25. B

Difficulty: Low

Category: Algebra

Getting to the Answer: Use the slope formula to find the slope of the line:

$$m = \frac{y_2 - y_1}{x_2 - x_1}$$
$$= \frac{-6 - 0}{0 - (-10)}$$
$$= -\frac{6}{10}$$
$$= -\frac{3}{5}$$

That's (B).

26. H

Difficulty: Medium

Category: Algebra

Getting to the Answer: This question seems long, but it actually isn't that complicated. FOIL the first pair of binomials, FOIL the second pair, then add the results by combining like terms:

$$(x + 4)(x - 4) = x(x) + x(-4) + 4(x) + 4(-4)$$
$$= x^2 - 4x + 4x - 16$$
$$= x^2 - 16$$

(If you noticed the difference of squares above, that will save you some time.)

$$(2x + 2)(x - 2) = 2x(x) + 2x(-2) + 2(x) + 2(-2)$$
$$= 2x^2 - 4x + 2x - 4$$
$$= 2x^2 - 2x - 4$$

Finally, add the two polynomials by combining like terms:

$$\boxed{x^2} \boxed{-16} + \boxed{2x^2} - 2x \boxed{-4} = 3x^2 - 2x - 20$$

Choice (H) is correct.

27. D

Difficulty: Medium

Category: Geometry

Getting to the Answer: To find the distance between two points that don't have either the same x-coordinates or the same y-coordinates, plug the points into the Distance formula and evaluate:

$$\text{Distance} = \sqrt{(x_2 - x_1)^2 + (y_2 - y_1)^2}$$
$$= \sqrt{(-2-3)^2 + (6-(-6))^2}$$
$$= \sqrt{(-5)^2 + 12^2}$$
$$= \sqrt{25 + 144}$$
$$= \sqrt{169}$$
$$= 13$$

Choice (D) is correct.

28. G

Difficulty: Medium

Category: Number and Quantity

Getting to the Answer: Look for shortcuts; you could write an equation and solve for h, but is there a faster way? Examine the two percents: 30% is half of 60%, so 30% of h will be half of 60% of h, or half of 80, which is 40. That's (G).

29. C

Difficulty: Medium

Category: Statistics and Probability

Getting to the Answer: Because the integers in Set A are consecutive, their average must equal their middle term. In a set of 7 integers, the middle one is the fourth term. To find the smallest term, count backward from 46: 46, 44, 42, 40. That's (C). You can also answer this question by using Backsolving. Start with (C). If 40 is the smallest integer of Set A, then the next 6 consecutive integers

must be 42, 44, 46, 48, 50, and 52. Take the average of these 7 integers:

$$\frac{40 + 42 + 44 + 46 + 48 + 50 + 52}{7} = \frac{322}{7} = 46$$

This matches the condition in the question stem: the average of these consecutive integers equals 46, so (C) must be the correct answer.

30. J

Difficulty: Medium

Category: Functions

Getting to the Answer: Test the sum for 2, then 3, then 4, then 5 terms of the sequence to see if a relationship can be determined. If $n = 2$, the sum is $1 + 3 = 4$. If $n = 3$, the sum is $1 + 3 + 5 = 9$. If $n = 4$, the sum is $1 + 3 + 5 + 7 = 16$. If $n = 5$, the sum is $1 + 3 + 5 + 7 + 9 = 25$. The sum is always equal to the square of n. Therefore, the correct answer is (J).

31. D

Difficulty: Medium

Category: Number and Quantity

Getting to the Answer: To multiply two matrices, the sizes (# of rows by # of columns) must match in a certain way. Here, the size of the first matrix is 2×2 and the size of the second is 2×1. If you multiply a 2×2 matrix by a 2×1 matrix (which is possible because the middle dimensions match), the result will be a 2×1 matrix (the outer dimensions when the sizes are written as a product). This means you can eliminate A, B, and C, which are all 2×2 matrices. To multiply the matrices, multiply each element in the first row of the first matrix by the corresponding element in the second matrix and add the products. Then repeat the process using the second row of the first matrix:

$$\begin{bmatrix} -2 & 0 \\ 1 & -3 \end{bmatrix} \cdot \begin{bmatrix} 2 \\ 2 \end{bmatrix} = \begin{bmatrix} -2(2) + 0(2) \\ 1(2) + (-3)(2) \end{bmatrix} = \begin{bmatrix} -4 \\ -4 \end{bmatrix}$$

Choice (D) is correct.

32. G

Difficulty: Medium

Category: Geometry

Getting to the Answer: This is an area question with a twist—you're cutting a piece out of the rectangle. To find the area of the remaining space, you will need to subtract the area of the sandpit from the area of the original playground. Recall that the area of a rectangle is length × width. The dimensions of the original playground are $x + 7$ and $x + 3$, so its area is $(x + 7)(x + 3)$ which FOILs to $x^2 + 10x + 21$. The sandpit is a square with side x, so its area is x^2. Remove the pit from the playground, and the remaining area is $x^2 + 10x + 21 - x^2 = 10x + 21$. Choice (G) is correct.

33. E

Difficulty: High

Category: Number and Quantity

Getting to the Answer: Because $m > 0$, m is a positive number; likewise, because $n < 0$, n is a negative number. Consider each answer choice and decide whether the expression must be positive, negative, or could be either depending on the values of m and n. Keep in mind that m and n can be even or odd integers.

Choice A: $-n^m \rightarrow$ If m is even, n^m is positive so $-n^m$ is negative. However, when m is odd, n^m is negative, so $-n^m$ is positive. Eliminate this choice.

Choice B: $-mn \rightarrow$ Because one number is positive and the other is negative, the product mn must be negative, so $-mn$ must be positive. Eliminate this choice.

Choice C: $m^n \rightarrow m$ is positive, so m raised to any exponent will also be positive. A negative exponent simply means to take the reciprocal of the number, not to give the number a negative sign. Eliminate this choice.

Choice D: $-n - m \rightarrow -n$ equals $-(-\text{number})$, which is positive, and m is positive, so $-n - m$ is a positive minus a positive. If $m > -n$, then $-n - m$ will be negative. However, if $-n > m$, then $-n - m$ will be positive. Eliminate this choice.

Choice (E): $n - m \rightarrow n$ is negative and m is positive, so $n - m$ is a negative minus a positive. This must be negative, so (E) is the correct answer.

34. F

Difficulty: Medium

Category: Geometry

Getting to the Answer: Use the midpoint formula and the given midpoint to solve for m and n:

$$m = \left(\frac{x_1 + x_2}{2}, \frac{y_1 + y_2}{2}\right)$$

$$(-3, -2) = \left(\frac{1 + m}{2}, \frac{9 + n}{2}\right)$$

Once you have the formula set up and all the given information plugged in, separate the coordinates into two equations and solve for the variables:

$$-3 = \frac{1 + m}{2} \qquad \text{and} \qquad -2 = \frac{9 + n}{2}$$
$$-6 = 1 + m \qquad\qquad\qquad -4 = 9 + n$$
$$-7 = m \qquad\qquad\qquad\quad -13 = n$$

Thus, $(m, n) = (-7, -13)$, which is (F).

35. C

Difficulty: Low

Category: Functions

Getting to the Answer: When given a function and a value of x, plug in the number value for each x in the equation and simplify. Make sure you follow the order of operations:

$$f(x) = 16x^2 - 20x$$
$$f(3) = 16(3)^2 - 20(3)$$
$$= 16(9) - 60$$
$$= 144 - 60 = 84$$

Choice (C) is the answer.

36. G

Difficulty: Low

Category: Geometry

Getting to the Answer: To find the length of a line segment on the coordinate plane, you would normally need to use the Distance formula. This requires the coordinates of the segment's two endpoints. Because $A(1, 5)$ and $C(1, 1)$ have the same x-coordinate, a much faster way is to simply subtract the y-coordinate of C from the y-coordinate of A. The length of segment AC is $5 - 1$, or 4. Choice (G) is correct.

37. C

Difficulty: Medium

Category: Functions

Getting to the Answer: With nested functions, work from the inside out. To answer this question, substitute the entire rule for $g(x)$ for x in the function $f(x)$, then simplify:

$$f\big(g(x)\big) = \frac{1}{3}\big(3x^2 + 6x + 12\big) + 13$$

$$= x^2 + 2x + 4 + 13$$

$$= x^2 + 2x + 17$$

Choice (C) is correct.

38. H

Difficulty: Medium

Category: Algebra

Getting to the Answer: Perpendicular lines have negative-reciprocal slopes. Because the line in the question has a slope of $\frac{2}{3}$ (the coefficient of x), the line you are looking for must have a slope of $-\frac{3}{2}$. Eliminate F and G. The question also says that this line contains the point $(4,-3)$. Plugging all of this information into the equation of a line, $y = mx + b$, will allow you to find the final missing piece of the equation—the y-intercept:

$$y = mx + b$$

$$-3 = -\frac{3}{2}(4) + b$$

$$-3 = -6 + b$$

$$3 = b$$

With a slope of $-\frac{3}{2}$ and a y-intercept of 3, the line is $y = -\frac{3}{2}x + 3$, which matches (H).

39. D

Difficulty: Medium

Category: Algebra

Getting to the Answer: This looks like a chemistry or physics question, but in fact it's just a "plug in the number and solve for the missing quantity" question.

Be sure to plug 95 in for C (not F). To clear the fraction (rather than distributing it), multiply both sides of the equation by the reciprocal of $\frac{5}{9}$:

$$C = \frac{5}{9}(F - 32)$$

$$95 = \frac{5}{9}(F - 32)$$

$$\frac{9}{5} \times 95 = F - 32$$

$$F - 32 = 171$$

$$F = 171 + 32 = 203$$

Choice (D) is correct.

40. J

Difficulty: Medium

Category: Algebra

Getting to the Answer: First, translate from English to math: "3 times x is increased by 5" translates to $3x + 5$, and "the result is less than 11" translates to < 11. Put these together to write an inequality and then solve for x:

$$3x + 5 < 11$$

$$3x < 6$$

$$x < 2$$

This inequality is graphed with an open circle at 2 (because x cannot equal 2) and shaded to the left, where the numbers are less than 2. Your graph should look like (J).

41. C

Difficulty: Medium

Category: Geometry

Getting to the Answer: Because $\overline{QS} = \overline{QR}$, triangle QRS must be a 45-45-90 triangle and the hypotenuse is $5\sqrt{2}$. Remember that $\cos = \frac{\text{adjacent}}{\text{hypotenuse}}$. Therefore:

$$\cos R = \frac{5}{5\sqrt{2}}$$

$$= \frac{1}{\sqrt{2}}$$

$$= \frac{1}{\sqrt{2}} \times \frac{\sqrt{2}}{\sqrt{2}} = \frac{\sqrt{2}}{2}$$

Choice (C) is correct.

42. K

Difficulty: High

Category: Number and Quantity

Getting to the Answer: You need to find the ratio of angelfish to puffers. You're given two ratios: tangs to angelfish and tangs to puffers.

Both of the given ratios contain tangs, but the tang amounts (5 and 2) are not the same. To directly compare them, find a common multiple (10). Multiply each ratio by the factor that will make the number of tangs equal to 10:

tangs to angelfish: $(5:2) \times (2:2) = 10:4$

tangs to puffers: $(2:3) \times (5:5) = 10:15$

Now that the number of tangs are the same in both ratios, you can merge the two ratios to compare angelfish to puffers directly: **4**:10:**15**. So the proper ratio of angelfish to puffers is 4:15, which is (K).

43. D

Difficulty: Low

Category: Geometry

Getting to the Answer: This question is testing whether you can substitute into a formula correctly. Because you are told the diameter is 6, you know the radius, r, of the sphere is 3. Plug this value into the formula and simplify:

$$V = \frac{4}{3}\pi(3)^3 = \frac{4}{3}\pi(27) = 36\pi$$

Choice (D) is correct.

44. G

Difficulty: Medium

Category: Algebra

Getting to the Answer: To simplify the given expression, look for factors in the fraction term that will cancel. Use the denominator as a hint as to how to factor the numerator. Be careful—you cannot simply cancel the $x + 1$ in the denominator with the $x + 1$ at the end of the expression:

$$\frac{x^2 - 5x - 6}{x + 1} + x + 1 = \frac{(x + 1)(x - 6)}{x + 1} + x + 1$$
$$= x - 6 + x + 1$$
$$= 2x - 5$$

Choice (G) is correct.

45. A

Difficulty: Medium

Category: Algebra

Getting to the Answer: Don't let the language throw you—*greatest monomial factor* just means the greatest common factor. Look for the largest number that divides evenly into 60 and 45. (Use the answer choices as a hint.) The number is 15, so eliminate D and E. Next, look for the highest power of each variable that appears in *both* terms: a^2 and plain b. Thus, the greatest monomial factor is $15a^2b$, which is (A).

46. G

Difficulty: Low

Category: Statistics and Probability

Getting to the Answer: Percent change is calculated by dividing the amount of change by the original amount. In 1985, the population was 3,000; in 1995, the population was 2,000. Thus, the amount of change was 1,000. Divide this by the original amount (the 1985 population) to find that the percent change was $1,000 \div 3,000 = 0.3333$, or 33.33%. The population went *down* from 1985 to 1995, so this is a decrease of 33.33%, which is (G).

47. C

Difficulty: Medium

Category: Statistics and Probability

Getting to the Answer: This question requires brute force. You need to list the data value corresponding to each year, order the values from least to greatest, find the median (the middle value), match it to a year in the graph, and then select the correct answer.

85	86	87	88	89	90
3,000	1,000	5,000	5,000	4,000	3,000
91	92	93	94	95	
4,000	1,000	3,000	2,000	2,000	

Order the data, keeping the year labels:

86	92	94	95	85	90
1,000	1,000	2,000	2,000	3,000	3,000
93	89	91	87	88	
3,000	4,000	4,000	5,000	5,000	

The median of this group is the sixth value, or 3,000. The years 1985, 1990, and 1993 all had populations of 3,000. The only one of these years among the answer choices is 1990, which is (C).

48. F

Difficulty: Medium

Category: Statistics and Probability

Getting to the Answer: Identify which pieces of information from the table you need. The question asks for the probability that a randomly chosen person from the study is employed and has a college degree, so you need the total of both females and males with college degrees who are employed compared to all the participants in the study. There are 188 employed females with a college degree and 177 employed males with a college degree for a total of 365 employed people with a college degree out of 800 participants, so the probability is $\frac{365}{800}$, which reduces to $\frac{73}{160}$, (F).

49. C

Difficulty: High

Category: Statistics and Probability

Getting to the Answer: Distinct permutations are permutations without repetition. You need to find the number of unique orderings of the letters GEOMETRY. If all eight letters were different, the number of unique orderings would be 8!. Because the E is repeated, you must divide by 2! to account for the repeated E. The result is $\frac{8!}{2!}$, which is (C).

Note that this process is the same as using the formula for "indistinguishable" outcomes: $\frac{n!}{a! \times b! \times \ldots}$. The number of letters is 8 (so $n = 8$), and there are 2 indistinguishable E's, so $a = 2$ and there is no b.

50. J

Difficulty: Low

Category: Geometry

Getting to the Answer: To match an inequality to its graph, you need to consider three things: the equation of the line, whether the line should be solid or dashed, and the direction of the shading. You can use any, or all, of these things to eliminate choices. Here, the shading is below (or less than) the line, so the inequality symbol should be $<$. Eliminate G and K. The line is dashed, but all the symbols are strict inequalities, so this doesn't help. The y-intercept of the line is -4 and the line rises 4 units for each 3 units that it runs, so the slope is $\frac{4}{3}$. This means the correct inequality is $y < \frac{4}{3}x - 4$, which is (J).

51. E

Difficulty: Medium

Category: Functions

Getting to the Answer: Occasionally, you may encounter a function that is defined in terms of two or three independent variables. These functions behave just as you would expect them to. As with any function, substitute the given values for the corresponding variables and simplify. Here, $x = 2$, $y = -1$, and $z = 3$.

$$h(x, y, z) = 4xy^2 - yz^3$$
$$h(2, -1, 3) = 4(2)(-1)^2 - (-1)(3)^3$$
$$= 4(2)(1) - (-1)(27)$$
$$= 8 + 27$$
$$= 35$$

Choice (E) is correct.

52. K

Difficulty: Medium

Category: Geometry

Getting to the Answer: Write the formula for the area of a circle, using r to represent the radius of the original circle in the question: $A = \pi r^2$. This is the area of the original circle. Then, write the formula for the area of the new larger circle, using $3r$ as the radius:

$$A = \pi(3r)^2$$
$$= \pi(9r^2)$$
$$= 9\pi r^2$$

Now, divide the two areas (area of the new circle by the area of the original circle) to find out how many times larger the area of the new circle is compared to the area of the original circle:

$$\frac{\text{area of new circle}}{\text{area of original circle}} = \frac{9\pi r^2}{\pi r^2} = 9$$

Choice (K) is correct.

53. C

Difficulty: High

Category: Functions

Getting to the Answer: You don't really have to know anything about trig functions to answer this question. You just need to know the definition of *period:* the period of a repeating function is the distance along the *x*-axis required for the function to complete one full cycle. For a sine curve, this means one full wave (one up "bump" and one down "bump"). Here, that happens between 0 and π, which means the period is π. Choice (C) is correct.

If you happen to know the normal period of sine, which is 2π, you could also set the *x* term (2*x*) equal to that period and solve for *x*. You'll get 2*x* = 2π, which simplifies to *x* = π.

54. J

Difficulty: High

Category: Algebra

Getting to the Answer: Solving equations that involve radicals may seem daunting, but they work just like other equations. In fact, they're usually easier to solve than quadratic equations because you don't have to worry about factoring. As a general rule, you need to 1) isolate the radical part; 2) eliminate the radical by squaring both sides of the equation if the radical is a square root, cubing both sides if it's a cube root, and so on; and 3) isolate the variable. To solve the equation here, the steps are:

$$\sqrt[3]{4x-12} + 25 = 27$$
$$\sqrt[3]{4x-12} = 2$$
$$\left(\sqrt[3]{4x-12}\right)^3 = 2^3$$
$$4x - 12 = 8$$
$$4x = 20$$
$$x = 5$$

Choice (J) is correct. Note that you could also use Backsolving to answer this question.

55. D

Difficulty: Medium

Category: Geometry

Getting to the Answer: The chord is perpendicular to the line segment from the center of the circle, so that line segment must be its perpendicular bisector. This allows you to add the following measures to the figure:

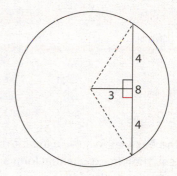

The two right triangles have legs 3 and 4, so they are both 3:4:5 right triangles with hypotenuse 5. This hypotenuse is also the radius of the circle, so plug that into the area formula to solve:

$$A = \pi r^2$$
$$= \pi (5)^2$$
$$= 25\pi$$

The correct answer is (D).

56. F

Difficulty: High

Category: Functions

Getting to the Answer: Don't let the function notation intimidate you. The graphs of two functions intersect when the function equations are equal. Therefore, you need to set the equations equal to each other and solve for *x*:

$$f(x) = g(x)$$
$$3^{3x+3} = 27^{\left(\frac{2}{3}x - \frac{1}{3}\right)}$$

When the equations have variables in the exponents, you must rewrite one or both of them so that either the bases are the same or the exponents themselves are the same. In this question, the two bases seem different

Practice Test

at first glance but, because 27 is actually 3^3, you can rewrite the equation as:

$$3^{3x + 3} = 3^{3\left(\frac{2}{3}x - \frac{1}{3}\right)}$$

This simplifies to $3^{3x + 3} = 3^{2x - 1}$. Now that the bases are equal, set the exponents equal to each other and solve for x:

$$3x + 3 = 2x - 1$$
$$x + 3 = -1$$
$$x = -4$$

Choice (F) is correct.

57. A

Difficulty: High

Category: Functions

Getting to the Answer: To solve a logarithmic equation, rewrite the equation in exponential form and solve for the variable. To rewrite the equation, use the translation $\log_b y = x$ means $b^x = y$. The left side of the given equation has two logs, so you'll need to combine them first using properties of logs before you can translate. Don't worry about the right-hand side of the equation just yet.

$$\log_b x - \log_b y = \log_b\left(\frac{x}{y}\right)$$

$$\log_3(5x - 40) - \log_3 5 = \log_3\left(\frac{5x - 40}{5}\right)$$

$$= \log_3(x - 8)$$

Now, the equation looks like $\log_3(x - 8) = 2$, which can be rewritten as $3^2 = x - 8$. Simplifying yields $9 = x - 8$, or $17 = x$. Choice (A) is correct.

58. F

Difficulty: High

Category: Functions

Getting to the Answer: Fortunately, "cannot be determined" is not one of the answer choices here, because that would be very tempting. There is in fact enough information to answer this question. You just have to use what you know about arithmetic sequences—specifically, that to get from one term to

the next, you add the same number each time. Here, you don't know what that number is, so call it n. The five terms in the sequence are:

$$4$$
$$4 + n$$
$$4 + n + n$$
$$4 + n + n + n$$
$$4 + n + n + n + n$$

These terms are already listed in order, so the median is the middle term, which is $4 + n + n$, or $4 + 2n$. The mean is the sum of all the terms divided by the number of terms: $\frac{20 + 10n}{5} = 4 + 2n$. Thus, the mean and the median have the same value, making the difference between them equal to 0, which is (F).

59. D

Difficulty: High

Category: Geometry

Getting to the Answer: You are given the cosine of $\angle BAC$ and the length of the hypotenuse of the triangle, so begin by using these and SOHCAHTOA to find the length of the side adjacent to $\angle BAC$ (which is AB):

$$\cos A = \frac{\text{adjacent}}{\text{hypotenuse}}$$
$$0.6 = \frac{AB}{15}$$
$$AB = 0.6(15) = 9$$

So the adjacent side, $\overline{AB}$, is 9, and triangle ABC is a right triangle with a leg length of 9 and a hypotenuse of length 15. Triangle ABC must therefore be a 3:4:5 right triangle (scaled up by a factor of 3), and $\overline{BC}$ must have a length of 12. Choice (D) is correct.

60. J

Difficulty: High

Category: Geometry

Getting to the Answer: The question states that the points lie on the graph of a parabola (which is a nice, symmetric U shape), so use what you know about parabolas to answer the question. Notice that the x-values in the table increase by 2 each time. To find the *y*-value when $x = -4$, you just need to imagine adding one extra row to the top of the table. Now, think about symmetry—you can see from the points in the table that $(2, -5)$ is the vertex of the parabola. The points $(0, -3)$ and $(4, -3)$ are equidistant from the vertex, as are the points $(-2, 3)$ and $(6, 3)$. This means the point whose *x*-value is -4 should have the same *y*-value as the last point in the table $(8, 13)$. So, when $x = -4$, $y = 13$. Choice (J) is correct.

Reading Test

Passage I

Passage Map Notes:

¶1: Countess Olenska (CO) no longer pretty

¶2: CO 1st in NY as little girl adopted by aunt Medora (M)

¶3: M repeatedly widowed, NY accepting of M's eccentricities

¶4: all kind to Ellen (E) [aka CO], M not follow mourning rules

¶5: E was well-liked, fearless child; E's odd edu.

¶6: E married Polish nobleman, ended in disaster

¶7: NY expected CO to be more stylish and vibrant

BIG PICTURE SUMMARY

Main idea: Ellen Mingott as a child and Countess Olenska as an adult did not fit New York society's expectations of her.

Author's purpose: To portray how a character changed from childhood to adulthood and the influences that shaped her

1. C

Difficulty: Low

Category: Detail

Getting to the Answer: Remember that the correct answer to Detail questions will be directly stated in the passage. Your notes should guide you as you locate specific references to the details in question. Line 23 mentions Ellen's parents' "regrettable taste for travel" in the context of lines describing what the people of New York thought. Predict something like "travel." Choice (C)

matches this prediction. Choice A is a misused detail; Medora does teach her niece to play the piano, but nothing in the passage suggests that this was undesirable. Choice B is a misused detail; Spanish shawl dances are described as "outlandish," but this is within the context of Medora and Ellen's eccentric, but accepted, behaviors. Choice D is a misused detail; while Medora often adopted children, this is never described as undesirable.

2. J

Difficulty: High

Category: Inference

Getting to the Answer: Consider how the author writes about New York society. In lines 24–25, she writes that "people thought it a pity that the pretty child [Ellen] should be in such hands," meaning that they did not feel the eccentric Medora was a good influence on Ellen. People call Medora "misguided" (line 30), and the author notes that she scandalized her family by not adhering to the "unalterable rules" of mourning (lines 31–32). All in all, New York society seems to have some rigid and snobbish rules. On the other hand, New York society "looked indulgently on her [Medora's] eccentricities" (lines 20–21) and "resigned itself to Medora" (lines 38–39). The author's view of New York society as it pertains to Medora seems to be mixed, which matches (J). Choice F doesn't take into account New York society's acceptance of Medora's odd behavior, G is opposite, and H is not mentioned in the passage.

3. A

Difficulty: Medium

Category: Inference

Getting to the Answer: To answer Inference questions, you will have to go beyond what is directly stated in the passage. However, the correct answer choice will be supported by evidence from the passage, so make sure you make a prediction that has solid textual support. You can predict, based on lines 56–66, that Ellen was unable to help her aunt because her own marriage to the immensely rich Polish nobleman "had ended in disaster." Choice (A) matches this prediction. Choice B is a distortion; since both Medora and Ellen left New York, their communication over the years is unknown. Choice C is a distortion; while the author tells you that Ellen had an incoherent education, nothing in the passage suggests that she resented this. Choice D is a distortion; though the passage makes it clear that Medora was eccentric, this is in no way related to receiving help from her niece.

4. F

Difficulty: Medium

Category: Inference

Getting to the Answer: Predicting an answer is particularly important for Inference questions like this. Make sure you can support your prediction with information in the passage. Lines 68–70 suggest that Newland has spent time thinking about Ellen, and lines 74–93 all describe Newland's observations of Ellen. Newland is not disappointed that Ellen is not as "stylish" as others expected (lines 84–86). You can predict that Newland is thoughtful and, unlike many of the other characters in the passage, nonjudgmental. Choice (F) matches this prediction. Choice G is out of scope; it might seem reasonable to conclude that Newland is likeable, but the passage does not provide any evidence to directly support this. Also, there is nothing to suggest that he is withdrawn. Choice H is opposite; Newland's observations about Ellen in the last paragraph clearly indicate that he is interested in her. Choice J is a distortion; Newland's observation that Ellen is not as stylish as New York society might expect says nothing about his own stylishness, nor does the author ever describe Newland's level of sociability.

5. A

Difficulty: Medium

Category: Function

Getting to the Answer: Wharton writes that Medora has "many peculiarities," (line 31), and that "New York looked indulgently on her eccentricities" (lines 20–21). This matches the first part of answer choice (A). Since you may not know what peripatetic means, hold on to (A) while you research the other answers. Though Wharton states that each time Medora returns to New York she looks for a less expensive house, indicating reduced circumstances, this doesn't necessarily mean that Medora is impoverished, and there is no suggestion that she is resentful. Eliminate B. Medora may be kind (she does, after all, take in orphaned Ellen), but loyal doesn't describe someone who "invariably parted from her husband or quarrelled with her ward" (lines 15–16), eliminating C. Choice D mixes up Medora with Ellen;

these words describe Ellen as a child, so D is incorrect. Choice (A) must be correct, even if you don't know that *peripatetic* means "traveling from place to place."

6. H

Difficulty: Medium

Category: Vocab-in-Context

Getting to the Answer: The word *flout* is used in the author's description of Medora wearing a veil considered too short for acceptable mourning and dressing Ellen in "a crimson dress and amber beads" (lines 36–37). Both of these are examples of Medora's "misguided ... many peculiarities" (lines 30–31), which go against accepted New York behavior. Thus (H), disregard, is a good match. Choice F is too strong to describe Medora's behavior, as she does partially follow, rather than totally eliminate, the rules of mourning. Choice G is opposite, and while J looks close to the word *flout*, it doesn't make sense in the passage.

7. C

Difficulty: Medium

Category: Inference

Getting to the Answer: Make sure you have good evidence for your prediction, and the right answer choice will be easy to find. Line 21 mentions Medora's *eccentricities*, line 31 mentions her *peculiarities*, and line 44 mentions the *outlandish arts* that Medora teaches Ellen. From these descriptions, you can predict that Medora is unconventional or eccentric. Choice (C) matches this prediction. Choice A is out of scope; although Medora does not adhere to conventions, as indicated by lines 31–32, there is nothing to suggest that this is attributable to arrogance. Choice B is a distortion; the description of the short veil that Medora wore to her brother's funeral in lines 34–36 might suggest immodesty, but the author makes clear that this is evidence of Medora's willingness to flout social conventions and never mentions any immodest dress or behavior. Choice D, which means following established practice, is opposite; you are told in lines 31–32 that one of her peculiarities is to "flout the unalterable rules that regulated American mourning."

8.   F

Difficulty: Low

Category: Detail

Getting to the Answer: Detail questions like this one are straightforward, but it can sometimes be difficult to find exactly where in the passage the relevant information comes from. Make sure that you are answering the specific question being asked, so that other details don't distract you. Medora teaches Ellen "drawing from the model" (line 49), which is described as "a thing never dreamed of before," so predict Ellen or Countess Olenska. Choice (F) matches your prediction. Choice G is out of scope; Newland is not described as having learned anything at all, let alone something controversial. Choice H is a distortion; Medora teaches Ellen, but the passage does not mention Medora learning anything herself. Choice J is a distortion; Count Olenska is only mentioned indirectly as the rich nobleman whom Medora marries. The passage makes it clear that Ellen is Countess Olenska; don't be fooled by this initially tempting, but incorrect, choice.

9.   B

Difficulty: Medium

Category: Function

Getting to the Answer: Locate where the author mentions Medora's mother and read the next few lines. The author writes that "her mother had been a Rushworth," (line 18), that Medora married "one of the crazy Chiverses" (lines 19–20), and that because of these two conditions, "New York looked indulgently on her eccentricities" (lines 20–21). In other words, given her mother and her marriage, people were not surprised by Medora's unconventional life, which matches (B). There is no support for A, so it is out of scope. Choice C is opposite; New Yorkers "thought it a pity that the pretty child should be in such hands" (lines 24–25), and D is true but not relevant to Medora's eccentricities.

10.   F

Difficulty: High

Category: Inference

Getting to the Answer: Remember that Inference questions will have details in the wrong answer choices that are meant to throw you off. Making a good prediction before reviewing the choices will guard against this. The beginning of the passage (line 4)

implies that Newland knew Ellen when he was young. Lines 54–60 state that no one had heard from Ellen for some time, and after a few years, she came back to New York, as Medora had done before her. Predict that at the dinner, Newland and Ellen had not seen one another for an extended period of time. Choice (F) matches your prediction. Choice G is extreme; although Newland is clearly paying attention to Ellen in the last paragraph, there is nothing to suggest that either of them is interested in a romantic relationship. Choice H is extreme; while Ellen's lack of *stylishness* (lines 85–86) might suggest that she is not interested in New York society's conventions, it goes too far to say that she is disappointed. Choice J is opposite; the passage clearly portrays Ellen and Newland's encounter as a re-acquaintance.

Passage II

Passage Map Notes:

> ¶1: climate change threat to FL economy: tourism + agriculture
> ¶2: S. FL storm damage (tourism)
> ¶3: Everglades
> ¶4: not enough water for citrus farms
> ¶5: livestock industry
> ¶6: plans to deal w/problems
> ¶7: more prep, diversify economy

BIG PICTURE SUMMARY

Main idea: Potential dangers to Florida's tourism and agriculture industries from climate change and ways Floridians plan to address them.

Author's purpose: To describe how climate change is likely to impact Florida's economy

11.   B

Difficulty: Medium

Category: Global

Getting to the Answer: This is a Global question because it asks for the purpose of the passage as a whole. Review your passage map and predict that the passage describes probable challenges to Florida's economy due to climate change and how the state is preparing to meet those challenges. The correct answer is (B).

Choice A is a distortion; while the passage does occasionally mention harm that has already occurred, it is primarily focused on future issues. Choice C is both out of scope and extreme; combating climate change itself is not addressed in the passage, and the author doesn't argue for any particular course of action. Choice D is also out of scope; the passage is focused on economic impacts, not on multiple ways climate change can impact people's lives.

12. J

Difficulty: Low

Category: Detail

Getting to the Answer: The clue "According to the passage" marks this as a Detail question. Locate where the passage discusses Hurricane Irma (in paragraph 2) and research what made it significant. The passage states that it was "the costliest hurricane in Florida's history," so (J) is correct. It is worth noting that this is a case in which absolute language ("more...than any other") does not mark a too-extreme answer; the passage itself does make that strong a statement.

Choice F is a misused detail; Irma could hypothetically have cost that much if it had hit Miami more directly, but in reality, it cost approximately $50 billion. Choice G is a distortion; the paragraph certainly suggests that climate change increased Irma's destructiveness but not that it was the first hurricane for which that was true. Finally, H is a misused detail; while the paragraph mentions the dangers of rising sea levels, demonstrating them is not what made Irma significant.

13. A

Difficulty: Medium

Category: Inference

Getting to the Answer: The word *implies* is a clue that this is an Inference question. Research what the second paragraph says about South Florida. It lost a great deal of money as a result of a hurricane, which could have been far worse if Miami, "Florida's second-most popular tourist destination" (lines 23–24), had been directly hit. You can predict that the area generates a lot of money from tourism. Choice (A) is correct.

Choice B is extreme; while the paragraph mentions rising sea levels as a concern, it does not suggest that South Florida is likely to become submerged. Choice C is out of scope; the passage does not discuss northern

Florida at all. Finally, D is incorrect because there is no evidence in the paragraph linking South Florida with agriculture.

14. G

Difficulty: Medium

Category: Detail

Getting to the Answer: "The passage makes clear" shows that this is a Detail question. Use your passage map to find where the passage discusses the Everglades and identify how climate change threatens it. Using paragraph 3, predict that the Everglades is likely to become submerged since much of it is barely above sea level. Choice (G) is correct.

Choice F is extreme; while paragraph 3 does mention salt water pushing inland, it does not say that this will poison fresh water. Choice H is a misused detail; the fifth paragraph mentions degradation of grasslands but not in reference to the Everglades. Choice J is a distortion; although paragraph 3 predicts problems for visitors, it does not suggest they will be entirely cut off from the park.

15. D

Difficulty: High

Category: Function

Getting to the Answer: The wording "author references ... in order to" identifies this as a Function question. Examine the surrounding text to understand why the author includes these references. The paragraph discusses how lack of water could harm agriculture; the EPA report explains how water shortages could come about, and the study demonstrates the impact of insufficient water on citrus crops. Predict that both provide support from scientific sources for the paragraph's main idea. The correct answer is (D). This choice doesn't match the exact wording of the prediction, but correct answer choices rarely will. Look for the choice that matches the general idea of the prediction rather than its specific wording. In this case, D includes supporting the main idea, and most readers are likely to find scientific studies and reports authoritative; thus, D fits the prediction even without exactly matching it.

Choice A is true of the study but not the EPA report, while C is true of the EPA report but not the study, so both are incorrect. Nothing in the paragraph is countering an argument, so B is also incorrect.

16. J

Difficulty: Low

Category: Detail

Getting to the Answer: "The passage states" is a clue that this is a Detail question. Since the question asks for a comparison between the two industries, research towards the middle and end of the passage, after both industries have been discussed. The fifth paragraph states that livestock brings in a smaller portion of Florida's agriculture revenue. Choice (J) is correct.

Although the passage mentions both water consumption and exports, it does not compare the two industries for either, so F and H are incorrect. The passage does not discuss pollution at all, so G is out of scope.

17. B

Difficulty: Low

Category: Detail

Getting to the Answer: The phrase "According to the passage" shows that this is a Detail question. The fifth paragraph discusses issues facing the livestock industry, including heat stressing the animals, loss of grasslands, and increased insect-borne diseases. Choice (B) matches the first of these and is correct.

Choice A is a misused detail; while the passage predicts reduced crop yields, it says nothing about these crops being used to feed livestock. Choice C is a distortion; the passage says that animals are likely to get sick because of increased mosquito populations, not because of the weather itself. Choice D is a misused detail similar to A; while water shortages may occur, the passage does not discuss their impact on the livestock industry.

18. H

Difficulty: Medium

Category: Global

Getting to the Answer: This question asks for the purpose of a paragraph, which requires an understanding of both the paragraph itself and how it fits into the passage as a whole. Thus, this is a Global question. While the passage so far has described problems raised by climate change, paragraph 6 discusses some potential solutions to these problems. Choice (H) is correct.

Choice F is a misused detail; only some of the paragraph is about infrastructure adaptations. Choice G is incorrect because this paragraph has moved on from describing the problems. Finally, J is a distortion; while parts of the paragraph involve directing water supplies, it does not refer to imbalances in rainfall.

19. C

Difficulty: Medium

Category: Detail

Getting to the Answer: The phrase "According to the passage" marks this as a Detail question. Paragraph 6 describes ways to counteract climate change problems; do some research there to find what solutions are being put forward for agriculture. The last sentence of the paragraph says that farms are switching to more water-efficient subsurface irrigation and mixed crop-livestock farms. The second part matches (C), which is correct.

Choice A may be tempting, but this answer choice says that subsurface irrigation is less efficient and being replaced, the opposite of what the passage states. Choices B and D are both out of scope; neither is discussed as a solution in the passage.

20. H

Difficulty: Medium

Category: Function

Getting to the Answer: The phrase *serves to* in the question stem indicates that this is a Function question. Read around the lines in question for context to determine why the author includes this detail. The paragraph states that policymakers want to diversify Florida's economy and international trade seems like a good way to do so. Predict that the fact that Florida already exports a great deal provides a reason *why* policymakers see this as a suitable area to expand. The correct answer is (H).

Choice F is extreme; although the passage makes clear that exports are important to Florida's economy, it does not suggest that they are a primary driver of expansion. Choice G is out of scope; the passage does not compare Florida's trade balance with any other state. Finally, J is a distortion; while the paragraph does explain the importance of diversification, that is not the purpose of this detail.

Passage III

Passage Map Notes:

Passage A

¶1: country music (C) born in central & southern Appalachians

¶2: originated in 1920s from multiple sources

¶3: the term "country" replaced "hillbilly"

¶4: Hank Williams 1st to take country national; artists

¶5: Nashville, TN = country home w/Grand Ole Opry (1925)

¶6: C relatives = honky tonk, Western Swing

¶7: C expresses Am. identity

Passage B

¶1: bluegrass (B) origin and description

¶2: B diff. from C: highlight 1 musician at a time, diff. instruments, vocal harmonies

¶3: own category in late 1950s, named after Bill Monroe's band

¶4: today: movies, festivals

¶5: B themes = working class; reflects Am.

BIG PICTURE SUMMARY

Passage A

Main idea: Country music is an American musical genre with a rich history.

Author's purpose: To describe the origins and history of country music

Passage B

Main idea: Bluegrass music is related to but distinct from country music, with its own cultural niche.

Author's purpose: To explain what makes bluegrass music unique

21. C

Difficulty: Medium

Category: Detail

Getting to the Answer: Use your passage map to locate this detail; the second paragraph should include the necessary information. Use the list of the sources of

country music ("spirituals as well as folk music, cowboy songs, and traditional Celtic melodies") to make your prediction. Choice (C) is correct because country music is not rooted in jazz. Rather, jazz was combined with country music to create Western Swing. Paragraph 6 states, "Additionally, Western Swing emerged as one of the first genres to blend country and jazz musical styles, which required a great deal of skill and creativity." Choice A is opposite; paragraph 2 describes the many sources of country music with the sentence, "Rooted in spirituals as well as folk music, cowboy songs, and traditional Celtic melodies, country music originated in the 1920s." Choice B is opposite; spirituals influenced the development of country music. Choice D is opposite; country music is rooted in cowboy songs.

22. J

Difficulty: Medium

Category: Inference

Getting to the Answer: The answer to an Inference question is supported by the passage. However, because all answer choices are in the passage, be careful to assess each one in terms of the actual question asked. A look at your notes or a quick scan of the passage should provide enough information to make a prediction about where to find the best country music. Match that prediction to the correct answer. Choice (J) is correct; in paragraph 5, the author writes "Country singers are considered to have reached the pinnacle of the profession if they are asked to become members of the Opry." To hear the best music, it makes sense to go to the place where those at the pinnacle, or top of their field, perform. Choice F is a misused detail; one would hear honky-tonk music, a derivative of country, but not country music itself, in these bars. Choice G is a misused detail; Ireland is the original home of the Ulster Scots, many of whom settled in Appalachia. Choice H is a misused detail; though country music had its origins in the mixture of music created in Appalachia, the author does not state that it is the place to hear the best music.

23. C

Difficulty: High

Category: Vocab-in-Context

Getting to the Answer: As with all Vocab-in-Context questions, use the surrounding clues to define the word in question. The word appears in paragraph 3, where the original term "hillbillies" is used to describe

"Appalachian inhabitants who were considered poor, uneducated, isolated, and wary." The more accepting word "country" has replaced "hillbillies," indicating that pejorative is a negative word, an adjective used to highlight the negative characteristics described in the paragraph. This matches (C), since disparaging means belittling, or bad. Choice A is a synonym for *original* rather than a word that means *negative*. Choice B is out of scope, as the author never expresses that the negative view is accurate, and D refers to where the people live rather than fitting the context of describing the term (i.e., it is not a "mountain-dwelling term").

24. F

Difficulty: Low

Category: Inference

Getting to the Answer: Both passages introduce several genres of American music, but this question refers to Passage B, so research the passage carefully. In the first paragraph, the author introduces bluegrass music and writes that it is "a mixture of Scottish, Welsh, Irish, and English melodic forms, infused, over time, with African-American influences" (lines 73–75), and that laments "are common themes." (lines 79–80). These are exactly the components of the song in the question, making (F) correct. The other answers refer to Passage A and are described as having different derivations.

25. A

Difficulty: Medium

Category: Detail

Getting to the Answer: Locate the paragraph in which bluegrass instruments are described, and match those descriptions with the correct answer choice. Your notes point to only one paragraph in which musical instruments are mentioned. Scan the answer choices, then reread the information in that paragraph to determine which answer choice characterizes the information given. Choice (A) is correct; musical instruments are described in the second paragraph and include typical ones such as "banjo, guitar, mandolin, bass, harmonica, and Dobro (resonator guitar)." But the paragraph goes on to include far less typical ones, such as "household objects, including washboards and spoons," which are not usually considered musical instruments, but are sometimes included in a bluegrass band. Choice B is a misused detail; African-American

influences are provided as one more source of the bluegrass genre but instrumentation is not referenced. Choice C is a misused detail; this is an example of a bluegrass piece used in a movie soundtrack. Choice D is out of scope; the reference to the Ozark mountains concerns the origin of bluegrass and has nothing to do with a description of musical instruments.

26. F

Difficulty: High

Category: Detail

Getting to the Answer: The answer to a Detail question is stated in the passage. Locate the paragraph in which the differences between country and bluegrass music are discussed. Paragraph 2 includes the information you need to answer the question. Be sure to keep straight which details describe each genre of music. Choice (F) is correct. Paragraph 2 details two characteristics of bluegrass music: first, that "bluegrass highlights one player at a time, with the others providing accompaniment," and second, that "bluegrass incorporates baritone and tenor harmonies." Choice G is opposite; country music features a single voice. Choice H is opposite; country musicians commonly play the same melodies together. Choice J is a distortion; which instruments are used is not cited as a difference between the music styles.

27. B

Difficulty: Medium

Category: Inference

Getting to the Answer: Locate the paragraphs that mention laments and high, lonesome sound, and consider what the author means by including these two details. The reference to *laments* is in the first paragraph and the reference to "high, lonesome sound" in the last paragraph are examples of "the hard-scrabble life of the American worker," which matches (B). Choice A is out of scope; the elements mentioned in the question stem do not necessarily reflect Irish music; bluegrass has multiple sources. Choice C is a misused detail; Shania Twain is an example of a country singer and is mentioned in Passage A only. Choice D is a misused detail; though bluegrass was originally called "hillbilly," this is the name for the genre, not the theme.

28. G

Difficulty: Medium

Category: Vocab-in-Context

Getting to the Answer: Vocab-in-Context questions require that you understand the context of a cited word or phrase. Locate the reference and focus your research on the text immediately preceding and immediately following the word or phrase in question. The introductory paragraph states, "One of the most enjoyable ways to analyze culture is through music." Look for an answer choice that indicates that music can provide specific insight about a culture as a whole. Choice (G) matches this prediction. Choices F, H, and J are distortions; *quintessential* does not mean old-fashioned, charming, or conventional (typical).

29. C

Difficulty: Medium

Category: Inference

Getting to the Answer: When asked to use a quote to find support in one paragraph for information in another, be sure to read the quote in the context of the paragraph. First find the paragraph in which the quote from Passage A appears, then match the quote to one in Passage B. Choice (C) is correct; Flatt and Scruggs are mentioned in Passage B, paragraph 3, in which they are characterized as "the foremost artists on their instruments." The best artists are certainly "talented and sophisticated." Choice A is a misused detail; this quote refers to bluegrass themes, whereas the question asks for one that supports talented and sophisticated musicians. Choice B is out of scope; the "pace and complexity" of the music does not necessarily relate to the skill of the musicians themselves. Choice D is out of scope; the relation between bluegrass and country music refers to the kinship of the genres, not the musicians.

30. H

Difficulty: Medium

Category: Global

Getting to the Answer: When looking for something on which both authors would agree, first determine what each one actually states in the passage, then consider what must be true based on those statements. The evolution, or gradual change, in music, as with anything else, must start from somewhere, so look to the parts

of each passage that detail the genesis of the music genres, then consider the progression from there. Choice (H) is correct; both authors detail the various music sources that became either country or bluegrass. In the first passage, the author mentions "folk music, cowboy songs, and traditional Celtic melodies," and in the second passage, the author refers to "Scottish, Welsh, Irish, and English melodic forms, infused, over time, with African-American influences." Both authors affirm that the two music genres are "indigenous." Thus, it must be true that both country and bluegrass music have evolved from their various roots to become American music, supporting agreement on the fact that music can evolve. Choice F is out of scope; each passage mentions how its particular music genre is popular (as explained in the next sentence in the explanation—the Czech festivals and international growth), but both authors don't describe why *both* genres are popular, only their own. Choice G is a misused detail; the Grand Ole Opry showcases country music only, not bluegrass. Choice J is out of scope; the passages don't each discuss both genres, only their own.

Passage IV

Passage Map Notes:

- ¶1: CubeSats good for space exploration
- ¶2: improved radios
- ¶3: testing for longer missions
- ¶4: consumer cameras → less expensive
- ¶5: less expensive → more experiments possible
- ¶6: plans to deal w/problems
- ¶7: CubeSats improve future space exploration

BIG PICTURE SUMMARY

Main idea: CubeSats offer many advantages for exploration and experimentation in deep space.

Author's purpose: To explore the benefits of using CubeSats

31. D

Difficulty: Medium

Category: Global

Getting to the Answer: The clues *author's attitude* and *main topic* identify this as a Global question. Review your notes to determine the author's tone and predict that the author is positive about the CubeSats and looking forward to their future. This matches (D).

Choice A is a distortion; the author is optimistic, but not cautious. Choice B is too neutral, and C is too negative.

32. H

Difficulty: Low

Category: Detail

Getting to the Answer: The phrase "According to the passage" marks this as a Detail question. Think about where in the passage you might find the original designers of the CubeSat and use your notes to help. The first sentence states that researchers at California Polytechnic and Stanford Universities "determined the specifications of the CubeSat design." This matches (H).

Choices F, G, and J all refer to other people in the passage who made use of the CubeSats, but who were not the original designers. NASA used the design for the MarCO mission, for which Joel Krajewski was a project manager and Cody Colley was a mission manager.

33. D

Difficulty: Medium

Category: Vocab-in-Context

Getting to the Answer: The clue words "most nearly means" show that this is a Vocab-in-Context question. Refer to the passage to see how radical is used in the sentence. It describes scientific experiments, so predict that it means ground-breaking. Choice (D) is correct.

Choices A and B refer to alternate meanings of radical that are not supported by the passage; there is no evidence that the experiments are ideologically motivated or involve militarization or aggression. Choice C, "primitive and organic," is the exact opposite of a scientific experiment in space.

34. F

Difficulty: Medium

Category: Detail

Getting to the Answer: The phrase "According to the passage" identifies this as a Detail question. Use your notes to find where the passage discusses communication technology. Research in paragraph 2 and predict that the satellites' radios and antennae were faster and more efficient. The correct answer is (F).

Choice G is incorrect because it describes the InSight lander's communication technology. Choice H is incorrect because it describes the MarCO satellites' cameras, not their radios. Choice J is incorrect because, although the passage mentions that the MarCO radios are the size of softballs, it does not discuss whether the radios were unusually small.

35. C

Difficulty: High

Category: Inference

Getting to the Answer: You can easily tell that this is an Inference question because of the word *Inferred* in the question stem. Research in the second paragraph to determine how the MarCO satellites compared to the InSight lander. The passage says that their communications are faster, but the answers to Inference questions are never explicitly stated in the passage. The paragraph goes on to say that they offered "more efficient monitoring of the landing process" and that their data would "help engineers design better landing technology for future missions." Since these sentences draw comparisons, you can predict that the MarCO satellites accomplished these tasks more effectively than the InSight lander itself. The correct answer is (C).

You may have had difficulty predicting for this question. If so, remember that you can eliminate incorrect answers to find the correct one. Choice A is out of scope; the passage does not discuss the resolution of photos or their distances. Choice B is incorrect because the passage does not mention miniaturized technology. Finally, choice D is incorrect because the satellites themselves do not land.

36. G

Difficulty: Medium

Category: Function

Getting to the Answer: The phrase *serves to* in the question stem indicates that this is a Function question. Review your notes to identify the purpose of the fourth paragraph and predict that it describes how using commercially available cameras made the satellites less expensive. Choice (G) is correct.

Choice F is extreme; the author is not arguing for anything in this paragraph, much less for using off-the-shelf components wherever possible. Choice H is too broad; the paragraph describes only one reason why the project was less costly. Choice J is a misused detail; although the paragraph does briefly praise the images, that is not its main purpose.

37. D

Difficulty: Medium

Category: Inference

Getting to the Answer: The words "Based on the passage" are a clue that this is an Inference question. In the fourth paragraph, where the passage discusses posting mission photos, it describes the scientists as proud and elated. You can predict that they were happy about how well the satellites did. This matches choice (D).

Choices A, B, and C are all out of scope; there is no evidence to suggest that the scientists had anything to prove or any demands to satisfy, and while they may have hoped to gain support, this is not stated in the passage.

38. G

Difficulty: Medium

Category: Inference

Getting to the Answer: The clue words "the passage suggest" show that this is an Inference question. The paragraph discusses how the CubeSats allow for an increased number and variety of scientific experiments than were previously feasible, so you can predict that these experiments were made possible because of the CubeSats. This fits with (G). Remember that correct answers will not always match the exact wording of your prediction, so you must be alert for equivalent meanings.

Choice F is out of scope; the paragraph does not discuss the experiments' creators at all. Choice H is incorrect because, while the passage does describe an experiment using linked satellites later on, it is not in these lines. Finally, J is opposite; the paragraph states that these experiments are in near-Earth orbit.

39. B

Difficulty: Medium

Category: Detail

Getting to the Answer: "The passage states" wording marks this as a Detail question. Consult your notes to find that the passage discusses linked satellite networks

and their advantages in the sixth paragraph. You can predict that these networks are flexible and less likely to fail. Choice (B) is correct.

Choice A is a misused detail; while the passage does say that CubeSats are less expensive, that is not an advantage of linked networks specifically. Choice C is incorrect because there is no evidence that the international cooperation mentioned was a result of the satellite network. Choice J is incorrect because the passage does not suggest that the thermosphere was previously inaccessible or that linked networks of satellites were necessary to study it.

40. H

Difficulty: High

Category: Function

Getting to the Answer: The clue "how the author" shows that this is a Function question, since it is about something the author does in the text. Review the lines in the question stem and determine what they have in common. In both, the author uses concrete numbers in order to drive home a point. The correct answer is (H).

Choice F is a distortion; while the author does juxtapose old and new, it is not for the purpose of dismantling old methods. Choice G is incorrect because not only does the author not use NASA or Stanford to increase the passage's authority, these institutions are not even mentioned in these lines. Finally, J is a misused detail; while the author does employ positive language in the first citation, she does not in the second one.

Science Test

Passage I

1. A

Difficulty: Low

Category: Using Data

Getting to the Answer: The question stem tells you that you're looking for a mineral composed of 32% zinc and 12% calcium. Table 1 lists the percentages of calcium and zinc in a variety of minerals, so look there for an answer. According to Table 1, hornblende is composed of 30%–35% zinc and 10%–20% calcium. Choice (A) is thus correct.

2. J

Difficulty: Low

Category: Interpreting Data

Getting to the Answer: The diagram presents the most common minerals in each soil horizon. A geologist digging down into the A horizon would encounter mostly quartz and mica. Quartz isn't included as a possible answer, but mica is. Choice (J) is thus correct. Choice F is incorrect because limestone isn't commonly found until the C horizon. Choice G is incorrect because shale isn't common until the final horizon. Choice H is incorrect because serpentine is commonly found in the B horizon.

3. B

Difficulty: Medium

Category: Interpreting Data

Getting to the Answer: Based on the diagram, you can see that the minerals are arranged in Table 1 so that the shallowest are at the top of the table and the deepest are at the bottom. However, as you move down the table, you'll notice that zinc content decreases, which indicates an inverse relationship between depth and zinc content. In other words, as zinc content *increases*, depth *decreases*. Choice (B) is thus correct.

4. H

Difficulty: Low

Category: Interpreting Data

Getting to the Answer: Based on the diagram, the only minerals geologists wouldn't commonly find at a depth of 30 feet or lower (to the bottom of the B Horizon) are limestone and shale. You can eliminate F, G, and J because each contain one of these minerals. Choice (H), then, is correct.

5. A

Difficulty: Medium

Category: Using Data

Getting to the Answer: The mineral content of granite is located in Table 2, so start there. Table 2 shows that granite is composed of feldspar, quartz, mica, and augite. If augite is found close to the other minerals in granite, then it should be located at roughly the same depth as feldspar, quartz, and mica. Now use the diagram to find the depths at which those three minerals

are most commonly found. Feldspar is found in the O horizon, at a depth of 2 feet or less, while quartz and mica are found in the A horizon, at a depth of 2 to 10 feet. So you should definitely expect to find augite at depths of less than 10 feet, as in (A).

6. G

Difficulty: Low

Category: Interpreting Data

Getting to the Answer: Zinc content percentage and calcium content percentage are found in Table 1, so examine it for an answer. Moving down the table, zinc content steadily decreases as calcium content steadily increases. The two quantities are inversely related, making (G) correct.

Passage II

7. D

Difficulty: Medium

Category: Using Data

Getting to the Answer: To answer this question, examine the formula that is provided at the beginning of the passage: $\Delta T_b = K_b \times m \times i$. This equation indicates that the boiling point will increase more if K_b, m, or i is increased. Item I would increase K_b, item II would increase m, and item III would increase i (because $CaCl_2$ splits into three ions, while NaCl only splits into two ions). Because all three items would increase the boiling point of Solution 5, (D) is correct.

8. H

Difficulty: Low

Category: Interpreting Data

Getting to the Answer: The results for Study 1 are presented in Table 1. Table 1 shows that for 0.171 mol of NaCl, the boiling point is increased to 101.75°C. Choice (H) is thus correct.

9. C

Difficulty: Medium

Category: Synthesizing Data

Getting to the Answer: This question asks about the melting point of Material 5. Table 3 provides data about when Material 5 melted, indicating that it did not melt in Solution 5, but that it did melt in Solution 6. Therefore, its melting point will be somewhere between the boiling points of those solutions. Table 1 shows that Solution 5 has a boiling point of 103.50°C and Table 2 shows that Solution 6 has a boiling point of 104.15°C, so Material 5's melting point must fall somewhere in between those values. Choice (C) is thus correct.

10. G

Difficulty: Medium

Category: Using Data

Getting to the Answer: Table 2 provides the boiling points for solutions consisting of various amounts of $CaCl_2$ added to water. The trend seems linear: for each increase of roughly 0.9 mol $CaCl_2$, the boiling point increases by roughly 1.4 degrees Celsius. The highest amount of $CaCl_2$ on the table is 0.631 mol, roughly 0.9 less than the amount in the question stem. Therefore, the increase will be roughly 1.4 degrees higher than 109.67°C, or 111.07°C. Choice (G) is thus correct. Choice F is between the boiling points for Solutions 9 and 10, which is too low. Choices H and J are too high.

11. A

Difficulty: Medium

Category: Synthesizing Data

Getting to the Answer: Table 3 gives an indication of the points at which each material begins to melt. Based on the information from Tables 1 and 2, a higher-numbered solution corresponds to a higher boiling point. It would be highly implausible for a material to melt at a low temperature but not at a higher temperature, which is the trend depicted in (A). The other choices are incorrect because they are all possibilities already revealed in Study 3's results: B corresponds to the results for Material 1, C to the results for Material 4, and D to the results for Materials 6, 7, and 8.

12. H
Difficulty: High

Category: Experimental Design

Getting to the Answer: The equation for boiling point elevation given in the passage indicates that the increase in temperature depends upon the molality of the solution. As noted in the explanation of the

equation, molality is defined as moles (mol) of solute over kilograms (kg) of solvent. Thus, the students recorded the moles of a solute, rather than its mass, in order to make the calculation of molality—and the subsequent calculation of change in boiling point—easier. Choice (H) is correct. Choice F makes little sense; measuring the solvent's mass does nothing to prevent measuring the solute's mass. Choice G is a false statement; moles are usually calculated on the basis of mass, so if anything mass measurements are more accurate. Choice J is true but irrelevant to the question.

13. A

Difficulty: Medium

Category: Synthesizing Data

Getting to the Answer: Table 3 shows that Material 7 melted in Solution 10, whereas Material 8 did not. That means that Material 7 must have a melting point of no more than 109.67°C (the boiling point of Solution 10), while Material 8 must have a melting point higher than that temperature. Thus, the results do support the claim that Material 7 has the lower melting point, making (A) correct. Choice B is incorrect because it reverses the results for the materials. Choice C is incorrect because the exact melting point of Material 8 does not need to be determined to support the claim—it only has to be shown to have a higher melting point than Material 7. Choice D is incorrect because the approximate melting point of Material 7 can be determined: it must be between the boiling point temperatures of Solutions 9 and 10.

Passage III

14. G

Difficulty: Medium

Category: Supporting Hypotheses

Getting to the Answer: According to Table 1, the concentrations of nitrogen, phosphorus oxide, and zinc all tend to increase as humidity level increases, regardless of which of the three data sources is considered. For potassium oxide, however, the trend is reversed: the concentration decreases as humidity increases. Choice (G) is thus correct.

15. A

Difficulty: Low

Category: Interpreting Data

Getting to the Answer: To answer this question, compare the System B data to the USGS data at 25% humidity for the 4 compounds given as answer choices. For nitrogen (N), the USGS concentration is 236 mg/L, while System B measures it as 408 mg/L, which is close to double. For calcium (Ca), USGS has 24.7 mg/L and System B has 23.2 mg/L, a much smaller difference, meaning B can be eliminated. For potassium oxide (K_2O), USGS has 9.2 mg/L and System B has 9.1 mg/L, a very small difference, allowing you to eliminate C, too. Finally, for phosphorus oxide (P_2O_5), USGS has 71.2 mg/L and System B has 75.6 mg/L, still smaller than the difference seen in nitrogen, meaning D can also be eliminated. Nitrogen shows by far the biggest difference, whether this is calculated in absolute or relative terms, so (A) is correct.

16. J

Difficulty: Low

Category: Supporting Hypotheses

Getting to the Answer: From Table 1, you can see that the potassium oxide concentration continually decreases from 9.4 mg/L to 8.2 mg/L as humidity increases from 10% to 80% in the USGS data, continually decreases from 9.4 to 8.0 in System A, and continually decreases from 9.5 to 8.3 in System B. Because the data from all 3 sources supports the hypothesis that potassium oxide levels decrease with increasing humidity, (J) is correct.

17. D

Difficulty: Medium

Category: Synthesizing Data

Getting to the Answer: The question asks you to determine which system is more accurate, so ultimately you're trying to find the one that is closer to the USGS data, which is described in the passage as "extremely accurate." Looking at the data for zinc, you can see that the measurements from System B are always closer to the data from the USGS than are the measurements from System A. Therefore, you know the answer to the question is yes, allowing you to eliminate A and B. Choice C, though, is incorrect because it gives the wrong

reasoning: System B does give lower measurements than System A, but that alone doesn't make it more accurate. The measurements from System B are more accurate because they are closer to the data from the USGS than are the measurements from System A. Choice (D) is thus correct.

18. H

Difficulty: Medium

Category: Synthesizing Data

Getting to the Answer: To answer this question, look at the row in the table that represents calcium concentrations for System B. You can see that the numbers gradually decrease from 10% humidity to 65% humidity, then increase quickly from 65% to 85% humidity. The only graph that shows values decreasing and then rapidly increasing is (H).

19. B

Difficulty: High

Category: Using Data

Getting to the Answer: Examine the System B data in Table 1 to answer this question. According to the table, a potassium oxide level of 9.1 mg/L falls between the values for 25% humidity (9.2) and 45% humidity (9.0), a calcium level of 17.3 mg/L also falls between the values for 25% (23.2) and 45% (11.6), and a zinc level of 0.57 mg/L likewise falls between the values for 25% (0.48) and 45% (0.62). Therefore, the level of humidity for this sample should almost certainly be some value between 25% and 45%. Only (B) falls within this range.

Passage IV

20. G

Difficulty: Low

Category: Supporting Hypotheses

Getting to the Answer: What are Scientist 1's and Scientist 2's viewpoints? Scientist 1 believes that type 2 diabetes is caused by excess sugar consumption, and Scientist 2 says that type 2 diabetes is caused by obesity as a result of a high-fat diet and lack of exercise. If new research suggested that 80% of people with diabetes have buildup of fat in the liver, this information would support the view of Scientist 2 only. The correct answer is (G).

21. B

Difficulty: Low

Category: Supporting Hypotheses

Getting to the Answer: Scientist 1 states that "the cause of type 2 diabetes is an overconsumption of sugar," while Scientist 2 states that "diets high in fat but not high in sugar are associated with an increased risk of type 2 diabetes." Thus, both scientists would most likely agree that the occurrence of type 2 diabetes in an individual is associated with the patient's diet. The correct answer is (B). Choice A is only mentioned by Scientist 2, and C is only mentioned by Scientist 3. Age is mentioned in the introductory text, but even though type 2 diabetes is more prevalent in adults, the passage does not suggest that age causes type 2 diabetes, so D is also incorrect.

22. H

Difficulty: Medium

Category: Supporting Hypotheses

Getting to the Answer: The passage states that type 2 diabetes occurs "when the body does not produce enough insulin," and explains that "Insulin is a hormone produced in the pancreas that helps regulate blood glucose levels." If the pancreas is removed, the body would not produce insulin, and would thus be unable to regulate blood glucose levels, thereby causing type 2 diabetes to develop. None of the answer choices state this explicitly, but (H) gives the major symptom of diabetes that was stated in the introductory paragraph: elevated blood glucose levels (hyperglycemia). Choices F and G are incorrect because they state the opposite of what you should expect. You can also eliminate J because you're given no reason to suspect a link between the pancreas and body fat content.

23. C

Difficulty: Medium

Category: Supporting Hypotheses

Getting to the Answer: According to Scientist 3, type 2 diabetes is inherited. Eliminate A and B, which correspond to the hypotheses of Scientists 1 and 2, respectively. Scientist 3 states that "Individuals have about a 15%–20% chance of developing type 2 diabetes if one of their parents has it and a roughly 50% chance if both parents have it." Since 18% falls within the 15%–20% range, Scientist 3 would probably predict

that an individual with an 18% chance of developing type 2 diabetes has one parent with type 2 diabetes. The correct answer is (C).

24. J

Difficulty: Medium

Category: Supporting Hypotheses

Getting to the Answer: Remember to keep straight who said what. If a 50-year-old developed type 2 diabetes, Scientist 1 would likely conclude the patient has a high-sugar diet, Scientist 2 would likely conclude the patient has a high-fat diet and/or lacks exercise, and Scientist 3 would likely conclude the patient inherited it from one or more parents. The only answer choice that correctly matches one of these predictions is (J).

25. A

Difficulty: High

Category: Supporting Hypotheses

Getting to the Answer: According to Scientist 1, the elevated blood glucose levels in individuals with normal insulin levels did not return to normal when they received small injections of supplemental insulin. It can thus be inferred that although insulin levels were normal, the body had a lowered response to insulin, indicating insulin resistance. Look for a choice that supports the idea that a high-sugar diet is caused by or otherwise related to lowered response to insulin. Choice (A) does just that. Choices B and D are incorrect because they mention fat intake and free radical production, respectively, which were only discussed by Scientist 2. Choice C is incorrect because Scientist 1 discussed the effects of a high-sugar diet, not a low-sugar one.

26. F

Difficulty: High

Category: Supporting Hypotheses

Getting to the Answer: Scientist 3 believes that "Type 2 diabetes is not caused by lifestyle or diet but inherited." To challenge Scientist 2's claim that the lack of exercise causes 7% of type 2 diabetes cases, Scientist 3 would have to explain how the actual cause of the occurrence of type 2 diabetes in these individuals is due to inheritance, rather than lifestyle. Choice (F) does precisely that: if the individuals who didn't exercise also had family histories of diabetes, then Scientist 3 could claim that the patients actually developed diabetes because of their genetics, not their lifestyles. Even though Scientist 3 actually states the information in G, it does not directly address Scientist 2's claim from the question stem. Choice H is incorrect because insulin injections are only discussed by Scientist 1. Choice J is incorrect because Scientist 2 does not suggest that type 2 diabetes solely results from lack of exercise, but also blames diets high in fat.

Passage V

27. A

Difficulty: Low

Category: Interpreting Data

Getting to the Answer: To answer this question, turn to the results of the studies in Table 1. According to the table, the lowest-density blood sample is 1.050 g/mL, that of Patient C. Looking at each column, you can see that Patient C has more platelets than Patient A but fewer than Patient B, fewer white blood cells than Patient A, the fewest red blood cells, but the most plasma. Choice (A), then, is correct.

28. H

Difficulty: Medium

Category: Experimental Design

Getting to the Answer: According to the passage, the purpose of the studies was "to determine the composition and mass of blood samples." Thus, the phlebotomist has an interest in avoiding anything that could alter the composition or mass of the blood on a temporary basis because it would skew the results of the studies. The passage also states that diet can affect the composition of blood, so it would make sense that the phlebotomist would try to control this factor by requiring the patients to fast. Choice (H) is thus correct. Choice F is incorrect because you're given no reason to suspect that taking blood is easier if a patient has fasted. Choice G is incorrect because if fasting could greatly change the composition of blood, then the phlebotomist would likely have made sure the patients avoided it by eating something beforehand. Choice J is incorrect because you're given no indication in the passage that anything the patient does can affect the ability of blood to separate in a centrifuge.

29. D

Difficulty: High

Category: Applying Core Knowledge

Getting to the Answer: According to Table 1, Patient C had a density of 1.050 g/mL, which amounts to a 10.50 g mass for a 10 mL sample. However, if you add up the masses of the components listed in Table 1, you get a total of less than 10.50 g (9.71 g, to be specific). The question is asking you to explain this discrepancy. To find the best explanation, consider each of the possibilities offered in the answer choices. Choice A does not offer an adequate explanation, because if some red blood cells remained in the plasma, then they would have been weighed along with the plasma, which means their mass would have been included. Choice B also falls short; the mass of the platelets would have been included when the white blood cells were weighed. Choice C suffers from a similar problem: if some of the formed elements remained in the plasma, their masses would simply be included when the plasma was weighed. By process of elimination, (D) must be correct. And this makes sense because the only components that were weighed were plasma, red blood cells, white blood cells, and platelets. If there were additional components, their masses would not be included in Table 1. This is also consistent with the opening of the passage, which claims that blood is 45% formed elements and 50% plasma, leaving 5% of the blood unaccounted for.

30. F

Difficulty: Low

Category: Interpreting Data

Getting to the Answer: Go back to Table 1 and look at the columns for total density and red blood cell mass. (Circle each column if you tend to get distracted by the other information.) Reading the table from the bottom up, you can see that, as total density increases, the mass of the red blood cells also increases, (F).

31. B

Difficulty: Medium

Category: Using Data

Getting to the Answer: The introduction to the passage states that "formed elements weigh approximately 1.10 grams per milliliter (g/mL) and plasma approximately

1.02 g/mL." Here, you have about 5 mL of plasma, so the total mass of plasma is roughly 5 mL $\times$ 1.02 g/mL = 5.1 g. You also have about 5 mL of formed elements, so the total mass of formed elements is about 5 mL $\times$ 1.10 g/mL = 5.5 g. The total mass of the sample would then be around 5.1 g + 5.5 g = 10.6 g. It may be a bit higher due to elements other than the plasma and formed elements, but the total mass is still likely to be between 10.0 and 12.0 g, as in (B).

32. J

Difficulty: Low

Category: Experimental Design

Getting to the Answer: The passage explains that the phlebotomist placed the blood samples in a centrifuge for 20 minutes in Study 2 and at a slower speed for 45 minutes in Study 3. Only (J) captures any element of this difference. Choice F is incorrect because you're told at the beginning of the passage that 10 mL of blood were taken from each patient. Choice G is incorrect because, while the mass of the blood samples did vary from patient to patient, the masses weren't intentionally varied by the phlebotomist from Study 2 to Study 3. Choice H is incorrect because a centrifuge was used in both Studies 2 and 3.

33. A

Difficulty: Low

Category: Interpreting Data

Getting to the Answer: To answer this question, simply compare the masses in the red blood cell column of Table 1. According to the table, Patient A has a red blood cell mass of 2.75 g, Patient B a mass of 2.70 g, and Patient C a mass of 2.65 g. Because Patient A has the greatest mass of red blood cells, (A) is correct.

Passage VI

34. G

Difficulty: Medium

Category: Interpreting Data

Getting to the Answer: Since the question asks about length and temperature, the simplest data set to consider is Table 1, because Table 2 includes another variable, type of material. Comparing the odd numbered trials (all conducted at 80°C) or the even numbered trials (all conducted at 20°C) shows that the shorter the rod, the higher the current, which is an inverse relationship. Choices F and J can be eliminated. Comparing any trials that hold length of the rod constant while changing the temperature, such as Trials 1 and 2, show that as temperature goes down, current through the rod goes up, which is another inverse relationship. Because both length and temperature are inversely related to current, (G) is correct.

35. C

Difficulty: Medium

Category: Using Data

Getting to the Answer: The passage states that voltage, current, and resistance are related through Ohm's law, $V = A \times \Omega$, where Ω stands for resistance in ohms and A stands for current in amperes. In the circuit used for these experiments, the voltage is held constant at 5 V, as indicated by the battery in Figure 1. This means that if current goes up, resistance must have gone down. Conversely, the lowest current will result from the highest resistance. Because each of the rods featured in the answer choices was tested in Experiment 2, to find the rod with the highest resistance, you merely need to find the one with the lowest recorded current in Table 2. The rod in Trial 9 conducted a current of only 20 mA, less than any of the others, so it must have the highest resistance. Choice (C) is thus correct.

36. H

Difficulty: High

Category: Using Data

Getting to the Answer: According to the question stem, conductivity uses the units of siemens per meter ($\sigma = $ S/m) and siemens are equal to inverse ohms ($S = 1/\Omega$). Putting these two equations together, you can see that the units of conductivity are equivalent to inverse ohms divided by meters ($\sigma = [1/\Omega]/m$), which simplifies to $\sigma = 1/(\Omega \times m)$. Choice (H) is thus correct.

37. B

Difficulty: Low

Category: Using Data

Getting to the Answer: According to Table 1, the rod in Trial 4 conducted 53 mA of electricity at 20°C. A rod of the same length was used in Trial 3, but it was heated to 80°C and conducted only 27 mA. Because 50°C is in between these two values, it is reasonable to assume that the current conducted will fall somewhere between 27 and 53 mA. Choice (B) is therefore correct.

38. F

Difficulty: Medium

Category: Using Data

Getting to the Answer: The introduction to the passage mentions Ohm's law, $V = I \times R$, which shows that voltage and current are directly related. Because the resistance values wouldn't change (the same rods would be used), the increase in voltage with the 10 V battery would lead to higher recorded values for current, regardless of the material of the rods. Thus, since both the copper and iron rods would conduct larger currents with a 10 V battery, (F) is correct.

39. C

Difficulty: Medium

Category: Using Data

Getting to the Answer: According to the results of Experiment 2, copper conducts electricity more effectively than iron. Thus, a 16 cm composite rod that was half-copper and half-iron would be expected to conduct electricity better than a 16 cm iron rod but worse than a 16 cm copper rod. According to Table 2, a 16 cm iron rod at 20°C conducts 40 mA, while a 16 cm copper rod at that temperature conducts 200 mA. Thus, the composite rod should conduct a current of somewhere between 40 and 200 mA, as in (C).

40. J

Difficulty: Low

Category: Experimental Design

Getting to the Answer: The variables that are directly manipulated in an experiment are the independent variables, so this question is asking for the one variable that is not an independent variable. In both experiments, the dependent variable—in other words, the variable that was observed and measured—was the current recorded by the ammeter. Thus, current was not directly manipulated by the student, so (J) is correct.

Writing Test

Level 6 Essay

I fully agree that pure scientific research is vital to increase our understanding of ourselves and our world, and that this research, even without specific goals, can result in important benefits to society. To fund this research, a consortium of government, pharmaceutical companies, and non-profit agencies should be formed, pooling money but giving no one group entire oversight or responsibility.

Many life-changing discoveries have been found without purposely looking for them. Alexander Fleming did not set out to discover penicilin, but in doing so accidentally saved millions of people from death. Putting a man on the moon did not help people on Earth, but it certainly taught us a lot about our universe. This kind of pure research must continue, and the cost should be shared by the government, drug companies, and non-profit groups. This type of research can be prohibitively expensive; thus, monies must be drawn from various sources, each contributing as much as possible. No single organization can completely fund ongoing research, especially if there is no stated goal other than to hopefully discover something beneficial. Tax payers, pharmaceutical company investors, and non-profit group members expect results, which may be long in coming, or, indeed, continually elusive. However, efforts must continue. As Thomas Edison said, "Just because something doesn't do what you planned it to do doesn't mean it's useless."

Consider also that pharmaceutical companies are always searching for new therapeutic drugs. They send scientists out into the field to come back with anything interesting, which is then researched and, if promising, developed into a new drug. Such is the relation between blood sugar and diabetes, leading to the insulin that my diabetic cousin takes; without insulin, he would not survive. If a drug company develops an important drug, it can make millions of dollars from the sale of it, leading to funding more research. Non-profit organizations also have a stake in pure research, since another accidental discovery could prove to be financially beneficial. Finally, if the government shares the burden of underwriting research, it is not at risk for being fully blamed if the research does not produce positive results. Taxpayers would be more liable to accept a minimal lose in a good cause rather than a major loss in an unsure endeavor. A partnership would ensure continued funding and the funders, as well as all citizens, would benefit from discoveries.

On the other hand, people who say the government should fund only research which has demonstrated its worth do not understand the function of pure research. It is not possible for researchers to say with certainty that they are going to find a cure for cancer. Researchers have to be able to say they are searching for something as yet unknown with the hope that it will be beneficial. And what is a clear and acceptable outcome? If cancer researchers find a cure for diabetes, but not cancer, is that acceptable if it is not the stated intention? A great deal of science is luck and perserverance. According to this perspective, if a researcher wanted government funding to work in the Amazonian rain forest with the general intent of exploring indigenous plants, the government would be unable to fund the project because there is no clearly beneficial objective. But that is exactly how quinine, a now widely-used treatment for malaria, was found, and the general exploration was certainly worth funding. Finally, it is unlikely that pure research, no matter who funds it, will result in disaster. Researchers are very careful to prevent this, and even if a disaster did happen, it would not be the fault of whom is funding the research.

It is quite clear that pure research is invaluable, as the examples of penicilin, quinine, and insulin support. It cannot be dependent on the whims, finances, and oversight of any one group but must be a concerted effort among all and for all who may benefit.

Score Explanation (6 in all domains)

This essay is clearly focused on the prompt, shows complete understanding of the issue, logically assesses the implications of all three perspectives, and puts forth the author's point of view in both the first and fifth paragraphs. This is a cohesive, critical analysis of the perspectives, with a solid, well-supported thesis.

Ideas and Analysis (6)

The argument is driven by strong and clear analysis of each perspective, with good examination of implications. The writer's consistent focus on the benefits of pure research makes the essay cohesive and precise: pure research is worth pursuing and, for economic and oversight reasons, must be funded by a consortium of groups. Keeping this focus, the writer is able to explore each perspective, identify pros and cons, and provide strong support for her point of view. Critical, logical thinking is clearly displayed.

Development and Support (6)

The writer introduces her argument with a strong statement supporting pure research in general, and she immediately follows up with her perspective. That perspective is developed through reference to "life-changing discoveries," the cost of research, specific discussion of drug company research and benefits, and what may constitute acceptable risk. Support is strong, referencing Alexander Fleming, penicillin, space exploration, quinine, and insulin, and inserting a relevant quote from Thomas Edison. Reasoning and support are well integrated, and the author never loses sight of the thesis. Both alternatives are discussed. One alternative is discussed in detail, while the other is given only passing, but still strong consideration ("And what is a clear and acceptable outcome?"; "Finally, it is unlikely that pure research, no matter who funds it, will result in disaster."). Development moves from the general to the specific, with excellent support for each point, and a clear and consistent perspective.

Organization (6)

There is a clear and strong introduction and a summary conclusion, both of which enlarge the specifics of the prompt to the larger issues involved. Each paragraph begins with a topic sentence, and the contrasting view is signaled with the phrase "On the other hand," while the third paragraph is introduced with the creative transition phrase "Consider also." The essay is cohesive and flows well, ideas are well-connected, and support is explicit, relevant, and well-positioned to enhance the argument.

Language Use (6)

The writing is mostly high-level, with the use of a rhetorical question and words such as "perseverance," "accountable," "consortium," and "pharmaceutical." Several sentences are varied and complex. The grammar and punctuation are mostly correct, though there are some spelling errors ("penicilin," "perserverance"). The writer's style is appropriately formal, even with a personal example, and her word choice is effective in characterizing the perspectives and writing a persuasive argument.

Level 4 Essay

Pure research is done for the purpose of discovery without a specific goal in mind. Even so, it has produced important breakthroughs such as treatment for Alzheimer's disease, and even the development of the GPS. Though scientific research is vitally important, people disagree about who should pay for it. Some people think that the government should fund the research if the goal is a good one. Others think that the government should only give money to research that can be shown will be helpful. Still others believe that the government and private companies should work together to give scientists the money they need, which is the best way to do it, and the perspective I agree with.

I know the importance of research because my little brother has asthma and requires daily medication. Though I don't know who paid for the research that helped make his meds, I'm quite sure that the research behind it took a long time and cost a great deal of money. Though the government may have enough money to fully fund research like this, it has other responsibilities as well and can't afford to fund research alone, especially if the outcome is unsure. However, with other money from drug companies and non-profit agencies, research can continue to be funded without any one entity eating into their finances earmarked for other purposes. Even if the research doesn't show results for many years, a group of funders can provide enough money so that scientists can keep working until they discover something helpful and then continue to develop it.

The government can't do everything on its own and companies shouldn't have to work by themselves either. If they team up, lots of research can get done. Asthma is now manageable, but there are plenty of other illnesses that are very deadly. Everybody is hoping for a cure for cancer one day, and scientists need time and money to find one. Groups working together can give those scientists the time and money they need, since no one group is responsible for an immediate, beneficial result from the research it funds. The government and companies should pick an amount of money they want to spend each year on scientific research and give it to a variety of research groups. Then, if any of the groups make a major discovery, they can earn more money and invest it back into ongoing research.

On the other hand, some people think that scientists should have to show the government that their projects will be helpful in order to get money. That would exclude a lot of past and future research that was done purely in the hopes of discovery but without assurances. Louis Pasture wouldn't have gotten money from his government to make penicillin since it was a total accident. Being able to pinpoint the exact purpose and result of pure research is precisely the opposite of what pure research aims to do.

Like all important things, research requires time, effort and money. The best way to fund it is to gather a group of government, private, and non-profit agencies who can pool their resources to let scientists keep working. Some research may fail miserably, but some may change the course of the world. That possibility is surely worth funding.

Score Explanation (4 in all domains)

The writer provides a minimal discussion of all three perspectives, but fails to fully consider the implications of the other perspectives. She doesn't fully consider counterarguments, but she does provide relevant support for her opinion.

Ideas and Analysis (4)

Ideas are clearly stated, if redundant. The argument centers around "time, effort, and money," with discussion of each taking up most of the essay. Her perspective is analyzed primarily through a personal anecdote about her brother, which is more related to research in general than to pure research. However, the author is consistent in her argument and able to critique another perspective while returning to her own point of view.

Development and Support (4)

The writer begins with a good statement defining pure research, immediately bringing in the examples of Alzheimer's and the GPS, though a brief explanation of their relevance would enhance the support. The first paragraph also introduces all perspectives. However, when the writer states her own opinion at the end of the introduction, she does not do so forcefully. The argument is developed with a personal statement about her brother's asthma, which leads into further discussion of funding. The writer continues this argument in the next paragraph, again referencing asthma and mentioning cancer, though both statements are fleeting and do not offer strong support. One other alternative is discussed in the fourth paragraph, nicely harking back to the definition of pure research (the incorrect reference to Pasteur and penicillin does not affect the support).

Organization (4)

The writer provides a clear introductory paragraph and a good conclusion, and she is able to tie the essay together by harking back to the initial definition of pure research at the end of the fourth paragraph with "Being able to pinpoint the exact purpose and result of pure research is precisely the opposite of what pure research aims to do." The first paragraph shows good connection between perspectives ("Some," "Others," "Still others"). However, there are few transitions other than the one introducing paragraph four; better use of transitions would make the essay flow more smoothly. The essay is nonetheless cohesive in its perspective.

Language Use (4)

The writing style is adequate, with some spelling and grammar errors. Word choice could be improved by avoiding very informal words and phrases ("eating into their finances," "total accident," "meds," "plenty of other diseases") and expressing ideas with more high-level vocabulary and complex sentence structure. Less use of contractions would also raise the language to a more appropriately formal essay level.

Level 2 Essay

Working with a real goal in mind is the best way to do a project and the goverment has lots of money, so I think the government should pay for research projects but only those which will succeed. I did a school sience project with too other kids but we ended up fighting and not finishing it, which is what would happen if lots of groups got together to fund something.

When my teacher assigns a sience project even though I get to choose which one to do she expects results. The goverment should think the same way because if they don't they will be spending money for something which could be useless. Just like my teacher does when she decides what grade to give my project, the goverment should think about how successful the research might be and save their money for research that will really come up with something important.

Like it says, "to many cooks spoil the broth" which means that when theres a whole group of people, chances are the end result is bad. That goes for the govement partnering with other groups also they should pay for research by themselves but only if it looks like the research will come up with something good.

Score Explanation (2 in all domains)

Though the author addresses the prompt and takes a side, this essay is very poorly written and supported, and ideas and analysis are weak with little clarity.

Ideas and Analysis (2)

This essay indicates a lack of understanding of the prompt and task, and poor reasoning and writing skills. The author has focused primarily on the issues of money and the negative effects of working with partners, likening the latter to working with others on a science project. She has not analyzed any perspective in depth; instead, ideas are repetitive, with shallow support. The author has not looked beyond her own school experience, thus her argument is weak and analysis of the prompt is superficial.

Development and Support (2)

The author fails to develop her thesis beyond general, poorly supported statements that repeat her two ideas that working together is detrimental to a project, and government money should be spent on projects with demonstrated success. Her support is weak and irrelevant, focusing on a school project, equating it with pure research, and suggesting that the government should determine its funding in the same way that a teacher determines a grade. The phrase that opens the third sentence is a trite platitude, again lacking any real thought and analysis. The author reasoning is inadequate and confused, and she fails to examine the argument logically.

Organization (2)

Though there are three separate paragraphs and the conclusion echoes the first paragraph's perspective, each paragraph is weak and disjointed, with no transition phrases to tie the essay together. Ideas are poorly grouped together; the author repeatedly compares a school project to governmental pure research funding.

Language Use (2)

There are numerous spelling and punctuation errors, word choice is simplistic, and the writing fails to be persuasive. "Government" and "science" are consistently misspelled, and there are several instances of improper pronoun/antecedent agreement. The author misuses the word "too," omits the apostrophe from "there's," and follows the missed apostrophe with a run-on sentence. Word choice and sentence structure are rudimentary, and the essay lacks the strength and style of writing that would make it persuasive and engaging.

Review Your Essay

You can evaluate your essay and the model essay based on the following criteria, which are covered in chapter 27:

- Does the author discuss all three perspectives provided in the prompt?
- Is the author's own perspective clearly stated?
- Does the body of the essay assess and analyze each perspective?
- Is the relevance of each paragraph clear?
- Does the author start a new paragraph for each new idea?
- Is each sentence in a paragraph relevant to the point made in that paragraph?
- Are transitions clear?
- Is the essay easy to read? Is it engaging?
- Are sentences varied?
- Is vocabulary used effectively? Is college-level vocabulary used?